Citizen Subject

Commonalities

Timothy C. Campbell, series editor

Citizen Subject

Foundations for Philosophical Anthropology

Étienne Balibar

Translated by Steven Miller

FORDHAM UNIVERSITY PRESS

NEW YORK 2017

Funding for this book was provided in part by the Helen Tartar Memorial Fund.

This book was originally published in French as Etienne Balibar, *Citoyen Sujet, et autres essais d'anthropologie philosophique*, Copyright © Presses Universitaires de France, 2011.

This work received the French Voices Award for excellence in publication and translation. French Voices is a program created and funded by the French Embassy in the United States and FACE (French American Cultural Exchange). French Voices logo designed by Serge Bloch.

This book is funded in part by a subvention from the Institute for Comparative Literature and Society, Columbia University.

Ouvrage publié avec le concours du Ministère français chargé de la Culture–Centre National du Livre.

This work has been published with the assistance of the French Ministry of Culture–National Center for the Book.

Cet ouvrage a bénéficié du soutien des Programmes d'aide à la publication de l'Institut Français.

This work, published as part of a program of aid for publication, received support from the Institut Français.

Visit us online at www.fordhampress.com.

Printed in the United States of America

19 18 17   5 4 3 2 1

First edition

Copyright page continued on page 395.

CONTENTS

Emily Apter

What is a citizen subject? A hyphenated subject, equal parts political citizen and subjected individual conscience? A freestanding agent capable of being federated with others? The ratifier of moral law, the self-punisher who dies by a thousand cuts at the hands of his or her own superego? The lead in a play about the psychic life of power in the era of weak states? The plebian legislator posed against the citizen king? A figure of possessive individualism reversed (which is to say, a self-dispossessed collectivist)? Or the *Untertan*, man of straw, anyone, "man without qualities," figure of *ressentiment*, silently resisting uniform commands? To whom or to what is the citizen subject subject? What comes after the subject when, to paraphrase Jean-Luc Nancy, the concept of "the Political" has been retreated? And what is left of the subject discursively posited as an effect of grammar, or as the product of a political philology of sovereignty? Who comes after the subject if not a process of becoming-subject and becoming-citizen, rethought from the philological ground up and across languages?

The "citizen subject" comes (historically and politically) after the obedient or "submitted" subject emerging from this philology, but the critical faculty never rests in Balibar's address of the problem of what a "citizen subject" might be. Each time the notion of "citizen" is called up, it recurs to "subject" and vice versa, in reciprocal, chiasmic, and dialectical relation. The doublet "citizen subject" emerges as a singular philosopheme, a calque on another, older doublet: the *subjectum-subjectus*, where *subjectum* referred in scholastic manner to an individual substance, a unity of body and soul, and *subjectus* (the "other name of the *subditus*"), was taken to refer to the human person, "subjected to" divine or princely authority. Reversing the latter and bracketing the former, Descartes defined as *ego cogito* or *ego sum* an antithesis to both of them, positing an "I" effect without foundation in a metaphysics of substance or a theology of incarnation. Much of this monumental book will be concerned with demonstrating the distortions produced, post Kant, by the imposition of a transcendental subject on the Cartesian *ego*, which fostered a projection of the subject as substantialized, self-prescribing of its freedom, guided by a teleology aligned with the construct of the "humanity" of man.

Balibar's comprehensive genealogy of the "citizen subject" began its life as a response to Jean-Luc Nancy's question "Who comes after the subject?" circulated in 1988–89 to a group of nineteen philosophers of different generations "in the spirit of eighteenth-century concourses and consultations" in order to "punctuate a theoretical *moment* and to highlight the *formulations* inherited from a recurring controversy."[1] The "moment" in question here concerned the pitting of "philosophies of the [*originary*] subject" (Descartes, Kant, Husserl), against [post]phenomenological or deconstructive critiques of the " 'metaphysics' of foundation"; "the structuralist 'decentering' of the immediate data of consciousness," and "the Marxist, Freudian, or Nietzschean critiques of the 'illusions' that beset the claims of consciousness to truth." These debates, for Nancy, could be situated within the even more capacious purview of a referendum on philosophy as such at a pivotal historical pass, a moment of self-questioning as fulcrum of Western civilization. This entailed interrogating how philosophical language would need to be transformed or supplanted in response to cultural shifts and critiques of Eurocentrism. "What between or beyond 'praxis' and 'theory' would this imply?" Jean-Luc Nancy would ask in his introduction.[2] Appearing in 2011 in a series titled "Pratiques théoriques" previously coedited by Balibar himself and fellow "Althusserian" Dominique Lecourt, one could say that *Citizen Subject: Foundations for Philosophical Anthropology* (*Citoyen Sujet et autres essais d'anthropologie philosophique*) in its French context could be situated in the framework of a broadly recognized, urgent need to study and critique the European lexicon of "praxis" and "theory."

Balibar reviews how the chapters, written over a long period, are each dedicated to the rereading of specific texts all circulating in different ways around the question of the subject, hinged to the notion of the citizen in the modern world. Balibar notes that the order of his reflection is sited within three interrelated modalities: the subject as self-identified, the subject as communally identified, and the transgressive subject as institutionally identified through law and judgment. Each part contains a series of deep meditations on and within carefully chosen philosophical and literary texts, named by author, but considered as texts that speak the subject: Descartes, Locke, Rousseau, Derrida, Hegel, Marx, Tolstoy, Freud, and Blanchot, to mention only a few. The readings of these texts are embedded in a general discussion of the specific "modernity" of the citizen subject under discussion, a modernity that is signaled in the final chapter of the book as "citizen-bourgeois." A map of this extraordinary intellectual territory might well adopt the *topos* discovered by Balibar in his reading of Rousseau's *La nouvelle Héloïse*, that *utopos* constructed through a triple geometry: triangle, couple, network. For the antinomies revealed in this structural diagram play continuously through the analyses, only to return, deepened, recast, and often estranged, to the initial question, the historical and theoretical complex, *subjectus/subjectum*.

If Balibar's procedures of interpretation are at times reminiscent of deconstruction, recalling the virtuosic way in which Jacques Derrida and Paul de Man would build up the history of certain tropes and figures, tracing their uses in classical arguments and glosses, only to baffle the possibility of making the arguments through a play of infinite reversals, double binds, or proofs about the unownability of language, they differ in their constancy to philosophically posed problems whose import takes precedence over difference effects and language play. Balibar will openly borrow from deconstruction its practice of dismantling "paradoxes of the universal," its dissolution of oppositions between universal and particular, absolute and relative, formal and material, one and multiple, same and other, but it is the philosophical problem of the universal that remains uppermost. Thus, it is the desire to give Locke his due when dismantling the myth of Descartes as "inventor of modern consciousness," or the impetus to unravel Hegel's "originary form of contradiction inscribed in linguistic usage" (which inflects his fiction of the quasi-subject who speaks in a subjectless voice), or the drive to demonstrate how philosophical expressions always already contain the seeds for deconstructing institutions of modernity, or the concern to unravel Freud's debt to Kelsen's juridico-political notion of hyperindividuality (*Über-Individualität*) in forging the Superego (*das Über-Ich*) and "theorizing the 'judicial moment' of subjection" that motivates the deconstructive move in *Citizen Subject.*

That said, as with deconstruction, Balibar's heuristic affirms distinct convictions about how to do things with texts: "Only singular texts articulate *determinate* theses and pose *determinate* problems of interpretation . . . an author *never writes the same text twice.*" We see this point illustrated in the reading of Rousseau, where any "doctrinal" reading of *Julie, or the New Heloise, The Social Contract* and *Emile* as three complementary models of one single system is abandoned in favor of a theory of each of these texts relationally competitive with the other two in trying "to resolve the unresolvable problem of community" or describe "a social bond compatible with the 'voice of nature.' " In this scheme, there are no universal descriptive terms; no metalanguage in philosophy prevails "that would make it possible to reformulate texts in universal, descriptive, or systematic terms, 'elevating' them above their letter in order to extract their rational kernel or to reduce them to an ultimate materiality, more fundamental than their own." If there is a task of the translator here, it is a very particular one, involving not the transference of roughly equivalent meanings from one language to another, but rather, bringing out the untranslatable singularity, the "only once" or singular occurrence *(hapax legomenon)* of the subject enunciated by each articulation or text in its own language.

In building a *translational* genealogy of the subject (or more specifically of the *subjectus-subditus*) that rivals the epistemological genealogy of modern subjectivity found in Foucault's *The Order of Things* (*Les mots et les choses*), Balibar develops a method drafted from an encyclopedic project *Dictionary of Untranslatables: A Philosophical Lexicon* (*Le vocabulaire européen des philosophies: Dictionnaire des intraduisibles*), spearheaded by the philosopher Barbara Cassin, in which "philosophizing in languages" became the watchword for rewriting concept-philosophy along the axis of mistranslation and endless retranslation. An author of or collaborator on the entries "Subject," the first person pronoun "I," "Soul," and, in the English edition, "Agency/Instance"), Balibar adopts a procedure consistently availed in *Citizen Subject,* one that, in addition to ensuring "the primacy of texts" and "the knot between writing and conjuncture," subscribes to "infinite translation imposed by idiom":

> To say that philosophers write in a particular fashion is to say that they write in a given language or in an "idiom" whereby they seek with an abundance of inventiveness (not necessarily jargon . . .) to compensate for the lack of universality. Today, there is general agreement on this point. This is why a portion of philosophical work has begun to shift toward the systematic examination of the effects of translation in philosophy, and thus also of the "untranslatables" and of the process of "translating the untranslatables" as a moment of conceptual "invention."

Unlike Hegel, whose *Phenomenology* aspired to an original, philosophical language that would allow "'spirit' to speak as such" and texts to dialogue among themselves in a discourse of absolute knowledge that dispenses with translation as a central problem, Balibar pursues an opposite tack, turning nubs of untranslatability into sites of resistance to any model of absolute knowledge and using a text, term, or specific grammatical usage that defies translation as an opening to collective participation in translational praxis. Untranslatability, as spur to philosophizing in languages, uses linguistic difference and the incommensurability among languages to question the universalism of any univocal idea of the subject, identifying instead singular subjects in singular texts, idioms, diction, and words. An example is the mining—in the discrepancies or voids of comparative translations—of Descartes's grammar, scrupulously parsed in order to examine what is the ego, who is an I" or a "me" (in the sense of being alive, existing, thinking oneself). Pondering the gap between Descartes's *"je pense donc je suis"* from the *Discourse on Method* (or *"ego cogito, ergo sum"* from *Principles of Philosophy*) and the far less well-worked proposition *"ego sum, ego existo"* from the *Meditations*, Balibar construes the early modern subject, self-doubting and alone, yet sustained in theophanic relation, alongside a subject-God who cannot think the human "I" since "he has no 'I'" and does not need it to exist. A similarly painstaking attentiveness to the grammatical specificities of the letter is applied to the analysis of Hegel's dialectical enunciation of subjectivity in the *Phenomenology of Spirit*: *"Ich, das Wir, und Wir, das Ich ist"* (I that is We and We that is I). It is the German language, which liaises the *"Ich"* to the *"das Ich,"* that brings out the "subject of the uttering within the utterance," thus allowing the voice (of subject as Spirit) to be heard in the text. And yet it is also this same grammar, with its "embarrassing" use of relative clauses, that overwrites the neuter *"Ich,"* threatening it with the return of a masculine or a feminine denomination that would install the "irony" of sexual difference at the core of the tautological formulations which dialectically convert the formal, empty reflection of the *"Ich"* (*Ich gleich Ich, Ich bin Ich*) into the "absolute" or "concrete" reflexivity of the *"Selbst"* (*"Selbst ist Selbst"*), for which no difference should remain unknowable. This allows in turn for an opening to the exteriority of a "we" (*Wir*) and from thence (through yet more reversals), to the conclusions that, first, the *"Wir* is not 'being'" (*Sein*), and second, the community, with respect to Being qua *logos* "lacks in being," condemning collective consciousness to a divisive historical objectivity. If there is a method or approach that comes to the fore in Balibar's readings of the text at the micro-level of grammatical singularities, it could be characterized as an intensive form of political philology that places the untranslatability of the subject and the unresolvability of the subject-in-community at the center of its praxis.

Does this insistence on singularity and idiomaticity imply that *every* examination of the universal is, for Balibar, foreclosed? Clearly not. But his "universalism" is at bottom a problematic one. For him, rather than *asserted* against its (logical and ideological) opposite ("particularism"), the universal needs to be *problematized* as a specific form of utterance. And this is not deprived of political implications. In contrast to a number of his contemporary interlocutors—Jacques Rancière, Alain Badiou, Jean-Luc Nancy, Slavoj

Žižek—who would seem to have abandoned the notion of the citizen along with the many other political specters put out of action by capitalo-parlementarianism and the "small p" politics of the mediocracy, Balibar holds fast to the "citizen subject," as lasting monument or remnant of historic, revolutionary inheritance and fulcrum of *equaliberty*. The portmanteau neologism *égaliberté*, to which he devoted the book *Equaliberty: Political Essays*, lays emphasis on "antinomies of citizenship" grounded in "moments of a dialectic that includes both historical movements and relations of force." These moments trace "a differential of insurrection and constitution lodged at the heart of the relations between citizenship and democracy" and take aim at neoliberalism's "unlimited promotion of individualism and utilitarianism" in response to the "crisis of the national-social state."[3] Dialectic and antinomy are equally heavy lifters within Balibar's technics in *Citizen Subject*, enjoined to produce a theory of the subject that is also an education in how to think the theory of the subject, starting with a close reading of *The Declaration of the Rights of Man and of the Citizen* (1789), where it is a question not only of determining "which is more foundational, man or citizen," but of defining an anthropological foundation of sovereignty that deals with the fundamental paradox of "*sovereign equality*." This paradox—also related by Balibar to a form of "intensive universality"—is grasped in a formula that he uses to emphasize the categorical stipulation of revolutionary equality: "The revolution will say: If anyone is not a citizen, then no one is a citizen" (which we could paraphrase as "if anyone is excluded from citizenship, then nobody has access to, or the right to citizenship"). The play here between the "anyone" citizen and the "nobody" citizen reproduces an aporia. This is citizen-becoming-subject (*devenir sujet*) that is "no longer a *subjectus* and not yet the *subjectum*." Upon this nascent subject equality will have to be unilaterally conferred, but she or he will always remain a subject of conflict, grappling with contradictions between the individual and the collective, rights and privileges, real and symbolic equality, active and passive participation in governance and systems of representation, egotistic, interest-driven forms of sociality (equal, but in their equality all the more susceptible to mimetic rivalry) and an undifferentiated equality that binds individuals into *a* polity, *a* society (dependent on exclusion of those not belonging). With this riven, suspensive figure of the citizen, vulnerable to destruction through struggles for equality and civil rights, we go, as one of the subheadings of this section on the *Declaration of the Rights of Man and of the Citizen* reminds us, from one subjection to the other. When the "citizen subject" occupies the place of both constituent of the State and actor of permanent revolution, it is subjected to different states of subjection, torn, as Foucault articulated so powerfully and as Balibar underscores, between the world of voluntary servitude and the world of right and discipline. For Balibar, *all of Foucault's work* is concentrated on the transition between these two worlds, a condition that returns us again and again to modalities of subjection in subjectivation, and that produces "a materialist phenomenology of the transmutation of subjection, of the birth of the Citizen Subject. As to whether this figure, like a face of sand at the edge of the sea, is about to be effaced with the next great sea change—that is another question. Perhaps it is nothing more than Foucault's own utopia, a necessary support for the enterprise of stating that utopia's facticity."

"A materialist phenomenology of the transmutation of subjection, of the birth of the Citizen Subject": This is the signature problematic of both Foucault and Balibar, with Foucault emphasizing the ambivalent force of subjectivation in the history of institutions and biopolitical management, and with Balibar excavating the "it" in the "I"; the strictures of sentient ego or consciousness; the force-field of the conscience directive within structures of moral intention; the self-defeating, tautological principle of "obedience to coercion" enshrined in positive law (one of Freud's principal points of contestation with the jurist Kelsen); the proprietary exigencies of "own-ness" (*Eigentum*) in self-predication and self-interest. These themes become loci for apprehending what is intractable in subjectivity. Tracking the semantic vagaries and overdeterminations of the Greek (*hypokeimenon*), the Latin (*subjectus/subjectum*), and the German (*Subjekt, Untertan*) of what we usually call in English a "subject," Balibar reveals the conformations of subjectivation in response to the vicissitudes of sovereign will (or its absent exercise); from princely *Willkür*, absolutism, and the *diktats* (the "oughts" and "shoulds") of instrumental reason to superegoic self-governance and the psychiatric blandishments of "therapeutic citizenship." This last establishes the psychotic as a subject of rights positioned exceptionally outside the jurisdiction of the penal apparatus yet exposed to a medicalized space of social relations that often confounds the determination of freedom within the sphere of patients' rights, ranging across the right to madness, abnormality, and difference and the right to care.

In, through, and beyond the meticulously expounded specificities of Balibar's readings, we apprehend in philosophically bolded characters: the forced hand of "internal 'conversion' towards divine truth" (Augustine); the submission of particular wills to the General Will (which "has the power to 'force subjects to be free'"); the subordination of the subject to the General Equivalent endowed with the brute capacity to dispose interobjectively of any thing or being in the form of money; the contagious urge to "obey the chief" expressed in *Massenpsychologie*; the judicial nature of guilt; the ego's self-management through protective shielding and defense (which puts it in crouch position); the sovereign state's autoimmunity; the adjudicator's determination of rightness, just cause, sufficient reason; the existential economy's rule by calculated risk and the extraction of profit from self-properties. Each of these suborning modes is starkly perceived as subject-constitutive in its dialectical relation to structures and institutions of law, ontotheology, primitive accumulation (capital), governmentality, carceral organization, heteronormative orders of sexual difference, racialized assemblages, psychopolitical economies, necropolitics. Viewed from this perspective, the book invites being read and taught as one seminar or as the catalyst of a cluster of canonical investigations into the role of subjection in subject-formation and the polarized parameters of the human.

No contemporary thinker has theorized the political fragility of modern citizenship-subjecthood in the continental philosophical tradition with greater critical nuance and rigor than Balibar. In the course of a career of writing and engagement that spans his participation as a student in the seminars of Louis Althusser in the 1960s and his most recent public tribunes addressing the crises of Europe in the wake of austerity economics, border closings, and Brexit, the citizen subject—in its vanishings and projective reappearances—has been a catalyst of Balibar's theoretical project. From his collaboration with Althusser on a symptomatic reading of Marx's *Capital* to a book coauthored with Immanuel Wallerstein devoted to the politics of race, classes, and nation; his reflections on universalism, force of law, and "equaliberty"; and the philological work on "subject" as a premier untranslatable, Balibar has demonstrated in a way that is particularly significant for Anglophone readers that the term "subject" (French *sujet*) does not just signify topical field or subject of the realm. It underscores how any construct of the freestanding individual or willing agent is flush with *poleiteia*, which is to say, imbued with a fully intersubjective I-ness/We-ness indissociable from the *polis* in the Political. Though there is no one sense of "the Political" (big P), it has been broadly construed as a constitutive sociality grounded in the solidarity of *communitas*; a prospect of Being(s)-in-common, whose aporetic, suspensive, inoperative structure means that it is fated to remain hypothetical, mired in antinomies, perpetually incomplete. It is this very incompletion, however, that represents for Balibar both an opening and an opportunity to think the subject as transindividual *subjectus* at once collective and singular, where the "I" (as Rousseau would have it), has "become a property that belongs to *each and everyone*, or to whatever citizen-subject . . . on the condition that he or she is 'indivisibly' part of the 'common.'" This catachresis of being(s) in common animates Balibar's notion of the "citizen subject," which must reckon with if not supersede in its materialization the conflict of conflicts that Balibar deduces from Hegel's *Phenomenology of the Spirit*: "the conflict of universalities" replicated in the "conflict of communitarian principles." It is the "citizen subject" (or subject citizen, as it is alternately conjured), a practical figure of pure *difference* and self-destroying essence, whose infinite task it is to sublate the irreconcilability of "'possessive' individuality and 'republican' citizenship" that for Balibar, it would seem, remains one of the great dilemmas of political modernity, just as it was for Hegel.

Though the Locke/MacPherson construct of "possessive individualism" has triumphed in regimes of extreme income inequality and distributive injustice and contributed to the virtualization of the subject of the demos (identified with the "movement beyond the divisions of a society produced by private property"), this does not of necessity preclude the invention of a subject of politics who could remake citizenship for a republic worthy of the name.[4] Thus, when Balibar purports to "trace the antithetical movements of the *becoming-citizen of the subject* and the *becoming-subject of the citizen*, which never cease to 'succeed' one another, but also, more profoundly, to precede and condition one another," this notion of mediated citizenship harks back to the French Revolution (and more generally, civic/democratic insurrections), particularly the moment at which the condition of being subject to the divine right of kings and held hostage to the caprice of absolutist regimes was changed out in favor of a citizenship vested with sovereign power and legitimacy. A comparable overturning would have to wait, residing perhaps in the prospect of a "citizen subject" finally released from sovereignty altogether. It might be said to coincide with what Miguel Abensour, using a Pocockian formula, calls Marx's "Machiavellian moment," qualified by Balibar as "the possibility of thinking an autonomous political practice that is not subjected to a sovereign instance," the possibility of a subject of "'true democracy' and nonstate politics." Though such a subject is only fleetingly glimpsed and remains a foreclosed hypothetical (confined to a messianic moment in Marx), it continues to flicker throughout *Citizen Subject* as some kind of as yet untapped resource of the "empty" rather than "full" subject of emancipation, a subject-nihilism if you will, that inverts and supersedes state sovereignty.

The complex structure and finesse of argumentation that is revealed as Balibar walks the reader through the paces of an immensely erudite philological and historical construction of the subject in the history of European philosophy, political theory, and psychoanalysis renders *Citizen Subject* immune to résumé or paraphrase. But stepping back, one ascertains that a central drama of *Citizen Subject* turns on the impossibility of perfectly reconciling universalism with anthropological difference: "abnormal and normality," "race" and "culture," "sex" as gender and orientation. As Balibar notes: "in 'bourgeois' modernity, anthropological differences realize the living paradox of an inegalitarian construction of egalitarian citizenship; or rather, that of a universalist limitation (founded about general or even generic traits of the human race) of what lends the 'political' universal an at least virtually unlimited scope." While the "citizen" part of the citizen subject exerts real pull on subjects toward the conjoint of a realizable universal (that may be extrapolated to a construct at one point attributed by Balibar to Judith Butler of a "*universalism of differences*," a "*more than two sexes*" or "*more than a single one*," situated beyond the binarism of masculine/feminine), it nonetheless becomes clear that each time it is a question of universalism, the remainders of anthropological difference—no matter how delocalized or desubstantialized—affirm their resistance to neutralization because of their own antinomic power of universalization.[5] This standoff bequeaths a misbegotten condition involving the complex interplay between inclusion and exclusion that Balibar calls the "ill-being of the subject of relation." As he announces in the final chapter, "within the framework of civic-bourgeois universality, the principal form of exclusion is *differential inclusion*" or, in a formulation that addresses the dis-ease or ill-fittingness of the universal in subjective interpellation: "The subject is here 'naturally' the bearer (*suppositum*) or the addressee (*subditus*) of the universal that overarches or constitutes it from inside; but, all to itself, the subject is also inevitably defined as 'lacking' universality." Ill-beingness (*malêtre*) as a category complicates univocal accounts of *Dasein* or, for that matter, any ontology posited in a generalist, generic, or neutral vein. It opens up the singular definite article of *the* Subject not just to plural, "otherwise" modes of being, but also to differently abled, non-normativized subjectivities and modes of cognizing worlds. In this sense, a new field of citizens' rights occupying the commons of differential intelligences might, through such readings of the subject, breach the philosophically enclosed, in-turned spaces of universal, monological ontology or of singular mathemes of truth (as in Badiou's axiomatic "I call the subject the local or finite status of a truth").[6]

Though *Citizen Subject* is in no way a work of political prescription, it seems to enjoin us to follow Rousseau in questing after a form of ego that might "exit its soliloquy" to inhabit a political space of "common being," a world of self inhabited by the other and socialized by means of attachments that supersede sovereign economies of subjugation, subordination, forcing, and *commandement*. "Our true *self* is not entirely within us," Rousseau wrote, thus prefiguring, with this concise observation, Balibar's "position" on what the citizen subject, as a philosophical construct, may be for—namely, the retreat of exclusion in the universal. As Balibar owns up with characteristic dialecticism, in what may be seen as his "last word" (at least in this book) on the subject: "My position, in other terms, consists in attempting to think the *conatus* of the subject-citizen as overdetermination: the overdetermination of the universal by contradiction, of contradiction by difference, and thus of conflict itself by exclusion, but also by what never gives up forcing exclusion to beat a retreat."

The retreat of exclusion in the universal and the intrication of this problem with subjectivation (caught in a perpetual conflict between subjection and emancipation) are among the predominant concerns of this magnum opus. This connects *Citizen Subject* to Balibar's greater oeuvre, where often it has been a question of demonstrating how, in its worst ascriptions, citizenship assigns normative rank to qualities and abilities of humanity, produces political exclusion, revokes the franchise, restricts the claims of extraterritorial noncitizens to the public good, and renders conditional and precarious the very right "to be" subject. We might say, then, that in an era of militarized security states, zones of detention, eroded cosmopolitan right, refusals of safe harbor, perpetual states of emergency, and sovereign autoimmunity, in which access to citizenship has been increasingly receded and retracted along with the old dream of cosmopolitan hospitality and frictionless border zones, *Citizen Subject*, while not itself addressing these punctual political issues directly, provides the philosophical underpinnings for rethinking the basic terms by which such issues are engaged with as theoretical practice.

FOREWORD

1. Editor Ermanno Bencivenga asked Jean-Luc Nancy to guest edit a special issue of the philosophy journal *Topoi* in 1988. It was then reprised in expanded form (with the addition of other essays, including Balibar's "Citizen Subject" and the longer version of Nancy's interview with Derrida), as the final number of *Cahiers Confrontations* in 1989. Eduardo Cadava and Peter Connor turned it into a book, *Who Comes After the Subject?* (New York: Routledge, 1991), supplemented with pieces by Sylviane Agacinski, Luce Irigaray, Sarah Kofman, and Emmanuel Levinas. The quotation is at page 2.

2. Jean-Luc Nancy, "Introduction," in *Who Comes After the Subject*, 1.

3. Etienne Balibar, *Equaliberty: Political Essays*, trans. James Ingram (Durham, N.C.: Duke University Press, 2014), 2–3.

4. On the untranslatable intrications of Lockean consciousness and Cartesian *conscience* in the invention of the modern subject and with respect to Macpherson's theory of possessive individualism, see Etienne Balibar, *Identity and Difference: John Locke and the Invention of Consciousness*, trans. Warren Montag (London: Verso, 2013). See too Stella Sandford's excellent introductory essay, "The Incomplete Locke: Balibar, Locke and the Philosophy of the Subject."

5. In his reading of Butler, Balibar is careful to point out that Butler's gender theory does not really pretend to have done with binarism. "It returns first with the fact that the anatomical uncertainty of gender . . . supports a melancholic relation to the proper body that never really comes to an end; and second with this other (much happier) fact that, without a 'law' or a 'truth,' the identification of 'masculine' and 'feminine' roles remains omnipresent in the 'fantasy' of

amorous desire. Instead of the binarism figuring the natural or symbolic 'code' that would be transgressed by the multiplicity of modalities of jouissance always threatening to the institution, it would be displaced upon the figure of the *couple*, which is always realized in a contingent fashion but remains binding in form because it never lets sexuality—or kinship—escape from the aporia of One=Two and to the displacements that it engenders."

6. Alain Badiou, "On a Finally Objectless Subject," in Nancy, *Who Comes After the Subject*, 25.

Citizen Subject

Introduction: After the Controversy

The present work is finally appearing in print after having been announced as forthcoming on several occasions by the publisher who accepted it for publication nearly twenty years ago. Exasperated though he must have been by my broken promises, he did not show it; and he never gave up asking for the manuscript. I am profoundly grateful to him. Without such unflagging interest and friendship I might never have pursued my original intentions, in spite of the stimulus that I received along the way from various meetings and collaborations. No less grateful am I to Bruno Karsenti and Guillaume le Blanc who, as the incoming directors of the "Pratiques Théoriques" series at Presses Universitaires de France, promptly offered that I should become an author at a press where, with Dominique Lecourt, I had long served mainly as a reader.[1]

It goes without saying that, over these many years, the conception and content of this book have evolved, even if the point of departure and method of selecting the essays that compose it remain largely unchanged. From the beginning, the idea was to gather several autonomous studies, some rewritten if necessary and some written specifically for this volume, that clarify and complement one another in such a way that they would test, complicate, and rectify the hypotheses that I put forward in an essay whose title, *Citizen Subject*, now extends to the entire book, and would measure how these hypotheses might help to understand the upheavals that modernity has produced in the field of philosophical anthropology. Today, of course, it appears that I multiplied questions rather than produced definitive answers. But I hope that I also clarified certain presuppositions, produced some knowledge, and—with the progression that I constructed—better elaborated the stakes of what at first remained essentially an intuition. I would like, then, to begin by saying a few words about my point of departure, about the order that I adopted, and about how I would reformulate the main question today.

I attach great importance, and great price, to the fact that, as I indicate in the full title—"Citizen Subject: A Response to a Question from Jean-Luc Nancy, Who Comes After the Subject?"—my essay was conceived in reaction to another's formulations rather than as an entirely autonomous elaboration. What makes this essay important are not only the memories of friendship and work that it still evokes for me today; more objectively, it is also that Nancy's question, addressed to a set of French philosophers from many generations and diverse orientations, in the spirit of eighteenth-century concourses and consultations, made it possible to punctuate a theoretical *moment* and to highlight the *formulations* inherited from a recurring controversy.[2] Indeed, one could say that the "critique of philosophies of the subject" (or, more precisely, the *originary subject*, referring to an ideal lineage that connects statements from Descartes, Kant, and Husserl) constituted the point of intersection (but also of friction) between the discourses of phenomenological (or post-phenomenological) deconstruction of the "metaphysics" of foundation, the structuralist "decentering" of the immediate data of consciousness, and the Marxist, Freudian, or Nietzschean critiques of the "illusions" that beset the claims of consciousness to truth.[3] With his paradoxical formulation ("Who Comes After the Subject?")—whose intentionally sophistic character I (along with other participants) underscore at the beginning of my essay—Nancy short-circuited the temptation to replace one "paradigm" with another (or one "positivity" with another), as if the moment had come to celebrate burials and births, or to pass in linear fashion from a philosophy "of the subject" to a philosophy "without subject." He conceded nothing to reactive formulations, which sought (and still seek) to defend the "endangered" subject (or to restore it) by upholding one or another of its absolutized theoretico-practical identities (consciousness, the person, individuality, responsibility, *praxis*, *Dasein*, freedom, *conatus*, power, agency, affect, body, and even flesh . . .), in more or less close connection with the values of *humanism* (and, in a usually more confused fashion, with the designation of the prime philosophical question as the "anthropological question").[4] Instead, he showed and even demonstrated two things: first, that the critique of the "sovereignty of the subject" (which, in his eyes, is an essentially a metaphysical category, although this can also be shown, *mutatis mutandis*, on the basis of a critique of juridical or psychological ideology) is an infinite, if not impossible task, since it can only be accomplished by articulating (or naming) the function of "overcoming" of subjectivity that ends up reproducing it as an imputed or self-referential figure (albeit displaced or disguised)[5]; second, that this critique has always already begun at the very heart of the definitions and institutions of the "subjectivity of the subject" (or, as Heidegger would say, its "subjectity," *Subjektheit*),[6] because these definitions and institutions are essentially unstable, translating not an affirmation or a negation, a *thesis* (of consciousness, existence, praxis, or personal identity), but a *question* without univocal response, a question in which Nancy's project itself participates. Accordingly, the only manner in which it is possible *philosophically* to call into question the dogmatism of subjectivity is, at the heart of subjectivity itself, to produce constitutive differences, irreducible gaps or disjunctions without synthesis, and thus to exhibit the points of heresy and the impossibilities of history, which will end up (but when? and how?) rendering it unrecognizable and carrying it beyond itself.

I must admit at this point that Nancy's tricky manner of reframing this question of the critique of the "constitutive subject," coming after others that marked our generation, profoundly troubled me at first, such that I was incapable of reacting, especially if it were a matter of reproducing or prolonging the sort of "nonresponse" to which, in a sense, my long-standing position in a certain school of philosophy had habituated me (and which would certainly have oscillated between formulas such as: the structure always already "operates" or the process "actualizes itself" *before* the subject).[7] When I finally managed to offer a response—"after the subject comes the citizen"—which, in many respects, simply turned the question back upon itself, I realized that it had transported me into unknown territory (even if, to all appearances, the terms that I employed were familiar).[8] Beyond an attempt to rectify the evidence adduced to show—in the wake of Kant, Hegel, and Heidegger (but also the historians of philosophy who were our professors: Alquié and Gueroult)—that the "philosophical constitution of the modern subject" goes back to the Cartesian invention (or, in a more historicist manner, to the cultural revolution of which Descartes was the exemplary mouthpiece), my response was founded upon three sets of hypotheses—each an inextricable mix of questions of philology, politics, and the philosophy of history:

1. I upheld that there is a *quid pro quo* (a nonarbitrary *quid pro quo*, founded on the presence, at the heart of Western philosophy and—as Vincent Descombes would say—of the "institutions of [its] sense," of an *objective play on words* deriving from the materiality of writing and the play of the apparatuses of thinking) between two etymologies of the "subject": that which derives from the metaphysical function of a grammar (the *subjectum*) and that which situates the word within the long history of the relation of sovereignty (the *subjectus*). The point is not that the first derivation is unimportant or irrelevant but that it cannot eclipse the second, nor a fortiori replace it, without rendering unintelligible the terms in which modernity formulated the question of freedom and the reasons why it implanted this question at the center of its reflection on "the being of the subject." I thus proposed to begin sketching a genealogy of the *subjectus-subditus*, moving from figures of its "subjection" to those of its emancipation, paradoxically thought as a "subjectivation."[9]

2. I posited that, in the European tradition that—rightly or wrongly—we have been taught to endow with more than provincial significance, the juridical and political antithesis of the "subjective function" has been represented by the figure (or rather, the successive figures) of the citizen, and by the "constitution of citizenship" (*politeia, civitas*),[10] to the extent that they operated a *reduction of verticality* that places the instruments of power and the law *at the level of the community* (ideally at least, but this ideality can, as Marx said, "take possession of the masses" and thereby engender material effects). More precisely, it transforms these instruments into instruments immanent to "co-citizenship" (and, when necessary, into offensive or defensive weapons): for, as conflictual as this community of citizens may be (or even precisely because it is conflictual, because "recognition" is the result of a struggle), the individuals or collectives that make up this community mutually

"confer" equal liberty upon one another, through a reciprocal procedure, always in an essentially horizontal manner.[11]

3. But I also posited (what, at bottom, was the mainspring of the philosophical thesis that I sought to formulate, even as it would prove the germ of many difficulties to come) that the relationship between the "subject" and the "citizen" (although this relationship is certainly inhabited permanently by a *conatus* of emancipation, which renews it and carries it historically ever forward, or ever "after") cannot be conceived as a linear succession or a teleological transformation: so that, in particular, the dialectical *Aufhebung*, whether Hegelian or Marxist, which obviously has a privileged relation to this relationship in both the history of ideas and the history of institutions, constitutes an *interpretation* rather than an *explication* of it. This great "sublation," it seems to me, is characterized at once by its *irreversibility* and its *incompleteness*—which is to say that it is unfinished, precarious, and insufficient. I posited that the *subjectus* whose vertical subjection is thrown into question by the co-citizenship of citizens always ends up "returning" at the heart of this sublation, not only because the modalities of subjection are multiple, tenacious, plastic, and irreducible to a single model or institution, but also because—as Rousseau saw with admirable clarity—co-citizenship is a "double relation" in which citizens are bound together in two modalities at once. The first modality affirms the collective sovereignty of citizens (and thus, as many have rightfully claimed, transfers sovereignty to a new "subject" rather than abolishes it), while the other individualizes their obedience to the norm of political power even as it constructs models for their "identity" and their "subjectivity" (including, of course, those which inhere in forms of disobedience and transgression).[12] I thus outlined a task for theoretical inquiry, indissociable from a group of philosophical, juridical, and literary texts that serve to document it (which, following Foucault's interpretation of Kant, I categorized as *philosophical anthropology*): to trace the antithetical movements of the *becoming-citizen of the subject* and the *becoming-subject of the citizen*, which never cease to "succeed" one another, but also, more profoundly, to precede and condition one another. Accordingly, I believed that I had, at bottom, rediscovered the essence of the "historial wordplay" on *subjectus* and *subjectum*, no longer in the modality of an unthinking *quid pro quo*, but rather in that of an object of analysis, brought to light through the mediation of the "citizen." And I still believe it, although the problem is now encumbered with relative clauses. I here offer the results of my work, by definition always provisional.

I must now resist two temptations, no matter their potential documentary or autobiographical interest: first, the temptation to interpret the conditions of time and place in which I was thrust toward my "response to Jean-Luc Nancy," or, in other words, the whys and wherefores (besides those I explicitly examined or critiqued in the course of my studies) of the privilege that I accorded to the theme of citizenship;[13] and, second, the temptation to give an account of the collective enterprises and research projects, associating them with so many recognitions of debt, to which I owe the chance to sharpen and rectify my previous hypotheses (although such recognition would bear witness to a dimension of intellectual work without which, for my part, I think nothing, and would acknowledge several university institutions that, today dangerously fragile, make such work possible).[14] I prefer to examine how, after twenty years of ruminations and explications of texts, sometimes issuing directly from the above questions and sometimes following byways without knowing in advance where they would lead, I believe that I might regroup my essays in order to found not a positive program of "philosophical anthropology," but a *discussion* of its stakes, its heritages, and its aporias. It will become obvious that I couldn't escape the academic law of organizing books in three parts; but also, so I hope, by respecting as scrupulously as possible the constraint of the situation (and the contextualization) that gave rise to each text, I victoriously disabused myself of any illusions of linear succession (and thus—I will return to this point—of the "history of ideas"). Without claiming to *exhaust* all the dimensions of a genealogy of the becomings that I just evoked (becoming-citizen of the subject, becoming-subject of the citizen), I grouped my essays under the following three rubrics: first, the auto-enunciation of the subject, whose guiding thread is the substantive and speculative usage of personal pronouns in different European languages and, in particular, of the "first person" (supposing that it can be separated from other pronouns, or from the other as such); second, the historicization of the communal "we," which Hegel problematized with unmatched depth, combining spiritualization and socialization, thanks to which one can go on to study the "reversals" that sustained thinking about the political subject in the epoch of bourgeois citizenship; and, third, the individualization of the subject by means of his subjection to the law and the institution of "judgment," which Freudian psychoanalysis interpreted in terms of the constitution of the "superego," and which it remains important to counterbalance with an analysis of an institutional *transgression* not only expressing the logic of desire but also the antinomies of knowledge, the dilemmas of social normalization, and resistances to the imposition of power.

I would like to add a few words on each of these constellations not in order to extract their lessons in advance but rather to describe their organization.

In the first part, I assemble studies of Descartes (the *ego sum, ego existo* from the *Meditations*), Locke (his invention of "consciousness" as the reciprocity of what I am and what I possess: *self* and *own*), Rousseau (not the Rousseau of *The Social Contract*, although it serves as a counterpart to everything that follows, but of *La Nouvelle Héloïse*, where he confers a revolutionary utopian form upon the classical analysis of the passions), and finally Derrida and the problematic of "sense certainty" (which he both prolongs and deconstructs by submitting it to the "law of genre"). Many other discussions would undoubtedly be necessary here.[15] My first thesis is that, in order to grasp what made the first-person enunciation "I think" (and, secondarily, "I want," or "I desire," "I believe," or "I sense") into the *focus imaginarius* of the representations of classical understanding,[16] one must begin with the great divergence between Descartes and Locke (today obscured both by the heritage of academic histories of philosophy and by the "spontaneous philosophy" of cognitivism): on Descartes's side, a *vindication of the subject* against the very divine omnipotence that creates and conserves it (the Third Meditation where the ego distinguishes itself logically and existentially)[17]; on Locke's side, a discourse on the *appropriation of things* by the work of consciousness, which incorporates disparate ideas into one and the same "personal identity." As I have done elsewhere, I claim in this book that we must completely dismantle the historiographic myth of Descartes as the "inventor of consciousness," give to Locke what belongs to Locke, and thereby free Descartes to occupy another position (ethico-political rather than ontological and epistemological), in order to frame appropriately the question of the "combined figure" whose effects run through modernity, in the form of transcendental psychology, analytics and phenomenology.[18] Rather than follow out this line of argument (which I certainly don't pretend is straight), I want to add a second thesis, which leads the reader down another path: the bypass or byway where the ego is always already constrained to find itself in the vicinity of an "*other*"—who is never, precisely, an alter ego (who does not become such without conflict)—and thereby to exit its soliloquy.[19] Accordingly, I borrow the title of the first section of the book from Rousseau's dialogue, *Rousseau Judge of Jean-Jacques*: "Our true *self* is not entirely within us."[20] As I will show, it is in the epistolary novel, *La Nouvelle Heloïse*, that I have found one of the subtlest expositions in the classical age of the problematic of the *passionate relation between subjects* (and its topological schemas: the triangle, the couple, the network). The necessary counterpart of this exposition is the explanation, in modern terms, of the relation between the question of the soul (or what "remains" of it after the theoretical revolutions of the seventeenth century) and the question of *sexual difference*, with its affective and social functions.[21] I believe that one can move from this point, not too arbitrarily, to the "postmodern" question of difference, which is no longer a matter of the transcendental subject, in a position-limit of interiority-exteriority with respect to the field of experience, but rather the quasi-transcendental relation immanent to acts of speech (I would also say, in classical terms: "commerce") whereby this experience is constituted through the conjunction and disjunction of subjects when they coexist and present themselves to one another. In our day, Derrida stands as the indefatigable interpreter of the responsibility that difference institutes and that transforms all "appropriation" into "expropriation."[22]

Is the relation to the other—and to the *différance* of the other—synonymous with *intersubjectivity*? Yes and no—as contemporary philosophical debates have amply shown. Nonetheless, it remains significant that the greatest French commentator on Hegel's *Phenomenology of Spirit* (Jean Hyppolite) read in it the upsurge of the problematic of intersubjectivity, right on the level of the extraordinary statement around which the entire book gravitates: *Ich, das Wir, und Wir, das Ich ist.*[23] Following his lead, I seized the occasion of an invitation from Pierre Macherey to research the provenance of this statement and to discuss the modality of its enunciation—work that allowed me to construct the entire second part of this book, devoted to the "communal subject" (and to the problem of the subject of community), as a commentary on Hegel and a few immediately posterior authors who offer a counterpoint to him (Marx, Tolstoy). Such commentary, I believe, offers the key to the problematic of "being in common" as the formation of a "common being" (and thus of a *reciprocity* of individual and social subjectivity), making it possible to grasp the prolonged dominion of this problematic and its difficulties.[24] It offers the key because the *Phenomenology* is both the most novelistic of Hegel's texts—perhaps the only one that rivals, in this respect, the great *Bildungsromanen* that were contemporary with it—and one of the most *political*. It is just as political, certainly, as *Elements of the Philosophy of Right* from 1820, although in a diametrically opposed fashion, since it is radically *non-statist*.[25] The singularity of the Phenomenologist is best appreciated by highlighting the connection between the intersubjectivity of the "I/We" to another problematic whose articulation is borrowed directly from social and political language: that of the "action [or the operation] of all and each" (*Tun Aller und Jeder*). Hegel aligns both under an enigmatic category that belongs at once to the dialectic of Spirit and its alienation (but can also be found throughout the work of those who carry it on—in particular, that of Marx and the Marxists): *die Sache selbst*.

I won't yet do a detailed examination of these articulations, each of which, in a sense, constitutes a "name of the subject." I would like to suggest, urging the reader to work out for himself the consequences that follow from the linkage between metaphysics and politics, another name under which one could try to think the "historical" matter, the "spiritual" substance, and the "social" effectivity of this *thing itself* upon which, within the chain of "figures" of consciousness, Hegel confers the decisive function of operating the return of consciousness toward historicity and concrete universality. It is quite simply the constituent power of subjects who act together, knowingly or unknowingly, sometimes by means of "national-popular" *praxis* (such as the praxis which, shortly before Hegel, a jurist-philosopher like Sieyès and the revolutionary inheritors of Locke, Spinoza, and Rousseau welcomed onto the scene of history), sometimes by means of productive "commerce" or the emergence of a civil society whose no less revolutionary effects were announced by the Scottish Enlightenment.[26] This notion of constituent power—troubled from within by duality or scission—is not only opposed to an "objective spirit" incorporated into morals and institutions; it also goes beyond or exceeds itself in the diverse directions that, in the *Phenomenology of Spirit*, Hegel attempted to relegate to the margins of his subjective equation. He aligns it, in particular, with the historical event par excellence—which, in the nineteenth century, would be either *war* or *revolution* (or a combination of both)—or with an *objective structure* that would be subjacent to the commerce among men, that is, the worldwide circulation of *commodities*.[27] This is why, in counterpoint to my rereadings of Hegel, I include in this volume analyses of Tolstoy and the two Marxes ("young" and "old"), which show that the same "thing" does not always correspond to the same subjects nor the same objects.[28]

In the third section of this volume, I explore new terrain (perhaps the other side of the preceding terrain?). Relying upon a play of syntax that will certainly remain untranslatable, I entitled it: "Du droit—à la transgression."[29] Within different contexts, I reflect upon the antinomies of judgment as figures of the becoming-subject of citizens. To introduce this new combination of texts and historical analyses, I would recall the order in which the chapters were composed, different than the order in which they are arranged here. The point of departure, chronologically, was the essay, "Private Crime, Public Madness," which I wrote in 1990 for a volume of the *Nouvelle Encyclopédie Diderot* entitled *Le citoyen fou*.[30] This is the third installment, then, of the research I was doing at the time on the institutions of "postrevolutionary" citizenship. I had personal reasons for investigating the disjunctions and recuperations of crime and madness: Althusser died alone and desperate, ten years after killing his wife and "benefiting" from a dismissal of his case accompanied by psychiatric administrative detention.[31] Most of all, however, I see retrospectively that, as a result of the Socialist government's project of reforming the penal and civil codes at that time, we were all (in our capacities as jurists, magistrates, psychiatrists, historians, philosophers, and sociologists) taking part in one of the last great "internal critiques" of the apparatus of *liberal* thought, which, born of postrevolutionary codes, would increasingly fall prey to the politics of "risk management," the "defense of society," and the "society of control."[32] This apparatus of thought (or this "knowledge-power"), which aims to maintain the theoretical difference between medical norm and penal law at the very heart of their practical complementarity, perhaps constitutes the major institutional condition of the political mode of subjectivizing "bourgeois-citizens," coordinating their *participation* and their *responsibility* (or, if one prefers, subordinating their access to rights to their ability to recognize their duties). Not only can liberalism not "defend" the freedom of individual subjects without controlling or limiting them, but, at the same time, it never ceases to threaten them, because the space that it concedes to such freedom is a narrow and uncertain path between the Charybdis of penalization and the Scylla of medicalization.

It might seem that such an approach to the question of the judging and judged subject, to which I was led by circumstances, represents no more than Marxist or Foucauldian "sociologism." One might claim that I take no interest in the inherent rationality of juridical norms, pay no attention to Freud, and only indirectly evoke the Kantian basis of the question of responsibility, articulating moral obligation in relation to legal constraints, which changes modality but never loses its effectiveness from classical idealism to modern positivism. Fifteen years later, an invitation from the Séminaire Interuniversitaire Européen d'Enseignement et de Recherche en Psychopathologie et Psychanalyse (directed by Fethi Benslama) would offer me the chance to correct the "impasse on Freud" and to exhume the part of the underpinnings of law that one might call, once again, quasi-transcendental. Following the method of historical epistemology, I centered my discussion upon a hypothesis concerning the "invention of the superego" (which Freud postulated as the unconscious authority to "discipline and punish" applied to oneself), which staged an "encounter" between psychoanalysis and law as a *conceptual* determination implicated within a *personal* altercation. Most of all, however, with the help of Freud and Kelsen I sought to clarify the mechanism of the "interpellation of subjects as individuals" that goes by way the internalization of guilt or the anteriority of punishment with respect to crime.[33] I thus found myself in a position to deploy (if not, properly speaking, to theorize) a constellation of secularized and democratized figures of subjection—typically *bourgeois*, undoubtedly—which reignites (for the last time? how to know?) the foundational millennial quarrel (in the West? or also elsewhere?) between "self-judgment" and "judgment of others" at the origin of the thematic of conscience, to which, by analogy, I give the name of reflexive individualism. But, even more unexpectedly—or so it would seem—I could redeploy in the same terms (or strangely neighboring terms) the political dimension of the idea of *public crime*, or what is thereby categorized as long as the State imposes upon the citizen its "monopoly of legitimate judgment" (which is ever since Hobbes's "Who shall be Judge?" one of the principal figures of the State's pretention to sovereignty). It is obviously not by chance that a writer such as Blanchot, when it behooved him to find insubordinate words to claim justice against the reason of State or reestablish the primacy of rights over duty (which is the very essence, as we know, of citizenship as an insurrectionary figure), went looking for these words in an inconvenient alliance between the republican traditions of resistance and the Sadeian discourse of transgression (whose blurry distinction between "crime" and "madness" would concern him once again a few years later). The transgression of the law, albeit the *law of transgression*, which can never be circumscribed once and for all within the bounds of the public or the private, is here thought as the necessary destiny of the subjectivity that "doubles" citizenship.

I would now like to enlarge the foregoing summary with a discussion of method, which I consider to be a matter of principle: almost all the essays in this volume consist of *readings*; they bear upon *texts* or traverse the interpretation of texts. These texts are always rigorously individualized not only in the sense they are authored but also in that, above all, they are each time unique. I compare these texts to one another but I do not discuss "works" in the sense that literary and university ideology gives this term, nor, even less, the "systems" or "tendencies" that would be represented in each product. I propose a re-reading of the *Second Meditation* and not of Cartesianism, of *Julie, or the New Heloïse* and not of Rousseauism, of the *Phenomenology of Spirit* (or a few moments therein) and not of Hegelianism, of the section from *Capital* on "commodity fetishism" and not of Marxism, and so forth. I thereby situate my work, of course, within the line of a "theoretical practice" of the relations between discourse and historicity, whose formation, at a certain moment, I basically had the opportunity to observe from the inside out and to attend the constitutive debates. This is my own manner of submitting the question—Must there be a theoretical practice?—to the test of time and discussion. More precisely, I would insist upon four points:

1. Only singular texts (whose borders, of course, immediately pose a problem: there is no reason why their limits must coincide with those of a book, which, in any case, are not always stable) articulate *determinate* theses and pose *determinate* problems of interpretation. This is due to the fact, especially in philosophy (although, in this respect, philosophy proves inseparable from literary activity, as does scientific thinking), that an author (before the invention of "cut-and-paste," which can always do without word processing . . .) *never writes the same text twice*. Variation is already the expression of a dialectic; it translates the "restlessness" of thinking outside of which there are no ideas. A good illustration of this can be found in the discussion that I devote to a statement from Descartes's *Meditations*: to write "*ego sum, ego existo*" is not to write "*cogito, sum*," even if an entire historiographical tradition proceeds as if this were the case and constructs its interpretation on such a basis (perhaps Descartes was the first to *interpret himself* in this sense, which reveals much about a philosopher's complex relationship with his own texts). A fortiori, one cannot work—as the representatives of the "analytic" tradition do—with simple *reconstructions of arguments*, substituting them for texts (although one can work, often fruitfully, upon such reconstruction itself, as a form of writing and a "secondary" philosophical invention).

2. Consequently, only with a singular text—or even with the singularity of statements in a text that is itself singular—can a reader and commentator, who might be a translator, enter into a dialogic relation (which I have constantly attempted to do) that comprises an element of imagination (e.g., imagine what Locke would have advised Pierre Coste to incorporate into his translator's notes in order to "avoid" Malebranche or what Freud would

have thought of Kelsen's objections to his theory of *Massenbildungen*) but that also must stand up to textual counterproof. In such a fashion, the commentator also attempts to insert himself as a third party and even to make himself, after the fact, into the (more or less "vanishing") mediator of an incomplete or interrupted dialogue between authors.[34] Who would believe that Rousseau wrote "the common ego" (*le moi commun*) as counterpoint to the "common good," in order to name the subject of the General Will, without reference to the fact that Descartes—followed by Pascal and Condillac—invented "this ego," "the ego" (*le moi*)?[35] Or that Hegel, without a conversation with Descartes, Locke, and Rousseau, could give the name *das Selbst* to the subjectivity of substance coinciding with its historicity or to the double movement of the internalization-memorialization (*Erinnerung*) and expropriation-appropriation (*Entäusserung* and *Aufbewahrung*) of the "objects" of consciousness? Or that Freud, without knowledge of Nietzsche (which he denied) or his documented reading of the Scottish empiricists, who invented the "impartial spectator" (Hume, if not Smith), could have "negated" the Cartesian gap between the *Ego* and the *Ille* in his conceptualization of an unconscious "Über-ich"? There must be traces of all this. Above all, an echo must resonate in *our own* interrogations or those of "our time."

3. Texts, much more than "authors" (and a fortiori "men"), have an intrinsic relation to conjunctures, whose contradictions they cast into relief and thus allow to be "problematized." I upheld this thesis in 1993 when I presented my work (which already included a provisional version of the present volume) for the university Habilitation, and I can only repeat myself here:

> Philosophy constantly endeavors to untie and retie from the inside the knot between conjuncture and writing. . . . I hold, then, that philosophy is never independent of specific conjunctures. It should be clear that I use the word in a qualitative rather than a quantitative sense, stressing by it the very brief or prolonged event of a crisis, a transition, a suspense, a bifurcation, which manifests itself by irreversibility, i.e., in the impossibility of acting and thinking as before . . .
>
> Such a notion poses the immanence of philosophical work to history, but it is resolutely opposed to all the variants of the notion of *Zeitgeist*, or of the "culture" or "spirit" of a time, including the form that Marx's concept "dominant ideology" gives it and the form Foucault gives it by means of the concept of *épistémè*. On the other hand, this notion seeks to link itself, freeing up the concept's critical and analytical potential, with Foucault's *points d'hérésie*—heretical points "shared by" a number of philosophies, insofar as these points designate in their very language what is at stake in the confrontation. Marx's "contradictions," Spinoza's "aporias," Descartes's "ambivalence," and so on, around which I have organized the study of their argumentations and concepts, should help to clarify one another as terms of a contradictory conjuncture and as reflection of these collective *points d'hérésie at the heart of* each philosophical discourse . . .[36]

This leads us to a second point: not only do philosophers always write *within a conjuncture*, but conversely, within the conjuncture, *they write*. The "think," no doubt (how could they not?), but only through writing and in constant confrontation with the problems writing poses for them, while also benefiting from the terms and conveniences it offers. All philosophy is essentially written, and philosophers have a particular relation to writing that necessarily includes the issue of its forms, "technical" modes or genres . . . or "styles." More: the philosopher's original relation to writing is determined by the fact that a singular experience of thinking is always an experience of writing, and that "philosophical practice" is one that, consciously or not, seeks in and by means of writing to go back to the very constraints that the latter imposes on thinking.

From that point in my presentation, I went on to examine a few modalities of this constraint: *aporia*, *dissemination*, and the *intersection of the signifying chain* (to which I will return).

4. If we uphold that it is the object—or better the interlocutor—that we encounter in texts, which are always "knotted" to singular conjunctures, when we rely upon them to discover the formulation of a problem (such as that of subjectivity), or the reasons for its evolution or permanence, the forms of its division into antithetical solutions, then we arrive at two new theses, which, I increasingly believe (along with others to whom I am often linked by work in common), are correlative.

The first thesis is that there is no "metalanguage" in philosophy that would make it possible to reformulate texts in universal, descriptive, or systematic terms, "elevating" them above their letter in order to extract their rational kernel or to reduce them an ultimate materiality, more fundamental than their own. Of course, this critique of metalanguage is quite prevalent, appearing in various modalities in a broad swath of contemporary philosophy—especially in Wittgenstein (although he and his inheritors often restrict the scope of their critique by denying the actually "philosophical" character of the questions that they address and the language games that they describe). In fact, this critique is already present in Hegel, once again in the *Phenomenology*, but in a very strange modality that must be deciphered and turned against itself: In order to let "spirit" speak as such, which he considers to be the common being of systems (and which he ends up calling "absolute knowledge"), Hegel refuses to describe and classify these systems;[37] he forges an original language that lets texts dialogue among themselves, albeit at the price, obviously, of a "translation" (a translation which, in practice, is shot through with these texts' own idiom). This is why—outside of rare exceptions (like Sophocles's *Antigone*)—his writing constantly draws upon prophets, orators, philosophers, and writers who always go unnamed. In my own book, all things being relative, I wished to do the opposite, because, since Hegel, Spirit is absent (except as a historically bounded philosophical concept): I thus replaced continuity with discontinuity, anonymity with the identification of authors and even their personification, the search for a unique idiom through attention to the particularities of each text (including linguistic particularities) that resist integration. I wished to practice what Deleuze calls "disjunctive synthesis." The result, I think, is not antidialectical. Beyond the discussions that I devote to Hegel in the central section of this book, perhaps the book might contribute to clarifying questions of how the dialectic is used in present day philosophy. My hope is that it offers access not to absolute knowledge but to a field of transformations and contestations where others will also be able to enter.

But this thesis is inseparable from another that concerns the relation between *translation* and *tradition*. To say that philosophers write in a particular fashion is to say that they write in a given language or in an "idiom" whereby they seek with an abundance of inventiveness (not necessarily jargon . . .) to compensate for the lack of universality. Today, there is general agreement on this point. This is why a portion of philosophical work has begun to shift toward the systematic examination of the effects of translation in philosophy, and thus also of the "untranslatables" and of the process of "translating the untranslatables" as a moment of conceptual invention.[38] In the chapters that make up this volume, I propose numerous applications of this idea (and, in point of fact, it is possible that none of my analyses can be separated from it). I took maniacal care to discuss philosophers' texts in their own language, a language confronted with other languages that they practice and transpose. In this respect, I have no fear of appearing pedantic or nostalgic for a "European order of languages" which is no doubt integral to an imperial project whose ongoing consequences we must evaluate and correct. What I do fear is that the weaknesses of my philology and the limits of my linguistic knowledge will be all too obvious. But it was necessary to take this risk in order to highlight, in particular, what a moment ago (citing my previous redaction) I called the relationship of texts to the signifying chains that they intersect (Nietzsche's *Zeichenkettel*)[39] and that determine in essential part their "material conditions of writing," provoking them and subjecting them to a mechanism of interpellation sometimes hailing from a very great distance. There is definitely nothing unexpected about the indices of such chains: the constant dependency of classical European philosophers with respect to a *scriptural* (biblical) basis at once relayed and redeemed by theology, and the recourse of theoreticians of modern citizenship to formulas of *ancient* republicanism and cosmopolitanism such as they were handed down by Aristotle and the Stoics. However, the objections that my readings have provoked (certain of which I have accepted since they come from specialists much more expert than I am on "my" own authors) bear witness that the *modality* of this intersection (the identification of the letter and the gauging of its effects) is always going to pose problems. I have no intention of reducing such complex problems to a single formula, whether it be Descartes's "repetition" of a foundational utterance of Jewish and then Christian monotheism, or Locke's "transmission" of the theme of the double personality from Augustinian religious morals to criminal psychology of the positivist age,[40] or Rousseau's "inversion" (within the framework of his enlarged familial utopia) of the relationship between activity and passivity that form the metaphysical horizon of ancient citizenship, or Freud's "return" to a theory of the "parts of the soul" that only frees itself from cosmological myth in order to deploy the allegory of theater and the tribunal. . . . On the other hand, I wish to acknowledge in advance, as friends have occasionally pointed out to me (in particular, Jean-Luc Marion, Jacques Derrida, and Bertrand Ogilvie), that many questions are left obscure or formulated in an imprecise manner, whether they concern the difference between the intersection with religious utterance and the repetition of an ontological thesis, or the difference between a metaphysics of substance (founded upon the speculative hierarchies of form and matter or active and passive) and an anthropology of the "condition" that is inseparable from a political order. What remains certain is that all of these questions radically escape the genre of the "history of ideas"; for, each element of method that I underscored above—the primacy of texts, the dialogic form of their interpretation, the knot between writing and conjuncture, and the procedure of infinite translation imposed by the idiom—constitutes a *condition of impossibility* for such a history. If I succeeded in extracting *philosophical* discussion of the subject from the *history of ideas* without thereby removing it from *history*, I would already consider myself quite satisfied.[41]

After recalling a "question" that I raised and the premature response that I thought it possible to offer, after summarizing the three paths that I took to interrogate the utterances of the subject of philosophy (autoreference, community, judgment), after sketching the rules of "method" that underpin my readings, what's next? Further questions, of course. For the moment, I do no more than sketch out their basic direction, which is illustrated in my concluding essay, "The Ill-Being of the Subject: Bourgeois Universality and the Anthropological Differences." Schematically speaking, what I tried to show is that the "site" of the *question of the subject* and its emancipation in the modern era (or better, in the field that we can only problematically call "modernity," to which we always belong, at least in part: this is ultimately *our question*, the question of "what we are" and, above all, what we are *becoming*), tends to coincide with the jointure of a political discourse on *the universal* (not only universal "values" but also universal *rights*) and a discourse of *anthropological difference* (itself divided into multiple schemas of identification and normalization, of which Foucault's reflection on the "abnormal" provides a typical albeit not directly generalizable example). This jointure, however, as necessary as it might always be, remains very deeply contradictory and, at the limit, untenable. *There is no way to sustain to this jointure*, or establish oneself therein, and yet *it is the place from which* the subject, indissociably individual and collective, *speaks itself as the question of its own "becoming citizen"* (or, as Arendt would say, its own "right to have rights").[42] The "care of the self" inherent to any subjective position, to any movement of subjectivation that would also be an emancipation, is thereby condemned not only to "disquiet" or a state of "unhappy consciousness," in the words of the classical philosophers who thus secularized the religious theme of the uncertainty of salvation, not only to translate the "discontents" (*Unbehagen*) of civilization that Freud taught us to derive from unconscious guilt or the "strangeness to self" (*Entfremdung*) that Marx and certain Marxists rooted in the alienation (*Entäusserung*) of labor power into conscious experiences or intersubjective relations, but also to seek the "being" of the subject in a much more objective (if not more fundamental) structure that at once *inscribes* it within the universal and violently *forbids it* from finding therein a "recognizable" place.

This is due, first of all, to the fact that this indefinite "place" (*topos aoristos*) of subjectivation is essentially a "place of relation" (or a place "for relation," for the institution of what, at a certain moment—at the turn of the nineteenth century—modernity began to call "the social relation")[43] and also to the fact that the privileged form in which universality is "knotted" to the subject or the multiplicity of differences that characterize the "human" is bound up with the recognition and revindication of rights is the *political community*. Such a community may or may not conceive of itself as particular or as absolutely universal, or derive the right to have rights from anthropological "characteristics," or ignore these characteristics in the name of the transcendental equivalence of all manners of "binding" human subjects to one another, or *fixate* differences within categories, classifications, or a hierarchized set of castes, or make them *fluctuate* at the whim of "pure" relations of forces or configurations of desire.[44] Such a situation, not contingent but structural, in which the double bind is the rule, affecting the very existence of subjects (their being of relation) is what—in an attempt to connect questions of civilization and its discontents to those of historical alienation in order to inscribe them within the determinations and differentiations of a structure—I call "ill-being" [*malêtre*] (or that which, if you will, makes a "being"—*Wesen*—into a "monster"—*Unwesen*).[45]

For good reason, one might ask: Why is this situation specifically "modern"? Mustn't we suppose that the condition or ultimate horizon of *all* subjectivation has always been the inscription of subjects within the universal via the problematic mediation of a real or, most often, and ideal community, and that all representation of the human is accompanied by a more or less immediate representation of "differences" whose function is at once *to mark the boundaries of the human* (or of belonging to the human "race": with respect to "animality" but also the "divine" or, generically, the "superhuman") and *to place humanity in relation to itself* in the person of the individuals or subjects who compose it (the women and the men but also the adults and the children, the healthy and the sick, the upstanding and the criminals, the compatriots and the foreigners, etc.)? This is certainly the case, even if the retrospective projection or the generalization of categories—such as that, precisely, of the "subject"—always poses problems. Accordingly, my goal is not simply to situate the "ill-being" of the modern subject and to mark its structural necessity within the perpetual difficulty of defining or instituting the universal, first inscribing community within it and then determining whether the role of anthropological differences is central or marginal to the constitution of that community. Instead, I relate this "ill-being" to a specifically "bourgeois" (or *civic-bourgeois*) modality of the institution of the universal, which makes of it a directly political objective, immanent to the institution of citizenship and simultaneously to a profound historical transformation—which is, in a sense, an overturning—of the function of "anthropological differences" and their definition. My discussion, as we shall see, turns upon a reading against the grain of Marx's famous critique of the universalism of the "rights of man and the citizen" (in "On the Jewish Question" from 1844) and its relation to the no less famous formula from the *Theses on Feuerbach* (1845) which declares that "the human being [*das menschliche Wesen*] is no abstraction inhabiting each single individual [*dem einzelnen innenwohend*], but rather, in its reality it is the ensemble of social relations [*das ensemble der gesellschaftlichen Verhältnisse*]." These formulas, it seems to me, do not so much function to "reduce" the idea of ("abstract") man in general, upon which modern political constitutions found the rights of the citizen, to *a bourgeois representation of the human* (which implies, in particular, the "naturalness" of possessive individualism or what the classical age called "egoism"), no matter the force of such a critical operation. They should be read as a manner of *posing the problem of anthropology* immanent to the bourgeois constitution of the political (adopting the term "bourgeois" in its institutional sense, which makes it the other name for citizen).[46]

It thus becomes necessary to ask: What singularizes *bourgeois universality* in relation to *theological* (or, more precisely, monotheist) universalities? The answer is precisely the fact of bringing the universal "from heaven down to earth" (or, as Marx shows, transforming the "heavens" into an alienated institutional construction at the very heart of earthly "social relations"). Or else, in relation to *cosmological* universalities (referred to the order of the *cosmos* as their ultimate being), the answer is the fact of passing from nature to the historico-political constitution or the "construction" of the universal (from *phusis* to *nomos* as the essence of the universal).[47] And these answers raise a further question: What charges political community (or, if one prefers, the *civitas terrena*) with the much more *direct, practical,* and *secular* task of the actualization (*Verwicklichung* and *Verweltlichung*) of universality (neither "given" in the natural order of the world or "hoped for" in an eschatological beyond) even as it renders this task much more problematic? This time, it seems to me, the answer is precisely the fact that, from now on, anthropological differences are at once *disqualified* as justifications for discrimination at the level of the fundamental rights of "human beings" (first or last among them, the right which harbors all others within itself, is precisely that of *access to citizenship*) and *disqualifying* as privileged means of legitimizing the internal segregations and exclusions that take citizenship (that is, full and entire, or "active" citizenship) away from a sector of human beings who are formally "equal by rights." In other terms, anthropological differences realize the living paradox of an inegalitarian construction of egalitarian citizenship; or rather, that of a universalist limitation (founded upon general or even generic traits of the human race) of what lends the "political" universal an at least virtually unlimited scope. We might well say that, on the level of "social relations," we witness the emergence of an *Unwesen* or "ill-being" of *Wesen* (of "being-in-relation") itself. And we could attempt to describe, logically and phenomenologically, the consequences that arise when the place of subjectivation, as a conflictual process of subjection and emancipation, is situated in the vicinity of this impossibility that must be ceaselessly deferred; or when the subjectivation of the citizen (and first access to citizenship) passes through a political confrontation with this contradiction.

Therefore, I reprised the schema of anthropological difference, which, in my essay, "Private Crime, Public Madness," I thought it possible to derive from the analyses whereby Foucault constructed the figure of the Abnormal during the revolutionary period. I attempted to delineate anew the limits of these analyses and their epistemological principle (focusing, in particular, on the uncertainty that affects the definition of the "abnormal"—and, consequently, that of the "normal" itself—when it is, from the outset, consigned to the registers of the pathological and delinquency) in order to extend them hypothetically to other "cases" of anthropological differences no less fundamental to the institutionalization of access to citizenship: that of sexual difference, of course, but also that of intellectual difference (or the difference between "body-men" and "mind-men"),[48] and, first of all, those of "racial" or "cultural" differences (which are, in the modern era, constantly shifting from one semantic code to another). At every turn, I attempted to hold different registers together: that of a discrimination or, at the limit, of an internal "exclusion," whose causes and effects can be entirely situated within the field of politics, and whose foundation—or, if one prefers, mode of definition—demands that *it precede itself* in the form of knowledge about the humanity of the human being, and which is less a matter of the demarcation of the inhuman than of the production of a "sub-humanity" or a *deficient* humanity; and that of a problematization of the subject that does not so much aim to make it into the support for a generic human essence or the addressee of a transcendental interpellation but rather the object of continual differentiation, in a sense that is never "settled" or "determined" in a univocal fashion, and that, sooner or later, emerges as the bearer of rebellion and the agent of a revindication of equality and access to citizenship who begins with the contestation of differences: either in themselves or in their institutional function.[49]

In this manner, I thought it possible to discover new terms to approach two classical philosophical questions that undoubtedly haunt the ensemble of these studies. I do not pretend to have addressed these questions as such, but perhaps to have displaced them from one formulation or one language to another. The first question is that of the possibility of *philosophical anthropology*, or rather the sense of the *anthropological question* in philosophy. This question is never independent from history—neither the "long" history of the metamorphoses of the universal and its languages nor the "recent" history of academic debates around the question, "What is man?" Once again, however, one must be wary of undertaking a *historicist* treatment of what is profoundly *historical*. The best way to proceed, then, is by repetition—that is, to ask why, for at least three generations and across two national borders (in the form of the great *translatio quaestionum* of German universities during the 1920s and 1930s to the French philosophical institution from the 1950s to the 1970s, and, in a different manner, American anthropology and political theory), *the anthropological question appeared inseparable from the question of humanism*, if not confused with it.[50] It is possible, however, that in the aftermath of this "humanist controversy," which lingered in the background of the debate over "the subject" a few decades ago (still going strong at the moment when, as I have recalled, Jean-Luc Nancy proffered his theoretical challenge), this confusion was gradually laid to rest.[51] Since then, it has become perfectly possible to reflect on the status of the anthropological question in philosophy without any position-taking for or against humanism, or rather with a retrospective understanding of why, only under determinate historical and intellectual conditions, could they appear to be two sides of the same coin.[52] I believe that the problem of the relation between "bourgeois universalism" and the "anthropological question" is rooted at much deeper and more general level than the humanism debate would suggest, no matter whether the humanism in question is moral or metaphysical. But this mutual inherence only becomes clear when, in addition to considering a *being in relation* (which Marx posited in the sixth of his *Theses on Feuerbach*) or a *subject divided* by repressing a part of its psyche (and thus defined by the impossibility of full "self-presence") that Freud systematized, we also take into account the *at once irreducible and indeterminable differences* that are implicated within the construction or institutionalization of any social relation and that "politically" overdetermine any unconscious scission or division of the subject. This is to say that the adjective "anthropological," more than a given field or a regulative idea, designates a critical question apropos of the necessary but ambivalent relation that exists between philosophical or sociological concepts and modern politics.

Thereby we trench upon the second question: What do we call "modernity"? How do we delimit it? How do we "find ourselves" within it or "find one another" (or not)? By what indices would we recognize (or not) the emergence of a "postmodernity"? In the essays that make up this book, I do no more, in a sense, that continually work on these questions.[53]

Of course, any response that limited itself to repeating or summarizing the themes of my argument would have a tautological character: modernity is the age or rather the "moment" defined by the overlapping and contradictory processes of becoming-citizen of the subject and the becoming-subject of the citizen; modernity is the "moment" at which the relation between the relation of the ego to the self (or to the "proper") and the relation of the ego to the other is perceived as a conflict or an internal contradiction; modernity is the "moment" at which the relation between the common and the universal can no longer be defined either as the inclusion of the common in the universal (which is fundamentally the position of ancient cosmopolitanism), nor as the universal extension of community (which is the revolutionary basis of Christian and Islamic political theologies), but rather becomes a *gap* at the heart of the universal itself (whether it be Hegel's constitutional State or Smith's "universal mercantile republic" or Marx's "division of labor at the stage of totality"[54]); modernity is the "moment" at which the assignation of social responsibility (the "judgment of others") must be referred back to an instance of "self-judgment," which makes the *antinomy* that used to characterize the "sovereign" (identity of morality and crime, the identity of respect for laws and their transgression) *the subject's own problem* (the object of its "care" and the "care" that it calls for); and finally, modernity is the "moment" at which the human can only become coextensive with the political (which no society has ever known) on condition that it be opposed to itself as the unity of a "species" and a division among "genres," the one always the condition of the other. The advantage of this last formulation above all the preceding ones (which it does not invalidate in the least) is that, even as it gives "modernity" a content that corresponds to *the affirmation of a new principle* (or at least a new question), it also obligates us never to grasp it independently from its *reverse side*, which contests it from the *inside*.[55] Most of all, this formulation obligates us to posit otherwise the question of the temporality wherein the conflict of bourgeois universality with itself unfolds: not as a time of succession but rather a time of precedence or a time of deferred action. Accordingly, the question (or controversy that marked the 1980s and 1990s as well as the humanist controversy of the 1960s and 1970s) that divides many of our contemporaries—and, on the horizon of this conflict, the wide field of "postmodern discourse" (Lyotard) or, on the contrary, the forward march of the "unfinished project of modernity" (Habermas)—is, in a sense, suspended. As Prime Minister Zhou Enlai is supposed to have said when asked about the meaning of the French Revolution: "it is too soon to tell"—that is, one day, the question will have to be posed otherwise.[56]

For their interest and their critical reflection on one or another of the developments contained in this book, I would like to offer my thanks to the philosophy students at the Universities of Paris I (Panthéon-Sorbonne) and Paris X (Nanterre, today called Paris Ouest), to the students in the Critical Theory Emphasis at the University of California at Irvine, at the Centro Franco-Argentino de Altos Estudios de la University of Buenos Aires, and at the Institute for Comparative Literature and Society at Columbia University, as well as to my colleagues and friends, Jonathan Arac, Fethi Benslama, Jean-Marie Beyssade, Christophe Bident, Olivier Bloch, Philippe Büttgen, Nestor Capdevila, Barbara Cassin, Michèle Cohen-Halimi, Janet Coleman, Alice Crary, Marc Crépon, Françoise

Dastur, Vincent Descombes, Françoise Duroux, Yves Duroux, Franck Fischbach, Didier Franck, Martine de Gaudemar, Suzanne Gearhart, Jean-Philippe Genet, Carlos Herrera, Maurizio Iacono, Claude Imbert, Christoph Jamme, Denis Kambouchner, Bruno Karsenti, Françoise Kerleroux, Pierre-Jean Labarrière, Sandra Laugier, Jean-Jacques Lecercle, Jean-Pierre Lefebvre, Alain de Libera, Béatrice Longuenesse, Pierre Macherey, Patrice Maniglier, Jean-Luc Marion, Giacomo Marramao, Natacha Michel, Jean-Claude Milner, Warren Montag, Michel Naepels, Soraya Nour, Bertrand Ogilvie, John Rajchman, François Regnault, Diogo Sardinha, Mariafranca Spallanzani, Gayatri Spivak, James Swenson, Emmanueal Terray, and Frédéric Worms.

Citizen Subject: Response to Jean-Luc Nancy's Question "Who Comes After the Subject?"

Both following Hegel and opposed to him, Heidegger proposes Descartes as the moment when the "sovereignty of the subject" is established (in philosophy), inaugurating the discourse of modernity. This supposes that man, or rather the *ego*, is determined and conceived of as subject (*subjectum*).

Doubtless, from one text to another, and sometimes even within the same "text" (I am primarily referring here to the *Nietzsche* of 1939–46), Heidegger nuances his formulation. At one moment he positively affirms that, in Descartes's *Meditations* (which he cites in Latin), the *ego* as consciousness (which he explicates as *cogito me cogitare*) is posited, founded as the *subjectum* (that which in Greek is called the *hypokeimenon*). This also has the correlative effect of identifying, for all modern philosophy, the *hypokeimenon* and the foundation of being with the being of the subject of thought, the other of the object. At another moment he is content to point out that this identification is implicit in Descartes, and that we must wait for Leibniz to see it made explicit ("called by its own name") and reflected as the identity of reality and representation, in its difference with the traditional conception of being.

The Myth of the "Cartesian Subject"

Is this nuance decisive? The fact is that it would be difficult to find the slightest reference to the "subject" as *subjectum* in the *Meditations*, and that in general the thesis that would posit the *ego* or the "I think/I am" (or the "I am a thinking thing") as subject, either in the sense of *hypokeimenon* or in the sense of the future *Subjekt* (opposed to *Gegenstandlichkeit*), does not appear anywhere in Descartes. By evoking an implicit definition, one that awaits its formulation, and thus a teleology of the history of philosophy (a lag of consciousness, or rather of language), Heidegger only makes his position more untenable, if only because Descartes's position is actually incompatible with this concept. This can easily be verified by examining both Descartes's use of the noun "subject," and the fundamental reasons why he does not name the thinking substance or "thinking thing" "subject."

The problem of substance, as is well known, appears fairly late in the course of the *Meditations*. It is posited neither in the presentation of the *cogito*, not when Descartes draws its fundamental epistemological consequence (the soul knows itself "more evidently, distinctly, and clearly" than it knows the body), but in the third meditation when he attempts to establish and to think the causal link between the "thinking thing" that the soul knows itself to be and the God the idea of whom it finds immediately in itself as the idea of the infinite being. But even there *it is not a question of the subject*. The term will appear only incidentally, in its scholastic meaning, in the "Responses to Objections," in the context of a discussion of the real difference between finite and infinite, and between thinking and extended substances, for which the *Principles* will later furnish a properly formulated definition. Along with these discussions, we must consider the one concerning the union of body and soul, the "third substance" constitutive of individuality, the theory of which will be elaborated in the "Sixth Meditation" and further developed in the *Treatise on the Passions*.

From consideration of these different contexts it becomes clear that the essential concept for Descartes is that of *substance*, in the new signification that he gives to it. This signification is not limited to objectifying, each on its own side, the *res cogitans* and the *res extensa*: It allows the entire set of causal relations between (infinite) God and (finite) things, between ideas and bodies, between my soul and my (own) body, to be thought. It is thus primarily a relational concept. We should understand by this that the essential part of its theoretical function is accomplished by putting distinct "substances" into relation with one another, generally in the form of a unity of opposites. The name of substance (that is its principal, negative characteristic) cannot be attributed in a univocal fashion to both the infinite (God) and the finite (creatures); it thus allows their difference to be thought, and nevertheless permits their dependence to be understood (for only a substance can "cause" another substance: this is its second characteristic). Likewise, thought and extension are really distinct substances, having no attributes whatsoever in common, and nevertheless the very reality of this distinction implies a substantial (non-accidental) union as the basis of our experience of our sensations. All these distinctions and oppositions finally find their coherence—if not the solution of the enigma they hold—in a *nexus* that is both hierarchical and causal, entirely regulated by the principle of the *eminent causality*, in God, of the "formal" or "objective" relations between created substances (that is, respectively, those relations that consist of actions and passions, and those that consist of representations). It is only because all (finite) substances are eminently caused by God (have their eminent cause, or rather the eminence of their cause, in

God) that they are also in a causal relation among themselves. But, inversely, eminent causality—another name for positive infinity—could not express anything intelligible for us except for the "objective" unity of formally distinct causalities.

Thus, nothing is further from Descartes than a metaphysics of Substance conceived of as a univocal term. Rather, this concept has acquired a new equivocality in his work, without which it could not fill its structural function: to name in turn each of the poles of a topography in which I am situated simultaneously as cause and effect (or rather as a cause that it itself only an effect). It must be understood that the notion of the *subjectum/hypokeimenon* has an entirely evanescent status here. Descartes mentions it, in response to objections, only in order to make a scholastic defense of his *realist* thesis (every substance is the real subject of its own accidents). But it does not add any element of knowledge (and in particular not the idea of a "matter" distinct from "form") to the concept of substance. It is for this reason that substance is practically indiscernible from its principle attribute (comprehensible: extension, thought; or incomprehensible: infinity, omnipotence).

There is no doubt whatsoever that it is essential to characterize, in Descartes, the "thinking thing" that I am (therefore!) as substance or as substantial, in a nexus of substances that are so many *instances* of the metaphysical apparatus. But it is not essential to attach this substance to the representation of a *subjectum*, and it is in any case impossible *to apply the name of subjectum* to the *ego cogito*. On the other hand, it is possible and necessary to ask in what sense the human individual, composed of a soul, a body, and their unity, is the "subject" (*subjectus*) of a *divine sovereignty*. The representation of sovereignty is in fact implied by the ideal of eminence, and, inversely, the reality of finite things could not be understood outside of a specific dependence "according to which all things are subject to God."[1] That which is valid from an ontological point of view is also valid from an epistemological point of view. From the thesis of the "creation of eternal truths" to the one proper to the *Meditations* according to which the intelligibility of the finite is implied by the idea of the infinite, a single conception of the subjection of understanding and of science is affirmed, not of course to an external or revealed dogma, but to an internal center of thought whose structure is that of a sovereign decision, an absent presence, or a source of intelligibility that as such is incomprehensible.

Thus, the idea that causality and sovereignty can be converted into one another is conserved and even reinforced in Descartes. It could even be said that this idea is pushed to the limit—which is perhaps, for us in any case, the herald of a coming decomposition of this figure of thought. The obvious fact that an extreme intellectual tension results from it is recognized and constantly reexamined by Descartes himself. How can the absolute freedom of man—or rather of his will: but his will is the very essence of judgment—be conceived of as similar to God's without putting this subjection back into question? How can it be conceived of outside this subjection, for it is the *image* of another freedom, of another power? Descartes's thought, as we know, oscillates between two tendencies on this point. The first, mystical, consists in *identifying* freedom and subjection: to will freely, in the sense of necessary freedom, enlightened by true knowledge, is to coincide with the act by which God conserves me in a relative perfection. The other tendency, pragmatic, consists in *displacing* the question, playing on the topography of substances, making my subjection to God into the origin of my mastery over and possession of nature, and more precisely of the absolute power that I can exercise over my passions. There are no fewer difficulties in either one of these theses. This is not the place to discuss them, but it is clear that, in either case, freedom can in fact only be thought as the freedom of the *subject*, of the subjected being, that is, as a contradiction in terms.

Descartes's "subject" is thus still (more than ever) the *subjectus*. But what is the *subjectus*? It is the other name of the *subditus*, according to an equivalence practiced by all medieval political theology and systematically exploited by the theoreticians of absolute monarchy: the individual submitted to the *ditio*, to the sovereign authority of a prince, an authority expressed in his orders and itself legitimated by the Word of another Sovereign (the Lord God). "It is God who has established these laws in nature, just as a king establishes laws in his kingdom," Descartes will write to Mersenne (letter of 15 April 1630).[2] It is this very dependence that constitutes him. But Descartes's subject is not the *subjectum* that is widely supposed—even if, from the point of view of the object, the meaning has to be inverted—to be permanently present from Aristotle's metaphysics to modern subjectivity.

How is it, then, that they have come to be confused?[3] Part of the answer obviously lies in the effect, which continues to this very day, of Kantian philosophy and its specific necessity. Heidegger, both before and after the "turn," is clearly situated in this dependence. We must return to the very letter of the *Critique of Pure Reason* if we are to discover the origin of the projection of a transcendental category of the "subject" upon the Cartesian text. This projection and the distortion it brings with it (simultaneously subtracting something from and adding something to the *cogito*) are in themselves constitutive of the "invention" of the transcendental subject, which is inseparably a movement away from and an interpretation of Cartesianism. For the subject to appear as the originarily synthetic unity of the conditions of objectivity (of "experience"), first, the *cogito* must be reformulated not only as reflexivity, but as the thesis of the "I think" that "accompanies all my representations" (that is, as the thesis of self-consciousness, which Heidegger will state as: *cogito = cogito me cogitare*); then this self-consciousness must be distinguished both from the intuition of an intelligible being and from the intuition of the "empirical ego" in "internal sense"; and finally, "the paralogism of the substantiality" of the soul must be dissolved. In other words one and the same historico-philosophical operation *discovers the subject in the substance* of the Cartesian *cogito*, and *denounces the substance in the subject* (as transcendental illusion), thus installing Descartes in the situation of a "transition" (both ahead of *and* behind the time of history, conceived of as the history of the advent of the subject), upon which the philosophies of the nineteenth and twentieth centuries will not cease to comment.

Paraphrasing Kant himself, we can say that these formulations of the *Critique of Pure Reason* form the "unique text" from which the transcendental philosophies in particular "draw all their wisdom," for they ceaselessly reiterate the double rejection of substantiality and of phenomenality that forms the paradoxical being of the subject (being/non-being, in any case not a thing, not "categorizable," not "objectifiable").[4] And this is valid not only for the "epistemological" face of the subject, but for its practical face as well: in the last instance the transcendental subject that effectuates the nonsubstantial unity of the conditions of experience is *the same* as the one that, prescribing its acts to itself in the mode of the categorical imperative, inscribes freedom in nature (it is tempting to say that it *ex*scribes it: Heidegger is an excellent guide on this point), that is, the same as the one identified in a teleological perspective with the humanity of man.

A Historial Play on Words

What is the purpose of this gloss, which has been both lengthy and schematic? It is that it is well worth the trouble, in my view, to take seriously the question posed by Jean-Luc Nancy, or rather the form that Nancy was able to confer, by a radical simplification, to an otherwise rather diffuse interrogation of what is called the philosophical conjuncture, but on the condition of taking it quite literally—at the risk of getting tangled up in it. Not everyone is capable of producing a truly sophistic question, that is, one able to confront philosophy, in the medium of a given language, with the aporia of its own "founding" reflection, with the circularity of its enunciation. It is thus with the necessity and impossibility of a "decision" on which the progress of its discourse depends. With this little phrase, "Who comes after the subject?" Nancy seems to have managed the trick, for the only possible "answer"—at the same level of generality and singularity—would designate the nonsubject, whatever it may be, as "what" succeeds the subject (and thus puts an end to it). The place to which it should come, however, is *already* determined as the place of a subject by the question "who," in other words as *the being (who is the) subject* and nothing else. And our "subject" (which is to say unavoidably ourselves, whoever we may be or believe ourselves to be, caught in the constraints of the statement) is left to ask indefinitely, "How could it be that this (not) come of me?" Let us rather examine what characterizes this form.

First of all, the question is posed *in the present tense*: a present that doubtless refers to what is "current," and behind which we could[5] reconstitute a whole series of presuppositions about the "epoch" in which we find ourselves: whether we represent it as the triumph of subjectivity or as its dissolution, as an epoch that is still progressing or as one that is coming to an end (and thus in a sense has already been left behind). Unless, precisely, these alternatives are among the preformulations whose apparent obviousness would be suspended by Nancy's question. But there is another way to interpret such a present tense: as an *indeterminate*, if not ahistorical present, with respect to which we would not (at least not immediately) have to situate ourselves by means of a characterization of "our epoch" and its meaning, but which would only require us to ask *what comes to pass* when it comes *after* the subject, at whatever time this "event" may take place or might have taken place. This is the point of view I have chosen, for reasons that will soon become clear.

Second, the question posed is "*Who* comes . . . ?" Here again, two understandings are possible. The first, which I sketched out a moment ago, is perhaps more natural to the contemporary philosopher. Beginning from a precomprehension of the subject such as it is constituted by transcendental philosophy (*das Subjekt*), and such as it has since been deconstructed or decentered by different philosophies "of suspicion," different "structural" analyses, this understanding opens upon the enigma into which the *personality* of the subject leads us: the fact that it always succeeds itself across different philosophical figures or different modes of (re)presentation—which is perhaps only the mirror repetition of the way in which it always precedes itself (question: Who comes *before* the subject?). But why not follow more fully the indication given by language? If a question of identity is presupposed by Nancy's question, it is not of the form "*What* is the subject?" (or "What is the thing that we call the subject?"), but of the form "*Who* is the subject?," or even as an absolute precondition: "Who is subject?" The question is not about the *subjectum* but about the *subjectus*, he who is subjected. Not, or at least not immediately, the transcendental subject (with all its doubles: logical subject, grammatical subject, substantial subject), which is by definition a *neuter* (before becoming an it), but the subject as an individual or a person submitted to the exercise of a power, whose model is, first of all, political, and whose concept is juridical. Not the subject inasmuch as it is opposed to the predicate or object, but the one referred to by Bossuet's thesis: "*All men are born subjects* and the paternal authority that accustoms them to obeying accustoms them at the same time to having only one chief."[6]

The French (or Anglo-French) language here presents an advantage over German or even over Latin, one that is properly philosophical: it retains in the equivocal unity of a single noun the *subjectum* and the *subjectus*, the *Subjekt* and the *Untertan*. It is perhaps for lack of having paid attention to what such a continuity indicates that Heidegger proposed a fictive interpretation of the history of metaphysics in which the anteriority of the question of the *subjectus/Untertan* is "forgotten" and covered over by a retrospective projection of the question of the *Subjekt* as *subjectum*. This presentation, which marks the culmination of a long enterprise of interiorization of the history of philosophy, is today sufficiently widely accepted, even by philosophers who would not want to be called "Heideggerians" (and who often do not have the knowledge Heidegger had), for it to be useful to situate exactly the moment of forcing.

But if this is what the subject is *from the first* (both historically and logically), then the answer to Nancy's question is very simple, but so full of consequences that it might be asked whether it does not underlie every other interpretation, every reopening of the question of the subject, including the subject as transcendental subject. Here is the answer: *After the subject comes the citizen*. The citizen (defined by his rights and duties) is that "nonsubject" who comes after the subject, and whose constitution and recognition put an end (in principle) to the subjection of the subject.

This answer does not have to be (fictively) discovered, or proposed as an eschatological wager (supposing that the subject is in decline, what can be said of his future successor?). It is already given and in all our memories. We can even give it a date: 1789, even if we know that this date and the pace it indicates are too simple to enclose the entire process of the substitution of the citizen for the subject. The fact remains that 1789 marks the irreversibility of this process, the effect of a rupture.

We also know that this answer carries with it, historically, its own justification: If the citizen comes after the subject, it is in the quality of a rehabilitation, even a restoration (implied by the very idea of a revolution). The subject *is not* the original man, and, contrary to Bossuet's thesis, men are not "born" "subjects" but "free and equal in rights." The *factual* answer, which we already have at hand (and about which it is tempting to ask why it must be periodically suspended, in the game of a question that inverts it) also contains the entire difficulty of an interpretation that makes the "subject" a nonoriginary given, a beginning that is not (and cannot be) an origin. For the origin *is not* he subject, but man. But is this interpretation the only possible one? Is it indissociable from the fact itself? I would like to devote a few provisional reflections to the interest that these questions hold for philosophy—including when philosophy is displaced from the *subjectus* to the *subjectum*.

These reflections do not tend—as will quickly be apparent—to minimize the change produced by Kant, but to ask precisely in what the necessity of this change resides, and if it is truly impossible to bypass or go beyond (and thus to understand) it—in other words, if a critique of the representation of the history of philosophy that we have inherited from Kant can only be made from the point of view of a "subject" in the Kantian sense. The answer seems to me to reside at least partially in the analysis of this "coincidence": The moment at which Kant produces (and retrospectively projects) the transcendental "subject" is precisely that moment at which politics destroys the "subject" of the prince, in order to replace him with the republican citizen.

That this isn't really a coincidence is already hinted at by the fact that the question of the subject, around which the Copernican revolution pivots, is immediately characterized as a question of right (as to knowledge and as to action). In this question of right the representation of "man," about whom we have just noted that he forms the teleological horizon of the subject, vacillates. What is to be found under this name is not *de facto* man, subjected to various internal and external powers, but *de jure* man (who could still be called the man of man or the man in man, and who is also the empirical nonman), whose autonomy corresponds to the position of a "universal legislator." Which, to be brief, brings us back to the answer evoked above: after the subject (*subjectus*) comes the citizen. But is this citizen immediately what Kant will name "subject" (*Subjekt*)? Or is not the latter rather the reinscription of the citizen in a philosophical and, beyond that, anthropological space, which evokes the defunct subject or the prince even while displacing it? We cannot respond directly to these questions, which are inevitably raised by the letter of the Kantian invention once the context of its moment is restored. We must first make a detour through history. Who is the subject of the prince? And who is the citizen who comes after the subject?

The Subject of Obedience

It would be impossible to enclose the "*subjectus*" in a single definition, for it is a matter of a juridical figure whose evolution is spread out over seventeen countries, from Roman jurisprudence to absolute monarchy. It has often been demonstrated how, in the political history of Western Europe, the time of *subjects* coincides with that of *absolutism*.

Absolutism in effect seems to give a complete and coherent form to a power that is founded only upon itself, and that is founded as being without limits (thus uncontrollable and irresistible by definition). Such a power truly makes men into subjects, and nothing but subjects, for the very being of the subject is obedience. From the point of view of the subject, power's claim to incarnate both the good and the true is entirely justified: the subject is he who has no need of *knowing*, much less *understanding*, why what is prescribed to him is in the interest of his own happiness. Nevertheless, this perspective is deceptive: rather than a coherent from, classical absolutism is a knot of contradictions, and this can also be seen at the level of theory, in its discourse. Absolutism never manages to stabilize its definition of obedience and thus its definition of the subject. It could be asked, why this is necessarily the case, and what consequences result from it for the "surpassing" or "negation" of the subject in the citizen (if we should ever speak of sublation [*relève*] it is now: the citizen is a subject who rises up [*qui se relève*]!). In order to answer this question we must sketch a historical genesis of the subject and his contradiction.

The first question would be to know how one moves from the adjective to the substantive, from individuals who *are* subjected to the power of another, to the representation of a people or of a community as a set of "subjects." The distinction between independent and dependent persons is fundamental in Roman jurisprudence. A single text will suffice to recall it:

> *Sequitur de jure personarum alia divisio. Nam quaedam personae juris sunt, quaedam alieno juri sunt subjectae. Sed rursus earum personarum quae alieno juri subjectae sunt, aliae in potestate, aliae in manum, aliae in manci pio sunt. Videamus nunc de iis quae alieno juri subjectae sint, si cognoverimus quae istae personae sunt, simul intellegemus quae sui juris sint.*

> We come to another classification in the law of persons. Some people are independent and some are subject to others. Again, of those persons who are dependent, some are in power, some in marital subordination and some in bondage. Let us examine the dependent category. If we find out who is dependent, we cannot help seeing who is independent.[7]

Strangely, it is by way of the definition (the dialectical division) of the forms of subjection that the definition of free men, the masters, is obtained *a contrario*. But this definition does not make the subjects into a *collectivity*; it establishes no "link" *among them*. The notions of *potestas*, *manus*, and *mancipium* are not sufficient to do this. The subjects are not the heterogeneous set formed by slaves, plus legitimate children, plus wives, plus acquired or adopted relatives. What is required is an *imperium*. Subjects thus appeared with the empire (and in relation to the person of the emperor, to whom the citizens and many noncitizens owe "service," *officium*). But I would surmise that this necessary condition is not a sufficient one: Romans still had to be able to be submitted to the *imperium* in the same way (if they ever were) as conquered populations, "subjects of the Roman people" (a confusion that points, contradictorily, toward the horizon of the generalization of Roman citizenship as a personal status in the empire).[8] And, above all, the *imperium* had to be theologically founded as a Christian *imperium*, a power that comes from God and is conserved by Him.[9]

In effect, the subject has two major characteristics, both of which lead to aporias (in particular in the form given them by absolute monarchy): he is a *subditus*; he is not a *servus*. These characteristics are reciprocal, but each has its own dialectic.

The subject is a *subditus*: This means that he enters into a relation of obedience. Obedience is not the same as a compulsion: it is something more. It is established not only between a chief who has the power to compel and those who must submit to his power, but between a *sublimis*, "chosen" to command, and *subditi*, who turn towards him to hear a law. The power to compel is distributed throughout a hierarchy of unequal powers (relations of *majoritas minoritas*). Obedience is the principle, identical to itself along the whole length of the hierarchical chain, and attached in the last instance to its transcendental origin, which makes those who obey into the members of a single body. Obedience institutes the command of higher over lower but it fundamentally comes from below: as *subditi*, the subjects *will* their own obedience. And if they will it, it is because it is inscribed in an economy of creation (their creation) and salvation (their salvation, that of each taken individually and of all take collectively). Thus the *loyal subject* (*fidèle sujet*) (he who "voluntarily," "loyally," that is, actively and willingly obeys the law and executes the orders of a legitimate sovereign) is necessarily a faithful subject (*sujet fidèle*). He is a Christian, who knows that all power comes from God. In obeying the law of the prince he obeys God.[10] The fact that the order to which he "responds" comes to him from *beyond* the individual and the mouth that utters it is constitutive of the subject.

This structure contains the seeds of an infinite dialectic, which is in fact what unifies the subject (in the same way as it unifies, in the person of the sovereign, the act and its sanctification, decision making and justice): because of it the subject does not have to ask (himself) any questions, for the answers have always already been given. But it is also what *divides* the subject. This occurs, for example, when a "spiritual power" and a "temporal power" vie for preeminence (which supposes that each also attempts to appropriate the attributes of the other), or more simply when knowing which sovereign is legitimate or which practice of government is "Christian" and thus in conformity with its essence becomes a real question (the very idea of a "right of resistance" being a contradiction in terms, the chose is between regicide and prayer for the conversion of the sovereign . . .). Absolute monarchy in particular develops a contradiction that can be seen as the culmination of the conflict between the temporal power and the spiritual power. A passage is made from the divine right of kings to the idea of their direct election: It is as such that royal power is made divine (and that the State transfers to itself the various sacraments). But not (at least not in the West) the *individual person* of the king: incarnation of a divine power, the king is not himself "God." The king (the sovereign) is *lex animata* (*nomos empsychos*) (just as the law is *inanimatus princeps*). Thus the person (the "body") of the king must itself be divided: into divine person and human person. And obedience correlatively . . . [11]

Such an obedience, in its unity and its divisions, implies the notion of the soul. This is a notion that Antiquity did not know or in any case did not use in the same way in order to think a political relation (Greek does not have, to my knowledge, an equivalent for the *subjectus subditus*, not even the term *hypekoos*, which designates those who obey the word of a master, who will become "disciples," and from whom the theologians will draw the same of Christian obedience: *hypakoè*). For Antiquity obedience can be a contingent situation in which one finds oneself in relation to a command (*archè*), and thus a commander (*archōn*).

But to receive a command (*archemenos*) implies that one can oneself—at least theoretically—give a command (this is the Aristotelian definition of the citizen). Or it can be a natural dependence of the "familial" type. Doubtless differentiations (the ignorance of which is what properly characterizes barbarism) ought to be made here: the woman (even for the Greeks, and a fortiori for the Romans) is not a slave. Nevertheless, these differences can be subsumed under analogous oppositions: the part and the whole, passivity and activity, the body and the soul (or intellect). This last opposition is particularly valid for the slave, who is to his master what a body, an "organism" (a set of natural tools) is to intelligence. In such a perspective, the very idea of a "free obedience" is a contradiction in terms. That a slave can *also* be free is a relatively late (Stoic) idea, which must be understood as signifying that on *another* level (in a "cosmic" polity, a polity of "minds") he who is a slave here can also be a master (master of himself, of his passions), can also be a "citizen." Nothing approaches the idea of a freedom residing in obedience itself, resulting from this obedience. In order to conceive of this idea obedience must be transferred to the side of the soul, and the soul must cease to be thought of as natural: On the contrary, the soul must come to name a supernatural part of the individual that hears the dignity of the order.

Thus the *subditus-subjectus* has always been distinguished from the slave, just as the sovereignty of the prince, the *sublimus*, has been distinguished from "despotism" (literally, the authority of a master of slaves).[12] But this fundamental distinction was elaborated in two ways. It was elaborated within a theological framework, simply developing the idea that the subject is a believer, a Christian. Because, in the final instance, it is his soul that obeys, he could never be the sovereign's "thing" (which can be used and abused); his obedience is inscribed in an order that should, in the end, bring him salvation, and that is counterbalanced by a responsibility (a duty) on the part of the prince. But this way of thinking the freedom of the subject is, in practice, extraordinarily ambivalent. It can be understood either as the affirmation and the active contribution of his will to obedience (just as the Christian, by his works, "cooperates in his salvation": the political necessity of the theological compromise on the question of predestination can be seen here), or as the annihilation of the will (this is why the mystics who lean toward perfect obedience apply their will to self-annihilation in the contemplation of God, the only absolute sovereign). Intellectual reasons as well as material interests (those of the lords, of the corporations, of the "bourgeois" towns) provide an incentive for thinking the freedom of the subject differently, paradoxically combining the concept with that of the "citizen," a concept taken from Antiquity and notably from Aristotle, but carefully distinguished from man inasmuch as he is the image of the creator.

Thus the *civis polites* comes back onto the scene, in order to make the quasi-ontological difference between a "subject" and a serf/slave. But the man designated as a citizen is no loner the *zōon politikon*: he is no longer the "sociable animal," meaning that he is sociable as an animal (and not inasmuch as his soul is immortal). Thomas Aquinas distinguishes the (supernatural) *christianitas* of man from his (natural) *humanitas*, the "believer" from the "citizen." The latter is the holder of a neutral freedom, a "franchise." This has nothing to in common with sovereignty, but means that his submission to political authority is neither immediate not arbitrary. He is *submitted* as a member of an order or a body that is recognized as having certain rights and that confers a certain status, a field of initiative, upon him. What then becomes of the "subject"? In a sense he is more really free (for his subjection is the effect of a political order that integrates "civility," the "polity" and that is thus inscribed in nature). But it becomes more and more difficult to think him as *subditus*: The very concept of his "obedience" is menaced.

The tension becomes, once again, a contradiction under absolute monarchy. We have already seen how the latter brings the mysterious unity of the temporal and spiritual sovereign to the point of rupture. The same goes for the freedom of the subject. Insofar as absolute monarchy concentrates power in the unity of the "State" (the term appears at this moment, along with "reason") and suppresses all subjections to the profit of one subjection. There is now only one prince, whose law is will, "father of his subjects," having absolute authority over them (as all other authority, next to his, is null). "I am the State," Louis XIV will say. But absolute monarchy is a *State* power, precisely, that is, a power that is instituted and exercised by law and administration; it is a political power (*imperium*) that is not confused with the property (dominium)—except "eminent" domain—of what belongs to individuals, and over which they exercise their power. The subjects are, if not "legal subjects (*sujets de droit*)," at least subjects "with rights (*en droit*)," members of a "republic" (a Commonwealth, Hobbes will say). All the theoreticians of absolute monarchy (with or without a "pact of subjection") will explain that the subjects are citizens (or, like Bodin in the *Republic*, that "every citizen is a subject, his freedom being somewhat diminished by the majesty of the one to whom he owes obedience; but not every subject is a citizen, as we have said of the slave").[13] They will not prevent—with the help of circumstances—the condition of this "free (franc) subject dependent upon the sovereignty of another"[14] from being perceived as untenable. La Boétie, reversing each term, will oppose them by defining the power of the One (read: the Monarch) as a "voluntary servitude" upon which at the same time reason of State no longer confers the meaning of a supernatural freedom. The controversy over the difference (or lack of one) between absolutism and despotism accompanies the whole history of absolute monarchy.[15] The condition of subject will be retrospectively identified with that of the slave, and subjection with "slavery," from the point of view of the new citizen and his revolution (this will also be an essential mechanism of his own idealization).

A Hyperbolic Proposition

The *Declaration of the Rights of Man and of the Citizen* of 1789 produces a truth effect that marks a rupture. It is nevertheless an intrinsically equivocal text, as is indicated by the dualities of its title and of its first line: rights of man *and* of the citizen, are born *and* remain, free *and* equal. Each of these dualities, and particularly the first, which divides the origin, harbor the possibility of antithetical readings: Is the founding notion that of *man*, or of the *citizen*? Are the rights declared those of the citizen *as man*, or those of man *as citizen*? In the interpretation sketched out here, it is the second reading that must take precedence: The stated rights are those of the citizen, the objective is the constitution of citizenship—in a radically new sense. In fact neither the idea of humanity nor its equivalence with freedom are new. Nor, as we have seen, are they incompatible with a theory of originary subjection: the Christian is essentially free *and* subject, the subject of the prince is "franc." What is new is the sovereignty of the citizen, which entails a completely different conception (and a completely different practical determination) of freedom. But this sovereignty must be founded retroactively on a certain concept of man, or, better, in a *new* concept of man that contradicts what the term previously connoted.

Why is this foundation necessary? I do not believe it is, as is often said, because of a *symmetry* with the way the sovereignty of the prince was founded in the idea of God, because the sovereignty of the people (or of the "nation") would need a *human foundation* in the same way that imperial or monarchical sovereignty needed a *divine foundation*, or, to put it another way, by virtue of a necessity inherent in the idea of sovereignty, which leads to putting Man in the place of God.[16] On the contrary, it is because of the dissymmetry that is introduced into the idea of sovereignty from the moment that it has devolved to the "citizens": Until then, the idea of sovereignty had always been inseparable from a hierarchy, from an eminence; from this point forward the paradox of *sovereign equality*, something radically new, must be thought. What must be explained (at the same time as it is declared) is how the concept of sovereignty and equality can be noncontradictory. The reference to man, or the inscription of equality in human nature is equality "of birth," which is not at all evident and even improbable, is the means of explaining this paradox.[17] This is what I will call a hyperbolic proposition.

It is also the sudden appearance of a new problem. One paradox (the equality of birth) explains another (sovereignty as equality). The political tradition of antiquity, to which the revolutionaries never cease to refer (Rome and Sparta rather than Athens), thought civic equality to be founded on freedom and exercised in the determinate conditions of this freedom (which is a hereditary or quasi-hereditary status). It is now a matter of thinking the inverse: a freedom founded on equality, engendered by the movement of equality. Thus an unlimited or, more precisely, self-limited freedom: having no limits other than those it assigns to itself in order to respect the rule of equality, that is, to remain in conformity with its principle. In other terms, it is a matter of answering the question: *Who is the citizen?* and not the question: Who is a citizen? (or: Who are citizens?). The answer is: The citizen is a man in enjoyment of all his "natural" rights, completely realizing his individual humanity, a free man simply because he is equal to every other man. This answer (or this new question in the form of an answer) will also be stated, after the fact: *The citizen is the subject*, the citizen is always a supposed subject (legal subject, psychological subject, transcendental subject).

I will call this new development the citizen's becoming a subject (*devenir sujet*): a development that is doubtless prepared by a whole labor of definition of the juridical, moral, and intellectual individual; that goes back to the "nominalism" of the late Middle Ages, is invested in institutional and cultural practices, and reflected by philosophy, but that can find its name and its cultural position only *after* the emergence of the revolutionary citizen, for it rests upon the reversal of what was previously the *subjectus*. In the Declaration of Rights, and in all the discourses and practices that reiterate its effect, we must read both the presentation of the citizen and the marks of his becoming-a-subject. This is all the more difficult in that it is practically impossible for the citizen(s) to be presented without being determined as subject(s). But it was only by way of the citizen that universality could come to the subject. An eighteenth-century dictionary had stated: "In France, other than the king, all are citizens."[18] The revolution will say: If anyone is not a citizen, then no one is a citizen. "All distinction ceases. All are citizens, or must be, and whoever is not must be excluded."[19]

The idea of the rights of the citizen, at the very moment of his emergence, thus institutes an historical figure that is no longer the *subjectus*, and not yet the *subjectum*. But from the beginning, in the way it is formulated and put into practice, this figure exceeds its own institution. This is what I called, a moment ago, the statement of a hyperbolic proposition. Its developments can only consist of conflicts, whose stakes can be sketched out.

First of all, there exist conflicts with respect to the founding idea of equality. The absolutism of this idea emerges from the struggle against "privilege," when it appeared that the privileged person was not ne who had *more* rights but he who had *less*: each privilege, for him, is substituted for a possible right, even though at the same time his privilege denies rights to the nonprivileged. In other words, it appeared that the "play" (*jeu*) of right—to speak a currently fashionable language—is not a "zero-sum" game: that is what distinguishes it from the play of power, the "balance of power." Rousseau admirably developed this difference on which the entire argumentation of the *Social Contract* is based: a supplement of rights for one is the annihilation of the rights of all; the effectivity of right has as its condition that each has exactly "as much," *neither more nor fewer* right(s) than the rest.

Two paths are open from this point. Either equality is "symbolic," which means that each individual, whatever his strengths, his power, and his property, is *reputed* to be equivalent to every individual in his capacity as citizen (and in the public acts in which citizenship is exercised). Or equality is "real," which means that citizenship will not exist unless the conditions of all individuals are equal, or at least equivalent: then, in fact, power's games will no longer be able to pose an obstacle to the play of right; the power proper to equality will not be destroyed by the effects of power. Whereas symbolic equality is all the better affirmed, its ideality all the better preserved and recognized as unconditional when conditions are unequal, real equality supposes a classless society, and thus works to produce it. If a proof is wanted of the fact that the antinomy "formal" and "real" democracy is thus inscribed from the very beginning in the text of 1789 it will suffice to reread Robespierre's discourse on the "*marc d'argent*" (April 1791).[20]

But this antinomy is untenable, for it has the form of an all-or-nothing (it reproduces *within* the field of citizenship the all-or-nothing of the subject and the citizen). Symbolic equality must be nothing real, but a universally applicable form. Real equality must be all or, if one prefers, every practice, every condition must be measured by it, for an exception destroys it. It can be asked—we will return to this point—whether the two mutually exclusive sides of this alternative are not equally incompatible with the constitution of a "society." In other terms, civic equality is indissociable from universality but separates it from *community*. The restitution of the latter requires either a supplement of symbolic form (to think universality as ideal Humanity, the reign of practical ends) or a supplement of substantial egalitarianism (communism, Babeuf's "order of equality"). But this supplement, whatever it may be, already belongs to the citizen's becoming a subject.

Second, there exist conflicts with respect to the citizen's activity. What radically distinguishes him from the subject of the Prince is his participation in the formation and application of the decision: the fact that he is legislator and magistrate. Here, too, Rousseau, with his concept of the "general will," irreversibly states what constitutes the rupture. The comparison with the way in which medieval politics had defined the "citizenship" of the subject, as the right of all to be well governed, is instructive.[21] From this point forward the idea of a "passive citizen" is a contradiction in terms. Nevertheless, as is well known, this idea was immediately formulated. But let us look at the details.

Does the activity of the citizen exclude the idea of *representation*? This position has been argued: whence the long series of discourses identifying active citizenship and "direct democracy," with or without reference to antiquity.[22] In reality this identification rests on a confusion.

Initially, representation is a representation *before* the Prince, before Power, and, in general, before the instance of decision making whatever it may be (incarnated in a living or anonymous person, itself represented by officers of the State). This is the function of the Old Regime's "deputies of the Estates," who present grievances, supplications, and remonstrances (in many respects this function of representing those who are administered to the administration has in fact again become the function of the numerous elected assemblies of the contemporary State).

The *representation of the sovereign* in its deputies, inasmuch as the sovereign is the people, is something entirely different. Not only is it active, it is the act of sovereignty *par excellence*: the choice of those who govern, the corollary of which is monitoring them. To elect representatives is to act and to make possible all political action, which draws its legitimacy from this election. Election has an "alchemy," whose other aspects we will see further on: as the primordial civic action, it *singularizes* each citizen, responsible for his vote (his choice), at the same time as it *unifies* the "moral" body of the citizens.[23] We will have to ask again, and in greater depth, to what extent this determination engages the dialectic of the citizen's becoming-a-subject: which citizens are "representable," and under which conditions? Above all: *Who* should the citizens be in order to be able to represent themselves and to be represented? (for example: Does it matter that they be able to read and write? Is this condition sufficient? etc.). In any case we have here, again, a very different concept from the one antiquity held of citizenship, which, while it too implied an idea of *activity*, did not imply one of sovereign will. Thus the Greeks privileged the drawing of lots in the designation of magistrates as the only truly democratic method, whereas election appeared to them to be "aristocratic" by definition (Aristotle).

It is nonetheless true that the notion of a *representative activity* is problematic. This can be clearly seen in the debate over the question of the binding mandate: Is it necessary, in order for the activity of the citizens to manifest itself, that their deputies be permanently bound by their will (supposing it to be known) or is it sufficient that they be liable to recall, leaving them the responsibility to interpret the general will by their *own* activity? The dilemma could also be expressed by saying that citizenship implies a power to delegate its powers, but excludes the existence of "politicians," of "professionals," a fortiori of "technicians" of politics. In truth this dilemma was already present in the astonishing Hobbesian construction of representation, as the doubling of an *author* and an *actor*, which remains the basis of the modern State.

But the most profound antinomy of the citizen's activity concerns the *law*. Here again Rousseau circumscribes the problem by posing his famous definition: "As for the associates, collectively they take the name *people*, and individually they are called *Citizens* as participating in the sovereign authority and *Subjects* as submitted to the laws of the State."[24]

> It can be seen by this formulation . . . that each individual, contracting, so to speak, with himself, finds himself engaged in a double relationship. . . . Consequently it is against the nature of the political body for the Sovereign to impose upon itself a law that it cannot break . . . by which it can be seen that there is not nor can there be any sort of fundamental law which obliges the body of the people, not even the social contract. . . . Now the Sovereign, being formed only of the individuals who compose it, does not and cannot have an interest opposed to theirs; consequently the Sovereign power has no need of a guarantee toward the subjects, for it is impossible that the body wish to harm all its members. . . . But this is not he case for the subjects toward the sovereign, where despite the common interest, nothing would answer for their engagements if means to insure their fidelity were not found. In fact each individual can, as man, have a particular will contrary or dissimilar to the general will that he has as citizen. . . . He would enjoy the rights of a citizen without being willing to fulfill the duties of a subject; an injustice whose progress would cause the ruin of the political body. In order for the social pact not to become a vain formula, it tacitly includes the engagement . . . that whoever refuses to obey the general will will be compelled to do so by any means available: which signifies nothing else than that he will be forced to be free.[25]

It was necessary to cite this whole passage in order that no one be mistaken: In these implacable formulas, we see the final appearance of the "subject" in the old sense, that of obedience, but metamorphosed into the *subject of the law*, the strict correlative of the citizen who *makes the law*.[26] We also see the appearance, under the name of "man," split between his general interest and his particular interest, of he who will be the new "subject," the Citizen Subject.

It is indeed a question of an antinomy. Precisely in his capacity as "citizen," the citizen is (indivisibly) *above* any law, otherwise he could not legislate, much less constitute: "There is not, nor can there be, any sort of fundamental law that obliges the body of the people, not even the social contract." In his capacity as "subject" (that is, inasmuch as the laws he formulates are imperative, to be executed universally and unconditionally, inasmuch as the pact is not a "vain formula") he is necessarily *under* the law. Rousseau (and the Jacobin tradition) resolve this antinomy by identifying, in terms of their close "relationship" (that is in terms of a particular point of view), the two propositions: just as one citizen has neither more nor less right(s) than another, so he is neither only above, nor only under the law, but *at exactly the same level as it*. Nevertheless *he is not the law* (the *nomos empsychos*). This is not the consequence of a transcendence on the part of the law (of the fact that it would come from Elsewhere, from an Other mouth speaking atop some Mount Sinai), but a consequence of its immanence. Or yet another way: There must be an exact correspondence between the absolute activity of the citizen (legislation) and his absolute passivity (obedience to the law, with which one does not "bargain," which one does not "trick"). But it is essential that this activity and this passivity be *exactly* correlative, that they have exactly the same limits. The possibility of a metaphysics of the subject already resides in the enigma of this unity of opposites (in Kant, for example, this metaphysics of the subject will proceed from the double determination of the concept of right as freedom and as compulsion). But the necessity of an anthropology of the subject (psychological, sociological, juridical, economic . . .) will be manifest from the moment that, in however small a degree, the exact correlation becomes upset in practice: When a distinction between *active citizens* and *passive citizens* emerges (a distinction with which we are still living), and with it a problem of the criteria of their distinction and of the justification of this paradox. Now this distinction is practically contemporary with the Declaration of Rights itself; it is in any case inscribed in the first of the *Constitutions* "based" on the Declaration of Rights. Or, quite simply, when it becomes apparent that to *govern* is not the same as to *legislate* or even to execute the laws, that is, that political sovereignty is not the mastery of the art of politics.

Finally, there exist conflicts with respect to the individual and the collective. We noted above that the institution of a society or a community on the basis of principles of equality is problematic. This is not—or at least not uniquely—due to the fact that this principle would be identical to that of the *competition* between individuals ("egotism," or a freedom limited only by the antagonism of interests). It is even less due to the fact that equality would be another name for similarity, that it would imply that individuals are indiscernible from one another and thus incompatible with one another, preyed on by mimetic rivalry. On the contrary, equality, precisely inasmuch as it is not the identification of individuals, is one of the great cultural means of legitimating differences and controlling the imaginary ambivalence of the "double." The difficulty is rather due to equality itself: In this principle (in the proposition that men, as citizens, are equal), even though there is necessarily a reference to the *fact* of society (under the name of "polity"), there is conceptually too much (or not enough) to "bind" a society. It can be see clearly here how the difficulty arises from the fact that, in the modern concept of citizenship, freedom is founded in equality and not vise versa (the "solution" of the difficulty will in part consist precisely of reversing this primacy, to make freedom into a foundation, even, metaphysically, to identify the originary with freedom).

Equality in fact cannot be limited. Once some x's ("men") are not equal, the predicate of equality can no longer be applied to anyone, for all those to whom it is supposed to be applicable are in fact "superior," "dominant," "privileged," etc. Enjoyment of the equality of rights cannot spread step by step, beginning with two individuals and gradually extending to all: It must immediately concern the universality of individuals, let us say, tautologically, the universality of x's that it concerns. This explains the insistence of the cosmopolitan theme in egalitarian political thought, or the reciprocal implication of these two themes. It also explains the antinomy of equality and society for, even when it is not defined in "cultural," "national," or "historical" terms, a *society* is necessarily *a* society, defined by some particularity, by some exclusion, if only by a *name*. In order to speak of "all citizens," it is necessary that somebody not be a citizen of said polity.

Likewise, equality, even though it preserves differences (it does not imply that Catholics are Protestants, that blacks are whites, that women are men, or vice versa: it could even be held that without differences equality would be literally unthinkable), cannot itself be *differentiated*: differences are close by it but do not come from its application. We have already glimpsed this problem with respect to activity and passivity. It takes on its full extension once it is a question of *organizing* a society, that is of instituting functions and roles in it. Something like a "bad infinity" is implied here by the negation of the inequalities which are always still present in the principle of equality, and which form, precisely, its practical effectiveness. This is, moreover, exactly what Hegel will say.

The affirmation of this principle can be seen in 1789 in the statement that the king himself is only a citizen ("Citizen Capet"), a deputy of the sovereign people. Its development can be seen in the affirmation that the exercise of a magistrature excludes one from citizenship: "The soldier is a citizen; the officer is not and cannot be one."[27] "Ordinarily, people say: the citizen is someone who participates in honors and dignities; they are mistaken. Here he is, the citizen: he is someone who possesses no more goods than the law allows, who exercises no magistrature and is independent of the responsibility of those who govern. Whoever is a magistrate is no longer part of the people. No individual power can enter the people. . . . When speaking to a functionary, one should not say *citizen*; this title is above him."[28] On the contrary, it may be thought that the existence if a society always presupposes an organization, and that the latter in turn always presupposes an element of qualification or differentiation from equality and thus of "nonequality" developed *on the basis of equality itself* (which is not on that account a *principle* of inequality).[29] If we call this element "archy," we will understand that one of the logics of citizenship leads to the idea of anarchy. It was Sade who wrote, "Insurrection should be the permanent state of the republic," and the comparison with Saint-Just has been made by Maurice Blanchot.[30]

It will be said that the solution to this aporia is the idea of a contract. The contractual bond is in fact the only one that thinks itself as absolutely homogeneous with the reciprocal action of equal individuals,[31] presupposing only this equality. No other presuppositions? All the theoreticians are in agreement that some desire for sociability, some interest in bringing together the forces and in limiting freedoms by one another, or some moral ideal, indispensable "motor forces," would *also* be required. It will in fact be agreed that the *proper* form of the contract is that of a contract of *association*, and that the contract of subjection is an ideological artifact destined to divert the benefits of the contractual form to the profit of an established power. But it remains a question whether the social contract can be thought as a mechanism that "socializes" equals purely by virtue of their equality. I think that the opposite is the case: that the social contract *adds* to equality a determination that compensates for its "excess" of universality. To this end equality itself must be thought as something other than a naked principle; it must be justified, or one must confer on it that which Derrida not long ago called an *originary supplement*.

This is why all the theories of the contract include a "deduction" of equality as an indispensable preliminary, showing how it is produced or how it is destroyed and restored in a dialectic either of natural sociability and unsociability or of the animality and human-ity in man (the extreme form being that of Hobbes: Equality is produced by the threat of death, in which freedom is promptly annihilated). The Declaration of 1789 gives this sup-plement its most economical form, that of a *de jure* fact: "Men *are born and remain* . . ."

From One Subjection to the Other

I think that, under these conditions, the indetermination of the figure of the citizen—referred to equality—can be understood with respect to the major alternatives of modern political and sociological thought: individual and collectivity, public sphere and private sphere. The citizen properly speaking is *neither* the individual *nor* the collective, just as he is *neither* an exclusively public being *nor* a private being. Nevertheless, these distinctions are present in the concept of the citizen. It would not be correct to say that they are ignored or denied: it should rather be said that they are suspended, that is, irreducible to fixed institu-tional boundaries which would pose the citizen on one side and a *noncitizen* on the other.

The citizen is unthinkable as an "isolated" individual, for it is his active participation in politics that makes him exist. But he cannot on that account be merged into a "total" collectivity. Whatever may be said about it, Rousseau's reference to a "moral and collec-tive body composed of as many members as there are votes in the assembly,"[32] produced by the act of association that "makes a people a people,"[33] is not the *revival* but the *antith-esis* of the organicist idea of the *corpus mysticum* (the theologians have never been fooled on this point).[34] The "double relationship" under which the individuals contract also has the effect of forbidding the fusion of individuals in a whole, whether immediately or by the mediation of some "corporation." Likewise, the citizen can only be thought if there exists, at least tendentially, a distinction between public and private: he is defined as a pub-lic actor (and even as the *only* possible public actor). Nevertheless he cannot be confined to the public sphere, with a private sphere—whether the latter is like the *oikos* of antiquity, the modern family (the one that will emerge from the civil code and that which we now habitually call "the invention of private life"), or a sphere of industrial and commercial relations that are nonpolitical[35]—being held in *reserve*. If only for the reason that, in such a sphere, to become other than himself the citizen would have to enter into relationships with *noncitizens* (or with individuals considered as noncitizens: women, children, servants, employees). The citizen's "madness," as is known, is not the abolition of private life but its transparency, just as it is not the abolition of politics but its moralization.

To express this suspension of the citizen we are obliged to search in history and literature for categories that are unstable and express instability. The concept of *mass*, at a certain moment of its elaboration, would be an example, as when Spinoza speaks of both the dis-solution of the (monarchical) State and its (democratic) constitution as a "return to the mass."[36] This concept is not unrelated, it would seem, to that which in the Terror will durably inspire the thinkers of liberalism with terror.

I have presented the Declaration of Rights as a hyperbolic proposition. It is now possible to reformulate this idea: in effect, in this proposition, *the wording of the statement always*

exceeds the act of its enunciation [*l'enoncé exceed toujours l'énonciation*], the import of the statement already goes beyond it (without our knowing where), as was immediately seen in the
effect of inciting the liberation that it produced. In the statement of the Declaration, even
though this is not at all the content of the enunciation of the subsequent rights, we can
already hear the motto that, in another place and time, will become a call to action: "It is
right to revolt." Let us note once more that it is equality that is at the origin of the movement of liberation.

All sorts of historical modalities are engaged here. Thus de Declaration of 1789 posits
that property—immediately after freedom—is a "natural and imprescriptable right of man"
(without, however, going so far as to take up the idea that property is a condition of freedom). And as early as 1791 the battle is engaged between those who conclude that property
qualifies the constitutive equality of citizenship (in other words that "active citizens" are
proprietors), and those who posit that the universality of citizenship must take precedence
over the right of property, even should this result in a negation of the unconditional character of the latter. As Engels noted, the demand for the abolition of class differences is
expressed in terms of civic equality, which does not signify that the latter is only a period
costume, but on the contrary that it is an effective condition of the struggle against
exploitation.

Likewise, the Constitutions that are "based" on the principles of 1789 immediately
qualify—explicitly and implicity—the citizen as a *man* (= a male), if not as a head of house-
hold (this will come with the Napoleonic Code). Nevertheless, as early as 1791 an Olympe
de Gouges can be found drawing from these same principles the *Declaration of the Rights
of Woman and Citizenness* (and, the following year, with Mary Wollstonecraft's *Vindication
of the Rights of Woman*), and the battle—one with a great future, though not much
pleasure—over the question of whether the citizen has a sex (thus, what the sex of man as
citizen is) is engaged.

Finally, the Declaration of 1789 does not speak of the color of citizens, and—even if
one refuses to consider[37] this silence to be a necessary condition for the representation of
the political relations of the Old Regime (subjection to the Prince and to the *seigneurs*) as
"slavery," even as true slavery (that of the blacks) is preserved—it must be admitted that it
corresponds to powerful interests among those who collectively declare themselves "sovereign." It is nonetheless the case that the insurrection for the *immediate* abolition of slavery
(Toussaint L'Ouverture) takes place in the name of an equality of rights that, as stated, is
indiscernible from that of the "sans culottes" and other "patriots," though the slaves, it is
true, did not wait for the fall of the Bastille to revolt.[38]

Thus that which appeared to us as the indetermination of the citizen (in certain respects compatible to the fugitive moment that was glimpsed by Aristotle under the name
of *archè aoristos*, but that now would be developed as a complete historical figure) also manifests itself as the opening of a *possibility*: the possibility for any *given* realization of the
citizen to be placed in question and destroyed by a struggle for equality and thus for civil
rights. But this possibility is not in the least a promise, much less an inevitability. Its con-
cretization and explicitation depend entirely on an encounter between a statement and situations or movements that, from the point of view of the concept, are contingent.[39] If the

citizen's becoming-a-subject takes the form of a dialectic, it is precisely because *both* the necessity of "founding" institutional definitions of the citizen and the impossibility of ignoring their contestation—the infinite contradiction within which they are caught—are crystallized in it.

There exists another way to account for the passage from the citizen to the subject (*subjectum*), coming after the passage from citizen to the subject (*subjectus*) to the citizen, or rather immediately overdetermining it. The citizen as defined by equality, absolutely active and absolutely passive (or, if one prefers, capable of autoaffection: that which Fichte will call *das Ich*), suspended between individuality and collectivity, between public and private: Is he the constitutive element of a *State?* Without a doubt, the answer is yes, but precisely insofar as the State is not, or not yet, a society. He is, as Pierre-François Moreau has convincingly argued, a *utopic* figure, which is not to say an unreal or millenarist figure projected into the future, but the elementary term of an "abstract State."[40] Historically, this abstract State possesses an entirely tangible reality: that of the progressive deployment of a political and administrative right in which individuals are treated by the state *equally*, according to the logic of situations and actions and not according to their condition or personality. It is this juridico-administrative "*epochè*" of "cultural" or "historical" differences, seeking to create its own conditions of possibility, that paradoxically becomes explicit to itself in the minutely detailed egalitarianism of the ideal cities of the classical Utopia, with their themes of closure, foreignness, and rational administration, with their negation of property. When it becomes clear that the condition of conditions for individuals to be treated equally *by* the State (which is the logic of its proper functioning: the suppression of the exception) is what they also be equally entitled to sovereignty (that is, it cannot be *done for less*, while conserving subjection), then the "legal subject" implicit in the machinery of the "individualist" State will be made concrete in the excessive person of the citizen.

But this also means—taking into account all that precedes—that the citizen can be simultaneously considered as the constitutive element of the State and as the actor of a revolution. Not only the actor of a founding revolution, a *tabula rasa* whence a State emerges, but the actor of a *permanent* revolution: precisely the revolution in which the principle of equality, once it has been made the basis or pretext of the institution of an inequality or a political "excess of power," contradicts every difference. Excess against excess, then. The actor of such a revolution is no less "utopic" than the member of the abstract State, the State of the rule of law. It would be quite instructive to conduct the same structural analysis of revolutionary utopias that Moreau made of administrative utopias. It would doubtless show not only that the themes are the same, but also that the fundamental prerequisites of the individual defined by his juridical activity is *identical* with that of the individual defined by his revolutionary activity: he is the man "without property" (*der Eigentumslos*), "without particularities" (*ohne Eigenschaften*). Rather than speak of administrative utopias and revolutionary utopias, we should really speak of antithetical readings of the same utopia narratives and of the reversibility of these narratives.

In the conclusion of his book, Moreau describes Kant's *Metaphysics of Morals* and his *Anthropology from a Pragmatic Point of View* as the two sides of a single construction of the legal subject: on the one side, the formal deduction of his egalitarian essence; on the other, the historical description of all the "natural" characteristics (all the individual or collective "properties") that form either the condition or the obstacle to individuals identifying themselves in practice as being subjects of this type (for example, sensibility, imagination, taste, good mental health, ethnic "character," moral virtue, or that natural superiority that predisposes men to civil independence and active citizenship and women to dependence and political passivity). Such a duality corresponds fairly well to what Foucault, in *The Order of Things*, called the "empirico-transcendental doublet." Nevertheless, to understand that this subject (which the citizen will be *supposed* to be) contains the paradoxical unity of a universal sovereignty and a radical finitude, we must envisage this constitution—in all the historical complexity of the practices and symbolic forms which it brings together—from *both* the point of view of the State apparatus and that of the permanent revolution. This ambivalence is his strength, his historical ascendancy. All of Foucault's work, or at least that part of it which, by successive approximations, obstinately tries to describe the heterogeneous aspects of the great "transition" between the world of subjection and the world of right and discipline, "civil society," and State apparatus, is a materialist phenomenology of the transmutation of subjection, of the birth of the Citizen Subject. As to whether this figure, like a face of sand at the edge of the sea, is about to be effaced with the next great sea change—that is another question. Perhaps it is nothing more than Foucault's own utopia, a necessary support for the enterprise of stating that utopia's facticity.

Translated by James Swenson

Annex: Subjectus/Subjectum

A. An Untranslatable Passage in Nietzsche

At the heart of the problems that are now raised by the use of the "subject" category—which has never been more central to philosophy, even though the twentieth century gave it a completely new orientation—there is a pun (intentional or otherwise) on two Latin etymologies: that of the neuter *subjectum* (which, like *suppositum*, has, ever since the scholastics, been regarded by philosophers, as a translation of the Greek *hupokeimenon*), and that of the masculine *subjectus* (equated with *subditus* in the Middle Ages). One gives rise to a lineage of logico-grammatical and ontological-transcendental meanings, and the other to a lineage of juridical, political and theological meanings. Far from remaining independent of one another, they have constantly overdetermined one another, because, following Kant, the problematic articulation of "subjectivity" and "subjugation" came to be defined as a theory of the constituent subject. That overdetermination can be overt, latent, or even repressed, depending on whether or not the language in question reveals its workings.

The best way to introduce these problems of modern philosophy is, perhaps, to read an astonishing passage from Nietzsche's *Beyond Good and Evil* (*Par-delà bien et mal*). I cite the most authoritative French translation and include the German terms in parentheses.

> Les philosophes ont coutume de parler de la volonté comme si c'était la chose la mieux connue au monde. . . . Un homme qui *veut* commande en lui-même a quelque chose qui obéit ou dont il se croit obéi (*befiehlt einem Etwas in sich, das gehorcht oder von dem er glaubt, dass es gehorcht*). Mais considérons maintient l'aspect le plus singulier de la volonté, de cette

chose si complexe (*vielfachen Dinge*) pour laquelle le people n'a qu'un mot: si, dans le cas envisagé, nous sommes à la fois celui qui commande et celui qui obéit (*zugleich die Befehlenden und Gehorchenden*), et si nous connaissons, en tant que sujet obeisant (*als Gehorchenden*), la contrainte, l'oppression, la résistance, le trouble, sentiments qui accompagnent immédiatement l'acte de volonté; si, d'autre part, nous avons l'habitude de nous duper nous-mêmes en escamotant cette dualité grâce au concept synthétique de 'moi' (*uns über dieser Zweiheit vermöge des synthetischen Begriffs 'ich' hinwezusetzen, hinwegzutäushen*), on voit que toute une chaîne de conclusions erronées, et donc de jugements faux sur la volonté elle-même, viendrait encore s'agréger au vouloir . . . comme dans la très grande majorité des cas, la volonté n'entre en jeu que la où elle *s'attend* à être obéi, donc à susciter un acte, on en est venu à croire, *fallacieusement*, qu'une telle conséquence était *nécessaire* (*so hat sich der Anschein in das Gefühl übersetz, als ob es da eine Notwendigkeit von Wirkung gäbe*). Bref, celui qui veut est passablement convaincu que la volonté et l'acte ne sont qu'un en quelque manière (*dass Wille und Aktion irgendwie Eins seien*). . . . 'Libre arbitre', tel est le mot qui désigne ce complexe état d'euphorie du sujet voulant, qui commande et qui s'identifie à la fois evecc l'exécuteur de l'action (*das Wort für jenen vielfachen Lust-Zustand des Wollenden, befiehlt und sich zugleich mit dem Ausführenden als Eins setzt*) qui goûte au plaisir de triompher des résistances, tout en estimant que c'est sa volonté qui les surmonte. A son plaisir d'individu qui ordonne, le sujet voulant ajoute ainsi les sentiments de plaisir issus des instruments d'exécution (*Der Wollende nimmt dergestalt dies Lustgefühle der ausführenden, erfolgreichen Werkzeuge*) qui sont diligentes 'sous-volontés' ou sous-âmes ("*Unterwillen*" *oder Unterseelen*), car notre corps n'est pas autre chose qu'un édifice d'âmes multiples (*ein Geselleschaftsbau vieler Seelen*). *L'effet, c'est moi*: ce qui ce produit ici ne diffère pas de ce qui se passe dans toute collectivité heureuse et bien organisée: la class dirigeante s'identifie au success de la collectivité (*dass die regierende Klasse sich mit den Erfolgen des Gemeinwesens identifiziert*).[1]

In Hollingdale's English translation:

Philosophers are given to speaking of the will as if it were the best-known thing in the world. . . . A man who *wills*—commands something in himself which obeys or which he believes obeys. But now observe the strangest thing of all about the will—about this so complex thing for which people have only *one* word: insomuch as in the given circumstance we at the same time command *and* obey, and the side which obeys know the sensations of constraint, compulsion, pressure, resistance, motions which usually begin immediately after the act of will; insomuch as, on the other hand, we are in the habit of disregarding and deceiving ourselves over this duality by means of the synthetic concept "I"; so a whole chain of erroneous conclusions and consequently of false evaluations of the will itself has become attached to the will as such. Because in the great majority of cases willing takes place only where the effect of the command, that is to say obedience, was to be *expected*, the *appearance* has translated itself into the sensation, as if it were here a *necessity of effect*. Enough: he who wills believes with a tolerable degree of certainty that will and action are somehow one. . . . "Freedom of will"—is the expression for that complex condition of pleasure of the person who wills, who commands and at the same time identifies himself with the executor of the command—who as such also enjoys the triumph over resistance involved but who thinks it was his will itself which overcame these resistances. He who wills adds in this way the sensations of pleasure of the successful executive agents, the serviceable "under-wills" or under-souls—for our body is only a social structure composed of many souls—to his sensations of pleasure as commander. *L'effet, c'est moi*: what happens here is what happens in every well-constructed and happy commonwealth: the ruling class identifies itself with the successes of the commonwealth.[2]

It is not a matter here of challenging the choices made by the translator (which would suggest that I intended to propose alternatives) but to point out the problems they raise. We attach particular importance to the fact that Nietzsche's text itself contains some thoughts about "translation" insomuch as it is a process of misrepresentation (*travestissement*) that has to be given a basic anthropological meaning. No less remarkable is the fact that, given the illusions of unity that are inherent in willing, the invocation of the political metaphor (if that is what it is . . .) goes hand in hand with the construction of a "French" phrase (which cannot be translated into French) that is a parodic version of the famous allegory of absolute monarchy attributed to Louis XIV ("*L'État c'est moi*").

Two striking features of the French translation are to be noted. It systematically introduces the word *sujet* (*sujet obéissant, sujet voulant*) because it makes the metaphysical assumption that an *Etwas* remains "the same" throughout the actions of commanding and the effects of obeying, and thus gets around the critique that Nietzsche's text is making, at this very moment, of the illusion of the "I" (*Ich*). But, in another respect, it thus provides itself with a generic term—playing on one of the connotations of the French *sujet* that is not present in the closest German philosophical equivalent (*das Subjekt*)—to express the ambivalence of the real or imagined relations of subordination (*arkhein* and *arkhesthai*) that exist between the "parts of the soul" (unless they are of the body) that constitute, for Nietzsche, the essence of the phenomenon of "will": *sujet obeissant* looks like a tautology, and *sujet voulant* almost like a contradiction. Or is it the other way around?

Far from being a curiosity, such a text brings us to the very heart of the linguistic tensions characteristic of the construction and use of the notion of *sujet*. Their essential characteristic derives from the Greek and Latin notions, which tend to produce two different paradigms for the interpretation of "*sujet*," one specific to the neo-Latin languages (and especially French) and one specific to German. In one case the simultaneously logical-ontological and juridico-political connotations of *sujet* are—thanks to a sort of "historial" wordplay on the meanings of *subjectum* and *subjectus*—exploited in a systematic investigation into the modalities of the "*assujettissement du sujet*" (subjugation of the subject). In the other case the relationship between the subject's mode of being and the register of law or power can be found exclusively in an ontology of freedom that contrasts it with nature, because the political dimension is immediately concealed by language or is, rather, relegated to the latent system. The two paradigms do not, of course, develop independently of one another, since they share the same classical references and because the more or less simultaneous translation of the works of European metaphysics is one of the main determinants of their history. In that respect it is striking that it should be the divergent readings of Nietzsche's work that bring this out.

B. The Sovereignty of the Subject: Bataille or Heidegger?

The first paradigm can be exemplified by Georges Bataille, who was probably one the first contemporary authors working in the French language to consciously exploit the possibility of inscribing a dialectical (or mystical) antimony at the heart of anthropology by defining the subject in terms of its "sovereignty," or in other words its nonsubjugation. According to Bataille this is just a bad pun—even though his construct obviously relies on it:

> If I have spoken of objective sovereignty, I have never lost sight of the fact that sovereignty is never truly objective and that, on the contrary, the term refers to a deep subjectivity . . . [in the world of things and their interdependencies] we see relations of force and, whilst isolated elements are of course influenced by the mass, the mass cannot *subordinate* [*subordonner*] them. Subordination presupposes a different relationship: that between subject and object [footnote: when sovereigns speak of "my subjects," it introduces an unavoidable ambiguity: the *subject* exists for me, the *sovereign*. The subject I am talking about is in no sense *subjected* [*assujetti*]. *The subject is the being as he appears to himself from within. . . . The subject who is different to the others differs from them in the way that the subject of labour differs from the object of labour.* The inevitable pun is unwelcome. I mean that the mass individual, who spends part of his time working for the benefit of the sovereign, *recognizes* him; I mean that he *recognizes himself* in him. The mass individual no longer sees in the sovereign the object he must be in his eyes, but the *subject* . . . the sovereign, who summarises the essence of the *subject*, is he for whom and through whom the instant, the *miraculous* instant is the sea into which the streams of labour flow.[3]

The obstacle Bataille comes up against here may have influenced his decision to abandon his book. But it also provides Lacan, Althusser, and Foucault with their starting point when they transform the impasse into an opening.

The second paradigm is exemplified by Heidegger's suggestion that Nietzsche's doctrine of the "will to power" should be seen as part of the "history of being" characteristic of Western metaphysics. Nietzsche characterizes the subject that designates itself "I" (*Ich*) or "ego" as a grammatical fiction (see in particular the fragments from 1887 to 1889 published under the title *The Will to Power*). Heidegger, however, is trying to demonstrate that it "is grounded in the metaphysics established by Descartes," to the extent that, although he makes body rather than "soul" and "conscience" the substance of thought, he identifies the latter more closely than ever with subjectivity and makes the criterion of truth the definition of man as subject.[4] Heidegger's problem it how is to determine, through a genealogical investigation into "metaphysics as the history of being," the preconditions for the moment of the ontological conversion (which is closely linked to the mutation in the idea of truth itself) that made *subjectum*, which Latin philosophers regarded as a "translation" of Aristotle's *hypokeimenon*, not just the simple presupposition of the realization of an individual substance in a particular form, but "the" very power to think, from which all representations stem, and which reflects upon itself in the first person (*cogito me cogitare* is the key phrase attributed to Descartes by Heidegger). The "sovereignty of the subject" (*Herrschaft des Subjekts*), on which we are still dependent, is for him basically the creation of the Descartes of the *Méditations* and *Principles of Philosophy*.

To begin to undo this tangle (and, in doing so, to elucidate at least part of the unsaid [*non-dit*] of late twentieth-century debates about the "philosophy of the subject" and the various critiques thereof), we must first reduce Heidegger's construction of the history of Being as the history of successive generalizations of "subjectness" (*Subjektheit, "I think"*) to the self-referentiality (or autonomy) of the transcendental subject and its retrospective attribution to Descartes, which made it the starting point for the specifically modern attitude in philosophy. Despite Bataille's embarrassment about what he calls a pun, we must then reconstruct a *longue-durée* semantics whose effects become ever more specific and conscious in the hands of his successors, whom it helps to unite, regardless of the obvious doctrinal disagreements. Let us begin with the first point.

C. The "Cartesian" Subject: A Kantian Invention

The expressions "Cartesian subject" and "Cartesian subjectivity" are so widely used and so often used to situate Cartesianism in a historical or comparative series (either in a French discourse, or between French and other philosophical idioms) that it is worthwhile expounding in detail the prehistory of this construct, which is also a translation error. That error reveals the extraordinary conceptual work performed by the language itself (because of the syntactic differences among Latin, French, and German). The error is sufficiently powerful and suggestive to induce a retrospective understanding of Descartes's text and the issues at stake in his philosophy, and we can no longer ignore the issue. Coming to Descartes after Kant's reading of him, we can at most see his *cogito* as an early form of resistance to the transcendental problematic but cannot divorce it from the language of "subjectivity." From that point of view, we cannot completely undo what Kant has done.

As Joachim Ritter judiciously reminds us, *Subjektivität* is already an important term in Baumgarten's *Aesthetics* (1750).[5] It refers to the field and quality of phenomena that, in the thinking, perceiving and sentient being, are the effect not of the external objects that affect it, but of its own dispositions (they are what Locke or Malebranche would call "second qualities"). Ritter's suggestion to the contrary notwithstanding, the use of *subjectum*, or rather *Subjekt* in German does not, however, precede this abstract conceptual formation; it comes later. It is in fact only with the *Critique of Pure Reason* that *das Subjekt* (variously described as the "logical subject," the "empirical subject," the "rational subject," the "transcendental subject," or the "moral subject") becomes the key concept in a philosophy of subjectivity. Kant's philosophy therefore simultaneously "invents" the problematic of a thought whose conditions of access to both the objectivity of the laws of nature and the universality of ethical and aesthetic values lie in its own constitution (the so-called Copernican revolution) and gives the name "subject" (i.e., the opposite of "object") to the generic individuality inherent in the interplay between the faculties of knowledge; for all finite minds, that interplay constitutes "the world" and gives a meaning to the fact of acting in the world. Even if we take into account its remarkable forerunners (such as that identified by Alain de Libera in the work of the radical twelfth-century Franciscan, Pierre Jean Olieu),[6] who were in all probability unknown to Kant, the only intrinsic connection between the *Subjekt* created by Kant and the scholastic notion of the *subjectum* or *suppositum* is that implied by the idea of the Copernican revolution: the categories, or in other words the most general modalities that the activity of judgment uses to attribute predicates to things, are no longer genera of being, but categories of subject, constitutive of the object (and, in that sense, of experience in general: "transcendentals").

Why, in these conditions, did Kant retrospectively project this discovery on to a "pre-cursor," namely Descartes? For over two hundred years, his work has lent credence to the idea that the subject is a Cartesian invention, and thus encouraged even the greatest thinkers to look for traces of a semantic mutation in terms that are almost never used by the philosopher of the *Meditations*. The answer lies, as so often, in the letter of the text itself. We will compare three passages from the *Critique of Pure Reason* ("Transcendental Deduction" and "Paralogisms of Pure Reason"). It has to be said that they are still not easy to translate.

1. *Das*: Ich denke, *muss alle meine Vorstellungen begleiten können; denn sonst würde etwas in mir vorgestellt werden, was gar nicht gedacht werden könnte. . . . Also hat alles Mannigfaltige der Anschauung eine notwedige Beziehung auf das:* Ich denke, *in demselben Subjekt, darin dieses Mannigfaltige angetroffen wird. Diese Vorstellung aber ist ein Aktus der Spontaneität, sie kann nichts als zur Sinnlichkeit gehörig angesehen werden. Ich nenne sie die reine Apperzeption . . . weil sie dasjenige Selbstbewusstsein ist, was, indem es die Vorstellung* Ich denke *hervorbringt, die alle anderen muss begleiten können, und in allem Bewusstsein ein und dasselbe ist . . . von keiner weiter begleitet werden kann.*[7]

The *I think* must be able to accompany all my representations; for otherwise something would be represented in me which could not be thought at all. . . . Thus; all manifold of intuition has a necessary relationship to the *I think*, in the same subject in which this manifold is to be encountered. But this representation is an act of *spontaneity*; i.e. it cannot be regarded as belonging to sensibility. I call it the *pure apperception* . . . since it is that self-consciousness which, because it produces the representation *I think*, which must be able to accompany all others and in which all consciousness is one and the same, cannot be accompanied by any further representation.[8]

2. Ich, *als denkend, bin ein Gegenstand des inneren Sinnes, und heisse Seele. . . . Demnach bedeutet der Ausdruck:* Ich, *als ein denkend Wesen, schon den Gegenstand der Psychologie . . .* Ich denke, *ist also der alleinige Text der rationalen Psychologie, aus welchem sie ihre ganze Weisheit auswickeln soll. Man sieht leicht, dass dieser Gedanke, wenn er auf einen Gegenstand (mich selbst) bezogen werden soll, nichts anderes, als transzendentale Prädikate desselben, enthalten könne. . . . Zum Grunde derselben können wir aber nichts anderes legen, also die einfache und für sich selbst an Inhalt gänzlich leere Vorstellung:* Ich; *von der man nicht einmal sagen kann, dass sie ein Begriff sei, sondern ein blosses Bewusstsein, dass alle Begriffe begleitet. Durch dieses* Ich, *oder* Er, *oder* Es (das Ding), *welches denkt, wird nun nichts weiter, als ein tranzendentales Subjekt der Gedanken vorgestellt =x, welches nur durch die Gedanken, die seine Prädikate sind erkannt wird.*[9]

I, as thinking, am an object of inner sense, and am called "soul." Accordingly, the expression "I," as a thinking being, already signifies the object of a psychology (342) . . . I *think* is thus the whole text of a rational psychology, from which it is to develop its entire wisdom. One can easily see that this thought, if it is to be related to a subject (myself), can contain nothing other than its transcendental predicates (A 343) . . . At the ground of this doctrine we can place nothing but the simple and in content for itself wholly empty representation *I*, of which one cannot even say that it is a concept, but a mere consciousness that accompanies every concept. Through this I, or He, or It (the thing) which thinks, nothing further is represented than a transcendental subject of thought = x, which is recognised through the thoughts that are its predicates (A 346)[10]

3. Der Satz: Ich denke, *wird aber hierbei nur problematisch genommen; nich sofern er eine Wahrnehmung von einem Dasein enthalten mag (das Cartesianische* cogito, ergo sum), *sondern seiner blossen Möglichkeit nach, um zu sehen, welche Eigenschaften aus diesem so einfachen Satze auf das Subjekt desselben (es mag dergleichen nun existieren oder nicht) fliessen mögen. Läge unserer reinen Vernunftsertkenntnis von denkenden Wesen überhaupt mehr, als das* cogito *zum Grunde . . . so würde eine empirische Psychologie entspringen.*[11]

The proposition "I think" is, however, taken here only problematically; and insofar as it may contain a perception of an existence (the Cartesian *cogito ergo sum*), but only in its mere possibility, in order to see which properties might flow from so simple a proposition as this for its subject. If more than the *cogito* were the ground of our pure rational cognition of things in general . . . then an empirical psychology would arise.[12]

Leaving aside the remarkable alternation among the pronouns (*Ich, Er, Es*),[13] we can see that Kant is doing one thing whilst claiming to do another. He attributes to Descartes a nominalization of the statement *cogito* or "I think" so as to make it the name of a self-referential operation whereby thought takes itself as its own object; the full formula should be "I am thinking that I am thinking what I am thinking." It therefore designates the "something" or the "being" that both intends and is intended by thought as a *subject* (*subjectum*, which Kant transcribes as *Subjekt*) in the sense that classical metaphysics defines a subject as a pole or support for the attribution of predicates. Kant thereby suggests to his successors (Fichte, Hegel) that the only conceivable subject (*hypokeimenon*) is a subject that thinks itself and whose predicates are its thoughts. From the Cartesian point of view, these two operations are contradictory, as we can see if we go back to the text of the *Méditations*. Strictly speaking, the simple phrase *cogito/je pense* is never nominalized in Descartes (its first appearance as "the *cogito*" is in Arnauld's *Des vraies et des fausses idées* [1683]), even if the way it reflects upon the properties of its own enunciation anticipates such nominalization. The transition to the metaphysical subject is, on the other hand, incompatible with the *cogito* in the strict sense (in the *Meditations*, it is reduced to the existential proposition "*je suis*," "*j'existe*"). The *cogito* is in fact inseparable from a first-person statement (*ego*), which Descartes contrasts with the he/it (*il/ille*) of God and the "this" (*hoc*) of his own body (in a problematic of identity or ego: "*Ce moi, c'est-à-dire mon âme, par laquelle je suis ce que je suis*"—"Thus this self [*moi*], that is to say the soul, by which I am what I am"; *Discours de la méthode, Sixième meditation*; *Philosophical Writings*, 32). "I think" is equivalent to "I am," which is then developed into "I am who I am," or in other words I am my soul (*mens*) and not Him (God) or that (my body). We have here a misunderstanding—which has very serious implications as, reading thought Kantian spectacles, the whole of transcendental philosophy, right down to Husserl and Heidegger constantly criticizes Descartes for having "substantialized the subject" in the very moment of its discovery.

The misunderstanding arises, basically, because Kant has difficulty situating in historical terms a philosophically revolutionary idea that encapsulates the entire originality of his own "transcendental dialectic" and that differs from both the "subjectivity" of Aristotelian metaphysics (*tode ti, hypokeimenon, ousia*) and the "ipseity" of the Cartesian "thing that thinks" (*ego ipse a me percipior*): that of the truth of the perceptive appearance inherent in thought. According to Kant, we cannot think (form concepts, subsume into categories, etc.) without our inner sense being affected and without, therefore, giving rise to the illusion that there is an "inner reality" which is itself the object of thought: the thinking "self" recognizes itself in its logical function (unifying experience) to the extent that it constantly misrecognises itself because it believes it can be known (as a phenomenon, literally a "that which appears": *erscheint*). Now, in Kant, "substance" is no longer of the order of being or of the Thing "in itself." Substance is no more than the concept of what which remains permanent in phenomena. Kant therefore explains to us that the *subject*, which in itself (qua potentiality or logical faculty) is nothing substantial because it is in no sense phenomenal, constantly *appears to itself* in the modality of a substance as it thinks (itself) and because it thinks (itself). In the *Transcendental Deduction* (§25), Kant writes: "I therefore have no cognition of myself as I am, but only as I appear to myself (*wie ich mir selbst erscheine*)" (B 158). The "I," which is given only in a form that is inseparable from an enunciation—"I think"—that also functions as its proper, or in other words generic, "name," can apprehend itself (while "affecting itself") only in an illusory mode. But this illusion or transcendental appearance (*Schein*) is the only thing that can deliver a primal truth, and the only possible form of ground. In one sense it is truth itself. *Subject* is the word that now denotes this astonishing unity of opposites. And Kant attributes to Descartes the metaphysical illusion he himself claims to have escaped. In the process of "being deceived," Descartes bears witness to the fact that the false is lodged at the heart of the true, or that illusion is constitutive of manifestation.

It does seem that we are dealing here exclusively with epistemological propositions and the experience of thought—and it should be noted that the enunciation's syntactic forms and the translations or transpositions play a determinant role. There is nothing to evoke openly a "practical" and, a fortiori, "political" dimension of the subject. This is not, however, certain when we look at two characteristics of the arguments we have just described. The first is that Kant's *subject* (the *Ich* or, to be more accurate, the *Ich denke*) is basically caught up in a relationship of ascription. The reflexivity ascribes to it, or it ascribes to itself, a representation that is both truth and error, recognition and misrecognition. The second is that this circle of apperception results in an injunction. It is not only tempting, but necessary to compare this injunction with the very form of the categorical imperative: We are enjoined to free our own representation from phenomenalism (or, which comes down to the same thing, substantialism) in order to relate it to the idea of "pure" intellectual activity. Now as such an idea is meaningless in terms of nature, and it is only as a correlate of freedom that it can acquire a meaning. This is the way the study of the "Paralogisms of pure reason" ends: the transcendental *subject* (the reflexive identity of the self or *Selbst*) is identified with the moral "personality" (*Persönlichkeit*): "a possible subject of a better world, which he has in its idea" (B 426).

In historical terms, one would like to be able to relate this substratum of Kant's thought to the "becoming a subject" of the revolutionary and post-revolutionary citizen, and especially to the establishment of the category of a "subject of law" (*Reichssubjekt*) of which we do not, as yet, have a sufficiently clear idea. In a recent study, Yves-Charles Zarka notes that in Leibniz, along with a problematic of justice and equity that requires everyone to "put himself in the place of all," we observe the emergence of the expression *subjectum juris*, in the sense of a "moral quality" that universalizes its bearer.[14] But we also know that, even when he seems to come closest to defining the idea of it (as in the *Theory of Right* of 1795), Kant (and Hegel after him) never uses the expression *Rechtssubjekt*, which seems to appear only with the *Historical School of Law* (Savigny, Hugo, Puchta).[15] These subjects (*Subjekte*), in "relation to whom" obligations can be conceptualized (and who "relate" those obligations to themselves) have strictly nothing to do with political *subjects* (*Untertan*, which Kant equates with the Latin *subditus*) who obey a sovereign (which may be the people, as constituted into a State). The encounter with the problematic of sovereignty and the law implicit in the idea of a liberation of the subject, and of the subject as "he who frees himself," therefore remains repressed. Only the young Marx, in his early critique of the Hegelian philosophy of the State, would be tempted to peek under the veil by lending credence to the *Staatssubjekt*.[16] But this manuscript would remain unpublished for more than a century.

D. *Subjectivity* à la française

It is, in contrast, possible to interpret the way in which contemporary philosophy—and especially contemporary French philosophy—understands the question of subjectivity: not as a question of essence, or as relating being to truth and appearance, or in the metaphysical opposition between nature and liberty, but as a political issue, a becoming or a relationship between forces that are "internal" to their own conflict.

From the point of view of the history of ideas and words, we should obviously establish a certain number of intermediary links, although we can do no more than evoke them here. First and foremost, there is Rousseau. The two sides of his work and the corresponding turns of phrase leave traces everywhere. Think of the way *The Social Contract* establishes a strict correlation between the figures of the "citizen" who is a member of the sovereign (or in other words the author of the law) and the "subject" who finds freedom in absolute obedience to that same law thanks to the "total alienation" of individual wills that gives rise to a general will. That will founds a "collective ego" that is reflected in every individual consciousness (in *The Phenomenology of Mind*, Hegel makes implicit reference to Rousseau when he speaks of *Ich, das Wir, und Wir, das Ich ist*). Think, too, of the way in which Rousseau's autobiographical works associate the theme of the authenticity of the ego with that of subjugation (*assujettissment*):

> There is not a day when I do not recall with joy and emotion that unique and brief time in my life when I was completely me, unmixed and unhindered, and when I could say that I was alive . . . I could not bear subjection [*assujetissement*], I was perfectly free, and even better than free since I was subject [*assujetti*] only to my own affections, and I did only what I wanted to do.[17]

We then have to take into account the revolutionary caesura, which not only has the effect of allowing the citizen (who is entitled to have political rights) to "take over" from the subject (*subjectus, subditus*) but also of allowing the subject (*subjectum*) to evolve into a citizen in the sense that his humanity is naturalized. This inscribes all anthropological differences (age, gender, culture, health, abilities, morality, etc.) in an "individual character," which determines the subject's social recognition, with which the subject identifies (to a greater or lesser extent) in the course of his education. Together with the Rousseauist theorem and the Hegelian or Nietzschean critiques that have been made of it, it is the historical and political precondition for Bataille's subversion of the relationship between sovereignty and subjectivity. Such (at least according to my hypothesis) is the genealogy of the identification of the *problem of subjectivity* with the *problem of subjection*, which will give a completely new meaning to the philosophical question of the subject (and at the same time our perception of its history). I would like to illustrate this new discourse on the "subject" with some typical examples:

Gilles Deleuze refers to this issue in his *Empiricism and Subjectivity*:

> It is the same difference [between the origin and the qualification of ideas] that Hume encounters under the form of an antinomy of knowledge: it defines the problem of the self [*moi*]. The mind is not subject: it is subjected. When the subject is constituted in the mind under the effect of principles, the mind apprehends itself as a self [*moi*], for it has been qualified. But the problem is this: if the subject is constituted only inside the collection of ideas, how can the collection of ideas be apprehended as a self, how can I say "I" under the influence of the same principles.[18]

Later (with Guattari), he carefully works upon the paradigms of servitude or slavery (*asservissement, servus*) and subjection or subjugation (*subjectus, subditus*) in order to explain the characteristic modernity of the capitalist subject:

> We distinguish machinic enslavement and social subjection as two separate concepts. There is enslavement when human beings themselves are constituent pieces of a machine . . . under the control and direction of a higher unity. But there is subjection when the higher unity constitutes the human being as a subject linked to a now exterior object. . . . It would appear, then, that the modern State, through technological development, has substituted an increasingly powerful social subjection for machinic enslavement. . . . In effect, capital acts as the point of subjectification that constitutes human beings as subjects; but some, the "capitalists," are subjects of enunciation that form the private subjectivity of capital, while the others, the "proletarians," are subjects of the statement, subjected to the technical machines in which constant capital is effectuated.[19]

Jacques Derrida discovers this constitutive amphibology from Rousseau onward:

> From then on, writing has the function of reaching *subjects* who are not only distant but outside the entire field of vision and beyond earshot. Why *subjects*? Why should writing be another name for the constitution of *subjects* and, so to speak, of *constitution* itself? Of a subject, that is to say an individual held responsible (for) himself in front of a law and by the same token subject to that law?[20]

He also finds it in connection with Levinas:

> The subordination of freedom indicates a subjection of the *subjectum* certainly, but this is a subjection that, rather than depriving the subject of its birth and its freedom, actually

gives [*donne*] it birth, along with the freedom that is therebty ordained [*ordonnée*]. It is still a question of subjection, but not in the sense of an interiorization; rather, the subject comes to itself in the movement whereby it welcomes the Wholly Other as the Most High. This subordination ordains [*ordonne*] and gives [*donne*] the subjectivity of the subject.[21]

But he also tries to force it to the point of implosion and, to adopt Artaud's neologism: "to derange the subjectile [*forcener le sujectile*]."

Writing at the same time as Bataille, Louis Althusser also emphasizes the paradox of sovereignty:

This God is a Subject-King, which is to say, a Slave-King. Hegelian freedom precisely delivers the subject from his subjection and converts his servitude into a kingdom. The concept is the kingdom of subjectivity, that is, the realm of the subject become king. . . . Such is the circularity of freedom in the concept: it is the conversion of servitude, the conversion of the subject into his reign.[22]

He sees this as the general mechanism whereby ideology "interpellates" individuals as subjects. The prototype is supplied by religious consciousness:

It then emerges that the interpellation of individuals as subjects presupposes the "existence" of a Unique and central Other Subject, in whose Name the religious ideology interpellates all individuals as subjects. . . . God this defines himself as the Subject *par excellence*, he who is through himself and for himself ("I am that I am"), and he who interpellates his subject, the individual subjected to him by his very interpellation, i.e. the individual named Moses. And Moses, interpellated-called by his Name, having recognised that it "really" was he who was called by God, recognizes that he is a subject, a subject *of* God, a subject subjected to God, *a subject through the Subject and subjected to the Subject*. The proof: he obeys him, and makes his people obey God's commandments.[23]

It is Lacan and Foucault who deploy the specter of subjectivity as a process of subjugation most systematically. But they do so in diametrically opposed ways.

Lacan draws upon the old heritage of two French phrases that are at once paradoxical and absolutely idiomatic: "the ego is hateful" (Pascal) and "I is an other" (Rimbaud). What is the subject according to Lacan? Nothing more than the sequence of the effects of the living individual's alienation by the "law of the signifier." While it has to be regarded as irreducible, the subject is never originary, but always already dependent. The subject exists only as an effect of the speech (*parole*) that constitutes it (and names it, to begin with) in a symbolic world of discourses and institutions that it cannot, by definition, master. This is how Lacan interprets the "misrecognition" that constitutes the unconscious. Because it is "subject [*soumis*] to the signifier" that irremediably cuts it off from itself, the subject must for ever oscillate between the illusion of identity—the narcissistic beliefs of an "imaginary capture" are resumed in the figure of the *ego*—and the unknown element in the conflict: the recognition of a question from the other (beginning with the other sex) as what is most characteristic about it. The subject is constituted in (and through) this impossible choice.

> If desire is an effect in the subject of the condition—which is imposed upon him by the existence of discourse—that his need pass through the defiles of the signifier . . . the subject find the constitutive structure of his desire in the same gap opened up by the effect of the signifiers in those who come to represent the Other for him, in so far as his demand is subjected to them.[24]

At best, analysis inverts the trajectory of the constitution of desire, which leads the subject to enunciate his own "lack of being" ("desire merely subjects what analysis makes subjective").[25]

Foucault, for his part, found in the methods used to obtain admissions and confessions (which migrate from religion and the inquisition to psychology and psychiatry) a model for the relationship between subjectivity, appearance, and truth (*Madness and Civilization, History of Sexuality*). In Bentham's panopticism he finds an ideal diagram of all the "fictive relations" (which are materialized in the working of institutions of social normalization) in which "a real subjection is born mechanically."[26] On this basis, he drew up a program for an investigation into the "modes of objectification that transform human beings into subjects," and especially relations of power."[27] But there is no power, either over the "self" or over "others" that does not involve the constitution of a knowledge (*un savoir*), and knowledge itself is not a purely theoretical activity: it is a social practice that produces objectivity. The question of the subject and that of the object, brought back to a twofold process of subjectivation and objectivation, of the subordination (*assujettissement*) of the individual to rules and to the construction of a self-to-self relationship that takes various practical modalities, the question of the subject and that of the object are therefore not opposed to each other. They are two aspects of a single reality:

> Foucault has now undertaken, still within the same general project, to study the constitution of the subject as an object for himself: the formation of procedures by which the subject is led to observe himself, analyse himself, recognize himself as a domain of possible knowledge. In short, this concerns the history of "subjectivity," if what is meant by that term is the way in which the subject experiences himself in a game of truth where he relates to himself.[28]

These are the very words that were used in Kant's Transcendental Dialectic; but their original meaning has been inverted. We can see that there is a circle of presuppositions; the *subject* is the set of subjugating or subjectifying structures (*dispositifs d'assujettissement ou de subjectivation*) that act objectively on the "subjectivity" of the individual. They presuppose, that is, the subject's "freedom," or ability to resist, and turn it against him. We are in other words talking about a power differential. It results in both a politics (trying to free the individual from certain disciplines and certain types of individualism) and an ethics (inventing "practices of freedom," "new power relations," and modes of *askesis* rather than of self-consciousness). Precisely because they are dispersed and conflicting, these propositions transform our reading of Europe's philosophical past. Because they reveal the associations and metaphors that underlie Nietzsche's text, they allow us to make different use of the subjectivity defined in the *Critique of Pure Reason*. Had the internal relationship not been established between the subject (*subjectum, Subjekt*) and personal subjection, and therefore with the political, juridical and theological power of which it is an effect and inverted image, we would not be able to recognize in the paradoxical combination of truth and transcendental appearance described in the "Paralogisms of Pure Reason" the sign of an originary difference (or *différance*) that concerns the ethics of internal obedience and *askesis* as much as the metaphysics of the mind and self-consciousness, if not more so. To conclude, they reopen the question of the active finitude specific to the Cartesian subject (or nonsubject), which is, perhaps, not so much a "nature" or thinking "substance," or in other words representation, as a "revindication" (as Canguilhem puts it) of the right to say "I," "between infinity and nothingness," or between God and the body.[29]

Postscriptum

In an essay published since the present article was completed ("Superanus," *Theory and Event* 8, no. 1 [2005]), Geoffrey Bennington in his own manner traverses the same "sites" of theory and writing—in particular, the relation between Bataille and Rousseau—starting from the Derridian question of the "drive of mastery" (*Bemächtigungstrieb*). A discussion between us (among others) would be necessary and welcome.

Translated by David Macey

PART ONE

"Our True Self Is Not Entirely Within Us"

"*Ego sum, ego existo*": Descartes on the Verge of Heresy

Mister President, you have imposed Draconian limits upon me. As a result, I must cut to the chase. The abstract that you might have received is not, as you no doubt grasp, a summary of my talk: not only because I hadn't yet given my text a definitive form but also because what I have to say, since it remains highly open to discussion, is very difficult to summarize. Rather than drawing conclusions, my goal today is merely to arrive at questions; and I would consider myself a very happy man if, to some extent, you were to concur that these questions can indeed be posed. Although I speak there of "sketching out what is, in certain respects, a renewed interpretation of Cartesian 'metaphysics,'" I make no pretense of articulating ideas that are wholly new. On the contrary, what I have to say, for the most part, has already been established thanks to the work of eminent Descartes scholars. But it seemed to me that these very ideas fare better, and, on a few important points, can be understood otherwise by restoring a key to their analysis that, to a remarkable degree, hasn't ever been elucidated—even if it occasionally shows up in what used to be called, in a now outmoded jargon, the "unsaid" of discussions.[1] On the basis of this restoration—"symptomatic," if you wish—I would like to attempt a rereading of a text that is constitutive of our philosophical culture, in which we have never stopped finding the unexpected, or even the unknown. In order to assure that this exercise wouldn't be without effects of *titillatio*, then, I lent my abstract a somewhat provocative form. You might surmise that this provocation, in the etymological sense, was addressed to myself first of all.

Absence of the Cogito

Let us begin, if you will, with what is already known. Commentaries on Descartes's *Meditations*, for a very long time now, have tended to isolate an argument that occurs at the beginning of the Second Meditation. This argument is what they designate under the name of the *cogito*, assigning it a fundamental place within the economy of the text, or within what Martial Gueroult, who borrowed from Descartes himself what has become the unavoidable formula, called the *order of reasons*. As a result, one speaks of "the *cogito*" and thereby designates: *either*, globally, the reasoning whereby, upon release from the "metaphysical doubt" that he instituted through various "hyperbolic hypotheses," Descartes discovers the certainty of his existence in the irreducibility of his own thought, the first truth necessary to reconstruct the other elements of science; *or*, more specifically, the phrase that, at the heart of this reasoning, presents us with the very moment when certainty is acquired, the cusp of the meditation; *or*, finally, the very utterance, isolated by Descartes himself, which can be said to be absolutely certain. From this point in the text onward, commentaries proceed in one of two complementary directions: on the one hand, to the study of the intimate relationship between this argument and the whole system of Cartesian metaphysics insofar as it privileges the subjectivity of the *Ego* and the being of thought; on the other hand, to the analysis of the utterance itself (often designated, today, as a "canonical" or "protocolary" statement) in terms of its structure and its discursive function—an analysis that was already well under way during Descartes's own lifetime in the discussions that he undertook with various readers and naysayers.

But this is where the difficulties commence. As we know, there is no doubt that the text of the *Meditations* features an utterance that one might call canonical, that even becomes the object of a particularly spectacular "staging," and that it is easy to suppose strategically governs the whole construction of the work. But this statement can only be called "*cogito*" by amalgamating it with statements from other equally "foundational" works in which Descartes elaborates similar arguments with more or less detail, and which actually contain, in Latin, the verb *cogito* or, in French, *je pense*. These other works are, principally, Part IV of *Discourse on Method*: "*je pense, donc je suis* [I think therefore I am]"; and the *Principles of Philosophy*: *Ego cogito, ergo sum* (translated back into French as "*je pense, donc je suis*"). But the utterance from the *Meditations* is different. It is simply *Ego sum, ego existo*—without any immediate, internal reference to *cogitare* or *cogitatio*. The designation of this utterance as the "*cogito*" or as the truth of the "*cogito*" is thus, at best, an interpretation. Naturally, this interpretation has been explained, even explained well. Although the *Meditations* does not contain the better known formulation, Descartes himself, in his *Responses to Objections*, had no problem discussing this text as if it could help understand whether the passage from *cogito* to *sum* entails a mediate or immediate inference or why the statement *cogito* ("I think") is privileged over other verbs that express subjective actions, such as *ambulo* ("I walk"). Moreover, there is no lack of evidence to suggest that the discourse of the *Meditations*, by virtue of its very singular form—that of a reflexive argumentation in the first person that reconstitutes or even constitutes the movement of thought—would be a sort of original version, or the reconstitution of the original version of the foundational argument, which was inscribed, not to forget, in a real intellectual experience and was inseparable from this experience. The "other" versions, expounded in the works that I listed before, can and must be presented either as the narrative of this experience or as a commentary on its metaphysical function; and, in this respect, they unambiguously indicate the place, indeed the very point in the written text of the *Meditations* to look for what they propose to call the "*cogito*." But it becomes difficult not to see that the more we accumulate incontestable reasons to identify the "*cogito*," or even the originary "*cogito*," with precisely *this* utterance from the *Meditations*—*Ego sum, ego existo* ("I am, I exist")—which Descartes called "necessarily true each time that I pronounce it or conceive it," the more the fact that it *does not* take the form of "I think, I am" (with or without *therefore*) becomes enigmatic and challenging.

Confronted with this enigma, as you know, the commentators have reacted very differently. I will quickly rehearse some of these reactions. Many of the greatest commentators purely and simply ignore it and, in order to discuss the *Meditations*, never fail to rely on a passage from Descartes's other works. Others notice it and treat it as a problem: either as the necessity of proving the equivalence of *Ego sum, ego existo* and (*Ego*) *cogito, ergo sum*, showing that "thought" and the "I think" are implied in the statement from the *Meditations*; or as the invitation to recognize the originality of the writing of the *Meditations*, the thought that is written in the *Meditations*, or even the thought of the subject who writes himself in the *Meditations*. The risk, then, is that the apparent and purposeful univocity of the Cartesian "system" would belie an insistent plurality, or, in any event, the singularity of his separate works, each of which must henceforth be considered as inherently self-sufficient, as a work that constructs its own language in its own way and according to its own "reasons."

Even such an approach, however, appears still to lack an element that would explicate this singularity, an element that would pertain to the very letter of the text, and that Descartes himself had no need to comment on, because, whether or not he was clearly conscious of it (not omitting to discuss what it means to be "clearly conscious"), this element can function as such only if it goes without saying. Or rather, I would prefer to say that it *goes with saying*; that is, it can only be understood (or read) in and through the text of the "meditation" itself and can never be extracted from this text nor made the object of a metadiscourse (unlike exactly what happens with "I think, therefore I am"), except at the price of immediately sapping it of its very effectiveness and signification. Nonetheless, this is exactly what I intend to do. I will explain.

Let us return to the *Meditations*, then, or rather to the *Meditationes*; for, what matters most, by necessity, is the first Latin text that Descartes *wrote*, and thus thought while writing, thought through writing. The translations of the text, whether the one that Descartes personally reviewed, or the modern one that Michelle Beyssade recently made available to us,[2] should come into play only when they reveal certain knots or textual difficulties. Let us make believe that we have never read this text; let us pretend, above all, that we know nothing about the "Cartesian system," or that, in order to gain access to it, we are strictly limited to the text of the *Meditationes*, which never presents itself as the description of a system but rather as the protocol of a singular reflection—a reflection that, nonetheless, by virtue of its writing, and precisely under the condition that this writing suits it perfectly, is open to the universal participation of all its potential readers. Let us turn to the beginning of the Second Meditation, to the moment when Descartes is about to discover what he himself calls the "Archimedian point," *vel minimum quid . . . quod certum sit et inconcussum*, making it possible to leave behind the "grave doubts" in which "yesterday's Meditation" had embroiled him. After he summarizes the arguments that found absolute skepticism (*Quid igitur erit verum? Fortassis hoc unum, nihil esse certi*), after recalling the hypotheses of the "deceptive God" and the "Evil Genius," here is what we read:

> Haud dubie igitur etiam sum, si me fallit; et fallat quantum potest, numquam tamen efficiet, ut hihil sim quamdiu me aliquid esse cogitabo. Adeo ut, omnibus satis superque pensitatis, denique statuendum sit hoc pronuntiatum, Ego sum, ego existo, quoties a me profertur, vel mente concipitur, necessario esse verum.[3]

In Michelle Beyssade's modern French translation:

> Il n'y a donc pas de doute, moi aussi je suis, s'il me trompe; et qu'il me trompe autant qu'il peut, il ne fera poutant jamais que je ne sois rien tant que je penserai être quelque chose; de sorte que tout bien pesé et soupesé, il faut finalement poser que cet énoncé, *je suis, j'existe, moi* toutes les fois que je le prononce ou que je le conçois mentalement, est nécessairement vrai.

Finally, in John Cottingham's English translation:

> In that case I too undoubtedly exist, if he is deceiving me; and let him deceive me as much as he can, he will never bring it about that I am nothing so long as I think that I am something. So after considering everything very thoroughly, I must finally conclude that this proposition, *I am, I exist*, is necessarily true whenever it is put forward by me or conceived in my mind.[4]

No major difficulties, it would seem. Nonetheless, a few remarks are necessary. Michelle Beyssade has good reason to want to underscore the insistence of the *Ego* (since the Duc du Luynes did not do so) which is not necessary in Latin to express the first person: "*moi aussi* je suis," "je suis, j'existe, *moi*." There is not the slightest doubt, upon an initial reading of this text, that the *moi* or the *Ego* supports the essential argument. It is he (me) who—being, existing, discovering (myself) and thus thinking (myself) as such—constitutes the "Archimedean point." But one little problem remains: *Ego* in Latin and *moi* in French do not at all function in the same manner; the reflexive pronoun *moi* could be read as the designation of the subject whereas *Ego* is the subject itself. Furthermore, I believe that we should take this insistence as far as possible, as Descartes himself did, translating the Latin in this way: "*Moi je suis, moi j'existe*" (or: "*je suis, moi, j'existe, moi*"—a formulation that better conveys the assertive *mode* or the *tone* whereby I exit from the fictive nothingness into which the hypothesis of the Evil Genius threatens to plunge me and affirm my existence against this supposed negation).

Let us now adumbrate an initial commentary. There are three main points:

1. Descartes presents us with an "utterance"—that is, a phrase that he pronounces himself (*hoc pronuntiatum*: my utterance, this utterance that I now proffer) and whose exact formulation he reproduces, as if between quotation marks; the

necessary truth or certainty of the utterance then inheres in its pronunciation or proffering. *Quoties a me profertur, vel mente concipitur* means very precisely: each time that I say it out loud or in my mind, each time that *it is uttered* in words or in an inner discourse.

2. How do we understand *quoties*? There is no reason that I can see, if we don't rely on what Descartes will say later, to interpret it as a restriction. On the contrary, it is a generalization: this statement is not only true at the moment, it is instantaneously true *as often as* it is proffered, which is always in my power to do; I can always repeat it *ad libitum* and there is thus no limit upon my ability to reproduce this punctual certainty.

3. How do we understand the duality *sum, existo*? A question of prime importance. It is hardly satisfying to see this duality as a "pleonasm" or a form of rhetorical variation. Up to this point in the *Meditationes*, *existere* has signified real existence: truly to be, really to be, to be as it were "in the real," in opposition to being merely in fiction, an imaginary being. At a minimum, then, *Ego sum, ego existo* signifies: *"je suis, je suis vraiment, moi"* ("I am, me, I truly am"), I am *in the sense of (real) existence*. This is why such an affirmation cannot but raise the question of nature or essence; for, what is it to think an "existence" or a "reality" when we do not know "of what" it is the existence? In any event, we cannot stop there: if this is in fact the meaning of *existere*, what good is the *sum*? Why begin with *Ego sum*?

And now, let us anticipate: the further we advance in the *Meditationes*, the clearer it grows that the problematic of *essentia* and *existentia*, which becomes explicit and dominant after the Third Meditation and culminates in the Fifth, is constructed precisely on the basis of the development and dialectical transformation of the statement *Ego sum, ego existo*. This problematic, then, does not come from the outside, from some scholastic tradition (even if there is some overlap); nor is it "conveyed" or "suggested" by our *pronuntiatum*, which would suppose that we know it already. It can be found, rather, *as a potentiality*, in an "indifferent difference," within this *pronuntiatum* whose formula will be scrupulously repeated many times. We can express this by saying that the very construction of the utterance exhibits an equivalence between *esse* and *existere* in which each term retains its own connotations and peculiar usage: *esse* refers to "being something" and not "being nothing" (*Ego sum* = *non sum nihil*); and *existere*, as we have seen, refers to "really being," not being a "fictive being" (*Ego existo* = I am not a being of reason alone, a dream or a delusion). We dare say, then: What emerges here in germ or in idea is something like the schema of a possible "ontological argument"; but this argument is about the *Ego* and is reduced to the immediate equivalence between terms that will later be formalized in terms of the categories of essence and existence. Tenuous as this indication might be, it remains important because it embroils the forthcoming question of *nature* or *essence* in what at least appears to be a circle: the essence or nature of the *Ego* can only be immediately identical to its existence, the essence of existing or of what exists as such. In truth, this identity entails a forceful constraint: no more than ten lines further on, Descartes will write, for example, that he is not, that *I am not a man*; which is to say that this *essentia* is not the *human essence*: *Quidnam igitur antehac me esse putavi? Hominem scilicet. Sed quid est homo?* Etc. And we know that it took a long time for *Ego* to be thought rigorously as "man," or rather as the spirit of a "man" . . .

But this does not prevent—quite to the contrary—another connotation from being present or at least suggested by the context: existence might well be identified with life, or better, less abstractly, with the fact of existing with the fact of *being alive*. This connotation comes into play from early in the First Meditation when Descartes includes among the illusions and forms of madness that generate skepticism, liable to be globally reprised as deceptions of an ill-willed God or evil genius, the idea of being dead, or of not being born; and the same idea resurfaces again in the descriptions of existing as *res cogitans*—that is, as *mens*, spirit, or as the *life* of this spirit, made up of the daily concatenation of all the thoughts that cover the entire field of its existence. Within the space of a few lines, as well, Descartes also elaborates the opposition between this existence and the nature of the *body*, the body seen as a *cadaver*, as always already dead. I am not "this assemblage of organs that one calls a human body"; neither am I "a fire" or "a breath"; but such is (at present) my life: I doubt, I know, I affirm, I negate, I want, I don't want, I also imagine and I sense. . . . Since Descartes did not formulate a metaphysical concept of the existential, shouldn't we understand *Ego sum, ego existo* as "I am, me who thinks, I am alive"— that is, as the singular being of the (thinking or thought) existence that is life assuring itself by itself in the first person? Perhaps. But, in our culture, which is also that of Descartes, there is a readymade if not omnipresent utterance that precisely equates *Ego sum* with "I am, I live"—meaning "I am the living being" (or even "I am life," which incontestably goes one step further). We don't yet have sufficient elements, then, to introduce such an utterance here and to hold it up to the Cartesian statement, but nothing can dissuade us from noting their strange similarity.

Who I Am

It probably seems that we are moving too slowly; but, in reality, a discovery is near. Everything that we have just said is, in a sense, an attempt to surmise how Descartes would treat his own utterance; that is, indeed, how he would understand it or himself raise the question of its understanding. Among the more original aspects of the text of the *Meditationes* is the way in which its own writing includes a moment of wonder and questions about the meaning of what has just been articulated. Every reader notices the pause that occurs after the *pronuntiatum*—a pause that translates nothing other than the emergent difficulty of understanding, the enigma of what initially appears to be a solution. The translators of the text (the first of whom was read by Descartes) have materialized this pause with a paragraph break:

> Nondum vero satis intelligo, quisnam sim ego ille, qui jam necessario *sum* . . .
>
> Duc de Luynes translation: Mais je ne connais pas encore assez clairement ce que je suis, moi qui suis certain que je suis.

Michelle Beyssade translation: Mais je ne connais pas encore d'une intelligence suffisante ce qu'est moi, ce que je suis, moi qui à présent de toute nécessité suis.

John Cottingham translation: But I do not yet have a sufficient understanding of what this "I" is, that now necessarily exists

None of these translations satisfies me because none is exactly equivalent to the Latin. At bottom, however, as I hope to show, the question has nothing to do with the weakness or confusion of translators. It does have to do with the fact that Descartes's sentence is untranslatable into French even though, in a sense, it was constructed on the basis of an element that comes from French or that passed through French (i.e., the *ego ille*, of which one possible equivalent is "*le moi*" or "*ce moi*," a Cartesian neologism that Pascal notoriously will reprise). I would go so far as to say—you will say that my reading is forced but such forcing is in the very syntax of the text—that this sentence, in its limpid simplicity and clarity, was *constructed in order to remain untranslatable*, to remain bound up with its sense and to exhibit it in an absolute singularity, one necessary component of which is the singularity of the language in which it is written, and in which—here I am anticipating—the model or mold that gives it certain effects was also written. Accordingly, the more one forces oneself to exactly render certain aspects of this sentence's syntax, *the less one manages to produce a simply equivalent sentence*: This is what happens when Michelle Beyssade attempts to get closer to the "letter" than de Luynes. She won't be angry with me, for we have already discussed it; in order to "render" the single *Ego* in the Latin sentence, she had to break it into three: "*ce qu'est ce moi, ce que je suis, moi qui*" (what is this me, what I am, me who). The impossibility of translating Descartes's sentence, which I consider an established fact until further notice, is the index of a problem that I will now try to pose. This problem also provides the guiding thread of our analysis.

Let us begin with the most obvious point. No translator has wanted or was able to exactly render *quisnam sim* (who I am); they all proceed as if there is a *quidnam* (what am I? What I am?). There is no need to have read Nietzsche, Heidegger, or Deleuze, to be sensitized to the difference between the question *who* and the question *what*, the philosophical stakes of the question of *Werheit* and the question of *Washeit*, in order to comprehend that this slippage is not negligible, especially at the moment when it arises in this text—that is, at the crucial moment when Descartes turns from the utterance of a primal certainty that is absolutely beyond doubt (I am, I exist) to further reflection upon this certainty, its "object" (*Ego*) and its signification. The question that Descartes poses, *poses to himself*, at the moment when he is certain of being and existing, certain that the assertion of being and existing that he pronounces is necessarily (the) truth every time that he pronounces it, is not *what am I?* but rather *who am I?* He poses the question to himself with a certain wonder, and for good reason. The question of essence properly speaking will come, undoubtedly, but it must first pass through the question of identity, which itself arises from the immediate coincidence of being and existing in *pronunciation*.

To understand this movement from the problem of identity or identification to the problem of essence or "nature" is also to understand why it is so difficult not to skip over it. The immediate context is, in fact, powerfully "deceptive." It entails a succession of ultrarapid oscillations between the neuter to the masculine within neighboring statements.[5] Throughout the entire passage, in fact, except precisely in the key sentence, Descartes writes in the neuter: Am I really *some thing* (rather than nothing)? *Which thing* am I exactly (and not some other thing, for example that thing I formerly [*olim*] believed myself to be until the moment when I began to think that I necessarily exist, notably the thing that the First Meditation associated with a *vetus opinio*, a long-standing opinion,[6] *Deum esse qui potest omnia, et a quo talis, qualis existo, sum creatus*, the "long-standing opinion that there is an omnipotent God who made me the kind of creature that I am"[7]—thus a *res creata*, a *creatura*, or rather a "man" as he will say once again).

It is no wonder that translators—not to mention general readers—are so attracted to this passage. If they know Latin, and the grammatical rule of *haec est mea culpa*, this could be the "attraction in gender" of the nominal attribute upon the demonstrative pronoun. But then why does Descartes write, five lines later, *quidnam me esse crediderim*? In reality, Descartes does *not* obey this rule; he deliberately chooses sometimes to write *who* and sometimes *what*. No only does he make no mistake, no "lapsus," but there is also a crucial effect of sense that is intrinsically bound up with the form in which he—which is to say, "I"—exit(s) from doubt (and from the fiction whereby which he constrained himself [i.e., whereby I constrained myself] to go to the extreme limit of doubt).

In order to verify this claim, let us extend our investigation to the entire Second Meditation. We soon discover a remarkable alternation at the same time as a remarkable insistence that punctuates the progression of Descartes's reflection. *Three times over*, the question *who* (*quisnam sim, quis sim*), which corresponds to the Ego's ever renewed experience of wonder before the certainty of his own *Ego sum, ego existo*, will set up, interrupt, and raise anew the question *what* (*quidnam sim*), to which one might respond either in the old way (I am a creature, I am a man, I am a body, I am a soul, etc.) or in the new way: *sum igitur praecise tantum res cogitans*, "I am therefore nothing other than a thinking thing." We thus find ourselves at the heart of the difficulty: if the translators were not able not to efface these three remarkable instances (but Luynes, as a gentleman of the Grand Siècle, twice skirts the issue by writing "*quel je suis*" [which I am]), it is not only because of the immediate context but rather, much more profoundly, because of *the retroactive effect of the response*, which they evidently know in advance: *sum res cogitans*, I am a thing that thinks, or perhaps, since the Latin in absolutely no way authorizes us to eliminate this reading (and, for the moment, there is only one), I am *the* thing that thinks. To the extent that I am, that I exist, and that I necessarily have this certainty, I am this and nothing but this: this very thing, the one that thinks. . . . The *Sache selbst*, one might be tempted to gloss in Hegel's language.

We are thus in a position to reestablish in Descartes's text a very simple dialectic—in some sense preontological or, better, presubstantial (since the notion of "substance," as we know, does not yet play a role in the Second Meditation): a dialectic of the *who* and the *what*, of the "I" and the "That." The reliance of this dialectic upon facts has the advantage of undercutting certain prestigious critical readings that are wholly founded on the idea that Descartes somehow "forgot" or never grasped the difference between being a person and being a thing, when, in fact, *it is this very difference that he is working on* and setting to work. But this observation, in reality, brings us much closer to the untranslatable singularity of the Cartesian sentence. What characterizes it is the internal reproduction, in a practically inextricable manner, of a similar oscillation, this time taking place *between the persons* who can be taken for the subject. Descartes's sentence is *unstable from the point of view of gender because it is profoundly undecidable from the point of view of persons,*[8] as if it superimposed or fused two concurrent statements:

1. I wonder what is this *Ego*, which, now, necessarily is (or about which we now necessarily know that it is or exists)—in (pseudo)Latin, something like: *quidnam sit "Ego" illud, quod jam necessario est.*
2. I wonder who I am, if it is now necessarily true that I exist—in (pseudo)Latin, something like: *quisnam (ego) sim, qui jam necessario existo.*

What I am trying to show, more or less well, is that the question of *quis*, that of the first person (*Ego*), and that of the third person or of substantivation (*Ille*) are inextricably mixed up with one another.[9] I hope that you will agree that this is much more than a grammatical curiosity, but rather a veritable symptom that pertains to the Cartesian text and the place in this text where the ontological implications of self-thinking, or thinking the "self" in the first person, were thematized—no doubt for the very first time, or at least for the first time in modern philosophy. Descartes's usage of *Ille*, which governs the hesitation between *est* and *sum* as well as between *quis* and *quid*, is profoundly *equivocal*. *Ille* is employed both as a demonstrative and as a personal pronoun: *Ego ille* is understood both as "this me" or rather "this I" ("this famous I," which we were taught in school to translate mentally each time we see it, in order not to forget the difference between *hic* and *ille*) and as "he," or "him," and thus "the other." If we decide to gloss or double Descartes's text, we should look more closely at "this I, he who" or at "I, this he (the one) who . . ." In the same way, after the antecedent *Ego ille*, if it signified *this "I"* or, if one prefers, *this "me,"* in nominalized form, Descartes should have written *est*, when, in fact, we read *sum*. Pascal did not write "the self am hateful" (*le moi suis haïssable*) but rather "the self is hateful" (*le moi est haïssable*); and, in *Discourse on Method*, Descartes himself wrote: "in such a manner that this self, that is, the soul, *whereby I am what I am, is* entirely distinct from the body"—a phrase that will literally be interpolated by the Duc de Luynes into the Sixth Meditation.

Inversely, there was in classical Latin an emphatic *Ille ego* that did not signify either "this I" or "this self," but was placed before the verb in the first person singular. In Virgil's *Aeneid*, for example, we find this exordium (later removed in the final version):

Ille ego qui quondam gracili modulatus avena
Carmen et egressus silvis vicina coegi
Ut quamvis avido parerent arva colono,
Gratum opus agricolis, at nunc horrentia Martis
Arma virumque cano

That man am I who once played his song upon a slender reed, emerging from the woods compelled neighboring fields to submit even to the greediest farmer, a work welcome to husbandmen, but now Mars's bristling Arms and the Man I sing.[10]

But Descartes (who, as we know, read Virgil) instead wrote something like "who am I, me, the one who now necessarily am?" We understand this sentence perfectly well even if we cannot really translate it.

The Theophanic Model

But why do we understand perfectly well? Because this paradoxical sentence has a—no less paradoxical—model or a "mold," which we know very well; it has a *precedent* that Descartes himself must also have known by heart: which is to say that he could reproduce it without needing to represent it or to remember it. Where did we read, where did he read *sum qui sum* (which, in indirect discourse—*sim . . . qui . . . sum*—becomes the primary components of the sentence: *quisnam* SIM *ego ille,* QUI *jam necessario* SUM)? It must have been in the only place where this exact formulation occurs—in the Bible or, more precisely, in Exodus 3:14, the episode of the "burning bush" that founds revelation as a personal relation between man and (his) God.[11] Let's be careful, however: It is not the man (Moses) who says *sum qui sum* (in the traditional Latin translation), but God; or rather, according to the traditional report, which allegedly transmits that of Moses himself, it is by saying *sum qui sum* that God communicates his divine Name, and that, therefore, he communicates himself as God through his Name, or as the God who is a Name. By communicating himself in this manner, however, God hides himself: Before becoming unpronounceable, this Name is unintelligible, or, at least, enigmatic. My object here is not to enter into a fresh discussion of the questions raised by the origin and the usage of this expression; it is only to verify that the letter of the Cartesian text remains inexplicable without this biblical reference, and to study some of the effects that this reference produces in this text. Étienne Gilson, as we know, upheld this biblical passage as the basis of the "metaphysics of Exodus," showing that it both opens up an originary ontology and thereby renders possible and necessary that a Christian philosophy exist.[12] We will see that, within the Cartesian context, the repetition of this utterance, by definition foundational within the field of Judeo-Christian sacred history, has quite different and even antinomial effects—which is undoubtedly yet another manner of making the confrontation between Descartes and Exodus inevitable.

Let us backtrack and recapitulate. If the structure of *sum qui sum* is indeed present within the *question* that Descartes poses after the *pronuntiatum*, which, as he underscores, functions as a necessary first truth, this does not amount to saying that Descartes "confuses himself with God." I will return to this point. In a sense, the exact opposite is the case: this structure is a moment within a reflexive progression that should ultimately render any such confusion absolutely unthinkable, albeit for reasons that undoubtedly do not leave unscathed certain traditional representations of "God." Nor does it mean, as various influential interpretations would have it, that Descartes reprises in his own name, as a response to the question *who am I?*, an utterance in the form *sum qui sum*, "I am he who am," "I am he who is," or "I am who I am." The question remains a question. But this means that *within the form of this question*, a form that is just as necessary as the proposition whose meaning it seeks to explicate, there insists—in a visible or, if one prefers, what comes down to the same thing, a "cryptic" manner—*the form of a possible answer*, in relation to which one will have to take a position.[13] If this virtual answer were finally recused, for instance, if the form of the question were thus *denied* in the answer given to it, the very meaning of this answer (whose first approximation, but only the first, is: *sum res cogitans*) will be intrinsically determined by what it excludes or, if one prefers, goes beyond.

But then it becomes necessary to take an extra step and to ask how recognizing the form of this question, which repeats and, as it were, "problematizes" the theophanic utterance, retrospectively clarifies and determines the utterance that occasions it in Descartes: *ego sum, ego existo*. It determines this utterance most obviously as *itself* the repetition of a repetition of the *same* utterance in the form of a "variant" that it incontestable because corroborated (traditionally, institutionally) by the very origin of these formulas. If *quisnam sim ego ille, qui jam necessario sum* implies a reference to *sum qui sum*—that is, if one could thus transform the question into an answer ("I am he who am" or "I am who I am" being something like the inner answer, or also, from another point of view, a nonanswer, induced in the question by its own formal repetition[14])—it is because *Ego sum, ego existo* itself implies a reference to . . . *Ego sum*, the single repetition of the *sum qui sum* from the sacred text, which the Evangelist places thrice in the mouth of Jesus (John 8:24, 8:28, 8:58).[15] This is what we intimated or glimpsed at the moment of discerning the germ of an ontological proposition in the Cartesian utterance, the moment of associating the notion of existence with that of real life or true life. *Egō eimi* in the Gospel of John means precisely this: the identity of existence and life, united in the element of logos, speech, enunciation, or proffering. As seductive as this analogy might be, however, it cannot suffice. When we read the gospel narrative, we *know* that the expression "I am" (in which the *Ego*, in both Greek and Latin, is already as insistent and self-referential as it is in Descartes: me I am, it is me who am, this me here who am) designates God in the first person because the text says so, or, more exactly, indicates it, lets it be seen through the situation in which it places he who proffers it, thereby highlighting the reprisal of *sum qui sum*. There is nothing of the kind in Descartes's text since it does not recount the words of a Man, a God, or a Man-God, but rather *the very speech* of a subject who thinks (written down, or transcribed, it is true, like all speech relayed by a tradition). This is why the attribution, here, must at first be no more than an intuition or a possibly fantastical hypothesis. But this hypothesis becomes certainty for us at the moment when, interpreting his own utterance, Descartes fabricates, at the risk of the untranslatable, if not the unintelligible, a second utterance that reproduces in structure and literally contains the *sum qui sum*. After having "produced" as a primary truth (foundational truth, wherein all metaphysical doubt is lifted) an utterance in the first person that repeats the one in the Gospel whereby Jesus, at the risk of blasphemy, declares himself God, attributes the name of God to himself, Descartes immediately *confirms* the nonaccidental character of this attribution. Anyone who wishes to interpret *Ego sum, ego existo* as a necessary truth is thus constrained by the very form of this necessity to repeat, in turn, the origin of this statement, which manifests itself in our culture as the self-referential name of a theophany. This is undoubtedly why, on the basis of its grammatical complexity, the *Ego ille* in our text (and in what follows, as I will discuss) is so loaded with meaning. The conceptual and grammatical novelty that it represents—the substantivation of the subject even before there is any question of thinking it as a substance—expresses the tension between two persons in one according to the very model, called "hypostatic," of the filial connection between "divine" persons.

We can now provisionally take stock of our reading so far. Beginning with the singularity of the text of the *Meditations*, its stylistic effects and difficulties of translation, we have noted that meditation, for Descartes, consists in a path of writing that intersects—at the point that he designates as the primary truth or "first principle" of his philosophy, as the very point of certainty—a signifying chain which comes from the very origins of the theological tradition: precisely, the chain of *transformations* and *displacements* of the utterance attributed to God (attributable to God alone, through which he designates himself—to the extent that he can designate himself), the utterance upon which, *from a theological point of view*, hangs all revelation, all belief, and thus all certainty. In writing the *Meditations*, passing from doubt to the affirmation of existence, and then from the affirmation of existence to the question of identity, before passing from this question to that of essence, Descartes follows this chain *backward*, as it were, toward what is considered to be its source. From there on, no doubt, many paths open up to us.

We can enter into this chain, following it from one time period to another, making an effort to supply its missing links, attempting to situate the singular place that Descartes—among others, philosophers and nonphilosophers—occupies within it, and to register the historical effects of his presence or, if one prefers, his intervention. Indeed, this chain is instituted upon an initial repetition: that which links the two *hapax*, the *sum qui sum* from the Old Testament and the *Ego sum* from the New Testament. Only this repetition makes it possible to consider, on the one hand, the theophany of the Burning Bush as the annunciation of the Messiah, and, on the other hand, the words of Jesus (*Ego sum via, et veritas et vita* [John 14:6] or, in brief, *Ego sum*) as the "primary truth" of the theological tradition—as Thomas Aquinas will do, for example, in the *Summa Theologica* (*De veritate*, Article 5: "Is God the Truth?").

"Between" the evangelical statement and the text of Descartes, of course, many other "repetitions" interpolate themselves. There is no reason to suppose that he knew all of them, or even any of them, since it is not a matter of citation, but rather the objective return of an utterance. The repetitions of Saint Augustine (the putative inventor of the *cogito*, which poses an entirely different problem) and Meister Eckhart (the inventor of *Ichheit*, destined for a great philosophical future) would deserve special attention. But I am not going to speak here of anything I only know partially and at second hand.

No less important, of course, would be the series of repetitions that come after Descartes, whether they be speculative, blasphematory, or parodical (or all at once): Voltaire's repetition ("I am a body and I think: I know nothing more"), Fichte's repetition (*Ich gleich Ich*, to be read as *Ich bin Ich*), Stirner's repetition ("I base my cause on Me: no less than God, I am the negation of everything else; I am the Unique"), Freiligrath's repetition in Rosa Luxemburg's voice ("I was, I am, I will be"), Nietzsche's repetitions ("*Ich bin kein Mensch, ich bin Dynamit,*" in a book entitled *Ecce Homo*), Rimbaud's repetition ("*je est un autre*"), Freud's repetition ("*Wo es war, soll Ich werden*"), the repetitions of Poe, Mallarmé, and Bataille ("I am dead"), Lacan's repetition ("Me, the truth, I speak"), etc. It thus becomes clear that the parodical repetitions are those that incorporate the name "God" or other Divine Name. The big question, however, is whether or not Descartes's "intervention" marks a point of decisive inflection after which the meaning and mode of such repetition could no longer be the same, since such repetition has a force of antinomy that, in a sense, turns the tables. In order to respond to this type of question, we still manifestly lack some essential elements.

Another line of inquiry would consist in looking for the commentaries and readings of Descartes, including the most recent, which might obliquely take into account the reference to the sacred text in the *Meditationes*—even if it remains unrecognized as such. I limit myself to a single example, privileged because it indirectly confirms the pertinence of the question that I have sought to pose here. In a recent contribution to a volume published by the Centre d'Études des Religions du Livre, *Celui qui est, Interprétations juives et chrétiennes d'Exode 3, 14* (He Who Is: Jewish and Christian Interpretations of Exodus 3:14),[16] Genevieve Rodis-Lewis examines Malebranche's critique of Descartes, showing that the rupture between the viewpoint of uncreated reason in his work and that of the finitude of created minds in Descartes is marked by the substitution of God's self-definition as "He who is"—with reference to Exodus 3:14—for the *cogito* as the function of primary truth, and by with the correlative transformation of the ensuing proofs of the existence of God. But should it be surprising that the *sum qui sum* (in one currently available translation) takes the place of the *cogito* (or what goes by that name) if the biblical dictum is, in reality, already present within it?[17]

Interesting as they may be, however, these various questions lead away from our principal object, which must be to trace the discursive fact that we have identified within the very unfolding of the *Meditations* and thereby to understand its signification for Descartes himself. I do not know whether you are now ready to grant, as I wrote in the abstract for this lecture, that the presence of the *Ego sum* and the *sum qui sum* in the very text of the *Meditations* is materially incontestable. But I am certain that, if so, you will also concur that the theoretical import of such a claim is—and perhaps is destined to remain—perfectly equivocal. More precisely, perhaps, it is destined to compel us to notice the profound ambivalence of Cartesianism with respect to the religious presuppositions and effects of philosophical reflection, an ambivalence that that we should certainly not hasten to dub masquerade or duplicity.

He Too, He Exists

It seems to me that this discussion should begin with a question, which I would formulate as follows. The fact that the collusion or coincidence between persons (the "first" and the "third," signified respectively by *Ego* and *Ille*) is inscribed at the heart of a question—"who am I, [if not] he who am?" or "who am I if not who I am?"—which is supposed to interpret why "I am" is necessarily certain, inevitably raises a further question: How does Descartes think the relationship between this necessity and the necessity that traditionally pertains to the *concept* of God as a being who necessarily is? In other words, this collusion leads us to examine more closely the relation between *Ego* and *Ille*, considering them as names for the divine, sovereign Person. Abstractly speaking, this relationship might prove to be one of identity, analogy, distinction, or even opposition.

Let us note that this problem traverses all of Descartes's *Meditations*, which is to say that it has already become a problem before the *pronuntiatum* that we discussed above, and that it will undergo new permutations beyond its apparent solution, the "proof of the existence of God" in the Third Meditation, often interpreted as the positing of a "second foundation," either anterior to the first foundation, emerging from a new return to origins, or competing or locked, as it were, in a metaphysical rivalry with it.[18] Indeed, within the First Meditation, at the moment when Descartes recalls the "old opinion" about the omnipotence of God that compels him to radicalize the process of doubt with the hypothesis of a deceptive God, which will then give rise to the Evil Genius, he writes: *Deum esse qui potest omnia, et a quo talis, qualis existo, sum creatus* (There is an omnipotent God who created me as I really am). This formula is opposed term by term, in advance, to the *pronuntiatum*: It does posit an equivalence between *esse* and *existere*, but only lodged between the being of God and his creative action; it is only as *creatus*, as the *creature* of divine potency, and not in an independent or much less necessary manner, that this formula allows me, within the register of opinion, to think my really existing being. Further, at the beginning of the Second Meditation, immediately before he announces that "I am," Descartes asks himself: "Is there not a God, or whatever I may call him [*aliquis Deus, vel quocunque nomine illum vocem*], who puts into me the thoughts I am now having? But why do I think this, since I myself may perhaps be the author of these thoughts [*cum forsan ipsemet illarum author esse possim*]"? By the same token, we can now grasp the radical consequences of positing the *pronuntiatum* as first truth within the examination of the "problem of God": we must suspend any initial reference to a creator and to creation (or perhaps, more precisely, to the direction in which "creation" moves: Who does the creating of what? Or even: Who does the creating of whom?) within the thought of my relation to God. On the other hand, The Fifth Meditation shows that only after developing the idea of a "truthful God," positing the conditions and limits of my certain knowledge of essences, may I reinterpret the existence of God as a necessary attribute of his essence (which is perfection or infinity in action)—or, in other terms, as the necessary being, knowledge of whom entails "the truth and certainty of all science." I must then consider that any demonstration or a priori knowledge of divine essence and existence would constitute, up until this point, a contradiction in terms. This contradiction introduces a new, very powerful discursive constraint, and leads to the well-known paradox of a "proof" that presents itself as self-sufficient even as it occupies a subordinate position within the "order of reasons." Between these two moments—which are generally agreed, respectively, to open and close the cycle of Cartesian *skepsis* in the *Meditations*—Descartes elaborates the dialectic of foundation, caught within the tensions that define the relations between thinking and being, time and eternity, creation and conservation, freedom and necessity.

I thus propose to approach a solution to these difficulties, which have provoked extensive debates, beginning with one textual detail from the Third Meditation that is unquestionably well known but has not always been radically enough taken into account. To the letter, the object of these arguments is not to "demonstrate the existence of God" or to "demonstrate that God exists," but rather to demonstrate *that God also exists*—or still better, *that he is and he too exists.* Everything turns upon the little word *etiam*, which Descartes persistently inserts into the formulation of his thesis:

> . . . *concludendum, ex hoc solo quod existam, quaedamque idea entis perfectissimi, hoc est Dei, in me sit, evidentissime demonstrari Deum etiam existere*: "And from this mere fact that there is such an idea within me, or that I who possess this idea exist, I clearly infer that God also exists."

> *Totaque vis argumenti in eo est quod agnoscam fieri non posse ut existam talis naturae qualis sum, nempe ideam Dei in me habens, nisi revera Deus etiam existeret, Deus, inquam, ille idem cujus idea in me est . . .* : "The whole force of the argument lies in this: I recognize that it would be impossible for me to exist with the kind of nature I have—that is, having within me the idea of God—were it not the case that God [he too] really existed. By 'God' I mean the very being the idea of whom is within me . . ."

Do these unambiguous formulas not effectively resolve the hotly debated question why does Descartes, as it is often framed, begin with an a posteriori proof of the existence of God, a "self-referential" version of the classical proof *a contingentia mundi*,[19] "before" offering an a priori proof, which would be his version of the ontological argument? The fact is that, in the Third Meditation, Descartes never actually offers to "prove the existence of God" as if in response to the objections of a skeptic or a naysayer ("I tell you that there is no God!" "And I will prove to you that he exists!"). What Descartes does do—which is neither more nor less, but something else—is to advance the proof that "God really exists outside of me," or better, that "God is really other than me," even though he is inseparable from me, in that, very precisely, the idea of God is always already within me, constitutive of the idea I have of myself as a *res cogitans* who becomes *res cogitans ideam Dei in se (in me)*—which is the true "*cogito*" of the *Meditations*, finally emerging at long last in a developed and complex form.[20] It is as if Descartes responded to an objection, not from an external naysayer, but rather *from himself*: wherein lies the proof *that I am not indiscernible from God*, I who am certain of existing and thus necessarily am each time that I—like God himself—say *Ego sum*?[21]

This question must obviously be inscribed within the lineage of virtual responses to the preceding *Who am I?*: "I am who I am," I am he who, being, exists. Let us no longer be surprised, under these conditions, to discover at the center of Descartes's "proof" a negative lemma, which, after all other possibilities are eliminated, leads to the necessary conclusion: *I am not God*, a proposition that is uttered in no uncertain terms, even if in a virtual mode: *atque ipsemet Deus essem*, to be understood in two parallel modalities both of which play a role in the proof: (1) I could be the author of my existence, engendering myself and conserving myself; (2) I could have forged myself the idea of infinite perfection on the basis of which I think and measure my own imperfection.

If we had sufficient time to follow it in detail, we might thus begin to clarify the trajectory of thinking and writing that constantly associates three moves:

On the one hand, we observe *the progressive dissociation of the "persons"* represented by Ego and *Ille* (further reinforced by the simultaneous introduction, in order to designate the first person, of the new formula *ego ipse*). This dissociation at the very heart of unity

(unity of the relation of causality or creation, unity of the relation of representation) culminates, at the end of the Third Meditation, with this:

> It only remains for me to examine how I received this idea from God . . . not that the mark need be anything distinct from the work itself. But the mere fact that God created me is a very strong basis for believing that I am somehow made in his image and likeness, and that I perceive that likeness, which includes the idea of God, by the same faculty which enables me to perceive myself [*per quam ego ipse a me percipior*]. That is, when I turn my mind's eye upon myself [*in meipsum mentis aciem converto*], I understand that I am a thing which is incomplete and dependent on another and which aspires without limit to ever greater and better things; but I also understand at the same time that he on whom I depend has within him all those greater things . . . actually and infinitely, and hence that he is God [*sed simul etiam intelligo illum, a quo pendeo, majora ista omnia . . . reipsa infinita in se habere, atque ita Deum esse*]. The whole force of the argument lies in this . . . [22]

On the other hand, we are presented with the systematic investigation, through enumeration and progressive elimination, of the only "thing," object of my ideas, about which I can be *certain from the outset that it also exists*, and thus that it does not leave me "alone in the world": *hinc necessario sequi non me solum esse in mundo, sed aliquam aliam rem, quae istius ideae est causa, etiam existere . . . quod me de alicujus rei a me diversae existentia certum reddat* ("it will necessarily follow that I am not alone in the world, but that some other thing which is the cause of this idea also exists. But if no such idea is to be found in me, I shall have no argument to convince me of the existence of anything apart from myself"). This "sole thing"[23] that "*also* exists," by which I am not alone (and which will end up restoring—as a bonus, in some sense—all the other "things" in the world), reveals itself to be *another thing that thinks*. I am tempted to say, in accordance with the language and logic of Descartes's argument: *the other thing which thinks* (because we do not and will not know of any other[24]): *et idcirco, cum sim res cogitans, ideamque quondam Dei in me habens, qualiscunque tandem me causa assignetur, illam etiam esse rem cogitantem . . . fatendum est* ("since I am a thinking thing and have within me some idea of God, it must be admitted that what caused me is *itself also* a thinking thing and possesses the idea of all the perfections which I attribute to God."[25]

Finally, we arrive at the identification of the cause thanks to which, being *now* with certainty, at every instant, *I will also be the next instant* with the same *res cogitans* other than me and "objectively" present within myself (yet again the *etiam: an habeo aliquam vim per quam possim efficere ut ego ille, qui jam sum, paulo post etiam sim futurus*: "I must therefore now ask myself whether I possess some power enabling me to bring it about that I who now exist will still exist a little while from now").[26]

Recapitulating this entire trajectory, then, we can see with maximum clarity the symmetry between Descartes's argumentation in the first two Meditations, which show that I too am (*ego etiam sum*, AT 24–25) as soon as (if I dare say: *si fas est dicere . . .*) one posits an omnipotent being—God or demon—capable of deceiving me, and the Third Meditation, which shows that *he also (that is, God) exists* as soon as one posits that I have within myself (even if, absolutely speaking, I cannot "comprehend" or encompass it) the clear idea of the infinite or the omnipotent. If God—or rather, the Evil Genius—is and deceives me, or, in a certain manner, thinks me, then I must necessarily be; his hypothetical existence implies my own, real existence. But if I am, and I have within myself the idea of God as an infinite being—which is to say that I think him—then he must also necessarily be, as another individual substance. My real existence implies his own, equally real. No more than the hypothetical omnipotent deceiver could *feign that I do not exist* could I deceive myself by *feigning that God does not exist* otherwise than I do, or that, in this sense, *I would be him.*

We are very familiar with the consequences of this formal dissymmetry within formal symmetry: my existence and my thought become dependent upon those of God, in an internal rather than external relation of dependence with respect to an Other to whom or to which I am immediately united, since I find him/it represented within myself and he/it is active within me at every instant. We are also familiar with the knot of difficulties that this dissymmetry presents: the difficulty of thinking my resemblance with another thinking thing that differs from me as infinity differs from finitude; the difficulty of thinking my freedom of decision (in Michelle Beyssade's excellent translation) not as an exception to this dependence but as its very reality and realization. Herein lies the entire question of the divine "mark" in the human. But it is worthwhile, before concluding, to take note of an aspect of this mark that is very closely related to the thematic of the *pronuntiatum*; and that undoubtedly makes it possible at last to grasp its sense.

Once Descartes has shown that God also exists—he as well; once he interprets this demonstration as the guarantee that God is not deceptive; once he finally produces the corollary of this thesis in the form of the assertion that *it is not God but I myself who deceives me* in the actualization of my also infinite will, and consequently that it is always in my power to decide not to be deceived, at least by abstaining from judgment, he will finally be able to arrive at a clear and distinct conception of the necessary link that binds the *esse* of God, or his essence, to his *existere*, or his existence. One might recall that he considers this link to have the same indissolubility and the same logical connection as that which binds the triangle to its angles and a mountain to a valley. But let us reread the text itself:

> There are many ways in which I understand that this idea is not something fictitious which is dependent on my thought [*illam non esse quid fictitium a cogitatione mea dependens*], but is an image of a true and immutable nature. First of all, there is the fact that, apart from God, there is nothing else of which I am capable of thinking such that existence belongs to its essence . . . For what is more self-evident [*ex se apertius*] than the fact that the supreme being exists, or that God, to whose essence alone existence belongs, exists [*quam summum ens esse, sive Deum, ad cujus solius essentiam existentia pertinet, existere*]?[27]

We thus find ourselves once again in the immediate vicinity of the *pronuntiatum* where we began. *There is, strictly speaking, no ontological "argument" but rather an identical proposition* (or, if you prefer, a "tautological" one).[28] More precisely, the whole argument of the Fifth Meditation is less an "ontological" *proof* than the dialectical preparation, through a comparative discussion of finite and infinite essences, for this new canonical statement, which expresses the veritable identity of infinite being and necessary existence with a certainty that is at least equal to that of mathematical truths, whose necessity is for me so binding that it renders all doubt impracticable.

What distinguishes such an utterance (in brief: *Qui est, Ille existit*) from *Ego sum, ego existo*? It is perfectly clear: the certainty of such an utterance is immediately established in the element of truth without any need to refer to the *Ego*. More precisely, it is without any doubt reflexive, expressive of the "sufficiency" or self-reference that characterizes the divine essence and is reflected in the idea that I have of it, but it is not "heauto-referential"; it does not comprise any idea of the first person positing or designating itself as such.[29] But it can and undoubtedly must also be read in the opposite manner: there is certainly an *analogy* between the bonding of being and existence that underlies the *Ego* and that which now underlies the idea of God, but there is also an abyssal difference, which derives from the fact that only a finite being, a single or the only "finite" *res cogitans*[30] can think and name itself as *Ego* or as *Ego ille*. This possibility is excluded for God—or better: it is excluded *from God*, to the precise extent that he is other than *Ego*. If God necessarily is, and if, although not "comprehensible," he is thinkable as a necessary being, not only is he not living in the sense that a finite thing would be, existing in duration, which is a pleonasm, but also he is not "I" or "me." In brief, he is *not a first person*; and he can neither think himself nor speak himself as such. Therefore, he cannot say, "I am the life," any more than "I am the truth" (or the "way" of truth) even though he may be the *true God* (an expression reprised twice by Descartes[31]), *the veracious God* that we contemplate, admire, and adore as an "immense light."[32]

Humanism of the Solitary Man

We can thus perceive the implicit and perhaps redoubtable consequences of the turns whereby Descartes inflected his writing from the Second Meditation onward. "By the idea of God," did Descartes really "not mean anything other than all men usually mean when they speak," as he wrote to Mersenne in July 1641? If you accept that the references to the biblical *sum qui sum* and *Ego sum* are not the products of my own fantasy, that they are truly at work in this text, then you must also reach the conclusion that it is not God, *that it was never God who designates himself in this manner*. From a reference or an intersection inscribed in a literary heritage, we have thus arrived at a rupture, a brutal *denegation*, probably unacceptable to the faithful of revealed religion and consequently to the theologians.[33]

We can express this rupture in diverse ways.

First, no one in reality (except perhaps madmen, but Descartes thinks himself unable to be mad), no one can say anything akin to "I am God." *I* cannot say it because *I* necessarily think God as other than me and myself, therefore, as other than God. But *God* cannot say it either because he is not an "I," he has no "I."[34] God entirely lacks this property, in addition to the "capacity" to deceive and to be deceived, and probably as well the "capacity" to doubt and then no longer to doubt. However, as with the causality of error, it must be understood—at the very limits of our faculty to "understand"—that, for God, this is not a lack, a *privatio*, but a simple *negatio*. Wouldn't it be necessary to claim that only the one (this "he") who says—and who, therefore, *is* "I"—can effectively deceive (himself), in the same way that he who can *be deceived*, insofar as he is an "I," can also absolutely *deceive*, which is to say that he can not be immutably and perfectly "veracious"?[35]

Second, me alone, the thing that thinks, and that thinks God, but also that doubts, that is deceived, that senses, that imagines, etc. (me in whom will, or freedom of decision, and intelligence remain irremediably unequal and distinct: only on this basis does Descartes talk once again of humanity, of human nature and "weakness"), I am the only one who can say *Ego, ego sum*, and, in a certain oblique and implicit or simply virtual sense, *sum qui sum*. I am obviously not alone in the world: but "in the world" (that is, at the heart of the world or transcending it, with a remarkable neutralization of this alternative), no matter whom I may be, I am alone, I am the one and only "I."

If we now permit ourselves a highly metaphorical and dangerously anthropomorphic language, we could conclude from this foregoing that, in the final analysis, Descartes removed or negated the *Ego* of God, the *ego sum*, or the *sum qui sum*—in brief, that which, in modern terms, we are in the habit of calling subjectivity. I am a subject, but God is not one. I am therefore *the* subject, which does not mean, for good reason, that I am *the* substance. *Ego ille*, myself or "the self" stands up, in a sense, in the face of God (as *its* other), in its very dependence, and in its absolute dependence. *Hier stehe ich, ich kann nicht anders. . . .*[36] Or rather, isn't it for us alone, reading Descartes today, that such a representation has a sense?

In any event, we should note the subtle ambivalence of this conclusion. The weakest and most contradictory manner of understanding it, if I have explained myself well, would consist in thinking that the "subject"—a fortiori: *man*—assumes in Descartes the mark of truth that the theological tradition identifies with God, bringing it down, as it were, "from heaven to earth," or bringing eternity into time.[37] On the contrary, the most satisfying way to understand it, I think, consists in saying: in this mark of truth, in this sacralized statement, which has been ascribed the effect of a revelation, there is, at bottom, *nothing more than the indubitable albeit quotidian (quoties . . .)*—and I would be tempted to say *"whatever"* [*quelconque*]—*truth* of a proffering or, if you will, a "performance" within reach of any *Ego* that utters itself as such, making reference to its own being. Descartes, or the Descartes of the *Meditations*, is no doubt an extremely radical "humanist," a philosopher of the autonomy of human freedom (which he calls "sufficiency") and of the essential goodness of human nature (foreign, it has often been remarked, to any concern with "sin"): He is a humanist, I dare say, *by definition*, and in his antagonism to everything that, following Henri Gouhier, we might call the "anti-humanism" of the seventeenth century. But he also completely barred in advance the road to this other humanism, the one most often recognized as such, despite its manifestly theological roots, whose mission, with or without reference to the "death of God," consists in projecting the attributes of God into man, or in forging a divine image (divinized, not to mention sacralized) of human nature.

"My Self," "My Own": Variations on Locke

In this lecture, I would like to tell a story about words. Or rather, two stories at once. The first is a public story, that of one moment within the great history of "personal" and "possessive" pronouns, which traverses the entire history of "Western culture," thanks to what has been called its colingualism, and determines its understanding of subjectivity.[1] The second and much more modest story is a private one, although it owes everything to public institutions of teaching and research: it concerns a stage in my own journey of initiation into the English language, from which, without indulging myself too much, I would like to derive a lesson. These two stories converge upon an error—a gross one—which I committed a few years ago, because I presumptuously imagined that my understanding of certain idiomatic properties of English was sufficiently advanced to allow me to frame an argument based on them. I wanted to clarify the reasons why it was in this specific European language and in the work of one of the greatest English philosophers of the seventeenth century that the terminological equivalence of *self* and *own*, and thus also *myself* and *my own*, was invented (along with the modern category of "consciousness") as the basis for a theory of personal identity that would go on to be considered and discussed as classical.[2] I committed and published (in France) an unmistakable error, which it took me a while to notice. But, in the end, I believe that I learned something new—and transmissible—from this misstep.

Lockean Untranslatability

When Barbara Cassin, along with a team of scholars from France and other countries, undertook the project of the *Dictionary of Untranslatables* (*Vocabulaire européen des philosophies*), and charged me with the task of organizing the group of articles on and around "subjectivity," she soon came up with the idea that this tome should be published alongside a series of smaller bilingual volumes, each focused on a single work (or a set of historically inseparable texts), in which the problems of *untranslatability*—the privileged object of the *Dictionary*—would be illustrated and tested through the experience of "translating the untranslatable."[3] For this collection, I proposed a new French translation of Book II, Chapter 27, of Locke's *Essay on Human Understanding*, entitled "Of identity and diversity," to be accompanied by an introduction, a historical dossier, and a commentary. Indeed, it was Locke who, in this chapter from his great work of the "theory of knowledge," in which the notion of the *self* is thematized for the first time, claimed that the "criteria" for personal identity should be the mutual implication of consciousness and memory, and elaborated the radical metaphysical, psychological, and political consequences of this claim.[4] This chapter—in truth, a sort of essay within the *Essay*—has unique consequences within the history of modern philosophy; but it does not so much draw its consequences from already established developments in the book on the operations of *mind* (a typically "untranslatable" word!) and *understanding*, but rather secures a new foundation for these developments. In fact, Locke added this chapter in the second edition of the *Essay* (1694) in order to respond to the theological criticisms according to which his conception of mind—by replacing the metaphysics of the substantial soul and its immortality with "empirical" (or phenomenological) descriptions of perception, reflection, and the association of ideas—could only undermine the foundations of personal responsibility, which are important for both morality and religion. His response, largely devoted to the formulation of what is today called the "Locke criterion" for personal identity, which strictly reduces identity to the continuity of consciousness, could only provoke a mass of further objections. Ever since Bishop Butler's denunciation of the circularity of Locke's reasoning, these objections have fueled philosophical debate, down to their most "technical" developments. Some (like Hume) would attempt to take Locke's "empiricism" further than Locke himself; others (like Leibniz) would seek, on the contrary, to renew the concept of "substance" (and with it the entire metaphysics of the subject).[5]

Alongside these debates, there are several reasons that impel me, in turn, to contend with the Lockean "untranslatable." The first reason pertains to the difficulty, materially inscribed within language, of understanding what distinguishes the *moi* of French classical philosophers (Descartes, followed by Pascal, and then Rousseau) from the Lockean *self*—for which Pierre Coste, Locke's first French translator (working in close collaboration with the author) proposed as equivalents *soi* and *soi-même*, neologisms in French themselves destined for great things. All of these terms, circulating between French and English, by way of repeated translation, obviously bear witness to a fundamental "turning point" in the history of philosophy (and even in culture). They are also symptomatic of the "point of heresy" that divides this history between empiricism and idealism. From this point, naturally, I arrived at the classical problem of philosophical anthropology and political philosophy: the Lockean notion of the individual as "Proprietor in one's Person" from the *Second Treatise on Government* (§§27, 44, etc.).[6] This notion replaces the classical notions of *dominium sui* (self-mastery) and *sui iuris esse* (autonomy, or independence with respect to every other—still fundamental in Spinoza, for example, where it is opposed to the *alieni iuris esse*), making it possible to institute a contractual order founded upon equality among subjects, or, in other terms, what MacPherson calls the "political theory of possessive individualism."[7] Finally, I was interested in the genealogy of the notion of the *subject* itself. In this connection, it was particularly important to me, very much against the tendency of philosophical discussions during the last fifty years (especially in France, where they have often taken a heated turn) about the "primacy" or the "sovereignty" of the subject in philosophy, *not to confuse the problems of subjectivity and consciousness.*[8] They have not only become distinct in the present epoch, when the influence of psychoanalysis and anthropology insist that the subject is essentially "unconscious," but were already and more radically so in the classical age, in the context of what is presented as the "birth" of the metaphysics of the subject. As proof, I would adduce the fact that the Cartesian theory of the "thinking thing" bears no intrinsic relation to the idea (nor, for that matter, to the term) of "consciousness" (and still less to that of "self-consciousness"). Only with Locke, once again, do we have the "invention" of a concept of subjectivity that implants it in the field of individual consciousness and essentially identifies it (much as Kant will do, despite the differences between them) with "self-consciousness." This is the way in which all of my interests converged toward the study of Locke—a philosopher whom I knew a little (even though his work was largely neglected in the French university curriculum when I was a student), though my knowledge was for the most part conventional and secondhand.[9]

None of this, however, suffices to determine the precise point at which the philosophical problem and the philological problem intersect, which is what led me to take the measure of Locke's work within language, examining the "translations" and "interpretations" that he required to make his conceptual distinctions, which, in their turn, would pose redoubtable problems of translation into French. As it happens, however, Coste himself already discussed these problems in relation to three key English terms, showing both why—despite appearances and the common reference of both French and English to Latin—they have no proximate French equivalent and how one might "invent" fresh translations, opening new pathways in philosophy. The first term that Coste discussed was the English *self*, for which he proposed to introduce into French the neologism *soi* or *soi-même* in order to distinguish this term from the terms *"moi,"* or *"le moi,"* which are fundamental to French metaphysics after Descartes. The second term was precisely *consciousness*, which he sought to translate as *"con-science,"* using a typographical artifice (like many in philosophy since then) designed to avoid any confusion with *"conscience,"* the cognate of the English *conscience*, a common term in moral discourse (as in the Shakespearean formula: "conscience doth make cowards of us all," which occurs both in *Hamlet* and *Richard III*).[10] And finally, the third term was *uneasiness*. In the early French translations of excerpts from Locke (which appeared previous to the publication of his book), this term was rendered as *"malêtre"* (or, if you wish, in more modern terms: *malaise*). Coste proposed that it henceforth be translated as *"inquiétude,"* thus setting in motion the great philosophical thematic of *disquiet* or *restlessness* (in German, *Unruhe*) that would dominate eighteenth-century literature and Romanticism.[11] On each of these points, Coste was never content to coin neologisms in order to surmount the untranslatability of Locke's English into the French of his time; but, whenever he did so, he entered into long justificatory footnotes, doubtless composed with Locke's blessing, which brilliantly show that, if philosophy does not simply take place (as much of today's so-called analytic philosophy would claim it does) in a "language of concepts" without idiomatic particularity, it becomes impossible to separate it from philology, and thus must pass through an experience of translinguistic writing.[12]

Identity/Propriety

Let me now try to explain the relationship between *self* and *own* at the origin of my error. The simplest thing would be to cite in their entirety the crucial passages from the *Essay*, no matter their length. Only if we appreciate Locke's near obsessional insistence upon these two little words and their recurrent pairing in his argumentation can we then perceive how, in and through the idiom of his writing itself, he produces an unprecedented signification (which, as we shall see, does not mean that it is without "sources" or preliminary conditions) and seeks to open a place for it within the field of philosophical discourse. In so doing, I also hope to show that Locke's English cannot be understood without referring to certain neighboring languages—in particular, the French of Descartes and Malebranche, who are his interlocutors, if not his adversaries. Because all of these sentences are literally "untranslatable" in one sense or another, there is no *equivalence* to help us overcome the *gulf* between languages—especially when the little words *self* and *own* are compared with their French counterparts, *"moi," "soi," "propre,"* and *"le propre."* We should also pay special attention to Locke's seventeenth-century English spelling, which, despite its slightly archaic look, remains easily understandable; it entails the possibility of writing composite pronouns either as single words or as the conjunction of two separate words, and thus of playing quite consciously upon two alternative syntaxes: the reflexive personal pronoun (*myself, itself, himself, oneself*) or the possessive pronoun (*my self*=this "self" that is "mine," that "belongs properly to me," that is *my own self*, or simply *my own*—but also, by analogy: it[s]self, this self that is "its" own, that "belongs to it"). These are not mere grammatical subtleties. I will attempt to show that these language games are essential both to Locke's semantics and to his theory of the "subject." This is why, no matter the difficulty of the task, which is generally insurmountable without recourse to paraphrase, we absolutely must attempt to make them pass from one language to another.

What follows are four passages from the *Essay on Human Understanding* that, I think, hold the key to our problem. The first is to be found in Book II, Chapter 27, §14, within Locke's discussion of whether different consciousnesses or memories, incommunicable to one another, would confer different identities upon the same individual; and, correlatively, whether the same consciousness (or continuity of memory), were it to pass from one individual to another (were we to imagine, for example, that Plato inherited not only the "thinking" but also the memories of Socrates . . .), would *ipso facto* make them one and the same person rather than a plurality of "men":

> Let any one reflect upon himself, and conclude that he has in himself an immaterial spirit, which is that which thinks in him, in the constant change of his body keeps him the same: and is that which he calls himself: let him also suppose it to be the same soul that was in Nestor or Thersites, at the siege of Troy . . . which it may have been, as well as it is now the soul of any other man: but he now having no consciousness of any of the actions either of Nestor or Thersites, does or can he conceive himself the same person with either of them? Can he be concerned in either of their actions? attribute them to himself, or think them his own, more than the actions of any other men that ever existed?

The second passage is part of the same discussion (Chapter 27, §17–18) but it moves from personal identity to the responsibility for actions:

> §17. *Self* is that conscious thinking thing . . . which is sensible or conscious of pleasure and pain, capable of happiness or misery, and so is concerned for itself, as far as consciousness extends. Thus every one finds that, whilst comprehended under that consciousness, the little finger is as much a part of himself as what is most so. Upon separation of this little finger, should this consciousness go along with the little finger, and leave the rest of the body, it is evident that the little finger would be the person, the same person; and *self* would then have nothing to do with the rest of the body. . . . That with which the consciousness of the present thinking thing can join itself, makes the same person, and is one self with it, and with nothing else; and so attributes to itself, and owns all the actions of that thing, as its own, as far as that consciousness reaches, and no further; as every one who reflects will perceive.

> §18. In this personal identity is founded all the right and justice of reward and punishment; happiness and misery being that for which everyone is concerned for himself, and not mattering what becomes of any substance, not joined to, or affected with that consciousness. For, as it is evident in the instance I gave but now, if the consciousness went along with the little finger when it was cut off, that would be the same *self* which was concerned for the whole body yesterday, as making part of itself, whose actions then it cannot but admit as its own now. Though, if the same body should still live, and immediately from the separation of the little finger have its own peculiar consciousness, whereof the little finger knew nothing, it would not at all be concerned for it, as part of itself, or could own any of its actions, or have any of them imputed to him.

The third passage is taken from §§23–24 where the "Locke criterion" makes possible the radical critique of substantialist ontologies:

> §23 . . . So that self is not determined by identity or diversity of substance, which it cannot be sure of, but only by identity of consciousness.

> §24. Indeed, it may conceive the substance whereof it is now made up to have existed formerly, united in the same conscious being: but, consciousness removed, that substance is no more it self, or makes no more a part of it, than any other substance; as is evident in the instance we have already given of a limb cut off. . . . In like manner it will be in

reference to any immaterial substance, which is void of that consciousness whereby I am my *self* to my *self*: if there be any part of its existence which I cannot upon recollection join with that present consciousness whereby I am now my *self*, it is, in that part of its existence, no more my *self* than any other immaterial being. For, whatsoever any substance has thought or done, which I cannot recollect, and by my consciousness make my own thought and action, it will no more belong to me, whether a part of me thought or did it, than if it had been thought or done by any other immaterial being anywhere existing.

Finally, we should also take into consideration §26, where the question of "self" is transferred into the sphere of jurisprudence ("Person a forensic term"):

Person, as I take it, is the name for this *self*. Wherever a man finds what he calls himself, there, I think, another may say is the same person. It is a forensic term, appropriating actions and their merit; and so belongs only to intelligent agents, capable of a law, and happiness, and misery. This personality extends it self beyond present existence to what is past, only by consciousness—whereby it becomes concerned and accountable; owns and imputes to it self past actions, just upon the same ground and for the same reason as it does the present. All which is founded in a concern for happiness, the unavoidable concomitant of consciousness; that which is conscious of pleasure and pain, desiring that that *self* that is conscious should be happy. And therefore whatever past actions it cannot reconcile or appropriate to that present *self* by consciousness, it can be no more concerned in than if they have never been done.

I apologize for these long quotations, but there is a linguistic materiality here that cannot be skirted, that must be seen and heard. I hope that you will agree with the following two suggestions. The first is that an essential part of the argument rests upon the idea that consciousness[13] is the operator of an "appropriation of the self" (or simply of *self*, treated as a proper name) by *itself*. But what does "to appropriate" mean? Two indissociable things: to identify with and to acquire, to transform into "private property." Accordingly, *itself* is nothing other than "its own self," *it self*, in a mirror construction, which becomes all the more obvious when the argument is transposed into the first person (or, precisely, when the "experience" that corresponds to this reflection takes place "in the first person"): "consciousness" is what appropriates *myself* to my *self* by appropriating all the ideas of which I am "conscious" (which I remember, which I keep within myself), and thus renders me the owner of myself by means of my thoughts. Whence my second suggestion: an equally essential part of Locke's argument rests upon the whole spectrum of uses and significations of the word *own*, which can be both an adjective ("my own thought and action") and a verb ("to own")—and thus becomes the "equivalent" of several French verbs (mainly *posséder* or *avoir*, to possess or be the owner of, but also *avouer*, to "recognize" that of which one is the author, whether it be one's sins or one's children, but, above all, one's thoughts). In reality, these two significations are not independent of one another, because one cannot avow or recognize something that is not one's "own" (or does not come "from oneself"); and inversely because the mere fact of avowing something or recognizing oneself as responsible for something, renders it ipso facto one's own, appropriates it, especially when it is a matter not of goods but of *actions* (wherein lies the knot that binds the juridical and the moral problem). The consequence of these verbal operations, loaded with an infinity of theoretical effects, is that they engender, at the very heart of Locke's foundational argument, an essential *circularity*, which links together, on the one hand, questions of identity and identification, and, on the other, those of the proper and property. These questions overlap to such a degree that they become practically equivalent. Accordingly, I might consider that what is "me," "myself," or "my self" is like a thing that I possess ("own") or that I avow ("own," once again); or which I avow that I actually possess because it is I who did it or thought it. It becomes "me"/"mine" as the moment when, doing or thinking it consciously, I "appropriate" it to myself. But what I thereby appropriate to myself is, circularly, what I identify with *self*—that is, with what is already "my own" or is indistinguishable from me, just as my thoughts are, because they form "my own self," etc. What is *my own* in the strong sense is always *myself* or *my self*, much as what is myself or "identical to me" is anything that I have or possess (what is my own) or that I can avow (what I can own).[14]

None of this, it seemed to me, is a mere linguistic curiosity. It is not merely a matter of Locke's skill at using the English language, but rather a "metaphysical language game," which proves no less important that the syntactic and semantic effects of the Greek verb *einai* and its cases and derivatives (*eimi, esti, ousia,* etc.) in the formation of a metaphysics of "being" or "essence," or than the "play of historial words" at work in the double Latin etymology of the "subject," combining a reference to the impersonality of the *subjectum*—the "support" of certain predicates or the "substrate" of certain properties—and a reference to the personality of the *subjectus*—an individual submitted to the authority or power of another person.[15] Upon this language game, I believed that it was possible to found, if not an explanation, then at least an interpretation and a theoretical localization of the relationship in Locke (and others) between a metaphysics of the subject whose consciousness becomes the mark of identity and a political theory that generalizes—or better, "universalizes"—the idea of citizenship, inasmuch as each individual can be considered as the "owner of himself" (or of "his own person"), and solely to the extent that he really exercises this ownership. With respect to this subject, C. B. MacPherson did not hesitate to speak of a "Western ontology of property." Perhaps, indeed, it is necessary to go so far; but, in any event, what is at stake is the heart of the subjective individualism that simultaneously unfolds on the psychological, moral, juridical, and political levels, and whose a priori structures transcendental philosophy seeks to articulate.[16] The reason for this intimate relationship between consciousness, identity, property, and citizenship would ultimately have to be sought in this metaphysics of *propriation*—as Jacques Derrida would say—whose circularity of meanings between *my self* and *my own*, or the fact that the meaning of *self* lies in its reference to *own* and *owning*, and vice versa, anticipates this relationship before becoming its privileged linguistic expression.[17]

So far, so good. But my intention was to go a step further—in fact, a step too far. I wanted to show that *self* and *own*, and thus, willy-nilly, *the self* and *the own*, *my self* and *my own*, are at bottom *one and the same—self-same concepts*, if you will. This would be a matter of speculative but also material identity, inscribed within everyday language and the rhetoric of a specific idiom. Locke would thus have founded European individualism because he was English and spoke English, by virtue of the speculative dimension inherent to certain usages of the expressions *my self* and *my own* and their synonymy. A certain historicism is always tempting, circulating at will from Greek to German to French examples, each time discovering a speculative element loaded with political intentions and metaphysical consequences. Why not English, too? I would observe, with textual support (viz. my previous citations), that the very letter of the *Essay* sometimes seems very close to articulating this equivalence, although it never purely and simply substitutes the expressions *my self* and *my own* for one another. Only implicitly, however, does it identify their meaning, by way of intermediate notions such as "appropriation," but also *concern*, or *attribute*, or *impute*, and so forth. The proof that I was seeking would require support from outside Locke's text.

"By the Fire Side"

At the moment when I was translating and studying Locke, by pure coincidence, I was also reading Gide's *Journal*. Gide is known for his admirable knowledge of English literature (he helped to introduce contemporary writers, such as Conrad, to a French audience and to get their works translated). His *Journal* includes citations in the original language; and, in the course of my reading, I stumbled across the following stanza from Robert Browning's poem "By the Fire Side" (which appeared in his collection, *Men and Women*, from 1855):

> My own, confirm me! If I tread
> This path back, is it not in pride
> To think how little I dreamed it led
> To an age so blest that, by its side,
> Youth seems the waste instead?

I will admit that I was very moved by these verses, no doubt because I mistakenly thought that the "age" in them is old age, which I am rapidly approaching. It was easy to make this mistake because of the context in which Gide cites these lines, and because they evoke the idea that one must work against the way in which vacillating memory troubles personal identity itself. I thought that the poem consisted in a rhetorical interpellation that the poet addresses to himself, taking himself as witness to his own life (a classical trope of lyric poetry); and I also must have said to myself, "my own, confirm me," seeming to speak to the "me" that at the same instant I was, echoed by my reading. Above all (and I recognize that this was not serious, that is was too fragile a basis for an interpretation with scholarly claims), I wrote that I had found an example in which *my self* and *my own* are pure and simply synonymous.[18] As it turned out, this was not the case at all (as I should have learned from the embarrassed reactions that I received from colleagues at the University of California, Irvine), but I only realized it after the fact, when I found the whole text of the poem, *By the Fire Side*, on the shelves of the library.[19] This is how it reads (I transcribe several stanzas that follow the one cited here, not only for their beauty but also because they are punctuated by the recurrence of the apostrophe, "my own," in a manner that lifts any ambiguity, and because they introduce an additional theme, whose importance will soon become clear—that of the tension between the one and the two—which tends to merge with a more troubling theme—the "possession" of a subject whose identity is subjugated to a double):

> My own, confirm me! It I tread
> This path back, is it not in pride
> To think how little I dreamed it led
> To an age so blest that, by its side,
> Youth seems the waste instead?
>
> My own, see where the years conduct!
> At first, 'twas something our souls
> Should mix as mists do; each is sucked
> In each now: on, the new stream rolls,
> Whatever rock obstruct.
>
> Think, when our one soul understands
> The great Word which makes all things new.
> When earth breaks up and heaven expands,
> How will the change strike me and you
> In the house not made with hands?
>
> Oh I must feel your brain prompt mine,
> Your heart anticipate my heart,
> You must be just before, in fine,
> See and make me see, for your part,
> New depths of the divine!
>
> But who could have expected this
> When we two drew together first
> Just for the obvious human bliss,
> To satisfy life's daily thirst
> With a thing men seldom miss?

Some brief notes on the content and circumstances of these verses. First, of course, "my own" does not designate the poet himself, but his wife, whom he lost not long after their first encounter. This romantic poem of love and regret, written long after the death of his beloved, directly evokes the bliss of a night of love under the starry sky in Italy. Henceforward, only the lovers' souls can penetrate one another as their bodies once did; and this new union will last for eternity, or rather, until the Last Judgment: *When earth breaks up and heaven expands.* If the poem refers to old age, then, it is only by anticipation, as the previous stanza shows, with its interesting variations on the theme of "possession":

> My perfect wife, my Leonor,
> Oh heart, my own, oh eyes, mine too,
> Whom else could I dare look backward for,
> With whom beside should I dare pursue
> The path grey heads abhor?

Allow me to keep playing the student for a moment longer: although only a careless beginner could fail to notice that, in the context of romantic love, "my own" is a common English expression, it remains quite idiomatic. There are similar expressions in French, in German, and in Italian (which is perhaps the closest to English): *mon trésor, Mein Schatz, mio bene*. None of these, however, exactly matches the English expression, which connotes all at once proximity, tenderness, and brutality or force. Let us not jump to the conclusion that English lovers are particularly "possessive," or that they force their language more directly to express the element of possession (*dominium*) in their passion, which might also be a manner of seeking in love the only form of possession that would be absolute, because reciprocal. "Personal-real," Kant says about marriage. Let us instead return to the construction of personal identity or "consciousness of identity" that Locke proposes, in an attempt to derive some benefit from the correction of my mistake. What would result from a joint reading of Browning's poem with Locke's essay from the viewpoint of the consciousness of identity as a phenomenon of *appropriation*? It promises, in particular, to provide a better understanding of the subtle and troubling modality wherein the construction of identity implies an interrogation of the *division* or *duality* of "self."

Why subtle *and* troubling? Because, in a sense, this modality is affirmed on one level (that of *enunciation*), even as it is denied on another (that of the *enunciated*). Language perpetually endeavors to annul the divisions that it is the process of positing. It never ceases to posit a divided and doubled self, both a "possessing self" and a "possessed self"; and it must do so in order to name the two poles, or "moments" in the process of identification that it describes. Theory, however, explains that the self is one and the same self, "the same to itself," since it possesses or recognizes itself (*owns itself*); and that it is "its own self." Let us not hasten to declare that this situation should be qualified as a mere "performative contradiction," or rather, at least, let us not misrecognize the extraordinarily productive use that the text makes of such a "contradiction" by linking it to the problem of personal identity as a end-oriented process of *becoming*. I underscore that Locke was fully aware of this contradiction himself, otherwise he could not have produced such a complex argument, imbued with such rhetoric and poetry, in order to explain there is no way to "judge" the identity of a person (and thus of his responsibility before any tribunal, whether it be that of men or of God) unless this person himself or herself avows, "owns up," and remains constantly conscious of having thought and acted in a certain manner. If Locke's text can mobilize in productive fashion the division and doubling that results from the simple fact of using *self* in English as a proper name, even as it theoretically affirms the self's identity with itself, this is obviously because his very writing manifests an acute consciousness of the "performative" effects of the *first person* (perhaps the only truly "Cartesian" element of this text).[20] But it is also inseparably because self is not, like the French *moi*, a pronoun; nor is it a noun like *le moi*. When I speak with Locke in English about myself, and thus about my "self," I place this self at such a distance—albeit fictitious—that I can *interpellate* it. And yet, the content of this interpellation is nothing other than an identification, an (ap)propriation, an avowal, or owning of self, not an expropriation or a disowning. It is, in sum, the discovery of the self's *inalienability*, which is nothing other than "my consciousness."

Although its sources can be traced as far back as the Stoic *oikeosis* and the Augustinian *confessio*, this entire argument is eminently "modern." It can be perfectly well articulated in Locke's vocabulary, and it is one of the most remarkable developments of the *Essay on Human Understanding*. Wishing to "confuse" *my self* and *my own* at any cost, to forge a nominal identity at the price of misinterpretation, what I effaced with my error was in fact nothing other than the element of disquiet, ill-being, or uneasiness that, in Locke, affects and defines this unity. The theory of *uneasiness* can be found in another fundamental chapter of the *Essay* (Book II, Chapter 21, "Of Power").[21] Locke explains, in a manner very reminiscent of Spinoza, that there is no consciousness without a desire that both deranges it and leads it toward new content and ideas. Accordingly, the idea of a stable or immobile self-consciousness becomes a contradiction in terms. Since consciousness is by definition *restless*, it must escape (from) itself in order to go toward new content. The self-identity of consciousness, then, is immanent to a perpetual flux or "train of ideas." The category that precisely designates this intrinsic association of consciousness and desire is that of *uneasiness*.[22] What I would propose here, then, both correcting myself and returning to Locke, is that there is indeed an identity or sameness of the *self* and the *own*, which is instituted in language, not given or acquired, but existing as a "troubled" identity (and, at the limit, as an identity trouble). And it is all the more remarkable that Locke does not really posit this trouble or this uneasiness as a *thesis*. In a certain respect, he expresses it and materializes it in the subtlety of his writing, which never ceases to *mimic* the movement of producing, losing, and regaining identity, or the process of the *differed* appropriation of "self," the dialectical process of self-consciousness doubling itself which arises only to negate or to annul itself as a "vanishing difference."

But there is more. Let us return for a moment to Browning's poem. At the source of my initial blunder was undoubtedly a repression of the "erotic" duality that differs from a pure and simple "instrumental" appropriation of the other; and that, in this text, refers clearly to sexual difference. If "what belongs to me" and thus forms "my own" is, according to Browning, my wife, it would be more generally the sexually different *other* with whom I may spiritually "be as one" to the precise extent that we are never physically indiscernible, he or she with whom I experience the uneasy relation of identity and difference, not only because this relation can become conflicted without abolishing itself, but because the "border" between what is shared or indivisible and what is divorced or distributed can never be established with any certainty. Traditionally, we give the name "love" to such uneasy relations; but this is nothing but the name for a difficulty or a problem in which both consciousness and desire play a part. In general, how can the idea of "sexual difference" be integrated with the concept of personal identity? Is there an element in Locke that opens in this direction and makes it possible to affirm, albeit obliquely, that *something of sexual difference* is always implicated in the uneasiness of the relation between *self* and *own*? This relation, then, remains haunted by a doubling of the one; it can only appropriate itself through permanent effort, through soliciting—perhaps fugitively— "doubles." How should we understand the fact that these doubles always metaphorize sexual difference: not only as the difference between supposedly given "sexes" or "sexualities," but more importantly as a *constitutive* differentiation, both *futural* and *residual*, whose description coincides with "the sexualized experience of myself" in which I differ "sexually" from myself as much as from the other? Such a question—if it is acceptable to consider it within an author from the "classical" age—opens toward a final series of textual comparisons. And it obliges us to take into account the relation between what Locke views as the "norm" or the "normality" of consciousness and what represents its exception, its monstrous or pathological horizon. To this end, one need go no further than Book II, Chapter 27, of the *Essay*, which, one will discover, contends at great length with such an exception.

The Vanishing Difference

Because I want to go right to the strangest figures of this relationship between the norm and the exception in the *Essay*, I will only evoke in passing the vast question of how the philosophical tradition has conceptualized this "vanishing difference"—whether it pertain or not to consciousness, personal identity, or more fundamentally to the unity of a "self" that only becomes an "itself" at the price of internal strife. In the modern era, this conceptualization would go by way of Kant's paralogism of pure reason, William James, Sartre, and Freud. But comparisons with Hegel, Adam Smith, and George Hebert Mead yield the most interesting interpretations of Locke. It is no accident that I have already flirted with Hegelian language to evoke the passage from a notion of property as result, or title, to a notion of appropriation as process or becoming. In Hegel, as we know, the experience of consciousness (in the *Phenomenology*) is described as a succession of disjunctions and reunifications in which the "self" (*Selbst*) emerges under the auspices of certainty and truth. But, above all, the movement of the experience of consciousness renders appropriation extraordinarily ambivalent: At each instant, it becomes a process of expropriation or disowning as well as one of identification; every identity turns out to be constitutively doubled by what takes place "behind its back" and thus remains *bewusstlos*. For Hegel, in the final analysis, the "subject" of the process is neither individual "self" nor an already constituted collective "self" (a *society* in the sociological sense) but rather the essentially uneasy relationship between the individual and the community (or "substance"), which perceives itself as an infinite process of "recognition."[23] Compared to Hegel, or the others whom we might convoke here—Adam Smith for this construction of the "supposedly impartial spectator" that sympathy engenders at the heart the "self,"[24] Mead for his dialectic of tendentious opposition between the Self, the I, and the Me, whose effect is to divide "me" into personalities each of whom represents a form of participation in the network of social communication[25]—Locke is remarkable because he does not theorize and thus does not *fetishize* the duality or dualism or the "moments" of consciousness in the form of dialectic *instances* or *poles*. With the rhetoric of his discourse alone, and with a play on words borrowed from language, he merely indicates the *essentially vanishing* nature of this duality, which consists in a purely temporal train of thoughts, constitutive of memory. All of this obviously comes from Saint Augustine and goes toward Hegel, as well as Husserl, Sartre, and above all William James.[26]

Now, what I have called the "subtlety" of the Lockean difference has its counterpart in another manifestation of the division of "self," which pertains to the fantastic but, to my mind, leaves no doubt about the sexual connotation of this division.[27] Locke's developments on the division and union of persons resulting from the dissociation or fusion of consciousnesses situate his work historically at the point of transition from ancient doctrines of the transmigration of souls, the reincarnation of the dead, and theologies of resurrection, to modern doctrines of psychic dissociation that, while seeming more "experimental," are not necessarily any less speculative. The psychological and psychiatric problem of what is today called "multiple personality disorder" is, in fact, purely Lockean, whether the authors who theorize it admit or deny the reality of the phenomenon of the "longitudinal" doubling of memory and time-consciousness, which leads to the conclusion that several "personalities" or "identities" coexist in the breast of the same physical (today: cerebral) individual. Each personality would possess his or her "own" experiences, memories, social and affective behavior, which results in the permanent discontinuity between "life" and social relations, in the adoption of several names and several different personal appearances, etc.[28] Let us re-read §23 from Book II, Chapter 27, the same chapter that I cited earlier:

> Nothing but consciousness can unite remote existences into the same person: the identity of substance will not do it; for whatever substance there is, however framed, without consciousness there is no person: and a carcass may be a person, as well as any sort of substance be so, without consciousness. Could we suppose two distinct incommunicable consciousnesses acting the same body, the one constantly by day, the other by night; and, on the other side, the same consciousness, acting by intervals, two distinct bodies: I ask, in the first case, whether the day and the night—man would not be two as distinct persons as Socrates and Plato? And whether, in the second case, there would not be one person in two distinct bodies, as much as one man is the same in two distinct clothings? Nor is it at all material to say, that this same, and this distinct consciousness, in the cases above mentioned, is owing to the same and distinct immaterial substances, bringing it with them to those bodies; which, whether true or no, alters not the case: since it is evident the personal identity would equally be determined by the consciousness, whether that consciousness were annexed to some individual immaterial substance or no. For, granting that the thinking substance in man must be necessarily supposed immaterial, it is evident that immaterial thinking thing may sometimes part with its past consciousness, and be restored to it again: as appears in the forgetfulness men often have of their past actions; and the mind many times recovers the memory of a past consciousness, which it had lost for twenty years together. Make these intervals of memory and forgetfulness to take their turns regularly by day and night, and you have two persons with the same immaterial spirit, as much as in the former instance two persons with the same body. So that self is not determined by identity or diversity of substance, which it cannot be sure of, but only by identity of consciousness.

This development illustrates quite well how Locke bids farewell to the old dualisms of the soul and the body, thanks to his radical application of the criterion of self-consciousness. However, because self-consciousness is characterized by an inner uneasiness or a vanishing difference, it contains the possibility of a *fantastic projection* of its duality into another domain. In this imaginary experience, the difference among "persons"—that is, "identities" or "selves"—joins up with the conflict between Day and Night, or the forces of Good and Evil, whose stakes might not outstrip our understanding but do escape our mastery.[29]

The Day-Man and the Night-Man

This will become clearer if we understand that Locke's text forms part of a chain consisting of ever new elaborations upon the division of the self expressed through the duality of consciousness (or consciousnesses). To conclude, I will address this subject merely by evoking a "point of departure" and a provisional "point of arrival." Saint Augustine's *Confessions*—Book X, in particular—is, I think, the origin of Locke's scenario of scission and opposition between the "Day-man" and the "Night-man" who embody antagonistic moral values and personify incompatible principles in the breast of the same human individuality. And I would suggest that the *Essay*'s formulations continue to resonate, along with the language of nineteenth-century criminological and psychiatric debates, in Robert Louis Stevenson's "fantastic tale," *The Strange Case of Dr. Jekyll and Mister Hyde* (1886). Locke is to be found midway between the one work and the other—albeit, as we shall see, upon his own path.

Here is the well-known passage from Augustine:

> Iubes certe ut contineam a concupiscentia carnis et concupiscentia oculorum et ambitione saeculi. Iussisti a concubitu et de ipso coniugio melius aliquid quam concessisti monuisti. Et quoniam dedisti, factum est, et antequam dispensator sacramenti tui fierem. sed adhuc vivunt in memoria mea, de qua multa locutus sum, talium rerum imagines, quas ibi consuetudo mea fixit, et occursantur mihi vigilanti quidem carentes viribus, in somnis autem non solum usque ad delectationem sed etiam usque ad consensionem factumque simillimum. Et tantum valet imaginis inlusio in anima mea in carne mea, ut dormienti falsa visa persuadeant quod vigilanti vera non possunt. Numquid tunc ego non sum, domine deus meus? Et tamen tantum interest inter me ipsum et me ipsum intra momentum quo hinc ad soporem transeo vel huc inde retranseo! Ubi est tunc ratio qua talibus suggestionibus resistit vigilans et, si res ipsae ingerantur, inconcussus manet? Numquid clauditur cum oculis? Numquid sopitur cum sensibus corporis? Et unde saepe etiam in somnis resistimus nostrique propositi memores atque in eo castissime permanentes nullum talibus inlecebris adhibemus adsensum? et tamen tantum interest ut, cum aliter accidit, evigilantes ad conscientiae requiem redeamus ipsaque distantia reperiamus nos non fecisse quod tamen in nobis quoquo modo factum esse doleamus[30]

What is most important about Augustine's description of the involuntary pollutions brought forth by the *incubae*, or the nocturnal "visitors" from a luxurious past that the saint renounced "once and for all" when he took a vow of continence, is that it contributes to a discussion of the limits of *conversion*. To what extent does turning away from self-love in order to devote oneself exclusively to the love of God (and thus to surrender absolutely to his power and his grace: *subjectio*) entail a radical *change of identity*, the birth of a *new man*? This is why Book X of the *Confessions* enters into the famous discussion of the relations between *memoria* (let us call it "memory" on condition that this term encompasses all the operations of the spirit, *mens*) and moral *concupiscentia* (the search for pleasure) in the constitution of the moral personality, the relation of self to self. But we should pay special attention to the fact that Augustine, telling the story of his life expressly in order to speak of the modalities of desire, always upholds the distinction between sexual and other desires, associated with different sorts of pleasure. Offering himself an example, he affirms that sexual desire can be completely surmounted or repressed (at least in the form of physical attraction caused by the beauty or sensuality of other bodies) while the pleasures of food and drink, or those that arise from the spectacle of beautiful landscapes or works of art, from the awakening or exercise of intellectual faculties, or from the praise that redounds upon virtuous actions, such pleasures are much more difficult to "forget."[31] They engender an interminable conflict, lifelong combat in which the "two men" associated with the "two loves" (human and divine), and belonging to the "two Cities" (or two worlds: hither and thither), coexist and never cease confronting one another. But the accidents of the night teach us that this dissymmetry can also be understood in another way. When he gets to the point of asking himself in the first person *who is the subject* of these forbidden pleasures and these involuntary acts, this subject for whom, to judge by their effects, memory traces are more real than the real itself, both possible responses to this question—"it's me" and "it's not me"—are equally troubling. But the ensuing uneasiness directly refers to Augustine's reflections on the involuntary element that inhabits the very heart of the will, bearing witness to the presence of evil as the "dormant" element that might always awaken and thwart our inclination toward the good. Worse, because the only possible explanation for this resilience of desire, and with it a "personality" or a "man" whom one believes to be gone forever, is that God himself wished to preserve the possibility of such a relation to pleasure, one must (following what Pascal called the "reason of effects") suppose that the *other man* inhabits exactly the same "place" as God and the truth—in other words, the very intimacy of the self, *interior intimo meo*. At this interior place arise both *alterity* and the *ambivalence of love*. In this sense, "Night-man" would incarnate the remainder of amorous or libidinal ambivalence that prevents the love of God from taking up residence in any "fortress" whatsoever, consigning every man to uncertainty about God's intentions with respect to His servant.

The text of Stevenson's tale, which constitutes the third term of our comparison, is also certainly open to more than a single interpretation. I presume that Stevenson, from a Calvinist family with several pastors, and benefiting from a good classical education (albeit intermittent and nonconformist), wouldn't be ignorant the Augustinian tradition, if only at second hand. This tradition is certainly legible in the title of the tale and the content of the final chapter, Dr. Jekyll's confession.[32] I have no evidence whether the Scottish novelist ever read Locke's *Essay*, but it is clear that his tale of two "personalities" represents a movement from Locke's second hypothesis (a single spirit or consciousness in two distinct corporeal individuals) to his first (two consciousnesses for a single body, as "repeated" by Augustine). For this reason, this tale does not present a "case" of multiple personality, but rather the play of imagination and thus, no doubt, of critical reflection upon the hypotheses at work in scientific literature.[33] The crucial passage can be found in the final "confession": Jekyll explains, shifting back and forth between the first and third person, how he discovered that the second self which he created using "transcendental medicine" in order *to externalize the double nature of man*, or to experience the actual separation of the man of good and the man of evil (the Day-man and the Night-man), no longer belongs to him or is no longer "him" (his own), no longer follows his intentions, *as if* it obeyed its own (ill) will, which he interprets as the unleashing of blind forces, forces of "bestiality" or "degeneration." It is at this precise moment that Jekyll's monstrous "thing," in which he condensed the whole desire that inhabited him to break free from social constraints (which he calls the "the very pink of the proprieties"), becomes a "person," because it becomes *the master of its master* (a transformation which the butler is the first to observe, commenting on it throughout the tale). This is also the moment when Jekyll declares himself incapable of identifying with Hyde and of continuing to say "I" to describe his double's actions. In reality, however—in the reality of fiction—this is the moment when the two identities become so deeply interlaced that only a "common" death can then dissociate them. In order to "kill" the Hyde in himself, Jekyll must kill himself.[34] This suicide, in any event, is so equivocal that we do not know whether it accomplishes an absolute dissociation or an ultimate identification. The question, of course, is: *Who will be judged?*[35] We might also find in it an allegory of the death drive, all the more fitting in that Jekyll is manifestly a melancholic character.

Witness the following passages:

> All things therefore seemed to point to this: that I was slowly losing hold of my original and better self, and becoming slowly incorporated with my second and worse. Between these two, I now felt I had to choose. My two natures had memory in common, but all other faculties were most unequally shared between them. Jekyll (who was composite) now with the most sensitive apprehensions, now with a greedy gusto, projected and shared in the pleasures and adventures of Hyde; but Hyde was indifferent to Jekyll, or but remembered him as the mountain bandit remembers the cavern in which he conceals himself from pursuit. Jekyll had more than a father's interest; Hyde had more than a son's indifference. To cast in my lot with Jekyll, was to die to those appetites which I had long secretly indulged and had of late begun to pamper. To cast it in with Hyde, was to die to a thousand interests and aspirations, and to become, at a blow and for ever, despised and friendless. The bargain might appear unequal; but there was still another consideration in the scales; for while Jekyll would suffer smartingly in the fires of abstinence, Hyde would be not even conscious of all that he had lost.[36]

> Thenceforward, he sat all day over the fire in the private room, gnawing his nails; there he dined, sitting alone with his fears, the waiter visibly quailing before his eye; and thence, when the night was fully come, he set forth in the corner of a closed cab, and was driven to and fro about the streets of the city. He, I say—I cannot say, I. That child of Hell had nothing human . . . He walked fast, hunted by his fears, chattering to himself, skulking through the less-frequented thoroughfares, counting the minutes that still divided him from midnight. Once a woman spoke to him, offering, I think, a box of lights. He smote her in the face, and she fled. When I came to myself at Lanyon's, the horror of my old friend perhaps affected me somewhat: I do not know; it was at least but a drop in the sea to the abhorrence with which I looked back upon these hours. A change

had come over me. It was no longer the fear of the gallows, it was the horror of being Hyde that racked me . . . but I was once more at home, in my own house and close to my drugs; and gratitude for my escape shone so strong in my soul that it almost rivaled the brightness of hope.

At all hours of the day and night, I would be taken with the premonitory shudder; above all, if I slept, or even dozed for a moment in my chair, it was always as Hyde that I awakened . . . I became, in my own person, a creature eaten up and emptied by fever, languidly weak both in body and mind, and solely occupied by one thought: the horror of my other self. But when I slept, or when the virtue of the medicine wore off, I would leap almost without transition . . . into the possession of a fancy brimming with images of terror, a soul boiling with causeless hatreds, and a body that seemed not strong enough to contain the raging energies of life. The powers of Hyde seemed to have grown with the sickliness of Jekyll. And certainly the hate that now divided them was equal on each side. With Jekyll, it was a thing of vital instinct. He had now seen the full deformity of that creature that shared with him some of the phenomena of consciousness, and was co-heir with him to death. . . . The hatred of Hyde for Jekyll, was of a different order. His terror of the gallows drove him continually to commit temporary suicide, and return to his subordinate station of a part instead of a person. . . . Hence the ape-like tricks that he would play me, scrawling in my own hand blasphemies on the pages of my books, burning the letters and destroying the portrait of my father; and indeed, had it not been for his fear of death, he would long ago have ruined himself in order to involve me in the ruin. But his love of life is wonderful; I go further: I, who sicken and freeze at the mere thought of him, when I recall the abjection and passion of this attachment, and when I know how he fears my power to cut him off by suicide, I find it in my heart to pity him.

How to interpret these variations? In Augustine as in Stevenson, doubling clearly has a sexual—or, at least, erotic—connotation, attached to the troubling presence of alterity at the heart of any consciousness that seeks to take possession of itself in order to identify with a "self." Herein lies a radical conflict that cannot be resolved in everyday life, only masked or avoided. Augustine describes it in terms of moral theology, Stevenson in terms of fantastic physiology; but the result, in both cases, is *the absolute expropriation of (or by) self*, which is also its disavowal or disowning. This expropriation is the same no matter if it appears as God's love implanted *in interiore homine*, there to speak the truth and incarnate the authority to whom one must submit unconditionally in order to be saved, or as the master of the master—death—who is also projected in the form of a both interior and exterior being, alternately identified with myself (my propriety) and my "monstrous" desire to flee all identity, and thereby all responsibility.[37] Where should Locke be situated between these two extremes? For him, the supreme principle is neither God nor death but perhaps something like *human life*; for, his philosophy clearly associates consciousness with life, elevating life to the rank of a principle. But Locke, a physician who became a great philosopher, is also a great writer. Even as he draws the furthest reaching consequences from the idea of a "self" that would not be defined by inner conflict or division, but rather by the *appropriation* or the virtual identification of "self" and "own," he cannot ignore that such an identity includes alterity, or that it must be defined by an intrinsic relationship to "its other." He thus separates two figures of difference, positing, on the one hand, *uneasiness*, the tension of self and own that maintains life and consciousness in a state of perpetual movement (which means that uneasiness is the *norm*, and that the *normality* of life is uneasy, troubled, or discontent); and on the other hand, the state of exception, or the limit-figure that arises when uneasiness merges with the monstrous, engendering a split between the corporeal and the mental, the radical dissociation of personality and individuality. In a sense, the latter figure represents the truth of the former, because it helps us to see that there is nothing natural or necessary in the identification of self and own, thanks to which being oneself can no longer be separated from owning oneself. This identification is merely a postulate, if not an injunction.

Postscript

I here reproduce the body of a letter that the linguist and philosopher Jean-Jacques Lecercle[38] wrote to me after I sent him the English version of this essay:

> The proximity of "self" and "own," despite the syntactical distance between the two terms, cannot be denied. What I can't manage to determine is whether Locke arrived at this proximity through the movement of language itself, or whether he was its initiator, or one of the initiators (which, when it comes to the transformation of the "self" from a grammatical morpheme into a noun, is clearly the case). Whence a few reflections of speculative linguistics. Semantically, the two terms are opposed. In Culioli's language, "self" is aligned with "be" as a marker of identification, but "own" is aligned with "have" as a marker of differentiation/localization. Except that language is never not in movement, whence the proximity, which I propose to formulate thus: with "self," the one divides into two (as one would say in the time of the blessed Chairman Mao), whereas with "own" the two meld into one. "Self," which is the reflexive pronoun, syntactically needs an antecedent in the same proposition, of which it provides the mirror image (this doubling is even clearer in the emphatic usage of "self," derived from the reflexive, e.g. "although I say it myself"). The "self" is thus the *ego* in the mirror. "Own," on the contrary, stems from a past participle (of "owe") transformed into a two-pronged verb (whence differentiation/localization): what I possess is localized in relation to me ("I own a car") and ego insofar as "own" results from the fusion of these two separate elements, such that "own" comes to designate solitude ("he is on his own"). I believe that this proximity must have emerged in the seventeenth century. My etymological dictionary whispers to me that the meaning of the verb "own"—"to recognize as belonging to oneself," and thus "to accept as true"— also appeared in the seventeenth century.

THREE

Aimances in Rousseau: *Julie or The New Heloise* as Treatise on the Passions

> I figure love, friendship, the two idols of my heart, using the most ravishing images!

> O divine friendship, sole idol of my heart![1]

The chapter that Paul de Man devotes to *Julie or the New Heloise* in his *Allegories of Reading* does not only represent a central moment in the economy of the book, where the category that guides his readings (the "allegory" from the title) is explicated and justified; it is also a particularly illuminating discussion of a knot of questions regarding *passion*, which are generally considered to hold the philosophical key to the novel. In order to understand how writing and theory are superimposed in *The New Heloise*, I draw upon two of de Man's assertions. The first says that "passion is not something which, like the senses, belongs in proper to an entity or a subject but, like music, it is a system of relationships that exists only in the terms of this system";[2] it is a *relational* notion. This also means that *love*, in the infinite variety of its modalities, as well as the correlative passions, can serve to elucidate (in part, at least) the nature of relations as such, not only from a phenomenological or existential viewpoint, but also from a logical one. De Man's second assertion defines the literary category of allegory as a "narrative of the second degree,"[3] which includes the deconstruction of its own immediate, apparently realistic signification. In this manner, allegory makes it impossible to dissociate fiction and reasoning, taking the text as an object of criticism from the position of an "impartial observer" situated outside of it.

This definition of allegory is pregnant with multiple consequences. In no way does it forbid us from recognizing that concepts are produced in *Julie or the New Heloise*, but only on the condition that we admit that these concepts can never be separated from the *literary experiment* in which they are presented. In another passage from his book, one will recall, de Man takes issue with the formulation whereby Louis Althusser concludes his essay on *The Social Contract*. The author of *For Marx* and *Reading Capital* suggests that, since the contradictions of the "original contract" cannot be resolved, Rousseau ends up abandoning theory and turning to "literature," in order to imagine—but without really thinking its conditions of possibility—a society endowed with the extraordinary capacity to restore the lost authenticity of nature.[4] Such brutal alternatives—"theory" or "literature," "concept" or "metaphor"—are untenable in de Man's eyes, and rightly so I believe (even if I remain dubious about such a "first degree" reading of Althusser). However, at the end of his chapter on *Julie*, which bears the same title as the book as a whole ("Allegory"), de Man is compelled to admit that his reading has left out a large part of what readers have traditionally found in it. Such a reading tells us nothing, in particular, about the novel's description (which has been judged both normative and subversive) of a utopian social order centered upon the family, or about its every equivocal relation to religion.

The Fiction of Correspondence

Rather than pursue a discussion of Althusser and de Man, I would like to move beyond the limitations that still hamper de Man's insight about the conceptual scope of allegorical writing, taking into account (as much as a single chapter allows) the entire system of the "passions" represented in *Julie*, and thus the whole world of subjects who are constructed through the writing of fictional letters exchanged between the characters in the novel. Without going so far as Alain Grosrichard, who claims that the character of Julie was actually the model for the Kantian *Ding an sich*, I will suggest that the system of intersubjective relations that *The New Heloise* presents to us effectively subverts the accepted dichotomies of passion and reason, and private and public; and that, in this sense, it represents Rousseau's most original attempt at reaching his ever "unattainable" philosophical goal, namely a type of social relation that would be both the *negation* and the *restoration* of the human being's inscription in nature; or that, in other words, would possess the characteristics of both "first" and "second nature."[5]

First, we must briefly characterize the traits of the novel's writing that manifestly command its form. One is a question of "style." It is the fact of Rousseau's having constructed the novel in an epistolary form, an exchange of letters between protagonists, leaving the reader to surmise their intentions and the effects of their reception, and to fill in what their account of events fails to tell. Rousseau models his novel very closely upon Richardson's *Clarissa*, a work that knew enormous success throughout Europe at the time.[6] But he also inscribes himself (in particular, through the allegory of his title) within a humanist tradition whose relation to fiction is more complicated.[7] The other aspect concerns the sequence of actions that emerges from the correspondence, or, in other words, the novelistic *plot* "proper": the characters in *Julie* who are touched by passion, subjected to social interests, and moved by sentimental or ideological motives, and so forth, evolve from the *initial situation*, in which the amorous liaison is formed between Saint-Preux and his student, provoking the ire of her family to which she appears to succumb in the end, and the profoundly ambiguous *final turn of events* in which Julie, now a wife and mother increasingly conscious of her dissatisfaction, comes to an accidental death that might be read as a bungled action, a renunciation, or a deliberate sacrifice. These two aspects of the novel—style and plot—are, obviously, imbricated deeply within one another.

The revival of the *roman par lettres* is at the origin of a glorious lineage of reprisals and reversals.[8] De Man recalls that this genre was criticized at first as an artifice insofar as Rousseau's invented correspondence, in large measure, *describes* events and states of their protagonists' inner lives or of the society where they evolve, but it only rarely constitutes *actions* that provoke other actions or reactions, as would be the case if a letter revealed to a character a fact that he would not otherwise know, or received a letter that was not meant for him,[9] or drew him into trumped-up feelings of love, jealousy, anger, or gratitude. This reproach of "artificiality" often implies the further claim that missives exchanged in *Julie* are not really "letters," or have no performative function—that is, they mention but do not enact the transformation of the thoughts and behavior of their authors and address-ees. In this regard, it has also been noted that letters from different characters are not really written in differing styles, which is understood to mean that they are less addressed to their "addressees" than *to the readers of the novel*, who become, in a sense, the social ad-dressees of a conventional form. I do not hesitate to make the opposite claim: Such a cri-tique is founded upon a much too conventional concept of the relations between subject and action; it fails to grasp that Rousseau's writing functions precisely to call this concept into question. The *correspondence effect* that we encounter within Julie is not limited to de-scribing or soliciting reactions from individuals; it must be conceived as a transindividual process. It is, in fact, the production and transformation of *the social relation itself* in and through the "commerce" of the characters it binds together, of whom one might say that Rousseau, as an "author," becomes the vanishing mediator. But this relation is made up of "passions" whose symmetries and dissymmetries, passive or active orientation, construc-tive or destructive consequences, or secret or public modality, never cease to raise ques-tions for the protagonists who, whether spontaneously or deliberately, produce a *correspondence* (in the sense of an object, a written trace, and a logical relation) which is *their own work* (or their common "property"). At times this correspondence brings them closer, at times it distances them, making them "strangers" to one another, or simply im-peding the unity of feeling that they yearn for. The performative dimension of the fic-tional correspondence that Rousseau offers the reader in *Julie* is thus not at all weakened but, on the contrary, much reinforced and multiplied by its mode of address. I would sug-gest that the phenomenological *experience* that the book seeks to account for (which, in an ironic mode, might be called "the science of the experience of passionate consciousness") exists only as the effect of the correspondence itself, produced or intensified by the ex-change of fictional letters. This is what distinguishes this experience, in particular, from a "specular" relation; it does not exist prior to *the writing of the letters*, which, in turn, is not "really" distinct from *the moment of their reading*. Of course, as de Man strongly un-derscores, this is because of the fact that Rousseau himself *reads the letters as he writes them* (or—in the case of certain letters that are reputedly borrowed from his own correspon-dence with Sophie d'Houdetot—as he *rewrites* them).[10] The experience that the *author* pursues—hiding behind the double mask of a denied anonymity and a disavowal without conviction[11]—by "identifying" with each of his characters in turn also depends on this fact; and this becomes especially clear when we notice that the novel has an open temporality, and thus an *experimental* dimension. Rousseau does not necessarily know the end in advance; or rather, he cannot decide *before writing* the letters whose authors he feigns—thereby lending them his own "style"—what the "meaning" of this end will be.

Let us take a further step. First of all, the usage of the epistolary form is linked to a fluctuating structuration of space and time, made up of variable "distances" between characters, "moments" of separation followed by moments of reunion, whose alternation plays a fundamental role in the novel's plot. Love and friendship both are affairs of imposed or accepted distances, which the imagination annuls in advance or seeks belatedly to compensate for with multiple declarations and avowals, but also of the spaces and gaps that letters open up at the heart of intimacy and presence, thereby interrupting the very enjoyment that they are supposed to prolong.[12] To the extent that letters are written, sent to and even imposed upon the other, expected, and read by one or many addressees, they materialize the complexity of the relationship between corporeal distance and the imagination, which, according to Rousseau, is nothing other than "community." Individuals either live at a distance from one another or they coexist in the same place (which can make it seem seems "artificial" that they need to write one another). This is why their "society effect" (as Althusser would say) cannot do without epistolary relations to "third parties" who, even if momentarily absent, are essential to the cohesion of the group. We might even suggest that what constitutes the "link" between characters (and thus subjects) *present* in the "same place" (*hic et nunc*) is ultimately nothing other than the set of letters whereby they remain connected to momentarily *absent* "friends." Should we say, repurposing Lacan a bit, that community here derives from an instance of the letter that transforms "relation" into a "nonrelation"? This remains to be seen.

A second remark might also be formulated. It is precisely because the characters in the novel communicate among themselves by means of written sentences that they are endowed, not exactly with *individuality* or *personality* in the social or psychological sense, but rather with a singular *voice*.[13] Is there necessarily a contradiction in the fact that the voice of a subject needs to be represented by the writing of a "correspondent" in order to distinguish itself as such? Isn't such a voice, on the contrary, the fundamental "grammatological" effect (as in Derrida, who might have sought evidence of this effect in the writing of *Julie*)? Not only do I think this second hypothesis is correct, but I would also relate it to the fact *the writing of each and every Rousseau work is implicitly or explicitly dialogic*, highlighting the contrast and on occasion the conflict among several "voices"—whence the division of the author function between the *different voices* that he adopts as his writing goes along. This is true of *The New Heloise*, Rousseau's unconventional "novel," but just as much of "theoretical" works such as the *Discourses* or *The Social Contract*, albeit in another manner, the philosophical consequences of which cannot be reduced to a single model.[14] Of course, "Dialogue" and "dialogic" form are complex notions, which is linked to the fact (to which I will return in conclusion) that the set of Rousseau's works dealing with the problem of community do not form the complementary pieces of a unified doctrine but rather *experimentations*, the various avenues whereby Rousseau sought to explore the same, fundamentally aporetic problem. However, *Julie* is a novel, a fact with extreme consequences. We can only access the meaning and results of its exploration through the relationship established between the "voices" that all bear the name of a character who is the "signatory" of a certain series of letters. *No sovereign voice*—which might be called neutral or absolute—steps forth in this dialogue to designate the path of truth; to engender what, after Spinoza, might be called *adequate ideas* (or perhaps "geometrical ideas") about the nature and effects of the passions that flare up between the characters. The only criteria at our disposal arise from the content and the sequence of letters, from the accord or discord between the judgments that different correspondents impose upon their mutual relationships. *For us*, such interpretations are destined to remain purely hypothetical. The importance of this fact appears as characters who are caught up in amorous passion—especially Julie and Saint-Preux—literally discover in and through writing that their physical and moral union actually constitutes a difference that drives them apart even as it unites them. There is a fracture in the reciprocity that renders two beings inseparable: "I seek ecstasy, and you seek love," writes Saint-Preux to Julie (Part I, Letter 55, 122). Is this the allegorical expression of a (Sartrean or Lacanian) thesis on the "inexistence" of the sexual relation? The description of an affect that generally follows upon masculine desire confronted with feminine demand (or vice versa)? The indication of one of the hero's character traits (about which he might well be mistaken)? We will never have any way to know for absolutely sure. As a result, every problem relating to the community that joins the characters will be formulated *in the plural*, through the contrast of many voices.[15] We might then ask whether the irreducibility of voices should ultimately be considered to be a sign of the *impossibility* of community or, on the contrary, whether it exhibits the difference without which there can be no transindividual reciprocity.

Transmuting Love into Friendship

Let us now consider the plot of the novel. It is often said that *The New Heloise* is divided into two large sections, the first dealing with love and the second with marriage. Rousseau himself underscores the caesura by explaining, at the beginning of Part IV, that the correspondence has now "resumed" after a six-year hiatus. More dialectically, the novel would describe the way in which the natural power of love destroys the foundations of a certain traditional (aristocratic) form of the family, in the wake of which the sublimation of love and its alliance with reason lead to the construction of a more stable and more authentic familial model, which can be called bourgeois.[16] The indications that Rousseau offers in his prefaces, in addition to the a posteriori reflections contained in his *Confessions*, lend support to this claim that the novel unfolds in two movements. But readers remain divided about the meaning of the final episode, which some see as a refutation of the idea that marriage and the rational feeling that founds it would be superior to amorous passion, while others find proof in it that for Rousseau the institution of marriage remained unsustainable without a religious supplement.[17] This episode consists of a sequence of interlinked melodramatic circumstances: Julie's "second conversion" from the religion of her childhood to a more "mystical" form devotion wherein she finds reasons to reenter to the familial order; the discord that results from this conversion between herself and her husband Monsieur de Wolmar (whereby the excess of religion seems to undermine what its own moderation can accomplish, unless the fault lies with irreligion); and finally her accidental—or providential—death, which most likely has a sacrificial dimension.[18] How precisely should this sequence be understood? I would like to advance a hypothesis that somewhat displaces the current interpretations of this sequence of events.

It seems to me that the source of the novel's drama, and the bearer of its philosophical import, lies in the project of achieving the transformation of one "passion" into another and "experimentally" studying the conditions of possibility for such a transformation. More specifically, it lies in the veritable *transmutation of love into friendship*—two passions that are certainly very close to one another, and yet radically heterogeneous. In order to capture the at once practical and theoretical aspect of this "problem," I rely upon a neologism—*aimance*—from Jacques Derrida's *Politiques de l'amitié* (1994) (a book that, unless I am mistaken, does not allude even once to Rousseau, although it discusses "fraternity" at great length). The English translators of the book have chosen to translate this word with a further neologism, *lovence*; but it seems to me that the French word might also be considered as an original translation of *libido*—especially with respect to Freud's usages of this term in his writings on culture."[19] For the moment, I leave open the question whether—in accordance with a schema of division often found in classical "treatises of the passions," which, at least in part, serve as Rousseau's model, even as he attempts to revolutionize their problematic—this *aimance* represents a *more originary and more indeterminate affect* than love and friendship, a "drive" at work in their respective vicissitudes, their increasing or decreasing intensities, the displacement of their object choices, their inversions of attraction and repulsion, etc; or whether it represents the *conjoined effect of love and friendship* (along with other passions as well) whose combination would account for complex "social" effects in which they can be seen competing with one another, substituting for one another, and passing from one subject to another.[20] Two observations help to appreciate the importance of this question for the interpretation of *The New Heloise*. First of all, the difference between love and friendship is traditionally difficult to parse for philological reasons that affect each individual language and especially the passage from one language to another: At stake is the notorious equivocity of what the Greeks called *philein* or the Romans *amare*, or the fact that we (modern French, but also English, and Germans) resort to "love" as the blanket translation for the words *eros* and *agape*, *amor* and *caritas*, and so on.[21] At the same time, as Derrida recalls in his book, the distinction between love and friendship has been of fundamental importance for political thought—before and after the "epistemological break" of Christianity.[22] Perhaps one might say that this distinction supports the difference of the political as such, to the extent that it intersects with the distinctions between the private and the public, domestic space (*oikos*) and the *polis*. Consequently, the simple fact that—at least in one possible reading—we might consider *The New Heloise* as organized around the idea of a transmutation of love into friendship, or around the question of knowing whether *such a transmutation is possible or not* (and under what conditions), is reason enough (although still formal) for us to read it not as a *marginally* but on the contrary as an *eminently* political text. Its subject matter would thus be nothing less than the *condition of possibility*—or of impossibility—for political society, which precedes the difference between regimes, their respective value, or characteristic institutions; and, for this reason, it is legitimate to read this text alongside *The Social Contract* and its concern with "what makes a people a people."[23]

Within the novel itself (by a *mise en abyme* that is very characteristic of eighteenth-century poetics, of which many examples can be found especially in the works of Marivaux: *L'Île des esclaves*, *La Double Inconstance*, *La Dispute*, etc.) this transmutation is given *the status of an experiment*.[24] Originally proposed by one of the characters—Monsieur de Wolmar, who represents the classical combination of *reason* and *authority*, thus incarnating the figure of the Master or the "living law" (*nomos empsychos*)—it is eventually adopted by all the novel's other characters who make it the very object of their *virtuous emulation*.[25] In a movement that might well be called violent, and even cruel, Wolmar suggests to his young wife—"You make cruel use of your wife's virtue," Julie writes to him[26]—that she invite her former lover, Saint-Preux, to their property, such that he might become not only a friend of the family, but also her closest and dearest confidant. Then he stages the crucial—and terribly risky—ordeal: in order to "cure" them of the obsessions of their imagination and to help them discover the possibility of a new kind of feeling, he brings them to the same *bosquet* (a clear enough erotic symbol, explicit in other languages) where, in a passionate embrace, they had declared their love for one another. But it was Julie herself who asked permission from Saint-Preux to disclose their past affair to her husband and offered friendship in exchange. And finally, Saint-Preux also adheres to this plan (or believes in all sincerity that he does so) when he accepts Wolmar's offer to take charge of educating his children (who are primarily Julie's, and so he must now "repeat" the situation of their former relationship with different results in view). The dimension of the performative utterance becomes very clear at this point: collectively adhering to the project of substituting the bond of reciprocal and sharable friendship for the exclusive love relations, and thereby even reducing conjugal love, or the affective relation institutionalized by marriage, to a single element in a larger and multilateral system of passionate friendship,[27] the three protagonists who write each other to discuss their common project are in fact *already in the midst of realizing this project* (leaving aside, for the moment, the other characters, who are also "friends," but played that role from the outset, and thus don't require conversion). The sequence of the novel's episodes thus hinge upon the following question: Under what conditions could such a plan—very much an "open secret"—be hatched in the minds of its participants, and what will be accomplished by the "real experiment" that Rousseau's fictional characters perform on themselves?

Let us know consider the questions that arise from the possibility of reading *Julie* as a "treatise on the passions" or even as a "natural history" of the passions in Locke's—and later, Fourier's—sense. Writing in the form of fictional correspondence is no mere literary device; it goes beyond the register of metaphor to become an allegorical resource of theory itself. If we start from the idea of a sentimental alchemy that transforms one passion into another (and thus one transindividual relation into another), then we should first examine what lends these passions their opposed qualities. Let us advance the following hypothesis: For Rousseau, unlike an entire tradition beginning with ancient Stoicism and perfected in the modern era with Descartes and Spinoza, and also unlike the seventeenth-century Augustinian "moralists," but closer to a wholly other lineage made famous by the French "tragedians" (Racine, Marivaux), the singular passions are not defined in terms of differences, derivations, and typologies, but rather of interferences and dialogue. What singularizes the passions is the way in which *they act upon one another* and thereby become "governable" or "ungovernable," and manifest themselves as transformable or untransformable. This difference, it seems to me, corresponds to a wholly other conception of *desire*, not oriented toward "the object" (as Descartes as well as Freud would say) but rather toward the response of the other "subject." The passions are formed within the microcosm of a small social circle. Moreover, they can only be described in the temporal form of a development or a transformation, which means that they entail a "historical" dimension that spontaneously assumes the form of a narrative of self, making the retrospective memory and imagination of sensations and past experiences into a feature of their present quality of feeling, and ascribing their "truth" to a series of *aftereffects*. This temporal dimension becomes manifest when friendship is presented not only as a *substitute* for lost or forbidden love, but also as the *actual affective relation* to a past love that it both preserves and transforms into something else ("He loves her in the past: that is the true answer to the enigma," Part IV, Letter XIV, Wolmar to Madame d'Orbe).[28] In other terms, *friendship repeats love*: there is an extraordinarily ambivalent relationship between them because it implies the trauma of reactivating old gestures in order to transform them. Whence the already mentioned episode of the *return to the secret (and sacred) grove* (or "profanation du bosquet") in which love was declared in such a way that it becomes possible, in the presence of a third party (that is, the husband), for the former lovers to kiss again, this time in friendship—which is also, of course, a sign of disillusionment that might well harbor an unconscious promise or the germ of desire's rebirth (Part IV, Letter XII, Julie to Madame d'Orbe).

A typical but theoretically troubling aspect of Rousseau's description seems to reside in *the elimination of negative passions*, and consequently in the turn away from the polarities of love/hate, joy/sadness, hope/fear, and so on, which play a determining, if not architectonic, role in the classical treatises, especially in relation to the question of the social or antisocial effects of the passions. It is as if Rousseau retained nothing but the good passions that can never be destructive unto themselves.[29] What confers this quality upon them is the fact that, in fiction, *there are only positive characters*, incapable of wishing one another ill, much less doing ill: the novel calls them "beautiful souls," using an expression which Rousseau did not invent but did make famous, and which Schiller, followed by Hegel, will make a determining moral and political category.[30] In *The New Heloise*, consequently, even if Saint-Preux initially emerges as a "vile seducer" (Part I, Letter IV, from Julie) and ends up as a "dangerous man" (Part V, Letter XIII, from Madame de Wolmar), there is no Lovelace or Marquise de Merteuil, not to mention Sade's heroes. Rousseau has now absolutely nothing in common with the seventeenth-century tragedians, in whose work the death drive always already inhabits each passion.[31] The results, however, are no less dramatic: in the form of "sad" passions (the jealousy and melancholy that generate a gap between the imagination of pleasure and the real experience of pleasure, the longing caused by the distance of the love object, etc.), the negative is not definitively excluded but rather is aligned with *the excess of the good*, forming the abyss or shadow that the good always has to conjure away. "Excess," however, is not the best term: it seems perfect to characterize what happens with sexual love, but it does not fit other forms of love that "moderate" themselves, or at least appear to do so, because they are compatible with reason and can combine with it. In more abstract and more general terms, we might speak of an *inadequation* inherent to the passions, the index of which would be the intrinsic distance between the experience of happiness, the very jouissance that passion brings, and the feeling of expectation and hope that it entails as the desire for a response from the other. This would certainly apply to sexual love, which Rousseau constantly describes as unappeased or inadequate to the imagination of it, unless it is replaced by a form of imaginary fusion.[32] But it would also apply to friendship: in the final analysis (and, of course, especially in the case of Julie, who thereby becomes conscious of something that everybody else dimly perceives) friendship is also fraught with unsatisfaction, fails to live up to its promises, and leaves behind a feeling of melancholy at the heart of happiness, calling for (reasonable or unreasonable) new arrangements. This also means that friendship and love both depend on the feeling of hope, especially if it is true that friendship feeds upon the hope to fulfill the expectations that love had disappointed.

In *The New Heloise*, Rousseau plays upon the broad and narrow meanings of the word *love*, and manages to distinguish at least five different varieties of it, experienced more or less thoroughly by the different characters: passionate sexual love (given to illegality), conjugal love exemplified by the successful marriage of convenience, maternal love,[33] the love of God or "devotion," and finally friendship as open-heartedness founded upon reciprocal sincerity. The novel invites us to follow to metamorphoses, displacements from one character (or from one *couple of characters*) to another. We reluctantly leave this phenomenology aside, retaining only the few aspects of it that illustrate Rousseau's understanding of the plasticity of desire and thus help to clarify how he deploys the aporetic structure of the novel—which is inseparable from its "allegorical" structure, which, in de Man's sense, means that the novel's articulations at once contradict and fulfill its intentions.

It is remarkable, first of all, that Rousseau describes friendship itself as a feeling, a "passionate attachment"[34]—no less passionate, in truth, than the sexual love that it is supposed to supplant, or rather displace, within the framework of the "plan" that the characters seek to actualize by forming a society of souls supposedly united by absolute mutual trust, permitting and even demanding that they *say everything to one another*.[35] I will suggest that the basis of friendship is passionate because, even as it *desexualizes love* or separates it from its sexual goal ("possession"),[36] in no way does it suppress or neutralize *sexual difference*. Actually, it does the exact opposite. This is bound up with the fact that friendship is essentially founded on the memory of the experience of love (or the desire to love), which preserves the sexed character of the subjects involved. In a sense, we could say that friendship, by halting the search for sexual pleasure and the imagination of amorous fusion, *intensifies* sex as difference or as distance. It is always colored, or determined, by the fact that it takes place between a man and a woman—or, as we shall see, between a man and a man, or a woman and a woman—but never between sexually "neutral" or "unmarked" individuals. Friendship is still expectation and desire, and there is no desire between sexless beings. Such is the unity of opposites or the "contradiction" that Wolmar, in a key letter (addressed to Claire), articulates with a Pascalian formulation: "I have made a discovery that neither you nor any woman on earth with all the subtlety one attributes to your sex would ever have made . . . that these two opposites should be simultaneously true; that they should burn more ardently than ever for each other, and that nothing more than an honest attachment should any longer prevail between them; that they should still be lovers and be no longer but friends; that, I think, you less expect, will have more difficulty understanding, and yet is in keeping with the exact truth. . . . Such is the enigma posed by the frequent contradictions you must have remarked in them" (Part IV, Letter XIV, 416).

But there is more. The metamorphosis that transforms sexual love into friendship is essentially destined to annihilate any possibility of *jealousy*: the sad, murderous passion, which the *Discourse on the Origins of Inequality* associates, in a dramatic description, with the desire for possession. But it does create new possibilities of transference and identification. One of the novel's mainsprings is constituted by the idea that a friend always tends to fall in love with the friend of his or her friend; and this idea is illustrated first by the case of Milord Édouard, Saint-Preux's friend, who falls in love with Julie, and next by that of Claire, Julie's cousin who becomes her friend and confidant, who falls in love with Saint-Preux. The complexity of the phenomena of transference increases when Julie, who is perhaps mistaken about the nature of her true feelings but remains capable of deploying a rational strategy of "distanciation," tries to convince her lover to marry her friend, thereby putting her in place of the love object that obsesses him so that she (Julie) could disengage (unless the whole point of procuring this ersatz love is to keep herself involved). All of the games, these substitutions, lead to the idea that the transformation of love into friendship is *reversible*, haunted by the possibility—always requiring new tactics to ward off—that the sublimated passion could return. There is thus an uncertainty that mounts as the novel comes to a close, the interpretation of which affects its "political" meaning. It seems that the elimination of jealousy and the metamorphosis of love into a passion that is no less intense, but that would no longer entail either ambivalence or instability, has no chance of succeeding unless a *supplement of transcendence* is added to the reciprocity of affects and the feeling of mutual trust (*confiance*) that engenders the confidences which the subjects share and make their common property.

What form does this supplement take? Either it is a *living eye* that itself belongs to the community and therein exercises an authority founded upon the superior power of rationality: such is Monsieur de Wolmar, whom many various commentators have likened to the "mortal God" of Hobbesian political philosophy.[37] Or it is the "devotion" to the hidden God of revealed religions, who can still be incarnated in the feelings and actions of a singular human being. This is what happens in Julie's final conversion (which is actually, as we know, her second conversion, since the first took place when, at the behest of her family and at grips with the guilt inspired by the death of her mother, she sacrificed the love that society considered illegitimate): increasingly ill at ease with her husband's atheism, she plunges into mysticism and ultimately sacrifices herself—or, at least, dies in manner that can be interpreted allegorically as a sacrifice, providing the community with a religious "basis" to found itself anew. Nonetheless, this "theological" moment is very strange: at the limit, it can only result in heresy and blasphemy, since it puts a woman in the place of Christ.[38] None of this is completely clear as such but remains suspended in an allegorical space: first because Monsieur de Wolmar's conversion to his wife's religion after her edifying death is only a vague rumor that the faithful Claire transmits in an final letter full of passion (Part VI, Letter XIII); but mostly, it seems to me, because Saint-Preux's own attitude remains obscure, while his "cosmopolitan" friendship with Milord Édouard—which unites, in spite of class differences, a modest Swiss preceptor and a rich English aristocrat—evokes an entirely other way, both more "social" and more "egalitarian," to put an end to the emotional instability of the community.[39] This essential uncertainty that besets the "conclusion" of *The New Heloise* on the level of its "intrigue" deserves to be interpreted on a theoretical level as well, but only if it is recognized that the novel itself incorporates a *"décalage"* (as Althusser would say) or an internal critique of its own utopia. On the one hand, indeed, when Julie saves her son from drowning at the price of her own life, this is the very type of the contingent event that, in the *Discourse on the Origins of Inequality*, happens to interrupt the continuity of a historical development, and in the *Second Promenade*, operates a subjective conversion to what is more profoundly "self" than "me" itself. But, on the other hand, this event reveals the absolute limits that affect the two competing models of transparency and clarity which might govern an "enlightened" society of friends: that of the *living eye* of a rational master educator and that of an *unreserved sincerity* among subjects. Neither the one nor the others can, in fact, foresee and know everything that constitutes their relations.[40]

Network: Doubles and Triangles

This brings me to my final point. The best way to elaborate it is to trace a geometric schema subjacent to the narrative of *The New Heloise*. What is particularly striking about the way in which Rousseau constructs the network of relationships among friends, integrating and displacing sexual love in order to reconcile affectivity with interest and reason, is his quasi-structuralist interpretation of intersubjectivity, entirely founded upon symmetries and oppositions. Let us then produce a diagram of the binary and ternary relations that support one another even as they retain a deconstructive tension.[41]

The structure that organizes the situation and governs the intrigue of *The New Heloise* at first appears as a triangle of relations; and commentators have not failed to notice its quasi-Oedipal character.[42] I say quasi-Oedipal because Monsieur de Wolmar, the "real" father of Julie's children, also seeks to incarnate an explicitly "symbolic" paternal figure with respect to the entire "family."[43] But all of the sentimental relationships are also reflected in Julie's "soul"; and they are thereby subsumed within the maternal love that she extends to the entire community. This virtual primacy of the feminine becomes legible in the confession that Saint-Preux writes to his lover: "O Julie! What is your inconceivable empire! By what strange power do you fascinate my reason!" (Part III, Letter XVI). The term *empire* is the one that Claire uses to confess to her friend what she finds irresistible in her, from which she cannot detach herself (Part IV, Letter II). The fundamental triangle, therefore, has two virtual points of sovereignty, one masculine and one feminine; and the subject occupying the third position, citizen Saint-Preux, happens to be subjected to both of them.[44]

However, Starobinski is the one who imposed a further remarkable displacement upon this reading, bringing out the logic of the *couple*, which is something else entirely: For him, the "principle of organization" or the "generative element" of the novel's intrigue does not reside in the place or the function of the individual, but rather in the couple formed by Julie and her cousin Claire; for, between them is established the bond of absolute trust or the relation of "transparency" that arises from the decision unreservedly to share their most secret feelings; and this decision will become the cornerstone of all the friendships, aligned in a kind of circle into which all the characters will gradually be drawn.[45] As a result of this brilliant idea, the ambivalence of the passion at the heart of each couple is brought from the margins to the center. It is risky, of course, to identify as the fiction's "first" couple not Julie and Saint-Preux but Julie and Claire: what they share and what binds them, initially, is not love but rather *the story of love*. This is, once again, the mainspring for friendship as the feeling that displaces, or defers, or reflects love. But it is also the point at which feelings become indecisive. These two cousins—the blond and the brunette, as in mythological couples—are, in reality, *Doppelgänger*: problematic "doubles," both one in two and two in one. They are liable to replace one another in various capacities: as spouses, as mothers. They certainly feel a homosexual love for one another that is only partially repressed. On this basis, they end up acting themselves as a couple of lovers.[46]

Taking this structural idea up a notch, we obtain the possibility of combining the novel's central "triangle" with the complete series of homosexual "doubles" that are bound up with it. Julie has her double in Claire, Saint-Preux has his double in Milord Édouard, and Monsieur de Wolmar himself has his double in the mute figure, akin to an "effigy," of Julie's father (the Baron d'Étanges), who always wanted to marry her off to his friend to settle an obscure debt (see accompanying figure).[47]

Such a presentation is interesting not only because it gives us the opportunity to elaborate the combinatory possibilities that underlie the different perspectives (or rather, as I suggested above, the different "voices"), both symmetrical and dissymmetrical, which make up the novel, and thus to conceptualize the necessity for the *disjunction* among the various positions, at a given moment within the novel's intrigue, of the characters who together hatched the project of collectively accomplished the conversion of love into friendship. It is also interesting because it allows us to manifest the *system*, or the complete network of transindividual relations that govern the movements or tropes of the characters' subjectivation. What it shows, in particular, is that the model of "community" that Rousseau pursues in *The New Heloise* is a system which combines relations (or "commerces") *pertaining just as much to homosexuality as to heterosexuality*. Even as he deploys the modalities of *aimance*—we might say, returning to Derrida's terminology—he also makes sex appear as *différance* (or a difference differing from itself).

Baron d'Etanges

↑

Monsieur de Wolmar

Saint-Preux   **Julie**

Milord Edouard   **Claire**

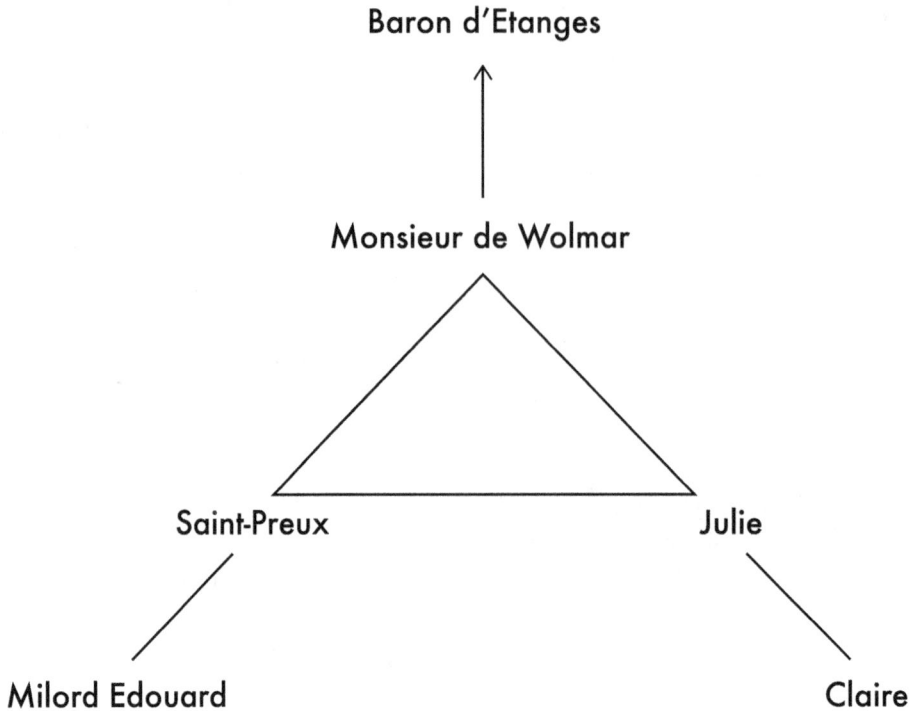

Binary and ternary relations in Rousseau's *Julie, or the New Heloise*

This radical consequence of the idea of a social transformation of the passions is un-doubtedly what is most remarkable. It would be necessary to compare in detail the struc-ture of differential subjectivations (itself essentially relational, and thus nonsubjective) inherent to *The New Heloise* with the definition in *The Social Contract* (I, 7) of the political community in terms of the "double relation" of each to each and each to all. Not only do we find here a challenge to any conception of friendship that would be founded on what, in *The Politics of Friendship*, Derrida calls "the double exclusion of the feminine"—that which denies the possibility of friendship between men and women as well as friendship between women (at least in the "public" or "social" sense of the category of friendship).[48] We are also in the presence of an alternative to the model of community that Rousseau proposes in *The Social Contract*, in which the discursive neutralization of sexual difference at each moment of the construction of the "sovereign" barely dissimulates Rousseau's purely homo-sexual conception of the constituent unity of the will of the citizens ("what makes a people a people").[49]

There are two ways, it seems to me, to formalize the "structure" that Rousseau elabo-rates in *The New Heloise* in comparison with that of *The Social Contract*: either one sup-poses that the system of relations is a "quasi-subject,"[50] which tends to liken *Julie* to *The Social Contract* on the level of the genesis of the "common self"; or, a more satisfying solu-tion to my mind, one thinks this system as a "nonsubject" distributing subjective places between which, according to different modalities of passion, the subjects must circulate in order to establish a "transparent" (or authentic) relation among themselves, and ultimately to experience the limits of such a relation. Faced with the alienation of the world of "possession" described in *Discourse on the Origin of Inequality*, *The Social Contract* seeks to think the quasi-transcendental conditions of possibility of an *antisociety*, while *The New Heloise* seeks to think (renewing the utopian genre along the way) a *countersociety*.[51] Unlike the schema of the subjective unity of the community of citizens explored in *The Social Contract* (the "common self"), the process of subjectivation and collective socialization described in *The New Heloise* (or more precisely, "performatively" operated by its epistolary fiction) turns upon the essential *heterogeneity* of its constituents. Heterogeneity of the fundamental passions, heterogeneity of the pairs of egalitarian sexuated "doubles" between which the quasi-hierarchical structure of the whole tends to decompose. Many readers of the novel, of course, have perceived this tension; but, conventionally, they tend to see in it the sentimental and private counterpart to the notion of the "contract," which pertains solely to public reason. Taking Rousseau at the word of certain among his statements, generally decontextualized, they have attempted to reduce *Julie* to the representation of a "family affair," without impact upon affairs of State. However, *Julie* is no more a "family novel" than it is a "novel of State" (to use Pierre-François Moreau's phrase for classical utopias): It subverts this opposition.[52] I propose, on the contrary, that each of the three great works that Rousseau wrote between 1760 and 1762—*Julie*, *The Social Contract*, and *Émile*—combine the concept and fiction each in its own way and in such a way that it enters into competition with the other two. Rather than make these works into the three wings of a single doctrinal system, I prefer to see in them Rousseau's various attempts to resolve the unsolvable problem of community: that of a social bond compatible with the "voice of nature," which the Second Discourse elaborated in radically negative, almost nihilistic terms. We must accept that, during these years when his productivity and inventiveness were nothing less than stupefying, Rousseau—always a writer, although a philosopher—was not one, but three in one.

FOUR

From Sense Certainty to the Law of Genre:
Hegel, Benveniste, Derrida

The present discussion is not exclusively devoted to the thought and work of Jacques Derrida. It is rather an attempt to bring the reading and discussion of Derrida in relation with other texts, and other heritages, in order to illustrate how his manner of philosophizing has transformed our understanding of certain fundamental problems. I would argue that what distinguishes his specific practice of deconstruction is the way in which it displaces the classical question of the "paradoxes of the universal," if only because it dismantles the metaphysical opposition between the universal and the particular, along with that of the absolute and the relative, the formal and the material, the one and the multiple, the same and the other.

However, I do not wish to address this question merely on a general level, but rather from a more limited and also more technical angle, which will make it possible to hear something of Derrida's voice in a less impersonal fashion. What I propose is to sketch a series of rereadings, beginning with the famous first chapter of Hegel's *Phenomenology of Spirit*, "Sense Certainty." Relating the Hegelian text to various texts by Derrida—passages from *The Post Card*, *Parages*, and *Monolingualism of the Other*—I will show that, taken together, in their dispersion and their kinship, these texts form what might be called "Derrida's sense certainty." Between Hegel and Derrida, however, a further mediation is necessary: that provided by Émile Benveniste's 1970 essay, entitled "The Formal Apparatus of Enunciation."

The Supplement of Speech

I begin with a passage from *Monolingualism of the Other*, a book in which autobiography and theory, which are never far apart in Derrida, much as in Montaigne or Rousseau, form an especially intimate unity. The general theme of Derrida's book is the paradox of a situation in which a man finds himself unable to consider as truly his own the only language that he can speak and write from the inside, with which he can identify subjectively, and to which he always refers back when he speaks and writes in other languages. In Derrida's case, this language is "French." It is the paradox of a relation that is neither pure and simple appropriation nor expropriation, but ex-appropriation, that Derrida analyzes on the basis of his own history, and that he ultimately asks that we consider as typical of the relation between any speaking subject and his or her "mother tongue," even if, in each case, it is in different degrees or modalities, irreducible to a single model. "Consequently, anyone should be able to declare under oath: I have only one language and it is not mine; my 'own' language is, for me, a language that cannot be assimilated. My language, the only one I hear myself speak and agree to speak, is the language of the other."[1] Who is this *other*, one might ask? In the case of a Jew from Algeria, violently stripped during his school years of his rights as a French citizen, as he recounts at length in this book and elsewhere, the other is the colonizer, the "master" of this land of Arabs and Jews—or, at least, this is what we would tend to suppose at first, at the price of a few historical simplifications.[2] But this master, we shall come to realize, also does not truly possess his "own" language—called the "mother tongue" or "national language"—because, in its letter and indeed its usage, this language is haunted by that of the colonized, who parasite it or limit it. Such a language, by definition, cannot be synonymous with absolute possession or mastery. Even more generally, *every language* is subjected to a permanent process of transformation by more or less violent interference with other languages; and thus, for every speaker or community of speakers, it exceeds any possible identification with the natural or historical property of a community.

Derrida proceeds to reflect upon the demonstrative value of his personal testimony, which exhibits in no uncertain terms the element of dispossession buried within his relation to a mother tongue that is both alienated and alienating. Therefore, he speaks *in the first person*, and he writes this: "What happens when someone resorts to describing an allegedly uncommon 'situation,' mine, for example, by testifying to it in terms that go beyond it, in a language whose generality takes on a value that is in some way structural, universal, transcendental, or ontological? When anybody who happens by infers the following: 'What holds for me, irreplaceably, also applies to all. Substitution is in progress; it has already taken effect. Everyone can say the same thing for themselves and of themselves. It suffices to hear me; I am the universal hostage.'"[3] The *other* is thus *any and every* other; and I am, in a sense, *any and every* other.

This is exactly what I call Derrida's "sense certainty," his own *Sinnliche Gewissheit*; and it is the point from which I will return to *The Phenomenology of Spirit*. As readers have often remarked, Hegel's short chapter on "sense certainty" is a very strange text.[4] It is supposed to resolve the aporia of *the beginning of dialectical progression*, whereas precisely such a progression recuses the idea of a fixed point of departure, of a *presupposition* that would claim to legitimize empirical or rational evidence, of an axiomatic decision, or, more generally, of an artifice exterior to the development itself. It is thus closely linked to a moment of skepticism constitutive of the idea of the dialectic. However, each time that Hegel contends with this problem of the beginning, we know that he resolves it by taking as a point of departure not a simple term, but a unity of opposites whose tension lies at the origin of an infinite development, unfolding in a succession of more and more concrete and more and more englobing figures, wherein the initial antithesis continues to be actualized, or figures as the trace of an initial contradiction. The most famous example, to be found at the beginning of the *Logic*, which is also considered to provide the *concept* of this figure of thought, presents the identity obtained by the inversion of *pure being* into *nothingness*, whose resolution is *becoming*—that is, the abstract concept of the dialectical movement itself. Contrary to a widely held opinion, the treatment of the question of beginning in the *Phenomenology* does not simply mirror that of the *Logic* in another terminology or another element (i.e., that of "consciousness"). It follows a much more complex path. Indeed, the "subject" of the dialectical development here is the *subject* itself (*das Subjekt*) presenting itself as consciousness—or rather, as on the path to consciousness insofar as this consciousness is destined to transform itself into "self-consciousness," and then into "self-conscious spirit," and finally into absolute knowledge; insofar as, ultimately, it retains nothing but the sheer form of the "self" (*Selbst*). In order to set this development in motion and infuse it with the principle of permanently overcoming the figures wherein, each time, consciousness believes anew that it has discovered the correspondence between certainty and truth; in order to set up an inaugural *restlessness*—that is, a *lack* within the relation between consciousness and its world, between its criteria of certainty and its representations of the true—Hegel offers a phenomenological description of what might be called *consciousness before consciousness*, the threshold upon which consciousness is yet essentially *bewusstlos*, deprived of the characteristics of representative consciousness: not only of self-consciousness, but also of the synthetic capacity to unify the properties of a "thing" in order to make it an object. This consciousness before consciousness does not so much pertain to the order of representation as to that of *presentation*; and its content is utterly formal (whence the irony of using the word "sense," which here functions as an instrument of the deconstruction of preexisting philosophical discourses). It is the immediate unity of a reference to an *I/Me* without qualities (we need two words there where German suffices with a single word, *Ich*) and to an "object" stripped of any stable properties, reduced to a *trait of identification* that might be any quality whatsoever of a nameable "entity," and that Hegel calls "this" (*Dieses*). As we see, what is at stake here are not cognitive contents, but pure indexical notions, at the limit of the notion of the "sign," theoretical and above all linguistic equivalents of the *gesture of showing* (a word that appears in the text)—in short, "word gestures"—which Hegel elaborates with a chart of quasi-structural oppositions. The three characteristic words of this originary language—*I, Here, Now*—are organized across three levels of successive correlations. The correlation of the *dieser* (that) and the *dieses* (this) that forms the first level gets divided, in turn, on both sides. *Dieser* becomes both *Ich* and *der andere Ich*, an astonishing formulation that is not a solecism (since *Ich* as a noun is normally neutral), but rather signifies "the other who is also I" (or even: who also says I), or inversely "I who is an other," and thus denotes the infinite repetition of always formally identical and always substantially different subjects of enunciation, even when it is possible to imagine that it is uttered by the same consciousness or the same individual. While *Dieses*, in turn, becomes both *Hier* and *Jetzt*, a correlation that functions both as a parallelism and as a complementarity: for, on the one hand, the dialectical reversals that can be exhibited with the Here are also valid in the case of the Now; and, on the other hand, the inevitable misunderstanding of sense certainty can be interpreted as the fact of always being elsewhere than where it says it is at the moment of saying it, and always in another time than that named in the place to which it refers.

In the course of the text, Hegel goes on to show that the essence of these correlations resides in a vanishing difference. The correlation of the two poles, *Ich* and *Dieses*, corresponds to a fleeting unity of these terms, which makes them seem inseparable, and which the philosophical tradition calls a pure sensation. It is not, strictly speaking, a perception, but rather an effect of the combined usage of the two correlative terms. The same will go for the correlation designated by the terms *here* and *now* and the effect of "presence" that it engenders. Inversely, one might conclude that the truth of these effects resides in the *separation* of terms: the *this* and the *that*, the *I* and its other, the *here* and the *now* and their respective others, and so on. But this would be an illusion as well, because *I* is nothing other than what I indicate; and what I indicate is nothing other than the intention of my speech gesture. Unity and separation are equally vanishing—at the limit of indiscernibility and of the power of these terms to draw distinctions. They are thus integral to the experience that constitutes the essence of sense certainty: the reversibility of the categories of the universal and the particular, the fact that each term paradoxically appears to be both absolutely singular and irremediably universal, that these two logical essences are one and the same thing. This is evidently what consciousness finds unbearable: the fact that I am myself, or that I am properly "my own," irreducible to any other, and that, nevertheless, as an "I"-sayer, I might as well be anyone and everyone, one moment in an infinite chain of substitutions; and that *this thing*, which is only itself, here and now, when I designate it, it becomes a mere random thing substitutable for any other, and consequently indefinitely other than itself. This is why consciousness wants to extract itself from this contradictory experience, or, more precisely, constitutes itself as consciousness by extracting itself from a sophistic discourse that it does not preexist, by radically dissociating the contradictory terms. It thereby becomes what it essentially is: a consciousness positioned over against a thing, a "thetic" consciousness of the thing, a consciousness that *posits* the thing.

I have spent some time on this Hegelian figure and its well-known characteristics not so much in order to rehash the thesis of the indiscernibility of the universal and the particular but rather to open the way toward what I consider to be the most interesting and also the strangest thing—that is, the *writing of Hegel's text*, the element of phantasmagorical fiction that it entails. Undoubtedly, Hegel's manner of presenting consciousness before consciousness as the origin of the dialectic is not absolutely without historical models or precedents (one might think of Hume and Condillac, of the Descartes of the First Meditation and the Plato of the *Theaetetus*, or of the Sophists themselves). Such comparisons are instructive but they do not touch upon the essential. Much more important is the way in which, at the end of the chapter, Hegel utters a hyperbolic thesis about the mutual implication of thought and language by way of a violently ironic critique of the notion of the inexpressible (or the ineffable, the unsayable: *das Unaussprechliche*), a notion that belongs as much to Platonism, where it connotes the transcendence of a noetic principle situated beyond essence, as to empiricism, where it connotes the irreducibility of sense data to abstract representation, as well as to the mystical tradition and the Romantic philosophy of art and religion. Hegel suggests that what has been decreed inexpressible in reality or beyond consciousness actually expresses the contradiction inherent to language, which cannot designate singularity without stripping it of determination and thus confounding it with pure universality. But this critique, which is decisive for the orientation of the dialectic to come, is possible only because, in what might be considered a circular fashion, the exposition of sense certainty initially takes place within the element of language, because it relies upon the exploitation of the properties of language that pertain to the fact of saying or enunciating (*sage, aussagen*), and upon the naming of the functions of enunciation. The experience called "sense certainty" has nothing to do with perception or with sensation in a psychological or physiological sense. It derives instead from a fictive linguistic experimentation. And the "contradiction" to which Hegel draws our attention here is not a contradiction of empirical consciousness but an originary *form of contradiction* inscribed in our linguistic usage, which precedes all of our experiences and structures them. After this beginning, however, it is especially notable that Hegel abandons any reference to language as a constitutive element of experience, only bringing it back again much later in the grand narrative of the genesis of consciousness, when it appears as a phenomenon of culture, a social phenomenon.[5] Of course, the language at stake in the chapter on sense certainty is absolutely elementary—or rather, it *appears* to be—because it is reduced to a single function, the function of designation or indication that inheres in the system of correlations between words that as such enact gestures of speech or gestures in speech.

How to characterize such a language on the level of logic and that of rhetoric? Rather than trying to find a more or less imaginary primitivity, I think that this language should be seen as an effect of writing, exactly in the sense that Derrida conferred on this term when he first took an interest in the "supplements of origin" that philosophers or anthropologists inscribe within their expositions.[6] At this moment in Hegel's text, then, what we have is a supplement of speech, and it is here that the text acquires a fantastic dimension. Hegel does not describe the experience in question from the outside; he constructs a fiction through writing; he acts as if it were sense certainty itself, transformed into a quasi-subject—or better still, into a subjectless voice traversing all subjects that itself enunciates the paradoxes of uttering the "I," the "Here," and the "Now." The narrative of the experience of sense certainty, a little narrative that precedes the grand narrative of the experience of consciousness and renders it possible, functions as an act of theoretical ventriloquism. It is, in a sense, phantasmagorical, but there is nothing arbitrary about this phantasmagoria; for, it is precisely what allows the paradoxical unity of the singular and the universal to appear as an incontestable property of experience. Sense Certainty (which might almost be an ancient Chinese lady's name, or an epistolary "screen name") speaks up and says to "us," to us who repeat it within ourselves: I *say I*, and I am already an other, either because I am myself no longer the same, because I have changed, or because another individual now occupies my subject position, speaks my own words with the same legitimacy and the same certainty. *I say this* and it is already that, some other thing, not identity but difference. *I say here* and it is elsewhere; *I say now* and it is already later; I repeat "day" and it is "night," "tree," and it is "house." The same nouns that endow experience with an elementary structure also inscribe contradictions within it—which it is very tempting to call "performative contradictions." However, if Hegel does not have recourse to such a category or its equivalent, it is because he wants contradiction to be spoken at the heart of experience itself; that is, because he stages it or writes it in the modality of a fiction. He thus writes I as if I unveiled to itself the contradictory nature of its speech act, as if the contradiction between the aim or intention (*Meinung*) of the utterance and the form of its uttering—or what he calls the *sprechen*—arises within language itself, forming its continuation, or its development. By combining the fiction of ventriloquist speech and the use of syntactical or syntactico-semantic categories, which concern the way in which the subject draws upon the resources of language to designate himself and to designate the presence of the objects he speaks about, Hegel produced this extraordinary text.

The Intercourse of the Subject

The moment has come to turn to the second text that I would like to reread with you—not a "Derridian" reading, but a reading oriented toward Derrida, and undertaken in view of an engagement with his work. Émile Benveniste's essay "The Formal Apparatus of Enunciation" dates from 1970 and constitutes, as might be easily verified, a synthesis or systematic recapitulation of the themes and analyses that are gathered, in the two volumes of the *Problems of General Linguistics*, under the general (and oh so problematic) title of "Man in Language."[7] Benveniste also employs an expression to which I will return: "subjectivity in language." All of these essays deal with the signification and usage of personal pronouns, beginning with the now famous definition of the two "correlations" that give meaning to this grammatical notion: first, the *correlation of subjectivity*, between *I* and *You*, the only pronouns that name "persons" in the strict sense—which is to say that, at the heart of the utterance itself, or more generally of discourse, they represent the agents or subjects of enunciation, the interlocutors; and second, they represent the *correlation of personality* between the I-You couple and any He(s) or She(s), between persons and a "nonperson" who cannot be an active participant in the interlocution, but rather becomes the other of whom the I and You discuss with one another, as if he or she were a thing, a third party, or, in any event, an absence.[8] The general topic of these texts, which must be reread in all their detail, is what Benveniste calls the *indicators* of enunciation, notably the relationship between the forms that mark verb tense—whence the remarkable distinction between the two modes of enunciating the past, which he calls the *historical mode* and the *subjective mode*, a distinction that parallels that between the impersonal and the personal.[9] These indicators encompass the reprisal and critical discussion of the Austinian concept of the *performative* utterance. How does the performative depend upon the status of the locutor? And under what conditions can its typical effect—the institutional efficacy of speech—be obtained or fail to be obtained?[10] I recall that these now classic articles, which "The Formal Apparatus of Enunciation" systematized and interpreted philosophically, were written in the 1950s and 1960s. They are thus exactly contemporaneous with the founding texts of "structural anthropology" in the work of Claude Lévi-Strauss, beginning with *The Elementary Structures of Kinship* (1949) and *Introduction to the Work of Marcel Mauss* (1950), which would require much time to examine in detail. When, in 1970, Benveniste gives systematic form to his analyses and thereby situates them at the point of intersection between linguistics and philosophy, he describes the function of personal pronouns, the signification of the different verb tenses, and the efficacy of the performative (such as *I promise, I decree, I swear, we swear not to disband without giving France a constitution*, etc.) as complementary aspects of a process situated at *within language itself*, and that, nonetheless, by means of purely linguistic forms and instruments, allows the subject *to appropriate language for himself*.[11]

What does "appropriate" mean? It means both that subjects *represent themselves* in the language that they speak, that they thereby acquire access to language *in its totality*, and that they define a condition of possibility for normal usage, the "proper" meaning of semantic categories. Of course, these acts of appropriation, which coincide with each time singular acts of speech, are entirely preprogrammed in their form, in their rules, and by the specific configuration of languages. In this respect, the crucial notion, for Benveniste, is that of the *sentence*. The subjects or subjectivities in question here are themselves functions of structure, which allows them infinitely to actualize themselves each time that the function of appropriation (enabled by the indicators of subjectivity) is fulfilled or, better, assumed by real locutors. We are dealing, then, with an inversion of the classical category of the subject, which obliges us to renounce a constitutive subjectivity in order to gain access to constituted subjectivity. Benveniste operates this inversion in his own field with the tools specific to linguistics, but the gesture—which can be found, at the same historical moment, in Lévi-Strauss's texts on kinship and Lacan's on the unconscious—is absolutely typical of the structuralist enterprise.[12]

In a marvelous essay on Benveniste, recently published in his book, *Le périple structural*, under the title *"Ibat obscurus"* (from Virgil),[13] Jean-Claude Milner argues that Benveniste's theorization of personal pronouns is not only *analogous* to Hegel's exposition in the chapter on "sense certainty," but directly issues from Hegel or owes its central inspiration to him. This becomes particularly obvious in Benveniste's manner of forming a correlation that associates the signification of pronouns and the demonstrative "this" or "that" with the indicators of presence "here" and "now"—which, in their turn, he associates in striking fashion with the interjections of affirmation and negation (*yes* and *no*) that, much like the personal pronouns, function as a forms of self-reference whereby subjects take a position at the heart of their own discourse. In Benveniste as in Hegel, "I" is nothing other than whichever person is in the process of speaking, who designates him or herself with a certain gesture inscribed in speech itself; and "You" is nothing or no one other than the person to whom the locutor who says "I" addresses him or herself materially, virtually, or fictively. This is what Benveniste calls the "correlation of subjectivity" or the correlation of subjects. Under Milner's guidance, then, we perceive a remarkable element of continuity between a segment of the dialectical tradition—albeit atypical—and structuralism, which deserves to be taken into account in studies of the genealogy of the latter "movement." But my own argument does not stop there.

What I would now like to attempt is a second reading of Benveniste, such as Derrida *would have done*, that subverts certain of his assertions; and that ultimately deconstructs the most characteristic positions of his anthropology without thereby—or so I hope—purely and simply annulling the question that he poses. Upon this basis, I could ideally return to "sense certainty" and attempt to show that it is itself, in a sense, "self-deconstructive." Naturally, this reading of Benveniste by Derrida is my invention or my extrapolation. Even if references to Benveniste are omnipresent in Derrida's work, from the devastating critique in *Margins* with respect to the question of the copula "is" and the "Indo-European" model of classical ontology (which is certainly not Benveniste's most original contribution) to the more nuanced readings in *Given Time* of the sections on the "gift" and "hospitality" from *Vocabulary of Indo-European Institutions*, these references—to my knowledge—never address what is most important for the question of Derrida's relation to structural linguistics and its conception of the effect of appropriation that links subject and structure. Our task, therefore, is to take the risk of reconstructing the confrontation—I dare not say, the dialogue—between Derrida and Benveniste.[14]

At the beginning of his essay, Benveniste defines enunciation, which he calls a "great process" or a "great phenomenon," both in terms of the *use* of language and of *action*:

> A fairly different thing is the use of language, which refers to a total and consistent mechanism that, in one way or another, affects the entire language. The difficulty lies in capturing this great phenomenon, so banal that it seems to be confused with language itself, so necessary that it is out of sight. Enunciation is the enactment of language through an individual act of use. It can be asked whether the discourse which is produced every time we speak, this event of enunciation, is not simply "speech." One must be careful about the specific condition of the enunciation: our object is not the text of the utterance but the very act of producing an utterance. This act is the act of the speaker mobilizing the language on her own behalf. The relation of the speaker to the language determines the linguistic characteristics of the utterance.[15]

This process of converting language into individual discourse, or enunciation, has different aspects, but most interesting to Benveniste is the formal framework: this consists in the formal conditions of what is essentially presented as an individual action. As the essay goes on to show, these conditions have a status that is very close to that of the *transcendental conditions* of the constitution of subjectivity in and by language—the status, in this sense, of an a priori. The first conditions, Benveniste tells us, those conditions that underlie the whole mechanism of reference to a world of objects and thus the possibility of appropriating signification, concern the introduction of the locutor into his or her own discourse, or the "presence" of the locutor in his own enunciation. This is why these conditions hang entirely upon the fact that the locutor says I and You, Yes and No, Here and Now, speaking in the first person and the present tense, the pivotal tense, the "absolute" tense. They are the "points" at which the act of saying refers back to the said, entering into it in circular fashion. Benveniste thereby comes very close to Hegel, even if his delineation of the correlations is broader and more precise. In one crucial respect, however, he rectifies what Hegel makes his "sense certainty" say: whereas the ventriloquist locutor from the *Phenomenology* is a solipsistic figure—irremediably so, because the I is engaged in a repetition that multiplies it to infinity—Benveniste's locutor is, from the outset, an interlocutor; it is constitutively "dialogic" and alternates between two names: *I* and *You*.[16] What this means is that meaningful speech can only take place in exchange or dialogue, even if the interlocutor remains abstract or imaginary (which is why Benveniste prefers the term *allocutory*, in order to emphasize that every discourse is an address and has an implicit *addressee*). Better said: all speech—every sentence in the first person—presents itself as the anticipation of a dialogue in which a subject addresses him or herself to a possible interlocutor or to *the possibility of an interlocutor*. The subject's twin names—I and You—are constantly brought back to life by the act of speech: "They are engendered again each time that an enunciation is uttered, and every time they designate afresh."[17] *But always together.* We could also assert, taking a distance from the author's terminology, that the process of appropriation, the introduction of subjectivity into the very structure of languages without which the concept of language would remain a dead abstraction, takes the form of "intercourse" in the classical sense of this old word (in German, *Verkehr*, and in French, *commerce*). Benveniste himself speaks constantly of communication. This communication or intercourse is symmetrical, because the I and the You are *destined to trade places* at a given moment, which means that the subjective appropriation of language exists only as a social process—in the general, anthropological sense. What is thereby constituted is *not an individual but a transindividual subject*. Accordingly, in no way does this symmetry mean that the two places of the subject are identical; nor that the corresponding pronouns are interchangeable signifiers. It is not difficult to perceive that what Benveniste calls a "personal pronoun," in the transcendental sense, is *the correlation of subjectivity itself*, such as intercourse puts it to work; and that this correlation is not the I or the You taken separately, but rather the *couple* that they form. This is real reason why *He* or *She* (*Er* or *Sie*, or *Es* in a language that has a "neuter" pronoun) are not personal pronouns, why they name "nonpersons" in order to describe their "personal" or "impersonal" character *from the outside*, as a *property*. (By way of anticipation, let us note that it is only on this level that it becomes possible to mark "gender"). The difference between pronouns, then, is manifestly due to the fact that, for Benveniste, the I does not form a couple with He or She, but only with You. In order for He or She to form a couple with I, the I must address them in the second person ("Where are you going, My Lord?"). But there is more. Initially, Benveniste's formulations give primacy to the I, which weakens the idea of a correlation of subjectivity: the locutor, he writes, "signals his position" in discourse by using the pronoun I, which *provokes*, at least virtually, a reaction or response from another person who will be called You. But his later formulations tend to *reverse the primacy of the I*, giving primacy to the You instead. Indeed, a locutor cannot enter language without *anticipating* or *imagining* a response on the part of an interlocutor, the idea of whom, or simply whose place, comes with the act of speech, no matter how oblique or indefinitely deferred it might be.

A Lacanian or Lacanizing interpretation of Benveniste would recall the famous formula: the subject receives from the other his own message in inverted form.[18] It would connect this formula to the fact that every act of speech unconsciously *reproduces* or *repeats* a primordial situation in which the subject would have been interpellated by the Big Other, named by name, no matter which this name is or which signifier functions as a name (and there are often very strange ones). But the Derridian interpretation that I am trying to envisage would go in another direction. It would insist, as we might surmise, on the idea that "the letter can always not arrive at its destination."[19] In order to acquire universal validity, in order not to allow for any exceptions, in order to remain open to any possibility or any *event*, it must not arrive at its destination, it must not get the anticipated reaction (i.e. a response) from the interlocutor. What is essential to communication, what I have preferred to call intercourse, is not or not only the fact of being successfully established, but rather the fact that it can be interrupted or broken, fail to garner a response, or an adequate—that is, personal—response. At the limit, it is the fact that an adequate response—in particular, when it is a matter of responding to a demand or a call—represents the impossible. Such a response, then, is always deferred; it is *différance* itself, and, for this reason, it is not enclosed within the dialogical symmetry of persons, but must be disseminated beyond their grasp, and thus exposed to loss. Such would be the new form—not "immediate" or "sensible" but formalized and indefinitely mediated—of the dialectical paradox instituting the coincidence of the singular and the universal.

Waiting for the Other

On the basis of this remark, which remains too schematic, it is finally time to let Derrida speak, Derrida "alone" (even if there is no writing less solitary than his, since it never ceases to cite, to dialogue, and to respond). After discussing what I call *the supplement of speech* in Hegel, and *the intercourse of the subject* in Benveniste, I would call this third section—for reasons to be clarified—*waiting for the other or the law of genre*. The always present possibility, or the possibility lodged at the heart of presence, of loss and indefinite waiting, of the impossible return of speech to its point of departure, becomes tangible by certain words—notably, certain forms of address—as they might be used in literature and beyond. In particular, this is the case with "Come" (*Viens*), which our grammar textbooks would formally designate as an "imperative," even thought it can also function as *the overturning of the imperative* (for example, in prayer, or in a declaration of love). It was thanks to Blanchot—in particular, *L'arrêt de mort* (Death Sentence), *L'attente l'oubli* (Awaiting Oblivion), and *Le pas au-delà* (The Step Not Beyond)—that Derrida insists upon the function of the "come," upon the way in which it organizes writing, and to carry it as far as possible in a direct confrontation with the philosophical tradition. After Blanchot, or rather along with him, Derrida invites us to hear in this "Come" the primacy of absence or the impossibility of being present that always overcomes the other's presence, even and especially when there is someone there, when there is someone whom we feel will never answer the demand to respond, but whom we persist in calling by the nickname or pronoun: "You," "Thou." In this manner, You and Thou tend to become not the name of the actually or supposedly present other, the actual or virtual interlocutor who might always materialize, but rather that of another whose absence can be sensed, as it were, and whose certainty is problematic. Allow me to cite, albeit much too briefly, a passage from *Parages*:

> —*Viens* [Come].
>
> *Viens*: what do you call what I've just, in French *je viens de*—what I just what? what I just said? Is *viens* a word? A word in French? A verb? On the face of it, it's an imperative, necessarily present, a mode here conjugated in the second-person singular. The definition seems to be as reliable as it is inadequate. . . . What did I do? I called. What do you call *that*?
>
> You've remarked how that, how '*Viens*'—let's say that strange word [*mot*]—in *Death Sentence*, right near the end, before those last two paragraphs that disappeared from one edition to the other and that provoke more, by their disappearance . . .
>
> —I have to interrupt you [*vous*]; you are losing me. Did you say to me 'come,' or have you already stopped talking to me in order for you to converse with whomever, about this—let's say this word [*mot*]—and about knowing what it—it what in fact? I'm lost.[20]

And in another book devoted to Blanchot, *Demeure*,[21] published in 1996 and then in an expanded edition in 1998, we find the logical consequence: *I become You.*

> But who is speaking here? Who dares proclaim, "I am alive"? Who dares reply "No you are dead"? Up until this point, as we noted, an "I" speaks of another, of a third: "I" speaks of him. "I" is me, speaking of the young man he was, and this is still me. This is called a narration. But for the first time, between the two instances of the narrator and the character, who are the same without being the same, there are quotation marks, there is speech that is being directly quoted. Someone is speaking to someone, a witness is speaking to the other for the first time, in a dialogue that is both an inner dialogue and, if I can put it this way, transcendent. "I" becomes "you" or addresses itself to "you," but we do not know whether the "I" is the one who says "I" at the beginning of the text: "I REMEMBER," or if it is the other, the young man. We do not know who "you" is, who says "you," nor do we know what is left out [*ce qui est tu*] of these two instances.[22] Like each of these sentences, this conclusion is singularly, that is to say, properly genial. One of the two, One of the Two, says to the Other, "I am alive," and would thus be the one who has survived. But it is the other, the one who has survived, who responds to him: "No, you are dead." And this is the colloquium, this is the dialogue between the two witnesses, who are, moreover [*au demeurant*], the same, alive and dead, living-dead, and both of whom in abidance [*en demeurant*] claim or allege that one is alive, the other dead, as if life went only to an *I* and death to a *you.*[23]

Here is how I would paraphrase this development: in the new "sense certainty," the ultimate reference, the groundless or substanceless ground is not I but You, the interlocutor who has always escaped yet again, whose presence is indefinitely deferred. As Derrida explains a little earlier in the same text, this reference irremediably *divides* the *subject.*[24]

Let us now compare these telegraphic indications to certain passages from *The Post Card: From Socrates to Freud and Beyond* in order to examine how this latter book treats the question of the correlation of subjectivity. When *The Post Card* was published in 1980, philosophers in France preferred to read it for the appendices—especially the famous critique of Lacan entitled "Le facteur de la vérité"—thereby disregarding the main section of the book (no doubt judging it to be too literary or foreign to the dominant demonstrative, dissertational, and argumentative genres in philosophy). You will recall that the first part of this book takes the form of a long fictional, amical-amorous correspondence ("envois"), much like that in *The New Heloise*, which revolves around the discovery at the Bodleian Library in Oxford of an odd postcard with a picture of Plato bending over a Socrates in the act of writing. I cite a brief excerpt from the letter dated June 5, 1977:

> You give me words, you deliver them, dispensed one by one, my own, while turning them toward yourself and addressing them to yourself—and I have never loved them so, the most common ones become quite rare, nor so loved to lose them either, to destroy them by forgetting at the very instant when you receive them, and this instant would precede almost everything, my *envoi*, myself, so that they take place only once. One single time, you see how crazy this is for a word? Or for any trait at all?[25]

You give me words: as Benveniste realized, it is thus "you," or rather "You," who gives words, who gives language to I, this language of which I is never the master. *It is "You" who makes "I" enter into language.* But something else emerges here as well, something to which Benveniste remains a stranger, or which by definition falls outside the oppositions that constitute his "formal apparatus of enunciation," even if, when we take into account the materiality of the dialogue's writing (this might be the function of letters, epistolary intercourse), it becomes impossible not to ask how formalism and its usage will be affected. Isn't there something more, a "law of genre" that is no less constitutive, in a *quasi-transcendental* fashion, of the "great process" or "great phenomenon" of the human being's entry into language?[26] Nonetheless, this thing, the fact is that the great linguist neglected it, which is not to go so far as to say that he repressed or disavowed it. What is this thing? It is not simply that all lived or "existential" communication is sexuated (or "gendered"— as the Americans would say). Sexuation, in this sense, would pertain to the imaginary. At stake is a structural characteristic that is much more material and thus constraining: the fact that it is impossible to engage in dialogue or enter into commerce via the pronouns "I" and "You" without ipso facto raising the *question of gender*—which is both momentarily neutralized in these pronouns and remains lurking, as it were, behind them. This "gender of pronouns" or the subjection of pronouns to the law of genre is thus an inherently paradoxical modality: gender is evoked only to be deferred, in such a way that it remains, at least for a time, undecidable. There is thus a "gender trouble" within the use of personal pronouns, which introduces a simultaneously erotic and enigmatic element within every real exchange of letters. Indeed, the correspondents are necessarily either of the same sex, or of different sex, or of yet another sex—as Balzac said in *Père Goriot* ("Bourgeois pension for the two sexes and others"). But language immediately represses the question that it itself raises. Rereading the passage from *The Post Card* that I just cited, along with many others, it is impossible not to notice the very insistent tonality of sexual difference that resonates in the use of I and You, not least because of the literary models that this text evokes (such as *The New Heloise*, which I mentioned before, with its very complex configurations). But can you *assign with any certainty* this difference? And, if so, *at what point*? It does not suffice, above all, to read the name of the author—Jacques Derrida—on the title page, apparently a man's name, to identify it "autobiographically" with the author of the fictional letters on Plato and Socrates, and to make the "normal" presumption that he is writing passionately to a woman. Even as the letter of writing both irrepressibly raises these questions, it forbids such a presumptuous response. In reality, we must wait for the moment (and the author of the book artfully postpones it) when the text offers up a masculine or feminine adjective or participle.[27] This is the point at which the suspension of gender in language comes to an end, albeit momentarily (which is definitely not to say that we can know with "certainty" the *real sex* of the interlocutors, since there are masks, disguises, pseudonyms, inversions of gender, and all the rest).

Derrida says the same thing, more speculatively, in *Parages*:

> This time, in *The One Who Was Standing Apart from Me*, it is to some "words" that "it would be enough for me to say" " 'Come.' "
>
> Reread at least the sequence that begins in this way: "I listen to this. Whom is he addressing? Who is involved here? Who is speaking? Who is listening? Who could answer such a distance? This comes from so far away and it doesn't even come . . ." Nothing I could say to you here can measure up to this. What he then calls *"paroles"* are not some mots, words, some discourse, or a figured designation of who would converse and pronounce some words [*mots*] in the proximity of his thought or his voice, not anything of what one things one recognizes under these words [*mots*]: paroles, mots, discourse, utterance or enunciation, and so on. Nor are they some things that we could oppose to words [*paroles*] or acts. Heard from the *come* they hear and emit, seeing that only "starting from" *come* could they cry out their name, they are part of the nameless. And yet, what marks and neutralizes at once sexual difference is that the anonymous, improper name (*thought, word*) given to the nameless is chosen so that its gender in French is feminine and its pronoun always *elle*. The whole transfer of the code (for example, *"je l'ai aimée et n'ai aimé qu'elle"* / "I have loved and only loved her/it") laterally causes, as in a silent accompaniment of the language, her/it—*la pensée* "thought" or elsewhere *la parole* "word"—to press toward, lean toward the feminine side; it is literally a *movimentum*, a feminine moment; it announces by unconscious pressure sexual difference before every other determination, every other identification. And as it—*elle*—is determined, called only starting from the *come* that it *launches* and *sends back*, the distance of the *come* instructs the non(pace) of sexual difference.[28]

When I asked one of my friends—not, to my knowledge, a militant feminist but certainly a brilliant linguist—the naïve question whether there are languages whose "true" personal pronouns, in Benveniste's sense, have a gender inflection (masculine/feminine), much as they have a numeric inflection (singular/plural), she responded with a certain vehemence: "Oh no! Language must retain an element of universality!"[29] However, might we suggest, along with Jacques Derrida, that this element is constitutively called into question by the *usage*, the *setting into movement*, the *movimentum* of linguistic forms, or, as Benveniste would say, their "engendering"? The universality of forms is inhabited by a singularity, or rather by an insistent *effect* of singularity, because it is always only a matter of the operation of formal correlations or oppositions. The question of sexual difference, which is also that of sexual indifference, enters into the neutrality of dialogue. Should we speak of an element of silence, of the *unsayable*? Yes and no. In any event, what is momentarily outside language is certainly not "outside the text." It would undoubtedly be tempting to suggest that we are touching upon the dark side of Benveniste's thesis that only I and You, in the form of a couple, are personal pronouns, whereas He and She, necessarily gendered, are not. Or that gender pertains to the "non-person." At least for a linguist, then, the "person" would be essentially deprived of gender, if not asexual. The structural description of the indices of subjectivity, and the relation between the saying and the said that they imply, seems unquestionable; but its flipside, or its underside, thus proves to be the repression of sexual difference, or rather its expression, in the "correlation of subjectivity." But isn't this to jump the gun a little bit? Rather than subjecting Benveniste—and, through him, linguistics or structuralism—to a wild psychoanalysis, or a lesson in political correctness, it would be better to proceed through displacement and supplementation, the deconstructive operations par excellence: the expression of gender is *deferred by language* and thereby becomes open to indetermination, to the play of speech and writing. At a certain moment, this expression will be called forth, inevitably: the "third person," necessarily differentiated or gendered, will enter the scene, or I and You will reenter the scene as He or She, as "nonpersons" or false persons, whose gender remains to come, and whom we are not sure (as with words or death) whether they still belong to the *human species* (*genre humain*).

This is very nearly what Derrida says in a remarkable passage from "The Law of Genre," once again a text written in the margins of Blanchot, or side by side with him.

> As the first word and surely most impossible word of *La folie du jour*, "I" presents itself as *self* (*moi*), me, a man. Grammatical law leaves no doubt about this subject. The first sentence, phrased in French in the masculine ("Je ne suis ni savant ni ignorant" and not "Je ne suis savante ni ignorante"), says, with regard to knowledge, nothing but a double negation (*not . . . not*; *neither . . . nor*). Thus, no glint of self-presentation. But the double negation gives passage to a double affirmation (*yes, yes*) that enters into alignment or alliance with itself. Forging an alliance or marriage-bond ("hymen") with itself, this boundless double affirmation utters a measureless, excessive, immense *yes*: both to life and to death.
>
>> I am not learned; I am not ignorant. I have known joys. That is saying too little: I am alive, and this life gives me great pleasure. And what about death? When I die (perhaps any minute now), I will feel immense pleasure. I am not talking about the foretaste of death, which is stale and often disagreeable. Suffering dulls the senses. But this is the remarkable truth, and I am sure of it: I experience boundless pleasure in living, and I shall take boundless satisfaction in dying.
>
> Now, seven paragraphs further along, the chance and probability of such an affirmation (one that is double and therefore boundless, limitless) is granted to woman. It returns to woman. Rather, not to woman or even to the feminine, to the female genre/gender, or to the generality of the feminine genre but—and this is why I spoke of chance and probability—"almost always" to women. It is "almost always" women who say *yes, yes*.

To life to death. This "almost always" avoids treating the feminine as a general and generic force: it makes an opening for the event, the performance, the uncertain contingencies [*aléa*], the encounter. And it is indeed from the contingent experience of the encounter that "I" will speak here. In the passage that I am about to cite, the expression "men" occurs twice. The second occurrence names the sexual genre, the sexual difference (*aner*; *vir*—but sexual difference does not occur between a species and a genre); in the first occurrence, "men" comes into play in an indecisive manner in order to name either the genre of human beings (the *genre humain*, named "species" in the text) or sexual difference.[30]

There is no appropriation of language without such an entry on the scene, such a *consequence* or *dissemination* of dialogue, which does not exist without I and You. Isn't this at least a part, but an important part, of the reason why Derrida forged the slightly barbaric neologism *exappropriation*, which oxymoronically combines the notions of appropriation and expropriation?[31] Benveniste is quite right to explain that speaking in the first person in the present tense is a way to acquire the totality of language all at once, which thus becomes an always reiterated *structural event*. There where Hegel described a loss of identity, basically the expropriation of the subject, Benveniste sees an appropriation, undoubtedly because the correlation of I and You entails a certainty that does not inhere in *this* and *that*. But the supplement of gender that Derrida inserts into the figure of intercourse (which is also that of the "gift" of language) takes us back, if not to the point of departure, then at least to a more ambivalent situation. In the appropriation something remains at once exigent and inaccessible, present and absent, given and withdrawn— namely, the *identity* of the subject (its sexual identity, but perhaps not solely that). Undoubtedly, for a "subject," things are much better this way.

I hope to have shown, going about it in my own way, that deconstruction is not merely a pure reversal, notably that of logical categories such as universal and singular. What it does is to make emerge at the very heart of these categories, in an irreversible fashion, an element of impurity or conflict that no dialectic can surmount. What, then, is the difference between Hegel and Derrida in this regard? A Hegel whom we could manage to contain within the limits of his point of departure; whom, in brief, we would ask to suspend his own teleology as he would have "us" do in order for the experience of sense certainty to be a true experience; a Hegel whom we would force to take seriously and literally the operations of fiction to which he turns in order to exit the metaphysics of the transcendental subject, would certainly not be very far from recognizing this element. The "supplement of speech" is precisely what, in Hegel, figures this impurity or conflict. This supplement itself immediately collapses into the effect of restlessness, however, perhaps because Hegel only accords an instrumental and provisional value to the symbolic forms that he relies upon. Are things otherwise with Derrida's "law of genre," which I have attempted to connect with a particular description of the retroactive effect of writing upon speech itself, insofar, of course, that it is not a matter of anthropology but structure? We have reason to think so, in particular because it ceaselessly introduces an uncanny (*unheimlich*) proximity between gender and mortality, the two sole determinations that are ultimately indissociable from a "You" marked by finitude to whom "I" address myself indefinitely saying *Come*!

PART TWO

Being(s) in Common

FIVE

Ich, das Wir, und Wir, das Ich ist: Spirit's Dictum

The present talk—and I offer my thanks to Pierre Macherey for the invitation to speak to his working group, which afforded me an opportunity to write it—should fit, not too arbitrarily, I hope, into this year's program devoted to exploring an discussing the category of "modernity." That said, my intention is not to contribute directly to this discussion, even if the problems of philosophy and history that I elaborate are generally considered relevant to our prevailing ideas of a "modern moment" and our manner of situating ourselves in relation to it. About these ideas, I will restrict myself to the following preliminary observation: there is no question that the category of "modernity" is differential, but it so in several senses that intersect and vie with one another.

The Thresholds of Modernity

Born of a "quarrel" in which it assumes the semantic value both of an alternative to the tradition and of a return to the sources that this tradition covers up, modernity does not just oppose itself to one or several "others," thereby opening an external space (e.g., the Ancient, the Tradition) where we can (with all the ambivalence that such a gesture might entail) project negative values or values in the negative; it is also divided against itself, internally, insofar as it assumes its own negativity and defines itself in terms of a continuous conflict between various incompatible interpretations of its progressive movement, interpretations that have as much to do with politics and institutions as culture or speculative thought. The new quarrel born from this division originates as far back as the movement of the so-called Anti-Enlightenment; and it will find an intrinsically "modern" figure in the thinking of the destructiveness of reason and the catastrophe of progress, such as Adorno's negative dialectics.[1] Today, as a result of a radical reversal of perspectives, the figure of this quarrel has been prolonged and displaced in the "postcolonial" critique of the grand narrative of worldwide modernization modeled on European rationality and governmentality as expressions of a structure of domination that belongs to a specific historical situation.[2]

Finally, "modernity" divides itself into a succession of moments separated by *thresholds* or corresponding to new *tendencies*, which one might conceive as periods of historical becoming (thereby redoubling, within its "fundamental period," the empirico-speculative problem that characterizes philosophies of history in general) or as the indices of a process of constantly calling into question of its presuppositions, a process with an entire history of its own, sometimes manifesting the finitude of its point of view and sometimes the uncertainty of its becoming. The most obtrusive index, today, of the way in which this second mode of internal differentiation opens up at the heart of the first and complicates it is constituted by the alternative between discourses of "postmodernity" (a category first proposed by Jean-François Lyotard in order to signal an "end" and then reprised as that of a "beginning" by philosophers of culture such as Zygmunt Bauman) and discourses of a "reflexive" or "second modernity" (which is also a "secondary modernity"), proposed mostly by sociologists and political scientists (such as Anthony Giddens and Ulrich Beck).[3]

My personal claim, articulated in a very schematic fashion, consists in positing all at once: that the theses which aim to "deconstruct" the institutions, presuppositions, and discourses of modernity are *always already present* at the heart of the philosophical expressions of modernity (which sought, in the first place, to "construct" it and, to that end, took the risk of thinking and speaking its conditions of possibility), meaning that postmodernity does not *put an end to* modernity, in accordance with the evolutionary schema that is privileged in discourses on the postmodern, but rather confers on it a critical allure that renders it intelligible; and that, on the other hand, the "phases" or "periods" of the historical development of modernity, which essentially correspond to displacements of its entire (political, cultural, and metaphysical) problematic, are separated by differential *thresholds* that must, of course, become traceable within social and institutional transformations—in inventions and discursive ruptures, and above all in the complex correspondences that should always be established between their different levels (such as, on the one hand, the political and industrial revolutions at the end of the classical age, and, on the other, the decline of metaphysics of human nature along with contractualist philosophies and their replacement by philosophies of historical evolution and juridical positivisms)—but that *are always repeated several times*. Or rather, the crossing of these "thresholds of modernity" (at once thresholds giving access to modernity, thresholds leading from one of its moments to another, and eventually thresholds opening beyond or toward the decomposition of modernity) occurs to us in the typical figure of indefinitely mobile *points of heresy* where certain typical oppositions are renegotiated. I am particularly interested in identifying such points of heresy and in understanding their precise relationship to the successive thresholds of modernity; and this is what I would like to discuss today with respect to a problem of reading and interpreting what I consider to be a privileged Hegelian text.[4]

From this essential differential point of view, the recourse to philosophical texts, or to certain details of their writing, becomes particularly interesting. I will not heighten the provocation by going so far as to claim here that we must prefer "philosophy in the restricted sense" to "philosophy writ large," but I will defend the idea that neither of these vectors is less important than the other. I entirely agree with Pierre Macherey both that "philosophy" does not have any preset limits (notably not those of the philosophical *genre* as the University has codified it) and that the meaning and stakes of philosophical discourses are unintelligible within a pure self-relation, when considered self-referential. Indeed, the meaning of philosophical discourses, which is eminently open and problematic, supposes an *exteriority*—singularly an exteriority of conflicts—in which they take an active part. But I also posit, correlatively, as I have said previously about Fichte and his theory of the "internal border," that "the philosophical text carries to the extreme the contradictions that go beyond it and yet nowhere else find an equally binding formulation." I would also add that the philosophical enunciation (that is, the production of a theoretical utterance in the context of writing, itself inscribed within a succession of texts that come up against one another) is our only means of access to what constitutes the singularity, radicality, the "timeliness" as well as the "untimeliness" of historical conflicts, whether they be social, political, religious, moral, or all of this at the same time.

Such an utterance, it seems to me, is constituted by the phrase—a strange phrase, as we shall see—that figures in the *Phenomenology of Spirit* at the end of the introductory section of Chapter 4 (and thus immediately before Section A: "Independence and Dependence of Self-Consciousness: Lordship and Bondage"): "*Ich*, das *Wir*, und *Wir*, das *Ich* ist." Hyppolite translates or tries to translate this sentence as follows: "*un Moi qui est un Nous, et un Nous qui est un Moi*" (a Me who is a We and a We who is a Me).[5] This is the sentence that I would attempt to explicate through an analysis of its sources and its effects, its immediate context and its theoretical scope within the whole of the work in which it appears. I would like to show that this sentence is an index *within philosophy* and through the specific means of philosophical writing that a *threshold* characteristic of modernity *has been crossed*; and also, of course, that it entails, or more precisely, the fact of *dwelling on this threshold* entails extreme tensions, if not insurmountable aporias. In reality, what makes Hegel's utterance indelible, in its prodigious density or consistency, is that it is also extraordinarily unstable; and it must be considered as always still on this side of and already projecting itself beyond such a threshold, or, in other terms, as caught up within the repetition of a perhaps very archaic past and calling for still largely indeterminate future repetitions.

I will say up front, in order to return to it later in my exposition, that I accord such privilege to the utterance in the "first person" in Hegel's text, in the form of a mirror relationship between I and We—or, if one prefers, the individual subject and the collective subject (as one of the sentence's rare commentators has said)—because it crystallizes in a single sentence three orders of problems that pertain to the essence of what we discuss under the name of "modernity":

First, this privilege of this sentence has to do with the relationship that it maintains with a metaphysics (which is also a grammar) of subjectivity and thereby with the more general anthropological problem of modes of subjection (or *asujettissement*, allowing this term to assume the ambivalence that contemporary French philosophy has restored to it), but also with the question of a "mutation" of subjectivity that would be proper to modernity (which is immediately signaled, here, by the association between the utterance of the person, at once single and doubled, and the arrival on the scene of the categories of consciousness and self-consciousness).

Second, this privilege derives form the properly "phenomenological" clue that this utterance furnishes with respect to problem posed by the constitution of a *community*: more precisely, of an "immanent" community whose principle of unity, going beyond simply adding up the individualities or subjectivities that compose it, does not presuppose the existence of the One, or the incorporation of a transcendent Law; it relies, instead, exclusively upon the reciprocity or mutual recognition, and thus also upon the conflicts, among its members. This is the precise point at which an engagement with Rousseau (who, as we will see, is invoked by the very letter of the text) proves indispensable.

Third, our utterance holds such privilege because it incisively raises the question of the difference between an *early modernity*—which an initial approximation might identify with the classical age and its problematic of sovereignty as transcendence (which encompasses thinkers as different as Descartes or Hobbes, with Rousseau at the outer edge, where an inversion begins to take form), and a *late modernity* (whose concurrent problematics of society, law, and historicity, refer in a complex manner to the preparation, the actualization, and the interpretation of the two great "revolutions" the quasi-simultaneity of which shook "European consciousness" to the core: the Industrial Revolution and the Democratic Revolution). To my mind, the fact that Hegel (or Hegel's writing) dwells here in such a vacillating fashion upon the "threshold" signifies that, in his own formulation of the exigencies of late modernity, he feels the need to "replay" ever so close to the letter of his text the tragedy of the inner inversion of theologico-political subjectivity into collective or social subjectivity, and thus ends up objectively inscribing at the very heart of a modern discourse the germs of a postmodern "deconstruction."[6]

Mirror Subjects

And now, having already spent much time upon rather formal preparations, we can begin to examine the problems of interpretation that Hegel's utterance imposes. I propose three orders of consideration. In an initial moment, I will concentrate upon the *letter* of the Hegelian sentence, relating it to its immediate and extended context within the *Phenomenology*. In a second moment, I will attempt to inscribe it within a "signifying chain" that features other utterances of the person as subject, each possessing both metaphysical and political implications—in particular, utterances of Christian religion and (mainly) utterances of Rousseau from *The Social Contract*. Finally, in a third moment, which I will have time only to sketch out, I will attempt to organize around the interpretation of this sentence a new suite of (well known) questions raised by the manner in which Hegel, in the *Phenomenology of Spirit*, seeks to problematize the immanence of community as well as its internal conflictuality.

Hegel's sentence (which I will on occasion abbreviate as "IWWI") is, read to the letter, *untranslatable* (as one may easily verify by examining the attempts to "translate" it in different languages, such as French or English). This is due to the use that it makes, in the same manner as the philosophical tradition that has been called idealism, of the idiomatic properties of the German language when it comes to the syntax of personal pronouns and notably the pronoun *Ich*.[7] It is due, in particular, to the possibility that German offers (as opposed to French, at least everyday, spoken French) immediately to turn the nonreflexive first-person pronoun into a noun (and, on this model, the other pronouns as well): *Ich* thereby becomes *das Ich*, thereby coming to function at once as "the subject of the uttering within the utterance," the entry of the person into language in Benveniste's sense, and as one of the names, even the proper name of subjectivity in general, and thus as a concept. Although French, after Descartes, Pascal, Condillac, and Maine de Biran, has *"le moi"* ("the me" or "the ego"), this is not at all the same thing.[8] It is due, correlatively, to the manner in which this sentence implicitly plays out in the text, by means of writing alone, a plurality of "voices" inherent to the phenomenological movement, whereby it realizes the ambition to "make speak" the subject whose constitution and history—that is, whose "consciousness" (*das Bewusstsein*, here on the way to transforming itself into *Selbstbewusstsein*)—it presents. Indeed, the text inserts (as least in the version that Hyppolite uses) in the midst of the presentation of what, according to Hegel's own expression, constitutes a "turning point" (*Wendungspunkt*) of the dialectical development, not a semicolon but rather a *colon*:

> With this, we already have before us the concept of spirit. What still lies ahead for consciousness is the experience of what spirit is—this absolute substance which is the unity of the different independent self-consciousnesses (*verschiedener für sich seiender Bewusstsein*) which, in their opposition, enjoy perfect freedom and independence: 'I' that is 'We' and 'We' that is 'I.' It is in self-consciousness, in the concept of spirit, that consciousness first finds its turning-point, where it leaves behind it the colorful show of the sensuous here-and-now (*des sinnlichen Diesseits*) [that is, this world down here] and the nightlike void of the supersensible [that is, the transcendent beyond, outside the world] beyond (*des übersinnlichen Jenseits*), and steps into the spiritual daylight of the present (*in den geistigen Tag der Gegenwart einschreitet*).

The sentence "IWWI" is not the simple conceptual explication of the "unity" that would form the concept of Spirit when it manifests itself for the first time "in the daylight of the present." (The theological connotations of "the present" are obvious: this First Day of spirit's appearance is, at the same time, the Last Day of alienation.) It is not inscribed on the same level as the rest of the phenomenological description where it appears, which, as we know, is uttered from the viewpoint of "absolute knowledge." It constitutes *the arrival on scene of another voice* that surges up in the middle of the text and speaks for itself in the first person—that is, *it speaks itself as this "spirit" that it really is*. This is why, contrary to what the available translations of Hegel would lead us to suppose, he did not write (although he could well have done so) something like this: "*ein Ich, das ein Wir ist . . .*" or "*das Ich, das auch das Wir ist . . .*" but rather, "*Ich, das Wir . . .*"[9]

The utterance in the first person entails a syntactic forcing that tilts toward explicit nominalization, and that, even in German, although it remains easy to understand, constitutes a singularity: if *Ich* and *Wir* are the marks of the first person expressing itself in person, making its own voice heard in the text, the relative clauses that refer back to it cannot be in the neuter (*das*); they must be in the masculine or the feminine (an embarrassing but interesting dilemma: *Ich der Wir . . .*, or *Ich die Wir . . .*); and, above all, the verb itself must be conjugated in the first person: not "*ist*," but rather "*bin*" or "*sind*." Fictively, the text thus makes heard two superimposed viewpoints, a concretion of voices: It produces an effect of identification and distanciation at the same time; it "exhibits" an utterance that, as such, should suffice to identify its subject (this is how Spirit speaks, this is what it says about itself, and it is on the basis of this "unique text," as Kant might have said, that we must, phenomenologically, seek to understand what it is and what it says to us, even and especially if it is in the form of a paradoxical utterance).[10] However, it already nominalizes this complex utterance, constituting it as an "object" of thought, and suggesting that we return to a descriptive formulation, to an elaboration of *figures* (the first that of the immediately subsequent "lordship and bondage"), which might be considered to explain the concept of such a personality, but which we must also ask each time whether they effectively grasp the essence (or the being: *Wesen*) that Hegel intends (knowing that, in reality, this will never happen . . . declining, for the moment, to take up the question of "Absolute Knowledge"). In order to transpose all of these concerns into a translation-commentary, we must ourselves ceaselessly play upon the two quasi-translations of IWWI that undo its syntactic anomaly without possible French equivalent: "*Un Moi qui est un Nous, un Nous qui est un Moi*," "*Nous que je suis, Moi que nous sommes*."[11]

Philosophy—in particular, classical philosophy—is not devoid of such utterances, but they remain rare; for, each time they occur is associated with revolutions in the writing and conception of subjectivity insofar as it is inseparable from an *act of speech* (*logos*, *legein*) against the background of an interminable confrontation (or polemical, "blasphematory" repetition) with the theophanic utterances of the Judeo-Christian tradition, always oscillating between an ontological perspective and an egological perspective. The most important example—which would take time to confront in detail, on the level of the very letter of the texts themselves—is, as I have attempted to show elsewhere, the "foundational" utterance that Descartes proposes in the Second Meditation: *ego sum, ego existo* (or, in the French version: "*je suis, j'existe*").[12]

I will leave this confrontation in abeyance for the moment in order to concentrate— once again, in schematic fashion—on a correlative question, that of the place occupied by the utterance from Chapter IV and the function that it serves within the entire development of the *Phenomenology*. This place is strategic, to such an extent that, in reality, one can argue that the whole structure of the book, its architectonic is constructed around this very utterance. Without the interpretation of this utterance, or rather of the relation that it maintains all through the *Phenomenology* with a series of others, which have in common with it a grammatical construction or a representation of the speculative concept and its function in the form of an equation whose terms are the self-references of the person (a representation the idea for which comes from Kant and especially Fichte, based on the originary "tautology" "*Ich = Ich*" or "*Ich bin Ich*"), the movement of this work is very difficult to make intelligible.[13] Or rather, let us say, more prudently, that it is in this relation that the sense of the work's movement is, *par excellence*, periodically signaled and reinitiated. A few indices might help understand how this is the case.

To read the *Phenomenology* as the progression of consciousness toward the absolute knowledge that is at once its ultimate figure and its surpassing (or the surpassing of its own finitude, the limits of its "experience") is to attend to the signification represented by a series of terms or expressions: first, *Ich* (the pure personal pronoun, at once singular and universal, sensible and abstract, whereby consciousness designates itself even before unfolding any content—that is, when, phenomenologically, it precedes itself as consciousness, in the chapter on "sense-certainty," *sinnliche Gewissheit*); second, *Ich gleich Ich*, or (with other connotations) *Ich bin Ich*, the "tautology" whereby Kant and Fichte (or rather, Fichte interpreting Kant) thought and articulated the logical structure of the unity of transcendental consciousness, and which Hegel never ceased to designate as an "empty," abstract form in which consciousness seizes hold of a unity devoid of any content of its own, making it impossible to understand how it must, through incessant movement, acquire new content through (individual and collective) experience, and prove the truth of this content and the specific contradictions that undermine certainty and constrain it dialectically to surpass any form of finite experience. The repetition of the equation, "*Ich = Ich*," occurs at intervals throughout the progression of the *Phenomenology*: it intervenes—always in a critical fashion, but also in relation to a new figure of consciousness of which it evokes, in a sense, a residue of abstraction—each time that Hegel crosses a *threshold* in the transformation of the experience of consciousness into a more effective modality of spirit, up to the ultimate repetition in the chapter on Absolute Knowledge, where its signification is suddenly revealed to be the exact opposite. What it evokes from that point onward is still a "tautology," but now it is, I daresay, a *concrete tautology*, not the pure and simple formal equality of the "I" with itself, but *the equality of the Self with itself* (or the fact that the Self is itself the adequate manifestation of its own content), which means once again (what Hegel marks explicitly in the text) that the "I" has become (a) "Self" (*Ich* names itself and it is itself Self) there where consciousness—whose proper name is *Ich* and whose formal structure is encapsulated by *Ich = Ich*—has passed into the element of self-conscious or "self-knowing" spirit, whose name is *Selbst*.[14] Indeed, the notion of *Selbst* is just as "pure"; its structure could be explained in the hypertautological form of a "*Selbst is Selbst*,"[15] which, for Hegel, contains the totality of experience in reflexive form, in incessant movement.

In the meantime, however, a mutation has occurred, without which these repetitions, these displacements that attend the diverse content of experience and the ultimate phenomenological reversal of *Ich* into *Selbst*, would remain unintelligible: this is the mutation that is signaled, and more profoundly defined by our utterance "IWWI," whose form—that of an equation mirroring itself—henceforth assumes its full meaning, at the precise moment when consciousness is transformed into self-consciousness, and when this self-consciousness shows that it itself already contains, "in itself," the structure and characteristics of spirit. This utterance says, literally, that *Ich* can be equal, adequate to itself as *Selbst* only on condition of "exiting" empty form toward the exteriority of a "we" (*Wir*), or better, on condition of finding within itself and internalizing through its own movement the figures of its own exteriority as "we"—beginning with the doubling of self-consciousness, the confrontation with another desiring self-consciousness, all the way up to the institutional and spiritual figures of culture, morality, and religion that constitute so many actualizations or concrete interpretations of the utterance "I am/is we." The guiding thread of Hegel's exposition is thus the presentation of the fact that *Ich* can only be reflected in "self," in *Ich*, on the condition of passing through an other that already includes it in advance, on condition of metamorphosing itself into *Wir*, and contemplating itself as *Wir*, and even as *Wir* who is *Ich*, who "says" *Ich*, who says itself and thinks itself as an individual and a subject, indivisibly. Each repetition of *Ich = Ich* is thus a repetition of "IWWI," which forms at once the critique of its formal abstraction and the actualization of its own dialectic, in a manner which each time "measures" the adequacy and inadequacy of this representation.

However, such a presentation is incomplete and, by the same token, imprecise. To present, as I have just done, the guiding thread of the *Phenomenology* as the progression from *Ich* to *Selbst* through the multiply reiterated concurrence of the "*Ich = Ich*" and the dialectic (or dialectics) of the "IWWI" is undoubtedly to anticipate and clarify our main concern—that is, the central function, within the development of Hegel's phenomenology, of the gradual elaboration of the concept of *community* (not *Gemeinschaft* but rather *Gemeinwesen* and, on occasion, *Gemeinde*), which is, at the same time, the critique of this concept, and thus its transformation, or its sublation within the idea of absolute knowledge (a very strange "absolute," since we know that it does not designate immobility or eternity, but rather, the incessant mobility that Hegel is the first to call *historicity*, which means, in turn, that the *Phenomenology* is essentially a critique of the way in which each community, or rather, each type of community—civic, sociocultural, moral, or religious—*perceives itself as absolute*, in the sense of an essential immobility or immutability).[16] By essence, this construction of community in the form of the deconstruction of its illusion of eternity, immobility, and self-sufficiency, must go by way of an elaboration of the conflict and tension that constitute the paradoxical alliance of finitude and infinity inherent to the double representation of the "I" as "We" and the "We" as "I"—to such an extent that one could go so far as to propose that the entire *Phenomenology* could be encapsulated in *the absolute historicization of the utterance "IWWI."* This is very important, indeed, but, I repeat, it always skips a step that must now be restored, a step that entails nothing less than the inscription of this entire development within the element of *universality* (or, if one prefers, within Hegel's terminology, within the element of *being*). Of course, this inscription must also be understood reciprocally as an elaboration of the concept of the universal as the dialectical development of becoming-"spirit," becoming-spiritual of "consciousness."

Spirit's Two Paths

What, then, is the step that I skipped? It is nothing less than the mirror image of the utterance "IWWI," which entails exactly (or almost exactly) the same grammatical singularities as "IWWI," and that appears in the very next chapter, Chapter V (itself symmetrical, the mirror image, of the chapter on "self-consciousness," which is already manifest in its title: *Gewissheit und Wahrheit der Vernunft*). After a fresh repetition of *Ich =Ich*, this time associated with the famous demonstration that the relation self/me and me/self (reflection) is always objectively determined (in the mode of objectification) by the "traversed and forgotten path" (*jener vergessene Weg*) that consciousness has "at its back," this chapter on "reason" (the classical name for the universal, the name for being as *logos*) passes through a astonishing variant upon the equation IWWI that, restored to its context, explicitly concerns the relationship between individual consciousness to the totality and unity of the *people* in the Rousseauist sense of the term (a people that is essentially "free" by virtue of its constitution and its self-sufficiency): *"Sie als Mich, Mich als Sie"* (Them as Me, Me as Them).[17] And finally, with respect to what Hegel calls the "Thing itself" or the "pure Thing"—that is, *the work*, identified with a "spiritual essence," *geistiges Wesen*, the (common) essence of all essences, *Wesen aller Wesen*, because it is an *active* essence, an action or operation "of all and each," *Tun aller und Jeder*—which, in another terminology, one might risk calling *praxis*—Hegel arrives at another synthetic formulation: "The pure Thing itself is what was defined above as 'the category,' being that is the 'I' or the 'I' that is being (*das Sein, das Ich, oder Ich, das Sein ist*), but in the form of thought which is still distinguished from *actual self-consciousness* (*vom wirklichen Selbstbewusstsein*) insofar as we can call them its content (purpose, action, and reality), and also insofar as we call them its form—being-for-self and being-for-another (*Fürsichsein und Sein für anderes*)—are posited as one with the simple category itself, and the category is thereby at the same time the entire content."[18]

We draw two possible lessons from this passage. (1) The *Wir* is not "being" (*Sein*). The radical "ontological insufficiency" of the *subject* as "we" becomes the permanent measure of its consistency or inconsistency, its consciousness or its unconsciousness. (2) Being (*Sein*) is also implicitly *logos*; and it is thus with respect to *logos* that community "lacks in being" (*manque d'être*). But what is logos? Divine Word? Natural Reason? Indissociable from its reflection upon "ancient" and "modern" community, the *Phenomenology* is always confronting the alternative between faith and Enlightenment; and, once again, this confrontation never comes to rest or to the "end of history": we move from individual or collective consciousness to a historical or institutional "objectivity," but the latter remains divided between two antithetical poles. It represents a *question* immanent to historicity, not a response.

We can thus propose a simplified chart that shows how one "proceeds" though the *Phenomenology* from the abstract viewpoint of *"Ich"* to that of *"Selbst,"* which includes within itself reflection upon all of the spiritual mediations in the mode of self-consciousness, passing through all the concurrent paths that must ultimately reunite within it, and that one might call respectively the "path of the *Wir*" and the "path of *Sein*."[19]

Ich = Ich

(s. 134) (PS, 104) (IV, intro., §166)

Ich, das Wir, und Wir, das Ich ist

(IWWI)

(s. 140) (PS, 110) (IV, intro., §177)

Ich = Ich

(s. 176–177) (PS, 140) (V, intro., §233)

Sie als Mich, Mich als Sie

(s. 258) (PS, 213–214) (V, B, intro., §351)

Ein Wesen, dessen Tun . . . nur Sache ist als *Tun aller und Jeder*

(s. 300) (PS, 251–252) (V, C, a, §418)

Das Sein, das Ich, oder Ich, das Sein ist

(s. 301) (PS, 252) (V, C, a, §418)

Diese Substanz ist ebenso das allgemeine *Werk*,

das sich durch das *Tun aller und Jeder* als ihre Einheit und Gleichheit erzeugt

(s. 314) (PS, 264) (VI, intro., §439)

Was darin dem Ich das Andre ist, ist nur das Ich selbst

(s. 383) (PS, 327) (VI, B, a, §537)

Ich = Ich

(s. 458) (PS, 395) (VI, C, c, §652)

Ich = Ich

(s. 461) (PS, 398) (VI, C, c, §657) (the beautiful soul)

Ich = Ich

(s. 472) (PS, 409) (VI, C, c, §671)

Ich = Ich

(s. 546) (PS, 476) (VII, C, §785)

Ich = Ich

(s. 553) (PS, 482) (VIII, §793)

Ich ist nicht nur das Selbst, sondern est ist die Gleichheit des Selbst

(s. 560) (PS, 489) (VIII, §803)

Ich = Ich

(s. 561) (PS, 490) (VIII, §804)

A very interesting counterproof, if we had the time to consider it, would consist in re-visiting the way in which Kojève, in his famous reading of the *Phenomenology*, elaborates the progression from internally divided self-consciousness to the unity of the people or the general will that offers this self-consciousness a collective and practical expression. Kojève does underscore that the *"Tun aller und Jeder"* supersedes the figure of "lordship and bondage" that he privileges in the exposition of the internal conflict of desiring consciousness. But he says absolutely nothing about the utterance of the "IWWI" that governs that figure (and already prescribes its objective) and, as a result, remains indifferent to the "repetition" of this utterance at the moment that the people emerge in the symmetrical form of the "ISSI."[20] He thus does not see that the collective being of the people is here *distanced* from the subjective form. Our examination would then proceed with Marcuse. In *Hegel's Ontology and Theory of Historicity*,[21] he refers back the "action of all and each" to its abstract prototype, the category of reason or the universal whose formula is "SIIS." But Marcuse, too, says nothing about the symmetry of this formula with "IWWI," which is consistent with his insistence upon the concept of *life* to the detriment of *consciousness* and *self-consciousness*.[22]

Models of Intersubjectivity: Rousseau and the Gospel of John

Let us now move on to the second stage of our attempt at interpretation, that which concerns the "sources" or, better, the "models" for Hegel's utterance. It is necessary to undertake an examination of the effects of transformation and recurrence that this utterance produces within a signifying chain, which can be broken down into precise statements—all constructed on the same model even if they vary greatly and appear in different languages—belonging to the same historical family. The scope of these statements extends well beyond philosophy into culture because they constitute the guiding thread for a certain anthropological approach to subjectivity. An utterance such as Hegel's IWWI (along with its internal variants), as one might suspect, even and especially if it constitutes an invention that is irreversibly *signed* in the name of its author, does not arise in the void but rather at the endpoint of a long series of historical repetitions, and at the point where this series intersects with texts and contexts that require a "return to origins" in order to rethink and perhaps completely overturn the utterance's signification. Never will we finish reconstituting such signifying chain, which Nietzsche called a *Zeichenkettel*, tracking down all of its turns and inflections. Let us then limit ourselves to the essential, or to that which, at the present stage of our investigation, seems to me to be the essential, even if it means relying upon conjectures that are, by definition, debatable.

Earlier I evoked the "Cartesian" model of *the ego sum, ego existo*. This utterance is indeed present in the background of the Hegelian text—not so much directly, however, but thanks to the intermediary of the "logicization" that Kant and Fichte impose upon it in the utterance "*Ich = Ich*"[23]; and it helps to show that there is a fundamental analogy between Hegel and Descartes that hinges on the way in which both have a quasi-divine *voice* (unless it is, as blasphemy or challenge, a *human parody* of the divine voice) intervene in the text.[24] Hegel underscores this relation once again when, in the dialectic that joins the "beautiful soul" to its own culpability, which becomes an obsession that constitutes it as such, transforms the other utterance of the tautology ("*Ich gleich Ich*") into the proffering of a haecceity: "*Ich bin's*," and "*c'est moi*," "I am so" (A. V. Miller) or "here I am, the Man you seek."[25] But this model—important as it may be for the history of modern subjectivity—is not immediately pertinent because it evidently lacks the two salient characteristics of Hegelian utterance: *formal reflexivity* (I=I, IWWI, SMMS, SIIS), mirroring, and the internal reference to *the difference between the individual and the collective* and then to the negation of this difference (or the inclusion of the common within the subject and the subject in the common).

This is why I would like to privilege two other models. The one is quite "distant" and yet, in a sense, eternally present, almost culturally intangible: the model of the theophanic utterances from the Gospel of John. The other is very close and immediately present in history, but also the object of a virulent controversy to which Hegel contributes in his own manner, all the more fascinating and subtle because it doubles for him as sort of self-criticism of the youthful convictions that he shared with Hölderlin: Rousseau's *Social Contract*. I will argue that Hegel explicitly and deliberately sought to "respond" to *The Social Contract* throughout the *Phenomenology*, but also to reprise Rousseau's question from within and to subject it to a radical transformation. This also reflects the fact that Hegel measures himself against Rousseau beyond the shock (and even the traumatism) of the event that he considers to be the implementation of Rousseauist discourse (and that was actually presented as such at certain crucial moments, in particular the moment of the Jacobin Terror)—that is, the French Revolution (or the part of it that had already taken place at the moment when Hegel was writing the *Phenomenology*: Everything depends on the way in which one chronologically "terminates" the revolutionary process and, as we know, the question of such termination is itself part of the controversy).

Let us begin with the Gospel of John. I hold that this text contains a direct and even the most direct model for Hegel's utterance; and that one can "see" it in the very letter of the text. Special glasses might be required, however. When I submitted this conjecture to two eminent Hegelians at our European university, Pierre-Jean Labarrière and Christoph Jamme, they immediately dismissed or refuted it as unlikely and even incongruous.[26] I would like, then, to document my conjecture in order to lend it maximum likelihood and thereby to open it wider to critique, if warranted.

Indeed, the reference to John does not pertain to the question of community in general, the return to the theological prototype that, after certain of Saint Paul's developments, is associated with the idea a "mystical body" which would raise all of its members into a unity or allow them to commune for all eternity within the same spirit. This idea, as we know, governs a large part of classical reflections on the State and political community, achieving its limit (but also, perhaps, its purest transposition) in the Rousseauist "contract" founded upon the emergence of the general will. The recurrence at stake here is, to my mind, much more literal, and less conceptual; it reactivates a series of evangelical statements that are open to theological elaboration, but that, more fundamentally, are integral to the inner discursive structure of religious consciousness.[27] This point is essential for understanding Hegel's later confrontation with Rousseau, who reverses from within the signification of the idea of the "mystical body" by substituting the people for the Church, foundational decision for eschatological hope, and finally the immanence of the law for the incarnated transcendence of the Word of God.[28] Hegel, struggling with this theologico-political model that is also a metaphysics of the "we" and its sovereign unity or indivisibility, must find his way back to the auto-enunciation of the subject whose own "voice" must be heard in order to disarticulate from within the apparent simplicity of political affirmation. The idea of the "mystical body" does not suffice and it is perhaps the very thing called into question here, along with its secular "translations."[29]

I here provide the pertinent passages from the Gospel of John (in the King James translation), accompanied by Luther's German translation, which Hegel was familiar with. All of the passages belong to Jesus's "farewell" to his disciples, beginning with the Last Supper, the betrayal of Judas, and the Passion, and ending with Jesus's prayer to God that he reunite men through him despite their sins (which the Lutheran tradition calls "reconciliation," *Versöhnung*, and which Hegel evokes on two occasions in his discussion of the "yes" that constitutes community: "*das Wort des Versöhnung*")[30]:

John 14:3. "I will come again, and receive you unto myself; that where I am, there you may be also" (*will ich doch wiederkommen und euch zu mir nehmen, auf das ihr seid, wo ich bin*).

John 14:10. "Believest thou not that I am in the Father, and the Father in me? "(*dass ich im Vater and der Vater in mir ist*).

John 14:20. "At that day ye shall know that I am in my Father, and you in Me, and I in you" (*dass ich in meinem Vater bin und ihr in mir und ich in euch*).

John 15:4. "Abide in Me, and I in you" (*Bleibt in mir und ich in euch*).

John 17:21. "That they may all be one; as thou, Father, art in me, and I in thee, that they also may be one in us . . . And the glory which thou gavest me I have given them; that they may be one, even as we are one" (*auf dass alle eins seien gleichwie du, Vater, in mir und ich in dir, auch sie in uns eins seien . . . ich in ihnen und du in mir*).[31]

It thus becomes evident that, following my hypothesis of a "transformation" within a single signifying chain, we must pass from a *Trinitarian* structure—men/disciples of Christ will be one in (with) him as he is in (with) them, in the image of his unity with the Father and the Father with him, or of his participation in the Father that is also the Father's in him—to a *dualist* schema, or rather the schema of a *double duality* ("I am who am We, We who are I," "I who am Being, Being who is I") whose final "reconciliation" is the Self (*Selbst* or *Ichselbst*), the absolute historicity of community. In the former case, the mutual belonging within a coming community passes through the transcendent relationship of the Master to his eternal Father (or the scission of the divine subject, followed by his incarnation and reunification beyond death). In the latter case, the construction of community (or perhaps the attempt at such a construction that can only end up going beyond the human, into "absolute knowledge") passes through mutual belonging or recognition of the Ego of consciousness with its "others" ("we") and the mutual belonging of this Ego with its "other" (being, or the objective world, or the universal), which are reconciled under the "name" of *Selbst*. Transcendence has thus been reduced to the plane of immanence. In order to understand the contemporary significance of this reduction, we must now turn to Rousseau. In John, Christ is the only one who says "I" (or "Me") *for all*, up close to the Father. In Hegel, but after Rousseau, the "I" has become a property that belongs to *each and everyone*, or to whatever citizen-subject, but on the condition that he or she is "indivisibly" part of the "common."

The decisive passage is Rousseau's presentation of the "pact" in *The Social Contract* (I, §6):

> In short, each giving himself to all, gives himself to no one; and since there is no associate over whom we do not acquire the same rights which we concede to him over ourselves, we gain the equivalent of all that we lose, and more power to preserve what we have.

> If, then, we set aside whatever does not belong to the essence of the social contract, we shall find that we can reduce it to the following terms: *Each of us puts in common his person and all his power under the supreme direction of the general will; and in return each member becomes an indivisible part of the whole.*

> Right away, in place of the particular individuality of each contracting party, this act of association produces a moral and collective body, composed of as many members as the assembly has voices, and which receives from this same act its unity, its common self (*moi*), its life, and its will.[32]

There can be no question, obviously, of an exhaustive commentary upon this central passage. No one would deny that, in the period that followed its publication, it has preoccupied not only political philosophy but also philosophy as such. From this viewpoint, we still belong to this period. The essentially political distinction between two types of collectivity or collectivization—the one external and artificial, dubbed an *aggregation*, the other intrinsic and quasi-natural (or producing the effect of an "second nature"), dubbed an *association*—will permanently remain on the agenda of philosophies (and sociologies or psychosociologies) of individuality, socialization, and being in common. For our purposes, it is necessary to highlight just a few implications of this passage that seem to directly govern Hegel's formulations.

In the first place, let us pay attention to the way in which the play of "voices" is set up in Rousseau's text. It is this play of the voice, which is to say this performativity of the "contract" that breaks *from below* (or from within) with any simple repetition of a theory of incorporation or inspiration. Whereas the unity of aggregation is imposed from an external sovereign, a "master" (as Rousseau had explained in the previous chapter), association (or "the people" in the strong sense of the term: we are responding here to the question, "what makes a people a people?") utters itself in the first person. In truth, association does not preexist the italicized utterance that Rousseau's text offers in the mode of the "we" that joins each and every "I" who proffers it on his or her own account. Accordingly, the constitution of the people (the emergence of the "general will") has an essential *performative* character. To *say* association in the required form (of unanimity) is to *do* it.

But the writing that reproduces at its heart the performative of the self-constitution of the people—in the form of a supplementary voice, as if transcribed from the original historical scene—is indissociable from the invention that arises "in person" within the text of *The Social Contract*, henceforth to govern its effects: the "common *self*" (*moi commun*). It is this "common self" that Rousseau's writing conveys before it is actually named. However, without this invention of writing, underscored with italics once again, which perhaps indicate a "citation" (self=I [who] say me myself, or rather, in fact: *we* [who] say *me* myself), but which also recalls the still exceptional character of this nominalization of the personal pronoun in Rousseau's time (only since Descartes, Pascal, and Condillac did "the me" [*le moi*] gain currency in French), there could be no immanence of the "constitutive power" to the "constituted power," of the sovereign (the people) to the State, and thus to the government. The people is thus this "being" who, having unanimously said "we" in order to "make [itself] a people," goes ahead and sovereignly says "I" at the heart of the State that is "its State." Fundamentally, this invention of *The Social Contract* is at once linguistic, speculative, and political.[33]

The "single-multiple person" (or the multiple in one) that Rousseau constructs in this manner has two essential characteristics:

In the first place, this person operates what I have elsewhere called a "reduction of verticality" or the incorporation of sovereignty into the people's "double relation" with itself[34]—at once sovereign and subject (*archōn* and *archomenos*), divisible and indivisible, equal and unequal, self-identical and different from itself.[35] Sovereignty is not thereby abolished (although the concept may be profoundly subverted and, at the limit, becomes contradictory) but rather it "descends" from the transcendental or eminent place where it previously resided (including in the form of the Hobbesian "mortal God") and becomes identified with the reciprocity of the *political relation* (which is why, incidentally, unlike the Leviathan that appears in the frontispiece to Hobbes's book, it is no longer representable in any sense of the term, not even allegorically). However, as we see in the later developments of *The Social Contract* (essentially Book II), this reciprocity also supposes the agency of a mediation, indissociable from a "dialectical contradiction" (total alienation as a condition of freedom). This mediation ("vanishing," as Fredric Jameson would say, because it should never detach itself from the general will from which it arises) is the *law*, the "act of all upon all," as it were.[36] The law is not anything else than the double relation, or the double relation "in act." But it confers on the "common self" a *subjective quality* that derives from the will and not only from an utterance (or else it renders explicit the immanence of an act of will to every utterance that operates a "fusion" of the one and the multiple, or the I and the We/All). Sovereignty is immanent to political association, to the people, on condition that the latter permanently enters into "relation" with itself through the intermediary of the law.

Whence the second characteristic: when Rousseau evokes the "common self" (liable to *speak*, or to utter itself as such in the form of the law on condition that this utterance always be preceded, in a transcendental fashion, by an *archi-utterance*, that of the "pact" that declares being in common as such), he both *does and does not* think it as a "natural individual." Outward, it certainly is a natural individual, in conformity with the jusnaturalist doctrine of international relations (Grotius, Hobbes) that Rousseau adopts or virtually upholds.[37] Inwards, on the other hand, which is the only aspect of the problem of sovereignty that the Social Contract addresses, the situation is much more ambiguous. The "moral and collective body" that Rousseau evokes is indeed a "political body" in the classical sense—a system of relations between parts and forces whose conflicts among themselves are presented as elements of sickness, degeneration, or dissociation—that will eventually be endowed with a "soul" (which Rousseau will never cease to seek, ending up with the aporia of "civil religion"). This presentation, which owes as much to Hobbes and Spinoza as to Montesquieu, dominated the *Discourse on Political Economy* and only begins to undergo change in the *Geneva Manuscript*, until, in the final version of *The Social Contract*, its antithesis appears: the concept of an indivisible or metahistorical "historical subject" that introduces freedom into the history of the world (hypothetically "reversing" the effects of alienation produced by history insofar as it unfolds as the forgetting and distancing of its own "natural" origin). This is the paradox—or, one is tempted to say, the miracle—of "total alienation." This collective subject that reconstitutes the equivalent of an origin against nature, or rather in opposition to what history has made of nature, is "improbable"; and, at the limit, it is *impossible*. In any event, it is not possible as the simple constitution of an organism but only as the development of an antinomy (one of whose extreme expressions concerns the relation between freedom and constraint: "which means nothing else than that he shall be forced to be free"[38]).

The Community Within Its Limits

In relation to Rousseau's construction (which he considers not only as metaphysical, as others will say after him, but the completion of metaphysics, or as the extreme point of its advance where it can no longer avoid transforming into dialectics or submitting to its own latent dialectic), and on the background of what he considers to be the experience of the Rousseauist theory of the French Revolution at work,[39] Hegel formulated a double critique:

1. He considered that the "reduction of the verticality" of sovereignty in the Rousseauist people, the transformation of a transcendence into an immanent unity, was a *fictive* or a contradictory reduction, and consequently an unfulfilled one, not because it only goes half way, but rather because it goes *too fast*: the mediation that it employs (the "law") vanishes too fast, but also remains inert, untransformable. With the representation of the law as equivalent of the double relation Sovereign/subjects, a materialized "abstraction" subsists at the heart of the totality. This representation cannot be reduced to its own movement and, above all, it keeps a distance from its internal conflicts and thus from its "life," both of which it always engages in an external, abstract, and formalist manner, oscillating infinitely between exhortation and constraint. Consequently, this representation does not construct community but rather destroys it—and this movement of destruction, or self-destruction, itself assumes a sinister figure within the French Revolution, leading to the Terror in which the law is no longer anything but the guillotine that forces the whole world to be free via equality in death. Not only have we lost forever the beautiful totality incarnated in the Greek city (or in the Hölderlinian *dream* of the Greek city, a dream that Hegel once shared) where the individual *immediately* becomes an "indivisible" part of the whole (I = We), but the attempt by Rousseau and the revolutionaries to recreate the "common self," instead of retrieving it or conjuring its impossibility, produces nothing but caricature.

2. He considered (something which is debatable) that, in the oscillation between a naturalism of the body politic and an absolute subjectivism of the general/ universal (*allgemein*) will—which makes up the whole originality of Rousseau's construction and its paradoxical relation to historicity (as the negation of a negation of natural origins)—the first moment always prevails over the second. This amounts to saying that *Rousseau did not have a concept of freedom as will* (and of will as freedom). In this sense, Rousseau in Hegel's eyes is always yet again a pre-Kantian; his concept of the will is trapped in a representation of the relation of forces (as Rousseau might well have wanted it). Rousseau's extreme voluntarism masks a persistent naturalism (a classical aporia of the "dualism," according to Hegel). Consequently, he misses out on the possibility of inscribing the universality of will in being and inversely on the sublation of the objectivity or "thingliness" (*Gegenstandlichkeit, Dinglichkeit*) of being in its spiritual becoming. He does not think, as Hegel claims to do himself, the "becoming-subject" of its own substance, whose emergence from the general will, or the collective will and historical figure of the *people*, constitutes one of the decisive moments of this becoming. Herein resides everything at stake in Hegel's elaboration of the *Tun Aller und Jeder* (or, if one wishes, of *praxis*, collective work), which Kojève addressed as an isolated question. But this elaboration also raises an ontological question which is immediately susceptible to a political translation—a matter of knowing whether the will is opposed, once again from the outside or in the form of quasi-transcendence, to the multiplicity of interests and their conflicts, or whether it *results* from these conflicts themselves, whether it constitutes their very movement, result, and supersession.

In the final analysis, it becomes possible to see that the two critical movements with respect to Rousseau that Hegel lodges at the heart of the *Phenomenology* and that form its guiding thread insofar as it is "political" from beginning to end (along with *Elements of the Philosophy of Right*, one of Hegel's *two* great political texts, profoundly different in so many respects and inserted into conjunctures that couldn't be more different), that these two movements are really one. In any event, they converge upon the same point—designated by a kind of monogram, the utterance IWWI. The critique of the "law" as the abstract media-tion of the relation of each to everyone and everyone to each demands the suppression of this mediation, or the sublation of its abstraction, and thus the construction and decon-struction of a juridico-political figure of the law as a *particular—inadequate and transitory— moment* of the constitution of community.[40] And this sublation can only take the form of a phenomenological elaboration of the *process* that produces the identification of I (Myself) with We (All) and the incorporation of We in each I (in the consciousness of each I), insofar as this is a process of recognition (and also, consequently, of misrecognition). Such a process is always conflict-ridden and even violent; it is animated by the whole violence of desire, interest, and the tension between life and the spirit within consciousness.

In the interpretation that I propose, this point of intersection is purely and simply iden-tical to the unfolding of the latent, inherently conflictual structure of the oxymoronic

formula IWWI (while the equation that it replaces, *Ich =Ich*, is "frozen" in a nondialecti-
cal immobility), insofar as it is the identity of identity and difference that the *Phenomenology* privileges (or whose *subjective* essence it manifests). This does not mean, of course, that
this formula should become the basis for a logico-grammatical ratiocination, but rather
that it is necessary to work toward its "fulfillment" and thus its "externalization" in the
passage through a series of *experiences* whose structure of subjective reflexivity it helps to
understand. One last time, however, it is necessary to underscore that, in order to explicate this formula of the dialectical movement of modern consciousness—profoundly "secular" and entirely directed, in particular, against the idea of a providential historicity
governed by a transcendent spirit that would survey it and assign it an end in advance—
Hegel had to espouse anew, beyond Rousseau and many others, a type of essentially theological utterance, albeit reduced to what remains most material and evental within it—that
is, the letter of its discourse. This is why I obstinately refer, by way of conjecture, to the
model of the Gospel of John. In this sense, Hegel's utterance, which stands on the threshold of our second modernity (or of the supersession of our first modernity, here symbolized by the *Social Contract*), is profoundly "untimely," "noncontemporaneous" with its own
context and its objective. This can help us to understand why, by the same token, this utterance entails the deconstruction of what it constructs, or the possibility of a "postmodern"
critique at the heart of modernity itself.

I can now see that it will not be possible for me to keep the promise which I made to myself, to save the most time and space for third phase of explication—that which should
allow us to return in more detail to the Hegelian reflection on *self-conscious community* in
the *Phenomenology* as the figure of figures, or the "generic" figure on the basis of which
the whole movement of consciousness might be grasped as the becoming-subject of spiritual
substance.[41]
   Without going into detail, then, I will programmatically evoke what are, in my view,
the most important stages of this movement. They all derive from the idea that the Hegelian attempt to transform the individual into the universal and to inscribe universality
within the element of the individual takes a specific form—for which Hegel appropriated
and displaced the metaphysical notion of *spirit* (by which I mean exclusively *spirit* in the
sense of the *Phenomenology of Spirit*, very profoundly different from what Hegel will later
designate with this term)—that authorizes him to make the difficulties, the obstacles, and
even the impossibilities of such a transformation or such an inscription into the very matter
of his elaboration (in this sense, too, the *Phenomenology* is an "experience" in and through
writing). This specific form is the equivalence between the notions of *subjectivity* and *community*; or, if one prefers, it is the idea, pushed to the limit, that *the only subjectivity is common or situated within the horizon of community* (of the possibility or impossibility of
community), and that, *there is community*—or better, "placing in common" of what can and
must belong to each and everyone—*only in the element of subjectivity* or by the effort that
subjectivity makes to go beyond its own limitations, its own finitude, without thereby laps-
ing into the objectivity and exteriority of a "substance" or even a "nature." Our discussion
of the monogram IWWI named and presented this equivalence but, at the same time,

from within it had already engaged us, in some sense, in its dialectic contradiction, as if we were ourselves its "subjects."

Ideally, we should start over again with a reflection, paying close attention to the text and its contexts, on what it means for subjectivity and for community to "say I" and to "say We," and thus to attempt to say both at the same time or in alternation (I-We). On this basis, there are three especially significant moments in Hegel's text to which we would have to return:

First, it would be necessary to examine the way in which Hegel himself—just after the utterance IWWI, that is, in the famous section on the independence and dependence of self-consciousness—problematized the relation between identification (identification of I with We and We with I) and community through the category of "recognition." It is not possible to repeat everything that is well known or disputed about this category, but only to underscore this: Recognition, as a movement of universalization whence emerges the first figure of the common (which could be called virtual), rests upon the idea that one of the self-consciousnesses, which can designate itself as I, or one of the sides of self-consciousness, ends up "contemplating" in the other (who is *its* other) not simply "He" (or "She") (a "He" or a "She") but precisely "We" or "the We" of which it is itself a part. For a consciousness that names itself *I* the other consciousness emerges as a virtual *We*, the anticipatory figure (still abstract) of *spirit*; and the We presents itself as an *other I* (with whose law consciousness must conform or identify in order to engage within the reality of the world). This is what lends the slave's (*Knecht*) viewpoint and his proper ethical "value" (work) their superiority over the master's viewpoint and his proper ethical "value" (the sacrifice of life or the acceptance of death). The Slave (that is, the subject), according to Hegel, can find the We or the community "wanting" in the Master, while the Master can never find it in the Slave. Here we already have an entire problematic of the "dominant ideology" and its critique "from below" by those constituted as a collective subject. . . . However, it is striking that the (provisional) outcome of the dialectic of recognition, at the far side of Chapter IV, which constitutes a sort of desperate return to the abstract form of the *Ich = Ich* (and the prototype for all of the ulterior returns)—that is, the unhappy consciousness—is described by Hegel as the "forced" turning of singularity in upon itself, or, if one prefers, as a singularity that constitutes itself (or despairs of doing so) *without community* or "deprived of *we*" (seeking a substitute in the astonishing figure of the "mediating minister" [*ministre médiateur*], as Jean Hyppolite translates the term [*den Vermittler als Rat*], to whom it abandons its will).[42]

Second, it would be necessary to examine how Hegel uses the reflection of the I in the We and the We in the I in order to think both *cognition and misrecognition at the same time*, or the fact that collective consciousness (all collective consciousness, in particular that of the people, the first figure whereby spirit exits abstraction and becomes "actually real") is both *Selbstbewusstsein* and *Bewusstlosigkeit* (which should be translated as "a-consciousness" or "consciousnesslessness" rather than as "unconsciousness" and a fortiori as "unconscious"), the one being the necessary flipside or counterpart of the other. In the course of the *Phenomenology*, the notion of consciousnesslessness always characterizes a still abstract universal or a universal that belongs to the register of being but not reflexivity.

Nonetheless, with the explicit arrival on stage of the problem of community (as a spiritual reality whose concrete manifestation is the people or its historical avatars—culture, religion), consciousnesslessness comes to designate what separates community from its own realization or from rising to its own concept, whether it be that of the Greek City, "Culture," the "General Will," or that of the community of believers (*Gemeinde*) unified in Christ by means of his "death." What we encounter here is, in a sense, the *resistance* of the "I" to coinciding with the "We" and, reciprocally, with perfect reflexivity that is tantamount to unity, to any "reconciliation" of the *same* self-consciousness.

Whence, third, the importance of moments that can be called "extreme," or that figure in the course of the *Phenomenology* as "limit-experiences" for consciousness when, we are tempted to say, *Selbstbewusstsein* is immediately converted into its opposite, *Bewusstlosigkeit*—which is to say that self-consciousness does not so much approach consciousnesslessness but rather *coincides* with it, concentrates itself within its own residue of inexpungable alterity. Two figures thus become particularly significant (and, of course, they have long polarized readers of the *Phenomenology*): *Irony* and *Terror*. These are radically negative figures of the impossibility of constituting a community as subjective community or "spirit," figures that impose a diehard limit upon the spiritual internalization of community as collective self-consciousness. It seems clear enough to me that the two figures symmetrically derive from our utterance (IWWI), which also makes it possible to understand their function. *Irony* is here understood in the sense that it assumes when, after Hegel's presentation of the conflict that divides the Greek city between the law of the heavens and that of the earth (or rather the law of the dead and that of the living) and his interpretation of Sophocles's Antigone, he writes that femininity (*die Weiblichkeit*), essentially "unbeknownst" or "consciousless," is the "eternal irony of community" (*ewige Ironie des Gemeinwesens*). Typically, then, Irony hinges upon an "I who is not We" (and resists the We without ceasing to be I). Inversely, Hegel describes *the Terror* both as the reign of "absolute freedom"—and thus the pure realization of Rousseau's idea of the General Will by the Jacobin revolutionaries—and as the delirium of equality imposed by law (which here "forces" us not only to be free but also to be equal to all others). Typically, it posits a "We who is not I" or that destroys the I even as it realizes a sort of monstrous and excessive construction of the We whose sole content becomes "summary" death stripped of any spiritual meaning. The annihilation of the We in its autonomization thus becomes perfectly clear. With the limit-experiences of Irony and Terror, Hegel seeks to show that the dialectic which hinges upon the identification of I with We and We with I entails a remainder that goes beyond what I just called "the flipside of misrecognition" (since all recognition has a side of misrecognition); for, it is a matter of absolute nonrecognition, or, if one prefers, the irremediably tragic element of historicity, which Hegel sought to uphold, in the *Phenomenology*, against the discourses of progress that characterize modernity past and future. At this point, we must, of course, ask why the Christ from Chapter IV ("the divine man") escapes this negative characterization but rather (*on condition of his death*) brings about a complete fusion of the I and the We;[43] and why this fusion remains, in Hegel's eyes, radically insufficient, perhaps the most insufficient of all (because it a mere *representation*).

SIX

The Messianic Moment in Marx

Im düstern Auge keine Träne,
Sie sitzen am Webstuhl und fletschen die Zähne:
Deutschland, wir weben dein Leichentuch,
Wir weben hinein den dreifachen Fluch—
Wir Weben, wir weben![1]

In the present essay, I would like to reexamine and, if possible, elucidate a question that often recurs in interpretations of Marx: What is the relationship between his concept of politics and religious (or theological) discourse? In view of the comparison that this issue of the *Revue Germanique Internationale* would like to draw, but also because of the strategic importance that, I believe, must be conferred upon this comparison, I will focus mainly upon *a single text*: the article, entitled "Zur Kritik der Hegelschen Rechtsphilosophie. Einleitung," that Marx published in the *Deutsch-Französische Jahrbücher* in March 1844. For the first time, in this text, Marx uses the name "proletariat."[2] I will show that, read to the letter and placed within its proper context, this text represents the "messianic moment" in Marx's thought, and it makes it possible to examine the permanence and the metamorphoses of this dimension throughout his work. Isolating a singular moment, on the level of its writing, I wish to position myself beyond debates about the "formation, "systematization," "development" of Marx's thought, grasped either as moments of continuity or discontinuity, because such debates tend to decontextualize his formulations and to substitute totalizing reconstructions for the necessary differential readings.

I choose the expression "messianic moment" to accord with that of the "Machiavellian moment" (borrowed from Pocock) that Miguel Abensour used in his landmark study centered on Marx's immediately anterior text, the "1843 Manuscript," known under the title, "Critique of the Hegelian Philosophy of the State," which he composed before his arrival in Paris, likely with the intention of making it into a book to which the *Einleitung* of 1844 would have served as an introduction.[3] What I would like to show is that, these two writings with almost identical titles diverge radically in style and in their basic concept of politics and their manner of *uttering* of its ends. This divergence is less a matter of an overturning of idealism into materialism, or in the transition from democratism to communism, although these questions deserve to be posed, than of the upsurge of an "impolitical" dimension at the heart of politics itself, associated with the redemptive function that the proletariat will assume.[4] Philosophically, it is entirely a question of understanding how the "Machiavellian moment" (eminently political, atheological, and radically democratic, if one follows Abensour) and the "messianic moment" are joined in a veritable unity of opposites—not only from the viewpoint of their linkage but also that of their conceptual correlation and, as it were, their *mutual presupposition*. If this is indeed the case, no matter the extreme diversity of figures in which this presupposition might appear in Marx's later writings and in those of his successors, what is at stake is an inherently irreducible structure of thought.

"The World Will Change Its Basis"

We will begin by describing the architecture of the *Einleitung* with emphasis upon its stylistic characteristics and its conceptual economy. Given our objective, of course, the best place to begin would be *the end*: "When all the inner conditions [i.e., the alliance between German philosophy or 'theory' and the proletariat, as the 'head' and 'heart' of human emancipation] are met, the day of the German resurrection will be heralded by the crowing of the Gallic cock [*wird der deutsche Auferstehungstag verkündet durch das Schmettern des gallischen Hahns*]."[5] Among the commentators who do not reduce the prophetic note in Marx to a journalistic effect, none, to my knowledge, indicates its exact provenance, which remains decisive.[6] This provenance does not rule out irony or demand that we attribute a univocal signification to this note; but it does forbid us from making it a mere accident of the pen. Give or take a verb, Marx reprises Heine's famous text celebrating the July Revolution, which evokes the same historical relationship between the Lutheran Reformation, the French Revolution and German Philosophy to be found in the *Einleitung*: "The Gallic rooster has now crowed [*gekräht*] for the second time, and in Germany, too, the day is coming. . . . What were we doing in the night that just ended? Well, we were dreaming in German fashion, that is, we were philosophizing. . . . Curiously, the practical actions of our neighbors on the other side of the Rhine nevertheless had a certain affinity with our philosophical dreams here in tranquil Germany. . . . Our German philosophy is nothing but the dream of the French revolution."[7] The crowing of the Gallic rooster that announces the day of emancipation thus signals an interpretation of modern revolutions as a trans-European historical and intellectual cycle whose imminent "resolution" Marx thought it possible to prophetize (as he did in the *Manifesto of the Communist Party* of 1847), at the same time as he hailed the upsurge of the proletariat as the savior of the world.[8] This conjunction also derives from an apparatus of writing—increasingly well known today—that is characterized by the brief but intense and reciprocal superimposition of Marx and Heine's singular "voices."[9] To what extent does this superimposition help elucidate the signification of this text as a whole? Schematically, I propose three keys.

The first key concerns the relationship between the conclusion of Marx's text and its much more famous opening formulations concerning *religion* ("opium of the people"):

> For Germany, the *criticism of religion* has been essentially completed, and the critique of religion is the prerequisite of all criticism. . . . The foundation of irreligious criticism is: *Man makes religion*, religion does not make man. . . . Man is *the world of man*, State, society. This State and this society produce religion, which is *an inverted consciousness of the world*, because they are an *inverted world*. . . . The struggle against religion is therefore indirectly the struggle against *that world* whose spiritual *aroma* is religion.
>
> Religious suffering is at one and the same time the expression of real suffering and a protest against real suffering. . . . The criticism of religion is therefore in *embryo* the *criticism of that vale of tears* of which religion is the *halo*.[10]

Let us leave aside, for the moment, debates about what these formulations owe to Feuerbach, whose "anthropological overturning" of theology, as we know, assumed prime importance for the young Hegelians in general, and to the atheism of the "radical Enlightenment," which Marx remained very close to and inspired his denunciation of the European monarchical and clerical restorations. Of more immediate interest to us is the theologico-political signification engendered by bringing together the opening of the article, which pronounces religion dead, and the messianic pronouncements on the proletariat that come at the end. This signification might be expressed in kitchen (or Church) Latin: *exit religio, adveniunt proletarii*. Relating religious illusion or mystification to the contradictory expression of the real, alienated world, Marx pinpointed a political problem, albeit a problem without immediate solution because it did not correspond to any actor or practical force. This "force" could only be found on the far side of complex historico-theoretical discussion, in the material figure of the proletariat (on the condition, to which I will return, that this figure is allied or organically fused with philosophy, which itself has achieved autonomy in the course of a long altercation with religion). The proletariat is thus the *other* (or the antagonist) of religion; but it is also the expression of its internal contradiction, the revelation of the secret that, as "protest" against suffering, it bears within itself. Here we have a schema that is much older than Marx and will live on beyond him: the messiah, or better, the "messianic force" reveals what religion betrays or perverts (the promise of emancipation or redemption), reestablishes it, and uses it to conquer religion itself. Let us take care, however, not to find here the dialectical "sublation" of religion; it is, much rather, a matter of interruption, even if this interruption is conceived as a return to originary authenticity.

This movement was at the heart of the Protestant Reformation, to the extent that it denounced the institution of the "visible" Church as a new Babylon prostituting revelation out to worldly powers, before it was repressed by the conflict between Luther and Thomas Münzer and by the Peasants' War.[11] It also manifests itself when "new Christianities" and romantic socialisms proclaim the advent of a religion of Man freed from theological superstitions.[12] And it remains as alive as ever in our own time in the way in which "liberation theologies" inveigh against the idolatry represented by the capitalist cult of money in the name of a "liberator God" who makes the poor collectively into the reincarnation of Christ, a sacrificial victim but also the figure of protest and revolt.[13] More significantly, perhaps, for the interpretation of our text, the same movement traverses Christian no less than Jewish (Kabbalistic) interpretations that, in antinomic fashion, identify the advent of the messiah with the abolition of the written, instituted law. In Marx, this interruption of religion by the messianic element, at the center of modern history on the way to becoming (once again) human history (or that of humanity in the making), is represented by the advent of a paradoxical, essentially *passive* (*Die Revolutionen bedürfen nämlich eines passiven Elementes*) and yet radically transformative force—a force inhabited by an "enthusiasm" for the new and capable of communicating it: the proletarian masses.

This is possible, obviously, only because these masses are invested with antithetical characteristics, conjoining the *nothing* of absolute dereliction, annihilation, and pauperization with the *everything* of a realization of human essence as "community" or plenitude of the "species" (*einer Sphäre endlich . . . welche mit einem Wort der* völlige Verlust *des Menschen ist, also nur durch die* völlige Wiedergewinnung des Menschen *sich selbst gewinnen kann*). This "negative representation of society" in the being of the proletariat is articulated in several idioms between which Marx never ceases to circulate. One among them goes back to the French revolutionary tradition and the political revindications that associate the sovereignty of the people with equality: "I am nothing, but I should be everything," writes Marx in a prosopopoeia of the revolutionary class, evoking the words of Sieyès that launched the French Revolution and prefigured a famous verse from the *Internationale*.[14] But these words themselves are already inscribed in a long signifying chain that traverses mysticism (the *todo y nada* or *nada per todo* of St. John of the Cross) and negative theology.[15] Marx will go on to associate them with a phenomenology of the crisis of bourgeois civil society, the terminology of which must be closely followed in order to understand its double historical and eschatological signification: *Auflösung* (the "dissolution" of society into the proletariat's conditions of existence, torn away from the conditions of life and forms of institutional recognition that "integrate" a class into the social order) communicates with *Lösung* (the "solution" or "resolution" of the political problem of emancipation that neither religious Reformation nor bourgeois political Revolution could provide); and, consequently, it also evokes redemption (*Erlösung*) and the redeemer (*die Rolle des Emanzipators*).

For the benefit of the proletariat, reduced by its oppression to the state of both elementary and generic humanity, stripped of all property or having nothing of its own (*Eigentumslos*), Marx can thus reactivate the biblical myth of liberating election: "radical" slavery turns into the redemptive mission of a "people of the people" working for all humanity. This mission is rooted in suffering and humiliation (and is thus, if you wish, the "Christly" aspect of the proletariat).[16] But it resides primarily upon the idea (which, this time, one would be tempted to consider as closer to Jewish messianism) of an injustice "in itself" or of an "absolute wrong" (*kein besonderes Unrecht, sondern das Unrecht schlechthin*") that determines the exit from history and the entry into humanity ("*welche nicht mehr auf einen* historischen, *sondern nur noch auf den* menschlichen *Titel provozieren kann*").[17] As in the Kabbala, and particularly in the "utopian revolutionary" variants of Jewish messianism, the resolution of historical injustice is conceived as the recreation of the world, at the price of its destruction (*"Auflösung der bisherigen Weltordnung"*), and not as a departure from earthly life or passage into another world.[18] From this viewpoint, in fact, Marx's extraordinary insistence on the term "world" (*Welt*) itself (and its cognates) from the beginning to the end of the *Einleitung* has an emblematic character: at the same time that it implies (in the very language of a theology which opposes the "sublunary realm" to the "heavens" and the "beyond") the radical critique of all dualism (characteristic, precisely of "religion," including the secularized forms thereof in bourgeois politics), it also insists upon the *materiality* of the Promised Land to which "human" emancipation would lead. But, of course, even as Marx never ceases to borrow from the eschatological traditions of "resurrection" and "redemption"—which are heterogeneous, although they remain historically linked—what he outlines here (or at least plays with, in a game which, caught up in his own "enthusiasm," he might not completely master) is a new messianism: that which the *Theses on Feuerbach*, one year later, will reformulate by identifying "revolutionary praxis" with the "transformation of the world," and that *The Communist Manifesto* will reprise in the form, once again, of a prophetic warning addressed to all the "ruling classes": "Let the ruling classes tremble at a communistic revolution. The proletarians have nothing to lose but their chains. They have a world to win."[19] Not simply militant, this messianism affirms that the transformation of the world is already well underway since a certain social order *forged* or "formed" unbearable chains, incompatible with its own survival. Under our very eyes, radical "passivity" is thus transformed into "activity." Potential being thus actualizes its passage to the act.

Demos: The Fullness of the Subject

Let us pause for a moment. What we have just described, abridging the citations while endeavoring to reproduce the most characteristic formulations, is a matter of rhetoric, or better, stylistics. Significant as such a description may be, however, it will never suffice to define a problematic.[20] In order to reach this level, comparative readings are necessary. Some would be concerned with the materials and formulations that specific sentences borrowed from the context in which they were written, along with the resulting effects of identification or, on the contrary, distanciation; while others would concern the relationship between these sentences and the entire set of Marx's writings from the same period, when his thinking underwent the most rapid evolution and crystallization. I provide no more than a schematic outline of these readings.

To begin with, it is necessary to measure the pregnancy of the theological and, most of all, the prophetic and apocalyptic vocabulary in European literature in the period from the French Revolution of 1789 to the revolution of 1848, by way of the "restoration" of the monarchy. This does not only apply to the productions of "utopian" socialism and communism, inspired or not by the idea of a "new Christianity," or, on the contrary, those of the "theocratic" counterrevolution, but also to nationalism. In this respect, there are great differences of tonality between the contexts—that is, between the aftermath of the great

French national affirmation, which opened, in Goethe's words, "a new era in the history of humanity," and the interminable wait for German national unity. It is not impossible that Marx (not far, on this point, from Moses Hess) relied upon French revolutionary rhetoric in order to elaborate a more "activist" discourse than that of German communists such as Weitling, who simply looked to the evangelical tradition for a model of society founded upon the community of goods.[21] However, in order to interpret Marx's formulations in the *Einleitung*—where it has been said that he "comes the closest to the preoccupations of a German nationalist thinker"[22]—the most decisive comparison would be with the idea of national salvation and the universal mission of Germany, by reason of the very idea that forms the guiding thread of his analysis. The blockage of the possibilities of antifeudal and anticlerical revolution after conservative turning point of the Prussian monarchy is compounded with the incapacity of the German bourgeoisie to transform itself into a "universal class," that is, to make itself the representative of the interests and rights of society as a whole (and of the "popular soul," *Volksseele*) against a regime of oppression. Whence the paradoxical possibility of projecting the whole of Europe beyond the bourgeois political regime. The analogies are striking between Marx's argument and the way in which Fichte, in his *Addresses to the German Nation* of 1807, described the German nation as a metapolitical spiritual force, whose liberation from foreign domination would also be that of all humanity, because it concentrates the moral energy of humanity as such. There are equally striking analogies with the way in which Cieskowski—the inventor of the philosophy of action that both Hess and Marx adopt—combined the idea of going beyond the antinomy between theory and praxis in universal history with the redemptive function of the Polish nation.[23]

Of course, the point of this comparison is not to *identify*, substituting one "subject of history" for another (the nation, the class), the discourses of national messianism and proletarian messianism (at least in its original, Marxian form)—as Voegelin tends to do too much. The point is rather to better understand, in a conflictual discursive context, how each messianism defines and pronounces itself against the other.[24] From this viewpoint, as well, the community of thought and writing that joined Marx and Heine during 1844 constitutes a fundamental argument: one finds therein the idea that "proletarians have no homeland," later to be placed at the center of *The Communist Manifesto*, where it figures both as one of the manifestations of the generalized negation conferring on the proletariat the status of a "class that is not a class of society" and as foothold for the internationalist slogan that expresses the universalism of the communist revolution. At the same time that Marx was composing the *Einleitung*, Heine might as well have been in the next room writing his great cycle of poems, *Deutschland: Ein Wintermärchen*, whose preface transforms patriotism into a cosmopolitan mission.[25]

In addition to the historical and literary context, however, we should also examine the context that is constituted by the sum of Marx's writings, published and unpublished, from the year 1843–44. Many have and will go on discussing, for a long time to come, the complexity of the theoretical configuration where, in the space of a few months, Marx's thinking undergoes a "mutation" from a "democratic humanism" to a "revolutionary communism" that is far from a return to unmediated community or a generalization of private property.

For my own part, I would like to draw attention to a remarkable characteristic of these texts: The fact that the constellation of concepts, generally considered to form the heart of the problematic of the "early Marx" (before the revelations of 1848)—i.e., *communism*, human or "social"[26] *emancipation*, *proletariat* as "universal class," "end of the political State," alienation (*Entfremdung*) and "externalization" (*Entäusserung*) of the general essence of man, revolutionary *praxis*—is never fully elaborated in any of the particular texts, each of which pertains to a different genre of writing and corresponds to a distinct destination (public or private).[27] This dispersion does not mean that there would be any pure and simple incompatibility between the concepts in question, but that any attempt to bring them together cannot escape a field of tensions between several viewpoints and discourses whose unity can only be problematic. Only by understanding these very tensions can one hope to find the keys to the mobility and intrinsic incompletion of Marx's thought, and thus also to its potentiality for reactivation at other conjunctures.[28] In order to conclude this necessarily partial analysis, as stated earlier, I will stick to one pertinent comparison: that which bears on the two "critiques of Hegel's philosophy of right," otherwise known as the *Manuscript of 1843* and the *Einleitung* of 1844, and that emphasizes the oscillation between the viewpoint of the "*demos*" and that of the "proletariat" as the bearers, respectively, of the political aspect and the impolitical aspect of the revolution.

I propose to unfold the sense of this comparison by reading the way in which each text relates the question of *activity* or *praxis* to the definition of a "collective subject," and consequently to the "transformations" (and the interminable decomposition) of the idea of sovereignty. There is no question of considering one or the other text as the more "materialist" by virtue of the accent that it places, on the one hand, on the empirical reality of the conflicts inherent to civil-bourgeois society, and, on the other, on the determinate condition for revolutions, the encounter between social forces and a radically critical theory. Instead, it seems to me that one must consider how the synthesis of the philosophy of praxis and materialism, which the *Theses on Feuerbach* will present as a dialectic that traverses all of modern thought, is suspended within this persistent tension between two points of view.

Miguel Abensour has very rightly shown that the critique which Marx developed in the margins of Hegel's *Elements of the Philosophy of Right* (one part of the section devoted to "internal public right," §§261–313) does not stop at demonstrating, through a reading of Hegel's texts that might be called "symptomatic," that the speculative dialectic fails to achieve its own objective: to make the constitutional State into the actual resolution, within the system of institutions, of the conflicts of "civil society" (as well as the family), and thereby to raise it up as a political absolute in which the idea of freedom (which is the very idea of right) would be both realized and autonomized.[29] From this reversal, whose target is the *abstraction* of the determinations of the modern State (as the State of "individual" property owners and their representation within the system of the division of powers), to which Hegel only added an apparatus of speculative deduction to produce the illusion of its necessity (thereby accentuating its analogy with the theological dualism of "heaven" and "earth"), Marx avoided deriving the inverse abstraction of a theory of "society" as the basis or "real subject" (the economic subject) of the figures of politics, as Marxism (and perhaps Marx himself, in his systematization of the principles of historical materialism) will be perpetually tempted to do later.[30] On the contrary, what he found in Hegel was the idea of a political subject who would both lie at the origin of a modern, fundamentally secular, and universalist State, opposed to the clerical and hierarchical institutions of the Ancien Régime, and of its eventual obsolescence or its predictable "end," inscribed in the untenability of its own limitations. Seizing hold of a resounding expression that surged from Marx's pen at the moment when he denounced the Hegelian attempt to isolate the manifestation of political sovereignty in the "moment" of monarchical decision (that is, on the part of the "head of State"), Abensour calls the institutive or constitutive subject the "total *demos*."[31] On the one hand, he relates it to Marx's thesis (once again produced through a reversal of Hegel's formulations) according to which, in the history of modern States, it is "legislative power" that has "brought about all of the great, organic, universal revolutions" (in opposition to "petty revolutions"—that is, mere reactions), and that, consequently, it is this power which, presenting itself as the representative of the totality of the people, *precedes* in right and in fact the constitution rather than simply forming its organ or legislating by its authorization. On the other hand, he relates it to the idea that the conflicts of civil society with itself, which, in the final analysis, originate in the "religion of private property," and for which the modern "political" State offers nothing more than a formal solution (catering to its own particular, bureaucratic interests), bear witness to the possibility of a *true democracy* (or of a nonstatist and nonrepresentative "democracy against the State") in which legislative power is "realized" by "abolishing itself"—that is, transforming itself into an *association*.[32] What Abensour calls the "Machiavellian moment" in Marx is the process that leads the people beyond *the State's formalization of social conflicts* (and thus beyond the bureaucratic control over the community political action, for which Hegel was the apologist) on the basis of the very potentiality that makes it exist through the history of revolutions. In other words, it is the possibility of thinking an autonomous political practice that is not subjected to a sovereign instance, whether it be transcendental or immanent, and that "institutes the social" in permanent fashion instead of reflecting passively upon the divisions thereof: "Marx, in a spirit akin to Machiavelli's . . . wants to acquaint us with the 'milieu proper to politics,' to help us think the essence of the political realm and bring out its particularity" (which lies neither in the State nor in Society).[33] Going down the narrow path between anarchism (to which one may attach the contemporaneous propositions of Moses Hess) and a socialism of labor that would absorb the political within "the administration of things" (as the Saint-Simonian school advances), Marx would like to make the emancipation of the popular subject into the permanent public place for its self-constitution, the upsurge of the "generic" dimension of human existence.

Abensour is well aware of the difficulties of interpretation that surround this figure of the subject—which finally underlies all the questions relating to "true democracy" and the possibility of thinking a nonstate politics. This is why, in the final pages of his essay, he finds it necessary to explain that Marx lacks the critical element to be found in Machiavelli in the form of a "finitude" essential to the thinking of the political. This is due to Marx's inability to think the people as a "totality" without, by the same token, ascribing to it the characteristic of *unity*:

There is no getting around the fact that Marx nonetheless thinks true democracy according to a model of unity, and that the self-identity of the people structures the 1843 Critique from beginning to end. In this respect, Marx's conception of democracy is at odds with a theory of democracy as a form of society that welcomes social division, and that distinguishes itself precisely by recognizing the legitimacy of conflict in society.

It seems a chasm is here deepened . . . between Marx and Machiavelli . . . he sees unity simply as a positive good, and does not appear to suspect either a link between certain forms of unity and despotism, or inversely links between social division, the rise of conflict, and liberty.[34]

It seems to me that the difficulty might be reformulated by saying that, in Marx's theorization of 1843, despite its critical function (or perhaps because of it—that is, because of the way in which he thinks this function starting from the Hegelian idea and its reversal), the *demos* as an essentially *full* or *effective* subject is—by default or excess, as it were—permanently menaced by two symmetrical dangers.[35] On the one hand, this subject remains *virtual*, projecting itself beyond the forms of its existence in the "pit" of contradictions that beset the political State, or as a movement beyond the divisions of society produced by private property, which Marx did not yet call the "class struggle" and whose modalities remain entirely nebulous. In other terms, the *time* of this subject's historical upsurge remains the speculative idea that the "movement of revolutions" will be set off again "from below," an idea that the *Manuscript* also identifies with that of "progress."[36] On the other hand, the same subject tends to appear not as a principle of the State's dissolution but as its inverted image, or at least as the inverted image of its *sovereignty*: not only because Marx upholds the constitutive tradition of the revolutionary people—those who sovereignly rise up "from particularity to domination"[37]—against the Hegelian corporatist compromise between liberalism and monarchy, but also because of people's own "consciousness" of their historical role, without which they could not liberate themselves from the political alienation incarnated by bureaucratic mechanisms of representation.

Proletarians: The Subject as Empty

What I would now like to suggest is that, in his "messianic moment," Marx does not properly resolve these aporias (which are perhaps inherent to any thought of democratization as an "uninterrupted" historical movement) but rather displaces them from one extreme to the other. Indeed, he confers on the proletariat, whose name is revindicated for the first time in this text, ontological characteristics and a historical function that are in many respects exactly the opposite of those that I have just elaborated following Abensour's lead: not those of a "full subject" but rather of an "empty subject," or even a *subject as void*. Nonetheless, this void, copiously expressed by the "negative" formulations in the *Einleitung* (first of all, that of the "dissolution" of civil-bourgeois society within the being of the proletariat, immediately assimilable to political nothingness) is in no way deprived of *practical* determinations. On the contrary, perhaps, this void is what allows certain dimensions of practice—understood as the revolutionary transformation of existing conditions—to be thought as such, albeit in a form that might be called "impolitical." This becomes apparent, it seems to me, at two points, where the discourse of the *Einleitung* sharply contrasts with that of the *Manuscript of 1843*.

It becomes apparent in the way in which the *Einleitung* represents revolutionary temporality, elevating to the level of structural generality what first seems to be a contingent exception: the "political delay" of Germany in the *Vormärz* years, and thus the anachronism that characterizes its both lagging and necessary relation to European evolution. Better, the *Einleitung* makes this contingency and this exception into the very structure of historicity, since it is what makes it possible to understand how a force of the past (or coming from the past) might be in a position to carry humanity into the future. It is tempting to claim that, in Marx's description, irreducible to any logic of progress (even "dialectical"), much as the proletariat is the "social class that does not belong to society," Germany is "a historical nation that does not belong to history"; and that, in the case of the German proletariat, these two negative determinations are one and the same. Because Germany, in a certain sense, "has no present," but rather crystallizes in aberrant fashion a "prehistory" and a "posthistory," it already represents the future at the heart of the past; it can only enter into the movement of history by exploding the "limits" of all its previous evolutions, which are the limits of politics as such ("*Deutschland als der zu einer eigenen Welt konstituierte Mangel der politischen Gegenwart wird die spezifisch deutschen Schranken nicht niederwerfen können, ohne die allgemeine Schranke der politischen Gegenwart niederzuwerfen*").[38] We now know that this condensation of delay and advance in the structure of the revolutionary event will be periodically reaffirmed in the Marxist tradition, sometimes as a programmatic thesis (Lenin on the Russian Revolution and, after him, the "Third World" Marxists), and sometimes as the matrix of a nonlinear and thus nondeterminist "concept of historical time," founded on the idea of "non-contemporaneity" to oneself (surprisingly, a concept that Ernst Bloch and Louis Althusser have in common: see *The Heritage of Our Time* [1935] and *For Marx* [1965]).[39]

It is also apparent in the way in which the *Einleitung* thinks the relation of the proletariat to philosophy through the famous metaphor of the "head" and the "heart," the metaphor that responds to what Marx calls the "principal difficulty" (*Hauptschwierigkeit*) facing the idea of a "radical German revolution": the absence of any "material base" for the theory of human emancipation to grab hold of, so that philosophy might become, in turn, a historical force after "overturning" the critique of religious authority into the critique of human alienation. "Just as philosophy finds its material weapons in the proletariat, so the proletariat finds its intellectual weapons in philosophy . . . The head of this emancipation is philosophy, its heart the proletariat."[40] Once again, these formulations must be interpreted in a context, or rather in a series of contexts. They have often been compared, in order to underscore the astonishing coincidence of terminology and date, to Auguste Comte's theses from the same year on the "alliance of the proletarians and philosophy."[41] On a formal level, however, it is just as interesting to compare them to the Kantian conception of transcendental synthesis ("Philosophy cannot realize itself without the sublation of the proletariat, and the proletariat cannot sublate itself with the realization of philosophy").[42] Undoubtedly, Marx's text represents the application, on this formal level, of an old philosophical schema designed to think the relation between the body and the soul, or the matter and the form, and thus the constitution of individuality, and which can be transferred to the intelligible and the sensible, the concept and intuition, theory and practice. The point is, however, that the "heart" is not exactly the same as the "body" (although a revealing lapsus among commentators has operated this substitution).[43] And what Marx seeks to think, or to designate allegorically, is less the *constitution of an individuality* (or a collective subjectivity endowed at once with matter and form) than *the fact of a historical intervention* resulting from the conjunction, on a world scale, of "consciousness" and "suffering" (or, at least, the imminence of this fact).[44] In this theorization of the overturning of passivity into activity, which is itself the heart of the messianic moment, "praxis" is thus not merely *one side* of the synthesis, but rather the *result* of the conjunction of the two conditions of possibility for action, each one of which in itself is mere passivity, or, yet again, a lack. The event (which Marx compares to a "the lightning of thought," *Blitz des Gedanken*[45]) no longer pertains to the order of representation but would rather constitute the limit thereof, the point of reality that dissolves the forms of representation, in the political no less than the metaphysical sense ("*die faktische Auflösung dieser Weltordnung*").[46]

The messianic moment is thus nothing other, in a certain sense, than the flipside or counterpart of the Machiavellian moment as soon as the latter gives rise to an aporia that does not simply concern the possibility of thinking politics beyond or even against the State, but rather the representation of the "political subject" to whom state action must be imputed, and who must be represented both as a totality (the people) and as a lack (the people of the people, always still to come).[47] It would certainly be erroneous to believe that the formulations which I have presented in this essay—so characteristic of the conjuncture of 1844, when Marx "changed place," in every sense of the expression—represent an endpoint. But it would also be erroneous to believe that the theoretical "differential" to which they bear witness is destined to disappear: on the contrary, one might advance the hypothesis that it will never cease to deepen, if only because of the persistent difficulty for Marxism to characterize the "class struggle" (compared in *The Communist Manifesto* of 1847 to a declared or undeclared "civil war") either as "politics" or as "nonpolitical" or "apolitical."[48] As for the messianic side of the definition of the proletariat, when it tends to gives way to a more "positive" definition of the working class or the "class of workers" (*Arbeiterklasse*) in relation to the mechanism of exploitation of labor power and the organization of surplus labor, it shifts onto the apocalyptic representation of the final conflict between revolution and counterrevolution, induced by state suppression of the popular and proletarian insurrections of the nineteenth century (see *The Class Struggle in France, The 18th Brumaire of Louis Bonaparte*). We can thus understand, it seems to me, both the interest and the limits of presenting Marx's theory as a philosophy of history that makes its own use of Hegel's secularized version of "salvation history," less to provide a realist equivalent than to intensify its "eschatological tension."[49] This presentation designates the place—or one of the places—of the discursive operations that Marx implemented, but it simplifies their stakes and, in a certain fashion, inverts their intentions by gathering them under the global category of "religion." In his construction (which is necessarily, at the same time, a deconstruction) of the "empty" figure of the revolutionary subject, given over to the "dissolution" of a world, Marx must encounter religious discourse and mobilize the resources of a "political theology." It is clear, however, to my eyes at least, that he immediately exceeds these resources with a surfeit of immanence—or better, *actuality*.

SEVEN

Zur Sache Selbst: The Common and the Universal
in Hegel's *Phenomenology of Spirit*

Certain great commentators on Hegel's *Phenomenology of Spirit* (Kojève, Marcuse, Lukács), in part inspired by Marxism and Existentialism, built their interpretations around the statement that defines spiritual "substance" (*Substanz*) as a "work" (*Werk*) resulting from *the activity of all and each* (*das Tun aller und jeder*).[1] Sartre should also be included, since one section of the *Critique of Dialectical Reason* comprises an explicit allusion to the "animal regime of spirit" and could be read as a gigantic attempt, in permanent altercation with Hegel, to reformulate the dialectic of "action in common" as the collectivized (and thus alienated) individual praxis which founds the passage from experience to historicity.[2] These commentators thus powerfully demonstrated that there is a reflection on *historicity* at the heart of the dialectic of "self-consciousness" and "praxis," such that the 1807 treatise would become an originary moment and permanent reference point for contemporary philosophy. An opposing strain of commentary, however, prolonging Hegelian discourse in the mode of "deconstruction," would attempt to *separate* the notions of *community* (or being-in-common) and *work* (or action, as the production of a work). I am obviously thinking about the thematic of the "inoperative community" developed by Jean-Luc Nancy on the basis of Bataille and Blanchot (who himself invented "inoperativity"), and about its echoes in Derrida's work.[3] The text that will form the "junction" between these differing readings of Hegel is Blanchot's essay, "Literature and the Right to Death," which explicitly refers back to Kojève, but—reprising the interpretation of the *geistiges Tierreich* as a satire of the world of "intellectuals"—displaces the dialectic from the "deception" inherent to the Thing itself toward writing and its capacity to "destroy language as we know it," thereby arriving at a reversal of the Hegelian interpretation of the Terror.[4]

In the present chapter, referring obliquely to these debates, I would like—in very schematic fashion—to outline a structural interpretation of the Hegelian statement (which I will designate as *TAJ*) and its function within the *Phenomenology*, which I hope will result in a better understanding of what at the heart of the "system," and sometimes against it, constitutes the irreducible singularity of this work. When I speak of the *Phenomenology*, what I mean, of course, is the 1807 text. The question of how Hegel revised this text in order to include it in the *Encyclopedia* as a "moment" of much reduced scope and different objectives, as well as the correlative question of how the writing of the text during the years 1806–7 somehow "escaped" its initial plan, are the object of numerous, ultimately inconclusive discussions.[5]

The Divided Center of the Phenomenology

Let us establish, first of all, that this stylized utterance (in accordance with Hegel's very characteristic writing habits, especially in the *Phenomenology*)[6] does indeed occupy a central place within the text, on the basis of which it would be possible to grasp its entire organization (naturally, not the only such basis, since other commentators have begun elsewhere, but it does, I believe, make visible a decisive problem that would otherwise remain occulted). I will proceed in two phases: first, I distinguish the contexts of this utterance, interpreting their interrelations; and then I signal certain of the significant correlatives of the idea.

The expression das *Tun aller und jeder* occurs at the end of Chapter V, Section C, §a ("The spiritual animal kingdom and deceit, or the 'matter in hand' itself"), and it is almost immediately taken up again in the Introduction to Chapter VI ("Spirit," *der Geist*). It thus encircles what might be considered *the principal break* in the construction of the work: that which operates the transition from "individual" or purely reflexive figures of consciousness, containing reminiscences of transcendental philosophy (perception, understanding, self-consciousness, reason), to "collective" or "historical" (*weltgeschichtlich*) figures (the ethical world, law, culture [*Bildung*], morality, religion). I speak of a break, but, of course, what's at stake is also a transition, which takes the form of an inversion (*Wendepunkt des Ganzen*, Otto Pöggeler writes). When consciousness manifests itself as "spirit" (*Geist*), it is tempting to characterize the viewpoint that it attains as "superior" or the "surpassing" of a previous viewpoint, namely that of "reason" (*Vernunft*): with this inversion, in fact, spirit "comes home to itself," actualizing in some sense what Hölderlin called a *vaterländische Umkehr*.[7] Nonetheless, we should not hasten to read this transition as a simple movement: the idea of an activity or an operation (*Tat, Tun*) that would be indivisibly attributable to the collective subject and to each singular subject (*aller und jeder*), or that is subjectively appropriable in two modalities *at the same time* (the collective and the singular), certainly holds the key to this transition. The discussion of the implications of this movement will show that it entails a complexity and a reversibility that will never cease affecting what Hegel, in 1807, calls the "concept" with a sort of inner aporia.

The formula *TAJ* first arises in the *System der Sittlichkeit* from 1802–3 to designate the contents of the "relation" that constitutes *the ethical life of the people* as a "totality" going beyond the opposition between indifference and difference.[8] Against the Kantian withdrawal into the "thing in itself" (*Ding an sich*), the *Science of Logic* ("General Concept of Logic"), in turn, will make the *Sache* or the "thing itself" into the very unity of thought and being and the presupposition of the dialectical movement. To my knowledge, only the *Phenomenology of Spirit* institutes a close reciprocity between these two themes.[9] In this text, *TAJ* first occurs during Hegel's elaboration of the strange figure designated as "the thing itself" (*die Sache selbst*), itself typical of what Hegel calls "individuality that knows itself to be real" (or that has the concept of its reality within itself). In other words, *living* individuality. Through this question—according to a tradition that is coextensive with the whole history of metaphysics—Hegel seeks to pose the problem of an *internal* relation between the whole and its parts. This relation in not accessible to external observation, not even if it is rational (*die beobachtende Vernunft*), for which the parts and the whole are represented as objectivities given in themselves. It implies an ability to rise to the viewpoint of a subjectivity that actually effectuates or realizes (*verwirklicht*) the objective unity that it reflects within its representation, and thereby presents itself for itself as an active or practical subjectivity. The result of its activity is what Hegel calls *Werk*, an operation or work—and a category upon which, as we know, the *Phenomenology* will endow with extreme breadth, since it will comprise labor (*Arbeit*) and artistic creation (*Kunst*), the transformation of external matter (Aristotelian *poiesis*) as well as the "formation" of self (which in Hegel becomes *Bildung*). This activity culminates with a return to the theme of the "political work of art," which comes from Hegel's Frankfurt period, in the description of "the religion of art" as the collective action of the ancient City that transforms the spirit of a people into a "spiritual work of art" (*geistiges Kunstwerk*) by means of public ceremonies and theatrical representations.[10]

However, in order for the *Werk*, both individualized and individualizing, to be thinkable in the universal modality demanded by reason (first emergence, in the Hegelian development, of the idea of a *concrete universality*), it must be conceived as a *cooperation*, the collaboration of multiple individualities upon a *common* work. In other terms, the work or operation of practical reason is for Hegel (as for all German Idealism from Kant to Marx) the immanent passage beyond its own particularity. At this moment, Hegel plays upon the etymological connotations of the German *Allgemeinheit* as that which is *all(en) gemein*— the common to all or the "being in common" of all—or, more exactly, he makes them serve his theoretical project.[11] By the same token, Hegel's work demands that we conceive a *transindividuality*, what he calls a "reciprocal fusion" or an "interpenetration" (*Durchdringung*) of particular actions. Unlike the figures of moral action evoked immediately beforehand (in particular, the "law of the heart"), which rely upon the opposition between the sphere of subjective "ends" and the objective "world" to which any means of achieving these ends would belong, the *Werk* presents itself (at least ideally) as a reconciliation of the subject and the object that would find both its ends and its means within itself.

Of course, what I have just summarized as the effective passage beyond a certain representative abstraction is, for Hegel, merely a problem, the solution of which is initially affected by a fundamental contradiction. For, the production of a universally valid work (in this sense, necessary or "true") on the basis of individual actions demands that the particularity of these actions be sacrificed, that their very contingency be negated (or that, as Hegel says, what is vanishing about them should itself vanish: "the vanishing of the vanishing," *Verschwinden des Verschwindens*),[12] and this cannot be taken for granted. It is the principle of this negation of the negation, as well as the contradiction that it entails, that Hegel designates using the coded expression *die Sache selbst*, which will be periodically repeated throughout the *Phenomenology*, and which he explicates by positing the schema of an "action of all and each" (indivisibly collective and particular):

> Consciousness experiences both sides as equally essential moments, and in doing so learns what the nature of the Thing itself really is, viz. that it is neither merely something which stands opposed to action in general, and to individual action, nor action which stands opposed to a continuing being and which would be the free *genus* of these moments as its *species* (*die von diesen Momenten als ihren Arten freie Gattung*). Rather is its nature such that its *being* is the *action* of the *single* individual and of all individuals and whose action is immediately *for others*, or is a Thing itself and is such only as *the action of all and each*: the essence which is the essence of all beings, viz. the *spiritual essence* (*das Wesen, welches das Wesen aller Wesen, das geistige Wesen ist*). Consciousness learns that no one of these moments is *subject*, but rather gets dissolved in the *universal Thing itself* (*in der allgemeinen Sache selbst*); the moments of the individuality which for the unthinkingness (*Gedankenlosigkeit*) of this consciousness were as good as a subject, one after the other coalesce into simple individuality, which, as *this* individuality, is at the same time immediately universal (*als diese ebenso unmittelbar allgemein*).[13]

As opposed to a complete *dissolution* of being in common into a confluence of separate individuals, which Hegel had previously characterized in Hobbesian terms as a "struggle of all against one another" (*ein allgemeiner Widerstand und Bekämpfung aller gegeneinander*),[14] but also as an immediate "vision" or intuition (*Anschauen*) of *the other as fellow man* in the unity of a given substantial community,[15] the "Thing itself" now in question is presented as a mediation, a system of determinate relations in which the negative does real work in view of an immanent end. The individualities have to sacrifice their particularity in order to construct what becomes their *own* universal end, but they cannot do so without conflict. This requires actual power, not just an ideality. In his translation of the *Phenomenology*, Jean-Pierre Lefebvre offers the best French translation for the term *Sache* (which Hegel carefully distinguishes from *Dingheit*, simple material thinghood): *cause commune* or *affaire commune* ("common cause" or "common concern"). Through one of the Latin usages of *res* (a judicial "cause"), as Jean Hyppolite suggests, Hegel rediscovers the Greek *pragma*. Accordingly, he shows how this problematic displaces the Aristotelian question of what is "proper to man": in order for individual activity to communicate with the universal, the *ergon idion*, the work proper to man that is also "particular work," must also become a *koinon ergon*, a "common cause actualizing itself in a work."[16] It is then a matter of testing the efficaciousness of this process and its immanence to action. In the section of the

Phenomenology on "individuality," Hegel examines this problem in two successive modalities, whose general significance we will discuss in a moment: (1) in terms of the appropriation of the result of activity of some by others and vice versa (consequently indissociable from an expropriation or an alienation, which Hegel describes as reciprocal "deceit," calling to mind the "invisible hand of the market" in Adam Smith and his contemporaries in the "Scottish Enlightenment," whom he studied assiduously);[17] (2) in quasi-Rousseauist or Kantian terms of obligation (*Pflicht*) and "general will" whereby the common cause is uttered (and puts itself to the test) as the universality of the *law*.

In the first pages of the following chapter (VI), however, the formula *TAJ* is reprised in a new context: the horizon of reason has been succeeded by that of spirit, which, in accordance with what is sometimes called *transcendental historicity*,[18] Hegel will forward the concept of the movement of the whole, leading from the "ethical world" of the city and its internal strife to the Protestant Reformation's "moral vision of the world" (thus following an order a bit different from the one which he will canonize later in his philosophy of "objective spirit"), and differentiating itself by itself through crises and resolutions. This movement also represents the entry into the sphere where subjectivity assumes a social and institutional character.[19] "Substance" and "subject" become categories that presuppose one another, which corresponds descriptively to the fact that every figure presented in the *Phenomenology* exhibits the certitudes of self-consciousnesses that think and live the finalities of historical institutions but also their conflicts (in particular, those institutions that carry forth the very utterance of the universal, as is clearly seen in the case of antagonisms between political law and religious law, or between faith and the enlightenment of secular reason).[20] Correlatively, a reflexive and critical thought measures from within the "truth" of these laws, their validity and their pretention to embody the absolute. Hegel then writes the following, which contains "in itself" the entire program for the second part of his work:

> But Spirit is the *actuality* of [ethical] substance. It is the *self* of actual consciousness to which it stands opposed, or rather which it opposes to itself as an objective, actual *world*, but a world which has completely lost the meaning for the self of something alien to it, just as the self has completely lost the meaning of a being-for-self separated from the world, whether dependent on it or not (*abhängigen oder unabhängigen Fürsichseins*). Spirit, being the substance and the universal, self-identical, and abiding essence, is the unmoved solid *ground* (*Grund*) and *starting-point* for the action of all, and it is their purpose and goal (*Zweck und Ziel*), the in-itself of every self-consciousness expressed in thought. This substance is equally the universal *work* produced by the action of all and each as their unity and identity (*Einheit und Gleichheit*), for it is the being-for-self, the self, action (*das Fürsichsein, das Selbst, das Tun*). As *substance*, Spirit is unshaken righteous self-identity (*Sichselbstgleichheit*); but as being-for-self it is a fragmented being, self-sacrificing and benevolent, in which each accomplishes his own work, rends asunder the universal being, and takes from it his own share (*an dem Jeder sein eigenes Werk vollbringt, das allgemeine Sein zerreisst und sich seinen Teil davon nimmt*). This resolving of the essence into individuals is precisely the *moment* of the action and the self of all; it is the movement and soul of substance and the resultant universal being. Just because it is a being that is resolved in the self, it is not a dead essence, but is *actual* and *alive*.[21]

Between the two instances of *TAJ* or in the gap of this "reiteration," what has taken place? Nothing and everything. A minimal interpretation would be content with suggesting that Hegel, in accordance with the mode of exposition he practiced throughout the *Phenomenology*, signals the dialectical "transitions" by elaborating each particular figure on the basis of the *recapitulation* of previous determinations, thereby showing their insufficiency and the necessity of going beyond them; and, correlatively, he characterizes each new moment as being "in itself" the internalization or recollection (*Er-innerung*) of the path traversed up to that point and the resolution of its contradictions. But this interpretation is far too formal. It does not take into account either the *strategic* character of this determinate transition (of which it would be possible to claim, without exaggeration, that it is the *Transition as such* that the *Phenomenology* would like to account for, since it marks the arrival on scene of its subject-object—spirit—as "Self" or *Selbst*) or the highly *problematic* character of the figure (or the practical schema) designated as *TAJ* and the internal vacillation that affects it. This is why I prefer the riskier interpretation that claims that the idea of *TAJ* is *divided* between its two successive utterances: as the *Sache selbst* or the "common cause" of individualities, and as Geist thinking itself and actualizing itself historically "all by itself." The *TAJ* is thus presented *"en abyme"* as the *very difference* between the two viewpoints of the "Thing" and "Spirit," or rather their *différance* in movement (the Derridian formulation here seems to me to be unavoidable). This *différance*, when we grasp on the level of Hegelian writing itself, also procures the possibility of designating what is at stake in the organization of the *Phenomenology* and constitutes its irreducible specificity: not only the result to which it leads (a certain neutralization of the antitheses of metaphysics, beginning with that of individual and collective), but also the strange modality in which it thinks—that of an opening and perhaps an aporia, intentionally reiterated at the end of the work under the paradoxical name of "absolute knowledge" (*das absolute Wissen*). The lesson of the *Phenomenology*, grasped anew on the basis of this turning point at which *Geist* must arise from the "thing itself" of which it is the spirit, as its truth and the transcendence of its contradictions, but also as its other, would thus be the following: the end of the movement of spirit (the becoming-subject of substance and the becoming substantial of the subject or self-consciousness), incorporating individual actions into the actualization of their common cause in a durable historical and universal figure of the universal, represents an end (or a teleological *process*) with any truly representable "end."[22]

I will now try to clarify and specify these propositions by underscoring three correlative developments convoked by the letter of our utterance. For lack of space, I can offer, at the very most, no more than a program for discussions to come.

The Equation of the Subject and Its Transformations

In his commentary on the *Phenomenology*, to which (no mystery here) my entire discussion owes quite a lot, Jean Hyppolite showed the necessity of closely associating the interpretation of *TAJ* with that of another set of remarkable utterances that punctuate the advance of the *Phenomenology*, working through a series of dialectical transformations and explications of the virtualities of the equation of the subject: "*Ich =Ich*" (or "*Ich gleich Ich*"). As we know, Hegel initially presents this equation (invented by Fichte) as the expression of a formalism of reflection as conceived by transcendental philosophy (that is, identifying the condition of possibility of experience with an "empty" or "tautological" form of self-consciousness, a mere *formal identity* that remains exterior to this experience, or independent from its phenomenal content); but, at the end of his work, he presents it as the expression of the self-determination of the *Selbst* (or of the spirit that has reached "absolute" knowledge of itself) that is foreign to no experiential content and that incorporates them all within its concept because it has acquired the ability to think itself *in its other* (natural, historical, and cultural objectivity) and has found the means to make this other inseparable from the meaning of a reflection upon its own differences, following the double movement of *Ent-äusserung* and *Er-innerung*. Between the extremes of this dramatic reversal, however, Hegel was not content periodically to repeat the statement of the equation *Ich =Ich* in order to register its changes of reference. He also proposed *transformations* of the equation, which are really alienations of it or ways for the "self" to contemplate itself outside itself, or to contemplate its own hither side (what happens, as the Introduction says, "behind the back" of consciousness).

In a play of alternating voices, the first of these transformations utters the reciprocity between the singular and the plural internal to the very unity of the subject: "*Ich, das Wir, und Wir, das Ich ist*," or (this) I that We are, (this) We that I am. Hyppolite initially reconstitutes this formula underlying the explication of spirit as "the operation of all and each." It allows him to make Hegel into the first philosopher to pose as such the question of *intersubjectivity*:

> Spirit here appears as the experience of a *cogitamus* and no longer merely that of a *cogito*. It presupposes both the transcendence of individual consciousness and the maintenance of their diversity within substance. . . . The universal self-consciousness which Hegel claims to reach, then, is not Kant's "I think in general" but human reality as an *intersubjectivity*, a we which alone is concrete. Spirit is this we precisely insofar as it simultaneously brings about the unity and separation of I's.[23]

In fact, the stylized expression "*Ich, das Wir, und Wir, das Ich ist*" (IWWI) never figures explicitly in the introduction to the chapter on spirit in which Hegel reprises the characterization of universal work as *TAJ*; but Hyppolite rightly inserts it or reads it between the lines, because it is what had earlier permitted Hegel to announce, from a distance, in the introduction to the chapter on the "Truth of Self-Certainty," the *coming on stage* of the concept of spirit as a structure of "recognition":

> A self-consciousness, in being an object, is just as much "I" as "object." With this, we already have before us the Notion of Spirit. What still lies ahead for consciousness is the experience of what Spirit is—the absolute substance which is the unity of the different independent self-consciousnesses which, in their opposition, enjoy perfect freedom and independence: "I" that is a "We" and "We" that is an "I." It is in self-consciousness, in the Notion of Spirit, that consciousness first finds its turning-point, where it leaves behind it the colorful show of the sensuous here-and-now and the nightlike void of the supersensible beyond, and steps out into the spiritual daylight of the present.[24]

But the joint reference to the "category" institutes a chiasmus of this formula (IWWI) with another remarkable variant of the equation of the subject, which is no less decisive than the other one even though its signification is apparently opposed to it, since the "other" who it posits in reciprocity with the subject in itself (*Ich*) is not also a subject (plural: *Wir*) but rather all the forms of objectivity encountered in experience, here designated as *being* (*Sein*). What Hegel calls the "category"—as we know, displacing Kantian terminology— is precisely the universal that is common to rational thought and to the "things" or "objects" that it comes to know; a universal that, he claims, cannot really exist if reason remains "observing," exterior to objects, but only if it becomes practical, internalizing things within the movement of its activity.[25] In the section on individuality, the "category" is thus identified with the *Sache selbst*, the "common cause" or "matter-at-hand" of agents who contribute to one and the same work; and, accordingly, the *TAJ* is defined as "being that is the I or the I that is being" (*das Sein, das Ich, oder Ich, das Sein ist*) (SIIS).[26]

In sum, what Hyppolite suggests is that the two formulas should be combined or fused: what makes it that *being is the I* is that *the I is we* (in the operation of all and each); but this must also be understood as the becoming-subject "for itself" of the community in action—*a we that is an I*—that as such acquires effective reality or actively actualizes itself in being (in things): it is then *I who am being* (SIWWIS). *TAJ* thus expresses well, in the modality of the "Thing itself" or alternatively in that of communal action, and in the modality of "spirit" or historicity, one and the same reflexivity, one and the same *Selbst* in itself and for itself; but the experiential reality or the phenomenological truth of this conceptual identity still hangs, precisely, upon the possibility of speaking or practicing *identically*, or *in-differently*, the language of the "we" and that of "being."

Das All-Gemeine: *The Dialectic of the Common and the Universal*

Will this ever actually be possible? It is doubtful, especially if what is posited speculatively and programmatically is not confused with what Hegel actually *presents*, inscribes, and describes. More precisely, it is evident that Hegel's solution consists in a repetition of the problem (which is properly what logicians call an "aporia"). This is my second observation. Once again, I am obliged to stop short: let us simply say that the *Phenomenology*, from its central "turning point" onward, can be read as a long inquiry into the possibility of *universalizing being in common* and, correlatively, of *instituting the universal* within the framework and modality of a community; and that the series of "historical" (or, as we would say today, "cultural") figures which this work reconstructs constitute so many attempts to actualize this possibility. This double movement is necessary for such a universal (moral, juridical, religious, political, pedagogic, and scientific) to become *concrete*, thereby going beyond mere utopia or pure ideality, and for a community truly to possess a power of unification within itself capable of transcending the differences and conflicts that it subsumes, not by repressing them outside itself but rather by "reflecting" them as *its* differences.

Formally, it is easy to see that the "We" of *Ich, das Wir, und Wir, das Ich ist*, which emerges from the schema of "recognition," is aligned with community, while the "being" of *Sein, das Ich, und Ich, das Sein ist,* is a transcendental determination of the "abstract" universal.[27] The forms in which Hegel describes the tension between these poles throughout Chapters VI and VII of the *Phenomenology*—from the figure of the "ethical world" (the Greek city, as interpreted by the tragedians) to that of "revealed religion" (Christianity founding the invisible unity of the church upon the event of the "death of God")—are clearly not at all uniform: they would not constitute interchangeable illustrations of the same, a priori "dialectical" contradiction." On the contrary, each time, in their modalities and in what has been called their *peripateticism* taking into account the narrative element that becomes essential to the phenomenological development and that delves extensively into the experience of literature (or extracts the truth inherent to its fictions), these figures depend upon *discourses* in which subjects who are also historical actors express their consciousness of the universal (and continue to express it in the speculative or spiritual present wherein all of these singular discourses subsist together, "for us"). It is as if, each time, Hegel, playing with repetitions and differences, *redefines the very terms of this recurrent problem*, a problem that historically confronts every "community" and determines every actual utterance of the universal. Rigorously speaking, the words of *community* (*Gemeinschaft, Gemeinwesen, Gemeinde*) and *universality* (*Allgemeinheit,* which must also be associated with all the terminology of the infinite and essence) are ultimately "historical" terms whose meaning can never be separated from the determinate discourses in which we find them (law, belief, science, culture). And the transhistorical metalanguage that we use to generalize the idea of this conflict only has philosophical meaning if it is returned to the heart of the singular configurations of spirit. But this metalanguage can still help to understand what is repeated in these configurations by means of an incessant variation, acquiring the sense of an ever renewed and always aborted (or always premature) attempt *to escape the finitude of representation, or to "liberate" its pure concept.*[28] This attempt alone is liable to produce the adequation of the common and the universal (to make *Allgemeinheit* into a "spirit" that would be *allen-gemein,* "common to all"). Were this attempt to succeed, however, it would deprive the concept of any dimension of experience or historicity and thus come to contradict itself.

What is repeated is initially the fact that, in general, the dialectic of community and universality constitutes the sublation (*Aufhebung*) of the dialectic which organized all the figures from the first part of the *Phenomenology*: that of "certainty" (*Gewissheit*) and "truth" (*Wahrheit*), or of the subjectivity and objectivity of the true. This sublation allows the earlier dialectic to be historically refounded, since community always entails a dimension of collective certainty that the individual must be able to experience; and the universal entails a truth claim that must be manifested in the objectivity of institutions and social practices. The irreducible tension between community and universality, which procures a substantial and not merely subjective existence for the difference between certainty and truth, does not abolish this difference, but rather effectively dissolves the appearance that it is simply a contingent or psychological difference, identifying it with a negativity inherent to the very movement of the spirit, that is with its reality. Once again, we must speak of *différance*: certainty as identical to truth and "differing" from it (or "deferring" its apparition), the community as identical to the universal and "differing" from it (or "deferring" its actualization)—in other words, *nothing less than spirit* as such.

Further, what is repeated is the fact that—by a sort of tragic fate of communities—the moment when they come closest to instituting universality, inventing for the universal an original historical or cultural language (for example, that of the "law" for the city, or that of intelligence or critical reason for the Enlightenment, or that of the "Protestant" moral vision of the world), is also the moment when they once again experience their particularity or finitude, as the other side of their claim to universality, the mark of the internal contradictions that might lead them to collapse. To utter the universal, or, more precisely, to utter it "for all," *sub specie universitatis*, is, by the same token, to determine it and thus to particularize it. Inversely—a very profound idea—due to the fact that the particularity of a determinate utterance of the universal does not exist "in itself," but only *for another*, in a conflictual relation or an essential process of *scission*, there is in the particularity *some universal* which exceeds it. The determination of the universal that is historically uttered (or proclaimed) within the framework of a community, therefore, does not destroy it, but rather exhibits an identity of opposites or an inherent paradox, which, in a sense, constitutes the very power of the demand—or the desire—for universality.[29]

This is also the point at which Hegel, pushing this dialectic to the extreme and producing its most striking developments, shows how the quest for universality (at once living *desire* and *spiritual* exigency) leads to the inversion of communal forms of consciousness into at least their apparent opposites. This quest also engenders the existential *solitude* that leads the subject back to the "empty" form of its tautology, or to *noncommunity* made up of incommunicable individualities: the "abstract person" under the law of the State, the "negative" and self-destructive freedom of the revolutionary Terror, the narcissism of the "beautiful soul," and the "unhappy consciousness" upheld by revealed religion and the theology of the "death of God."

Finally, all of these repetitions lead to a rather troubling "endpoint": the fact that the "absolute knowledge" in which truth and certainty would finally be reunited and become exactly coextensive (expressed in the terminological passage from consciousness, *Bewusstsein*, to "self," *Selbst*, and from experience, *Erfahrung*, to "knowledge," *Wissen*) *does not correspond to any noticeable, nameable, or describable figure of community*. In Hegel, actually, there is no "community of absolute knowledge"—such as Spinoza's philosophical community of *sapientes*, who have achieved the "third kind of knowledge," even if this community is highly paradoxical. In terms of Kojève's reading of Hegel, which, at this point, brings into the *Phenomenology* another component of the Hegelian system (interpreting it in his own way), the problem would be articulated thus: the discourse of "absolute knowledge" would be implicitly the discourse of the State in its complete form (or of the "end of history" in the concrete universality of the State, with its citizens as so many "functionaries"). Indeed, the (modern) State dissolves within itself all communities. Hyppolite, for his part, after rightfully noting that Hegel renounced the attempt to found a "philosophy of the Church" or a "philosophy of humanity" on the basis of a phenomenology of religious consciousness, concludes that, as a "moment of history reconciling this temporal moment with a truth in itself atemporal"—that is, the adequation of the common and the universal—absolute knowledge is "so vague" that it excludes any determinate solution.[30] Inscribed in this indetermination, he suggests, are *several* "post-Hegelianisms," in particular that of

Marx ("to change the world," taking up the idea of the *Sache selbst* within the perspective of revolutionary action). But, to remain faithful to Hegel, Hyppolite prefers to interrogate the idea of *logic* as the sublation of *phenomenology*—which comes down to following the path that Hegel began to indicate in the Preface to the *Phenomenology*, composed after the fact, but also to exiting the question that animated the entire work.[31]

This absence or perhaps this negation of community corresponding to "absolute knowledge," if this can still be considered a figure of spirit in the earlier sense, can be interpreted (in what is even the most traditional interpretation) as a *transcendence of the universal* with respect to the finitude of community (and therefore of the institution, representation, temporality, and conflictuality), which would be the ultimate result of the Hegelian process: Historical configurations of spirit would only designate, at bottom, so many errors or aborted attempts, even if they are inevitable, to grasp the unrepresentable within the framework of representation. Under these conditions, the *Phenomenology* would be not only a critical or even deconstructive enterprise but also an attempt to eliminate history through history, a veritable game of retrospective massacre. Once the endpoint had been reached, "there was history in the past, but there will be no further," as Marx would say in another context . . . And since the question of community, in the actual variety of its forms, constitutes the central stake of a reflection on historicity, it would be, in the final analysis, a *refutation of the very idea of community*, or of its intrinsic "falsity," in the name of an absolute knowledge "without community."

But since Hegel never fails to repeat that the "self" of spirit or absolute knowledge has no other content that the internalization (*Erinnerung*) of all these external figures by one another, and that, besides, the chapter on "absolute knowledge" does not contain any *positive* definition of the universal, but only a *passage to the limit* of the representative and temporal conditions of historicity, it is necessary to attempt another reading. This reading consists in supposing that the final "truth" of the *Phenomenology*, as I said earlier, possesses an aporetic character, which belongs precisely to the perpetual *différance* of the common and the universal, and which renders them forever indissociable and always re-opens a gap at their very heart. It is this *insurmountability of finitude*, in the multiplicity of its recurrent forms (for, in the final analysis, the "lesson" of the *Phenomenology*'s *grand narrative* is much rather the heterogeneous *contemporaneity* of the figures of spirit, no matter the initial "moment" of their upsurge, or that of their surmounting within a linear temporality),[32] that Hegel sought to illustrate, making universality into the at once immanent and impossible "end" of every community. Let us note that such a reading is not simply skeptical, but above all *critical*, much more profoundly than the simple "Platonic" antithesis between the speculative concept and representation; for, such a reading implicitly describes (or even demonstrates) the genesis of the *illusion of the absolute* specific to collective individualities throughout history (whence they derive their subjective consistency). This illusion is engendered precisely by the certainty which each such individuality cherishes (and which is the very condition of their transindividual possibility: *Ich, das Wir, und Wir das Ich ist*) of attaining and instituting the universal, or of having "finally found" (as Marx will say later about the Commune), the formula, different from all others, of the correspondence between community and universality as such. This reading also makes it possible to understand in what sense the *Phenomenology*, more than any of Hegel's other works, constitutes the model for the great projects of "ideology critique," or of *the effect of ideological misrecognition* as such. But this point calls for another discussion.

The Conflict of Universalities and Community Without Community

But this principle of the gap between community and universality, which organizes the whole second part of the *Phenomenology* (and thus orients its construction from the outset, or even encapsulates this construction within itself) could also be discussed otherwise, in such a manner that we rediscover the importance of *TAJ*. This will be my final observation. If we concede that there is no metalanguage of the absolute, or "universality of the universal" to measure the "community of community," one Platonic idea used to measure another Platonic idea (the True and the Good?), we might still forge the hypothesis of a *conflict of universalities* or "principles" of universalization (such as the republican *law* that applies equally to all, the *value* of commodities or general equivalent, rational or experimental scientific *truth*, the human *person*), and of a *conflict of communitarian principles*, whose manifestations the *Phenomenology* would unfold in such a way that each one represents for the other (in the hollow of its finitude) its own *lack of being*, or its *inability to attain the absolute*. The reason for this conflict does not reside in the fact that each falls short of some distant universal "in itself" (for the absolute, Hegel says, is always already *close by us*, the whole question being *how*), but solely in that the only absolute is contradiction, the work of the negative reflecting itself "for itself."[33]

As I recalled earlier, the schema of the "common cause" (*Sache selbst*), as the activity of all and "identically" of each (*TAJ*), becomes the object of a double elaboration in relation to the theoretical and institutional models that it generalizes and raises to the level of the concept. The passage to the vantage point of *Geist*, which might be expected (and perhaps Hegel expected it himself) to unify these models (or, what comes down to the same thing, to *subordinate* them to one another), actually just sets up their repetition in an amplified form. But the development of spirit in the course of Hegel's writing is not yet without its surprises; for it soon becomes clear that he is obliged to supplement these two models with another (that of "reconciliation" or *Versöhnung*), such that, by the end of the *Phenomenology*, we find not two but *three* typical configurations of being in common, each implying its own definition of individual and collective subjectivity, each striving *to say, to think, and to do* the universal, and nonetheless *failing to grasp* the universality that others present; and this reiterated "contradiction" is the only one that can be called historical. Let us attempt to clarify this last point.

It is obviously very striking that, in the section of the *Phenomenology* on "individuality," Hegel could uphold for so long the symmetry between the two configurations of the "work" (*Werk*), which, on the one hand, is associated with a "civil society" founded upon the division of labor and competition, in which the activity of particular individuals—each acting as a "party" (*Partei*) to his own interest—complete one another and can be exchanged against one another; and, on the other hand, with the idea of a "general will" or "pure absolute will of all" (*der absolute reine Wille Aller*), whose ultimate consequence is the actual sacrifice of the particular will and the production of a pure obedience to the law, distinct from "service" (*Dienst*) to a master. What thus emerges from Hegel's text is the fundamental *equivocity* of the idea of *TAJ*, in which the *Phenomenology* will tarry for a long while; which means that it will develop the means to explore "phenomenologically" the structures of this equivocity, describing its behavior, its signification and value, its traces in history, and the existential crises that it occasions. By the same token, the *Phenomenology* is an unequaled interpretation of the anthropological dilemmas of a modernity torn between "possessive" individuality and "republican" citizenship, so that it should come as no surprise that its effects are legible throughout contemporary thought, even beyond the intellectual traditions that consider themselves Hegelian.[34]

We should not be misled at this point by the fact that the "moments" of the dialectic appear to occur in *linear succession*. It is true that, *at first*, Hegel proposes a phenomenology of the "animal kingdom of spirit," which revolves around a mechanism of alienation or "deception" (which is first the *self-deception* of individuals who are contributing to the production of a common social value—their own cooperation—even as they believe that they are doing no more than pursuing their own particular or egoistic goals), before *defining* the Thing itself as "spiritual essence" immanent to the activity of all and each, and only then moves on to a phenomenology of the operations of the "legislative reason" and "verifying reason" which function to assemble the individual self-consciousnesses around a sovereign representation of the *law* by means of imperatives or rational determinations of "virtuous" action. The law thus appears as the horizon at which the contradictions of commerce will be surmounted. But—even as it puts in place the fundamental principle of civil liberty or the self-determination of the members of the community, "the obedience of self-consciousness is not the serving of a master whose commands were arbitrary, and in which it would not recognize itself"[35]—the critical tonality of this last description (allusively taking aim at Rousseau and Kant) is so strong in the text, often verging on derision, that we cannot but wonder whether the conclusion to draw is truly that the general will represents the surmounting of the invisible hand of the market. Isn't it rather that the latter (at least at this stage) entails a much higher *degree of reality*, or of the inscription of subjectivity in *being*, than the politico-moral principle of the will, even if (according to Hegel) it always poses an unresolved "spiritual" problem of the representation or the consciousness of its result (or of the "cause" that it serves)? In reality, it seems to me that what Hegel wants to say is that the categories of "real" universality (value, exchange) as well as those of "symbolic" universality (law, equality) *both institute communities* in which the difference between the part and the whole, the individual and the collective is mediated or relativized, and yet always fails to make this community into a living "individuality of individualities" in which consciousness would no longer see anything in its own actions except the inner expression of a being in common conceived as a unique and absolute essence.[36]

It is instructive to compare this development with later Hegel texts in which the expression *die Sache selbst* occasionally reappears (but without being explicated as *TAJ*), in particular the famous passage in the *Introduction to Lectures on the Philosophy of History* on the "cunning of reason":

> In fulfilling their grand designs as necessitated by the universal spirit (*dem allgemeinen Geist notwendig*), such world-historical individuals (*die welthistorischen Menschen*) not only attained personal satisfaction but also acquired new external characteristics in the process. The end they achieved was also their own end (*das Ihrige*), the hero himself is inseparable from the cause he promoted, for both of these were satisfied (*die Sache und der Held für sich, beides wird befriedigt*). . . . Nevertheless, since the subjective factor is of a purely particular character, and since its ends are purely finite and individual, it must necessarily subordinate itself to the universal. But in so far as it implements the Idea, it must also help to sustain the underlying substance.[37]

The process at stake here does not correspond exactly to the functioning of civil society in general, although it does rely upon the schema of the contradiction between the representation that individuals have of their own interests, the desire that moves them, or the "position" that they take, and the result to which they actually contribute, involuntarily. More specifically, it is the historical action of "great men" who, through the "crimes" inspired by their ambitions, become the *instruments* of the progress of civilization or of the "universal spirit." However, the notion of the instrumentality of human actions is profoundly foreign to the exposition of the *Phenomenology*; and the same goes for the teleology known as "cunning," which makes no room for the problem of the construction of a community, but wholly inscribes individual actions (independently of their "consciousness" and their reciprocal perception or "recognition") into the spheres of the particular and the universal, whose hierarchical articulation is assured by the State as the historical representative of the spirit of the people. By contrast, we see that the "thing" in the *Phenomenology*, as Hyppolite correctly understood, pertains to the modalities of intersubjectivity, which cannot be divided (at least immediately) into the particular and the universal, but rather can be, in turn, "particular" or "universal" for one another. What could be shown, in particular, is the thread that links this nonhierarchical treatment of the opposition between the *Phenomenology*'s two specific modes of assembling individuals to the opening of Max Weber's *Economy and Society* that treats *Vergesellschaftung* ("socialization") and *Vergemeinschaftung* ("communization") as two modes of regulating conflict (designated as *Kampf*) that are both concurrent and constantly overdetermining one another.[38]

This is why, when Hegel folds the problematic of the *TAJ* into the horizon of *spirit* that knows itself as a historical and collective universal, we see this debate *begin anew* in a certain manner, within a different order and on a vaster scale, perhaps several times over: Herein lies the whole question of *alienation* or *foreignness* (*Entfremdung*) inscribed at the heart of Chapter VI, in which, I suggest (without justifying it), one might include not only the paradigmatic development on *culture* (*Bildung*), with its characteristic conflict between the universals of faith and reason, which both tend to "form the individual" with an emphasis upon his intellectualization and autonomization, but also the *entire set* of the figures of social conscience from the ancient city to modern morality, or from the submission to destiny to submission to duty. Nonetheless, this development has a surprise in store for us: It opens toward the upsurge of a third collective schema, as foreign to the reciprocal action of material interests as to the unity of "legislative" wills. As a result, Hegel will *defer* the moment of "absolute knowledge" for one entire section of the book, even as the long development on "morality" and the consciousness of evil *already* reached, in the same text, the "yes of reconciliation" (*das versöhnende Ja*) and the identity of opposites:

> The word of reconciliation is the *objectively* existent Spirit (*der daseinende Geist*), which beholds the pure knowledge of itself *qua universal* essence, in its opposite, in the pure knowledge of itself qua absolutely self-contained and exclusive *singularity*—a reciprocal recognition which is *absolute* spirit (*ein gegenseitiges Anerkennen, welches absolute Geist ist*).[39]

This leaves a choice between two interpretations: (1) the study of religious community, which is the object of Chapter VII, corresponds to the necessity of *positively enrooting* the ultimate critique of representation in a description of religious consciousness (which, in a sense, forms the triumph of this critique since it pertains to an infinitely more concrete, and *sensible* representative universe than that of morality and its abstractions: good and evil . . .); (2) this study corresponds to the necessity of critiquing the most powerful *absolute pretention* of all, that of religion. An old debate: Hegel the Christian (or spiritualist) versus Hegel the atheist (or even materialist). . . . Everything depends on knowing whether "absolute spirit" should be understood as the same thing, in substance, as "absolute knowledge." Or rather as its radical other: both the closest and furthest. In any event, however, it is necessary for Hegel—phenomenologically—to *problematize* the notion of reconciliation, and the notion of community spirit that it implies, instead of accepting it as the "final word." And this would require nothing less than the complete rewriting of the "history of religions" (which goes back as far as primitive peoples and the ancient Empires, to the cult of sunlight and the invention of sacred statuary) in order to inscribe within the very genesis of religion the irreducible specificity of the "religious community" that culminates in "the Christ," the institution of the common (*Gemeinde* rather than *Gemeinwesen* or *Gemeinschaft*, which Hegel used previously) on the basis of the symbolic event of the "death of the man-god." The semantic opposition between *Gemeinde* and *Gemeinschaft* also subtends the long development on "community"—that is, the theory of the Church as the "realm of Spirit" that concludes the theoretical introduction to the section on "Complete or Manifest Religion" in *Lectures on the Philosophy of Religion*. But more time would be required to examine the (considerable) distance between these two viewpoints.

Nothing is more equivocal, in reality, than the notion of religion, which is why this genesis entails, under the heading of spirit, a new interpretation of most of the previously traversed moments that seeks to inscribe them within the perspective of a "manifestation of the divine," or of a "representation of representation," as the mediation necessary for consciousness of the absolute. The composition and publication of the *Phenomenology* slightly predates those of the magisterial work that, within the German (and European) university, will found the history of religions as an anthropological discipline: Friedrich Creuzer, *Symbolik und Mythologie der Alten Völker, besonders der Griechen* (1810). On the other hand, Hegel's work is contemporary with the at once historical and speculative work of Schelling on the philosophy of mythology and revelation (*Philosophy and Religion*, 1804), from whom, since their early association with Hölderlin, Hegel continually sought to diverge. This divergence is marked here, in particular, by the *total elision* of the notion of "monotheism"—central to Schelling's work—in Hegelian discourse.[40]

It is obviously not possible for me to offer, here and now, a reading of this long historico-dialectical discourse on religion and the modes of religious consciousness. But I would like to conclude by asking how its ultimate result, the invisible community of Christ, might be connected to the problematic of *Tun aller und jeder*, which, as I have attempted to show, bears within itself the possibility of the two previous communities (that might also be called *commerce* and *association*) and their respective institutions of the universal. What "universal," then, would be instituted by "absolute religion," which makes the world and its violence or its inherent "evil" into the means of the collective redemption of men? Is it a new sort of activity, producing a "work" such as utility or the law? Or rather, does it entail the vanishing of this practical schematism? Does there remain a *trace* or a "remainder" of the *Sache selbst* in this reconciliation? Consequently, what is to be done with this community that arises *over and above* the institution, or with this excess of community that revelation institutes in relation to the alternatives of *TAJ*?

The answer to this question, I think, is that we are confronted here with a *paradoxical community*, if it is measured in terms of the foregoing criteria; and that, in this sense, Hegel wished precisely to carry these criteria to their limit.[41] At first sight, the faithful, who believe at once in the reality of the event represented as death and the resurrection of the man-god, do not "do" anything; they are not "active," not even in the sense of a *Bildung* (the sociopolitical question of religious education and its project of producing moral individuals has been carefully examined elsewhere). They do no more than "appropriate" a negative idea, that of the death of God, or even the simple, paradoxical utterance: "God himself is dead." However, it is possible to say that, by relating to the event of his death in the mode transfiguration ("death becomes transfigured from its immediate meaning, viz. the nonbeing of this particular individual, into the universality of Spirit who dwells in His community, dies in it every day, and is daily resurrected"),[42] the faithful *make themselves into "Christ"* and correlatively make Christ into the community (or the spirit of the community—rather than, we note, his "body," unless this opposition is no longer relevant here: conciliated or reconciled in a "mystical" fashion). The schema of this community is neither reciprocal utility nor an association of wills; it is truly a *unification of consciousnesses* that rests upon the way in which each subject or subjectivity "revives within himself" the same symbolic event, or operates on his own account the same "resurrection" or rebirth. The commentators who have studied the sources of the Hegelian problematic of *Versöhnung*, comparing it to the theological discourse and scripture[43]—in particular, Françoise Dastur and Christoph Jamme—have showed that it harkens back to the *Vereinigung* elaborated by Hölderlin at the time of his friendship and collaboration with Hegel. In reality, Hölderlin's philosophical novel, too, finishes upon the "word" (or the "dictum": *Wort*) of reconciliation: "Like lovers' quarrels are the dissonances of the world. Reconciliation is there, even in the midst of strife, and all things that are parted find one another again (*Wie der Zwist der Liebenden, sind die Dissonanzen der Welt. Versöhnung ist mitten im Streit und alles Getrennte findet sich wieder*)."[44]

But wouldn't this spiritual unification, from another viewpoint that quite simply represents its critical underside, actually be a *dissociation* or a *disjunction*, meaning that religion *radically isolates subjects in their very communion*, forming a sort of "community without community" (which is to be distinguished from the *absence of community*, or of *determinate* community, that I associate with "absolute knowledge")? What Hegel describes as a third collective schema of recognition, or of the identification of the "I" and the "We," is a shared certainty with an at once sensible and supersensible character, a "distribution of certainty" that each individual would effect in a certain way on his own, in a purely internal fashion. This sharing unifies him invisibly with everyone. In other terms, each and all are now one, just as they are one with the "resurrected" Christ. But Hegel hastens to tell us that his representation remains always again *severed* between the present of faith and the to-come of eschatological waiting, the presence and the absence by my side of this other whom I am "in spirit." This representation is thus further away than ever, in a sense, from a "satisfaction" or a *repose* of spirit within its own substance. This is why the affirmative reconciliation (the *Ja der Versöhnung*) that singularizes it gives rise, upon its intimate withdrawal, to the infinite recurrence of the "unhappy consciousness," which, from then on, will be associated with the negativity of an experience of imminent death that was never neutralized, but rather generalized and "placed in common," by the religious work of symbolization, the ultimate and perhaps the most powerful form of representation or utterance *sub specie universitatis*:

> The death of this representation contains, therefore, at the same time the death of *the abstraction of the divine Being* which is not posited as Self. That death is the painful feeling that God Himself is dead. This hard saying is the expression of innermost simple self-knowledge, the return of consciousness into the depths of the night in which I = I, a night which no longer distinguishes or knows anything outside of it. This feeling is, in fact, the loss of substance and of its appearance over against consciousness; but it is at the same time the pure subjectivity of substance, or the pure certainty of itself which is lacked when it was object, or the immediate, or pure essence.[45]

Versöhnung or "religious" community (which I called excessive) must always yet again prevail over its contrary, unhappy consciousness; it is always yet again to be made or operated beyond itself, because of the void (or the lack) opened up at the heart of its presence. However, beyond itself there is properly speaking *nothing*—nothing, at least, that can be said and be lived "in common."[46] This "residual" (or "final," fully accomplished) negativity is, for Hegel, the very *experience* of all and each—whereby it is also radically distinguished from Irony and the Terror.

It is much too early, obviously, to "conclude" an inquiry of this type. My only intention, today, was to show, on the level of the text of the *Phenomenology* itself, that a certain constellation of terms and syntagms that are totally idiomatic and, for the most part, specific to this work—the *Sache selbst*, the *Tun aller und jeder*, and the equations of the type, "*Ich, das Wir, und Wir, das Ich ist*" and "*Sein, das Ich, und Ich, das Sein ist*" (and even *Sie als Mich, Mich als Sie*)—dialectically organize its construction around the elaboration of one and the same problem, which concerns the *inadequation* (surprisingly resistant to being surmounted, but never fixed once and for all in a formulaic opposition) of the correlative notions of community and universality in their multiple historical figures. This problem, I have suggested, is destined in Hegel (within this state of his thought, in many respects still the most provocative, that which remains for us the most *urgent and timely*) to remain open or unsolvable. This is the aporia that is registered, or better, *thought as such* in the form of "absolute knowledge," which elevates it above particular forms of representation in order to conceive it in general as finitude and historicity. Should this aporia come as a surprise? Hegel, of course, did not uphold it as such when, later (as already the Preface, composed after the fact, bears witness) he will consider the developments of the *Phenomenology* to be both his greatest achievement as a writer and his deepest morass as a philosopher. . . . It is not likely, today, that we would define exactly the same figures of community (or inversely those of solitude) by privileging the same categories, or that we would associate them with the same names of the universal, because, among other reasons, we see now what Hegel could not see: the "unpredictable" excesses of the logics of the marketplace, the law, and communion, which take shape *behind their backs*, and the "geophilosophical" (Western) limits of a certain experience of spirit (or sense). But it is probable, if we attempt to rethink the "thing itself" in a conceptual, concrete, and critical fashion, that we could hardly find anything better to propose philosophically than such an open multiplicity of conflicting utterances. We "Hegelians," therefore . . .

Men, Armies, Peoples: Tolstoy and the Subject of War

This chapter reprises several elements from a course taught at the University of California, Irvine, entitled "Politics as War, War as Politics" (January–March 2006). In this course, I opened to discussion the claim, frequent in contemporary discourse, that the "new wars," which have broken out since the end of the Cold War and collapse of the world divided into "blocks" determined at the end of World War Two, would be essentially "non-Clausewitzian"—in that their protagonists are no longer solely territorial nation-states, operating by means of regular armies, or that they present an essential dissymmetry, or that they make it impossible clearly to distinguish politically or juridically between the "state of war" and the "state of peace," to list a number of characteristics that are more or less inevitably bound up with one another.[1] Such a claim supposes that there is in Clausewitz an analytic concept or perhaps an ideal type of war in the Weberian sense, both inseparable from certain historical conditions and formalizable (even axiomatizable), on the basis of which it would be possible to elaborate comparisons, distinctions, and conjectures.

A first epistemological question arises at this point, the question whether this concept or ideal type exists as such in Clausewitz himself, and in what form, or whether it is the result of a secondary elaboration, taking up and making use of the work (notoriously unfinished, and perhaps, on certain points, contradictory) of the author of *Vom Kriege* on the basis of questions that pertain to an ulterior epoch and the logical or political exigencies that it imposes—if need be, measuring the distance between the one and other.[2] But this first question, as Raymond Aron notably affirmed in his extensive comments on Tolstoy in his book on Clausewitz, raises a second, less epistemological than genealogical. With

Claude Lefort's famous book on Machiavelli in mind, it might be called the question of "Clausewitz in the making" [*le travail de l'oeuvre Clausewitz*]; and it would bear upon the *becoming* of Clausewitz's formulations, as well as the concepts and theses that they call forth in a long series of reprisals, transformations, and inversions, which began upon the (posthumous) publication of this author's works and continue until this day. Ineluctably, this question makes our theorizations of politics and war into *post-Clausewitzian* conceptions, even when they go against Clausewitz's formulations or call into question the presuppositions of his work.

Within this genealogy, it is important to include Leo Tolstoy's novel *War and Peace*, which first appeared in five installments from 1865 to 1869, universally considered one of the masterpieces of world literature, not only because Tolstoy used elements from Clausewitz in preparation for writing the novel,[3] but more specifically because the narrative echoes one of Clausewitz's most famous theses: that which concerns the "strategic superiority of defense over offense." Tolstoy's new interpretation of this thesis goes back, in a certain sense, to the "source" of its elaboration in order to draw new philosophical consequences from it.[4]

Novel and Antinovel

Before any reading or rereading of Tolstoy's work, it would be useful to recall a few aspects of the author's biography and chronology. First of all, as a member of the high Russian nobility and thus destined for service in the Russian Empire in one capacity or another, Tolstoy himself spent many years as a professional soldier. His experiences of war span the colonial wars in the Caucasus[5] (1851–52) to the Crimean War (1855), from which he derived his famous story about the siege of Sebastopol. These extremely violent experiences gradually wrought a change in his attitude toward war. But this change is overdetermined by the way in which he considered the question of patriotism and the "historical mission of Russia" during the European conjuncture of 1850–60. *War and Peace* was elaborated and published at the historical moment when a new "Napoleon"—reissuing the coup d'état of the "18th Brumaire"—came to power in France, and, on its side, the Russian Empire, under the reigns of Alexander II and Nicolas I, positioned itself as the guarantor of the European order established at the 1815 Congress of Vienna. The Crimean War ended in defeat for Russia at the hands of the Franco-English alliance, in the wake of battles that shocked contemporary witnesses because of the high numbers of dead and the cruelty of the wounds that resulted from the revolution in weapons technology. This is the background of the theoretical debates about the "efficient causes" of history and the relationship between wars and the politics of nationalities and the confrontation of Empires. At this period, Tolstoy was not at all a *pacifist* or an advocate for *nonviolence* (which implies the nonresistance of a people to invasion or foreign aggression) in the sense that he would theorize during his final years; but he was radically opposed to Russian expansionism and hegemonism in Europe; and, in the service of this position, he enlisted a political and philosophical thesis on the "patriotic war" of 1812. For Tolstoy, this war ended in 1813, upon the complete liberation of Russian soil by Kutuzov's victorious armies; or rather, this war changed nature at the moment when, under a new commander, the Russian troops and their allies attempted to pursue Napoleon back to Paris, and thereby to modify the regime of the French Empire, in accordance with a movement of the flux and reflux of "historical" masses, the concept of which he would develop in *War and Peace*. The relationship between his positions on contemporary history and the philosophical lesson that he attempts to derive from his reconstitution of the great war through which the Russian nation succeeded in saving itself from annihilation, however, is not simple: Rather than serve as an illustration of previously elaborated theses, the novel is the means to pose problems of the relation between wars, the existence of peoples, and the sense of history as they emerge from the contemporary epoch. This is why it is impossible to dissociate the two orders of equally complex questions raised, on the one hand, by the ideology (or the philosophy) of Tolstoy, and, on the other hand, the mode of the writing of *War and Peace* that also governs its mode of reading. The first set of questions addresses the heterogeneous complex of populism and patriotism (very far from "Slavophilia," albeit founded upon the hypothesis of an essential difference between East and West of the European continent), "anarchism," and historical "fatalism" that preceded Tolstoy's invention of a "New Christianity" and his conversion to a prophetism of nonviolence in which the law of love must prevail over the law of war.[6] The second set addresses the thorny problem of knowing "who speaks" in the text of the "novel." How to interpret the combination of an apparently classical novelistic narrative, in which characters presented in a more or less favorable light utter opinions or incarnate attitudes about life and politics, and a theoretical reflection presented in an impersonal fashion, and thus credited to the "author" and thus supposed to represent his own philosophy? Between the one and the other, should we see the complementarity of an abstract thesis and its narrative "incarnation"? Or should we look for a more complex, more uncertain relationship between them, pertaining to what Bakhtin will call "dialogism," thereby making writing not into the simple transcription of a theory but the experience of exploring it and calling it into question?

This question, of course, is relevant not only to the work of Tolstoy. It concerns the form of the modern novel as such to the extent that it pertains to what Pierre Macherey calls "literary philosophy," in which *War and Peace* would seem to be situated somewhere between Victor Hugo's *Les Misérables* (written between 1845 and 1862) and Robert Musil's *The Man Without Qualities* (Book One, the only one published, appeared in 1930 and 1933), by way of rival Dostoevsky's *The Brothers Karamazov* (1880).[7] But it was perhaps Tolstoy's work in particular that, for the first time, as soon as it was published, raised the question of the "genre" in relation to that of "thought" or "lesson": Initially, it took the form of "stylistic" critiques denouncing the *heterogeneity* of the book and its departures from the models established by novelists in the previous half of the nineteenth century, to which Tolstoy would be led to respond in an appendix added to the complete edition of the novel in which he lays claim to a specifically "Russian" manner of setting aside the laws of the genre (which might also be interpreted as the claim to a "nonnovel" or an "antinovel," were it not that, in a sense, *War and Peace* is also, as Lukács asserted, the *perfect novel*); and later it took the form of a long series of reactions from critics and writers (Virginia Woolf)[8] who would compare the novel to Homer (whose legacy Tolstoy also claimed for himself), to Hegel, or to Proudhon (who provided the very title of the novel, "borrowed" from his 1861 work, *La Guerre et la Paix: Recherches sur le principe et la constitution du droit des gens*).

Two schemas of analysis seem to me useful for understanding the philosophical problems that this book poses. The first is what Pierre Macherey presented through an engagement with Tolstoy and Lenin's reading of him in his book *A Theory of Literary Production* (1965).[9] Borrowing Lenin's image of the "broken mirror" in which the Russian Revolution (of 1905) was reflected and divided into contradictory "flashes," Macherey examines the literary effect produced by inserting or encasing ideological utterances within the framework of a narrative that distributes them among a multiplicity of subjects; and he characterizes it as the critical effect of "distancing" with respect to ideological content. This interpretation applies to the "characters" and their problematic relationship to the identity of the author; but it apparently neglects to account for precisely that which constitutes the singularity of Tolstoy's novel (and, in the eyes of many early readers, its "weakness"), the exposition—resumed and interrupted many times over, culminating in the second part of the Epilogue, and thus placed in the position of the "conclusion"—of the theory of the forces of history applied to Russian national war, which is not encased within a narrative (and which is generally condemned by literary critics who see it as a sequence of "dissertations" and by philosophers who see it as a compendium of confused opinions on free will and necessity).

More recently, Gary Saul Morson has independently returned to this question in what is certainly one of the best commentaries on Tolstoy's novel, *Hidden in Plain View: Narrative and Creative Potentials in War and Peace*.[10] He begins with Bakhtin's critique of Tolstoy as the representative of a "monological" writing, opposed to Dostoevsky as the virtuoso of "dialogical" writing, and he attempts to turn this critique against its author, precisely by studying dialogism or the play of plural voices at work in Tolstoy's novel that makes it impossible to attribute to any among them the privilege of objectivity or neutrality, but rather transfers meaning (or the effect of meaning) into their permanent conflict. The sole exception to this dialogism would seem to be what Morson calls "absolute language," that which Tolstoy employs precisely to present his philosophy and his interpretation of Russian history—what might also be called a "subjectless" language, the language whereby the subject absents itself from the fiction because it exactly coincides with the author's language. But it remains possible to surmount this apparent exteriority, which produces the illusion that the novel mechanically juxtaposes two genres or two styles. Indeed, not only can the "absolute" language be identified with a *supplementary voice*, which would mix up with the fictive voices and enter into dialogue with them (thereby illustrating what Morson calls "the dialogue of the author with the novel"), but it can also be supposed that Tolstoy sought to institute a permanent confrontation (a "dialogue," if one prefers) between the novel's "theory" and its "fiction" in a sort of *hermeneutic circle*, in which the discourse on causality, on meaning and the absence of meaning in history, and the narration of collective and individual "lives" in search of happiness, or salvation, function as touchstones for one another. The relation between these elements cannot be characterized as subsumption. Far from it. On the contrary, there is a critical reciprocity between them, internal to the very writing of the novel, which absorbs the philosophical genre and, to this precise extent, goes beyond its own limitations as a "fiction." This is the direction one must follow to understand, on the one hand, how *War and Peace* could figure, in the eyes of certain contemporary historians, as a "precursor" to more recent visions of "total history"[11]; and, on the other hand, how to identify the questions situated in the interstice, or the point of divergence, between the two types of discourse (the question of the reciprocity of private lives and public or political history; that of the interpenetration of "war" and "peace," apparently contradictory states whose dilemma only exists precisely within a "total" experience that alternates or imbricates them).

It is within the perspective of generalized dialogism, which includes the discourse or the voice of "theory" itself, that I will seek to interpret *the politics of war* as Tolstoy thinks it in *War and Peace*, or, more precisely, the "impolitics" of this novel (employing an expression accredited by the works of Roberto Esposito). What I mean by this is indeed an inversion of the interpretation of war as the "continuation of politics" in the Clausewitzian sense, but one that is paradoxically effectuated through generalizing and pushing to the extreme a certain Clausewitzian thesis: the famous "superiority of defensive strategy" over offensive, which will also figure at the heart of Mao Zedong's very different reprisal of this thesis within the framework of his own theory of the "war of the people." In Tolstoy's conception—so much so that Morson can speak of a "negative history (or historiography)"—defensive strategy is transformed (or retransformed, if we admit that Clausewitz's model for his own theorization was precisely Kutuzov's apparent "inaction" in the Russian campaign) into *negative strategy*, which calls into question the conceptions of power or the *archè*, as much in the sense of a chain of command as of the influence of will upon the course of history. And this leads (via a reflection on the significance of partisan war as the privileged form of popular war) to rethinking also in negative fashion the relationship between the "people" and the "army," which is essential to Clausewitz's idea of war as the "continuation of politics by other means." In the final analysis, precisely because it constitutes the principal force of history, the "people," which manifests itself in the crucial ordeal of the war of liberation or of public salvation, is deprived of the metaphysical characteristics of the subject, even if its collective essence emerges symbolically within an episode that might be called "mystical"—the providential encounter between the hero Pierre Bezukhov and the peasant Platon Karataev, reduced to a state of equality through the common condition of imprisonment, exposed to the extreme violence of men and nature.[12] Let us attempt to explicate these four points in succession to demonstrate their connection.

Negative History

Morson develops at length the idea of negative history and puts it in relation to Tolstoy's critical use of his Russian and French historiographical sources. This idea pertains, first of all, to the work of deconstruction that Tolstoy undertakes with regard to the relations between the course of war and the episodes into which it is typically divided (notably, battles, supposed "decisive," which constitute the pivot upon which Clausewitz's rational analysis of war turns). On the basis of this work, it entails the critical interrogation of this rationality itself, concentrated in the figure of the "duel" or the confrontation between adversaries who can be represented as symmetrical collective actors. Consequently, the only "laws" of war (and, by the same token, of history) would be "negative," inseparable from the refutation of the illusions that it inevitably produces itself.[13]

Within Tolstoy's denunciation of "positive" historiography, it is important to note the extraordinary richness of information that he used for his "total" reconstitution of the conditions of Russian politics at the turn of the century: from the history of freemasonry to that of the reformism of the Speransky government, from the morals of court life, the city, and the country, to the details of party struggles and foreign alliances and so on. But all of this information, which turns upon the articulation of military episodes, strategies, the moments and the aims of political action and their material and moral repercussions upon society and the subjects who constitute it, ultimately leads to a double denunciation of the illusions of narrative: the illusions of the "heroic war" waged by a nation considered as a single historical individual, and those of "the rational conduct of war." Heroism is dissolved by the observation of the suffering of individuals; it only belongs to the humble, "negligible or insignificant men." While armies neutralize or destroy one another on the battlefield of mass war, critical observation, always subjective, discerns a few improbable and unperceived "decisive" actors (the type of which is Captain Tushin with his little battery at the skirmish at Schöngrabern). As for the idea of the rational or rationalizable conduct of war, undertaken by generals who draw up battle plans and therefore believe that they are in control of war, or can rectify its execution, thereby operating a synthesis of concept and intuition, it is a mystification. The same goes for the idea of military "genius," which is a mere appearance resulting from pure luck. Tolstoy affords himself the luxury of making appear on the future battlefield of Borodino a German officer by the name of Clausewitz, whose prognostics will be rigorously refuted by real developments. This is what Tolstoy sets out to show by establishing, on the basis of his engagement with sources, a map of the unfolding of this battle that contradicts that of the history manuals.[14] This critique is linked to a generalized "perspectivism" (considered untenable by most commentators: Aron, Gallie, Münkler) realized by attributing the perception of events only to the characters who participate in them and who thus have a necessarily partial and contradictory view of them. Tolstoy remarks in the appendix to *War and Peace*, added in order to respond to his critics, that enemies never see the same "battle" in the same way, even when it comes to judging who won (the example of Borodino, known in French historiography by the name of the Battle of the Moskova, is eloquent in this regard). But, in reality, this false perception or false consciousness is part of the "relation" as such: it can be generalized to war itself as a doubly dissymmetrical relation. *At bottom, the adversaries or the "actors" never wage the same war at the same time*; it might even be said that they are "noncontemporaries." And this is why war is indeed a relation; it is not a duel in which attack and defense would be the mirror images of one another. The idea of calculating or anticipating the actions or reactions of the adversary in order to oppose them with a determinate strategy or tactics is devoid of sense. War is thus not anything like a "game." This favorite metaphor of war theorists—*Kriegsspiel*—is in reality the result of a rationalization of the element of subjective symmetry that resides within the passions of war, and, in particular, within *hostility*. And even on this point, it would be necessary to introduce a critical correction (see the crucial episode of the destruction of Smolensk, after the French invasion: III.ii.2).

From this critique, we move, by way of a further generalization, to a calling into question of the categories of "consciousness" and "will," and, consequently, of the metaphysics of freedom and necessity. Tolstoy proposes a "fusion" of these two elements in a schema of the "differential" of historical movement—which he claims, in his correspondence, to have borrowed from Pogodine, the Russian "Schellingian" philosopher.[15] Consequently—and we will never cease discovering new equivalents and consequences of this thesis—it is not "politics," understood as an intentional action (*Zweckrational*, as Weber would say, himself a great deployer of the Clausewitzian distinction between the plane of "goals" and that of "ends": *Ziel, Zweck*), which "makes history." It would thus no longer possible pure and simply to adopt a providentialist vision according to which politics is no more than the manifestation of history, such as it was renewed precisely in relation to the great European revolutionary war by one of Tolstoy's inspirations, the "theocrat" Joseph de Maistre.[16] The philosophical comparisons that are most relevant here (but that also serve to mark a distance) are with Spinoza (for his critique of the illusion of free will and its confusion with freedom), and with Hegel (of whom it is difficult to know how much textual knowledge Tolstoy was likely to have gained through the teaching of German philosophy at the Russian universities or through the reading of "Left Hegelians" such as Bakunin or Herzen). It is particularly interesting to compare the theoretical epilogue of *War and Peace* with the final section of Hegel's *Philosophy of Right*: There, where Hegel (briefly) explicates the sublation of politics within a history based on perpetual war and with States (or peoples organized into States) as actors, Tolstoy explicates (at length) the dissolution of politics within a naturalized history whose quasi-law is the infinite cycle of war and peace, and whose quasi-actors are not so much individualized peoples as the elementary components of popular force, the multitude of active and mostly passive comportments of "little men." There is also a comparison between Tolstoy and the post-Hegelian theory of the class struggle as the motor of history that Marx and Engels were developing at the same moment, in which the action of the masses is formally substituted for that of States and great men. At such a price, the subordination of the concept of politics to the concept of history makes it possible to reconstitute a rationality. But this rationality supposes that the masses are not only active but also organized or organizable (which leads to the practical idea of the "party," in the general sense of the term), and that they can be attributed an immanent "intelligence," over against the "personalized intelligence" that for Clausewitz represents the function of the State in war, or a tendency to become "for themselves" conscious of the sense of their own action.

Deconstruction of the Archè

There are thus two complementary illusions—that of the agency of the will and that of the sense of history—the crucial test of which comes in the experience of war. Inverting the sense that his predecessors—whether rationalists or "idealists," philosophers or historians—gave to these illusions, Tolstoy's critique opens toward a generalized calling into question of the privileges of the *archè*, as commandment and as commencement (or decision), which means that his own philosophy as elaborated in the novel would be, in the literal sense of the term, a "theoretical an-archism." This anarchism develops itself on several levels.

The most immediately evident among these levels and the most effective from a literary perspective is the description of the commandants (those whom might generically be called *archontes*), represented in the novel by Alexander and Napoleon and their ministers, counselors, and strategic advisers, who figure as marionettes—that is, as actors who never cease deceiving themselves that they are the ones who make decisions and master the course of things, while, in reality, they are moved by their interests or passions, and, more profoundly, by the effects of the power structures in which they are inserted and of which they serve as agents. Tolstoy suggests that the basis of this determination is the effect of mimetic rivalry or the "duel" between "men of power" themselves, mediated by the admiration that they seek from their subjects, in which they are invested by virtue of the charismatic nature of power. Our reading of the novel must be prudent at this point because its description does not resemble the type of cynical satire or moral pessimism practiced by the materialists in the age of Enlightenment. On the one hand, Tolstoy offers a substantial analysis of the real social stakes of the politics of the State and of the alternative between reform and reaction (his novel is contemporary with the abolition of serfdom and constitutes a taking of position on relations of dependency between the nobility and the peasantry, which must be replaced in order to assure the reconstitution of a mutually beneficial order). On the other hand, the analysis of the patriotic passions and the feelings of personal devotion, or the sacrifice that the person of the leaders inspires in the subjects who make up the people, revealed precisely by wars, cannot be reduced to a theory of mystification or of voluntary servitude. Once again, it is necessary to take into account a dissymmetry, constituted by the authenticity of such feelings on the part of those of experience them and by their mystificatory character for those who inspire them and claim to make use of them.

At bottom, however, the question is about the insufficiency of the concept of "power"—which might be considered the key concept of political thought from the Greeks to the modern confrontation between revolutionaries and antirevolutionaries—to explain the historical enigma par excellence, the movement of the "masses," the fact that a multitude of human beings act at the same moment in the same way, thereby actualizing in practice what Rousseau called the general will, placing it at the root of what "what makes a people a people." In reality, the concept of power is tautological. It projects causes and effects into the abstraction of the "eternal circle."[17] The only way to break this circle, or to exit the tautology, if one wants to avoid deferring to the intervention of a transcendental instance (divine will, Providence), is to extract from the analysis of the effects of power the idea of a *constituent force* that resides in the unconscious movement of the people, or rather, once again, in the differential relation between the movement of the masses and the always conditional effects of direction that they produce, and that seem, in turn, to guide them. In a manner to which, in general, a Marxist might formally subscribe, but also a historian such as Michelet imbued with a national mysticism, Tolstoy thus derives an (essentially negative) "law" which states that the participation and the representation of individuals and the masses in the power "relation" are always in *inverse* proportion to one another. This law, as we shall see, is closely linked to the representation of the historical cycles in which power is caught up, but the principle of which is a quasi-natural succession of war and peace that does not truly have a "subject."

The critique of the idea of the *archè* leads back to the phenomenology of war. This is where Tolstoy radicalizes Clausewitz's idea of the "superiority of defensive strategy," removing it from its context, going back to its historical sources, and pushing it to the extreme. At the center of the description of Napoleon's defeat in Russia is the figure of General Kutuzov and his permanent conflict with the politico-military *establishment* that is nonetheless obliged to trust him at the hour of greatest danger. In the guise of impotence and indecision (which his adversaries hold against him, incapable of understanding his essentially nondiscursive thought or the sources of his energy, which do not reside in his person but in his contact with the people whose strengths and weaknesses he knows well), Kutuzov is actually the only one who can see that *resistance* is not only a "tactic" but also a "strategy," and thus the only one capable of *preparing himself* mentally and materially for long-term resistance, conserving and concentrating his forces. This intelligence of strategic resistance obviously has effects upon the definition of the "political goal of war"; for, it calls into question the instrumental character of war. War can no longer serve as a means to any end whatsoever; or better, as soon as war ceases to manifest itself as a resistance and must become counteroffensive, *and thus offensive*, it must cease or destroy itself. Tolstoy's entire art consists in *delaying the moment when the counteroffensive should begin and thus invert the course of the war*, such that a time lag is produced. It thus offers a sort equivalent to what Clausewitz calls "friction" (a fiction of friction). Upon Napoleon's defeat, or rather his lack of victory at Borodino (followed by the torching of Moscow, which transforms the occupation of the capital, "the seat of power," into a demonstration of impotence), the movement of the masses physically reverses course—that is, the French army stops advancing and begins to retreat while the Russian army puts a halt to its retreat and begins to advance. But only upon reaching the border, the outer edge of the historical territory of the Russian people, does Kutuzov's strategy cease to constitute "resistance," or more generally nonaction (whereupon Kutuzov himself disappears, because he is totally identified with this strategy, nothing more than its instrument). Commentators often refer to this moment when they discuss Tolstoy's use of Clausewitz's descriptions and his interpretation of the new historical figure of the *guerilla* ("small war," invented by the Spaniards fighting against Napoleon) or partisan war, illustrated by the convergence in the novel of "regular" and "irregular" forces respectively commanded by two of its heroes, Denisov and Dolokhov. Guerilla actions (which Tolstoy does not at all idealize, underscoring the cruelty shown by the partisan forces) constitute, in a sense, the moments of offensive tactics subordinated within the grand strategic defensive. The essential point, as we know, is the idea that Kutuzov's genius managed permanently to rein in his generals' temptation to attack the routed French army, because this action would have exhausted his own troops, or resulted in failure, because they were themselves severely weakened. What then becomes decisive is a *negative goal*, accessible only in the form of inaction or nonaction—that is, the preservation of the army's "consistency," or its character as a community founded upon the unity of the "people" of whom it is constituted, in opposition to its *decomposition* in the form of a simple "herd" (a metaphor that Tolstoy draws out at great length, first in relation to the Russian army, routed by the French attack at the battle of Smolensk, and then a second time and on a greater scale, which one might call "total," in relation to the French army and its progressive decomposition during its hasty flight through the Russian winter, marked by the famous Berezina episode).[18] (Re)composition (in popular resistance) or decomposition in being routed, such is the alternative corresponding to the two historical movements of the masses, which determine the political meaning to give to military operations. At the limit, the idea of defensive action joins up with that of inaction; or, more precisely, it makes it necessary to subvert the representations—which might be called "Western"—of effectiveness as the domination of the means and events of war by a voluntary subjectivity that configures them in terms of its own goals.[19]

The Subjectivity of the People and the Encounter Among Its Bearers

It would be tempting to object that, in reality, Tolstoy didn't at all abolish the concept of political subjectivity, that he only transposed the leaders or directors of the State into the collectivity of the people in a democratic-leaning or, tautologically, "populist" fashion, upholding the people and its capacity for historical rebirth as the final instance of explication, and consequently as the constituent power or *the power of power*. It would be vain to contest that this populist strain exists and is even insistent in Tolstoy; but one might also suggest that it is itself submitted to the work of internal critique, by means of a dialogism that ultimately prevents it from producing anew the univocity of the "subject of history." What might appear to be such is, in really, merely a quasi-subject. It is in the description of the relations between the people and the army—that is, two modalities of the existence of the people, as a mass of individuals and as an organized institution—that this question becomes most acute. It became an urgent question, precisely, during the "patriotic" wars of the Revolution and the Empire in which, first on the French side, and then on the German (or Prussian) or, more generally, European side, national defense required that professional armies founded on discipline be replaced with conscript armies founded upon the "moral factor" and enthusiasm for a goal or a leader (or both at once).[20] Clausewitz clearly perceived this revolutionary change and made it the distinctive trait of the emergence of a new form of war, now "absolute" rather than "relative," in which it is the people and not mercenaries who do the fighting; a form of war that concretizes the theoretical hypothesis of a "passage to extremes" in which the very existence of the people (or of their State) is at stake rather than merely the acquisition of one or another competitive advantage (territory, colonies, tribute states). But this change also posed a formidable political difficulty, which Clausewitz attempted to solve by imagining a "fusion" of the old institutional forms of war with their new social and ideological content (i.e., of the bureaucratic power of the State and the nationalism of the masses), for which he never managed to elaborate the definitive formula.[21]

In Tolstoy, there is a critical delimitation of the problem: The army and the people become unified or form a single historical individuality only under determinate conditions, that of a defensive strategy in the service of a negative objective, the liberation of the homeland; and, in the absence of these conditions, this unity dissolves in favor of one of its two constitutive terms—that is, it gives rise to peace or reinstalls the hierarchical appearance of a State power dominating the people by means of the army. But there is also, once again, a "negative" reading of the question that opens the possibility of going beyond it, even if this would entail the interrogation of the accepted concepts of politics. It is not in the power of the State to control or "discipline" the people by compelling it—albeit virtually—to participate in the army or "military service." But it is also not in the power of the people—nor in its interest—to constitute itself a counterpower by spontaneously providing itself with an army or transforming itself into an army. Such a transformation is only the product of exceptional or transitory circumstances.

The most significant moment, once again, is that of the transitional or "differential" form incarnated by the fugitive action of partisan corps, which is never totalizable even while it expresses the essence of the people's capacity for resistance and its maximum effectiveness. In the description that Tolstoy offers of the partisans, in fact, which allows him to insist upon the paradoxical virtues of insubordination, the coordination of their actions is never the result of obedience to a "chain of command" but the omnipresence of an *idea* (that of liberation) coming "from below," along with the luck or fortune of circumstances that favor the cause. We are thus quite far from what with Mao or Guevara—both educated in the Leninist tradition of political organization—will become the discipline of the party at the heart of popular war. Tolstoy fully believes in horizontal coordination; but he also does not hide the fact that it cannot exclude the agency of "private" interests, from vanity to profiteering. The people are constituted in a movement that subtends the great unconscious historical forces. It is, as such, the expression of a "mass movement"; but, on the level of the individual, it is always on the verge of decomposition, or even of turning into its contrary. Its existence, which is metaphysically necessary for history to happen at all, is thus inevitably a matter of miracle.

What takes shape through the vast phenomenology of war as individual and collective ordeal that Tolstoy undertakes in *War and Peace* is an extremely paradoxical and improbable philosophy of the unity of opposites, which might be characterized as a mysticism of immanence, or even a materialist mysticism (if materialism resides precisely in the fact of situating the motor of history in the process of the composition and decomposition of the masses). Not only did Tolstoy assume this extremity, he gave an allegorical representation of it in a central episode (often considered one of the keys to understanding the novel), which also allowed him to keep it at a distance (or to afford us, his readers, such distancing). The episode in question is the encounter between Pierre Bezukhov and the peasant Platon Karataev—who is at once "simple" and "inspired" by popular wisdom. If we consider that Pierre (along with his friend Prince André, destined to die) is the novel's principal male figure, with whom the author multiplies the traits of identification, we can say that the alternative of war and peace plays a role in the three "positive" couples that Pierre spontaneously forms in the course of the novel (in opposition to the negative couple formed with his first wife Hélène, arranged by society): the war couple (or the fraternity in war and politics) that he formed with Prince André; the peace couple and the conjugal love that he formed with Natasha (Prince André's former fiancée); and, between these two couples, the "accidental"—but thereby all the more essential—couple that he formed with Platon.[22]

It would be false to say that this couple has no moral, or even religious value, and no political character. On the contrary, it delivers a truth for politics that is situated in some sense beyond politics or at its extreme edge, which is encountered when institutional bonds are dissolved. Pierre meets Platon and becomes like a brother on the shores of death, in the conditions of deprivation and extreme violence to which Russian prisoners were subjected in the column that the routed French troops dragged with them. A herd within the herd, since the French no longer have any power other than the power to oppress a few prisoners at their mercy when, in reality, they have already been vanquished by the Russian army and people. Platon will be severely beaten because he can no longer follow, after having illustrated a certain Christian charity ("love thine enemies") by fashioning a shirt for one of his captors. What matters in this encounter is that it brings together the representatives of the two extremities of society: not only a (very) rich man and a (very) poor man, but also, most importantly, an *intellectual* (and this is par excellence Pierre's character throughout the novel) and a *simple* man; for, this is the difference that can never be effaced even in a situation of extreme deprivation where there is no longer rich or poor, because suffering is generalized (according to a type of analysis that will return in the description of the camps in the twentieth century).

It might be supposed, consequently, that Tolstoy is returning to the idea of a national unity, or a unity of the "whole people," cemented by the patriotism that wars and, more generally, states of exception muster against class conflicts and particular interests. But this is not at all the case. First, there is no neutralization of class differences, but rather the pure and simple *disappearance* of their pertinence. Pierre and Platon become one in suffering and goodness, humanity. But this experience is as fragile as it is fleeting. Produced by war as a miracle of harmony, in a moment of suspense between defeat and victory, defensive and counterattack, life and death, this experience is reserved for two individuals then marginalized by the course of history; it crystallizes and symbolizes the vital element that constitutes the people as a community, beyond the opposition of its internal interests; but it does not exhibit any permanent substance of this people, and a fortiori does not make possible any institution. This experience thus translates the ambivalence of the at once constructive and deconstructive relation that war maintains with politics. Unto themselves, "the two of them," in their *Zweisamkeit*, Pierre and Platon are what is essential to the people; but they would not have become two (or one in two) except in the messianic "clearing" of tragedy at its darkest moment.

The Social Contract Among Commodities:
Marx and the Subject of Exchange

> *. . . so closely do these properties of being invisible adhere to reality until some
> circumstance removes them*
>
> —MARCEL PROUST, *Sodom and Gomorrah*

From the first, Marx's theory of commodity and money fetishism formed one of the most
admired and contested aspects of his "critique" of political economy. In an astonishing
fashion, it restores the correlation of sovereignty and subjection to the heart of the modern "social relation" that appears to herald the triumph of free individuality. To this end,
it was necessary conceptually to reinscribe the classical schema of the "contract" into the
representative and practical space of commodity exchange, whose immediacy he explodes
by showing its latent metaphysics, which is also an anthropology and a politics. I will attempt in this chapter to unfold the moments of this critical construction of the universal,
still almost unparalleled.

The Dialectical Movement of the First Section

The position that the development entitled *Der Fetischcharacter der Ware und sein Geheim-
nis* occupies within the economy of Section I of the first book of *Capital* is clearly very well
thought out.[1] But it remains rather surprising with regard to the order of the dialectical
exposition that Marx worked to construct, to which it is known that he attached special
importance, and upon which he never managed to confer a fully satisfying form. This
development at first seems to be a sort of scholium to the other developments in the first
chapter, adding to them a historico-philosophical reflection on the "meaning" that social
relations derive from the forms of generalized commodity exchange. On the other hand,

this development is attached to a final moment of the dialectic of commodities, which deals with the transformation of the *general equivalent* into *currency or money*. However, this transformation, in Chapter III, will become the starting point for a new dialectic, which traverses the successive figures of "measure" (which Marx calls "ideal") and circulation (in which money tends to be represented by a "sign" of itself), finally to return to a "corporeality" (*Leiblichkeit*) that circulates in autonomous fashion on the world market. From then on, exchange appears as a double circulation, or a double flow in opposite directions: that of particular commodities and that of the "universal commodity," which is offered and demanded as such. These two circulations are correlative, each functioning as the "middle term" for the other. But each can also become autonomous; and, in particular, the quantity of money in circulation can become independent of the commodities produced and consumed—thereby appearing as "wealth" as such, or, on the contrary, becoming brutally devalued, the extreme of the uncoupling occurring in the form of economic crisis.

It would thus seem that, by inserting the section on commodity fetishism at this precise point, Marx sought to elucidate this double movement: on the one hand, to show that "the riddle of the money fetish is therefore the riddle of the commodity fetish, now become visible and dazzling to our eyes,"[2] and that the circulation of commodities, as products of social labor and results of a division of labor, determines in the last instance the apparently autonomous, and irrational, forms of monetary circulation; and on the other hand, to show that "money as a measure of value is the necessary form of appearance (*notwendige Erscheinungsform*) of the measure of value which is immanent in commodities, namely labor-time,"[3] and that, without this formal autonomization, which also bears the germ of an at least temporary material independence, the reproduction of the conditions of social production would remain impossible (at least within given historical conditions: those of mercantile and, more specifically, capitalist society). It would be important to show that the "laws" of monetary economy are, at bottom, *nothing other* than those of commodity production and that the enigmas or contradictions of such economy (including when its contradictions lead to a "crisis" resulting from an underlying turmoil, a counterfinality of the freedom of exchange) can be "rationally" understood on the basis of the contradictions that initially characterize the "commodity form," or the fact that the products of labor historically have become commodities. But it should also be shown that the circulation of commodities—contrary to what various "utopian" or "scientific" socialists, such as Proudhon, might believe—*cannot dispense with* (faire l'économie de) *monetary abstraction* (or supplementary abstractions to which this one eventually gives rise: credit, fiduciary currency, etc.), and thus with an "external" mediation that necessarily escapes its instrumental function in order to stamp its authority, apparently deriving from its own inherent power, upon the whole of society. The quasi-phenomenological description of this double movement would thus be at the heart of "commodity fetishism" and would also make it possible to clarify notorious difficulty of Marx's analyses.

The section on "commodity fetishism" is localized, in that sense, not in the margins of the text, but as close as can be to its dialectical "center," at the point occupied by *mediation* in the Hegelian model to which Marx essentially adheres. Accordingly, it should not come as a surprise—on the contrary, it becomes extremely significant—that this development also constitutes, within the context of *Capital*, the first and perhaps the most significant approach to the problem of *subjectivity*, to the form in which human individuals and collectivities, at a certain moment or stage of universal history, represent their own social universe and their mutual dependency. Indeed, Marx, in the course of his constant and controlled rewriting of *Capital*, scattered indices in his text of a progression that identifies the empirical immediacy of the commodity as a first *phenomenal form* (*Erscheinung*) and the "world market" as the very site where the *concept* of commodity circulation is actualized, with the concrete figure of this concept.[4] It would thus be possible to reconstitute a wholly typical dialectical progression, a perfect example—leading, by way of a moment of reflection or subjectivity, from abstract being or sensible immediacy to concrete universality.

This coincidence would not be less significant because of the fact that Marx wished to confer upon this entire analysis a *critical* function, designed to highlight both the historical limitation and alienating character of the forms of commodity production (a fortiori when they become the forms of capitalist production). For, precisely, such a critique must not take the form of an external denunciation but rather traverse a deployment of the very form of the scrutinized social relations that respects their own "logic" (the dialectic, Hegel said, should not be limited to the "external activity of subjective thought" but rather must express "the *very soul* of the content").[5] The dialectical moment of mediation, in which the initial idea must be alienated in separation, the reciprocal exteriority of the subject and the object, the particular and the universal, consists here precisely in the presentation of an "alienated subjectivity."

Figures of Subjectivity: Economy, Law

The idea of considering the theory of commodity fetishism as a necessary moment in the dialectic of the "commodity form" (or in the passage from the commodity to money), as seductive as it may be when considering the formal organization of Section I of *Capital*, still leaves unsolved several difficulties with regard to the organization of the text.

The first difficulty, which we will do no more than evoke in general terms, concerns the relation of this "dialectic" to the whole of the work. For a century, it has given rise to innumerable discussions; and it becomes even more difficult to parse taking into account the fact that, despite the various outlines for the whole of *Capital* that Marx left behind, the work remains unfinished. The theoretical "circle" in which it would become possible, in the final analysis, to discover the ultimate meaning of Marx's actual point of departure, was never traced. Worse, the outline to follow, it seems, was drawn up in a number of contradictory versions, which leads to the conclusion that the reason why the work was left unfinished does not only reside in lack of time—because the task was too large, because one stage or another proved unexpectedly difficult, or because of the author's perfectionism—but rather in an intrinsic aporia that pertains to the concept of "capitalist society" (or capitalist social formation) as a "concrete totality" or a "synthesis of multiple determinations" (Introduction to *Contribution to the Critique of Political Economy*, 1857).[6]

The development within the first section on "fetishism," since it is precisely there where Marx attempts to classify various social formations and to discuss their ability or inability to grasp the mechanism of their own functioning and their place in history, also promises to reveal a difficulty that affects his entire project. In truth, the presentation of this development as a separate "supplementary" section could be understood as the indication—at the very heart of Section I or the dialectic of the commodity—of the difficulties he kept encountering in his attempt rigorously to articulate what he considered to be his two great "discoveries": (1) the elucidation of the "logic" of the value form and (2) the analysis of the successive forms of exploitation (or class antagonism) leading to the emancipation of social work, contradictorily generated by capitalism itself.

A second difficulty, however, is of more immediate concern. It resides in the very relation between the theory of fetishism and the question of money. We have already mentioned that, in the course of his studies, Marx began with a very classical identification of the modern "fetish" with money and went on to deepen and extend this metaphor to the entire commodity form, and then to the whole set of economic categories. On the other hand, we have said that Marx's analysis of commodity fetishism implies a double movement consisting of (1) the "reduction" of the specificity of money to elementary form of the commodity and (2) the "projection" of the contradictions inherent to this form into a specific abstraction or ideality that corresponds, in the final analysis, to the properties or powers that the monetary instrument appears to possess "by nature." However, such a presentation seems to miss an essential thematic that populates Marx's developments (and that it would be extremely reductive to consider as a mere rhetorical form): that which aligns fetishism with the production of a *mystique* or a *mysticism*, or, more precisely, a "profane mysticism" proper to mercantile society.

Whoever reads Marx attentively will notice that he employs a double terminology in order to evoke the itself double character—"sensible supersensible" (*sinnlich übersinnlich*)— of the value laden "thing," that is, the commodity: on the one hand, a terminology of the secret or the enigma that must be penetrated or discovered to possess a rational signification; and on the other hand, a terminology of the "mystical veil" or the "phantasmagoria" whose effects of suggestion upon individual spirits or souls must be understood. Passage between these two registers is assured by a certain use of the word "mystery" and by the tracing of a certain analogy between fetishism and the history of religions—which functions to designate fetishism as a new stage in this history, at once more abstract (as the ultimate stage in the secularization or a laicization of beliefs) and paradoxically more irrational, turning back to an identification of the divine with a magic power in things themselves, or, more precisely, to certain things invested with supernatural functions. The universal quantification of the relations of exchange would thus accomplish not so much in a "disenchantment" of the world but rather a "reenchantment." But, at bottom, this historical and cultural analogy does little more than displace into other regions the duality that causes such difficulty—the fact that Marx uses the same word to designate a *phenomenon of expression* (a "hieroglyph to be deciphered," a "language" to be understood beyond its initial obscurity) and a *phenomenon of symbolization* that entails both a dimension of idealization and a dimension of incorporation (the extraordinary powers that belong to the thing insofar as it immediately incarnates, in its sensible or "visible" materiality, *social power as such*, thereby allowing everyone to dream of appropriating it). Obviously, it seems that the first aspect refers to the phenomenal form in its particularity, much as the proportionality of value between commodities both expresses and dissimulates (as a "sign" does) the "social substance" constituted by the work needed to produce them; whereas the second aspect refers to money as the manifestation of the universal in the phenomenal sphere itself—that is, to the fact that a certain thing somehow exhibits its own ideality, "makes it visible" as the expression of the "invisible" (which forms the "mystical" moment as such). In other terms, the first aspect refers to what Marx calls "the conversion of persons into things" (*Versachlichung der Personen*) while the second refers to the "conversion of things into persons" (*Personifizierung der Sache*).[7] If one brings into play the metaphor of the language of things that Marx pursues at length in this section (but is it a metaphor? Isn't it rather a way of reflecting the very possibility of metaphor?), the first aspect would refer to the fact that *commodities are (like) signs*, which display the characteristics of human work, while the second would refer to the fact that *certain commodities are (like) speaking subjects*, ghostly or "spectral" subjects (as Derrida would say) lending a voice or a power of interpellation to what in itself is without voice or deprived of voice (men as workers or producers).[8]

But this ever reborn division of fetishism between the pole of the simple commodity and that of the money commodity makes us wonder whether Marx really did achieve what he always vaunted as his greatest discovery—a dialectical "passage" from the commodity to money, or, to speak the language of economists, from the theory of value to the theory of money.[9] There is still uncertainty about the function of the famous development. Is it the sought-after elucidation of dialectical mediation? Or rather, is it the displacement into a philosophical space of the very difficulty of finding a mediation, or of "dialectically" operating this passage, which would suppose the immanent constitution of a symbolic element absent from the very notion of value, and which depends upon the emergence of precisely this element to be able to present itself as the general interpretation of the form of social relations in the bourgeois world? In brief, what theoretical *difference* results from the adjunction, in the "genesis of money," of a critique of the fetishist *illusion*, essentially incarnated in the monetary symbol and its imaginary powers? And to what extent must we conclude that, without this "illusion," which Marx compared to a religious "delusion," the economic form itself would never function?[10]

This difficulty, in turn, ushers in a third. We just said that the analysis of fetishism formally occupies the dialectical place of reflection on *subjectivity*, in the sense that it unfolds the field of representations (at once realist and delusional) in which the "bearers" (*Träger*) of determinate social relations live their lives (the relations of exchange, or better, the relations of "commodity production") and thereby interpose themselves as a necessary middle term (which, for Marx, is also a "veil," a veil that lets itself be seen as such) between individuals and their own social activity or their work in common. However, the "place" of this mediation is *already occupied*, in Marx's exposition, by a development about which we have not yet said anything and that appears in Chapter II: "The Process of Exchange."[11]

This brief but very dense chapter has never attracted much attention from commentators, with a few rare exceptions (such as the unfortunate jurist Pashukanis, a victim of the

Stalinist terror, who made it the basis for his theorization of *bourgeois law*),[12] although its tenor is actually quite remarkable. Formally, the progression that Marx follows in Section I is this: (1) commodity, (2) exchange, and (3) money. In other words: (1) the *elementary form* of the mercantile world, then (2) the *process* whereby this form is constituted and by which it always extends to new objects or domains, and finally (3) the *concept* that contains in itself the "concrete" unity (historical and institutional) of the form and the process, which can be called the market (or, in Marx's analysis, the world market).

Such a dialectical progression can be read directly—as if the putting into movement of the form and its historical totalization resulted from the tension or contradiction contained "in itself" in the initial form itself. But, as in Hegel, it is better to read it retrospectively, as a movement that returns from its end to its origin. It would then be the presuppositions of the structure or the figure of the market that are progressively put in place, moving from the most "abstract" to the most "concrete." From this perspective, the content of Chapter II becomes particularly significant: Once again, we are contending with figures of subjectivity, but now in a totally other register. First of all, Marx introduces the juridical categories of the *person* (property owner) and the *contract* (unity of wills) as the correlative or the "reflection" of the economic categories of exchange, without which exchange could never occur, because "commodities cannot go themselves to market and perform exchanges in their own right."[13] Marx then endeavors to show, in a brief historical sketch (or rather, in the ideal genesis of the circulation of commodities that provides the general sense of historical evolution), how the practice of exchange between communities and between individuals rendered progressively necessary and ultimately irreversible the development of the commodity form and then the institution of money. It requires not only structures or forms, after all, but also men, or, more exactly, men progressively acquiring the quality of juridical persons and recognizing each other as such, in order for the commodity form to become socially dominant through a specific *action*, an individual and collective practice, what Hegel called *ein Tun aller und jeder.* Herein resides a new characterization of the "subject," this time no longer as the bearer of economic relations and their corresponding representations, but as the subject of law, individualized and represented in the language of juridical institutions. Nonetheless, what is the nature of the relationship that unites these two figures of subjectivity? Should we consider them concurrent? Or rather, should we conclude that, after juxtaposing a phenomenology of "economic representations" and a phenomenology of "juridical representations," both linked to the idea of a market structure, either as a form of "inner" (and fundamentally illusory) "consciousness," or as the institutional reflection (and as such lending a social objectivity to thought itself), Marx wished thereby to think their articulation as complementary aspects of the *subjectivity of the market* or subjectivity such as it is constituted by the social relations of commodity production?[14]

Constitution of the General Equivalent

Let us then keep these general problems in mind (although they demand much more extensive study) as we concentrate our attention upon the development that concerns, properly speaking, the universality of money and its relation to certain classical models of political philosophy.[15]

Commodity "fetishism," in one sense, has no other function than to theatricalize and to place in a comparative historical perspective the phenomenon of the inversion of "real" relations that Marx considers as inherent to "the mode of commodity production"—that is, to any organization of social production in which the necessary labor of individuals is divvied up between different branches and processes of production, not as a result of the communal decision of the producers, but rather of the indirect mechanism of buying and selling products whose exchange value is "measured" immanently by the quantity of labor socially necessary for their production.

In fact, what's at stake is a double inversion, or two successive inversions, because Marx wanted to show two things at the same time. On the one hand, he wants to show that social labor, in a consumer society, only exists as "private labor," executed independently by individual or collective producers who do not know one another. The correspondence, in quantity and quality, between the labor that society has at its disposal and the needs of its own reproduction cannot be established directly but only through a blind adjustment calibrated by an "exterior measure," the exchange value of the products of labor. There is an inversion because, for Marx, in the final analysis, labor and needs remain social realities, and because the true "subject" is society, or rather the *ensemble* of individual practices that, unbeknownst to them, fulfill the necessities of its existence.[16] But Marx would also like to show that, in the quantitative form or "value-form" of the commodity, and particularly in the monetary form, another inversion takes place. Instead of social relations of mutual dependency between producers being presented as relations between human persons or groups, who together form a collectivity united by a common interest, they are presented as spontaneously or automatically instituted relations between the things themselves by virtue of a "social property" that commodities seem to possess "by nature": a determinate exchange value prescribing the proportions in which they may be exchanged for one another. A fortiori, when this social property is concentrated in money, which also seems to possess the natural capacity to measure the value of commodities and to determine their mutual relations, the relations of individuals to their own conditions of social existence (and thus to themselves, since, in the final analysis, it is a question of how their labor contributes to the satisfaction of their needs) becomes entirely projected into a figure of external objectivity: "to the producers . . . the social relations between their private labors appear as what they are, i.e. they do not appear as direct social relations between persons in their work, but rather as material [*dinglich*] relations between persons and social relations between things."[17]

These two successive "inversions"—the one described in terms of the overturning or dissolution of social relations into private relations, the other described in terms of the turning of human or personal social relations into relations between things or "objective" relations—play a decisive role in Marx's text. It must be understood right away that, in Marx's eyes, the second inversion in no way annuls the first; on the contrary, it is what makes it possible to understand why—under given historical and material conditions—fetishism is insurmountable, why there is an "enigma," a "mystery," an "obscurity," an obscurity that is radically impenetrable because it is expressed in the form of absolute clarity. If this were merely a matter of the division of social labor, in which individuals somehow "negotiate" among themselves for the social recognition of their labor, we could continue to imagine that the social bond would appear to them as a product of their own work. In a certain sense, this would even be the ideal schema of a contract or convention, in which individuals would confront each other's force and interests. However, as soon as things as such incarnate social necessity, and particularly this fetishized "Thing" par excellence—both sensible and supersensible, material and immaterial, particular and universal (and thus immediately presented as a "unity of opposites," much as Christ, in the theology of incarnation, is immediately presented as both man and god, or much as a specter is presented as both dead and living)—all that individuals can see in their mutual relations, always determined by their engagement with the "value" of things and the constraints that they impose, is the consequence of the social property or power of things. In other terms, they must contend with what Hegel called the "Thing itself" (*Sache selbst*).[18]

This is what leads Marx, in a manner that might at first seem paradoxical, to posit fetishism as the expression of a certain "truth" of commodity production: Such production *effectively* dispossesses individuals of their social identity, of their belonging to a collective of production, and thus, in this sense, "the social relations between their private labors appear to the producers as what they are" in the market relation that opposes them to one and other and places the representation of their community outside of themselves. At the same time, however, the incarnation of value (which is in itself a social relation) in the material form of a thing signals the impossibility for individuals of "seeing anything but what they see"—that is, looking for the explication of the regularities (or catastrophes) of economic life in a determinate historical relation. This is also why Marx specifies that, even if the theory of "labor value" articulated by classical economists marks "an epoch in the history of mankind's development," because it ascribes the value of commodities to the quantity of labor that is socially necessary for their production, it "by no means banishes the semblance of objectivity (*gegenständlichen Schein*) possessed by the social characteristics of labor,"[19] because it does not change anything in the social structure of this semblance. On the contrary, the theory tends to reinforce the semblance because it presents what is only the result of a long historical evolution as a mechanism inscribed within the nature of things whose eternal laws it attempts to articulate. In truth, the discourse of the classical economists can only oscillate between scientific explication and the reproduction of semblances, or produce a demystification in the very form of mystification, as shown by its tendency to present "labor" either as an internal determination or "substance" of value or as one commodity among others whose own universality would cause to function as the "measure of values."[20]

Following Marx's indications, we can represent the relation that substitutes for the simple division of labor in mercantile society as a *social contract* that would be sealed tacitly or in practice *between commodities themselves*. Such would be the figure that emerges from Marx's exposition of the constitution of the "general equivalent" (*allgemeines Äquivalent*), which presents itself as the collective action of "things." In the initial presentation of this notion, Marx writes:

The new form we have just obtained expresses the values of the world of commodities through one single kind of commodity set apart from the rest, through the linen for example, and thus represents the values of all commodities by means of their equality with linen. Through its equation with linen, the value of every commodity is now not only differentiated from its own use-value, but from all use-values, and is, by that very fact, expressed as that which is common to all commodities. By this form, commodities are, for the first time, really brought into relation with each other as values, or permitted to appear to each other as exchange-values.[21]

When each commodity expresses its value in an isolated or contingent fashion in exchange with one or several others, it is "the private task (*das Privatgeschäft*), so to speak, of the individual commodity to give itself a form of value, and it accomplishes this task without the aid of others."[22] As soon as the generalization of exchange between all products of labor gives rise to the need for a single expression for all values, or for a "general equivalent," the very process of expression changes nature:

> The general form of value, on the other hand, can only arise as the joint contribution of the whole world of commodities (*gemeinsames Werk der Warenwelt*). A commodity only acquires a general expression of its value if, at the same time, all other commodities express their values in the same equivalent; and every newly emergent commodity must follow suit. It thus becomes evident that because the objectivity of commodities as values (*Wertgegenständlichkeit*) is the purely "social existence" of these things, it can only be expressed through the whole range of their social relations; consequently the form of their value must possess social validity.[23]

Pursuing his analysis, Marx explains that the mechanism of forming the general equivalent is a mechanism of *exclusion* that extracts a single commodity from the universe or "world" of multiple commodities (their *Mannigfaltigkeit* or qualitative diversity). This commodity will, from then on, have "monopoly" on the representation of value; or it will represent value as such "for" all other commodities, which, inversely, can only express their own value in this single form. This means that commodities will cease to be *directly* exchangeable for one another; that they now can only be exchanged through the intermediary of their relation (albeit purely "ideal") to the general equivalent (in other words their "common measure" in the objective language of the general equivalent, which, in practice, is money):

> The last form . . . gives to the world of commodities a general social relative form of value, because, and in so far as, all commodities except one are thereby excluded from the equivalent form. A single commodity . . . therefore has the form of direct exchangeability with all other commodities, in other words it has a directly social form because, and in so far as, no other commodity is in this situation.[24]

This might also be expressed by saying that the duality which inheres from the outset in the very form of the commodity, and is present in each commodity as the "elementary form" of social wealth—the duality of the particular character of the commodity (its materiality, its utility with respect to a determinate need) and its universality (its "generic" character as a product of social labor, which renders it commensurable with all others)—becomes dissociated. It is as if each commodity had extracted or projected outside of itself its own generality or genericity in order to confer it upon the sole "equivalent" commodity, which, from then on, is charged with representing *for each commodity* what it has in common with all other commodities, or its "equivalence" with respect to all the others. It thus becomes a "real abstraction," or a transcendental essence, which, nonetheless, *also* figures as such within "empirical" reality or within the field of perception.

But after the discussion of fetishism, Marx will explain that this universalization must be considered as the common action of commodities themselves, which always already unfolds (in an "anteriority" more structural than properly historical, even if the trace of it might be sought within history) behind the back of their human owners (or the producers-exchangers) and by the intermediary of the movements that this action prescribes to them:

> The owner of a commodity is prepared to part with it only in return for other commodities whose use-value satisfies his own need. So far, exchange is merely an individual process for him. On the other hand, he desires to realize his commodity, as a value, in any other suitable commodity of the same value. It does not matter to him whether his own commodity has any use-value for the owner of the other commodity or not. From this point of view, exchange is for him a general social process. But the same process cannot be simultaneously for all owners of commodities both exclusively individual and exclusively social and general. . . . In their difficulties our commodity-owners think like Faust: "In the beginning was the deed." They have therefore already acted before thinking. The natural laws of the commodity have manifested themselves (*betätigen sich*) in the natural instinct of the owners of commodities. They can only bring their commodities into relation as values, and therefore as commodities, by bringing them into an opposing relation with some one other commodity, which serves as the universal equivalent. We have already reached that result by our analysis of the commodity. But only the action of society (*gesellschaftliche Tat*) can turn a particular commodity into the universal equivalent (*allgemeines Äquivalent*). The social action (*gesellschaftliche Aktion*) of all other commodities, therefore, sets apart the particular commodity in which they all represent their values. The natural form of this commodity thereby becomes the socially recognized equivalent form (*gesellschaftlich gültige Äquivalentform*). Through the agency of the social process it becomes the specific social function of the commodity which has been set apart to be the universal equivalent. It thus becomes—money.[25]

Here we would seem to have the three typical characteristics of the "contract" form such as the philosophers of the classical age developed it within the tradition of "natural law" (which Marx knew either directly through his readings of Spinoza, Locke, and Rousseau, or indirectly through Hegel's critique of this tradition). First, social universality is the product of the *common action* of individuals (and thus of their decision or will, which might well be "tacit," and even is necessarily so in the case of a truly originary contract) and, in return, it qualifies them as members of a social body (as "citizens")—that is, it guarantees their mutual recognition (or their "equality"); second, this common action institutes the *representative power* of social individuals, at once "idealized" and "incarnated" in an individual or a "body" of individuals who thereby find that they *belong to society to the precise extent that they transcend it* (including to the extent that they are excluded), and who present themselves in the figure of the "double body" (or of the "mystical body," both carnal and spiritual) inherited from theology and secularized; and third, the whole process obeys the logical schema of *presupposition*, since its result—the recognition of a civic or social community, the passage from particular existence or interests to universality— is always already the condition of its actualization, at least as a formal necessity, a "natural law," or tacit intention.

Obviously, however, what lends the Marxist conception of the contract as it is elaborated in *Capital* (or the Marxist variant of the contract form) a very singular signification is that the "individuals" who intervene as the contracting parties are not human subjects but individual commodities; and that the "action" at stake (*Tun aller und jeder*) is the action of commodities (or, at least, the action of human beings as the mere bearers of the commodity form and executors of the logic of circulation). Accordingly, the "society" that is formed here must be considered not as a society of persons but as a society of animate "things" (or things whose soul and intentions are incarnated in the form of human will) and the "contract" that institutes it as a true social relation among commodities. This is, it would seem, the sense in which we should interpret Marx's reference to "the great commercial republic" in the first French translation of *Capital*, which he reviewed:

> It is in the commerce between nations that the value of commodities is universally actualized. Therein, as well, they come face to face with figure of their value in the guise of universal currency—the "money of the world," as James Steuart calls it, money of the great commercial republic as Adam Smith would say after him.[26]

In this "republic," it is first the commodities themselves that are the "citizens"![27]

The "Mystical" Supplement

However, such a reconstruction cannot be completely satisfying because it leaves aside precisely the element of "mysticism" (or, as Derrida would say, the "spectral" element) that, in Marx's description of fetishism, is added to simple mystery; for, it exhibits mystery in the materiality of an immediately ideal or idealized thing. In Marx's description, what specifically characterizes this supplement, it seems, would be the effect produced by the difference of "form" between a simple general equivalent—which, in principle, could be any commodity whatsoever, provided that it occupies the empty place of the "excluded commodity" set aside for it by all the others—and money properly speaking, materialized in the "body" of precious metals. The task before us, then, is to figure the specific power of money, both as the real or practical power to place commodities into circulation and as an imaginary power. We will see that what is specific to money is its excess of power over the simple "commodity," even when the latter is conceived as a universal form. The risk is, obviously, that the adjunction of this excess of power might subvert the "egalitarian" schema of social contract among commodities and might replace the "commercial republic" with a *monarchy* of money whose origin would remain, in the final analysis, inexplicable. Herein lies the ambivalence of Marx's discussion, which is always seeking to reduce the "power of money" to that of commodities themselves, of which it is always merely the delegate, and to show how the money form is irreducible to the simply "functional" notion of one commodity excluded from the "society" of all the others. This ambivalence is not at all diminished by the fact that this discussion situates us in the world of social *appearances*. On the contrary, by a sort of redoubling, only among these appearances themselves does the question arise of how to decide which of these two forms should be considered as the "truth" of the other.

Although, in a certain sense, Marx took a position, on the economists' own terrain, against monetarism in all of its forms, he still sought essentially to show that the money form is more than the simple "generalization" of the value form of commodities.[28] Money itself has an exchange value that allows it be exchanged for all other commodities; its value, like theirs, is determined "in the final instance" by the labor time socially necessary for its production. In this sense, it could be said that money is "in" the commodity form and the world of commodities, among which it circulates. In another sense, however, since money alone incarnates value "in itself," and since, consequently, it alone becomes the universal measure of the values and means of payment for all commodities, these commodities can only actually circulate with the introduction of money or the exercise of its universal buying power. The *Contribution to the Critique of Political Economy* says that money alone is the object of "universal need": an astonishing notion (contradicting the "materialist" anthropology that posits need as a vital function) that connotes *excess*, or rather inscribes excess within everyday experience itself.[29] But within a society whose individuals only ever produce with the market in view, a commodity is only ever offered in view of satisfying such a "universal need." Not only is the universal circulation of commodities necessarily monetary, but the "social" character of commodities (their value) is only manifested in contact with money; and it is thanks to its intervention that commodities actually go into movement (or at least they do so with the anticipated supposition that the operations of buying and selling will be "settled" in money or with an acceptable representative of money, such as paper bills). This autonomization of the social power of money, of course, will reach its height with the development of the capitalist mode of production, since it is only with the accumulation of money and in view of its unchecked growth that all the operations of buying and selling become "factors of production."

In Marx's analysis, we can find three reasons for the excess of "sovereign" power that it seems to draw from its nature alone but that, in reality, must be ascribed to the various functions of circulation. The first is the fact that the crystallization of the general equivalent in the form of money corresponds to the actual formation of a world market. It might be said that the form of the general equivalent already sketches out a virtual universality, a form of equivalence for all particular commodities (and the labor that produces them) whose extent remains unknown. But, on the contrary, money is effectively and concretely universal. (The *Contribution* from 1859 had explained that, "gold and money help to create the world market in that the very concept of money contains the anticipation of its existence," because money is not limited by any borders, or because it transgresses all restrictions linked to representations of community, and, prefiguring the terminology of the analysis of fetishism, "the magical effect of gold and money is by no means confined to the period of infancy of bourgeois society but is a necessary outgrowth of the completely inverted image that agents of the commodity world have of their own social labor, is shown by the extraordinary influence exerted in the middle of the nineteenth century by the discovery of new gold fields").[30] The second reason is that only money, precisely insofar as it consists of a "determinate" material, historically incarnated by precious metals, can be "dematerialized"—that is, conventionally represented in circulation by a "monetary sign" (such as paper money, letters of credit, a check, etc.). In Chapter III of *Capital*, Marx explains that this metamorphosis requires the intervention of the State and the institution of its "monetary sovereignty." It would thus seem to contradict the foregoing representation of a money whose existence is linked to the world market, since there is no world State. But this disparity is resolved if we are willing to admit that, in reality, "the society of commodities" must be identified neither with a "universal commercial republic" as a global space without borders nor with a purely national space but rather with the interconnection of multiple state sovereignties at the heart of the world market.[31] The process of the materialization-dematerialization-rematerialization of money thus corresponds precisely to the concrete figure of the emergence of the nation-state as the institution of the world market and of the world market as the transcendence or relativization of particular sovereignties whose respective power is "measured" by their capacity to impose their own representation of money in some part of the world (upon a given "territory" and sometimes beyond).

That said, the figure of the social contract of commodities does seem to reach the limit of its validity with the third determination of money's autonomy with respect to the form of the general equivalent: the capacity of money to create commodities that are not immediately "parties" to the contract because they are not initially products of social labor or branches of the division of labor (that is, if we continue to advance to the same metaphor, the capacity to "create new citizens" in the republic of commodities). This capacity is principally exerted in two directions, one evoked in the first section of *Capital* and the other later in the book.[32] In the first instance, this capacity appears in the constitution of "fictive" commodities whose value is called "irrational" because they are not products of labor but only enter circulation as a result of the appropriation or the monopolization of *natural* objects that form the conditions of possibility for all production— above all, the *elements* (water, earth [minerals, etc.], air, and so on). In the second instance, this capacity is found at a deeper level, closer to the very "substance" of value, when human labor is itself transformed into a commodity, which cannot happen unless individuals exchange usage of their labor-power for money, with which they then seek to procure on the market the means of their own subsistence. Just as, in Rousseau, the General Will has the power to "force subjects to be free," the General Equivalent in the form of money possesses the capacity to put any "thing" or any "being" that becomes an object of need into circulation and, with this end in view, to represent it as a quantity of value.[33]

Money

General Equivalent

Land   A   B   ( )   D   E   Human
Labor Force

            Commodities   Commodities

Social Labor

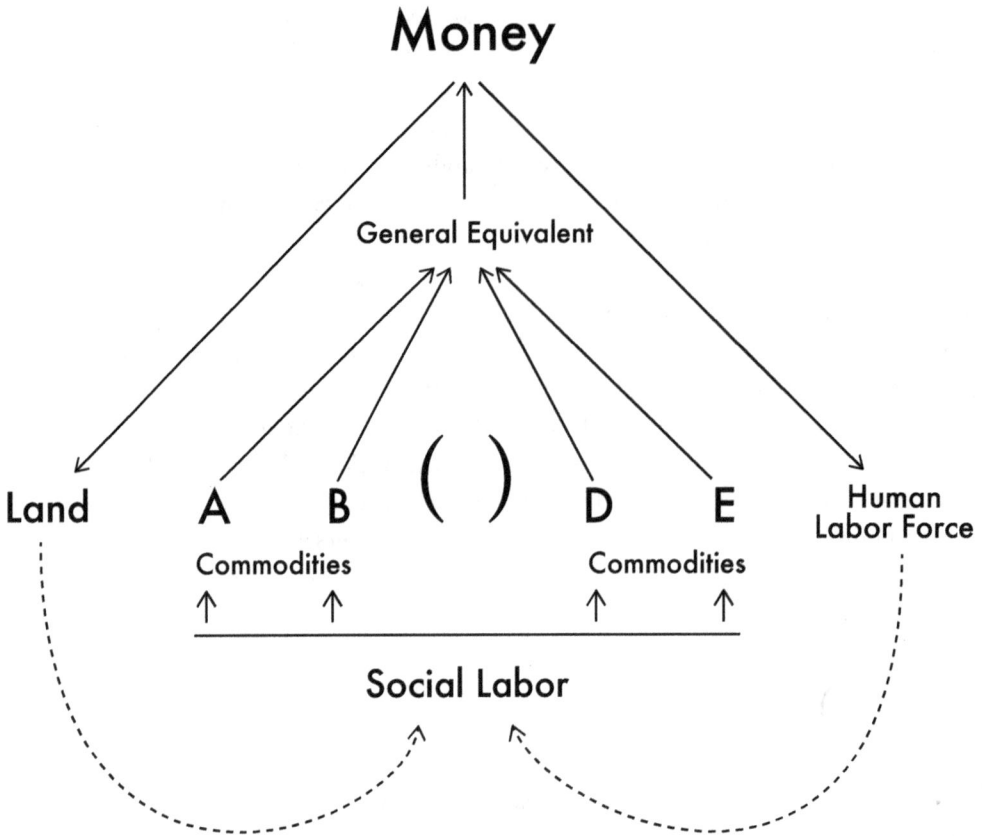

The social contract among commodities

    The dissolution of the "social worker" is exhibited, in turn, through the intermediary of money, which then becomes the middle term in the "self-relation" or the subjectivity of each individual in the reproduction of his capacity to work and its utilization for productive tasks. At the same time, the "supernatural power" of money is manifest through its capacity to transform persons into things, or, at least, to shift the distinction between person and thing into the heart of the individual himself (thereby allowing the producer to appear as the "owner" of his own labor power—his body and his brain as labor powers—which he is "free" to alienate).[34] As we see, then, money does not only express an extensive universality, that of the means of circulation on a world scale, but also becomes the agent of an *intensive* universality, in the sense that the commodity form encompasses the *totality* of possible objects, including those that were not included in its initial definition, letting "nothing" escape its grasp. These are the indications of the sense in which it is possible to say not only that commodity production extends to the entire world (destroying or absorbing all the other modes of production) but also that the commodity form itself constitutes a world, or represents a form of the constitution of the world as the totality of humans and things under the domination of "things"—which is also to say, "ghosts."

Postscriptum: Interobjectivity

Three remarks might help better situate the foregoing analysis within an inquiry on the problematics of modern subjectivity, notably in their relation to Hegel's propositions.[35]

1. In the first place, it might be said that the structure described as a "social contract of commodities" figures not an "intersubjectivity" but rather an "interobjectivity," since it is on the level of objects (commodities), insofar as they bear the power of social labor, that relations are established that induce what Althusser called a "society effect."[36] This said, however, it should be remarked that this interobjectivity itself constitutes a *mode of subjectivity* or a *constitution of the subject*. It is what Marx calls "alienation," in the sense of a "becoming stranger to oneself" of the subject (*Entfremdung*). An alienated subjectivity is still a subjectivity, perhaps even the *typical* subjectivity within a given social structure, that which historically generalized this notion and conferred upon it an ontological scope. But this raises the question of the relationship between interobjectivity, whose structure he described and interpreted historically, and the category of the "person," diametrically opposed to that of the "thing." Here we run up against the amphibology that governs the references to the "person" in Marx's text. On the one hand, this category is applied to subjects before their alienation (thus, in practice, commercial relations), or, on the contrary, to the subjects who emerge with the hypothetical overcoming of alienation to whom their "social relations" would no longer appear in the "inverted" form of relations between things (i.e., with "communism"). On the other hand, however (especially in "The Process of Exchange" [*Capital*, Vol. 1, Chap. II], which, as I recalled before, is founded entirely upon categories of "abstract right" in the Hegelian sense), the "person" designates the other face of the fetishism of things, the human (not to say humanist) "double" thereof, configured by the right to property and exchange necessary for the circulation of commodities. This is why I have spoken of a "fetishism of persons" that parallels the "fetishism of things"—although, in all rigor, for Marx, the first is merely an aspect of the second. Of course, this amphibology is not tenable: one must *choose* one sense or the other of the category of the "person" and thereby to incline toward one of the two possible readings of the phenomenology of alienation. If one chooses to use the word "person" for *subjectivity freed of alienation* (either before or after the generalization of commodity exchange), one provides oneself (theoretically) with the means to evoke a *disalienated sociability* in which pure "intersubjectivity" would be reconstituted at the expense of interobjectivity, by a negation of the negation. If one makes the "person"—as Marx says elsewhere—into a "juridical mask" that subjects must wear who fulfill the functions prescribed by the "social contract of commodities," one no longer evokes disalienation (at least as long as the historical conditions for the emergence of this structure of representation, which renders it necessary but also places limits upon it, are not specified), but rather analyses *the subject effect of a structure*.[37] This second possibility is no less critical than the first, since it reveals the logic of subjection, but it is much less "revolutionary." Accordingly, it should be noted that it best describes the theoretical (or conceptual) result of Marx's construction, but perhaps does not correspond to what he consciously sought to prove. The "cunning of reason," ironically, also goes about its work within philosophical writing.

2. In the second place, we should return to the analogies between the Marxist and the classical models of the "social contract," offering a more nuanced interpretation that, in particular, takes into account the "overturning" that Rousseau wrought within the problematic of "total alienation" that Hobbes initially constructed to account for the genesis of *sovereignty* and its "absolute" character. As I suggested above, the phenomenology of the *Tun aller und jeder*, which Marx transferred from "persons" to "things" in order to account for the subjection of the former to the latter, begins by describing a (structural) procedure of *authorization* (the constitution of the general equivalent by "extraction" of one commodity from the society of commodities, which results from their simultaneous decision to be exchanged for it alone) followed by a procedure of *representation* (the incarnation or materialization of the general equivalent, which is as such a pure function, within the "body" of money, coinciding with its autonomization as an object of universal demand, and with the development of its own power *to create new commodities*). Marx thus operates (in relation to Hegel, who modeled the *Sache selbst* in part upon Rousseau's "general will") a paradigmatic regression *from Rousseau toward Hobbes*, which corresponds to the elucidation of the imaginary powers (mythic, phantasmatic) of sovereignty, for which the best word is precisely "fetish." This elaboration of the deep affinities that link the constitution of sovereignty to the representation of the "supernatural power of things," rather than to an effect of will or consciousness, becomes all the more striking because Marx's description otherwise remains attached to the "democratic" schema of mercantile socialization, in which the powers of the "whole," even when they become autonomous, are never anything but the expression of a collective constitution.[38] But, at this point, another ambiguity arises, or another amphibology analogous to the earlier one in that it concerns Marx's *critical objective* (and even his political objective, in the sense that of a politics of "disalienation"). Is the point, as he sheds light on the *process* of authorization and representation that subtends the constitution of interobjectivity, to diminish the fascination of the "fetish," and thus, in some sense, intellectually to liberate subjects from the "thing" that is implanted at the heart of their relation to the other and that monopolizes this relation? Or is it rather to *deduce* the effects of quasi-transcendental illusion that result from the fact that social labor is subordinated to exchange, or from the fact that the social utility of the products of this labor is expressed in the "value form," which necessarily leads to the development of money, and to imagine (and perchance to dream) the freedom and solidarity (or mutual recognition) that would result for them from going beyond commodity exchange? This alternative is nothing less than secondary if, following Marx's own indications, we attach the analysis of fetishism to a problematic of the difference between mercantile society and communist society.

3. This precisely would be the object of my third remark, bearing on the indetermination that affects, on this level, the question of the relations between *community and the universal* in Marx. The question is no less insistent in Marx and no less essential for orienting the dialectical progression toward an "overcoming of contradictions" than it is in Hegel (especially in *Phenomenology*). However, whereas in Hegel the "common" and the "universal" constitute *two antithetical poles*—that of the *Wir* (the "we") and that of *Sein* ("being" or the "category")—and intersubjectivity moves between them,[39] it seems that, in Marx, the

idea of "the end of history" emerges as *the conflict between two concurrent universalities*: The one *radically excludes all real community*, if not all "society" or "sociability" (this is the universality proper to circulation and the production of commodities whose "medium" is money, or, in other terms, the materialization of a generalized quantitative equivalence between abstract labors); the other is *identified with the actualization of authentic community* as the "rational organization of productive operations" and the "transparency" of the mechanisms for distributing labor and its products among subjects (or, if one prefers, among the "citizens" of the community of producers). It is true that this conflict might be reduced to a *definitive scission* between universality and community in itself, if the former is thought as indissociable from representative abstraction and the latter, on the contrary, as the extreme limit of a quest for the concrete universal, in which the "common" is as such the law of freedom and equality that places every individual in relation with every other. Even this outcome, however, would be a "resolution" of the dialectic of the common and the universal, which is founded not on the increasing indiscernibility of the two terms, as in Hegel, but rather upon their irreducibility. Nonetheless, in Hegel, at least in certain texts (above all *Phenomenology*, which is careful not to propose the State as the objective synthesis of this dialectical movement but rather concludes upon an at once aporetic, tragic, and mystical figure of the community that turns upon the identification of individuals with a symbolic death and the reconciliation that it promises),[40] this "proximity" of community and universality is in some sense a lure, or it obscures a lack whose satisfaction is indefinitely deferred by history. Inversely, in Marx, the only way that history might only promise the overcoming of the oscillation between antithetic modalities of the universal is by an act of faith (or, not very different, by the *dialectical presumption* of the necessary effects of the class struggle, of the development of contradictions internal to the capitalist mode of production founded on the extension of the commodity form to the very reproduction of human beings, and of the long-term superiority of "socializing" tendencies over "utilitarian" countertendencies of the collectivization of labor).[41] The question of knowing which of these two *aporias*, in the strict sense, is the more untenable obviously does not pertain to logical argumentation. It could also be that, taken together, they call for a new mode of defining the common and the universal, which would necessarily correspond to another concept of the "subject."

PART THREE

The Right to Transgression

Judging Self and Others: On the Political Theory of Reflexive Individualism

In French and several other languages, the notion of judgment designates both a "faculty" or "capacity" and an action that takes place within the sphere of public or private relations. It can have a general neutral signification (that of an evaluation about the adequacy of means to ends or to the quality of the ends themselves). But more often it designates, in dissymmetrical fashion, the determination of a deserved or undeserved sanction upon the action of a subject, especially when the action in question is a "crime" or a "delict."

Judgment thus possesses both an anthropological side and an institutional side. How are they linked to one another? This question, as we know, is one of philosophy's constant preoccupations, but it is also an obstacle, even an enigma, at the intersection of the metaphysical, moral, and political dimensions of any theory of the subject. With this tradition in mind, through a rereading of a series of classical texts I would like to associate two sorts of preoccupations. I will seek to rethink the question of "responsibility" for actions as an agency of the individualization of the subject, which one must never assume is established a priori. But also, interpreting "responsibility" as an index of the *rights and duties* of the citizen, I will seek to characterize the democratic function of the "faculty of judgment." This function might appear endangered today, especially in a society that tends contradictorily both to expropriate the citizen's "capacity to judge" in favor of juridical automatism and expert decision making and make urgent appeals to this capacity in the name of "social defense" and the "protection of victims." It is eminently political, in that it combines the individual's own judgment with collective deliberation. And the constitutive paradox of judgment is carried to the extreme if we admit that only the individual subject can be the judge of his own intentions but he cannot *be his own judge* with respect to the social value of his actions, no more than he can *do justice to himself*. There is thus a permanent risk that morality will be divorced from justice.

The title that I chose for this task explicitly recalls the formulations of contemporary philosophers who have sought to problematize the imbrication of autonomy and heteronomy. Foucault's final course at the Collège de France in 1982–83, for example, was entitled *The Government of Self and Others*.[1] But also, one of Paul Ricoeur's principal works bears the title, *Oneself as Another*.[2] Importantly, Ricoeur rereads a text by Kant—one of the "well known" texts whose details always pack surprises—on "man's duty to himself as his own innate judge," from the Doctrine of Virtue (§13) in *Metaphysics of Morals* (1796).[3] This text places us at the heart of the tradition that associates "conscience" with the political model of an inner "tribunal" (what, in French, is called the *for intérieur*, derived from the Latin, *forum internum*).[4] It thus becomes especially clear how the reference at least to an ideal sovereignty (which might be called "God") makes it possible to resolve the tension between a reflexive foundation of the capacity to judge and the necessity that its result be communicated or made common property.

I cannot enter into a complete genealogy of these formulations.[5] But I would like to highlight a few of their implications in three distinct phases: (1) to go back to the Greeks (and notably to Aristotle) in order to designate the political dimension of the activity of judgment; (2) to examine a few characteristics of what I call "reflexive individualism," illustrated in Locke, Rousseau, or Kant, by the problematic of the "judgment of oneself"; (3) to indicate, on the basis of a reading of Hegel, how modern liberalism (of which Hegel is as valid a representative as many others, in spite of certain legends about him) transformed the *sharing of judgment* into a function regulated by the State, if not wholly a State function. In conclusion, I will evoke a few anthropological monstrosities or horrors that have been covered up—more or less successfully—by this double-faced structure of the "internal" and "external" tribunal or of the "judgment of self and others," which can obviously be applied in various ways (whether it be "judge yourself as others would judge you" or "judge your neighbor as yourself . . .").

Archè Aoristos: *Judging and Deciding*

Let us begin with the *Greek* idea of the citizen capable of judging. My reference point will be a fundamental text by Aristotle, in Book III of the *Politics* (1275a). This text defines the citizen as such (*polites haplos*) by the exercise of an "unlimited office" (*archè aoristos*).[6] This generic name, with its negative and certainly ambivalent form (since it connotes both the element of the citizen's "omnipotence" and the risk of excess that it entails)—which, as Aristotle immediately specifies, designates a reality that "mainly exists within democracy," there where "a people" (*demos*) is to be found—combines two functions: that of *boulein* (willing, deciding) and that of *krinein* (judging, discriminating). Citizenship as an institution thus founds the correlation between participating in the assembly of the people (*ekklesiastes*) and being a member of a tribunal or a judge (*dikastes*). How to interpret this?

We should begin, I think, by observing that Aristotle reduces sovereignty to immanence: *dikè* here is no longer the cosmotheological "justice" that is the privilege of a "sovereign" or a "master of justice"; it is not even any longer, as in Plato, a transcendental idea, but rather is brought within reach of the citizens, becoming a reality through their own practice. By the same token, this concept of justice ought to be seen as the "egalitarian" expression of the freedom that is characteristic of a democratic idea (shared at least by certain Greeks) insofar as it is inseparable from the praxis of the citizen who "judges by himself" the felicity of actions that tend to bring the common good into existence.[7] This democratic citizenship combines three striking characteristics. There is a correlation between the two generic "offices" or *archai* exercised by all citizens: passing from *boulein* to *krinein*, the citizens who make the law also oversee its application. This is why their citizenship is "unlimited." Next, there is a reciprocity between citizens: they "judge one another" (but, let us underscore, not *simultaneously*: one cannot be judge and judged at the same time, because of the principle of noncontradiction). This reciprocity concretizes the relation to the law, whose existence it presupposes, but which it avoids sacralizing or autonomizing in relation to civic life. Finally, this entire construction of citizenship implies the idea of collective rationality, both deliberative and communicative: the citizens are "competent" on condition that, constituted as a tribunal, they "represent" a movement beyond inevitably partisan individual opinions (*doxai*) toward a collective practical wisdom (*phronesis*).[8]

This conception (largely inspired by Athenian institutions from after the reforms of Cleisthenes) remains one of the sources for the legitimacy of the institution of the "popular jury" and of the link between the idea of the jury and that of democracy.[9] But we ought not mask the fragility of this legitimacy. It is already called into question within the Roman practice of justice as a technique of professionalized arbitration (which does not necessarily make it a function of state).[10] The Roman institution of justice rests upon a rigorous distinction between *civil justice*, relating to property litigation (*suum cuique tribuere* as a rule of justice) and *criminal justice*, relating to forms of violence that do harm to persons and thus infringe upon the public order and, at the limit, throw into question what it means *to belong* to the social body (the "public" enemy or the internal enemy of "all and each," a threat to the whole community).[11] These comparisons also make it possible to form an idea of the degree of violence, potentially subversive, implied within the very idea of the "unlimited office" of the citizen. In another recent collection of essays, Ricoeur echoes Foucault when he notes, "Action implies a capacity to do something that gets carried out on the interactive place as the *power* exercised by an agent *on* another agent who is the recipient of this power. This *power over others* offers the permanent occasion for violence in all its forms."[12] This power is particularly extensive (or even maximal) in the case of the "power to judge," to elevate oneself as judge, even under the supervision of a "universalist" juridical system (which assures that a judge is not a *dealer of justice*). It thus comprises a gray zone in which power cannot be distinguished from excess of power and degrades the one who exercises it. It might well be concluded that Aristotle's notion of the *archè aoristos*—which might be considered the trace of sovereignty within citizenship—thereby reveals its other face: not only the system of democratic powers but also the "indeterminate"

208 The Right to Transgression

or "unlimited" office that is only accountable to itself and thus entails the possibility of tyranny.

Internal Right, External Right

Let us now move on to the second phase of this discussion, which concerns what I have called "reflexive individualism." Inevitably, this can be no more than a sketch. Returning to the problems raised by Kant's text, I would now like to place them within the perspective that becomes dominant in the classical age, linked to the emergence of a certain "subjective right" but entailing consequences that go well beyond such right. What I call *reflexive individualism* is the other face of what has been called *possessive individualism*.[13] It lends content to the idea of a "sovereignty of the subject" that consists precisely in the absolute right to judge oneself. Any other right to judge can only be derivative with respect to this originary right. But this is only true—it must immediately be specified—on the express condition that the individual *bears the community within himself*, or better, the *law of the community* (which is precisely what makes him a "subject"). The subject, therefore, is doubled with respect to the instance of the *law*, which is one and the same time universalized and internalized. From this doubling, principally, derive all the "dualisms" of the empirical and the transcendental (or the "subject of fact" and the "subject of right"), the moral and the juridical (respectively related in Kant to the obligation of conscience and state coercion), and the general and the particular (or community and individuality).[14]

More time would be necessary to discussion the extent and limits of reflexive individualism, comparing it to other forms of reflexivity, which, coming from the humanist tradition, did not have the same privileged destiny within the constitution of classical subjectivity, or were relegated to a single side of the divide between exteriority and interiority, for pragmatic as well as political reasons. Many of these forms of reflexivity are obviously fundamental: in particular, the idea of being "one's own doctor" (still present in Descartes) and that of being "one's own educator" (the trace of which runs from Montaigne to Rousseau, forming a sort of contestatory hypothesis with respect to the development of educational institutions that revolve around the figure of the "master," thus situated in the margins of the conflict over such institutions between religious and secular authorities).

Leaving aside (unfortunately, because this is the most decisive point) the question of the "mad" idea of engendering oneself, I will concentrate on the problem posed by the notion of "defending oneself." We know that this problem has not at all disappeared from modern political culture (witness the virulent debates on the *right to bear arms* in a country such as the United States). It does not represent something *impossible*, at least in every circumstance, but rather a *prohibition*, or else the object of a *sacrifice* made by the individual in exchange for greater security, which might also be identified as the passage from politics to the police. This is a central argument in Hobbes, who also discusses its limitations: No one can be coerced (even by the sovereign) *to accuse himself* of a crime, whether he committed it or not. Correlatively, no one has the right *to defend another man* against the sovereign, whether he is guilty or innocent.[15] In *Leviathan*, Chapter 28, Hobbes recalls how, by the Covenant at the origin of civil society, each man abandons the right to defend the others but not the right to defend himself. Accordingly, he may certainly come to the assistance of the sovereign against another entity but not against himself. This is why the guilty subject who revolts, who refuses his punishment, is not punished as a *citizen* but rather as an *enemy* of the State. Correlatively, the question arises whether it suffices, in order for the citizen to remain a citizen throughout his punishment, to submit and stifle his pride.[16] It thus becomes clear that the sacrifice of self-defense and the absolutization of self-judgment are two faces of the same constitution of subjectivity.

Above all, however, it is necessary to investigate the role of the upsurge of this self-referential instance of justice in the remaking of the judicial institution that made it not only the emanation of state power (as is massively the case in Hobbes, where self-judgment maintains only a residual, negative function, but thereby all the more significant) but also the institutional expression of "moral personality"—or, as Foucault would say, the *empirico-transcendental doublet* that makes the individual, bearer of moral and social universality, into the constituent power of the State and the subject of the historical community. This is what I had in mind a moment ago when I spoke of the implantation of the universal—in the form of the law (or its "imperative")—at the heart of subjectivity itself. Whence a dialectic of judgment whose mainspring, as we know, is the idea of a self-doubling, but also the idea that moral education forms an essential condition of autonomy, necessary to the foundation of "man" as well as the "citizen."

It is interesting in this respect to examine the similarities and differences between Rousseau's formulations and those of Kant. It can be convincingly shown, by rereading the lines from the *Social Contract* on the "double relation" between the individual and the law (as an obedient subject and as a citizen member of the sovereign) that everything is thought in terms of *judgment*. In order for the law as an expression of the general will to "come from everyone in order to be applied to everyone" (Book II, Chapter 4), *it must be applied to all and to each*. Nonetheless, in Book III of the *Social Contract* (Chapter 1), Rousseau rejects the idea of an autonomous judicial power: in the strict sense, there are only *two powers* (the legislative and the executive). Is this not a way of saying that the "faculty of judgment" is inseparable from the idea of subjective right, and the responsibility that accompanies it, remains strictly internal and individual? In Kant, on the contrary (§45 of the *Doctrine of Right*), one finds the classical doctrine of the "three powers," determined according to the tripartite schema of the sovereign (legislator), the government (executive), and the judge (judiciary), which are like the "three propositions of a syllogism."[17] The elements of the empirico-transcendental doublet are thus in place. Self-judgment is the fundamental expression of the autonomy of the moral subject. In Section II of *Groundwork for the Metaphysics of Morals* (1785), Kant anticipated this doubling in his theorization of each subject's confrontation with the maxim of his action with the moral intention. The condition for it is the neutralization of interest, which makes it possible to represent the subject as a member of the community of reasonable beings. In the *Metaphysics of Morals* itself what becomes manifest, however, is that the counterpart of this capacity of the subject to judge himself as an empirical individual from the perspective of an ideal community, which he upholds consciously or unconsciously, is the difficulty of *absolutely judging others*.

As I have alluded, the Doctrine of Virtue includes a development on "man's duty to himself has his own innate judge."[18] Within a democratic perspective analogous to that of Rousseau, one would expect that the Doctrine of Right would include a symmetrical development on the right of individuals *to judge others*, corresponding to the external relations that subjects maintain with one another as "subjects of right." But this does not at all prove to be the case, even though, visibly (in conjunction with the discussion of French revolutionary constitutions), this problem would be at the heart of the institution of the jury and its generalization. The possibility for the people to judge itself goes by way of representation, which is here taken in the classical double sense: (1) juries are themselves instances formed of the "representation of the people," and (2) the mainspring of their activity is the law's rational capacity of "representation" (that is, the relation of subsumption of the particular case under the general rule).[19] In order to actualize Rousseau's democratic intention, it was thus necessary to go by way of precisely the institutional mediation that he recused.[20] Not before Hegel's *Elements of the Philosophy of Right*, however, will the perfect correlation of "internal right" and "external right" be actualized, which means that they must be taken in reverse order, and that the relation between conscience and the idea of God or the "kingdom of ends" must be replaced by an immanent relation between the "self," the "universal," and the "community" (which Hegel calls spirit and, in the *Phenomenology* of 1807, never ceased trying to resolve its aporias).

The Honor of the Criminal

We thus arrive at the third phase of my discussion: after the citizen's competence we are going to address his relative incompetence; after the foundation of reflexive individualism, we observe its limitation in the form of a judiciary that is essentially a social institution. The subject "individualized" by his responsibility is the *middle term*: the both indispensable and relativized mediation, destined to be surmounted by his belonging to a concrete community. But such a community is defined more than ever as a community of citizens, especially when it takes the form of the universalist nation.[21]

Is it paradoxical to use Hegel to discuss these problems that are typically those of "liberalism"? I do not think so. Hegel is indeed a liberal, in the "organic" sense; his constant problem is the possibility of instituting liberalism in the form of a State.[22] The guiding thread of *Elements of the Philosophy of Right* (1821) is a profound reflection on the function of the tribunal in relation to crime and injustice, or the "delict" (*Unrecht*), and the right to punish. Through the judicial function, right reproduces (and thus quite simply produces) the belonging of the individual to the community as an autonomous individuality. This is the heart of the ethical signification of right. This reflection comprises two correlative examinations: on the one hand, it is necessary to ask how does it happen that the individual becomes "the judge of himself" (like he can be "the owner of himself" through the intermediary of culture, which neither Kant nor Hobbes would admit) by taking part in a community and acting to transform it into an institution of the universal; and on the other hand, it is necessary to ask what "disposition of self," what form of responsibility conditions this civic belonging. The thorough examination of these philosophical and political questions will lead Hegel to look closely at the problem of the *jury*, at what enables the citizen to consider it an honor to submit to judgment and to the collectivity's right to punish (the problem of recognition par excellence). But it will also lead him philosophically to delimit the task of the police, especially with respect to the distinction between reason and madness (which, from a liberal perspective, is inseparable from the imputation of responsibility).

Three key moments in *Elements of the Philosophy of Right* pertain to this series of examinations. First, §100 on the *honor of the criminal* (which anticipates §220 on his reconciliation with the law, an indispensable moment within reconciliation with right itself). This notion has two sides: every citizen is potentially guilty because he must be able to violate the law and thereby "effectuate right" (or confront it with its real conditions of application); he has, in a sense, the "right to punishment"; but whoever is recognized as guilty must also be a citizen, co-responsible for the validity of right (and not an enemy of society or a "public enemy").[23] Next is §120, which concerns precisely the exclusion of children, the feeble-minded, and the mad: Hegel—for whom the sovereign nation-state has become analogous to a "second nature"—seems completely to ignore the question of foreigners or residents who would have a different conception of law and justice than that in the name of which their "recognition" is demanded by the State. . . . This new development will lead Hegel (remark §132) to posit that the State "attenuates or suppresses responsibility"—by virtue of what Foucault would certainly call "power-knowledge." We thus return once again to the function of the *police* as correlative to *justice*, such as it was defined in the section on "civil society."[24] Finally, the last moment is proposed by §228 in which Hegel justifies *the mixed composition of tribunals*, associating the rival principles of the popular jury and the magistracy composed of professional jurists: a jury without legal experts is blind, perhaps tyrannical, but legal experts without a jury are oppressors—whose position Hegel compares with enslavement! This is, therefore, another development of the dialectic of the "master and slave" whose conflict (struggle for recognition) is revolved in the liberal State (or constitutional State, what we will call a "State of right").[25]

By undertaking this vast and summary trajectory, my intention was not limited to putting in place a "dialectic" of the function of the citizen and constitutive subjectivity, which, through its many vicissitudes, forms a experience of civilization that seems to us to be inherent to the democratic tradition. This objective is important to the extent that, as I began by saying, it seems that technocratic and technological evolution of contemporary societies leads to the increasing expropriation of the judicial function and more generally of the citizens' own capacity to judge. One ought to ask in what forms, under what conditions, according to what anthropological foundations, or within what "cultural" or "multicultural" framework could such a capacity be defended, even extended in such a manner that its "unlimited" character would be regained.

But I also wanted to draw your attention to the contradictions and even the dimension of inhumanity that inevitably affects this capacity. This "pathology" of the judicial faculty (without which, in truth, it would only have a symbolic function) becomes manifest in the case of the distinction between reason and madness, or more exactly between crime and madness, which is the very type of the fundamental anthropological difference, at once ineluctable and indefinable (which means that "human" society, in the two senses of the term, cannot be abstracted from this difference or claim to have fixed it once and for all using "objective" criteria).[26] But perhaps it is also more secretly at work in the constitution of a subjectivity for which responsibility is inseparable from the internalization or the becoming-unconscious of the judicial function, in the form of this hyperbolic culpability that Freud called the Superego and that he made into the point of articulation between individuation and civilization.[27] Whereas, for Kant, the risk inherent to the "pathological" constitution of moral conscience is that the subject would be permanently tempted to acquit himself, "forgetting" the universality of the categorical imperative, for Freud (who, on this point, draws both from clinical experience and from literature) the "psychic tribunal" in front of which each person becomes (unconsciously) the judge of himself before judging others is a manifestation of the death drive. The risk, or rather the fatality, is that *each person has always already condemned himself* and even compelled himself to transgress the law in order to be punished in its name. This is, obviously, a paradoxical (but perhaps no less determining) justification for the necessity of external tribunals, instituted by the State in "reality": not only do they maintain social order, but they also protect individuals from their own unconscious tendencies, by limiting their desire to "judge themselves" in order to be better condemned and better punished.[28]

ELEVEN

Private Crime, Public Madness

To clarify the questions raised today by the relations between madness and justice, with reference to the heritage of the French Revolution: such a project, if not confined to the stylistic exercises that typify certain commemorations, is paradoxical in several respects. Indeed, what prompts current discussions on the function of the psychiatrist in the courtroom or on the role of judgments of civil capacity in the treatment of mental illness, is yet again the perspective offered by the reframing of the Penal Code (including the famous Article 64, which makes "insanity"—or, in the more recent version, "psychic or neuropsychic disturbance"—into the principal operator of the nullification of a crime or a delict, either in its juridical reality or in its penal consequences). Such a perspective is opened today by the modification of the law of 1838 (stopping short of its pure and simple suppression as a law that *excepts* the mad or the mentally ill from the rights that normally accrue to persons).

The fact is, in a first paradox, that this juridical corpus does not date from the revolutionary period; nor is it even the direct prolongation of its political and discursive practice. The penal code derives, on the one hand, from the imperial regime's erection of a great armature of "codes" designed to reorganize the administration of civil society on the hither side of that political torment and the momentary collapse of public order; and, on the other hand, from the July monarchy's setting up of institutions of French liberalism whose "culture of government" came with the slogan "Finish the revolution." Naturally, nothing is settled by the mere observation of a gap between the orientation of the revolutionary moment and the real origins of the "modern" psychiatric and judicial apparatus. One can and must ask what irreversible constraints the Revolution imposed on all subsequent practices of instituting social relations (which is precisely a practice of reorganizing society, carried out by men who were forged in revolutionary experience or emerged from it, whether it be Pinel or Napoleon, Guizot or Esquirol). And one should also ask how much of the real continuity, or of the symbolic effectiveness of government is due to the way in which, for nearly two centuries, every movement of reform that rises up against the institution invokes the principles, spirit, and logic of the Revolution or of its typical moments (beginning with, what is the foundational reference par excellence, the Declaration of the rights of man and of the citizen).

But precisely, this is the *second* paradox. As many commentators have been content to repeat for decades, the system of social and institutional practices that "treat" what has come to be designated globally as *deviance* (a term that we will have to discuss) no longer much resembles what it was at the start of the nineteenth century—neither from the viewpoint of its material infrastructure, nor from that of the behavior and education of its personnel, nor from that of the principles of its administration, nor even, strictly speaking, from that of its juridical nature—as soon as its pivotal utterances ("Article 64," "Law of 1838") are no longer taken solely in abstract isolation but rather as the pieces of an ensemble.[1]

To what must we attribute, then, the veritable fixation of the debates, at regular intervals, upon the letter, signification, and origins of these utterances (a fixation that never fails to produce contradictory effects, often within the same speakers, since at times the abolition and the modification of these texts are demanded *in order to align the law with practice* and at other times *in order to lift the obstacles impeding transformation of practice*)? Perhaps this fixation must be viewed as the symptom of a recurrent contradiction that is constantly displaced at the behest of social, political, or technical transformations, and of "progressions" as well as "regressions," but also constantly revived (since it is essentially unsolvable): a contradiction that is not so much *between* practice and law as *within* practice itself, but that emerges by virtue of *practice's internal relation to law*—in other words, of the constitutive role that law plays within the very institution of psychiatry. Periodically, then, discontent among the participants in the drama of mental health (doctors, but also patients and their *proches* or "intimates"[2]) will become fixated upon the demand that the texts, which confer upon mental health an official status, be rewritten. Why, then, such irony? Perhaps it must be admitted that, if the incriminated texts have not sufficed to create the institution of mental health, with the set of its social functions, or to determine the history of its successive configurations, their astonishing resistance to change is indeed the index of a structure, which remains invariable beneath the evolution of morals, practices, and forms of knowledge, and which, with irresistible force, *reintegrates* any transformation, shearing away its "excesses," within a certain social norm. In brief, if the attempts to "go beyond" Article 64 and the law of 1838 always fail, or prove incapable of producing anything truly *other*, is it certainly not because the letter of these texts, and the coupling officially established between them, contains certain of the *real conditions* that allow a society or a given type of social formations to assure its continuity (or, as one used to say, its "reproduction")?

The Conflict of the Faculties

Perusing even a small portion of the reflections that attempt to specify the objections to the psychiatric apparatus and the judicial and penal apparatus and the initiatives to re-form it, one cannot help but notice a striking circularity that first shows itself in the sym-metrical positions upheld by jurists (notably lawyers) and by psychiatrists. At the limit, one has the feeling that each protagonist, sensing the inhuman and ineffective aspects of the field in which he operates, somehow expects salvation from his counterpart. Accord-ingly, lawyers such as Robert Badinter will attempt, if not to conserve Article 64 of the penal code in its original form, then at least to transform it in a manner that increases the possibilities of transferring the authors of crimes and delicts from a penitentiary system into a medical system, to replace punishment with treatment.[3] They undoubtedly think that treatment is less destructive of the individual, or that it represents an opening toward possible evolution, whereas, in practice, penal sanction leads to a life of recidivism and asociality. But the psychiatrists who demand that hospitals or clinics for the treatment of mental illness be abolished or updated also refer increasingly to the authority of law: either to denounce the different forms of exclusion from the rule of law (at the extreme limit, the state of legal incompetence or disenfranchisement) that reduce the "mentally" ill subject (unlike all others) to the status of a minor, at once protected and sequestered, and to demand his reintegration into society as a "legal subject"[4]; or—once wardship, assistance, or the restriction of freedom have become inevitable due to the critical situa-tion that madness produces for individuals and groups—to demand the institution of more effective and democratic measures for assessing psychiatric practices.[5] We thus get the strange feeling of watching a replay, but in reverse this time, of the "conflict of the faculties" that marked the origins of the institutions of mental health and modern justice. Instead of the psychiatrist and the judge vying for control over deviant or "dangerous" individuals and for mastery over their arraignment, it is almost the opposite that takes place: The judge increasingly demands more from the psychiatrist and the psychiatrist more from judgment or from justice.[6]

In truth, the real situation is a bit more complicated. Within each "camp," there is an insistent division along the lines of this conflict of the faculties that produce divergent eval-uations of what the law and the institution are and what they produce. Neither for the same reasons nor at the same moment do the reformers of the penal system see a need for psychiatric treatment. Generally partisans of involuntary hospitalization, they consider this measure to be either a substitute for impracticable imprisonment, with a view toward normalizing, even rehabilitating the deviant individual, or a preventative, prophylactic, and even hygienic measure designed to lower the risk of criminal "passages to the act," or fi-nally as an indispensable measure to accompany or compensate for most forms of incar-ceration, without which they become practices not of the rehabilitation but rather the demolition of the personality (they ask to send psychiatrists into the prisons).[7] Likewise, all for different reasons, the spokespeople for psychiatric reformism turn to the law as a recourse against the impasse of institutionalization, even when it is transformed by grad-ual insertion into the apparatus of the "sector."[8] The double function of the psychiatrist

as bearer of knowledge and power, as representative of medical ethics and of the exigencies of public security, is at times denounced as the very root of psychiatry's reduction of
the "mad" to the status of an object,[9] and at other times, on the contrary, as an occasion
to establish—by subversion, if need be—an institutional link with the "outside" of the hospital world, that is, a link with the exigencies of society. The idea of the patient as a "subject of law" or, more recently, as a "citizen," is presented either as a preexisting limit that
ought to forbid psychiatry to turn into an undeclared enterprise of repression (even if it
is in the name of normality or of assistance and help for suffering), or as means and foothold
for therapeutic action itself (since what the psychotic must first regain, what he has foreclosed, is precisely the instance of the law that governs access to the "real").[10] In the one case,
then, the mentally ill patient is declared to be a subject of rights in order to liberate him from
a certain imposition of the law that oppresses freedom and the personality; and, in the other,
the point is to allow the patient to rediscover the sense of the law. This divergence is well
illustrated by the antithesis between the positions of Drs. Franck Chaumon and Philippe
Rappard, and it enters into their respective attitudes toward the law of 1838. Finally, it is no
longer possible to misrecognize how the references to "therapeutic citizenship" imply radically divergent orientations, depending on whether they accompany a plans to reconstitute
social relations in the "fictitious" space of the medical community, or whether they participate in the demand to dissolve this community within a "real" environment, whose capacity
for tolerance of the abnormal obviously must be systematically ameliorated.

Might we say that these crossovers manifest the persistence of a vicious circle from which
psychiatrists and jurists alike prove incapable of extracting themselves? Yes and no. Even
though they can be seen as the reflection of professional positions and ideological options,
it is also difficult not to recognize in them more profound determinations.

In the first place, what unfolds in this reformist debate is the *constitutive equivocation* of
the notions of "subject," "subject of right," and "citizenship." No matter how their therapeutic approaches diverge from one another, all the reformists remain humanists, in that
they oppose the reduction of the individual to the status of punishable, rectifiable, and
medicatable matter (even and especially under the pretext of his "dangerousness"); and that
they claim that any treatment which society proposes and imposes upon him must recognize his freedom. This position of principle doubtless becomes particularly important at
a moment when the use of psycho-pharmacological techniques is on the rise, coupled with
a new extension of psychiatric objectivism. But it does not determine whether the "freedom of the subject" consists in the individual's unconditional right to oppose any constraint
that he does not recognize as legitimate, or whether it consists in the right to guarantees
against the arbitrariness of instituted powers. Nor does it make it possible—as soon as one
enters into an ambivalent situation, at the limit of the very notion of illness, characterized
at once by the demand for help and the refusal to change (oneself), or even quite simply to
communicate—to determine whether the "rights of patients" must be interpreted as a
"rights of madness"—the right of an individual history to preserve its singularity, the right
of "abnormal" speech to be heard as such[11]—or rather as a "right to care" inscribed within
a conception of the community as a bond of solidarity. Indeed, it seems that, within the
discourse of contemporary humanism, there where the category of the "subject" once

encompassed the subject of rights as well as the subject of the unconscious, the moral person as well as the right to difference, the "citizen" is now the category that harbors the same series of contradictory determinations. "Citizenship of the mad" (or even of madness) and "therapeutic citizenship" prove to be inverse notions.

But the circularity of reformist discourse also expresses an even deeper constraint. It is not by chance that the psychiatric and judicial authorities take turns incarnating, each for the other, the figures of freedom and constraint. This oscillation is inscribed within the longstanding structure (which must well be called specular) of *madness* and *crime*. There is no crime, indeed, that is not haunted by the possibility of madness, either as its condition or its consequence. This is even a reason why, no matter the criminologists who would deny it,[12] "crime" and "delict" *are not* purely interchangeable or even roughly equivalent notions: whereas the notion of delict or even delinquency cannot help but evoke the infraction or the transgression of *positive* law (so much so that that, at the limit, it is the idea of a society without delict or delinquency, and thus without ill will, without human weakness, that appears abnormal and "mad"—and that becomes explicitly so when one evokes a program of the total eradication of delinquency), the notion of crime—as soon as one admits the relativity of the behaviors and acts that are classed as "criminal" in one society or another, from one historical epoch to another—inevitably raises the question of evil as such, conceived as the negation of human nature or as the negation of human destiny—in brief, an absolute—that cannot be treated or even thought without bringing into play the hypothesis of a cut separating the individual from the human community. This is also why, within the tradition of French democracy, the distinction between delict and crime coincides in principle with the two utterly distinct modalities of judgment and sanction, of the correctional and the assizes. The one is purely technical, the affair for professional jurists who establish the facts and apply an instituted norm to them; the other is moral and political, the affair of the representatives of the people (enlightened perhaps by the technicians) who forge an "intimate conviction" and take only their individual "soul and conscience" as judge, shifting from positive to natural law. The passage from one sense of infraction to the other, from the category of crime to that of delict (example of blasphemy) or vice versa (example of rape), is thus not a question of degree, or gravity, but rather a question of principles and of civilization, which distinguishes two regimes of truth.

Accordingly, there is no madness—in the strong sense of the term: dementia, psychosis— that is not haunted by the possibility of crime, already transparently inscribed within the institutional category of "dangerousness." More precisely, there is no madness that does not confront the individual, his "intimates," and the collectivity with the eventuality of death, even with its imminence, neither as "natural" nor as "accidental" death, but rather as "unnatural" death, the turning of life against itself. Distinctions should probably be made. Which death? And *whom* does it threaten? (Or even: *what* does it consist of?—since there are "slow deaths" compared to which the arrest of physiological functions seems insignificant . . .). But isn't the eventuality of death in psychosis, beyond nosographic types, characterized precisely by the way in which it obscures the identity of the potential victim? Suicide or homicide are "opposites"; but, if the chain of causes that leads to them, or the structure that implies them, were radically heterogeneous, it is likely that the psychiatric or institutional formula for a person who is "a danger to himself and to others," which is inscribed in the law of 1838, would not have endured as long as it has. Crime thus appears as one of the possibilities, or one of the vicissitudes of madness, which no one has the power to exclude a priori (since there is madness in the very attempt to exclude it, just as, symmetrically, today we find something demented in the naturalist enterprise of nineteenth-century organicist psychiatry and criminology to exclude a priori the eventuality of suicide by forging the category of the "born criminal").[13]

The Structure of Alienation: How to Explain It?

It seems fairly obvious that, on an institutional level, crime and madness are always already situated in the vicinity of one another, such that each term becomes the other's virtual cause or consequence. What is less clear is why these terms should have the status of an unavoidable *alternative* that excludes any "third possibility" and that assigns the individual to one or the other category as soon as violence comes into play (or to be more specific: illegitimate violence—not only individual but also contrary to social norms, which illustrates the relativity of the *conditions* in which this alternative is applied and produces its effects, effects that become all the more absolute as their rationale becomes less explicit). Institutional alternative: what Dominique Coujard, speaking of the "choice" offered by Article 64 of the Penal Code, excellently calls a "medico-legal Yalta."[14] Existential alternative—the properly *alienating* alternative, as Lacan would say, because it restricts the individual (the "subject") to a choice between two modalities of destruction, to two vicissitudes of exclusion: either to be unapologetically criminal (which could mean identifying with someone who must be a criminal or someone who will always become a criminal once again), or to claim one's innocence, in no way the author of the act committed by the "other" who is oneself.

It is fairly obvious that it is precisely this alternative (alienating for the individual, for his "intimates," for the collectivity itself, since it precludes any possibility of "recuperation" and thus of salvation for its fallen members, in an epoch that institutionally no longer believes in a beyond) which reformisms, especially those of psychiatrists, seek to dislodge, calling into question either the function of expertise that the courts impose on them or the judicial and penal element inscribed within their function and their therapeutic practice. It is no less evident that this constantly scuttled undertaking is basically a failure, in the sense that there are ultimately always insurmountable obstacles to any radical reform of the institutional apparatus, such that this apparatus always ends up being reproduced in practically unchanged form. It is even possible to uphold that *the more* that Article 64 of the Penal Code and the law of 1838 are updated, so as to avoid the condemnation of nonpunishable individuals, *the more* the alternative "either insane or criminal" will be effectively implemented, and thus become unavoidable. . . . Once again, therefore, we must ask whether this alternative might not be a veritable *structure*: which does not mean that it is transhistorical, and thus absolutely impossible to transform, but that, since it functions as the invariant or common presupposition of a range of practices, individual and social, symbolic and material, it is not possible to envisage its modification without first or simultaneously displacing an entire set of correlative representations and social relations.

Let us suppose that it is in fact the case that the alternative between crime and madness, inscribed within the fabric of innumerable individual existences, is the structural knot that institutions have materialized in history for a long period from which we have yet to emerge. How could we account for it? First, there are three types of explanations that might be called metahistorical. Without a doubt, these explanations each highlight different aspects of the structure (that is, they add new dimensions to the idea that we could form its necessity, they "tighten the knot" a little, and they thereby allow us better to understand why it is so difficult to loosen). But each of them, it seems to me, stops short of explaining the structure's *mode of functioning* within our most familiar institutions forms.

There is, first, a theological explanation (even and especially if it takes the form of a philosophy of the history of modern societies that characterizes them in terms of "disenchantment," "secularization," or the "decline of the sacred"). It is the theory that Dostoyevsky adumbrates in *The Brothers Karamazov*, which hinges upon the claim that crime and madness represent two "remainders" left behind after the *disappearance of sin* from the institutions and beliefs of the West (at least insofar as it is an incontestable absolute, a "normal" and normalizing term). The criminal and the madman (the alienated, the mentally ill) can thus be thought within a moral register or in the register of nature (of the spirit or the body); but they remain specially human, anthropological notions that elude the supernatural dimension of sin in which the upsurge of evil is both explained and condemned by a transcendental injunction. Precisely because of this disappearance of sin from our *objective* intellectual horizon (as Hegel would say) we would seek *subjectively* to understand the enigma of what used to be called the "sinner's" culpability as a sort of combination of the consciousness of crime and the unconsciousness of madness. But this disappearance is also what might clarify the *opposition* between the two secularized figures of evil that now confront us. Indeed, without any transcendental instance to unify them, each of the two notions retains a single aspect of transgression, either the transgression of law or that of meaning, either evil affecting the will or evil affecting reason and understanding. However, it might be suggested, at least formally, that this *dissociation* is at the same time what necessarily *binds* the notion of crime and madness to one another, thereby instituting them as a veritable alternative, unavoidable as soon as the question of evil is effectively posed for modern man. Accordingly, the "sin" absent from crime and madness would not be totally abolished but rather repressed, which means that the secularization or laicization of our societies is less a matter of abolishing the theological horizon than of displacing its location and its function. Rather than functioning as a "plenitude," this horizon now functions as a "void," taking the form of a negative justification rather than a positive "foundational norm" exhibited by institutions themselves. Since men cannot *really* be sinners, they must become madmen or criminals when they represent evil for other men or for themselves. No matter how illuminating this explanation may be on the symbolic level—constituting, in a sense, the corollary to an elucidation of the paradox of "the sanctity" of laws in secular societies—it has the drawback of not helping at all to understand the various modalities in which the theological returns or is disavowed within judicial and psychiatric practices, always rife of paradoxes. Isn't the judicial apparatus that employs the most "rationalist" (if not the most "utilitarian") procedures for defining and sanctioning responsibilities the one that cannot avoid perpetuating the forms of the sacralization of power? Isn't the criminology informed by biology and psychiatry the one that comes the closest to reconstituting the unitary theological figure of sin by producing the myth of the "criminally insane" or the "born criminal," albeit to inscribe this myth within an wholly positivist framework?[15]

The next explanation would be sociological or, more precisely, an explanation in terms of the class struggle: at the bottom of the medico-legal structure's astounding resistance to change, and of the complementarity of the categories of crime and madness, should be discerned a strategy of domination by the bourgeois classes, utilizing the State in order to discipline or hegemonize civil society. From this viewpoint, the analyses proposed or prompted by Michel Foucault's *History of Madness* and *Discipline and Punish* are in no way incompatible with a certain Marxist tradition. Indeed, these analyses continue to show that the categories of "mental illness" and "delinquency" are structurally inapposite categories, clumsy with respect to their explicit object: Conceptually and institutionally, they *fail to grasp* a large share of "madness" and "illegality" (actually, the essential share, in both cases), amalgamating them into a mass of behaviors incompatible with the social order, generally ascribed to the lower classes, or to situations of individual "exclusion" or insecurity that, for underprivileged people, result from the ferocity of this same social order. Accordingly, it should come as no surprise that prisons and psychiatric hospitals are populated by the lower classes. How to interpret the risk of abnormality and dangerousness that, in the form of mental illness or criminality, effectively hangs over the potentially rebellious exploited populations? One might attempt a functionalist reading, explaining that this risk is part of a strategy of intimidation and disqualification, which essentially functions in the margins, and by means of marginalization: Not every proletarian is labeled a madman or a criminal, but every proletarian, if he commits a crime or goes mad, is in danger of falling into the subproletariat—that is, into a state of insecurity and nonright that, in turn, are supposed to be the breeding ground of "crime" and "madness." Further, this force of this explanation can be multiplied by showing the mechanism whereby the ideological effectiveness of this strategy is produced. Since class conflict is not represented as such, questions of public order no longer pertain to politics but rather to hygiene and "social defense." But there is also an unwished-for result, a compromise formation between the demands of social control, the "disciplinary" objectives, and the forms of rationality in which the bourgeois elite perceive the meaning of their own domination and their own social organization as a progressive and normalizing work: "abnormality" can permanently be relied on to prove how well founded the enterprise is and to indicate the type of resistance (deliberate or not) that it must always confront. Within this perspective, however, even if it is not difficult to interpret the omnipresence of the imaginary of social danger and pauperization in the criminal type and in taxonomy of the symptoms of madness, at least two questions remain. In the first place, the very question of the differentiation between the "madman" and the "criminal," the question why these two complementary figures, constantly associated in practice, are conceptually opposed to one another. They might be expected to merge within a single category analogous to "unreason" in the classical age—correlative to what Foucault called the "great confinement," which, as we know, *anachronistically* provided the model of the critical notion of exclusion such as it was globalized, and simplified, by anti-institutional discourse in the 1970s. In the second place, there is the question of why this conceptual couple has been perpetuated beyond the social conditions of its formation, while the direct confrontation between the dominant class and the "dangerous classes" gave way to a much more individualized and much more technicized system of social control. For several decades, it has been periodically announced that the installation of a differentiated, welfare-oriented, and normative network for the "management of risk" (to borrow the title of a notable book)[16] would result in the withering away of the great psychiatric and judicial apparatuses. However, even if we have the technical means to bring about such a withering away, there is no evidence of a univocal evolution in this direction, but rather the superposition of old and new forms. Everything proceeds as if "crime" and "madness" were unavoidable notions.[17]

The third type of explanation is completely different: it inheres within the very logic of juridical form. At the beginning of the nineteenth century, there was an inversion within the hierarchy of "cases" that call for a distinction (and thus a confrontation) between crime and madness.[18] But this observation should not make us lose sight of the fact that the alternative of crime and madness, along with the logic of the "excluded third" that it implies, corresponds exactly to the binary form of the juridical problems of competence, property, and responsibility. Of course, such a form (well before the emergence of the notion of a "subject of law") does not predetermine the modalities whereby the juridical personality is attributed and recognized, whereby situations of conflict are resolved, or whereby the guilty are processed. Nor does it even imply that responsibility and irresponsibility are absolutely exclusive, external to one another (or cannot be combined to various degrees). For a long time, in fact, the opposite was the rule, destined to be reintroduced with the more recent notion of "attenuating circumstances." But this binary form imposes two fundamental constraints: (1) that any possession of a right or a property also implies responsibility for the consequences of its exercise or its use; (2) that any person who is not responsible for his acts himself becomes the responsibility of an other person (whether it be a physical person or a moral person, that is an institution).[19] This is why, if the treatment of "unreason" in the classical age becomes a problem for the police and is thus situated in some sense outside the law, the provisions of Article 64 of the Penal Code, which bind the alternative of crime and madness to the question of responsibility along with its correlatives and its placeholders (imputability, culpability, punishability), are already contained within the provisions of ancient law (Roman—and thus private—law, and canon law). Even the formulation, "in a state of insanity or coercion by an irresistible force," which does not proceed directly from it, becomes evident because the distinction between "internal" coercion and "external" coercion is a logical part of the structure (as the dual fashion of disjoining the actor from the juridical author of an action).

Nonetheless, this binary form is not capable of explaining why the two antithetical situations must each be essentialized within a human type (the madman, the criminal), or why they must be conceived as mutually exclusive inversions of the "normal" human condition, whereby they turn into individual destinies. Only when such a transformation occurs, however, is the law invoked, not only to decide upon the competence or incompetence of persons, but to orient the "invalidated" subject toward the "total" institutions, at once segregating and orthopedic, of the prison and the psychiatric hospital, respectively saddled with the infinite task of restoring morality, as well as rational thought or the ability to communicate. There is, then, if not a break in the form of the law, then at least a revolution in its usage that this form cannot account for.

The Great Bourgeois Divide

Before attempting my own response, which would not invalidate these three explanations, but rather would open a trajectory beyond what remains doubtful in them, we must specify how, historically and logically, the structure of "crime and madness" is liable to vary in the process of its application.

Indeed, it is possible to imagine three different ways of treating this alternative. The first consists in thinking it as essentially incomplete, reserving for the individual or for part of himself the possibility of *neither* being accused of madness *nor* of criminality. The second consists in thinking that the two terms of the alternative might be fused or even might derive from a fundamental unity—that of a form of individuality which is *both* mad *and* criminal—potentially called "abnormality," "asociality," or "deviance."[20] The third, finally, consists in keeping the alternative in the form of a reciprocal exclusion: *Either* the dangerous or abnormal individual is mad *or* he is criminal, but he cannot be both at the same time. It is immediately obvious that these different possibilities not only correspond to distinct psychologies or social analyses but also crystallize political visions of the world. They derive from such visions (as if such political ideologies were definitive) than perpetually contribute to constituting them and to dissociating them from one another.

Neither mad nor criminal: This is, we might say, the formula of utopian critique of segregative institutions, in the sense that they uphold the existence, among individuals who "pass to the act" of violence (and sometimes also undergo such acts), of "cases" that are irreducible to this dichotomy and that are consequently not susceptible to being "treated" by the procedures that it implies. Better yet, this formula upholds that there is a part of *every individual* that cannot be understood either in terms of pathology or of transgression of the established order; and that can only be engaged apart from the rituals prescribed by these institutional types or essences. Such engagement is only possible on the basis of a metaphysics of the soul or the subject—which might be personalist or, on the contrary, structuralist (as in the psychoanalytic tradition) but is always linked both to an affirmation of the irreducible singularity of individuals and to a critique of the distinction between normality and abnormality, either recusing any use whatsoever of the idea of abnormality or on the contrary insisting on the virtual pathology universally present in human individuality, the actualization of which is circumstantial not constitutional.

Both mad and criminal: This is, conversely, the formula of conservative positivism, for which the distinction between the normal and the pathological becomes truly constitutive.[21] It is illustrated particularly well by the criminological and psychiatric variants of organicism; but it also reemerges in behaviorist objectivism, because what can be said in the language of "degeneracy" can also be said in that of "maladjustment." The usage of the terms of abnormality and deviance are probably those that best characterize this position. Subsuming crime and madness under a single signifier, they make it possible perpetually to renew the process of explaining guilt in naturalistic terms. This becomes even clearer if we suppose that the authoritarian or disciplinarian treatment of individual violence—including that which is directed against the individual himself, never inconsequential for his entourage since it is basically impossible to find individuals *whom no one needs*—presupposes and calls into question the law as an absolute good, the absolute value of society as a totality. If this absolutization of society (or the institutions that represent it) were not a problem, there would be no place for the *overdetermination* of the asocial individual in terms of the strangely cumulative double register of the pathological and the judicial, which, in turn, entails the instrumentalization of institutions in the service of a single program of "social defense." In his courses from the 1970s, Foucault studied the gradual installation of the "models" of such overdetermination—monstrosity, incorrigibility, perverse infantile sexuality—but he also illustrated its conceptual instability.[22] There is, indeed, something untenable about the notion of the "criminally insane" or in the combination of determinism and condemnation, which leads to the oscillation between different forms of anti-utopia: the abolition of the juridical moment as such (replaced by the automatism of the division between "curable" and "incurable" cases), or inversely the reinforcement of a juridico-penitentiary apparatus armed with legal certainties and harboring practices of elimination. As opposed to critical utopianism, whose principled refusal of the categories of "exclusion" always tend to turn into a projective inversion: the individual as such is neither insane nor criminal; *it is society* that produces these situations, first by categorizing them; and, at the limit, it is *to society itself* that the predicates "mad" and "criminal" should be attributed.

Between these two extremes, we can better understand why the "liberal" formula par excellence is that of *the alternative: either mad or criminal*. It is a closed alternative, in the sense that it imposes the forced choice (an "alienating" choice, as I described earlier) of one term or the other. But it is also an open alternative, in that it always necessarily confers upon an a posteriori examination—that is, to an expertise, if not a process of deliberation—the burden of determining individual destiny. The paradox (and the violence) of expertise is that it fixates a destiny and, at the same time, proclaims it to be contingent, revisable. But the very form of the alternative—which can very well coexist in practice with a whole range of more or less repressive practices—excludes the idea of predetermination. It is part of a system of "guarantees" that function to confirm that society does not save or condemn the individual in advance; that the individual retains the formal, theoretical possibility, even in limit situations that entail segregation, of choosing his role. This explains, it seems to me, why the medico-psychiatric structure is part of an ensemble that includes, on the one hand, the institution of the popular jury, and on the other, the principled insistence upon the possibility of a "moral treatment" of madness. The *border* between crime and madness, responsibility and irresponsibility, punishment and treatment, must never be drawn once and for all, but is must be as such (that is, as a posed and debated *question*) unavoidable, or "regulative," as Kant would say. This is why discussions on the conditions of expertise, the designation of those who exercise it, the moment of its intervention, and the adequacy or in adequacy of the categories it deploys, are not (or not only) symptoms of the inadequacy or blockage of the system, but also and above all the modalities of it s real functioning in time. Around these modalities might always be reconstituted, if not a consensus, then at least a regime of equilibrium between powers and social forces.[23]

This would explain the double historical dissonance within the construction of the medico-legal system whose astonishing resistance to change is on display today: on the one hand, the fact that Article 64 comes *before* the law of 1838, even though both are products of juridical "rationalism"; on the other hand, the fact that they are both *posterior* to the events of the Revolution and the formulation of its principles. The point is not that a general disposition, which addresses the very definition of a "subject of law," should have preceded a disposition of the exception that extracts certain individuals from the "common law," nor that a pure legislation of public order (the first function of the State) should have preceded a legislation that combines public order and welfare, the function of "sovereignty" and the "social" function of the State. It is that this is precisely the logical order of the *constitution of the subject* corresponding to the institution of liberal society—or better, corresponding to the becoming-subject of the universal "citizen" (promised rather than truly promoted by the French Revolution) within a liberal society, which is to say a society that relies upon law to regulate social conflicts, anthropological differences, and cultural tensions. Such a society might be more or less repressive in practice, and "social defense" remains one of its main concerns (especially because, incontestably, it always considers antagonisms as a threat or a form of violence); but it must always begin by giving *itself* a regulative law of *correspondence* between the universality of citizenship, which defines belonging to a political community, and the particularity of individual differences, which defines subjectivity with respect to the law. This is precisely what supports the institution of a medico-legal system that is encapsulated in the formula, "either mad or criminal," and in this sense, even if it is repressively applied to the dominated classes, it retains a more general scope, which might be called "hegemonic," constitutive of the relation between the two roles that the liberal State assigns to the individual—a member of the "sovereign" collective *and* a subject of the law (who ought to be permanently confronted with the problem of his own "will" to obey the law, or, if one prefers, his voluntary servitude toward a purely abstract and symbolic master, and with the moral and existential "choice" that such a obedience implies).

It is surprising that Michel Foucault—pursuing by turns the study of the constitution of the psychiatric apparatus and the penitentiary apparatus little by little discovers the forms of their similarity (the objectification of the subject) and of their complementarity (the "conflict of the faculties" that opposes medical power to judicial power, and that ultimately arranges for the latter to grant the former the greatest possible breadth, but at its very heart, under its hegemony)—would end up eluding the question of the relation between the institutions that arose immediately or mediately after the revolutionary rupture and the political and anthropological constraints imposed by this same rupture upon the construction of liberal society.[24] Indeed, the "man"—who must be constituted as a subject by his relation to the different institutions of the State—is not only the man of bourgeois society; he is also, indissociably, *the man of citizenship*, the different spheres and different degrees of the exercise of citizenship. The revolutionary rupture itself only implies the universalization of citizenship; and negatively, it thereby ruins the possibility of any compromise between the formalism of law and religious anthropologies, as well as purely discretionary police practices. By the same token, however, it opens, in two phases, the task of an institutional construction of the "subject" corresponding to this citizen, intended to precede it and render it possible, within the conditions of a bourgeois society and sociability.[25]

Among these conditions, it is clear, by way of conclusion, which one should be emphasized. Michel Foucault described at length the moral and social grip of the family in the institutional transformations that took place at the end of the eighteenth and the beginning of the nineteenth centuries. Notably, he recalled that the institution of the asylum, which will contribute to the objectification of madness, was only set up after a previous initiative to found a mode of treatment upon the participation of the family, the "family courts," had failed, and as a substitute for this initiative. Likewise, he describes the way in which the alternative of crime and madness is inherently bound up with familial violence, especially murder perpetrated against family members. He thereby shows the intimate solidarity that links the bourgeois institution of the border between the "normal" and the "pathological" within moral behavior to the sociological and juridical distinction between the public and private spheres. Within this very volume,[26] Jean Bart and François Hincker remind us, against the tenacious legends dredged up within many current discussions around "citizenship" and "exclusion," that the repressive dispositions inherited from *interdiction* and perpetuated within *incompetence*, and then within wardship, always proceeded *from private law toward public law* (not the inverse), and most often instituted a civil incapacity while maintaining political capacity. The essential thing was patrimony, paternal power, not the right to vote. However, this private incompetence, which is systematically associated with the irresponsibility of the madman or the forfeiture of the criminal, is entirely codified and decided upon by the State, henceforth the grand tutor of all the families upon which it is directly imposed within its role as guarantor of the social order.

This is why I would be tempted to propose that the great bourgeois divide between crime and madness is also one of the forms, or one of the moments, of the new divide between the public and private spheres. From this moment on—at least virtually, because there subsist more or less "active," more or less "passive" citizens who are the stakes of a permanent political conflict—every individual exists as a subject within the public sphere *and* within the private sphere. How does this distinction not only not disappear but even come to be reinforced?

One answer might be "property," which is incontestably a part of the solution. Another answer might be the family itself, insofar as it is a basic institution of the national "community" by means of sexual difference. Yet another answer, on a wholly other level, would be the unconscious: because a society in which, *in one way or another*, the distinction between the public and private sphere is not assured, is a society in which the "passions," the vicissitudes of love and hate, demands for the satisfaction of desire, would never run up against an institution of the "reality principle." This would be a "savage" society. At the junction of all these functions, in order to sanction the separation of the public and private spheres, whose modalities are purely historical and social, and in order to operate the collective repression of "primary processes" (as Freud calls them), we find precisely strategies and institutions for defining "responsibility." However, the medico-legal apparatus put in place at the beginning of the nineteenth century is clearly an apparatus designed to publicize crime and to privatize madness: One might even say that it is an apparatus designed to confer (through the procedures of investigation, judgment, and punishment, not to mention the integral role of the press) a supplement of publicity upon crime and symmetrically a supplement of privacy upon madness (by assigning it purely familial causes and, in the end, logically, by offering the family of the psychotic treatment as a group for "its problem," or by reconstituting within institutional space a community of the family type rather than the civic or professional type). *Private* property, *private* passions, *private* madness—these constitute the poles of a certain sphere, which has its own forms of objectivity and subjectivity. *Public* crime, the *public* functions of family ties themselves: the bounds of another sphere (still sometimes haunted by the ghost of "civil death," derived from the Napoleonic Code).

Here again, we can hesitate between a functional explanation and a conjunctural explanation. Either we presume that the formal logic of the rule of law confronted with violence and internal danger consists in distributing cases between the public and the private or rather, as history shows, that the very uncertainty of this border requires its reinforcement with a second degree exclusion, an exclusion within the exclusion, which is indeed, in a sense, the alternative (that I have called liberal) between crime and madness. On this basis, we might better understand both why the structure that appears in the institutional forms of Psychiatry and Justice is so resistant to change, and why it still appears ever more "in crisis." How indeed do we maintain this categorization, this symbolization of "evil" (and misfortune) when its bases—individual citizenship and property,[27] reciprocity of the institution of the State and the institution of the Family within the constitution of the "subject"—become largely ungraspable? Why, as well, wouldn't we expect new fluctuations in the notion of responsibility or in the distinction between the public sphere and the private sphere as we witness the increasing importance of forms of social "pathology," both individual and collective, which lend themselves less and less easily to being thought and classified within the properly liberal alternative between crime and madness? In this respect, one might invoke drug use, but also the set of "handicaps" now codified by law and entrusted to the care of the state, or again the conundrum of racist and sexist "aggressivity,"[28] the prevention and sanction of domestic abuse, and so forth. To some degree—not by chance—these "pathologies," for approximately the last twenty years, have subtended reformist politics and libertarian utopias. But they also give us reason to fear that they serve as justification, or pretext, for the resurgences of organicism and authoritarianism united within a new culture of "social defense." *Private crime, public madness*: In the end, this inversion of the "normal" order of things does not seem so improbable.

The Invention of the Superego: Freud and Kelsen, 1922

On the occasion of the 150th anniversary of the birth of Sigmund Freud, speaking in an amphitheater that bears the name of Jean-Martin Charcot, the theoretician of hysteria who was his teacher, I would like to present a synthesis—and thus inevitably a mere summary—of the initial results of the research that I have been conducting over the last several years, primarily within the framework of the seminars that Bertrand Ogilvie organized at the Université de Paris X–Nanterre. These seminars led me to reconsider what I believed I knew about the evolution of Freud's thinking, in particular with respect to the constitution of the "second topic" and its relation with a specific historical conjuncture, but also with contemporaneous debates in political and legal philosophy. I say "results," but it would actually be better to speak of hypotheses, for nothing of what I have to present is certain—far from it—and its most immediate effect is to reopen questioning in a range of directions.

These hypotheses bear upon what one might call the invention of the superego (the term adopted in English, both capitalized and not, with or without a dash, in order to translate the Freudian term *Über-Ich*) and simultaneously upon the relation between psychoanalytic discourse and the problem of the political: not as a relation of application, a philosophical analogy, or simply of their mutual dependence on a common anthropology or theory of "culture," but rather as a veritable reciprocity of perspectives, manifest in a recurring question that both fields recognize as their own. This reciprocity, I would argue, is manifestly evidenced in Freud's very introduction of the concept of the "superego," which thus becomes the representative of the political at the heart of the theory of the unconscious just as it is or could be the representative of the unconscious psyche at the heart of political theory. Indeed, I believe that it is possible to explain this reciprocity both chronologically and by interpreting its signification with respect to what should be considered the crucially important encounter in 1922 between Freud and Hans Kelsen, which has not gone entirely unnoticed by historians and philosophers but has never, to my knowledge, been considered as a decisive event (except perhaps in the research undertaken, some time ago, by Enrique Mari).[1]

An Encounter

A few precautions are necessary at this point. First, there is no question of claiming to pull out of a hat the heretofore unknown "reason" why Freud, in his famous essay *Das Ich und das Es*, published in April 1923 and composed throughout the previous year, decided to introduce the word *Über-Ich*, which had never before appeared in his writing,[2] without taking into account the internal evolution of Freudian thinking, indissociably theoretical and clinical. The invention of the superego—at once conceptual and verbal—functioned to crystallize Freud's rethinking of his representations of the psychic apparatus, a dissociation of the functions of consciousness (*Bewusstsein*) and of the ego (*Ich*),[3] and a definition of the ego as an essentially unconscious agency of the personality, divided between the contradictory exigencies of the libido, feelings of guilt, and the reality principle. This rethinking had already been underway for several years; and it might even be claimed that it could already be found in germ in the attempt to inscribe the vicissitudes of the drives and their specific ambivalence within the Oedipal scenario. But the meaning of this evolution can only be grasped by restoring a "missing link" that is particularly decisive because it bears upon the emergence of a name ("superego") for the concept, and because, as we know, in any theory the effectiveness of rethinking and the new problems that it opens hinge upon the cognitive and performative event of this *naming of the concept*.

Whence a second point of clarification. The encounter between Freud and Kelsen, which takes place in 1921, is clearly marked by the publication in 1922 in *Imago* of Kelsen's long lecture (first delivered within the framework of the Vienna Psychoanalytic Society on November 30, 1921) entitled "The Concept of the State and Social Psychology, with reference to the Freudian theory of group psychology" (*Der Begriff des Staates und die Sozialpsychologie. Mit besonderer Berücksichtigung von Freuds Theorie der Masse*), in which, for forty dense pages, he comments on Freud's essay from the previous year (*Massenpsychologie und Ich-Analyse*). My hypothesis—perhaps too simplistic, but it aims to highlight a largely underappreciated element—is that this encounter must have pushed Freud toward a theoretical inflection if not an outright turning point.[4] Nonetheless, this is not the aspect of this encounter that has been privileged by commentators on the event, who have preferred to investigate what Kelsen sought from psychoanalysis during the preparatory phases of his "pure theory of law"—going on from there, by way of a theory of the imaginary, of "fictions," or of the symbolic order, to enhance applied psychoanalysis with aspects of a Kelsenian philosophy of law.[5] For my own part, following Kelsen's interpellation to the letter, I will seek to reconstitute the implications of his commentary and to imagine its impact upon Freud's thinking, upon which I believe that the effects are immediately observable. Freud had more than a momentary reaction to Kelsen's argument, in which, claiming that he found in Freud an attempt to construct the concept of the State by means of psychoanalysis extended from the individual to social relations, he proposed to establish both the critical function of this concept and its limits of validity. It prompted him to do real work within the field of psychoanalysis, bearing precisely,[6] as I will show presently, upon the unconscious articulation of the relation between guilt and obedience or coercion, and upon what exposes the subject of law to "voluntary servitude," a question raised by Kelsen that Freud wanted to reformulate and restore to its proper place. The point is not only to make the encounter with Kelsen into the occasion to make an argument of political philosophy but, more important, to show how, for the first time, a properly political question was made to play a constitutive role within the theorization of the psyche.[7] If one adopts such a hypothesis, the encounter between Freud and Kelsen, which lends its language to the first "political moment" (there will be others) in the history of psychoanalysis, no longer appears merely as an occasion or a incitation but clearly contributes directly to the framing of a problem, to the inventing of a terminology, and to the determination of a conceptual content.[8]

Critique of Political Psychology

I presume that we are all familiar with the content of Freud's 1921 essay on "group psychology."[9] It is organized in three sections. The first is devoted to a critical reading of theories of social psychology that revolves around the hypothesis of *suggestion* and the distorted expression that it gives to the way in which libido circulates within the construction and decomposition of institutions. The second is devoted to the elaboration of the properly Freudian category of *identification*, of which Chapter VIII features a graph built around the analogy between the structure of social relations and that of the phenomena of "fixation" or "object choice" in hypnosis and the state of being in love. Finally, the third section is devoted to the attempt to discover the genetic foundation of the previously described phenomena with reference to the anthropological theory developed in *Totem and Taboo* (1912), and thus in terms of the regression to an archaic prototype of the relations of dependency upon an authority figure of the "paternal" type. In addition to this ternary progression, the essay features two developments that are very important from a methodological viewpoint: (1) an introductory chapter that raises the question of going beyond the opposition between individual and collective psychology, and (2) an "afterward" (*Nachträge*) that proposes a typology of *Massenbildungen* or "mass formations" (which are also, per definition, formations of the unconscious) which distinguishes between formations that put two subjects into relation (or a subject and an object, and vice versa) as in hypnosis and being in love, formations constituted by a multiplicity of subjects linked to one another and to their "model" through the mechanism of identification, and finally, in an antithetical manner, formations that pertain to a subject deprived of social relations or whose social relations are inhibited, as in neurosis or a fortiori in autism. This afterward, whose theses bring to mind certain aspects of Simmel's work (a comparison set aside by Freud but that Kelsen will outline in his commentary) suggests a possible development of the problematic of the *Massenpsychologie* very different from that which hinges upon the idea of archaic regression—but this is another matter that I must leave aside for now.

It should go without saying that *Massenpsychologie* belongs to the history of political philosophy and even constitutes a turning point within this history, to be situated in a series that begins with Plato's *Republic* and goes up to Arendt's *Origins of Totalitarianism*, passing by way of *The Prince* (Machiavelli), the *Leviathan* (Hobbes), *The Social Contract* (Rousseau), *Elements of the Philosophy of Right* (Hegel), *Capital* (Marx), *The Concept of the Political* (Schmitt), and so on. But this does not prevent Freud's essay from being a work of psychoanalysis—*theoretical* psychoanalysis, a term that I adopt to finish once and for all with opposition between "pure" and "applied." But we need to be more specific: *Massenpsychologie* occupies the terrain of a preexisting discipline that might be called (and that today, notably in English-speaking universities, is still occasionally called) "political psychology" in a critical fashion that is not without analogy to the way in which Marx occupied the terrain of "political economy." In particular, this means that—as Marx did with Quesnay, Smith, or Ricardo—Freud *appropriates* a good many of the notions and the problematics from the discourse that he criticizes even as he displaces and sometimes overturns it. His writing remains to an essential degree a *paraphrase*.

The prehistory of political psychology goes back as far as Plato and notably to his ferocious critique, in Book VIII of the *Republic*, of democracy and the manner in which it turns into tyranny. The properly modern tradition of political psychology—in the nineteenth century—is inseparable from the conservative reactions to the French Revolution and liberalism (in Le Bon, Taine, and even Tarde) that find in mass movements with a popular basis, and especially in socialism, a form of social pathology, a decomposition of authority and a return to barbarism at the heart of civilization that threaten political order and that bear witness to the proximity between the soul of the crowd and that of primitives, women, children, and criminals, in whom the allegedly irrational element prevails over the rational element. It is precisely in order to designate this analogy and to enroot it in a biological evolutionism oriented by a racial determinism that political psychology, especially in France, makes use of the term *unconscious* and associates it with the superimposition of medical language upon the description of social phenomena. This is all familiar to us today thanks to the work of Michel Foucault and others.[10]

The central problem of political psychology, especially in Le Bon, is that of the enslavement of the will or the *desire to obey* a chief, "guide," or "leader," which it articulates in a very ambivalent critical modality that fascism will eventually exploit for its own benefit. In what I interpret as his own critique of political psychology, Freud also upholds a reversal of perspectives, but one of a very different nature. Playing one version of political psychology (McDougall) against another (Le Bon), and destroying in this domain and others the pivotal antithesis between the normal and the pathological, he shows that the phenomena of suggestion—or better, the fixation of the libido upon the person of the leader (*Führer*)—accompanied by the feeling of collective omnipotence and disregard for the ordinary rules of morality, are comparable to hypnosis specifically in that they entail an *abandonment of the critical mentality*, or of the "reality principle," in favor of the dictates of the holder of authority. However, such psychologies are not only concerned with uncontrollable crowds or masses, dubbed "spontaneous" or "transitory" (that is, insurrections, mass movements, or revolutions), but first, and above all, the functioning of the institutions of the established order, among which Freud singles out the Church and the Army. The "artificial masses" (or perhaps the "constructed masses": *künstliche Massen*) are the true primary or primitive formations. Consequently—and this is one of the most remarkable aspects of his analysis—Freud assigns to collective psychology, founded not upon a racial concept of the unconscious but a sexual concept in the enlarged sense, the task of understanding both what cements the permanence and order of institutions and what happens or becomes explicit when these institutions collapse or dissolve but that had always already haunted them to such a degree that they could hope to twist it to their advantage: panic and fear of death in the case of the Army, fanaticism and intolerance in the case of the Church.[11]

Identification and Its "Models"

When Freud moves on to a "positive" construction, the duality of the institutional "types" represented by the Church and the Army (which might also be conceived as two *tendencies* within the functioning of any political institution) is absorbed into the presentation of a single schema of institutional functioning. It is the schema of identification, the definition of which culminates in the graph from Chapter VIII, designed to help "see" the dimensions and problems that a linear discourse cannot fully account for. Three brief remarks on this point.

First, what the concept of identification designates and the graph makes blindingly clear is a *transindividual* structure in which the opposition between an individual and a collective psyche is radically surmounted (even though Freud's introduction to his essay remains content to relativize it and on the level of his writing to uphold a dissymmetry between the two sides, in a sort of methodological "relational" individualism). What is

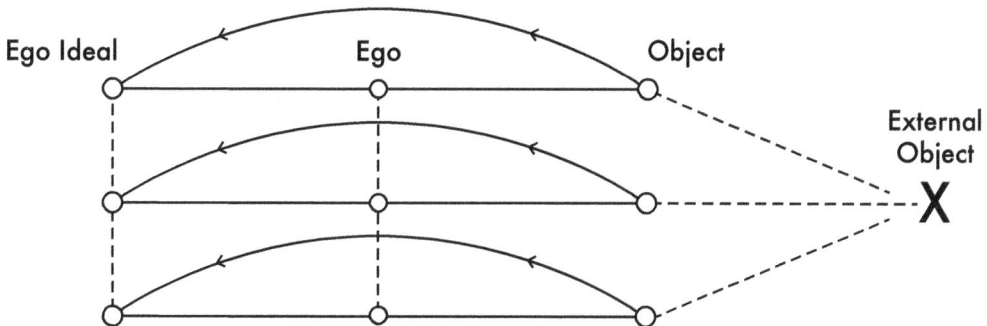

Freud's graph of identification from *Group Psychology and the Analysis of the Ego*

here called *Ich*, "ego," is just as much the result or the product of a mechanism of identi-fication described as a "placing in common" of the love object as it is the point of depar-ture or source of this mechanism. Inversely, what is called the "external" object, figured as the "spot" marked by a cross or an X is not only *the object placed in common* by preexist-ing egos, themselves external to one another, but is also the condition of possibility of their own constitution. The arrows of retroactivity in the graph are thus what indicate, for each parallel line of individuality, the origin of a doubling of each personality or subjectivity into an *Ich* and an *Ich-ideal* and makes this doubling into the condition of its object choices. It would actually be necessary, at this point, to comment on each detail of Freud's graph. The essential point to grasp is the constitutive circularity whereby the ego's essential characteristic, an internal doubling always liable to become a scission, emerges from the "placing in common" that doubles all objects with a quasi-transcendental dimension—or, as Freud writes, an internal exteriority—of which it forms the unconscious condition.[12]

From this point on, we can articulate the two sides of what Freud, scrupulously playing upon the traditional significations of the word, calls "identification": (1) intersubjective mi-meticism or the reciprocal assimilation of individuals (*Imitation, Gemeinsamkeit*), and (2) the reproduction of a superior model (*Vorbild*) that he finds respectively in the descriptions of the crowd offered by political psychology and in his own analysis of the process of introject-ing lost objects. These two dimensions, which might be called horizontal and vertical—or to better respect the graph, transversal and longitudinal—are correlative and condition one another. There is thus a flagrant analogy between this schema and those of classical politi-cal philosophy that institute the political upon the ideal form of a foundational contract—which "makes the people a people," to cite Rousseau—whose constitutive paradoxes have also demanded recourse to a graphic or allegorical elaboration (as in Hobbes, for example).[13] At stake is indeed the ability to think a *double relation* of all to each and each to all that hinges upon both the indivisibility of the common and the distribution of multiple subjec-tivities, the equality of subjects to one another and their originary relation to authority or the law. On the condition that we understand that this contract is not an historico-juridical conjecture but a transindividual unconscious structure, this analogy is decisive. So much so that, in Freud as well, when the relation to an "external" *Vorbild* is what constitutes subjects as such, or as so many "egos" attached to their ideal, the "place" of the *Vorbild* itself is still nothing other than the effect of the common desire of these subjects, who thus become the origin of what subjects them (much as, in Hobbes, the contract that institutes the place of the sovereign is sealed outside of this place, between the subjects of this contract). This is why Freud, who thereby distinguishes himself from theoreticians of the leader's "prestige" such as Le Bon or even Max Weber with his concept of "charismatic power," is practically indifferent to the supposed virtue or power of leaders (or the idea that might substitute for them: what is called a *führende Idee*); or rather, he reduces these attributes fundamentally to the projection of the desire of subjects.[14] Measuring the consequences of this analysis for the constitution of the ego, it becomes clear that Freud is laying the groundwork for a problematic of the circuit of imaginary identifications and a reinvestigation from a psycho-analytic perspective of the old theme of multiple personality.[15]

Whence my third remark. The ego that is externally (or "mimetically") redoubled and multiplied has a relationship to the *Vorbild* that undoubtedly adheres to a general schema (that one should describe at greater length as well as study its relations with an entire Western philosophical and religious tradition: think, for example, of the *imitatio Jesu Christi* and of what, in *Religion Within the Limits of Reason Alone*, Kant calls the communitarian "prototype" or *Urbild* of morality). But it is also marked, from the outset, by a profound ambivalence. The question arises of the relation between the problem of the relation between binding and that of unbinding or the decomposition of bonds, which, as I have recalled, Freud inscribed at the limit of the institution or of the *Massenbildung* itself. More specifically, what relation is there between, on the one hand, the breaking of the bonds that tie egos to one another and to their common object functioning as a model and, on the other hand, the fact that there are common objects of hate and fear no less than common objects of love and desire? The negative or destructive passions, aren't they factors of collective identification as powerful as the "attractive" passions, if not, on occasion, more powerful? Are these two types of passions separable? The question also arises, in another register, whether Freud's schema is complete even from the perspective of his own libido theory, especially with respect to its ability to take into account sexual difference: Left at the fringes of his descriptions and examples, sexual difference seems not so much ignored as denied, which could be put in relation to the problematic of the homosexual object choice, which intensely concerned Freud at the time. "Groups" and "Institutions" cemented by identification are quasi-exclusively made up of male subjects such that the feminine ends up hidden in the place of the "object."

I will leave aside these fundamental questions and instead evoke another duality whose relation to our problem is more immediate. This is what might be called the ontological and political duality of the model. The distinction between the two institutional types—the "Army-type" and the "Church-type"—is incorporated into the concept of identification, but in a manner that is troubled, or at least held in suspense. Freud does indeed tell us that the common object whereby the "egos" are retroactively assimilated and internally doubled *can either be a "real person" or an "idea,"* if not an ideology—an object of trust or faith, given in one case in the mode of life and presence and in another case in that of abstract representation and absence. And he aligns this alternative, at bottom, with the great alternative between the narcissistic (at work in hypnosis) and its obverse the melancholic (figure of impossible mourning) modes of ego constitution. But what Freud claims as the very type of the *idea*, in relation to the example of the Church, is the *imaginary person* of Christ along with his teaching. There is only a short step from this claim to the supposition that the love of an idea or the fact of letting an idea become the measure of reality is always the love of a dead person or a specter; and it relies upon the fantasy of a speech that would be uttered from the very place of death, from which it would derive all its power—which shows Freud's dependence upon a certain Christian myth of community. But it might also be concluded that the effectiveness of a model in general is linked to its doubling, to the internal duality that permits it to function both as personification and as abstraction, presence and absence, visibility and invisibility, idealization of life and of death. Accordingly, on the level of the institution, it might be said that there is something like an army in every church but also something like a church in every army. And thus something war-like in every conversion, something crusade-like in every national war. . . .

Let us now turn to Kelsen's essay. The fact that Freud, after inviting Kelsen to present his work as a jurist, philosopher, and theoretician of politics to the Psychoanalytic Society of Vienna, wished so urgently to publish a (perhaps expanded) version of his intervention that same year (1922) within the journal that he directed, *Imago*, and then had it translated in order to publish it (in 1924) in *The International Journal of Psychoanalysis*, directed by Ernst Jones, shows that he accorded it an importance well beyond a desire to dialogue with his "colleagues" and to be recognized by the queen disciplines at the University.[16] It suffices to read the whole of this wonderfully conceived and argued essay to perceive that it suddenly transfers Freud's attempt to theorize social and political phenomena as a transindividual organization or economy of unconscious desire into a political context whose high stakes will be loaded with consequences for the whole history of twentieth-century thought. This context is that of the interrogation, in the aftermath of World War One, of the traditional concepts of imperial and national sovereignty, experienced throughout Europe as a collective trauma and crisis of civilization, and of the collapse of the models of authoritarian, militaristic, and clerical states, which opened the way, on the one hand, to revolutionary and then counterrevolutionary attempts to overthrow parliamentarianism, and, on the other hand, to endeavors to redefine democratic constitutionalism, of which Kelsen himself was among the foremost protagonists within the whole space of Mitteleuropa. During this period, Kelsen, the principal drafter of the new Constitution of Austria, appointed at a very young age as a professor at the University of Vienna and as a member of the Constitutional Court created by the Austrian Republic,[17] was working upon the elaboration of what would become, in 1934, the foundational work of juridical positivism, the *Reine Rechtslehre* or "pure theory of law."[18] This work comprises a detailed engagement with all the currents of political and juridical philosophy and sociology of the period, including Marxism, and it makes extensive use of certain of Freud's ideas, as can be seen in his other major published work from the period, *Der soziologische und der juristische Staatsbegriff*, and in a series of complementary articles.[19] Gathering all of these elements and engaging with their content, it is difficult to avoid the impression that this encounter constitutes an extraordinarily intense moment of confrontation and crystallization, of which Kelsen's essay on Freud forms an integral part. But it also impossible not to see how this confrontation would destabilize the author of *Totem and Taboo*. The image that his new friend, the Viennese jurist, would cast back to him will have been one of the instruments of his destabilization.

Freud's Error According to Kelsen

Kelsen's essay comprises three parts of equal length. Only in the second part is Freud named and discussed; but it is clear that the whole construction of the essay hinges upon this carefully delayed entry on stage.

The first part of the essay is a critique of psychosociological theories of the State, judged in terms of their capacity to account genetically and formally for what constitutes in Kelsen's view (very Rousseauist on this point) the essence of the State as a supraindividual or supra-personal (*über-individuell, über-persönlich*) modality of social bond—that is, the immanent reduction of the multiplicity to a unity (a multiplicity of persons but, above all, of actions, since the State is less a unique "person" than a unified *actor*). Anticipating his turn to Freud, Kelsen underscores the importance of sociological theories of *conflict* as constitutive of society (notably Simmel's interactionism) but also the inability of these theories to account for what renders conflictuality compatible with the unification of society in the form of the State and even provides it with an essential resource, namely the *forgetting of conflict* or its repression outside the consciousness of social actors. He explicitly raises the question of how class conflict can "disappear from consciousness within the community of a state" (§5) and consequently in what sense there can be no political State without a structure of unconsciousness. This question is inseparable from that of the supraindividual unity and its "internalization" by individuals who enter into a political grouping and thereby surmount—relatively—their own "individualism." It would be fascinating to examine in more detail the way in which, in this text and others, Kelsen combines this problematic with a reflection on the question of *fictions* and on that of *ideology*.

At this point, in the second part of the essay, Freud will make his entrance. At first, it seems that Kelsen considers that Freud's theory of *Massenbildungen* is intrinsically superior to all other theories of supraindividual unity because it dissolves the abstraction of the notion of power or replaces the element of exteriority that it contains with a principle of internal subjection (and thus Kelsen correctly interprets the Freudian notion of the "external object = X" as a reference to an internal exteriority or an imaginary externalization produced from inside). Only such a theory makes it possible properly to think "relations" or "bonds" (*Verbindungen, Bindungen*). But this superiority has its immediate counterpart in what Kelsen does not hesitate to call "Freud's conceptual slippage": *eine Verschiebung in der Begriffsbildung* (§16). Even as Freud rectifies the abstraction of the sociologists whose concepts are "too weak" (that is, too external, mechanical, such as the concept of *Wechselwirkung*, reciprocal action) in order to think the unification of the state, Freud immediately undermines his own insight by subsuming it under a concept, that of *identification*, which is "too strong" (because it overstresses interiority and even organicity). What is strange, in a sense, but in no way arbitrary, as we'll see, is that Kelsen does both the questions and their responses. It is he who attributes to Freud the ambition to construct a theory of the State that would in a certain sense form the metonymical horizon or goal of his analyses of army-type and church-type institutions and their complementarity as structures of idealization or fiction. And it is he who, consequently, declares that Freud had failed in his ambition, or at least failed to rise to the level of his supposed objectives, by virtue of the fact that the essence of the State resides first of all in the positing of a *juridical norm*, and that the concept of such a norm as well as its mode of effectuation are utterly irreducible to modalities of "belief" or "love" toward a person or personified idea and a fortiori to the mechanisms of affective *fusion* and mental *regression* which, for Freud, combining the lessons of his critique of political psychology with the anthropological thesis of *Totem and*

Taboo, would form the deepest unconscious cause of these modalities. In brief, the theory of the State as a "juridical order" that is also an "coercive order" (*Rechtsordnung ist Zwangsordnung*—Kelsen's absolutely symmetrical thesis, readable both backward and forward, which is at the heart of the contemporaneous work, *Der soziologische und juristische Staatsbegriff*, and which the *Reine Rechtslehre* will ultimately found within a transcendental philosophy of the norm in general and its bilateral reality: obligation and sanction) requires an underside of unconsciousness, but it must not be identical with a theory of the unconscious as such.[20]

Otherwise, the consequences would be epistemologically and politically disastrous. And Kelsen insists upon this point. First, such a representation of the State as a "mass" makes it impossible to differentiate its unity (and thus its authority) and the unity or authority of the partial, subordinate "groups," whether permanent or transitory, that constitute society and endow it with its specific multiplicity (what Hobbes will call *systemes subject* or what an entire sector of contemporary sociology calls *communities*). If such groups must indeed entail a concrete principle of binding, their imaginary dimension being constitutively affective and personal, the State can only be founded upon the effectiveness of an abstraction, a "real abstraction" in a certain sense, and upon its own universality and impersonality. Kelsen is a republican, let us not forget; he is even the author of the first republican constitution in the history of his country. But the difficulty goes much further: Freud, in his view, annihilates the idea of a citizenship that represents the subjection of individuals to a juridico-political order. This is indeed how Kelsen interprets Freud's description of the "thirst for obedience" that binds the subjects of the mass to their model.[21] For Kelsen, Freud does not much critique Le Bon than he exacerbates his theory; he generalizes Le Bon's description of revolutionary crowds and transposes it to the institution in general, thereby rendering the State indistinguishable from a dictatorship or a form of totalitarian domination.[22]

The Injustice of the State as Political Fantasy

But Freud's conceptual error (or the one that Kelsen attributes to him by extrapolating his intentions) immediately turns back into a potential strength with the idea of a practical use of psychoanalysis in the service of the Rule of Law, which might even make psychoanalysis indispensable for the preservation of a State governed by such a principle. The third phase of Kelsen's essay, then, addresses a sort of offer of mutual aid to Freud: You recognize that the juridical order is always situated beyond the sphere of collective identities and subjective identifications, and I will show you how constitutional democracy needs applied psychoanalysis and, at the limit, cannot do without it. In large part, this new development is devoted to a critique of Durkheim's theories of society and religion (to which Kelsen opposes the Freud of *Totem and Taboo*). The object of this critique is both to reject any *sociological* conception of the norm, which sees it as evidence of immanence of society and its moral imperatives within individual actions and feelings, of which the State would be the organ, and then to explain what precisely is the psychological need to which the norm corresponds, describing it in terms very close to those that come from Kant's "transcendental dialectic": the transformation of functions into substances, the personification and even the divinization of State authority.[23] Psychoanalysis is then invited to fulfill, in the practical domain, the same function that Kantian critique fulfilled in the speculative domain: It is supposed to indicate the genesis of the substantialist illusions that affect the representation of State authority, showing that these illusions represent the incessant return or reactivation of a repressed archaic mentality that considers society to consist of a "substance" common to social subjects, "shared" among them like the body of the omnipotent father was shared in the myth (which Freud took up in 1912) of the "primal horde" and its violent dissolution. Such a critique will certainly never abolish the substantialist illusions inseparable from what must be called, from Kelsen's viewpoint, the fantasy of sovereignty or of the omnipotence of the State. But it can indeed help to combat the in no way benign theoretical expression of these illusions, which amounts to a certain political theology or mythology. The danger inherent to the Freudian viewpoint—the fact that it makes the State itself unto the manifestation of a process of *regression*—is thus converted into its opposite, or turned positive, putting psychoanalysis at the service of the modern democratic State as the privileged "therapeutic" instrument of defense against the regressive archaism that never ceases to threaten it from within. Many psychoanalysts today, or philosophers with or without a psychoanalytic formation, would not disagree with such a perspective that the experiences of fascism and totalitarianism seem to have rendered even more urgent. But why is archaic regression, or the hypostasis of State power, such an ineluctable danger? Kelsen gives two reasons closely linked to his own theory of the juridical unity of the State and its identity with a coercive order, such as that generalized and founded anew in the *Reine Rechtslehre*. At least the second of these reasons—formulated in the final lines of his 1922 essay and developed in the exactly contemporary work, *Der soziologische und der juristische Staatsbegriff*—could not fail to shake Freud's reflections to the core.

The first reason is formal; it is simply that the State must be represented as itself a subject of law[24] or as a *juridical person*—that is, as a collective that an institutional fiction endows with a corporate "personality." Juridical personality, no doubt, is merely a functional notion that makes it possible to impute properties, actions, decisions, and delegations of power *to the State*, but it also permanently leads the subjects of the State to "believe" that beneath the fictional person lurks an intention, and thus a personal entity, or a moral, social, and historical substance, and so on—in brief, a *real identity*—and thus to project metaphysical, "anthropomorphic," "subjectivist," and "voluntarist" representations back upon the juridical order.

To this initial mechanism, which closely follows Kant's schema of the hypostasis of the subject or the moral person in the "Paralogisms of Pure Reason," Kelsen adds a second much more troubling and even subversive mechanism. It is the idea that a juridical order as a coercive order which entails a *sanction* (and indeed the threat—or promise—of sanction for infractions of the law) necessarily passing through the courts and thus making judicial power into the very organ of the law's effectiveness, confronts the individuals who are subjected to the law, even if they are its collective "authors," with a power that they are not entitled to dispute, with which they cannot negotiate, and which for them, in actual practice, incarnates an omnipotence. There is thus a specific fantasy that is inherent to the relationship of subjects to the State: Although the idea of the injustice of the State, distinct from a simple mistake committed by its functionaries in the process of applying the law, is a contradiction in terms (Kelsen thus adopts one of Hobbes's fundamental ideas),[25] the subjects of the State cannot prevent its omnipotence and especially the omnipotence of its sanction from appearing to be potentially arbitrary. *They cannot not wonder whether the State is unjust toward them*, whether its declared good will does not hide deep cruelty or risk turning into cruelty.[26] More profoundly, it is this phantasmatic supposition—juridically irrational but psychologically incontrovertible—which forms the underside of the idea that the State constrains us to assume juridical autonomy, "forces us to be free," or explains that we cannot resist the illusory tendency to make it into a "person," if not a God. Or a demon—called Leviathan or Behemoth.

I would like, here, at my own risk and peril, while searching for any evidence available within the texts themselves, to attempt to reconstruct what must have been Freud's response to Kelsen's critique, which he had himself solicited, as well as, the offer for mutual assistance that accompanied it. I believe in fact—even without focusing on all of the details—that he could only have taken it very seriously, in spite of the fact that it appeared to consist in a quid pro quo, but behind which was hidden a truth.

An Alienating Choice: The Unconscious or the Political?

Freud certainly did not intend to propose a theory of State institution, even if this idea haunts the association of the Church and Army, which lies at the heart of a unified theory of the institution—in particular in the imperial or postimperial context. In *Group Psychology and the Analysis of the Ego* (*Massenpsychologie und Ich-Analyse*), one might say that Freud limits his discussion to *certain* "apparatuses" of the State. Reversing Le Bon's theory, he makes identification (personal, ideological) not only the force behind the anarchical *disorganization* of the masses but, most importantly, that of their *organization* into "communities" or "systems" of belonging. Preferring to compare the processes of identification with being in love and hypnosis, he goes so far as to introduce them within the topography of the psychic personality as the quasi-transcendental condition of individual self-recognition (the "ego"), as well as that of the mutual recognition of subjectivities (which one could call the "we"). However, he does not ask how such systems of identification become mutually compatible, nor correlatively, which new investments of ideal objects, whether positive or negative, would most likely unify these systems within a politics and an economy of the unconscious.[27] What once again appears to take the place of this synthesis or this unity of assemblages (as conflictual or problematic as it may be) is *regression*—that is, the common root of all identifications and their characteristic ambivalence within an *archè* arising from the depths of the generations (the *Urvater der Urhorde*: the Primal Father of the Primal Horde).[28] However, this archaic model, which allows Freud in *Totem and Taboo* to think together the origin of social violence (*Gewalt*) and that of the law (*Gesetz*), is in reality *antipolitical*, both because it dissolves the specificity of all institutions within a generic "prehistory" of humanity (prehistory without history, to which we relate in the mode of repetition), and because it identifies—albeit in the form of a myth or a conjecture—the essence of authority with the persistence of an "immortal" substance of tyranny, slavery, and vengeance that is necessarily misrecognized as such, and that is, by definition, not susceptible to any *deliberate action*, whether collective or individual.[29] Because he accepted the Freudian theory of the affective constitution of social relations and of the feelings of belonging to collective institutions (*Bände, Bindungen, Verbindungen, Verbände*), and, at the same time, argued that political and historical unities of the state type, founded upon the "normative" constraint of the law and the "monopoly of legitimate violence,"[30] no matter the intensity of the attachments that they generate (especially nationalism) or the drives that they unleash, remain irreducible to such a libidinal economy and even precede it—since, otherwise, it would be impossible to prefer one political regime to another and to make it the objective of a "constitution"—Kelsen, therefore, presented Freud with a veritable challenge. And Freud could not ignore this challenge without abandoning the terrain that he had just begun to secure in *Group Psychology and the Analysis of the Ego* (*Massenpsychologie und Ichanalyse*) and its new formulation of the relation between the unconscious and "culture"—or, in reality, between the unconscious and politics.

In order to take up this challenge, it would be necessary to account for a paradoxical type of identification, or a limit of identification, which is strictly speaking neither "positive" or "negative" but rather "empty," since it does not entail any imaginary *representation* of an object of love or hate that individuals (or their "egos") might "hold in common" but only a pure principle of *obedience*. But then he would have to acknowledge that the "subjects" of the political institution as such (the "citizens," if we were to adopt the terminology of the republican tradition) *are not subjects in the psychoanalytic sense*— that is, individuals whose thoughts and behaviors depend more or less predominantly on unconscious psychic formations. *The unconscious or the political—this would be the choice.* In a sense, this is precisely what Kelsen hoped Freud would admit to, but not without making room for a "return" of the subject of the unconscious in the *failure* or *corruption* of any "pure" juridical order, in order to understand why the constitution of citizenship (membership within a *politeia*) needs a mythical supplement that seems to emerge from the most archaic constitutions of authority and that provides fodder for pathological representations of sovereignty (including, of course, the sovereignty of the people).[31] Freud no doubt found it unsatisfying to have to think the unconscious as the system of the "psychic" or "cultural" determinations of behavior (and of individuality itself) whose influence would extend no further than the gates of the "city"; but it was hardly little more satisfying to have to align such a separation—which is not without relation to the ancient dichotomy of the "domestic" and the "public" spheres, and perhaps even reflects modernity's tendency to repress within the unconscious those conflicts spawned by their interaction—with the dualism of the "normal" (the normative order) and the "pathological" (or the abnormal), which his entire critique of political psychology as well as the orientation of his clinic rejects!

"A State Inside the Head"?

Within the space of just a few months, then, I am convinced that Freud sought a thoroughgoing response to Kelsen's objection, which would comprise a development and perhaps even a reorganization of his own theory of the transindividual "bond." We would thus be well advised not to ignore the "external" or rather conjunctural factor here—namely, the singular historical moment, which both Freud and Kelsen were aware of, and which they certainly discussed.[32] This is certainly a question that would require further research relying upon correspondence and individual testimony. But it is very likely, I believe, that the juridical ideal of the formation of a constitutional State, equidistant from the two "extremes"—the authoritarian State, which the prefascist movements of the 1920s strove to reinvent, and the "non-State State" of the dictatorship of the proletariat, in the form of a communist (Soviet) system of "council" democracy, to which many psychoanalysts closely tied to Freud rallied with greater or lesser enthusiasm[33]—is the perspective that Freud and Kelsen shared and that becomes the basis for their collaboration, and perhaps, on Freud's side, already the source of a more emphatic pessimism.

However, the urgency to "respond to Kelsen," which I am hypothesizing here, did not lead Freud to reframe as such the question of the relation between Church and State, or of the two main types of institution and community belonging, but rather *to turn back upon Kelsen his own question about juridical coercion* (or better, *of obedience to juridical coercion*), and consequently to call into question the concept of the "norm," which renders the juridical order irreducible to a mechanism of the masses or of psychological identification. Kelsen upholds that the law is an *a priori* synthesis of imperative and coercion, and that this synthesis sustains itself, except when it must be defended against resurgences of the archaic and the theological. In this respect, he directly inherits Kant's concept of the law but separates it from its relation to a transcendental morality.[34] For Kelsen, positive law constitutes its own *Grundnorm*, or produces from within itself the foundation that it needs, at least in the mode of "fiction." The question Freud poses—to himself and to Kelsen—aims at bursting this fictive self-sufficiency: it asks *what it is to obey* and, more precisely still, *what it is to obey coercion*, to be deprived of the inner capacity to resist it, *to renounce any revolt* against it—with certain exceptions of course—and what is the "structure" in which such renunciation or privation is rooted, such that it is always already presupposed by the functioning of the social order.

However, let us be prudent and therefore as precise as possible. Freud does not say that individuals subjected to the power of the State or to the positivity of the law *do not revolt*. He does say that such a revolt, which is radically illegitimate in the eyes of the State that has claimed a "monopoly" on the codification and the sanction of the law, can only be enacted, when it escapes inhibition, in the mode of anxiety and guilt, or maniacal challenge and delusions of grandeur, all of which postulate the inevitability of punishment and even seek it out.[35] In this sense, Freud does not install, as one might hastily conclude, "an image of the State in the head"—that is, in the individual unconscious—known as the Superego.[36] He does not *legitimize* the State or the law by means of the unconscious, nor does he project the phantasmatic double of political authority within the structure of the unconscious (as many of his readers, whether psychoanalysts or not, have believed to their satisfaction or dismay). This would do no more than displace the question, *redouble* a political utterance with a psychological interpretation, and enter into infinite regression. In a much more troubling fashion, however, Freud describes a fundamentally *antinomial* psychic process that forms the counterpart within the unconscious to the State's monopoly upon legitimate violence. It is as if obedience to legal coercion were *produced on two scenes at once* (or on a public scene and on "another scene") in modalities that are both inseparable and radically heterogeneous, each the condition for the other. The terms, as will become clear, are the same: law, authority, obedience, transgression, crime, punishment, guilt . . . but the series bifurcates at the notion of coercion. Consequently, if Freud's theoretical invention confirms the universality of the juridical order postulated by Kelsen (an order made up of multiple hierarchies of specialized orders, which, in this sense, have no outside, or from which it would be impossible for a subject to claim any escape), it also, paradoxically, tends to locate a contradiction at the heart of this order's purchase (*Bemächtigung*) upon individual psyches, and, in this sense, renders its legitimacy radically uncertain. We are thus led into the vicinity of a reflection on the paradox of "voluntary servitude," which admittedly remains in circulation, in search of a theoretical position as well as a name, among all the protagonists of this great debate opened by political psychology. However, the modalities of this reflection would be very specific, against the grain of accepted ideas, showing both the ineluctable character of voluntary servitude and the impossibility of making it an instrument of power, whether by "excess" or "lack." This is the complex that I would like to try to describe, taking as my guiding thread the *terminology* that, in Freud, crystallizes the "encounter" between the juridico-political question and existing psychoanalytic theory.

What Freud names the principle of obedience is the "superego," *das Über-Ich.* "All of us have a superego," or better, we are ourselves "superegos," insofar as the singular histories of the psychic apparatus—what Freud increasingly refers to as "psychical personalities" (*psychische Persönlichkeit*, a term that it would not be inordinate to include in a series with "moral personality" and "juridical personality," and that also entails, of course, an element of fiction). Better yet, *we are* "the superego"; we unconsciously become its representatives and agents in relation to ourselves (which also means that we become its subjects, in the typical form of a *division*).[37] There is nothing simple about the choice of the term *Über-Ich.*[38] It undoubtedly stems, among other things, from Kelsen's insistence upon the formation (*Gebilde*) of a *Über-Individualität* and upon the *über-individuell* and *über-persönlich* character of the juridico-political norm that demands obedience to the universal, or, if one prefers, to the law. But it also pertains to a vast paradigm, upon whose idiomatic resources Freud always relied (*Übertragung, Überdeterminierung, Überschätzung, Überarbeitung . . .*[39]). In this instance, it is most important to retain that the combination of the preposition, *Über*, and the pronoun, *Ich*, produces two meaning effects at the same time: *über-Ich* is that which maintains itself "above" the *Ich* within a hierarchy of authority positions and it is what Freud appears to privilege each time that he associates the function of the superego to the idea of an agency of observation, surveillance, and critique, which emerges from the tradition of moral empiricism (the *impartial spectator* in both Hume and Smith—both of whom Freud read extensively in his youth).[40] But the superego is also, literally, a "super-ego"—a superior—greater, stronger—ego, at least in imagination and fantasy, much as one says "supermale" (Jarry) or "superman" (Nietzsche): a meaning more directly associated with the entire thematic of the constitution of the superego in the image of the father or the parents and of their absolute power over the child who experiences, with anxiety, his own inability to resist them, his own "littleness."[41] In this sense, the superego is something within me that is greater than me, or better *it is an ego greater than my own ego*, an ego that fashions or fictions itself as "greater than itself."[42] At the intersection of these two paradigms in *Das Ich und das Es* (Chapter 5), one finds this "redundant" expression: *das überstarke Über-Ich* (the superpowerful Superego).[43]

The second key term that must serve as a guiding thread is of course *Zwang*, usually translated into English as "compulsion," and inserted by translators into the entire series of Freudian concepts linked to it, from the *Zwangsneurose* ("obsessional" or "compulsive" neurosis, whose paradigm is the Rat Man), to the *Wiederholungszwang* ("repetition compulsion") that *Beyond the Pleasure Principle* associates with the ongoing effects of traumatic experiences and their indefinite displacement, their conversion into sources of paradoxical pleasure, which together form the enigmatic unity of the "death drive" (*Todestrieb*). I am close to thinking, and I do indeed think, that the question of the *Zwang* (*What is a compulsion?* How does it operate? How does it manifest itself? And what "good" is it? Why does it impose itself? But also why does it form the irreducibly anxious modality of the relationship to authority?) is the very point of intersection between the problematics of Kelsen and Freud; and that it is the catalyst for theoretical invention, at least for one of them. On one hand, there is Kelsen's idea that the law, insofar as it establishes an *order*, or a system (which, going a step further, it would be tempting to call "systematic coercion"), establishes the equivalence between obligation and coercion, or the perfect coextension of the two, with the exception of certain lapses, or even *by means of a constant recuperation of its lapses*. On the other hand, there is the Freudian elaboration of the problematic of the *Zwang* which gradually takes over the entire phenomenology of the manifestations of the unconscious in normal or pathological life (that is, which defines normality as the scant freedom or illusion of freedom that coercion allows for, as one clearly sees in *Inhibition, Symptom, Anxiety* and in *New Introductory Lectures* of 1932), and which, in any event, forms the kernel of the manifestations of the "superego": from the pole of surveillance or critical observation (that is, self-criticism), to that of *severity* or *harshness* as such, the anticipation of punishment in its arbitrariness for crimes that were never committed "in reality," which Freud discovered through the study of the *Zwangsneurosen*, the veritable laboratory for the development of the superego from a clinical perspective.

Only by holding together both of these terminological threads—the one of "over", *Über*, and the other of compulsion, *Zwang*, which is inseparable from the law and especially the right to punish—is it possible to understand how Freud proposed to Kelsen, not, as is all too often assumed, the refoundation of the Kantian concept of the "categorical imperative" as a structure of the unconscious, which would reestablish, in another modality, the subordination of law to morality, but rather an analysis of the ambivalent effects produced in a subject's unconscious by coupling the idea of law with that of State coercion.[44] Without such a coupling no social norm would be effective, nor would the respect for norms produce the "excessive" guilt (*Schuldgefühl*) and the "need for punishment" (*Strafbedürfnis*) which Freud describes as characteristic of the "severity" or "cruelty" of the Superego, which derive from its "instinctual" nature or from the retroactive effect of the "id' at the heart of the "ego" that it represents, and that ends up instituting the absurd equivalence between obedience to the law and the transgression of the law.[45]

Let us now turn to the text of 1923, *Das Ich und das Es* (supplementing it on occasion with a few later developments that directly refer back to it); and let us attempt to reconstruct the progression that leads to Freud's fundamental antinomianism.

The Psychic Tribunal and the Interpellation of Subjects as Individuals

In *Das Ich und das Es* (1923), Freud introduces the Ego Ideal/Superego pair by recounting its "genesis" from the series of identifications that follow upon one another within the history of each individual and that thereby contribute to the formation of personality (or to the different relational characters of the "ego"): in order not to result in a pathological multiplicity of identities, an organization or a synthesis is required, the condition of which, Freud tells us, resides in a "primary" identification that derives from the resolution or the decomposition of the Oedipus Complex ("normally," it is an identification with the father, at least for the little boy—*das männliche Kind*—who, as usual, is the focus of Freud's attention). The Superego would thus be the *first ideal*, even if the genetic anteriority of the model is already fraught with a series of paradoxical characteristics: above all, the fact that the superego is concentrated in an *injunction*—at once exhortation (*Mahnung*) and interdiction (*Verbot*)—that entails a characteristic double bind ("Be like your father!" "Don't do as your father does!") (Chapter III) transferred from the father to other "authority figures" (especially, educators, *Lehrer*) who take up the paternal function of commandment and interdiction (*Gebote* und *Verbote*). How could the subject (the unconscious ego) not feel guilty of failing to reconcile what is both enjoined and prohibited? As soon as these injunctions are internalized, at once repressed and appropriated by the subject identified with the paternal model, there arises the idea of an inevitable and inextinguishable sense of guilt (*Schuldgefühl*) that constitutes the unconscious affective modality of the ego's subjection to the superego. However, Freud will only return to the analysis of this complex in the final chapter of *Das Ich und das Es* (Chapter V) after a long excursus upon the dualism of the drives (*Eros* or the sexual drive and the death drive that he does not himself call *Thanatos*) and after formulating the hypothesis of a "defusion" of the drives that opens the possibility of a "desexualized" libido that might take the form of a sublimation (moral, intellectual, aesthetic) but also that of the ego's tendency to self-destruction, or, what comes down to essentially the same thing, to inhibit its own capacity to seek and find pleasure, whether in external objects or by taking itself as a narcissistic object.

The return to the problem of guilt occurs by way of a clinical observation: that of "negative therapeutic reactions" in which the patient resists the interpretation that would allow him to liberate himself from his symptom and the suffering it causes and ultimately resists the cure itself or "refuses" it. Freud begins by interpreting the *Krankheitsbedürfnis* ("the need for illness" and thus for suffering), which constitutes the manifest aspect of this supplementary symptom, as the effect of a "moral factor," the extreme consequence of the feeling of guilt.[46] And then, with a remarkable extrapolation (undoubtedly suggested by the clinical material, but also certainly by the "paradoxical logic" of unconscious causality), he transforms the feeling of guilt itself into an obstinate attachment to "suffering as punishment" (*Strafe des Leidens*), which the subject neither wants nor is able to renounce, and which, in turn, proves to be a displacement of a more fundamental "need for punishment" (*Strafenbedürfnis*) ("more fundamental" in that it is always present in the unconscious, even when it is largely neutralized or defeated by Eros). From this moment onward, "ordinary" logic (that of common sense, but also that of socially observable behaviors) will be inverted. Wrongdoing or crime would no longer engender the feeling of guilt or occasion sanction and punishment, as in a healthy distribution of roles between the judged and the judge. On the contrary, the perpetually recurring need to be punished or the *punishment compulsion*, which confuses these two roles or attributes them alternately to the same person, is what engenders guilt and produces, on demand, criminal intentions (or intentions that are lived as criminal), interdictions to be transgressed, and passages to the act that unendingly "justify" and sustain the need for punishment.

Freud is not satisfied with merely providing this logic with a name. Instead, he proposes a model whose meaning is much more than allegorical: that of a *psychic tribunal*, the subject of which is split into distinct "agencies," each acting against the others, and plays every role at once (accused and accuser, judge and victim).[47] It is a "Kafkaesque" tribunal before which it is all the more impossible to defend oneself since the origin of the crimes committed cannot be pinpointed or always lies further in the instinctual depths of the subject; and it seems that the "cruelty" of this tribunal's sentences must never acquit the criminal of his debt. The correlate of this tribunal's domination or mastery over the conscious and unconscious ego (or more precisely, over any possibility of "treating" unconscious conflicts by means of consciousness) is a permanent susceptibility to *anxiety*, to which Freud devotes the remainder of the work ("the *ego* may be considered the very site of anxiety," *die eigentliche Angststätte*). Freud's interpretation of the constitution and functioning of the superego as a paradoxical or excessive judicial instance, which exacerbates the dimension of arbitrary and moral violence that is more or less completely neutralized or counteracted within the functioning of "real" or "external" tribunals, clearly shows how far he departed from his previous models of idealization or sublimation linked to the theory of the "ego-ideal." It marks the arrival on stage of what, to cite Foucault (who himself, in *The History of Sexuality*, Volume 1, discusses a certain Freudian posterity), might be called *the repressive hypothesis*. And finally, it entails a series of notable consequences whose "political" implications must also be elaborated.

The analogy between consciousness and a tribunal or an "inner space" (*for intérieur*) is, of course, as old as classical (Stoic and then Christian) conceptions of morality. It remains central in Kant. And it supports the model of *self-judgment*. However, Freud puts significant pressure this idea, bending it toward a "general" theory of *norms* or of the normative as a pure compulsion to do wrong and thus of punishment or sanction. It is not by chance that the text refers to "duty" or "having to be" (*Sollen*).[48] In general, all of these developments (and comparable ones in Freud's subsequent writings, especially in the *New Introductory Lectures* [1933], where he discusses "the judging activity of conscience," *die richterliche Tätigkeit des Gewissens*)[49] primarily concern moral conscience, interpreted as both conscious and unconscious, personal and impersonal ("internalized" and "external- ized," especially under the influence of religious institutions); but they always describe it as a passage to the limit of the juridical process. What characterizes such conscience (and here we are already within the register of antimony) is the excess morality that must reign in the unconscious (*Übermoral, hypermoralisch*) in order for individuals to recognize the existence and the necessity of norms. By the same token, this "hypermorality" is situated not only "beyond good and evil" (in the sense that every good is also, from another point of view, an evil, *Übel*) but also beyond the metaphysical distinction between autonomy and heteronomy and, consequently, at a point that *precedes* the distinction between law and morality.[50] The "tribunal" that this conscience delineates, then, is not so much analogous to real tribunals, pushing their functioning would to the point of absurdity; it is, instead, the unavowable archetype, at the border between the normal and the pathological, which accounts for the universal applicability of real tribunals.

It is, therefore, worthwhile to reconsider the models of identification that Freud had previously associated with the examples of the Army and the Church and to ask what more or different the ultrajuridical authority of the superego brings to the discussion. It offers, evidently, a third institutional schema of identification that is just as closely linked to the problematic of the State (and of the relation between subjects and the State) but that does not at all accentuate the same components of belonging. The models of the Army and of the Church, as I have recalled, correspond to two modalities—presented as complementary—of identification as a (double) relation to a *Vorbild* and to "fellows" [*sem- blables*] or "brothers": their function is thus essentially to *collectivize* and to produce an "egalitarian similitude" (*Gleichheit*) among individuals belonging to the same group.[51] This is why these models cannot be completely excluded from the analysis of state formation, especially when it is linked—as it must be in the modern period—to the rise of nationalism and patriotism. The first of these modalities—which I have called "ideological"—would appear to have a certain privilege, because it emphasizes the *melancholic* side of the ego ideal, wherein love is associated with the feeling of the irremediable loss of a perfect ("over- valued": *überschätzt*) object that we somehow made happen, and that ultimately confuses reality testing with capacity to repress the drives, to frustrate desire, and to find satisfac- tion in this frustration. This is the point at which we come closest to the characteristics that Freud ascribes to "moral conscience" and its excesses, hastening to underscore, as Nietzsche does, their religious origins as well as their social function. What "we" must internalize and, to this end, unconsciously elaborate on the basis of our earliest relation- ships (to our parents) is not the law of the living leader (of the "sur-vivor," as Canetti would later write) but rather, as happens in the Church, the law of death or of the Sacrificed.

However, Freud's actual description of the formation of the super-ego also refers to the effects of a brutally physical—or better: corporeal—authority (that of the parents and particularly the father) even if he does not describe familial discipline as a discipline of the "military" type. The combination of a feeling of guilt and the need for punishment produced by the repression of the fear inspired by an authority of the "judicial" type (who would judge us as the actors of our acts, even the virtual ones, that is, for our desires) inverts the relation between the subject and the group, or of the "ego" to a "we": it does not so much produce an effect of identification as an effect of disidentification and of disassimilation, or of *individualization*, by rendering each subject "responsible" for a wrong that would be his very own. The superego is by no means less of a transindividual structure than the ego-ideal of which it constitutes a new elaboration; but what is specific to it—to parody Althusser's well-known formula—is the *interpellation of subjects as individuals* and thus the production of their isolation, their solitude (and their anxiety of solitude) at the heart of the crowd.[52] What is constituted here, it is not difficult to see, is at least one condition for the formation of a *subject of the law*, whose obedience, even if it corresponds to a general rule, becomes the object of a judgment or threat of punishment that concerns him alone, confronting him with himself or, as one says, with the responsibility that, no matter what he does, "cannot be escaped." One might add that the superego establishes a *negative bond* between individuals: neither love nor brotherhood, neither hate nor hostility, but rather the inhibition of the other-directed destructive drives or of the *Bemächtigungstrieb*, whose counterpart is the development of the self-directed "destructiveness" and "aggressivity" inseparable from the feeling of guilt.[53]

As Pierre Macherey does in his remarkable commentary on *Civilization and Its Discontents* and its critical relation to the ideals of modernity, it would be plausible to see this development as Freud's reprisal, on his own terms, of the Kantian problematic of "unsociable sociability," which combines the attraction and repulsion, the association and disassociation of individuals within a single "unit."[54] But it is also necessary to see that, within these contradictory forms, the question of *belonging* is posed with great acuity; and that the analyses of "the formation of the masses" (*Massenbildung*) and its corresponding schema of identification seem to provide a homogeneous and definitive answer to this question, which is precisely what allowed Kelsen to point up its insufficiency with respect to the functioning of a juridical order. What does it mean to belong to a "tribunal" or a State that defines itself primarily as a tribunal, incarnating and monopolizing all judicial functions? It is, so it seems, *individually and personally* to pertain to the sanction of the tribunal, to its "jurisdiction," and therefore, to have been institutionally *positioned there* as "one and all" (*omnes et singulatim*) without being able to withdraw from it or misrecognize it, to challenge it. This question has ceaselessly preoccupied the philosophy of right, never failing to mark its political orientation, as we can see in Hobbes, Hegel, and Kelsen himself.

For Hobbes, as we know, the fundamental question posed by social relations at the heart of every organization ("system") or association is the following: *quis judicabit*? "Who shall be Judge?" Which judge or tribunal shall take up the legal disputes that arise and the crimes committed within it? In the final instance, the judge of judges ("Supreme Court") is the sovereign, the one who is himself judged by no one and who handles all the procedural matters: This is why subjects can only submit to the law if, dissolving all personal allegiances or subordinating them to the sanction of the State, and if each one, within his own inner tribunal [*for intérieur*], relinquishes his capacity to defend himself against the sovereign authority—that is, the "fictive" or "impersonal" person of the State—and recognizes its absolute right to judge every transgression of the law (under the strict condition, however, that the latter be *promulgated in advance*: *nulla poena sine lege*, which might be seen as an expression of the "rule of law," more or less felicitously translated as *Rechtstaat* or *État de droit*). It is not difficult to see that this is the model for what Kelsen will describe as the institutional hierarchy of norms within the juridical order and their ultimate dependence upon a "fundamental norm" (*Grundnorm*) that legitimates all the others.[55]

For Hegel, in a fundamental passage from *The Philosophy of Right*,[56] the condition for the tribunal's effectivity is that the criminal (or more generally, the "delinquent") *wants his own punishment*: the context shows that this is a logical proposition and not a moral or psychological one because it intervenes at the moment of "abstract law" when the juridical form is exhibited apart from the "person" of the subjects who are its bearers. To assume that the subject who commits a delict or an injustice (*Unrecht*) waits for a sanction to come and reestablish order is at once to make the offender into an instrument for the actualization of the law and to reintegrate him, by acquitting him of his "debt to society," into the community from which he had excluded himself by infringing the law (which also means, with all the ambivalence of such an idea, that no one is ever truly "outside the law"). *There is no such thing as* transgression: or, if one prefers, transgression is the individual appearance of the rational process by which the law imposes itself, validates itself (the manner in which it appears to the "finite" individual).[57] This same idea can be found in Kelsen, despite everything that would distance Kelsen from the Hegelian dialectic; except that, in Kelsen, *contradiction as appearance* has been turned into the *appearance of contradiction*: as the *Pure Theory of Law* explains, in opposition to the tradition of "natural law" on this point, the delict or injustice (*Unrecht*) is not a "negation of law"; it is an action that the law prohibits and consequently sanctions in advance. As a result, he who commits the delict does not "step outside the law," which is an expression devoid of meaning (one might say that he does not possess the "power" or the "faculty" to do such a thing); he actually allows the law to exist or confirms its validity (*Geltung*), "through the reaction of the juridical order in the form a sanction."[58] But in reality—and such is also the significance of the equation *Rechtsordnung ist Zwangsordnung*—without delicts no sanction would ever need to occur and the coercive character of law would remain a pure fiction. It thus becomes plausible to conclude that the delict, which does not contradict but rather *affirms* the law as an obligatory norm, is in fact necessary to the very existence of the law. One can also see that the "belonging" of individuals to the juridical order, always already given within it and constantly verified by its functioning (at least as long as this order is perpetuated), is the *subjectivity effect* proper to sanction.

I would like to propose that Freud, in his own theorization of the "judicial moment" of subjection (that is, of the superego as a structure, a system of social relations that individualize by means of guilt), by shifting the entire "logic" of negative identifications onto the scene of the unconscious (wherein the pathology of obsessional neuroses, of melancholic delusions, and of moral masochism only ever provide him with an aggrandized and one-sided representation of what is "normally" at work in the conflictual constitution of the personality),[59] reached the inverse conclusion: *There is only transgression*, and this is why *there can be belonging* to such an "impersonal" order as the juridical order. However, in order to develop this last point we must take up once again, albeit in broad strokes, the unconscious mechanism of belonging to the social order (which is also a mechanism of unconscious belonging to this order) such as Freud organizes it in *Das Ich und Das Es* in the form of the "genesis" of the superego and the state of "dependency" that it imposes upon the ego.

The Genealogy of Authority and Transgression

Unquestionably, Freud's entire presentation of the superego, which systematizes the "second topic" of the psyche, is governed by a genetic schema centered on the "dissolution of the Oedipus complex" and the *repression of the very repressing agency* that it entails; or, in other words, by the way in which an "external" coercion is transformed into an "internal" coercion in order to resolve the conflicts that arise, for the "little child" as both the subject and object of desire, from the family situation that Freud describes as a triangle of libidinal relations. In this manner, the new notion is brought into relation to the theory of sexual development, the clinic of the individual neuroses, the interpretation of the "formations of the unconscious," and the idea that thoughts and affects which emerge within consciousness or manifest themselves within symptomatic behavior are based upon intolerable or unacceptable experiences of desire whose effects we experience and express *after the fact*. The superego thus appears as the final "stage" in the construction of personality, whose specific modality is responsible for our "character" and imposes the law of repetition upon our lives. However, we know perfectly well that the *linearity* of this scenario— even when it is corrected by the recognition (practically constitutive of psychoanalysis) that there is no standard development, uniformly reproduced by everyone, but only singular variants, or, if one prefers, the subject's own "interpretations" of his personal history and its constraints—immediately presented a problem that crystallized theoretical divergences and revisions. In Freud's text, many of these difficulties are revealed through corrections and shifts in emphasis produced in the process of writing, either within the parameters of a single work or in the series of developments that it engenders. I would like to recall two of these shifts that would seem to concern how we understand the idea of a correlation between the "feeling of guilt" and "the need for punishment" that derives from coercion and, in turn, engenders coercion. The point is not to invalidate the schema of "deferred action," which makes the individual into an unconscious subject or a subject at odds with his history; it is rather to show that this schema entails relational and institutional dimensions whose specific conflictuality overdetermines the divisions that constitute the personality and endows them with the effectiveness of a structure.

The first shift that I have in mind is one that leads Freud in *The Ego and the Id*, and even more clearly in subsequent works (*Civilization and its Discontents*, and *New Introductory Lectures on Psychoanalysis*), to replace the reference to the Oedipal "father" whose "threat of castration" his son fears by virtue of the sexual desire he feels for the mother, and with whom he will seek to identify in order to displace the conflict, with a collective reference to "parents."[60] The implications of this shift are obviously complex, since the latter formulation includes the mother alongside the father, or places her in competition with him, and implies an authoritarian familial structure with its own social history.[61] However, at the same time, it is striking that Freud insistently inscribes "the parents" within a larger series that he designates as "the authorities" (*Autoritäten*) and which also includes "educators" (*Erzieher*), "teachers" (*Lehrer*), "models" (*Vorbilder*), and "heroes" (*Helden*).[62] At times (from the genetic perspective), the power of these authorities and their specific contribution to the superego's mastery or to its reinforcement are linked to the fact that they take turns occupying the "position" initially set aside by the dissolution of the Oedipus complex or filling the "paternal function." At other times (from the institutional perspective), it is, inversely, the father and, more generally, parental authority, which is presented as the primordial bearer of the social function of authority and coercion, repressing the drives in favor of "civilization," using their own instinctual energy against them (which is, properly speaking, guilt); and this anteriority would explain why the parent-child (and more specifically the father-son) relation constitutes the "primary" identification that gives rise to unconscious representations of authority and crystallizes their affects. This inversion comes to the fore once again in the politico-cultural essays—for instance, *Warum Krieg* ("Why War?" [1932], written in response to Einstein's interpellation)—where Freud's reflection on the dualism of the life and death drives is intimately bound up with an analysis of the function of the law and institutions. The parent-child relation is thus explicitly inscribed within a set of relations of domination that the law functions to perpetuate in the guise of equality: men and women, parents and children, winners and losers, masters and slaves. . . . [63] In summary, the paternal function is conceived according to a twofold register or is twice inscribed: (1) in a personal history with a genealogical structure and (2) in a system of social relations that are simultaneously power relations. Must we not suppose that the traumatic violence to which Freud attributes the "repetition compulsion" exerted by the superego arises precisely due to the overlapping and mutual reinforcement of these two forms of dependency?

A complementary lesson may be drawn from the other shift, which can be found in Freud's texts concerning the superego as the "model" for exerted and undergone authority, especially in *The New Introductory Lectures on Psychoanalysis* (1933). This model is never direct but must be inherited and transmitted, precisely in the mode of guilt, which thereby functions as the "operator" of the permanent "reproduction" of a repressive or punitive structure. From the need to be punished, one passes to the need to punish, and so on and so forth, indefinitely. It is the idea according to which, "As a rule parents and authorities analogous to them follow the precepts of their own super-egos in educating children. . . . Thus a child's super-ego is in fact constructed on the model (*Vorbild*) not of its parents but of its parent's super-ego . . . and it becomes the vehicle of tradition and of all the time-resisting judgements of value (*Wertungen*) which have propagated themselves in this manner from generation to generation."[64] Several commentators underscore the significance of Freud's revision of this schema of the Oedipal incorporation of the "castrating" father: Lagache, then Lacan; Laplanche and Pontalis in their entry on the "superego" from *The*

Vocabulary of Psychoanalysis; and Jean-Luc Donnet. . . . [65] The significance of this correction appears all the more clearly, it seems to me, when one conceives of it as a redoubling of the genealogical schema: superimposed upon the "father" is the "father of the father" as the bearer of the injunction and of the model of authority on the basis of which each "generation" will decide how to educate the next, and as the ideal judge before whom one must account for the successes and perhaps, above all, for the failures of education. At first glance, this correction is the inverse of the previous one: whether one narrowly interprets this genealogical redoubling, in terms of a strict paternal lineage, or more expansively, in terms of the succession of generations, what it signifies is that the superego is a guilt which is passed or "transferred" from those who have been subjected to authority to those that exert it and thus something which subjects, knowingly or not (but fundamentally not), "turn" against their sons (or their children) because they inherited it from their fathers (or parents). It then becomes clear that this transmission is freighted with anxiety and primed for all the excesses of self-criticism; for, not only is it the sign, for each subject, of civilization as a task he can never fulfill, but it also brings him face to face with the possibility of evil (and destruction) that he himself—or the tyrant that he harbors within—is liable to produce even as he makes himself an instrument of the good.

Considered together, these corrections inscribed in Freud's text already evoke a "relational" configuration more complex than the simple interiorization of the paternal authority as an unyielding judge to whom the ego must unconsciously account for all his actions. The psychic tribunal reveals itself to be constituted *at the same time* by a personal instance inscribed within a genealogical succession and an impersonal instance constituted by a network of institutions or apparatuses of domination and of coercion (the "family" constituting par excellence the point of intersection between the two, where they exchange places and injunctions, to the extent that one is tempted to say, both at once: "The superego, it's the family!" "The family, it's the superego!").[66] The fact that Freud always designates the guilt-complex knotted together with the punishment-complex as the site of an excess of "severity" might suggest that this disproportionate violence is fuelled by overdetermination: The genealogical constraint is excessive with respect to institutional constraint, which it charges with instinctual energy, but the logic of the apparatuses of power is also that which makes the father or "parent" into a sovereign despot or an absolute master of the house.[67] From this perspective, the theory of authority originating from the *Urvater der Urhorde* also functions, in an allegorical mode, as a fusion of the two models of authority or the two relations of power that Freud combines in his descriptions of the superego, and which allow him to make it, at once, the pivotal point in the history of individual personality and the guiding thread of an interpretation of the ambivalence of the phenomena of civilization, or of the element of ineradicable archaic violence within the march toward "progress."[68]

From this point of view, it becomes possible to grasp the full significance of the characteristic that Laplanche places at the center of his reading of Freud's texts on the genesis of the superego and its topographical inscription: the superego is a "contradictory" instance.[69] I will venture a little further and assert: *the superego is the instance of contradiction*—both in the sense of *ambivalence* and of *antinomianism*. Relying from start to finish on the logical (or rather "paralogical") figure of a double contradictory injunction, Laplanche deciphers in Freud the passage from a first level of complexity, corresponding the fact that Oedipal conflict stirs up ambivalent affects (love and hate, admiration and fear) that are simultaneously presented or activated, to a second level corresponding to the fact that the law prescribes both obedience and transgression and thereby engenders the very guilt that it sanctions. This union of opposites is properly what one may call *antinomianism*, in the precise sense that this notion has assumed in the theological tradition with respect to the question of the origin of the law and of sin, which places the subject "under the law," and where it forms a thematic parallel to that of the "theodicy" to which Kelsen refers.[70] Antinomianism can be read as the radicalization of the idea that subjection occurs by means of a delict implied in the very utterance of the law, the law as *interdict*—such that this delict is not a matter of contingency but of necessity. It can also be read on the side of the law itself as the expression of the fact that law has no raison d'être other than the "production" or "imputation" of the evil (violence, injustice, transgression) that it interdicts or sanctions. The idea of a psychic tribunal (or of an ultrajudicial psychic apparatus whose model would be both genealogical and institutional, fusing in some sense the "private" and "public" figures of power) whose functioning is governed by antinomianism thus becomes indistinguishable from the idea of the *unconscious* itself, which, Freud tell us, disregards the contradictions that usually orient the perception of reality.[71] As a result, in particular, the superego treats with equal "severity" both intentions and actions; it "punishes" obedience to the law no less than its transgression, both of which, from its perspective, are no different; and, consequently, it simultaneously utters the interdict as an injunction.

In his essay, "Dostoevsky and Parricide," published in 1928 as a preface to a collection of drafts and letters which formed the final volume of Dostoevsky's *Works* in German, Freud gives clearest expression to the idea of the correspondence between the superego and the antinomianism of the unconscious. In fact, this essay combines the interpretation of Dostoevsky's neurotic symptoms with that of the criminological fictions of his novels—in particular, *The Brothers Karamazov* (which Freud aligned with Sophocles's *Oedipus Rex* and Shakespeare's *Hamlet* as literary elaborations of the Oedipus Complex). These fictions would have allowed the writer to express the feelings of guilt implied by his murderous jealousy toward his father and to displace his need for punishment, producing, by other means, the same paradoxical sense of relief or cure that he experienced thanks to the agony of deportation that the tribunals of the Tsar (a figure of idealized paternal authority) had inflicted on him. However, Freud uses the intrigue of *The Brothers Karamazov*, wherein another person (a half-brother) ends up murdering the father rather than the person who unconsciously wanted to do so, in order to introduce a supplementary dimension of antinomianism:

> It is a matter of indifference who actually committed the crime; psychology is only concerned to know who desired it emotionally and who welcomed it when it was done. And for that reason all of the brothers, except the contrasted figure of Alyosha, are equally guilty. . . . Dostoevsky's sympathy for the criminal is, in fact, boundless . . . and reminds us of the 'holy awe' with which epileptics and lunatics were regarded in the past. A criminal is to him almost a Redeemer, who has taken on to himself the guilt which

must else have been borne by others. There is no longer any need for one to murder, since *he* has already murdered; and one must be grateful to him, for, except for him, one would have been obliged oneself to murder.[72]

A supplementary aspect of identification is here incorporated into the theory of the superego, in the sense of *Gleichheit* (egalitarian similitude, or mimetic equality). This point might be developed by noting that—from the viewpoint of the psychic tribunal—not only does the crime or delict (real or virtual) incorporate its authors to the juridical order, but also the crimes of *certain* people *incorporate us all to the juridical order*. It should not be surprising that, under these conditions, we have such a need for the existence of "criminals" and "delinquents," whom to shower with combined hatred and pity, or that the State and its representatives need them *for our sake*. But also: by taking on the responsibility of identifying and punishing these criminals, the State short-circuits the function of the "personal" superego, or provides us with tools for evading the severity of the superego that we are to ourselves—for which we have every reason to be grateful, albeit not without misgivings (what if the State was mistaken? What if it was to change its mind and discover that "we" are none other than the criminals by delegation . . .).

The Political and the Impolitical

Having thus delineated the main threads of our hypothesis (which I believe can be grouped under the heading of the Foucauldian formula of the *repressive hypothesis*, in a somewhat modified sense), we must now turn toward some conclusions, which are not obvious, because they attribute to Freud's metapsychology a scope and practical consequences that are perhaps far removed from what he might have advanced as a psychoanalytic intervention within the field of politics. In this respect, the situation does not appear to be fundamentally different from the one that already characterizes all the social effects of psychoanalysis, especially in the field of mental health governed, yesterday as today, by the belief in a natural difference, "objectively" locatable, between states or behavior described as "normal" and those which are described as "pathological."[73] Everything, it seems to me, derives from the effect of subversion produced by comparing Kelsen's equation—*Rechtsordnung ist Zwangordnung* (the order of the law is equally an order of coercion)—with the Freudian equation: *Schuldegfühl ist Strafbedürfnis* (the feeling of guilt is equally a need for punishment, thus a call to transgression). In order to explain the significance of this comparison, I will take the liberty of borrowing Kelsen's own manner of developing the implications of his equation and of confronting them, one last time, with what I have called the antinomianism of the Freudian superego.

In the *Reine Rechtslehre* (1934), Kelsen devotes a paragraph to the question of what motives lead individuals to juridical obedience (in particular, obedience to the law) (*Motive des Rechtsgehorsam*).[74] It is admittedly difficult to claim that it is indeed, factually, the threat of coercion (the representation of an act of coercion—*Zwangsakt*—as the a consequence of a delict—*Unrecht*) which induces subjects to obedience, as would do a strict juridical positivism that supposes the law to be a mere "technique," a system of means at the service of any given social order. In many cases, the fear of punishment or the execution of a sentence does not suffice, and "completely different motives" (*ganz andere Motive*) must come into play: religious, moral, social, and more generally, "ideological" motives that associate the representation of a dreadful "evil" with that of the "good," a desirable social state. By the same token, it would seem that the juridical order can only appear "complete," including the conditions of its proper effectiveness (*Wirksamkeit*), to the extent that it entails the definition of certain values. Yet, it is precisely this reference to substantial values that a "pure" theory of the law, both independent of political ideologies and of religious or metaphysical beliefs must "critique" in order to arrive at a positive definition of the juridical norm.

It is by perfecting his theory of the articulation between a "primary norm" and a "secondary norm" that Kelsen thought he was able to give an account of the law's autonomous consistency.[75] In order to be able to speak of an effective norm, which fulfils its function of organizing individual behavior while establishing their personal responsibility, what is required is both a unity of *form* (that is, the logical coherence of a system of juridical obligations) and a unity of *content* or of a material coercion that compels respect of these juridical obligations. This unity does not arise retroactively but must already be inherent to the concept of the law itself; it must, in other terms, be established a priori. It is a sort of equivalent to "transcendental schematism" that Kant used to think the unity of mathematical ("conceptual") form and experiential (or "phenomenal") content in the constitution of natural phenomena. It thus becomes possible to apply to law the formula employed in *The Critique of Pure Reason* to show *a contrario* the necessity for two components and their synthesis: those norms that do not take the form of obligations inscribed in a constitutional order (dominated by a "fundamental norm")—are "blind," arbitrary, or illegitimate; but those that are not accompanied by coercion or imperatively put into effect are "empty" or deprived of effectiveness from a juridical point of view.[76] Neither of the two terms can be analytically "deduced" from the other. The operation that unites them (Kelsen speaks of identity, exactly as he does with respect to the relation between the "juridical order" and the "order of coercion," or the "law" and the "State," of which we have another formulation here) has a "synthetic" character. Contrary to what one might think, however, the norm that Kelsen calls "primary" is not *obligation*; it is precisely *coercion*, especially in the form of a definition (within a "penal code") of a type of behavior that becomes the object of an interdict and will bring a determinate sanction or punishment (*Strafe, Bestrafung*) upon its author.[77] *Obligation* appears as its correlative: as the "second norm" that prescribes behavior that would make it possible to avoid punishment.

The schema of the law, therefore, harbors at its core a moment of *negation*; but Kelsen hastens to specify that it this negation is something other than *contradiction*. There can be a contradiction between propositions describing facts that are not produced simultaneously or between norms with different logics; but there cannot be a "contradiction" between facts and norms, which derive from two heterogeneous universes, even in the instance of an "illegitimate act" or delict—as seen above in our discussion of the way in which crime is folded into the juridical order itself as a "negation of law" (*Unrecht*). The juridical order, therefore, appears as a synthesis of codification and of judicial sanction, from which contradiction is excluded, but whose effectiveness permanently depends upon negation. However, this is only possible on one condition, which can indeed be called *political*: It is that the constitutional norm or *Grundnorm* should be backed up by the "monopoly on the power" to coerce (or violence: *Gewalt*) that belongs to the State. Under these conditions, right becomes State and State becomes right: there is no individual "liberty" that is not the flipside of an interdict and thus there is no such thing as non-juridical conduct; but all violence or coercion that does not correspond to the State's protection of a norm of law is illegitimate and must itself fall under the sway of coercion. It is, surprisingly, the political unity of the State that saves the law from logical contradiction.

An order defined in such a manner possesses an absolute character, since it isn't possible to get outside of it or legitimately to resist it. I believe, more precisely, that according to Kelsen, such an order forms a *fiction of the absolute* in the mode of an "as if," since it entirely depends on the *institutional supposition* of the juridical, obligatory, and coercive character of the "fundamental norm" that grounds it. This is the very point at which the Freudian reversal, whose potentially subversive nature I have indicated, would intervene. What the analytical experience reveals, according to Freud, is that the relation of a subject or an unconscious "ego" to a universe of coercion and obligation, without exterior or means of escape, is not merely a world of negation and interdicts but much rather a fabric of insoluble contradictions. It is as if, on the psychic scene ("the other scene" of the unconscious), Kelsen's *two norms* collapsed upon one another, fusing the threat of punishment with permission or obligation, and unleashing the contradiction that had been set aside by the dualism of "facts" and "norms." In order for the juridical order to be deployed and respected, it is necessary not that the unconscious contains a "psychological" counterpart to the juridical order, a "State within the mind" that would permanently redouble the prescriptions of law and the orders of State with additional moral (or better: "hypermoral") force, thereby producing a phenomenon of "voluntary servitude," but rather, more profoundly (if the actions regulated by the law must be the actions of "human" beings), that the juridical order's underside of disorder or *an-archy* should be repressed and thus preserved, or redirected toward other symptoms or other individual behaviors (at the risk, in "pathological" cases, of paralyzing the very capacity to act). It is necessary that the radical "feeling of guilt" engendered by absolute coercion should be repressed and perpetuated, and along with it, the paradoxical equivalence of intentions and acts, behaviors of obedience and movements of transgression.

The emphasis placed on the relation between the idea of a juridical order and its unconscious opposite that is rather akin to an instinctual disorder, organized around the representation of the absolute legitimacy of coercion (which Kelsen intuited when he found that individuals are haunted by the injustice of the sovereign), certainly does not signify that *there is no juridical order*. It also must not lead us to attribute anarchist convictions to Freud (even if many anarchist revindications have fed upon the Freudian doctrine of the superego—but, we must note, so have many "orthopedic" and "normalizing" programs). What this signifies, I think, is that the juridical order envisaged from a psychoanalytical perspective is, strictly speaking, "groundless," and that one can no longer really act "as if" it had a ground, unless one were to *believe in a fiction* or to "realize" this fiction, which is indeed a form of myth or of illusion. If the juridical order is "founded" on something, it would rather be upon the permanent possibility of its decomposition and thus upon the very conflict that it sustains through repression. It is preferable to read this not as a Freudian *political* thesis, which would oppose that of Kelsen much as Kelsen opposes other theoreticians of law and the State, but rather as an *impolitical* thesis that shatters the fictive autonomy and self-sufficiency of the political. But it could be that the only "concepts of the political" worthy of the name are precisely those that one way or another show the dialectical relation of the political to a contradictory "other scene" that overflows or delimits them. In truth, an equation such as *Rechtsordnung ist Zwangsordnung*, if one were to draw every consequence from it, really leaves no other possibility.

THIRTEEN

Blanchot's Insubordination: On the Writing
of the *Manifesto of the 121*

The title of this chapter derives from a metonymical displacement. Blanchot himself never authorized any confusion between his role as a drafter of the *Manifesto of the 121* and that of the draft dodgers, deserters, and militants whom, along with his cosignatories, he intended to support and defend before the law. However, as we shall see, the word *insubordination* encompasses both a narrow and a broad sense; it connotes a community of action and feeling, evoked in what the *Manifesto* calls "the cause of all free men." My point of departure is a footnote in Christophe Bident's book *Maurice Blanchot partenaire invisible* (which was an essential resource for me throughout the preparation of this talk) citing Marguerite Duras from an interview in 1985:

> *The Declaration of the Right to Insubordination* did not order men to insubordination with respect to the State. It did not order at all. It did not demand; it did not demand that the individual refuse to obey the orders of the State. It taught the individual that he bears within himself every reason, both clear and intelligible, to be an insubordinate and at the same time not to be. . . . It confronts men who have been "called up" with their essential responsibility: their sovereignty . . . [1]

It has been said, even though he was not the author of the first version, written by Dionys Mascolo and Jean Schuster, that Blanchot was principal drafter of the Declaration, revising it sentence by sentence, negotiating details with his coauthors, responding to or even anticipating the objections from certain signatories whose collaboration seemed indispensable.[2] He was always intent upon marking the collective character of the final text; he had no desire to be its "author," either in the sense of the classical myth of the author or in the sense of what, very soon afterward, Foucault would call the "author function"; and yet, we have every reason to believe that, without him, the Declaration would never have possessed the same *effectivity*, or assumed the character of a work of writing producing a political effect. This character of the text poses a double problem— that of its signature and that of its composition.

For the moment, I will offer just a few suggestions about signature to which I will return later. At the two poles of the specter conjured by the list of signatories on the Declaration, without neglecting to mention anyone—for each name is that of an intellectual or an artist whose authority mattered, of a conscience whose decision was in no way automatic—there is a visible signature, even very visible, that of Sartre, and an invisible signature, or barely visible, not because it is anonymous (what would an "anonymous signature" be? Even if certain writers have dreamed of such a possibility, it is obviously impossible) but rather because it is numerous or multiple. The paradox, if there is one, would be that Sartre did not write a single bit of the Declaration and Blanchot wrote or rewrote all of it. This distribution of roles becomes inverted within institutional memory. If you are curious enough to consult a standard history book, you would find the following account, which I extract from the work of René Rémond, a historian whose competence and honesty have been unanimously praised:

> Instead of building upon his success,[3] de Gaulle gave the impression of hesitating about which path to take. He temporizes: never so much as in 1960 did one have the feeling of losing time. He undertook a "mess hall tour" to galvanize the army and to restore its morale. There are divergent accounts of what he might have said to the troops, but most give the impression that he revisited certain of his declarations and let his audience know that France would never give up Algeria, whence the subsequent reproaches that he spoke out of two sides of his mouth. In metropolitan opinion, meanwhile, confidence in his initiatives, which had recently been reinforced by his determination during the Week of Barricades [in Algiers], was on the wane. An increasing number of sectors of French society were aligning themselves against the continuation of the war. The Union Nationale des Étudiants de France (UNEF) . . . was no longer afraid to declare its solidarity with the Union Générale (UG) of Muslim Students of Algeria, which had been banned. Intellectuals, journalists, and professors close to Jean-Paul Sartre and his journal, *Les Temps Modernes*, signed on to the so-called Manifesto of the 121, which legitimized insubordination and adjured young French people not to combat a people struggling for its independence. A few would go as far as providing direct aid to the FLN: these were the "briefcase handlers" ("*porteurs de valise*"), in particular the network constituted by Francis Jeanson. The longer it went on, the Algerian War became a seed of discord that undermined the cohesion of the French nation and broke down the social body.[4]

This account thus gives the impression that the project and the text of the Declaration came from *Les Temps Modernes*, no less than the acts of insubordination, desertion, and support for the FLN, whereas, in fact, the causal order is the opposite. Visibility trumps invisibility. It was Sartre who polarized the emotions of public opinion and the State response.[5] But the words that triggered them came from Blanchot.

There is no question that we must take seriously Blanchot's constant affirmation: The Manifesto is a "collective" text whose formulations do not express the ideas and positions of *one* individual but rather of a movement—and, even more, of a *moment*—which means that they operate a temporal cut at the heart of the present day and insert a dividing line at the heart of opinion. But we must also weigh the full significance of the fact that Blanchot is the one who *found the right words* for this collective expression: words of "consensus" and even of "compromise" between neighboring discourses, but also and above all words of *decision* and *interruption* that will prove to be historically "performative." Otherwise, these words would not have been so often echoed, supported, doubted, criticized, attacked, and vilified; nor would they have given rise to so many judicial proceedings.[6] However, Blanchot could only have "found" them because, for the most part, he already had them at his disposal, among the words he employed as a writer, albeit in an entirely other context. This brings me closer to the problem that I would like to address. In order to specify it further, I cite another protagonist, Pierre-Vidal Naquet, the famous classicist and Greek historian:

> At the beginning of the summer, I received a visit from Jean Pouillon, the bearer of a text whose vigor sharply set it apart from the usual petitions. This manifesto did not call for insubordination or desertion but rather "respected" them and judged them "justified." It solemnly proclaimed that the cause of the Algerian people is that of all free men. . . . I was called in by Laurent Capdecomme, director of higher education. He had been rector of the University of Alger at the moment of the Audin affair and was still in the position at the moment of the barricades on January 24, 1960. . . . Then and there he made me specify in a dictated letter that the manifesto I signed at the beginning of the summer was simply called an "appeal to public opinion." It was, I believe, Blanchot who had radicalized the title and [Jerôme] Lindon [the publisher] who limited the number of signatories to 121.[7]

Radicalized—this is the important word in the preceding passage, not to be confused with violence or vehemence, since in no way does it exclude measure, exactitude, or rightness.[8] What I would like to analyze is the encounter between the radicality of the Manifesto, which accounts for its immediate political effects as well as ongoing relevance, and the specific radicality of Blanchot's own thinking and writing.

I will divide this analysis, as is only right, into three phases. First of all, I adhere to the letter of the manifesto and discuss the implications of its key words and expressions, which, not by chance, are concentrated within its title: "insubordination," but also "declaration" and "right." Next, I examine the intersection between the idea of a "declared right to insubordination" and other of Blanchot's formulations that, even in a different context, refer to the idea of a refusal or negativity that under certain circumstances might be carried to extremes; in particular, the 1948 text on "Literature and the Right to Death," already discussed at this conference by Vanghélis Bitsoris,[9] and the 1965 text on Sade, first published under the title "L'inconvenance majeure" ("The Main Impropriety")[10] as a preface to the section of *Philosophy in the Bedroom* entitled "Frenchmen, yet another effort if you wish to be republicans . . ." Finally, I will outline two concurrent hypotheses that can be formed with respect to the idea—which, in certain respects, the Manifesto drafted by Blanchot has in common with slightly later texts by Hannah Arendt inspired by American resistance to the Vietnam War—of a "foundation without foundation" of the law, which is evidenced precisely by the need for civil insubordination or disobedience.

Insubordination as a "Right"

I presume that one has reread or will reread the text of the Manifesto. If one cannot find François Maspero's now extremely rare 1961 edition of the text, it can also be found in *Lignes* 33 (1998). It is also available on the Internet, on the site of *Le monde diplomatique*, along with a useful introduction by Dominique Vidal. My commentary will not stray far from the famous title itself, adducing passages from the text that sometimes confirm it, sometimes infirm it, or complicate its interpretation. First of all, why is this title so changeable? Beginning as an innocent "call," it became, thanks to Blanchot, a "Declaration," but the annals of history finally transformed it into a "manifesto."

There are reasons for this last formulation, but it is disfiguring and restrictive: whether one thinks of the *Manifesto of Equals*, *The Communist Manifesto*, the *Manifestos of Surrealism*, or the *Situationist Manifesto*,[11] each expresses a worldview, projects, and the doctrine of a *movement* that, might claim to be either minoritarian or majoritarian, but always claims to be "revolutionary," if only within the order of culture, or it might already exist or remain to come (or better, might be in the process of manifesting itself, passing from obscurity to publicity, and affirming its conquering intentions: change life or transform the world). What probably encouraged the perception of the 1961 declaration as a "manifesto" is that many writers and artists who emerged from surrealism played a role in its drafting, but also and above all that a number of those who signed it or diffused it were inscribed within a revolutionary perspective, often *against* the political party that at that time aspired to a monopoly on the revolutionary idea (the Communist Party). Indeed, they proposed to replace the proletarian struggle with the anticolonialist struggle, which would soon become the "third-worldism" of which the Algerian revolutionaries would figure as the avant-garde, or to regenerate the former through the latter. But the "movement" to which the Declaration refers, from its first phrase on, is not a revolutionary movement in this sense; it is a movement of "refusal," "revolt," "protest," and "resistance"—the most insistent term (not to forget that the government in place was that of General de Gaulle)—whose bearers are "the French" (which is to say, the citizens of the French Republic in general). It is also a movement of support, characterized as "aid and protection," for the combatants of the Algerian war of independence, but the words here are calculated as precisely as possible: The anticolonialist struggle for liberation is in the background, its universal signification is noted, but this is not what is directly at stake—not least because this national struggle has no need for spokespeople chosen from among French writers and professors.

All of this might appear restrictive but the actual title reverses the situation—at least within the French conjuncture. "Declaration of the right . . ." evokes a lineage that goes back to the Declaration of the rights of man and the citizen; it is a way to inscribe the "movement" that expresses itself in such terms not within the perspective of a revolution to come, but rather within the permanence of the revolution that has already been done, and yet must always be redone, begun anew, or reactivated. Thanks to the ambition sustained by such a formulation ("Frenchmen, yet another effort . . ."), the Republic is disengaged from the constituted powers that claim to incarnate it but, in fact, "betray" its principles, and moves toward a certain constitutive power, to the acts and voices that momentarily represent its permanence, incarnating "right" as opposed to fact. As for the "right to insubordination," the expression has a very strong conjunctural resonance, because de Gaulle himself declared that the Algerian population possesses a "right to self-determination" (speech of September 16, 1959, which would lead to the referendum of January 8, 1961). The declaration of a right to insubordination thus responds to the proclamation of the right to self-determination, or rather it denounces the flagrant contradiction between such a proclamation and the pursuit of the war, in the course of which one can only think—and I have always thought—that the mobilization of young French people is destined to falsify the application of such a discourse in one way or another.[12]

Taken together, these two systems of reference produce a quite remarkable supplementary result. The original *Declaration* from 1789 inscribes a fundamental "right"—it is even one of the rights that Article 2 calls "natural and inalienable"—which has a striking affinity with the "right to insubordination": the "resistance to oppression," a revolutionary version of the right to resistance, is a notion as old as it is controversial in political philosophy.[13] *By declaring a right to insubordination*, even under particular conditions (which illustrate the type of circumstances in which it must be exercised), the manifesto of the 121 reestablishes the right to resistance at the heart of the universal that articulates the relationship between humanity and citizenship, or makes the one an expression of the other. But, in so doing, it recalls or specifies a double implication revealed by history. On the one hand, the right to resistance is not only exerted against an external oppressor but also and above all against internal abuses of power; on the other hand, it is not only exerted for the benefit of a people who struggles for *its own rights* but also a people who defends *the rights of the other*, or who rises up against the role of oppressor that it is being made to play toward an other and thereby discovers the solidarity or indivisibility of their respective rights. Or better still, it discovers the fact that *the rights of a people* (its "self-determination") come from *an other* whom determinate circumstances have made precisely "its other."[14] Here we touch upon the interweaving of "rights" and "duties," to which I will return.

Let us now examine more closely the problems posed by the terms of insubordination and right, as well as their paradoxical, or even antinomic, conjunction. As I have said, "insubordination"—*hic et nunc*—is first the standard term for young conscripts refusing to carry out their military service or to rejoin the units to which they were assigned.[15] This word was not chosen but rather imposed by reality. But it immediately unveils immeasurable implications. We should linger for a while, texts in hand, over the examination of the whole specter of terms with which "insubordination," considered as an idea or a principle, is liable to be associated or exchanged. I have already cited refusal, resistance, revolt—to which might be added rebellion and, above all, disobedience (understood as dis-obedience: not only the absence of obedience but its cessation, the interruption that turns it into its opposite). In a moment, I will return to the question of insurrection. Cutting this discussion very short, I would only pick out two aspects of the phenomenon thereby designated, I repeat, on the basis of what is *said* on the level of historic conflict.

Insubordination is first "in-subordination," the overturning or interruption of subordination. And subordination is the same thing in general as *subjection*, the *subjectio* of Roman law of which *manumissio*, "manumission," is one particular case. The insubordinate in general is thus the one who refuses and thereby annuls the condition of being a subject (subject of the law, subject of power, subject of the sovereign).[16] This helps account for Duras's use of the term "sovereignty," in a register that might evoke Bataille but that primarily refers to the traditional Lockean or Rousseauist conception of a freedom that founds citizenship, without which there would be no valid form of consent but only a "pact of subjection," a voluntary servitude. The gesture of insubordination constitutes a return to an initial moment that conditions the very possibility of obedience as free consent. There is a fundamental dis-obedience that precedes and renders possible *both at once* subordination to authority, to the law, to instituted power as the doing of *free men* (as the Declaration says), and insubordination when it is called for by the degeneration or disqualification of authorities, or the perversion of the law: what occurs when these authorities give free rein to the army, or sponsor the practice of torture, or decree a war whose object goes beyond national defense (modern, enlarged forms of what classical discourse called *tyranny*). When it comes to such choices, it is in-subordinate or dis-obedient citizens who become judges before the State, not vice versa. At stake is the revindication and restoration of a freedom; but it is a freedom that has the character of necessity and that has an affirmative value in its very refusal. Should we think of the *great refusal*, the quasi-Nietzschean expression that Blanchot will employ later? This is a delicate question because, in the context of 1959, this expression has a pejorative character (as in the famous passage in Dante's *Inferno* from which it ultimately derives). It is impossible not to notice the ambivalence of the term "refusal" in Blanchot's political texts that precede the drafting of the *Declaration*.[17] But the Declaration itself is concerned with proposing, under the name of insubordination, a "non-negative" modality of refusal. In order to highlight this refusing affirmation or this affirmation immanent to refusal, it is important to consider the "clarification" ["*mise au point*"] that Blanchot wrote in response to critiques of the Declaration[18]: at the same time as the *non possumus* of the Apostles John and Peter, he refers to Luther's famous declaration at Wittenberg: *Hier stehe ich, ich kann nicht anders*, adapting it in French:

> At each of humanity's decisive moments, a few men, sometimes a large number, have always known how to safeguard the right to refuse. '*We cannot.*' '*Here I stand, I cannot do otherwise.*' [*Je m'en tiens là, je ne puis autrement.*] This refusal is a fundamental recourse. We should all watch over such a right, watch over it so that it won't be used without rigor, watch over it so that, reaffirmed and upheld, it remains what it is: the ultimate recourse as the power to say no.

It is understood, I think, that this no is also a yes, and perhaps even the most essential yes since it is the yes of man to his own freedom.

But *insubordination* is also something else—that is, *illegality*. At this point, we touch upon the paradoxical idea of a right against right, against the law, and upon the question of whether there is a right outside, beside, or above the law. I believe that it is important to tread carefully upon this decisive point, making sure to draw upon discussions of it that revolve around the notions of *incivism* and *anarchy*. Dionys Mascolo and Jean Schuster circulated a text in 1958 entitled, "Project for popular judgment and the first executive measures,"[19] which was aimed at the project of a referendum to ratify the Constitution of the Fifth Republic and concludes upon the following formulations:

> We declare as illegal the De Gaulle government and Charles de Gaulle himself as a usurper. We do not recognize the results of the referendum that we hold to be null and void. Expelled from French nationality by the Vichy regime, the free French people were yet the only really free French people.[20] Our relations with the pseudo 5th Republic can only be analogous to the relations of those French people with the government of Marshal Pétain: *resistance to oppression*. Civism today cannot be anything but subordination without honor to an extant regime that we have little more reason to accept that the one formerly imposed on us by foreign occupation; in truth, this regime has also been imposed on us *from outside, by ultimatum, and by the military*; and the conspirators of Algiers and their counterparts based in Paris are just as foreign as any foreigner. *We call for a union of free consciences to make INCIVISM the order of the day, to obstinately refuse to serve, to propagate the spirit of insubordination in every sector of society, to resist in every possible manner and by any means necessary a power that is busy laying the groundwork for the rise of fascism in France.*[21]

I will overlook the partially erroneous character of this text's political diagnosis, common among many on the Left at the time, and not only among militants of the extreme Left,[22] in order to note that, if we consider the 1960 declaration in line with this text, it becomes clear that the latter inverts the former's conclusions about civism and incivism:

> Is it necessary to recall that fifteen years after the destruction of the Hitlerian order, French militarism . . . has managed to reinstate torture and make it like an institution in Europe once again? It is in these conditions that many French people have come to question the meaning of traditional values and obligations. What is civism when, under certain circumstances, it becomes a shameful subordination?[23]

Incivism is neither vindicated nor urged but the accusation of incivism is disqualified (much like, later in the text, that of treason). The quality of the citizen—I would say his "virtue"—is thus highly vindicated for the signatories and the insubordinate themselves. Civism and insubordination are identified *modo temporum*.

This demonstration extends to the question of anarchy, which is bound up with the army's claim to incarnate by nature republican legitimacy, which recalls the Dreyfus affair; and with the question of the equation between insubordination, the refusal to bear arms, desertion, and anarchy, which is denounced on the Right and vindicated by certain groups on the Left.[24] This question comes to the fore in Blanchot's interview with Madeleine Chapsal for *L'Express*, censored but included in François Maspero's book:

M.C.—Aren't you afraid that speaking of insubordination will lead the country to anarchy?
M.B.—But anarchy lies in the fact of letting the army become a political power as well as in the fact that the current regime owes its rise to a military coup d'état that thereby sealed from the beginning the illegality of the imperious order that in its august manner it claims to represent and to impose upon us. Since May 1958, we have been in a situation of anarchy; this is the truth that everyone has vaguely grasped. For since May 58, everyone has known that the army has become a political power with the intention of determining national destiny in its entirety. We know that the army, with its enormous material force, and because of the importance that the Algerian War has given it, has the power to overthrow governments, to change regimes, and to impose decisions of its own choosing. This transformation of military power is a capital fact of unprecedented gravity. Well, we are saying that henceforth the refusal to assume military duty takes on an entirely different meaning. For, in claiming the right to have a political attitude, the army must recognize, in turn, in each young Frenchman the right to judge whether yes or no he accepts being enrolled in the kind of political party into which its high-ranking representatives have sought to transform it. Some accept that there is nothing to be said about it. Others refuse: this refusal is henceforth a fundamental right.[25]

In a central position within the declaration itself, one reads:

Neither a war of conquest nor a war of "national defense," the Algerian War has almost completely become an action specific to the army and a social caste that refuses to yield before an uprising whose meaning even the civil power, realizing the general collapse of colonial empires, seems ready to recognize. Today, it is mainly the will of the army that maintains this criminal and absurd combat, and this army, by the political role that many of its high ranking representatives make it play, sometimes acts openly and violently outside of any legality, betrays the ends that the entire country entrusts to it, and compromises and risks perverting the nation itself by forcing citizens under its orders to make themselves accomplices in a factious and degrading action. Is it necessary to recall, etc.[26]

The word "anarchy" is not to be found, but there is a description and analysis of its causes. And in Blanchot's interview with Madeleine Chapsal, one finds:

In fact—and it is important to point it out—the Declaration is not a claim to anarchy, denying or contesting State authority in all circumstances. Here too, those who would have wanted the Declaration to affirm more, affirm the right to refuse any military obligation in general, were really only looking for an alibi, the refusal always offered to good conscience by a theoretical expression of an absolute right, disconnected from reality.[27] What is important, what is decisive, is to affirm that, in the situation precisely defined both by the Algerian War and by the transformation of military power into political power, traditional civic duties have stopped counting as obligations. This is what the Declaration essentially reminds us.[28]

If we return for an instant toward the political tradition from which Blanchot emerges (and with which, many years before, he had completely broken), that of the nationalist extreme Right, the term *anarchy* acquires a particular resonance. In his fairly tendentious book, Philippe Mesnard cites editorials that Blanchot published in 1933 in *Remparts* where he diagnoses signs of a "general political crisis," in which the State falls under the control of private interests ("The State is no more"), and calls for radical solutions "in order to put an end to this decadence" and "in order to restore France to itself, to rediscover the State without statism, a society without socialism, and a government without anarchy."[29] *X sans X*: already the schema is there, or rather *almost* there . . . For Mensard, it shows the permanence, beyond all of Blanchot's reversals of opinion, of his "revolutionary" political rhetoric. He rightly highlights the polyvalence of the argumentative schemas that are situated within the perspective of a "state of emergency" or a "state of exception" and invoke legitimacy against legality; and that historically pertain to the Left as well as the Right, to good or ill effect. But he completely misrecognizes the difference between a discourse that refers to the State as a synonym for order (sooner or later, a "new" order [Ordre Nouveau])[30] and a discourse that refers to the citizens as the recourse of "democratic institutions" when they are taken hostage by public powers. Herein lie not only a political but also a logical abyss. At stake in this opposition, naturally, is the meaning of the idea of the "nation," in suspense ever since the statements in the *Declaration on the Rights of Man and the Citizen* from 1789 on the "principle of sovereignty."[31]

This brings us to the theoretical heart of the Declaration, insofar as it discovers within the singularity of an exceptional situation evidence of a fundamental right: what can and should be called the antinomic structure of political freedom. Such freedom is certainly not opposed to right, to law, or more generally to institutions; one might even say that it has no other place of actualization and existence than the life of institutions (to anticipate, I invoke the title of Saint-Just's work—impregnated with Rousseau and Montesquieu—that Blanchot will cite further on: *Republican Institutions*). Nonetheless, only through frontal opposition to legality does political freedom periodically constitute or conquer itself anew, such that the institutions that organize it or regulate it become *its* institutions, the "institutions of freedom" (*constitutio libertatis*, Arendt will say in *On Revolution*); only then, in other words, does it take the form of *a right exercised against right* or, even more radically, *a right without right, X without X*—this time, rigorously posited.[32]

In this essential antinomianism, we have the germ of several fundamental discussions. I can only evoke them briefly, in order to reach—already very late—my second objective, which is to weave a network of associations between the words that Blanchot wrote in the name of everyone and his personal writing, for which he always sought to achieve a certain neutrality.

First of all, I think that this is the key to understanding Blanchot's famous insistence on the fact that the Declaration utters a right and not a duty, which might appear to contradict the fact that, in the body of the text, he makes rather solemn reference to a double "duty": the "sacred duty" to refuse obedience to an authority that betrays its own mission and the "duty to intervene" of citizens and especially intellectuals when the authorities pursue those who carry out this refusal. Blanchot and Duras insisted that one should absolutely refrain from prescribing a conduct that pertains to freedom, from making it a new obligation at the very moment when the principle of obligation is being called into question. But there is more. This same debate already took place during the drafting of the *Declaration of the Rights of Man and the Citizen* of 1789 when it was a question, in conformity with the jusnaturalist tradition, of entitling this document "declaration of rights and du-ties" before this symmetry was recused by the revolutionary National Assembly.[33] What Blanchot and his cosignatories rediscover, then, is the priority of right over duty at con-junctures when it isn't a matter of legitimizing in advance an established order or a social order but rather of instituting a political community in view of emancipating individuals and the government of the people by the people. The consequence of this discovery is pre-cisely the antinomy of the right, "right without right," which is not founded in advance upon anything other than its vindication and its exercise—along with the risks that they entail—and not genetically or teleologically upon the duties and obligations that they make possible. In other words, such right is not founded upon anything preexisting, given, or substantial.

A second debate would open up at this point, of capital importance for the political phi-losophy of our time: it would compare the "right without right" of Blanchot and his comrades—an idea that I once called *insurrectionary*, already referring to his 1965 essay[34]—to Arendt's "right to have rights," or better yet, to the couple formed by Arendt's idea and Schmitt's conception of sovereignty as the suspension of legality in view of restoring the legitimacy of the State and the decision on the state of exception at the heart of constituent power. What I call right without right in Blanchot is indeed a suspension or interruption that pushes toward the limit where the juridical order turns against itself. This limit, how-ever, cannot be defined as an absolute (at once in the metaphysical sense and in the sense of the strictest juridical tradition: *ab legibus solutus*); instead, it materializes a contingency or an intrinsic fragility and a *finitude* of the juridical order, which can only derive validity from a praxis that itself takes forms which cannot be prescribed, something like an *inter-nal outside* which is freedom itself. What becomes manifest here—something which should become the object of an entire discussion of its own—is the equivocity or even the con-tradiction within the idea of sovereignty to which one must inevitably refer. Reference to Arendt's work is important precisely because it pushes this contradiction to the extreme. There is a profound affinity between *right without right* and *the right to have rights*, each of which is the flipside of the other, the negative face (bearing a power of affirmation) and the affirmative face (fully constituted by a dispossession). In Arendt, as well, the institu-tion proves to be deprived of any guarantee other than the process of emancipation that it formalizes—or not. Nonetheless, only after her own reflections from the 1960s on civil disobedience, in the context of another colonial war and the insubordination that it pro-vokes, does Arendt uphold dissidence and a constitutionally guaranteed right to insubor-dination (an obvious contradiction in terms, at least from the viewpoint of a juridical positivism for which "the law is the law") as the condition of possibility for a democratic order, as I have explained elsewhere.[35]

This brings us to the third type of debate that I would like to evoke without entering into the argumentation itself; the debate about the reference to "inalienable rights" or right superior to the positive juridical order (such as the famous "unwritten laws" of Antigone, *agrapta nomima*). Such a reference is singularly absent from the Manifesto drafted by Blan-chot, unless perhaps one were to "generalize" or "universalize" the principles underlying its denunciation of torture and the colonial oppression. Perhaps this absence is partly the pragmatic consequence of the fact that, in order to utter such principles, it is necessary to convoke an ideology or a metaphysics, upon which the signatories would not be able to agree—whether it is a matter of divine commandments, the prescriptions of humanity, or an inscription within the sense of history. With all of this evacuated from the Declaration, it produces once again the strange effect of contingent necessity, without any foundation other than its utterance. In his commentary on this text, Christophe Bident refers to a few sentences that I wrote much later, in 1997, in the name of the movement of disobedience to the Debré bill on the denunciation to police authorities of immigrants, relying—*mutatis mutandis*—to the precedent of the Manifesto of the 121. In order to explain, in my own turn, why it is necessary within a limit-situation to refound a political community against the official powers that govern it, I spoke then of "the higher laws of humanity" which require obedience beyond and against that which is due to positive laws, and I cited "the respect for the living and the dead, hospitality, the inviolability of the human being, and the inalienability of truth."[36] At bottom, this constituted a return to the primacy of duties over rights, as well as, inevitably, to a philosophy of natural law. I am not sure whether it is possible to avoid such a return, which opens the door, of course, to an infinite dispute over the "substance" and "provenance" of the invoked values. With Blanchot's text—as with Arendt, perhaps, in another manner—we have, inscribed *hic et nunc* within the urgency of a conjuncture, the pure vindication of a negative right against the negation of right. Herein lies the sole "guarantee," the absence of guarantee as guarantee, the infinity of finitude.

Insurrection, Death, Literature

On the level of his own experience of thought and writing, what could have prepared Blanchot for such formulations? This is, one suspects, not a psychological or biographical question. Nonetheless, it is reversible: what results in Blanchot, often a good distance from the moment of declaration, from the identification with what Bident calls (and I will join him in doing so) the *point of inflexibility* or the *inflexible point*?[37]

Because I need to go more quickly now, I will limit myself to evoking the possible relations between the declaration of 1960 and two of Blanchot's well-known texts, chronologically situated at disparate moments. My goal is to formulate questions, not to find answers. The first text is the essay, "Literature and the Right to Death" (1948), which has already be discussed at length at this conference. The second is the essay "Insurrection, The Madness of Writing," previously published as "The Main Impropriety" (1965). Both texts deal with literature, or an extreme form that it can take, and the paradoxical relation—immediate proximity and irreducible distance, conjunction and disjunction—that aligns it with extreme moments in politics. They deal with the fact that "poetics" in an expanded sense contains the sole possibility of expressing what in politics exceeds politics—or exceeds its normality, precisely because politics as such is *not* purely "political."

To begin with a word about "Literature and the Right to Death,"[38] it seems perfectly clear to me that the two syntagms—the "right to death" and the "right to insubordination"—cannot be understood independently of one another. But what is the relation between them? We might respond by trying to show that each term is implied by the other, in one sense or another. If we recall that the expression "right to death," or rather *right to die* comes from Hölderlin's poem "The Death of Empedocles," which Blanchot does not cite in 1948 (there is a different reference to Hölderlin in the text) but must have known and thought about, lingering over it in later texts (*Ich will sterben, das ist mein Recht*),[39] we can then suggest that death, or chosen death, is the ultimate form of insubordination. In "The Great Refusal," Blanchot speaks of the "outside" and of the "absence of work" as words that must be held in reserve "knowing their fate is bound up with the writing outside language that every discourse, including that of philosophy, covers over, and obscures through a truly capital necessity. Which necessity? The one to which everything in the world submits."[40] A few pages later, under the title, "We have lost death," in order to complicate the idea of "refusal," he goes on to specify: "the force of the concept does not reside in refusing the negation that is proper to death, but on the contrary in having introduced it into thought so that, through negation, every fixed form of thought should disappear and always become other than itself" (which is indeed a manner of discerning a thematic of insubordination in Hegel, whose radicality he is attempting to reestablish against Bonnefoy).[41] Death, and more generally negativity, is in-subordination, dis-obedience to the laws of necessity, to which all obedience refers, including obedience to nature.

But the major reference point in "Literature and the Right to Death" is not Hölderlin but rather Hegel, as we know, and more precisely a certain reading—at once derived directly from Kojève and, I believe, subtly deviating from his philosophical intentions—of the account of the *Terror* in the *Phenomenology of Spirit*, the background of which is the thematic of the struggle unto death and combat for recognition, or more generally that of the encounter with death, the "absolute master," as a both necessary and impossible, or unbearable, ordeal of the spirit.[42] Since Hegel associates the phenomenology of Terror with the presentation of "absolute freedom" (leaving aside the question whether, following Hegel, with or against Kojève, this moment must be seen as a dialectical transition toward absolute spirit or, on the contrary, toward a historical abyss he risks getting forever lost), we might try again to operate a subsumption of the two "rights," but this time in the other direction: insubordination only has the sense of an absolute affirmation of freedom to the extent that it is *unto death* or is included within the horizon of death. Not only in the sense of the danger of death imposed by a "master" but in the sense of mortal "punishment"— or the equivalent thereof—accepted in advance by he who, upholding right against right (which is obviously what a revolutionary does), positions himself as a "criminal" with respect to the established order. This is actually what he is, within the finitude of his action. Herein lies, we should note, a nonnegligible interpretation of the nature of the "risk" inherent to the exercise of the right to insubordination. We might even go so far as to posit that insubordination becomes a right in the strong sense if and only if it constitutes a moment of the right to death, if it is anchored in an acceptance of death that goes to the point of upholding it as a "right." This recalls the formula of Olympe de Gouges from her Declaration of the Rights of Woman from 1791: "woman has the right to mount the scaffold; she also has the right to mount the tribune [and take the floor]."[43]

But these two movements of subsumption do not seem entirely satisfying. It think that it is necessary to go beyond the alternative that they delineate and attempt not a *reduction* of one term to the other (insubordination, death) but rather an *articulation* of their respective significations at the heart of the more general problematic of "right," precisely as the entry point where individual freedom joins the community, notably the political community. Entry point: this is tantamount to a point of maximal exposure where the possibilities of affirmation and annihilation are permanently in play. Blanchot's text itself provides the means to do so, at least allegorically, by addressing the question of literature and the effects of writing in terms of the Hegelian dialectic of the *Sache selbst*. (But is it really an allegory? Wouldn't be rather what Philippe Lacoue-Labarthe calls a "poetics of history"?[44] The *Sache selbst* is the "thing itself" not in the sense of a given material object but rather in the sense of the "common cause" or "work in common" that individuals seek to realize through many methods of instituting the community, whether it be that of the commerce of goods and ideas, even books, or that of the political recognition of a general will that confers the characteristics of universality and autonomy upon obedience to the law.[45]) This will become the very object of the "unworking" or *désoeuvrement* the prodromes of which can be found in this text. It would be necessary to take the time to read in detail the entire development that begins by elaborating the Hölderlinian and Mallarméan idea of a negativity of words that metaphorically "kill" the things and persons that they name, and then turns this negativity against the speaking subject (or especially the writing subject) himself, showing that he sacrifices his own being or cedes to the power of death that "speaks within him." Let us posit—but we will have to return to this claim at greater length some other time—that the horizon of Blanchot's text is the following thesis: literature—which, Blanchot writes, "sympathizes with obscurity, with aimless passion, violence without right, with everything in the world that seems to perpetuate the refusal to come into the world"[46]—is the counterproductive activity that "destroys language in its present form and create it in another form."[47] In destroying language, however, albeit virtually or fictively (or rather, *especially* if it is fictively) literature does not only make "the reality of things" exist in the modality of their "unknown, free, and silent existence,"[48] it also "shatters the world"[49] or institutes a "mode of the end of the world,"[50] which I interpret as the dissolution of our belonging and thus of our community insofar as it is founded upon a belonging that is *given* or received from history as "necessity." Literature radically "insubordinates" the world and the community—if I may adopt Foucault's verbal neologism.

Insubordinating the world, including the social world, isn't this also what's in question in Blanchot's essay on Sade from 1965? Isn't this what's at stake in the idea of "impropriety" associated with the insurrectionary practice of politics, which we would attempt to uphold as another equivalent, a privileged manifestation of the idea of insubordination, and one of the conditions of its effectiveness? Sade already figured at the heart of Blanchot's 1948 essay, alongside Hegel, as a "man who identified perfectly with the revolution and the Terror" but who identified with them to the extent that he is "the writer par excellence" and "unites all the contradictions" of the writer—in particular, the contradiction that consists in writing *for everyone and no one*.[51] This writer thus figures at the center of the 1965 text; or rather, it is the couple that he forms with Saint-Just, in which each of the two characters, both of them writers and political actors, procure the sentences that speak the truth of the other. Let us note the reprisal of the theme of the "right to death" in a development against the death penalty as a legal procedure, a procedure of the normalization of society:

> *"It is only at the moment when the law is silent that great actions burst forth"* . . . [If] we must
> have laws . . . never let the law encroach upon life itself, on this point compromise is
> impossible: for how can a people delegate its right to exist, that is, finally, its right to
> death, if it cannot communicate its right to be sovereign?[52]

In this text, Blanchot's argument—which I do not claim to summarize and I am cognizant that its movement, its very writing, is destroyed by cutting it apart—passes through three moments.

The first moment identifies in Sade a pure expression of the revolutionary thesis or of the constituent process that only has reality on condition that it never stop, that it be endless:

> It says that living in a republic will not suffice to make a republican, nor will a republic be
> made by having a constitution, nor, finally, will laws make this constitutive act that is the
> creative power endure and maintain us in a state of permanent constitution. We must
> make an effort, and still always another—this is the invisible irony. Hence the conclusion,
> barely hinted at, that the revolutionary era is only just beginning. But what kind of effort
> will it be? Who will require it of us? Sade calls this permanent state of the republic
> insurrection. In other words, a republic knows no state, only movement-in this it is
> identical to nature. This perpetual perturbation is necessary, first of all, because the
> republican government is surrounded by enemy governments that hate it and are jealous
> of it (the thesis of being closed in); there is no peace for man once he has been roused:
> revolutionary vigilance excludes all tranquility, thus the only way to preserve oneself
> henceforth is never to be conservative, that is to say, never at rest.[53]

The restlessness or disquiet that appears first to be linked to external circumstances ultimately proves to be the intrinsic modality of the exercise of power within a revolutionary perspective—that is, within a movement of emancipation that incorporates, "Hegelianly," its historical conditions and its obstacles into its own infinity. In its final articles (33–35), the so-called "Montagnard" *Declaration of Rights* from 1793 proclaimed that the "right to insurrection" is applicable as long as there is "oppression against the social body"—that is, as long as "a single one of its members is oppressed."[54] The direct heir to Sade and Saint-Just, in this regard, is a certain Marx, the one of the "declaration of permanent revolution."[55] Therefore, we have a relativization of the law and the institution with respect to a political *praxis* that, in accordance with the moments of a revolution that its adversaries themselves push to radicalize, can make use of the framework of law or, on the contrary, subvert it.

In a second moment, Blanchot describes Sade's unveiling, this time by him alone, of the radically antinomic character of the constitutive act distilled by his specific use of the word "crime":

> The virtue that all its legislators place at the basis of the Republic would be in keeping with
> it only if we were able to achieve it without the past—outside history and beginning history
> with it. But he who is already in history is already in crime, and will not escape from it
> without increasing both the violence and the crime. (A thesis we may well recognize—but
> calling it Hegelian and being scandalized by it does not suffice to keep it from being true.)[56]

Let us not forget that "crime" is the keyword in the denunciation by the revolution and particularly by the Terror of the counter-revolutionaries.[57] But, in this case, it is not a matter of denouncing crime and praising virtue; it is, on the contrary, a matter of that which makes Sade's discourse subversive and intolerable at the heart of the very revolutionary process in which he participated, even if he draws perfectly reasonable and politically moderate conclusions from his own argumentation: the substitution of "crime" for "law," and even a sort of hyperbolic absolute of crime, the "crime of nature," the intrinsically criminal movement that is nature itself, the very foundation of the "natural law" invoked in democratic constitutions. Sade is not satisfied to invoke natural law as a transcendental foundation against positive law; he also "destroys" the positivity of nature. Crime is, metonymically, "the law above the laws": it is their radical suspension not only on the level of the letter but also that of the "spirit," the very spirit that obeys and that, according to Montesquieu and others, is rooted in morals:

> Let us again read Saint-Just: "*The solution is in the real insurrection of minds.*" And Sade: "*Insurrection . . . ought to be the permanent state of the republic.*" What is it that distinguishes, I will not say these two men, who are as foreign and as close as two contemporaries can be, but these two equally absolute sentences? It is clear. For Sade, insurrection ought to be as much an insurrection of morals as an insurrection of ideas; it ought to reach all men and the whole of every man; still more, it ought to be permanent, all the while being excessive. Subversion should constitute the only permanent feature of our life; it should always be carried to its highest point, that is to say, always closer to its term, since where there is energy as a reserve of force, there is energy as an expenditure of force: an affirmation that is accomplished only by the greatest negation. I understand that one will wish here to denounce this utopia, and the danger of utopia. . . . But let us leave judgments aside.[58]

But it is the third moment that, in a certain manner, commands everything. What precisely is this freedom whose exercise Sade upholds against every law, and for which he is ready to pay the heaviest price (life imprisonment)? We do not gain access to this freedom through the perpetration of some "sadistic" crime but rather solely in the freedom of writing as the unconditional freedom to "say everything," which constitutes properly speaking what must be called the interruption or the "vacancy of history":

> With Sade . . . we have the first example (but is there a second?) of the way in which writing, the freedom to write, can coincide with the movement of true freedom, when the latter enters into crisis and gives rise to a vacancy in history. A coincidence that is not an identification. For Sade's motives are not those that had set the forces of revolution into motion; they even contradict them. And yet without them, without the mad excess that the name, the life, and the truth of Sade have represented, the revolution would have been deprived of a part of its Reason . . . For this is surely Sade's truth . . . "HOWEVER MUCH MANKIND MAY TREMBLE, PHILOSOPHY MUST SAY EVERYTHING." Say everything. The line alone would have sufficed to render him suspect, the project to condemn him, and its realization to imprison him. And it is not Bonaparte alone who is responsible. We always live under a First Consul, Sade is always pursued, and always by reason of the same exigency: the exigency to say everything. One must say everything. Freedom is the freedom to say everything, a limitless movement that is the temptation of reason, its secret vow, its madness.[59]

In this passage, we find a new expression of antinomianism: The extreme limit of reason—its "consequence," as Althusser would say—is the extremity of madness, the point of inflexibility where the difference between them is neutralized.[60] Only Sade, by means of a fiction that he puts into practice, and which remains imperceptible but leaves an indelible trace or promises to return, effectively operates the "suspension of the law," and thus only he radically identifies with the act of insurrection, because only he inscribes an absolute insubordination at the very heart of insurrection, which is the condition for it to become, if it can, a "permanent state." This insubordination does not necessarily consist in the fact of disobeying all laws but rather in the fact of "saying everything." And this fact does not depend (or not only) upon a legislation relative to the freedom of opinion and expression but more fundamentally upon a capacity to write within the horizon of death—that is, an impersonality, one might also say a universality, beyond all proprieties, which are by definition constituted, particular, and restrictive. Herein lies the "transgressive" foundation of right, with the proviso that this foundation does not found anything, or at least does not consolidate anything, but always already undermines the claim that what it founds would have an absolute solidity.

We thus obtain the reciprocal proposition to the one that seemed to result from "Literature and the Right to Death": Literature is political not only in that it gives rise to an impersonal power that destroys everything but also in that, from the depths of the destruction of the world, it gives rise to an "indestructible." For, this "indestructible" has nothing to do with a necessary foundation or nature of things, whether it be purely anthropological or the reflection of a divine order, whose basis would be invulnerable to the vicissitudes of history and the risks of political action. On the contrary, it is essentially contingent, "aleatory" and permanently exposed to its own overturning. It thus derives from precisely the same uncertainty that, at almost the same period, Blanchot articulates in his commentary on Robert Antelme's *The Human Race*, which features the expression par excellence of the fragility of resistance: "man is the indestructible that can be destroyed."[61] By way of a perhaps problematic short circuit, I would also be tempted to say: Sade shows Blanchot that the freedom to say everything—that is, to write everything—is the insubordination that can be subordinated, the indestructible freedom that can be destroyed. There is nothing optimistic about this assertion, only an ethics of liberation from fear beyond the annihilation of hope.

On the basis of these intersecting readings, and the phrases that they provide, we can now return to the *Declaration of the Right to Insubordination in the Algerian War* and ask whether it has gained in intelligibility. I do not only mean that these phrases would provide a hermeneutic apparatus but only that they might offer a guiding thread to pose the question: What is to be done with this declaration beyond its historical "moment"? Especially after reading Sade as the more radical double of Saint-Just, do we risk suggesting that the right to insubordination, as an individual and collective activity responsive to the democratic state of emergency, this extreme moment at which politics turns against its own institution, would only exist as such within literary space?

This is not, it seems to me, the conclusion we need draw, but on condition that we assent to linger at least for a long moment within *uncertainty*, perhaps a very profound philosophical ambivalence, which is certainly not without practical effects. *Two schemas*, and not a single one, of the unlimitation and hyperbolization of freedom, of the exercise of right against right, or constitutive insubordination, might be, if not derived from the texts we have just read, then at least associated with their letter. The first is a schema of transgression that, for simplicity's sake, I will associate with a doubtless problematic and heterogeneous series of names: Bataille, Benjamin, and thus Derrida. There is no democracy or right that defends against its own instrumentalization by power without transgression or the possibility of transgression. The second schema is that of a certain *resistance* whose necessity Foucault inscribed within an "agonistic" conception of the political (a metaphorical extension of the idea of the political as "the continuation of war by other means"). This resistance—or better, *resistances*—constitutes the force liable to foil the set of "immunitary" mechanisms for the *defense of society*. These two schemas are profoundly heterogeneous and, at the limit, do not inspire the same practices of politics. Perhaps, too, they correspond to profoundly different *conjunctures*. The point is not to choose between these schemas but to analyze and to understand. What they have in common, however, on the formal level, is that they are both radically opposed to the positivist conception of the law whose formula can be reduced to the famous tautology, daily invoked in order to invalidate the very idea of insubordination: "The law is the law" (*Gesetz ist Gesetz*). This assertion conceals the inner link between authority and coercion that makes it permanently possible to reestablish unconditional subordination when its legitimacy or power is compromised. The *Manifesto of the 121* contains *in nuce* both the developments of transgression that annul the law in order to reestablish a transcendence and those of resistance that attempt to foil the effectiveness of power (but can also, by the same token, give it the means to perfect itself). Indeed, the period immediately following the Manifesto will have extensively illustrated these two types of developments.

PART FOUR

The Ill-Being of the Subject

FOURTEEN

Bourgeois Universality and Anthropological Differences

Everyone is a citizen, or must be, and whoever isn't must be excluded.[1]

For the State amputates itself whenever it turns a citizen into a criminal.[2]

In this concluding chapter, I want to articulate the relationship between the political categories of modernity and the question to which its metaphysics always returns: that of subjectivity, endowed with consciousness—perhaps affected with unconsciousness—and with rights, duties, or individual and collective missions.[3] Not only will I examine this relationship on the level of the history of ideas, morals, and social relations, but I will also articulate it as a *conceptual* unity that helps to clarify certain existential and institutional problems and, in so doing, ask whether they are still our problems (and why) or whether they are already on the wane (and how). This discussion will thus be schematic, incomplete, and preliminary, not only in its "conclusions" but also in its formulations, which it is my main goal to render more precise.

The Other Side of the Citizen: The "Bourgeois"?

My working hypothesis is that political modernity comprises two antithetical movements with respect to "anthropological differences"; and that thanks to this antithesis the project of modernity remains active and relevant, albeit *otherwise*—incomplete in its very completion.[4] On the one hand, modernity promoted or invented a notion of the citizen that implies not only that an individual belongs to a community but also that he has access to a system of rights from which *no human being can be legitimately excluded*. This universalism does not signify that differences are irrelevant in the lives of individuals and collectivities; but it does seem to require that they be repressed into the sphere of "particularity" that politics, as such, seeks to neutralize. On the other hand, modernity enlarges as never before the project of *classifying* human beings precisely in terms of their differences; it generalizes the concept of difference and, more importantly, transforms it—using it to designate not hierarchical status or complementary genders but primarily *possibilities of human actualization* among which the individual must "choose" and that, each time, represent *differentials* of power, value, and ability. These movements conflict with one another when human variation becomes the means (in fact, the only "logically consistent" means) *to deprive individuals* (and collectives or classes)—who, as Arendt writes, possess a *"right to have rights"*—of their natural rights, thereby compelling nature to annul itself or to produce *"nonpersons."* [5] But conflicts can also arise—and this eventuality demands that we invert our formulation of the problem—when de facto exclusions are claimed to be, in principle, universal on the basis of supposed "quasi-transcendentals" such as life, nature, the history of humanity as a species, or the general conditions of civilization. *Because the human and the political* (the "rights of man" and the "rights of the citizen") *are coextensive "by right," the human being cannot be denied access to citizenship unless, contradictorily, he is also excised from humanity.* Therefore—and I apologize for the brutality of a formulation that is nonetheless all-too-relevant in reality because of past and present exclusions based on race, sex, deviance, pathologies, to mention only a few—the human being can be denied such access only by being reduced to subhumanity or defective humanity. "Difference" is often only a euphemism for this exclusion and the forms of discrimination based on it, soon becoming, in addition, thanks to a "performative reversal," a slogan—one whose political modality remains inherently problematic—that upholds and demands rights, dignity, and recognition. Thereby, it comes to designate a unity of opposites or an antinomic political function.

Du côté de chez Karl

In order to understand the internal tension among the categories at work here, it might be clarifying to return to Marx's "critique of the rights of man," especially as he formulated it in a famous passage from "On the Jewish Question" that has become the model for attempts to "demystify" modern humanism and the anthropology that underlies it. [6] Marx begins by refuting the thesis of his adversary, Bruno Bauer—for whom the constitution of a "secular" state entails the suppression of particularisms (or bonds to specific communities, especially religious ones), which means that the Jews must renounce their religion if they want a chance to benefit from political emancipation. But he ends up asking why, and "in which sense of the category," the "modern political State" posits the rights of the citizen as the expression of the rights of man that precede and exceed him. [7] His response, as we know, comprises two propositions: (1) that the autonomy of the "rights of the citizen" belongs to a community of "generic being" that exists only in the "heaven" of ideas and state institutions, whereas the principle of such a community is constantly negated "on earth" by the reality of the conflicts and the competition that take place between "egoistic" individuals in *social relations* and in what Hegel calls *bürgerliche Gesellschaft*;[8] and (2) that the "natural and inalienable" rights of "man," which constitute the foundation and horizon of the rights of the citizen, are in no way forms of universal emancipation but rather modalities of actualizing the primacy of *private property*. The generic man whose advent these rights proclaim is, in fact, the "bourgeois"; he corresponds to the absolutization of what MacPherson later calls "possessive individualism" and that Marx himself designates as "egoism."[9] These two propositions are correlative because the primacy of private property, contradicting the essentially "social" character of human activities (or "relational" character: *die Verbindung des Menschen mit dem Menschen*, Marx writes), produces a conflict of interests which, in their turn, spur the imaginary reconstitution of community in the form of an institution projected above civil society. Accordingly, the subject of this institution (the "citizen") is distinguished from the human being (which is to say, from the bourgeois) through his abstraction or reduction to a purely juridical universality. The *citizen* is thus a *bourgeois* who imaginarily separates himself from his own social condition by calling this condition *human*.

Underlying this analysis is a lesson that I consider learned. There is no need to explain again the constitution of the "empirico-transcendental doublet" (the germ of which lies in the correlation between the idealism of the citizen and the materialism of the bourgeois) or the constituent function that Marx assigns to the regime of property. And yet, even this elementary lesson is fraught with perhaps ruinous ambiguity, linked to Marx's twofold usage of "man." Jacques Rancière forcefully underscores this ambiguity in his book *Disagreement* at the moment when he posits that Marx's discourse is not strictly *political* but *metapolitical* because it situates the reality and stakes of emancipation either on the near or the far side of real episodes of conflict; and because it represents emancipation as a ("class") struggle rooted in the *social*. Marx's concern, Rancière explains, is to reveal that the democratic constitution is constituted by a gap between "an ideal identified by a Rousseauist figuration of the sovereignty of citizenship and a reality conceived in Hobbesian terms as a war of all against all."[10] But, in the course of Marx's text, the treatment of this gap "undergoes a significant inflection": At first, "the gap signifies the limits of the political, its powerlessness to achieve the properly human part of man. . . . But, along the way, this truth about man trades places. Man is not some future accomplishment beyond political representation. He is the truth hidden beneath this representation: man of civil society, the egotistical property owner matched by the non-property owner whose rights as a citizen are only there to mask radical nonright. The inability of citizenship to achieve man's true humanity becomes its capacity to serve, by masking them, the interests of the property owner."[11] The name of "man," in other words, serves two antithetical functions within Marx's text: It designates both the subject and the objective of true emancipation— that is, emancipation that *directly* engages the "essential forces" of man (which Marx does not hesitate to call "communism") rather than deferring to the institutions and mystificatory representations of the State; and, at the same time, it refers to the alienated form of social existence where competition is the rule and where human nature is molded into whatever figure favors the triumph of property.[12]

This amphibology results in profound uncertainty about the critical usage of the category of "man" and about humanist discourse in general. Does the mystification of such
discourse reside in the fact of imagining liberation by means of a term that designates alienation or in the fact of covering up the alienation using a term which functions as a name
for authentic essence? This uncertainty can be dispelled if we bring it into relation with
the typology of "emancipations" that Marx proposes in the same text. There are four:
"religious" emancipation (displaced into an imaginary domain), "political" emancipation
(actualized by the institutions of the modern democratic State), and the "human" and
"social" emancipations to come. This enumeration reveals two things, obviously related:
on the one hand, political emancipation entails an amphibology of its own, or, at least,
remains caught between the poles of a contradiction (which Marx, especially in his essay
on the "Jewish question," interprets as a *historical differential* or as a characteristic of the
"present moment"),[13] because it must be considered both as *real with respect to religious
emancipation* and as *imaginary with respect to human emancipation*; and, on the other hand,
human emancipation (freed from the alienations of politics) is nothing other than *social*
emancipation. This does not only mean that such emancipation must take place in a region of "society" distinct from the political sphere (thereby confirming Rancière's critique) but also that it consists in a movement toward socialization (not only productive but
also moral, aesthetic, and affective) that dislodges and quells the utilitarian individualism
of bourgeois society where the egoism of property reigns. The "human" and the "social"
are thus always identical, whether it be in the authentic forms that make it possible to
realize the transindividual capacities of man through "commerce" between all men, or in
the alienated, inverted, and self-destructive forms of a society bent upon countering the
conditions of its own blossoming. Furthermore, this identity always has a political signification, either in the sense of a politics of emancipation or in the sense of a repressive
politics (whose "subject"—*subjectum*—is the State which "appropriates to itself" the forces
of its subjects—*subjecti*—in the manner of a Leviathan). As embarrassing as it may be
from a theoretical viewpoint, Marx still endows the amphibology of the notion of "man"
with an essential dialectical function, because it encapsulates the secret affinity between
the forms of servitude and those of freedom, or of egoism and communism, and thereby
designates the alienation that must be left behind.

   This elucidation of Marx's text, however, remains incomplete if we do not also examine the symmetrical amphibology that structures the notion of the "citizen"—or, more
precisely, the "interlinguistic" usage of the terms *Bürger* or *Staatsbürger* (in German) and
citoyen or *bourgeois* (in French in Marx's text). This is a significant duality that allows Marx,
once again, to highlight a historico-political differential with anthropological stakes.[14]
This amphibology signifies that the two "sides" of the dualism that constitutes modern
society—which is precisely called "bourgeois"—along with its institutions and its models
of "social relations," as well as the forms of *individuality* that it promotes, maintain the
same relation to one another as the two words in French—*citoyen* and *bourgeois*—which
correspond to the single German word *Bürger*. Let us risk a quasi-tautology: The *citoyen*
is nothing other than the *Bürger* of a *bourgeois* but, inversely, the *bourgeois* is nothing other
than the *Bürger* of a *citoyen*. This language game implicating several neighboring idioms

actually goes a long way and is of crucial political importance. It plays upon the possibility of a conceptual reversal inscribed within the very etymology of the word "bourgeois" and its institutional uses, going back to the constitution of urban and commercial communities as autonomous political entities and then traversing all of modernity with its "bourgeois revolutions" (from the insurrections of the *popolo* in Italian cities to the Dutch, English, American, and French revolutions). Historically speaking, in fact, *Bürger* designates the "citizen of the cities" whose "franchise" is founded upon the new regime of property that "shatters" traditional bonds of dependency, whereas *Bürgertum* (in French, the *bourgeoisie* or *droit de bourgeoisie*) would be equivalent to "citizenship."[15] Without this tradition, Marx could never have revived the critical edge of the term, submitting it to a decisive torsion. Working within its parameters, he restores the *field of struggle* that links the two spheres which, after the French Revolution, are ideologically designated as the "rights of man" and the "rights of the citizen"; for, it is the separation of these spheres that functions to dissimulate and to "manage" (or to "police") this struggle. Likewise, the same tradition demonstrates the necessity of coupling the political question with the anthropological question. If we went no further than elucidating the amphibology inherent to the concept of "man," we could debate forever whether Marx "sociologically" reduced the signified "man" (or "human being") to its bourgeois actualization or whether he idealized the bourgeois by upholding him as a unified anthropological type. The semantic equivalence that promotes such a debate, it would seem, remains solely within the "social" sphere situated beneath the intangible realm of politico-juridical citizenship:

$$\frac{\text{Citizen}}{\text{"Man"} = \text{"Bourgeois"}}$$

Returning to our previous amphibology, however, we find ourselves in the presence of a "continuous proportion" structured in such a way that each side is liable to pass into the other:

$$\frac{\text{Citizen}}{\text{Bourgeois}} = \frac{\text{Bourgeois}}{\text{Man}}$$

This proportion, it seems to me, should be interpreted as follows: "Citizenship" is not immunized (whether it be theoretically, through its definition, or practically, through the institutions of such and such a State) against the contradictions that derive from its "organic" insertion into "bourgeois society" whose conflicts, relations, and processes it functions to formalize. Nor is it immunized against the exigencies of the "real," "radical" equality and freedom to which it owes its legitimacy. This proportion is thus, from beginning to end, one of the poles of a political struggle for emancipation within the State and society. The counterpart of the "becoming-subject" of the citizen is, at least potentially, the "becoming-citizen" of the subject. But this thesis on politics necessarily has its own counterpart. Initially, Marx's equation of Man with the Bourgeois exposed the manner in which the bourgeoisie used the name "man" to idealize and universalize its own conditions of existence and, more generally, the form of individuality that makes it possible to believe that private property is something "natural." When read "against the grain," moreover, this thesis comes to signify that bourgeois society "transforms human nature."[16] But bourgeois society could not operate such a transformation unless it maintained a constitutive relationship with its other—the State, public power—that both dominates and structures it (in particular, by means of juridical categories and practices). Every anthropogenesis or anthroponomy is at once "social" and "political." This concurrence becomes especially clear through the various "characters" that individuality may assume (and which, if need be, it must become conscious of or submit to in the form of a condition and its corresponding *habitus*) in order to get recognized, accepted, and "enacted" as the individuality of a *citizen* (either male or female).[17]

The examples of such characters that come immediately to mind derive—to borrow Max Weber's terminology—either from the *Vergesellschaftung* (process of socialization) or from the *Vergemeinschaftung* (process of communitarization). These processes can never be completely disassociated; they do not give rise to two physically distinct individuals who, under "normal" conditions, would acquire and assume the moral personality traits that are necessary for an individual to exercise the responsibilities of a property owner, worker, "parent" or "child," soldier or housewife, etc., and to develop the convictions or "prejudices" that cement a sense of belonging to a religious, professional, or, above all, national community.[18] Nonetheless—even if it remains difficult, except for the sake of analysis, to separate the questions of *normality* and *identity* that arise with respect to all the great "anthropological differences"—multiple personality here is the rule rather than the exception: *homo nationalis*, *homo oeconomicus*, and *homo juridicus* are two or three in one (and many more). The *anthropological question* that is immanent to the historical establishment of the double proportion that structures the relations between "citizen," "man," and "bourgeois," and to the conflicts which it formalizes, does not lead back to some *anthropologia perennis*. Anthropology becomes less monolithic because it concerns forms of "subjectivity" that suppose, develop, and reproduce the universalism of bourgeois citizenship; it becomes a question about the "scissions" or differences that constitute the human being and that characterize the *political* institution of a communitarian bond, even a "fictive" one, between individual property owners (who are, first of all, "owners of themselves" or "their person").

Frantz and Mary: The Missing Voices

Relying upon a rereading and amplification of the Marxian themes of the "critique of the rights of man" and of the articulation of the relationship between the "State" and "civil-bourgeois society," the preceding discussion has certainly justified the idea of a "political anthropology" of modernity. Along the way, however, we drifted away from the objective of constructing a genealogy of the "exclusions" that characterize modern universality and their specific violence. Why this drift? There are, it seems to me, two reasons for it.

First, there is something inherently pedagogical about discussing the individual human being's formation or acquisition of a "character" who would appear on the scene of the world and in relations with other actors in the "mask" of the bourgeois and the citizen. The function of this pedagogy is to construe any deviation from the norm or any counteridentity as "failures" in the individual's formation (imputable either to the individual himself, to society's demands, or more "dialectically" to the maladjustment or discordance between the one and the other) rather than as differences, in the strong sense of the term, manifesting diverse modes of actualizing "the human."[19] The problematic of alienation in Marx—which governs the importation of categories of political anthropology into his work—only escapes this pedagogism because he relies upon a relatively timeless table of the "historical figures of individuality" that belong to each social formation or mode of production, and because, to some degree, Marx measures the failure of these figures not with reference to a norm but rather to the "absent finality" of humanity reconciled with itself.

But the second reason, one might say, is that Marx's historical scene, with its dramaturgy of social roles and their human masks, is missing voices.[20] We would obviously not impute to Marx a sociological conception of the "process" or "mechanism" whereby social relations are reproduced within bourgeois society, a conception of society as a mechanism of *inclusion* or *integration* governed by laws of equilibrium and regulation. Nonetheless, the exclusion that mattered to Marx (whose forms he characterized, especially in his analyses of the violence of the "factory system," by means of a phenomenology of difference modeled upon the "difference between manual and intellectual labor") is both global and homogenizing. Marx tends to grasp the forms of subjectivity that he discovers through the politics of the exploited in the field of bourgeois universality in terms of a new empirico-speculative doublet: Either the subject is a "worker" under conditions of class domination or a "proletarian" who extracts himself from those conditions through a radical negativity that is essentially founded in objectivity.[21] *Other differences* are condemned to be assimilated into the great phenomenology of the class struggle, appearing only as variants of an "absolute wrong," to disappear from the political scene, or to remain voiceless; they are paradoxically *excluded from exclusion* (and thus from the vindication of the "right to have rights" that historically responds to this exclusion).

This limit (which is the constitutive limit of Marxism or, as Althusser would say, reveals its character as a "finite theory") is not only the source of a potentially disastrous political blindness; I would argue that it also tends *to obfuscate the modern anthropological question*—which it is necessary to raise because there are "borders" or "limit points" where civic-bourgeois universality turns into a procedure of exclusion or disqualification, and because *differences* (and consequently the exclusions that they determine) *are irreducible* to any single model or procedure.

In order to call this obfuscation into question, it is less important—at least immediately—to perform analyses that illustrate the *particularity* of certain "typical" differences or exclusions (those that might be upheld or defined by a more or less unified "movement" within the framework of a "pluralism" of political subjectivities) than directly to *make heard* voices that utter contradiction. In their very singularity (because each voice is, precisely, that of a "subject" or a *subjectivation* under determinate conditions), these voices demonstrate that the contradiction manifested in exclusions (and voiced by the excluded themselves) is exactly what allows universality to be "verified" as such, because it prevents it from compromising on its principle and devolving into a more or less accommodating hege-mony. Most of all, these voices show that the great "anthropological differences" (whether it be sex, intelligence, "race," or—as we will see—abnormality) are never simply a matter of *particularity* (nor of its defense or celebration in the form of "particularism," to say nothing of "communitarianism"). They derive, on the contrary, from a *conflict of univer-salities*. Each anthropological difference as such traverses humanity as a whole; and each *represents the universal* against utterances that, in attempting to "neutralize" it, end up "com-munitarizing" it, since such attempts always end up instituting citizenship as a restricted community solely of "normal persons," "civilized men," "responsible subjects," and so on. This is why such rebel voices evoke, *in fine*, nothing less than the differential of subjectivity by means of which the universal becomes (or rather becomes anew) a political figure, quali-fying a constitutive citizenship that can be neither regulated nor imposed from on high.

Among innumerable such voices, I will discuss two who belong to different eras. Both, however, are equally timely, because they possess the remarkable particularity (like Marx himself, in a sense) of having put in writing the "tropes" that operate the inversion whereby universality turns into and against itself.[22]

The first voice is that of Mary Wollstonecraft in *A Vindication of the Rights of Woman* from 1792.[23] Wollstonecraft wrote her book (which opens with a dedicatory epistle to Talleyrand) in response to the decision on the part of Constituent Assembly to inscribe in the Constitution of 1791, after the Declaration of the Rights of Man and the Citizen, a distinction—which Sieyès proposed—between "active citizens" (only voters and eligible voters) and "passive citizens" (which include women who benefit from nationality but are deprived of political rights).[24] After the Introduction, where she elaborates one of the guid-ing themes of her work (that the education of girls disqualifies rather than prepares them; and that society—that is, men and more specifically men of the ruling class—relies upon this deficient education to prevent them from gaining access to intellectual profes-sions and public positions, shutting them in their ignorance and priming them for seduc-tion that belittles and enfeebles them),[25] she illustrates the paradoxical use of names for the difference between the sexes:

> . . . I have sighed when obliged to confess that either Nature has made a *great difference*
> *between man and man*, or that civilization which has hitherto taken place in the world has
> been very *partial*. I have turned over various books . . . the result [has been] a profound
> conviction that the neglected education of *my fellow creatures* is the grand source of the
> misery I deplore, and that women in particular are rendered weak and wretched by a
> variety of concurring causes, originating from one hasty conclusion. *The conduct and*
> *manner of women*, in fact, evidently proves that their minds are not in a healthy state. . . .
> One cause of this barren blooming I attribute to a false system of education, gathered
> from the books written on this subject *by men* who, considering females rather than
> *human creatures*, have been more anxious to make them alluring mistresses than affectionate
> wives and rational mothers; and *the understanding of sex* has been so bubbled by this
> specious homage, that the civilized women of the present century, with a few exceptions,
> are only anxious to inspire love. . . . In a treatise, therefore, on *female rights and*
> *manners* . . . it is asserted, in direct terms, that the *minds of women* are enfeebled by false

refinement . . . and that, in the true style of Mahometanism, they are treated as a kind of *subordinate beings, and not as a part of the human species,* when improvable reason is allowed to be the dignified *distinction which raises men above the brute creation,* and puts a natural scepter in a feeble hand. Yet, *because I am a woman,* I would not lead my readers to suppose that I mean violently to agitate the contested question respecting *the quality or inferiority of the sex.*[26]

In the opening sentence of this passage, one can see that "man" is generic (as *homme* has remained in French, while German distinguishes between *Mensch* and *Mann*), as it is later (when Wollstonecraft claims that reason, not force, elevates men in general above "brute creation"). Soon after, however, a "partition" occurs (which is transformed into "partiality"): a partition between "Men" and "Women"—the latter also designated as "females" or the author's "fellow creatures" when she stands forth as a subject, thereby designating the "place" from which she speaks to vindicate equality or "parity" of rights and "manners." The most remarkable sentence, however, is still the first, which speaks of "a great difference between man and man," because it renders the name "man" constitutively equivocal. On the one hand, the affirmation is inherently contradictory; it consists in the negation of a tautology (man is man no matter his particularities). On the other hand, it asserts a historical given founded in "nature" by the dominant ideology: all "men" (humans) are not equal in rights since some of them, "men" (males), ascribe reason (and thus power) to themselves while the others, "women" or "feminine men" (females), are carefully excluded.

This is precisely what I call the *synecdoche of the universal,* relying upon the classical definition of this trope (substitution of the part for the whole). On the one hand, man is the whole of man; on the other, man is half of man. What is more extraordinary in Wollstonecraft's text, however, is the presence of a further synecdoche mirroring the first: it is the trope that, in English and in a certain "bourgeois" French, authorizes the use of the noun "sex" to designate not a *relation* (in the various senses of the term), but the feminine subject herself, who becomes identified with the organ (or faculty, distinctive quality) that she bears or, ultimately, with sexual difference itself. Man, on the contrary, tends to neutralize sexual difference; for men (males) can only appropriate the universal at the price of losing the sex attributed to woman.[27] Nothing "remains" of man but reason and power— which are supposed to be asexual. In order to regain sex, he must *take possession of the woman* who bears it, which is why he educates her to offer it to him.

Already expressed here, in extraordinary fashion from a "symbolic" viewpoint, we find one of the guiding threads of modern feminism, which does not so much contest universalism as unveil its inherent contradictions.[28] At the origin of the feminist movement is a triple conflict: the conflict arising from (1) the representation of feminine sexuality as essentially "passive," culminating in submission, (2) the relegation of women to the domestic sphere, limiting their activities to motherhood and housework, and finally (3) the symbolic inferiority that—beyond exceptions that prove the rule or actualize it in antinomic fashion—excludes women from achieving "excellence" in the field of knowledge and from serving as representatives of the people.[29] These conflicts are in no way mutually exclusive; each one, to a greater or lesser degree, supposes the others. This does not imply, however, that determinations of the "feminine" form a coherent whole. In order to bring them together as a whole, it is necessary to name them as multiple components of a single *defective relation* inscribed within woman's very *being* and, at the same time, to "suppose" woman (and sex itself) as a figure of the universal.[30] In the language of politics, this feminist logic can be articulated in the following manner: men made the "public" into their "private" property—and thereby, without realizing it, they introduced a contradiction into the institution of citizenship, reducing it to a corporate privilege. In the language of semantics, it becomes: Instead of constituting a differential "mark," the masculine gender is supposed to be "nonmarked," or representative of the "human" as such, whereas the feminine becomes the sole bearer of sexual difference.[31] In the language of dialectics, finally, it implies that one of the sexes is inscribed two times within the universal: once as "part" and once as "whole" (both as represented and as representative). Wollstonecraft's language anticipates all of these discourses. She does not say, "I am, I exist," nor "we women," but rather "I am a woman"—and she does so at the precise point where the designation of "sex" (often qualified as "fair" or "weak") divides "man from man."

Let us now turn our attention to another voice, this time closer to us: that of Frantz Fanon. In *Black Skin, White Masks*,[32] we encounter a trope that is not unlike Wollstonecraft's synecdoche because it too entails both the appropriation of language (that Fanon discovers in culture or literature in general but also, more important, in the colonizer's institution of norms of pronunciation that make it possible to mark creole or "negro" speech and to relegate it to the status of an infantile or barbaric subhumanity)[33] and the identification of the White with the universal to which he claims exclusive access ("civilization"). But Fanon's trope also differs from Wollstonecraft's because, unlike "sex," the "color" that the white allows the black to own and to represent does not consist in anything that might, in return, evoke their "common" humanity.[34] This difference can once again be articulated in the language of Lacanian psychoanalysis (whose early developments Fanon knew well and cited them in his book). In the case of the difference between the sexes, we might say that anthropological difference becomes the object of repression. In the case of racial difference or "color," however, it becomes the object of foreclosure followed by a hallucinatory return. For "bourgeois" man, woman is a subservient subject (*subjectus*); whereas the black, and especially the former slave (which is precisely the overdetermination that Fanon describes), is precipitated into a state of *abjection*, which often appears in the form of fantasies of animality. At the point where these positions overlap, we encounter precisely the figure that postcolonial studies calls "the subaltern"—who is typically a subaltern *woman*.[35]

In the opening and concluding pages that frame Fanon's book, it is thus particularly striking that he would articulate the "dialectic" of the contradictions of humanism in the form of a *double bind* that forbids blacks—but also whites—from taking part in the "partition of the human" (either . . . or . . .) whose absolute character they affirm:

> What does man want?
>> What does the black man want?
>> Running the risk of angering my black brothers, I shall say that a Black is not a man.

There is a zone of nonbeing, an extraordinary sterile and arid region, an incline stripped bare of every essential from which a genuine new departure can emerge. In most cases, the black man cannot take advantage of this descent into a veritable hell . . .

Blacks are men who are black; in other words, owing to a series of affective disorders they have settled into a universe from which we have to extricate them.

The issue is paramount. We are aiming at nothing less than to liberate the black man from himself. We shall tread very carefully, for there are two camps: white and black . . .

We shall show no pity for the former colonial governors or missionaries. In our view, an individual who loves Blacks is as "sick" as someone who abhors them.

Conversely, the black man who strives to whiten his race is as wretched as the one who preaches hatred of the white man . . .

The black man wants to be white. The white man is desperately trying to achieve the rank of man.[36]

But, on the final page of the book, Fanon writes:

I, a man of color, want but one thing:

May man never be instrumentalized. May the subjugation of man by man—that is to say, of me by another—cease. May I be allowed to discover and desire man wherever he may be.

The black man is not. No more than the white man.[37]

And then, the very last lines:

My final prayer:

O my body, always make me a man who questions![38]

Between the beginning of the book and the end with its Nietzschean overtones, of course, a transformation or a transvaluation has taken place, albeit only on the level of thought (but if it were to take place in reality, it would first occur by means of thought). The modality of this transformation can only be defined as a language game—provided that we presume the language of this game to be "performative" rather than cognitive or "theoretical." Moreover, when we listen to this voice, which proffers the universal in the face of the very community that has taken possession of it—the "colony"—and thus dooms itself to imposture, it must be loaded with a rage of color and a rage against color, which, it says, is nothing less than hell. One could certainly claim that Fanon's uses of the word "man" reveal a contradiction that is close to the one that structures Marx's use of the same word in "The Jewish Question." "Man," in Fanon, designates both the denatured and phantasmatic humanity that whites uphold in the name of a community without blacks (both in their own eyes and those of their masters) and another generic and egalitarian humanity that would just comprise individuals, or even bodies, and not "colors." In Marx, however, the amphibology remains something unsaid in his analysis of alienation; whereas, in Fanon, it appears as a violent contradiction among *uses* of the name of man that enter into colonial (or postcolonial) practices and representations; a contradiction *between* what he calls "camps" and *at the heart* of each individual that destiny lodged within one camp or another, inheriting an identity (and thus a "discontent") from it. This contradiction does not take place between abstractly distinguished historical stages (alienated bourgeois society, communism or human emancipation); it is at work within each use of language, each "encounter" between subjects, in order—all at once—to manifest impossibility and to instill a feeling for the intolerable which might eventually give rise to transformation. Once again, this has nothing to do with a contradiction between "universalism" and "particularism"; it is a matter of the contradiction that affects the very utterance of the universal.[39]

The voices of Frantz and Mary do not speak *about* difference in order to define it, justify it, or combat it; they speak *in* difference (or *out of* difference) of the contradiction that it induces. From this unstable point—which is a matter of "ill-being" rather than "being" and thus disorients all ontology (even an ontology of "relations")—I would now like to begin anew, sketching a sort of typology of anthropological differences as *universal differences* through a few contemporary readings on texts and institutions.

FOREIGN BODIES

Following the trajectory that Fanon's "interrogation" opened up, what my initial discussion seeks to address is precisely the incarnation or incorporation of community identities in modern societies, essentially organized as *nations* with certain *empires* among them. What interests me, in other terms, is the genealogy of the citizen as *homo nationalis*. However, my goal is not to undertake such a genealogy on the level of abstract generality, discussing different theories of the origins, marks, and functions of "human ethnic diversity" considered as a timeless trait of human history, but rather to articulate it in terms of a specific debate that runs through contemporary critical thought. The participants in this debate assess the relative importance of the notions of "race" and "culture" in order to understand the existence and the mechanism of relations of *domination* between "communities" that are represented as *foreign* to one another on the basis of character traits that can be generalized to an entire population and transmitted from one generation to another. Rather than attempt to summarize this omnipresent debate, I limit myself to remarking that it gives rise to inverse reductions that divide up critical thought. Oscillating between antiracism and multiculturalism, either it explains that "culture" is the *new name* under which a conception of the "diversity of human races" and their inequality is perpetuated and adapted to a new conjuncture, even as this conception's central notion is disqualified, or it shows, retrospectively, that "race," a pseudo-biological notion founded upon natural history and evolutionary theory combined with the eugenic program of European nationalism, was never anything but a naturalist projection of a "cultural" concept or a historical myth. The vector of critique, of course, cannot be inverted in this way without changing the sense of the *concepts* themselves.

First of all, it is necessary to examine the conditions under which the notion of the "foreigner" refers, properly speaking, to an anthropological difference. This does not appear to be the case, at first glance, if the notion of the foreigner is understood in a strictly ju- ridical sense. The foreigner (*l'etranger, der Ausländer*) would be "simply" the citizen of an- other State. His rights and the constraints that impinge on him have nothing to do with the human condition; they appear to be superimposed on it. The anthropological dimen- sion of this distribution only emerges when the division among nations is thought as the differentiation of humanity itself and thus appears as a quasi-transcendental trait (the human species only exists in the diversity of its languages, cultures, and communities, etc.). Ethnology, in turn, undertakes to describe and interpret this trait, often starting from an extra-European space, in order to show that it is a "natural" dimension of political multi- plicity. Most important here, however, is the way in which the figure of the "foreigner" informs the representation of inassimilable differences (or differences whose assimilation becomes *problematic*) at the heart of political space. In other words, the *inner foreigner*, con- stituted by his or her very "foreignness"—ascribed various causes (essentially race and culture and, eventually, ideology, religion, and political position), but, in the last analysis, identified with a *displaced alterity*—is the one who "should not be where he is," and who functions both to reveal collective identity to itself and to call it into question, if not to threaten it. Not only the simple *foreigner* but the *stranger* or the *Fremde* . . . [40] Such a prob- lem emerges as soon as citizenship and nationality are imposed as two sides of the same equation, which happens in the course of the revolutionary process whereby the *nation*, the "collective subject" of insurrection, is transformed into a new type of "sovereign," internally and externally at war. Already in his "Manifesto" from 1789 (*Qu'est-ce que le Tiers-État?*), Sieyès had defined the nation as a totality that is constituted by deducting the inassimilable "foreign" element—identified with the ci-devant nobility—whom he proposed to "expunge into their German forests," thus inverting the aristocratic myth of "race war."[41] Symmetrically, in what remains one of the most profound contributions to the anthropology of *homo nationalis*, the *Addresses to The German Nation* of 1807, Fichte introduces the notion of the "internal border" (*innere Grenze*): a border can actually sepa- rate communities only if it "withdraws" and is redrawn within a space that is moral and intensive but not extensive (cartographical or territorial).[42] Although such a border founds the institution of the state, it must remain transcendental: the *Kulturnation* precedes the *Staatsnation*. For Fichte, the former German "Jacobin" infused with civic universalism and fundamentally opposed to the racialist conception of the nation (that of the "populists" of the *Volkstum*), the subjective identity that founds the national community, and functions as a reference point in times of crisis, is located in the common language, or better, in a certain *usage of common language*.[43] But the transcendence of linguistic identity is itself apo- retic: it must be protected or restored against the foreignness that penetrates it in the name of the communicability or translatability of idioms. It is thus necessary to draw other borders at the heart of interiority; and these borders might well coincide with other anthropological differences, if there were a means to exempt them from continuous alteration.

With this idea, we touch upon the point where the representation of the foreigner as the *other of the citizen*—the other to whom he necessarily exists in relation—turns into a mechanism of exclusion: and thus, the notions of *purity* and *hybridity* make their entrance.

They are an obsessive concern in the self-representation (*Selbstthematisierung*) of colonial societies; but they are already inseparable from the nationalist idea of a "We" who would be radically distinct from the "Other."[44] No need to insist at length on their intrinsic ambivalence: from the viewpoint of *identity*, purity is "normally" privileged, whereas hybridity (or what is purported to be such, since it depends upon the ability *to define and isolate purity*) is dreaded, devalorized, and even exterminated. But this order of things can be inverted into desire for and valorization of hybridity, or of *métissage*, which, in turn, gives rise to an imaginary attempt to "generalize the hybrid."[45] The important point for us is that the antithesis of the pure and the hybrid can always be configured either in the language of race or that of culture (especially the culture of language whose *purism* guarantees the integrity of culture in general) as conditions of immunity with respect to the foreigner, giving the nation permission to protect itself against him or to neutralize the effects of his "internal" presence, and thus to exclude him materially or symbolically (through elimination or assimilation). Herein resides a sort of chiasmus between two languages ("race," "culture") that function as alternative means of thinking the tension between anthropological difference as *identitarian difference* and the universalism of bourgeois "citizenship."

The debates concerning the relationship between race and culture, as I recalled earlier, have markedly changed direction during the last half century. This political and discursive complex could never be encapsulated in a single formula. But we may highlight two of its striking aspects. In the first place, it was shown that, from the 1980s onward, genetic racism was replaced by a *neoracism*, which was not only another language to legitimate discriminations and hierarchical representations of humanity but also a reflection of the new configurations of racism linked to the multiplication of diasporas and what one might call the normalization of "population mixing."[46] This neoracism—illustrated, in particular, by the discrimination against foreigners or citizens of foreign origin—has been variously qualified as "cultural" or "differentialist," or sometimes as a "racism without races." Second, the need to understand the mechanism of this replacement and to negotiate between opposed interpretations of it[47] led to a reexamination of the opposition between "race" and "culture." In the work of anthropologists, the effort to articulate these notions always results in a third term: fundamentally, that of the *ethnic group* (or *ethnicity*). However, today, long after the historical moment when colonizer-nations sought an ideal, mirror image of their own identity in the supposed simplicity and homogeneity of colonial populations, do we know what an "ethnicity" is?[48] My feeling is that theoretical discourse and common perception alike are caught within a characteristic double bind, equivalents of which arise with respect to other "differences": It is impossible to *deny* (or absolutely repress) *ethnic differences* (no matter their "marks," whether autoreferential or heteroreferential); it is impossible to *circumscribe* them and to posit them as *absolute*. Whether implemented against individuals or groups, extreme violence is potentially present on both sides of the alternative. The historical—or ideological—oscillation between the language of "race" and that of "culture" would be primarily the symptom of this uncertainty.[49]

Nonetheless, it remains important to describe the rhetoric of substitutions whereby these concepts cross one another. It is necessary to bear in mind that this rhetoric is always *contextual* (linked to conditions such as decolonization or the intensification of migrations, their economic function, as well as their capacity to spark "struggles for recognition"); it is always *institutional*—that is, linked to administrative or cognitive procedures whereby the community (nation, people, State) may *gain knowledge of what it is* or recognize itself in the mirror that institutions hold up to it; and finally, it is ambivalent, which means that it functions to stigmatize but also to claim freedom and destabilize domination.[50]

However, it seems to me that the plasticity of strategies of "translation" of the racial into the cultural and vice versa, or the employment of the genealogical schema to think both the "hereditary" transmission of biological characteristics and that of "cultural heritage," always leave behind a *residual dissymmetry* on the basis of which the antithesis can be reconstituted—relegating, in particular, *universality to one side and difference to the other*. Today, no matter the apparent triumph of "culturalism," the tendency is toward the universalization of genetics, through notions of the "genetic diffusion" that destroy the idea of absolutely homogeneous populations, and toward the particularization of cultures as endangered (or indigenous) "traditions," which international programs undertake to protect. But this tendency can also be inverted: the universalism of genetics is also what permits the formation of a new positive or negative "eugenics" that would make it possible to pinpoint "at risk" individuals or populations. Delineating symptoms, one might seek to *identify* the point of resistance to the wholesale substitution of one code for another: one could say that this point is the "somatic," insofar as it is radically distinguished from the "biological," because it no longer pertains to the order of science or even pseudoscience but rather to that of perception and affect. There is no doubt that the fusion of populations effaces (and renders ridiculous) the various groupings of characteristics that used to be taught in schools in order to define "human types," but it does not efface the "aesthetic" phenomenon of *perceived differences between bodies*, no matter their markings and no matter how overdetermined they may be by cultural practices. This point is important because it prohibits one from limiting anthropological difference to a single social relation or a single domain of meaning, the search for which would underlie the process of subjectivation as identity construction or the belonging of individuals to a community. Obviously, the identification of the "somatic" as a site of intersubjective differences is always inherently sexualized.[51] The "body" as such—a fortiori the *speaking body*, conferring on speech a hallucinatory visibility—is neither "universal" nor "particular," but always irremediably singular.

THE ABNORMAL

I will now discuss a second "case" pertaining to any entirely other mode of exclusion (even if there were common ideological sequences organized around the notion of *degeneracy* and, more generally, the influence of the evolutionary paradigm): I take it up from Michel Foucault's manner of presenting the question of "abnormality" and "abnormals" in the course he offered at the Collège de France in 1974–1975, culminating in the lecture that he gave in Toronto, 1978, at the *Law and Society Symposium*, "The Dangerous Individual," which reprises and hones many of the course's themes.[52] His principal object is to elaborate the technologies of power that bring the development of a new form of knowledge into relation with methods of "governing" industrial society. Obviously, these technologies do not exclude violence and repression, but they do subordinate them to disciplines of behavior whose objective is less to *prohibit* or to *inspire fear* than to *prescribe* and to *normalize* (or to configure, to select "normal" modes of conduct). To this end, it is necessary not only to institute models but also to make it so that subjects recognize these models.[53] This is precisely the function of a system of institutions that include law and medicine but also the schools (in other words, the great "amenities" of bourgeois society). All of these institutions function by upholding the opposition between normality and abnormality and by exercising *judgment* that could be called *discriminating*, in the dual sense of a differentiation among individuals separated into various social—but also "moral"—categories (in particular that of *character*, as in Kant) and of a distinction among the modes in which the norm might be negated by different manners of overturning, abolishing or "deviating" from normality.[54]

This is the point at which things become more complicated and the very notion of normality proves terribly equivocal. This is not simply because the normal is liable to be negated in many different ways and to varying degrees. What destabilizes the norm— and, at the same time, institutes it in practice—is the fact that heterogeneous and ultimately incompatible "abnormalities" are treated as a continuum and end up fusing with one another. This is fundamentally the history of the alliance between psychiatry and criminology, which results in the recurrent conflation of the types of the madman and the criminal. What especially drew Foucault's attention was the convergence of two processes that unfolded throughout the nineteenth century and into the twentieth century, the first on the level of institutions and power struggles and the other on the level of anthropological knowledge and discourse. On the one hand, there is an evolution that leads from the competition between judges and doctors—analogous to Kant's famous "conflict of the faculties"—to determine which "power" (psychiatric or judiciary) would preside over the arraignment of the "great criminals" whose atrocious actions (parricide, infanticide, regicide, anthropophagy) were haunted by the specter of madness, to a close collaboration between these same powers at the heart of the penal process. From this moment onward, the psychiatrist would intervene as an "expert" whose knowledge is required to determine the justiciability, responsibility, and punishability of any and all criminals. He thus judges before the judge (or he "pre-judges").[55] This collaboration is crucial, Foucault shows, in order to define a criminality that is no longer simply a matter of an objective infraction of the law or defiance of the sovereign but rather the expression of a *personality*; and that, therefore, gives rise, in advance and at the origin of any actual crime, to the psychosocial figure of the "criminal" as a *subject capable of committing it*.[56] On the other side (that of knowledges), negative categories are invented that undermine and permanently threaten to breach the bounds of normality—in particular, the category of *perversity*.[57] The "pervert" links up the earlier notions of "monstrosity" and "monomania," thereby authorizing the deployment of an entirely other problematic: that of "dangerous individuals"—dangerous at once to society and to themselves—against whom a system of anticipatory defenses must be developed. From then on, judiciary and medical determinations converge at the heart of a crimino-pathological continuum. Passing from the Sorbonne to the Palais de Justice (if not the Préfecture de Police), psychological knowledge undertakes to elaborate the causes of perversity by tracing it to the pathogenic disorders—especially those of a sexual nature that generate *instincts*, with children as their victims or agents, who, at the same moment, became the focal point of the moralizing discipline of the bourgeois family.[58] A speculative biology, in turn, to which Foucault often refers using the remarkable expression "meta-somaticization," inscribes these perversions within the horizon of a *species degeneration* that must be combated with "eugenic" and "pedagogical" barriers—both medical and racial, thus (bio)political.

But the danger to the species—a return of the inhuman or the infrahuman at the heart of the human—becomes an obsessive theme only to the extent that it crystallizes a question that the subject must consider as a citizen, in the exercise of his functions as an "juror" that characterize the new egalitarian constitution. Foucault insists on the fact that the process of modern assizes, in which (albeit by delegation and cooperation with a complex apparatus for interpreting and applying the laws) the people takes responsibility for its own "security," constitutes a locus of truth.[59] At the same time that citizens "defend" themselves, they seek to grasp *who they are* as men acting in the public or private sphere, what they are "one and all" (*omnes et singulatim*) capable of, and which fragile barriers (including, of course, the barriers of social class) protect them (or not) against perversion.[60] Anthropological difference—which is a matter of normality, responsibility, property, judicial capacity, and citizenship (everything that could be grouped under what in seventeenth-century English was called *propriety*, the "moral" doublet of *property* and the inheritor of the Stoics' *convenientia* or *oikeiōsis*)—acquires a reflexive function within the framework of collective introspection; or, alternately, it becomes the object of a question whose plethora of responses barely hides an anxiety-inducing aporia. The "sovereign" is defined by a specific answer to the traditional question, *quis judicabit?* ("Who shall judge in the last instance?"), which Hobbes placed at the center of his *Leviathan*. The democratic regime, in turn, answers this question with a set of interlocking categories, at once reflexive and prescriptive: the people, the majority, and the regime of normality. But it always seems that the final category is presupposed in the first.

The relationship between judgment, reflection, and self-possession (the condition of *propriety* in general) is here fundamental. For my part, in a text that I wrote in response to interdisciplinary debates in France about the plan to reform the Penal Code and the law of 1838—which declares the mad to be irresponsible and subjects them to administrative authority by derogation of their rights as persons—I attempted to incorporate Foucault's analyses (only partially available at the time) into a reflection upon the discursive strategies of bourgeois politics designed to make intelligible both penal responsibility and society's relation to "deviance." By means of three simple logical operators—disjunction, conjunction, and simultaneous negation—aligned with three characteristic political "tendencies," I produced three particular cases of a combinatory that reveals the system of the "ideologies" of modernity.[61] The idea that the individual can be *either insane or criminal* (but not both at the same time, even if discriminating between them remains problematic), corresponds to a *liberal* politics. The idea that he can be *both insane and criminal* corresponds to a *conservative* politics that is periodically reactivated by ideologies of "social defense" layered upon biological or sociological determinisms.[62] Finally, the inverse idea that the individual "in himself" is, at bottom, *neither insane nor criminal*, because these forms of deviance result from pathogenic and criminogenic social conditions that must be abolished in order to establish the possibility of free and happy life, which would escape the alternative between the "normal" and the "pathological," corresponds to a socialist or anarchist *utopian* politics.[63] The "liberal" position is, of course, the unstable point upon which the whole system pivots; it is both politically fragile and profoundly ambivalent. The endeavor to separate the criminal and the madman relies heavily upon the possibility of collective "discernment," which is very important for democracy within the framework of a society whose members remain inherently "fallible"; for, such discernment potentially enlarges the field of "normality" in which individuals watch out for themselves rather than being watched over in an authoritarian fashion. But this separation also makes such normality into a mechanism of ordinary exclusion *at the very heart* of civil society, by means of the feeling on the part of subjects of *not being others* (or of being appreciably different from those who are "others"). This feeling obviously is all the more troubled, and potentially violent, as its negative counterpart is more equivocal.[64]

At this point, we rejoin the implicit lesson in Foucault's analysis: The power-knowledge of psychiatry and that of law maintain a fundamental *uncertainty* about the nature of the danger that threatens the subject within his "self-possession." Returning to the question of anthropological differences, this lesson can be expressed as a *double bind*. What characterizes these differences is not only that they are *unavoidable* (which is to say that it is impossible to imagine the human *deprived of such differences* or subsisting outside of them without inflicting intolerable violence upon it); it is also that they are indefinable or impossible to localize (which is to say that one cannot—once again, not without extreme violence—draw a bright *line of demarcation* between concepts and the classes of humans that correspond to them; one cannot, for instance, absolutely define what separates a "normal" subject from a "mentally ill person" or an "honest man" from a "criminal," and divide "abnormal people" without remainder into these two faces of the inhumanity within humanity). This is why liberalism itself has a utopian side that more or less successfully resists its own antithesis, the "reduction of complexity" operated by the collective fantasy of perversity.

"Bourgeois guest house for both sexes and others"

At this point, I would like, no less schematically, to consider a third "case": that of sexual difference.[65] Why, one might well query, did I wait so long when sexual difference is the only true "anthropological" difference, or, at least, the only foundational one? Even if we relativize all the differences used to classify individuals, it is impossible to do without the idea that humanity is sexuated (or, in more recent terminology, "gendered").[66] Nor could one give up asking in what sense and up to what point *the revindication of sexual equality* calls into question not only the *interpretation* of sexual difference but also *the very fact of this difference*. There are several reasons.

Earlier, I recalled how the feminist contestation of the persistent (and even rationalized) *triple oppression* of women in bourgeois society might end up deconstructing of the very terms of the problem of female "inferiority" (or their "passivity" with respect to male "activity," all the more inevitable because it is inscribed in the law of the State itself). In order to take a supplementary step and to call into question the very idea of a natural difference, it would be necessary to superimpose critiques of *heteronormativity* upon feminist critiques of male domination. As a result, the problem of anthropological difference and its political functions would no longer be posed exclusively in terms of identity or identification *but conjointly in terms of identity and the norm*. Relations of domination should be analyzed in terms of these two dimensions of subjectivity at the same time.

In order to bring this debate together with a reflection on the contradictions of the universal, I will limit myself to evoking certain of the difficulties that beset psychoanalytic conceptions of "bisexuality," going back to Freud's own formulations. These formulations are a feature of his work from *Three Essays on the Theory of Sexuality* (1905) to his 1931 article on "female sexuality" and the chapter on "femininity" in *New Introductory Lectures on Psychoanalysis* from 1933. Since they do not always have the same content, the most convenient approach, then, would be to follow Freud's presentation of bisexuality in Chapter 3 of *The Ego and the Id* (1923).[67] In what he calls a "digression," Freud characterizes the problem of articulating the relation between identifications and object-choices on the basis of a double relation: "The intricacy of the problem is due to two factors: the triangular character of the Oedipus situation and the constitutional bisexuality of each individual."[68] The little boy (*das männliche Kind*) concurrently develops an identification with his father and a love for his mother who is his first "object-choice," until such a moment when these relations come into conflict with one another. The resulting Oedipal crisis is then resolved by "dissolving" the Oedipus complex in one of two ways: either "normally" by reinforcing the identification with the father, which must entail a renunciation of any claim upon the mother and thus opens the way for new feminine love-objects, and which would ultimately "consolidate the masculinity in a boy's character,"[69] or (in an implicitly deviant fashion) by an identification with the mother that other texts uphold as one of the bases for homosexual object-choice, through the subject's fantasy of replacing her as the object of the father's love. In a symmetrical fashion, the little girl develops an identification with her mother and a love for her father, but the situation is complicated by the fact that *for the girl as well* the mother remains the first object of libidinal fixation. The girl's "secondary" identification with her mother, which will determine her femininity, must then entail the renunciation or elaboration of a loss. Freud seems to think that the virtually melancholic character of this relation—or, at any rate, its intrinsic ambivalence—is what accounts for the "quasi-normality" of an identification with the father *even in girls* and thus for the completely different signification of homosexuality in men and women.[70] This series of arguments shows how uncertain Freud's work remains on this question: uncertainty about the assignation of *normality* to certain identifications or certain object-choices over others, about the function of *ambivalence* at the heart of each identification with a parental model, and about whether the antithesis of "masculine" and "feminine" can be mapped onto "active" and "passive" roles in the configuration of the libido.[71]

Everything is debatable (and eventually was debated) in this scenario that introduces into its theoretical construction and into its interpretation of clinical observations and experiences a great number of prejudices about "normality." Nonetheless, it is also worthwhile to recognize the critical lesson that it has to teach with respect to the status of difference. Even if sexual difference must be "propped up" and "invested" at every instant of individual history, it is not—any more than the libido itself—a biological reality. At the same time, however, it is not simply "sociological" or "cultural," a matter of convention or power.[72] In reality, relying upon a quasi-structuralist approach, it becomes clear that sexual difference depends upon a *combinatory* that offers or imposes upon the subject *two possibilities of "choice"*: on the one hand, a choice between "masculine" and "feminine" and, on the other, between "heterosexual" and "homosexual" orientations. By definition, all the combinations are of the same nature, which is why Freud unambiguously declares that homosexual orientation is constituted in exactly the same manner as heterosexual orientation (and that, in reality, all human sexuality entails a specific distribution of homosexuality and heterosexuality between the conscious and the unconscious).[73] This means that there is no "natural" determination of sexual identity (masculine or feminine), but only an unconscious historical construction (of which each stage "reinterprets" previous investments and thus puts an indetermination back into play). However, one might claim, Freud never gives up circumscribing preferred forms of identity in the course of a given "development," the prototype of which is access to genital sexuality built upon the virtually "perverse" phases of infantile sexuality. True enough. Freud often presents this development as a law that the individual must uphold in order to join the social order. At other times, however, he describes the same development as a constitutively pathological process. In reality, the subject falls short of the "maturity" or the ideal anthropological "fulfillment" which orient the teleology of classical pedagogies (themselves linked to conceptions of access to citizenship). On the contrary, this development signifies that adults *in reality always remain children* whose relation to the anatomical difference between the sexes results from identification with the members of the parental couple, in whom this difference is projected as the "cause" of love or hostility. And so on and so forth to infinity—because the parents themselves only base their own identity upon identification with the model of "their sex." At bottom, it is thus the *parental couple* that upholds the law of binarity (the obligation to make the always risky—if not impossible—choice between two times two possibilities) and imposes it. This is close to what Lacan will call "familial complexes," drawing upon the institutional models described in contemporary anthropology.[74]

Summary as it may be, this brief account of Freud's approach to sexual difference makes it possible to perceive where Lacan's innovation resides and why his thesis—"There is no sexual relation"[75]—is important for our problem. Two aspects of Lacan's argumentation are immediately apparent. The first is his intransigent but profoundly atypical defense of the binary structure of sexual difference, presented in terms of antithetical "constructions" of universality (as "all" and "not-all," which can be interpreted as, respectively, a *conjunction* and a *disjunction* of the categories of the *universal* and the *community*). The second is his extreme formalism, which means that, in the final analysis, the causes of identification pertain neither to psychology nor sociology but only to the symbolic efficacy inherent to the *institution*, the prototype of which is language, and which necessarily subsumes "experience." For Lacan, the experiences in question must always be *thought*, even if they are situated at the limits of the representable. And there is no thought (even unconscious) outside the structures of language or even logic. What is "divided" between the two "sides" of sexual difference is not the human species but rather the *speaking being*. But, as in Aristotle, there are only speaking beings (*zōon logon ekhōn*) within the institutions of the city (*zōon politikon*).[76]

Going one step further, we soon recognize that the two sides of Lacan's table of sexuation have an *identical* logical structure, give or take a "double negation." On the side that formalizes the dilemma of masculinity, the subject is torn between the universal realization of the phallic function, which is common to all individuals gendered "male," and the exception that would constitute a "noncastrated" identification with the phallus itself, whereby the subject no longer *possesses* but *is* himself the phallus, ultimate object of feminine desire. In other words, the virile "excess" whereby the community of males is constructed only becomes perceptible from the perspective of "woman," or from the other side of the table, which bears witness to its inconsistency. On the side that formalizes the dilemma of femininity, the subject is torn between the general impossibility (for all women) to *not* be subjected to masculine ("phallic") jouissance and the impossibility for *all* to fall under this law of enunciation: whence the inevitable consequence that feminine jouissance—"lawless" and thus "cityless" (*apolis*)—should represent to men an irremediable lack, a line of flight with respect to the domination of sexuality under the phallic order or community signifier.[77] Nothing substantial or material distinguishes the masculine from the feminine: *for every "x"* (that is to say, for each and every one of "us," subjects to come whom the unconscious obliges to make "choices" about sex), two contradictory attitudes toward the phallic function are possible, both equally misleading: the one believes it possible to *take possession of phallus*, the other to *escape it* (thereby transforming the "not all" of femininity into a rival or alternative "all").

One can read this elaboration of sexual difference either as Michel Tort proposes, as a "logicized" remnant of an archaic *paternal dogma*, essential theological and patriarchal, or as Joan Copjec does, relating it to a typically *modern* (or perhaps even "Rousseauist") conception of the relation between the subject and the law, situating the law *on the same level as the subject*.[78] Suffice it to say that the political ambiguity of Lacan's approach is abundantly illustrated by the divergent interpretations of his work (which is probably the result that Lacan deliberately sought to effect). More than any other post-Freudian, Lacan defends the idea that *there is only one sexuality* (or, we might say, *sex* as a relation that is a nonrelation) although it comprises two different "modes of entry," and that this sexuality is dominated by the "masculine" phallic function (which has no antithesis).[79] However, since this function is only that of a signifier in relation to which any subject position is inherently aleatory, males suddenly find themselves dispossessed of "property rights" over the function itself, except as an institutional *fiction* undergirded by a phallic imaginary that keeps them happy and the fantasies of power or impotence that they attach to it. Herein

lies the paradox of Lacanian discourse: Because it posits that the only domination is masculine, it can be read either as a Machiavellian justification of this domination or as the
anarchist project to ruin it and thereby to expose it to ridicule.

Moving very quickly to the positions of Judith Butler, we notice right away, of course,
that—taking up the critiques of dominant masculinity and heteronormativity spearheaded
first by gay and lesbian movements and then by the queer movement—she destroys as radically as possible the privileges of binarism, showing that the representation of "gender" as
an alternative limited to two possibilities is nothing but the *retroactive effect*—impacting
the very definition of sexual identities—of the normative structure that obliges us to choose
between two predetermined antithetical "sexualities": the one presented as normal, and
the other presented as deviant (or, in the best cases, subversive).[80]

It is generally admitted (whence a certain number of the critiques, sometimes virulent,
addressed to her) that Butler incarnates a relativist and culturalist epistemology. I would
uphold, however, that the "absolute relativism" at stake here (much like the "absolute historicism" that I discussed elsewhere in reference Gramsci) is indiscernible from a universalism. This becomes manifest in the elaboration of an emancipatory discourse, liberated
from the norms that give rise to the violence that society exercises against "deviant" bodies and behaviors, that one might call a *universalism of differences.* [81] And it becomes even
more manifest in her recognition of the political fact that claims of minority rights cannot dispense with the language of civic universalism if they want to avoid producing "ghet-
toized" mentalities and mutually exclusive groups, even if these revindications do not
hold this language to be "natural" or univocal in its effects. Butler thus aligns herself with
the notion, derived from Arendt, of a universalism that is an "antifoundationalism." Accordingly, she is not far from Rancière when she describes how the demand to extend
freedom and equality to a "monstrous" humanity, rendering the human a "stranger to
itself," poses a challenge to universalism.[82] Going even further, one might discern in Butler's work a sort of turning of Lacan against Lacan: no pleasure "matters" more or better
than another because any objects invested with fantasy (the "object a," in Lacanian code)
awaken and fixate as such the desire of the subject. Once again, this idea is profoundly
egalitarian. But it is also entirely compatible with the thesis (in truth, adapted from
Hegel) that (since all desire is "the desire of the Other") we receive our identities as subjects *from the Other* with whom we exist in a relation of lack, dependency, and loss. This
means that the manner in which we construct our behavior and configure our bodies is a
function of the manner in which we imagine a (masculine or feminine) Other in order to
make ourselves loved by her (or him).[83] More than ever, we find ourselves in the domain
of innumerable multiplicity or the difference of sexualities which necessarily implies that
there are *more than two sexes*—and, a fortiori, *more than a single one.* An attentive reading of
Butler's texts shows, however, that this is not her last word: "binarism" has radically
changed its status, but it has not entirely disappeared. It returns first with the fact that the
anatomical uncertainty of gender—although it may do nothing to justify moral, social,
and political classifications coupled with repressive measures and cruelty—supports a
melancholic relation to the proper body that never really comes to an end;[84] and second
with this other (much happier) fact that, without a "law" or a "truth," the identification of

"masculine" and "feminine" roles remains omnipresent in the "fantasy" of amorous desire.[85] Instead of the binarism figuring the natural or symbolic "code" that would be transgressed by the multiplicity of modalities of jouissance, always threatening to the institution, it would be displaced upon the figure of the *couple*, which is always realized in a contingent fashion but remains binding in form because it never lets sexuality—or kinship—escape the aporia of One = Two and to the displacements that it engenders.[86]

Reread side by side, Freud, Lacan, and Butler seem to show once again that anthropological difference—the less localizable and the less substantial it becomes, never allowing individuals to be "classified" without remainder into "pure" types—can never, much like civil status, be neutralized or avoided when it is a matter of understanding what it means for several subjects *to join together in the realization of the universal*, whether it be "passively" or "actively." It is perhaps the reverse of Foucault's lesson about the normal and the pathological. Are we thus in a position, if not to conclude, then at least to characterize the general situation that results from the three compared cases, at once on the level of the institution and that of subjectivity?

Ill-Being or the Subject of Relation

Incapable of being stripped of human essence nor purely and simply identified with it, what I have called "anthropological differences" (which, I have attempted to show, are always also *differences within differences*) form at the very most a site for problematizing the human and what it is supposed to "place in common." The result is a very strange configuration of relations between gestures of exclusion and those of inclusion. Clearly, then, the representation of anthropological differences is immediately linked to violent forms of *exclusion*, which it appears to found or justify after the fact. Race (along with culture, religion, etc.), sex and sexuality, illness and more generally the pathological, the criminal personality, or simplemindedness, either separately or in conjunction with one another, make certain individuals both human and less than human; and, marked as such, they become objects of care, protection, redress, surveillance, punishment, and isolation that are gathered up and banished from public space or the right to intimacy and barred from the array of educations, professions, exchanges, associations, and communities which constitute citizenship in the "material" sense. Foucault, however, he who has done so much to elucidate this multiform reality of exclusions and confinements within modern history, went out of his way to insist that *there are differences among these modalities of exclusion*.[87] The figure that increasingly held his attention is that of an exclusion that presupposes an inclusion or even is actualized *in the form of an inclusion*: the continuous surveillance of individuals in the name of the various "risks" that they represent, both to others *and to themselves*, makes it possible to dissociate them from others without thereby consigning them to the other side of a border or confining them in "camps," and entails a positive counterpart in the generalized practice of "governing individuals." For my part, I indicated above that certain differences crystallize in the upsurge—in a literal sense—of what can be called the *foreign body*,[88] that which appears at the heart of a space where, normally, it has *no place*, where *it should not be* if reality were what it is supposed to be. All the figures of the strange foreigner—the neighbor distinguished by color, race, culture, or quite simply his name, who can seem perfectly integrated even as he remains an *alien*—provide the clearest examples of this body. But the abnormal and the pervert are foreign bodies within the moral sphere; another is the representative of the "third sex" who troubles binary codes. Femininity, for men, is a "dark continent."[89]

These examples—which will be called "metaphorical," there where, in reality, everything is metaphor—lead straight to the idea that, at least within the framework of civil-bourgeois universality, the principal form of exclusion is *differential inclusion*. Universalism cannot be materially separated from institutional forms that display the foreign body, define it, and control it. By the same token, the foreign body incarnates the two opposing poles of every definition of the human: it is the inhuman against which society fights and defends itself, just as we all do—each and every man and woman—as we try to become human. This immanent alterity, it must be said once again, has nothing to do with particularity, because it always already affects the belonging of the subject to a common "species." But religious and secular philanthropy also teach us that this alterity *as such* (or this difference *as such*) is inherently *human*; and that we must always know how to recognize this humanity in order to remain "human" ourselves. Nothing calls for identification more than the criminal, the handicapped person, the sick or insane, the illegal alien, the oppressed aboriginal, the unreasonable woman (hysteric, jealous, mystic), the homosexual, the hermaphrodite, and—above all perhaps—the *child*.[90] Ultimately, it will be the supposed "model" or "dominant" type of citizen (the famous "white heterosexual adult male") that ends up as the figure not only of the exception but the "straw man."[91] And it is "normal" that things are like this. Every simple, "positive," "generic" form of *humanism* is thereby shattered without everyday language offering a substitute term. "Antihumanism" works only on condition that it articulates from within humanism a form of *contradiction* or *resistance*.

Today, as we know, the thematic of the internal exclusion and the construction of alterity as expulsion is ever more widely shared. But if we have any hope of understanding the forms of subjectivity (or better, the modalities of subjection and subjectivation) that "answer" to the dynamic of universalization, an additional step is no doubt necessary. What "anthropological differences" denote, without ever managing to pin down, is less a matter of *differences between individuals or subjects*, the unequally recognized "place" that they occupy within the framework or at the edges of the human species or society, than of the originary dissymmetry of "bonds" or "relations" themselves: the relations by means of which *individuals socially and politically constitute the human* (and which, reciprocally, individualize it). This is why it remains insufficient, and essentially impracticable, to attempt to divvy up universality and difference by assigning them, respectively, to the ideality of the species or genre (that is, to the "human community") and to the concrete reality of the individual—or perhaps, to the transcendental and to the empirical. In a manner that I have several times called "quasi-transcendental" (with Foucault and Derrida), both universality and the difference that impedes it and fosters its realization are always already situated, *at the same time*, on the side of the species (or the community) and the side of the individual, because they are inseparable from a phenomenon that is much more originary that these artificially distinguished names: relation itself, in the (inter)active sense of the term.

In order to render this idea more explicit, along with the philosophical question that it implies, it would be useful—if not indispensable—to begin one last time from the Kant's and the Marx's formulations at the point where their respective "critical" intentions appear to intersect: the correlation of the problem of the bourgeois universality of rights (with their correlative duties) with the formalism of realized abstraction. The Kantian subject (from the *Critiques* but also from *Anthropology from a Pragmatic Point of View*, which provides the other face of this subject) is "transcendental" insofar as it finds within the "I think" inhabiting consciousness the idea of the universal immediately linked to rationality, morality, and the historicity of indefinite progress. There is probably no need to demonstrate at length the relation between this philosophical figure and the political institution of civil-bourgeois universalism, because the figure itself insists upon this relation and the decisive transformation that it operates (at least in theory): a movement from a relation of vertical subjection to a monarch or a transcendent God (who is "sovereign" or "seigniorial," positioning men at once as "subjects," "children," and "creatures") to a subjection with respect to the law (moral, juridical, and social) and to the individual responsibility that it imposes: "the human being's emergence from his self-incurred minority" by his own means.[92] On the other hand, Marx's formulation in the *Theses on Feuerbach*, when he opposes the "essence of man" whose only reality resides in the "ensemble of social relations" to the abstract notion of the *species*, seems diametrically opposed to Kant, although it is also closely linked to a "cosmopolitical" perspective.[93] This formulation does not only abolish transcendence but also transcendental subjection by situating the anthropological question (which it explicitly addresses) on what Deleuze will call a "plane of immanence."[94] What then happens to the category of the subject? Must we conclude, in line with a specific reading of Marx (which is always useful, especially in order to set aside the presuppositions of *theoretical humanism*), that this category no longer has a constitutive place but only, at most, that of an ideological *supplement*? Or rather, must we seek to reformulate this category *beyond* what, in Marx, appears to disallow such a move, without thereby abandoning the idea of a conversion or a *reduction of verticality*—which we are tempted to call democratic and also secular? What should we say of a subject who would not merely be the subject "of" a relation (and thus subjected), or placed by experience, life, history, and institutions "within" a relation or a set of relations, but would itself be "as such" a relation, exposed to the *retroactive effects* of the relation that always already constitutes it and *caught from behind*, as it were, by its intrinsic inequality?

The two parts of the famous Sixth Thesis on Feuerbach are both important for our problem: *Aber das menschliche Wesen ist kein dem enzelnen Individuum innewohnendes Abstraktum. In seiner Wirklichkeit ist es das ensemble der gesellschaftlichen Verhältnisse.* "But the human essence is not an abstraction that inhabits [or comes to lodge] in each individual": here we have a critique of metaphysical individualism, in which two heterogeneous philosophical traditions are fused, both from Antiquity but closely associated in philosophy of the modern era: the tradition of "substantial form" (or of individuation as the combination of form and matter) and that of the interpellation of the subject by an inner voice that reveals its truth.[95] The subject is here "naturally" the bearer (*suppositum*) or the addressee (*subditus*) of the universal that overarches it or constitutes it from inside; but, all to itself, the subject is also inevitably defined as "lacking" universality. This is even more the case when the form of the subject is that of a "humanity" to be realized in history and when the interpellation comes from the inner voice of moral conscience. Marx thus inverts the perspective in order to give a positive value to a relation that, little by little, extends universality to the whole "world" of reciprocal interactions among individuals, whom he essentially conceives as "producers" (which is to say that, as they fabricate the means of their own existence, they also make the universal exist socially and politically instead of being content to receive it as an externally imposed form or to welcome and harbor it as a call).[96]

"In effective reality, it is the ensemble of social relations." This formulation calls for several remarks. The ensemble of which it speaks is not a "whole" or a closed totality, circumscribed in advance (*Ganze*), but rather an open totality or a indefinitely extendable network; it only exists in the form of a practical realization or a common "work"; and, above all, it proposes to identify the social itself as a *relational* mode of subject constitution that grants primacy, once again, to horizontality over verticality. Along these lines, I elsewhere proposed to adumbrate Marx's "ontology of relation," comparable to various philosophical attempts to reintegrate the individual within the transindividual (thereby signaling his agreement with the tradition that links the insurrectional moment of bourgeois revolutions to communism).[97]

Nevertheless, we should underscore that while Marx keeps a decisive critical distance from bourgeois universalism and naturalism, whose essentialist individualism ("possessive" as well as "reflexive") he denounces, he does not depart from its abstract representation of the human, making "relation" (*Verhältnis*) into a generic activity that is fundamentally *reciprocal* and, in this sense, undifferentiated, even when it is presented as intrinsically *conflictual*. Dissymmetry or difference would only enter this relation as a secondary factor, more likely in the form of alienation or a socio-political obstacle to the realization of human essence rather than as a condition of its effectivity or a mode of its power of transformation. What happens to such an idea when we take into account—as we have been doing here—the fact that anthropological differences are not merely *added to the universal* in a contingent fashion, arbitrarily *limiting* it or *overturning* its signification, but rather *contradict and thereby actualize it*, placing it into a determinate relation with itself and opening one or many abysses at the very center of universality that also usher inhumanity back into the human?

On this point as well, Kant can serve as guide because of the use he makes of symptomatic terminology; he is not unaware of anthropological differences even if he conceives of them in an very conventional manner as "characteristics" of each person, each sex, each people, each race, and finally of the human species as a whole (see *Anthropology from a Pragmatic Point of View*), but he "represses" these differences outside of reason (and consequently outside of the emancipatory perspectives that it prescribes) and thus installs them alongside what in the *Critique of Practical Reason* and *Groundwork for a Metaphysics of Morals* he calls the "pathological." However, the pathological is not simply the empirical or the sensible, even when it refers to "motives" that are opposed to morality. It is rather the *other* of reason that returns to impede reason's exercise by virtue of the free will that characterizes it, thereby "perverting" its use by inverting its values.[98] In many respects, the pathological is like a *foreign body* that reason discovers within itself; it tends to divide the human subject at the same time as it furnishes a material basis for the perpetual combat that this subject must wage in order to join the rational community of "citizens of the world." Reading Kant with Marx, however, while submitting both to the radical decentering operated by phenomenology and an analytic of anthropological differences, makes possible a further step—or rather a lateral step. This reading allows us to pass from the idea of a divided subject or a subject endowed with a "dark" side (analogous to a malefic force) to the idea of an *ill-being of the subject*, or that of an intrinsically "discontent" subject or "malformed" subject: not on the level of psychological or moral interiority but on that of the very exteriority and immanence of the social relation that it upholds with every other subject and thus with the "quasi-transcendental" conditions of its own humanity.

It would no longer be sufficient, then, to posit anthropological differences as "constitutive of the human," which is fully compatible with the idea that they would always be *complementary* with one another or would be distributed among individuals "without remainder"—which reduces universalism to a supplement of ideality that would allow the subject to resolve the dilemmas that such differences provoke, often by eliminating everything that imposes itself as perversion, alienation, or simply alterity. Instead, we should say that anthropological differences in their unstable multiplicity are the only site where subjects can exist who raise the question, without preset answer, what it means to regard—*or not regard*—other subjects (who are also *others as subjects*) as human, and thus practically to confer on them an equal right to have rights. Because this site is unstable, perpetually changing its configuration, and because it is most often constituted of unacceptable forms of discrimination and their rationalization, it is not really "habitable." Nor is it *acceptable* or *tolerable*, although it is also the site of astonishment, excitation, identification—or of rebellion. It is precisely the place of ill-being: the *Wesen*, "being" or "essence," which Marx still invoked at the far edge of his critique of "individualist" bourgeois abstraction, is only ever a "nonbeing" or rather a "monster" (*Un-wesen*). The monster does not correspond to any type, norm or substance, does not derive from privation or absence, and does not foretell any superman, but it can be reduced to a certain "thing": an ensemble of instituted relations and bonds that alter, differentiate, and annul themselves as they transfer (or return, ghostlike) from one subject to another. Accordingly, the monster carries onward, without assignable limit, the *conatus* or the possibility of a multiplicity of transformations: passages from activity to passivity, from isolation to community, from the becoming-subject of the citizen (that is, its construction at the heart of institutions that never include one within the universal without excluding others or even the same ones under a different guise or capacity) to the becoming-citizen of the subject.

The formulations that I have attempted to refine here, always in a provisional fashion, showing that anthropological differences intervene in an irreducible but equivocal fashion in all the processes of "normalization" and "placing in common" that serve to mediate between the subjectivity of the individual and the universality of transindividual relations, do not only tend to represent this becoming as a process "without origin or end" (as Al-thusser said), a perpetually renewed task, a multiplicity without unity, but also to show that these processes hold the key to the constitution of the universal in its civil-bourgeois form—that is, in the form of a politics of immanence that is characteristic of modernity, to which Marx fully belongs (because he attempted to carry it to extremes). We are very aware that there is no universality without dialectics, without contradictions that breathe energy and movement into it; and that these contradictions result from the fact that a *political* institution founded upon the equal access of everyone to the freedoms and powers that are called the "rights of man" never ceases, at the same time, to deny such rights or restrict access to a select number, which is *also* a manner of defining their "humanity." The power of this contradiction, its capacity to "make history" (or to generate *historicity*) becomes manifest in a range of emancipatory movements, both "majoritarian" and "mi-noritarian" (assuming that such a distinction is not questionable, as it is in the case of feminism). In a sense, however—this is also a lesson that we have learned—the power of contradiction thus understood remains abstract and, consequently, impotent. What en-genders the capacity to defy the institution of the universal in its own terms cannot sim-ply be contradiction; it must also be difference—and, more precisely, the universalizing difference that intersects with contradiction. Through modalities that are never reduc-ible to a single model, anthropological difference is not only the site of "troubled" identi-fications and normalizations; it is also the point that gives rise (with as much trouble) to upheavals of power, displacements of belonging, counteridentifications, and the invention of alternative norms that Foucault called "counterconduct." My position, in other terms, consists in attempting to think the *conatus* of the subject-citizen as overdetermination: the overdetermination of the universal by contradiction, of contradiction by difference, and thus of conflict itself by exclusion, but also by what never gives up forcing exclusion to beat a retreat.

INTRODUCTION: AFTER THE CONTROVERSY

1. Neither Michel Prigent at Presses Universitaires de France nor Helen Tartar at Fordham University Press was able to see the fruition of work they had so strongly and generously encouraged in their respective languages. This is a tragic coincidence. I think of it with sadness, but also with immense gratitude. I am proud to have been considered a friend by these two great editors of our time.

2. Nancy's question, along with responses from Badiou, Balibar, Blanchot, Borch-Jakobsen, Courtine, Deleuze, Derrida, Descombes, Granel, Henry, Lacoue-Labarthe, Lyotard, Marion, and Rancière, appeared in French in *Cahiers Confrontation* 20 (Paris: Aubier, 1989), and, in English (adding texts by Agacinski, Franck, Irigaray, Kofman, and Levinas), in *Who Comes After the Subject?* ed. Eduardo Cadava, Peter Connor, and Jean-Luc Nancy (New York: Routledge, 1991). Jean-François Courtine makes reference to the "scansion" represented by this debate in his preface to the dossier "Moi qui suis le sujet" published in *Les Études philosophiques* (January 2009). For another characterization of this philosophical "convention" and the question that provoked it, see Gayatri Chakravorty Spivak, *A Critique of Postcolonial Reason: Toward a History of the Vanishing Present* (Cambridge, Mass.: Harvard University Press, 1999), 27–29.

3. See my essay, "Structuralism: A Destitution of the Subject?" *differences: A Journal of Feminist Cultural Studies* 14, no. 1 (Spring 2003): 1–21.

4. I will only provide two examples of such reactive productions (albeit not devoid of talent and teaching) dating from the same period: Manfred Frank, *Die Unhintergehbarkeit von Individualität* (Berlin: Suhrkamp, 1986); Alain Renaut, *L'ère de l'individu: Contribution à une histoire de la subjectivité* (Paris: Gallimard, 1989).

5. *Aufhebung*, Hegel would say; *relève*, Derrida would say. Nancy is content to inscribe the word "after," affecting it with a question mark that, rightly understood, contests it from within: erased in the title of *Cahiers Confrontation*, it subsists and even triumphs in the English volume.

6. On the medieval origins of these variants, see the analyses of Alain de Libera in *Archéologie du sujet: I. Naissance du sujet; II. La quête d'identité* (Paris: Vrin, 2007) that he magisterially distilled in his contribution to our coauthored article for the *Dictionary of Untranslatables*, of which I provide an excerpt later herein. Starting from the problem of the passage from the Greek *hypokeimenon* to the Latin *subjectum*, de Libera reconstructs the entire concurrence between the Aristotelian lineage centered upon the relation between form and matter in individuation and the Augustinian lineage centered upon inner certainty and the analogy between human and divine persons, pursuing the consequences of this concurrence all the way into contemporary debates between analytic philosophy and cognitivism.

7. Among the reference points common to the entire classical "critique of subjectivity," it is necessary at least to cite Cavaillès from *Sur la logique et la théorie de la science* (written in 1943, published in 1947): "It is not a philosophy of consciousness but a philosophy of the concept

that can provide a doctrine of science," and Canguilhem's articles "Qu'est-ce que la psychologie?" (1956, republished in *Études d'histoire et de philosophie des sciences*, 1968) and "Mort de l'homme ou épuisement du cogito?" (*Critique* 242, 1967), between which would be situated Althusser's "Freud et Lacan" (1964–65, republished in *Écrits sur la psychanalyse* [Paris: Stock-IMEC, 1993]), in which he compares the critiques of *homo psychologicus* and of *homo economicus*. In addition, it would certainly be necessary to include—retroactively elucidated by Deleuze—Sartre's *La transcendance de l'ego* (1934). See also the studies that Pierre Cassou-Noguès and Pascale Gillot collected in *Le concept, le sujet et la science: Cavaillès, Canguilhem, Foucault* (Paris: Vrin, 2009).

8. Nancy kept his own "response" in reserve: "being in common," the horizon of an ontology of "us" (see *Being Singular Plural*, trans. Robert Richardson and Anne O'Byrne [Stanford: Stanford University Press, 2000]). I intend to return to this ontology, addressing together with other attempts to think the "common" and "communism" (many of the most essential among them, in France and elsewhere, arising from the encounter between Nancy and Blanchot, which, in 1983, occasioned two intertwined books: *The Inoperative Community* [Nancy] and *The Unavowable Community* [Blanchot]). But, for the moment, I cannot avoid turning away from this task, even as I entitle the second section of the present volume—focused on the development and antitheses of the Hegelian *Ich, das Wir, und Wir, das Ich ist*—with an expression that, in fact, comes from Nancy: "Being(s) in Common." I say "turn away," but the distance is not so great, since it seems to me that Nancy never stops meditating on Hegel and dialoguing with him on this point. See Jean-Luc Nancy, *Hegel: The Restlessness of the Negative*, trans. Steven Miller and Jason E. Smith (Minneapolis: University of Minnesota Press, 2002).

9. The antithesis between subjection and subjectivation runs insistently through Foucault's work but characterizes all French philosophy from the second half of the twentieth century, since one of the guiding threads of this philosophy is what we could call the problematic of "modes of subjection." See "*Subjectus/subjectum*," in this volume. In a very interesting work, partially inspired by Judith Butler's analyses in *The Psychic Life of Power* (Stanford: Stanford University Press, 1997), Yoshiyuki Sato related the insistence of this antithesis to the omnipresence of the concept of "resistance," which has clear historical connotations in the period under consideration (*Pouvoir et Résistance: Foucault, Deleuze, Derrida, Althusser* [Paris: L'Harmattan, 2007]). For my part, I would suggest a duality of resistance and transgression, which leads me, as one will see, to confer crucial significance upon Blanchot's formulations in various contexts.

10. One of the things that I did not take sufficiently into account with these formulations is the internal *doubling* of this category, which is not only a function of its Greek and Latin roots, but also of the fact that, beyond this historical difference, there insists, on the level of the very *language* that names institutions, an alternative within the representation of the link between "subjects" and the "community," as Benveniste showed in "Deux modèles linguistiques de la cité," in *Problèmes de linguistique générale* II (Paris: Gallimard, 1974), 272–280.

11. My work thus dovetailed with the "proposition" that, at the same historical moment, I was attempting to inscribe at the center (mobile, problematic, and contested) of the demands and extensions of citizenship in the modern era. See "La proposition de l'égaliberté" (1989, republished in *La proposition de l'égaliberté* [Paris: Presses Universitaires de France, 2010] and in English as "The Proposition of Equaliberty," in *Equaliberty: Political Essays*, trans. James Ingram [Durham: Duke University Press, 2014]).

12. One might be tempted to oppose the Rousseauist model of the constitution of the citizen with a Spinozan figure, representative of another modernity (or an "anti-modernity," as Negri writes). See my essay, "Jus, Pactum, Lex: sur la constitution du sujet dans le *Traité Théologique-politique*," *Studia Spinozana* 1, no. 1 (1985): 105–142, which I have not reproduced in the present volume despite my original intentions, at once in order to avoid making it even bigger and to focus upon a single line of questioning at a time.

13. It suffices to say that it would be necessary to reflect on an overdetermination characteristic of the 1980s, particularly in France, which gave rise, precisely in 1989, to a sort of symbolic interpellation. On the one hand, this date is the anniversary of the insurrection from which republican institutions derive their legitimacy (and whose trace is reactivated in their inner conflicts). It became the object of intense controversy between those (such as the communists) who have always claimed the "Jacobin" heritage and those (such as François Furet and Marcel Gauchet) who, diametrically opposed to them, see in this heritage the source of Marxist-Leninist-Stalinist totalitarianism that it is high time to "bring to an end." But, on the other hand, in an unforeseen if not unpredictable fashion, this date coincides with two events that—each in its own way—call into question our entire representation of the *historical process* that gave form to the discourse of modern citizenship (which one may call "bourgeois": I will later discuss the extended sense in which I understand this term): the first is the development in Europe (and especially in France) of a *postcolonial conflict* in which a modality of "subjection" and a particular category of "subjects" began to concern "citizens" about the ownership and usage of their rights (see my study, "Sujets ou Citoyens? Pour l'égalité" [1984], reprinted in *Les frontières de la démocratie* [Paris: Éditions de la Découverte, 1992]); the other is the "revolution of 1989" in the Socialist world, that is, the peaceful insurrection (in some places, victorious: Warsaw, Budapest, Leipzig, and Prague; in other places, repressed: Tiananmen Square) which came to reactivate a notion of popular citizenship or sovereignty *against* one of its most characteristic historical "derivatives," held up as a global example.

14. Nonetheless, I will mention five collectives where, directly or indirectly, most of the writings collected in the present volume were prepared and presented: the project of the European Science Foundation, "The Origins of the Modern State in Europe, 13th to 18th centuries," in which I collaborated on Theme F: "The Individual in Political Theory and Practice," under the direction of Janet Coleman (See *The Individual in Political Theory and Practice* [Oxford: Oxford University Press, 1996]); the Vocabulaire Européen des Philosophies, a research unit at the Centre National de la Recherche Scientifique under the direction of Barbara Cassin, whose results were published in 2004 by Éditions de Seuil and Le Robert (and ten years later in an English translation—revised and expanded with further entries written originally in English—entitled *Dictionary of Untranslatables: A Philosophical Lexicon* [Princeton: Princeton University Press, 2014], ed. Emily Apter, Jacques Lezra, and Michael Wood); the working group "La Philosophie au sens large," under the direction of Pierre Macherey at the Université de Lille III (UMR [Unité Mixte de Recherche], "Savoirs, Textes, Langages"); the group "Penser le contemporain," under the direction of Catherine Colliot-Thélène and myself, convened within the UPRESA [Unité Propre de Recherche de l'Enseignement Supérieur Associé] of the CNRS, "Philosophie Politique et Sociale" (Université de Paris X and École Normale Supérieure de Fonetenay-aux-Roses); and, finally, the anthology of contemporary French philosophy that I co-edited with John Rajchman and Anne Boyman for the series Postwar French Thought at the New Press, under the direction of Ramona Naddaff.

15. I sketch a few of them in the articles that I composed for the *Vocabulaire européen des philosophies*: in particular, "Je-Moi-Soi," "Conscience," and "Âme-Esprit." On autoreference, I can only signal the importance of a book by Vincent Descombes, *Le complément de sujet: Enquête sur le fait d'agir soi-même* (Paris: Gallimard, 2004), which we had the occasion to discuss at the Collège International de Philosophie when it was first published, bringing to bear the lessons of Benveniste and Tesnière.

16. As Kant will say about the ideas of reason in general: *Critique of Pure Reason*, Appendix to the Transcendental Dialectic. Immanuel Kant, *Critique of Pure Reason*, ed. and trans. Paul Guyer and Allen W. Wood (Cambridge: Cambridge University Press, 1999), 591.

17. I borrow this formulation from Georges Canguilhem, who makes it into the culminating point of his last great published text, "Le cerveau et la pensée" (1980, reprinted in *Georges*

Canguilhem: Philosophe, historien des sciences [Paris: Albin Michel, 1993]): "In this sense, the *I* surveying the world of things and men is also the *I* of Spinoza and the *I* of Descartes . . ."

18. Étienne Balibar, *Identity and Difference*, trans. Stella Stanford (New York: Verso, 2013). Vincent Carraud, who just published a work in which, with different conclusions in view, he discusses the same set of texts, has pointed out certain factual or interpretive errors that, he claims, invalidate my position. I do not agree, but, of course, I will take into account the rectifications that seem incontestable in a future edition of my book.

19. I adopt the term "soliloquy" from an article by Jocelyn Benoist where he refers—with a generosity for which I thank him—to my intervention before the Société française de philosophie, "Ego sum, ego existo," which is reprinted herein. See Jocelyn Benoist, "Les voix du soliloque. Sur quelques lectures récentes du cogito," *Études philosophiques* 4 (1997): 541–555. Benoist recalls that the genre of the "soliloquy" began with Saint Augustine; that it is distinct from both monologue and dialogue; and that it is designed to stage the "originary duplicity of the ego."

20. "Our sweetest existence is relative and collective, and our true *self* is not entirely within us. Finally, such is man's constitution in this life that one never is able to enjoy oneself well without the cooperation of another." Jean-Jacques Rousseau, *Rousseau, Judge of Jean-Jacques: Dialogues*, trans. Judith R. Bush, Roger D. Masters, and Christopher Kelly (Hanover, N.H.: University Press of New England, 2012), 118. Here as well as in the passage from *The Social Contract* that describes the formation of the public person by an "act of association" as the upsurge of a "common *self*," Rousseau always italicizes the substantive form (*moi*) of the first-person reflexive.

21. This is what I elsewhere call "the remains of the soul" in the classical philosophers who eschewed the hierarchical schemas of correspondence between the parts of the soul and the cosmological order: the Cartesian "substantial union," Lockean "uneasiness," and Kantian *Gemüt*. See *Dictionary of Untranslatables*, "Soul," 1009–1022.

22. *Responsiveness* or *answerability* rather than formal *responsibility*. This is not to say that others have not also theorized responsibility, each in his own fashion: Deleuze, Althusser, Lacan, Lévi-Strauss, to cite only contemporary French thinkers. Rather than drawing up a conventional table of structuralism and poststructuralism, I would prefer, if I had the time, to study what they all owe to the reading of Rousseau (and to different aspects of Rousseau).

23. "Je que Nous sommes, Nous que je suis" ("I that We are, We that I am"). Or else, in another attempt at translation [into French]: "Un Moi qui est un Nous, un Nous qui est un Moi" ("A Me that is an Us, an Us that is a Me"). See Chapter 5 of this volume. [A.V. Miller's English translation of the statement has a strictly chiasmatic structure: "'I' that is 'We' and 'We' that is 'I.'"]

24. This problematic proceeds essentially from Hyppolite's reading of Hegel: in his commentary on *The Phenomenology of Spirit*, and in the courses that I had the opportunity to take one year (1960–61), he never ceases to emphasize the importance of the Hegelian text to discuss the problematics of intersubjectivity. What is it that, going "beyond" Hegel, remains nothing other than the autonomization and reversal of a moment within his discourse? What is it that assigns untransgressable *limits* upon this discourse and thus assigns us an other aesthetic, an other politics, and an other logic of "relation" or "rapport"?

25. Or rather: *a-statist*, and thus already pushing the limits of the hypothesis of a "concept of the political" that would not be subordinated to the constitution of a State, even by anticipation. The interpretation of the *Phenomenology* on this point divided the disciples of Kojève from those of Rosenzweig. Hyppolite tried not to choose, but is this possible?

26. It is notable that the syntagm "constituent power" was invented by Sieyès (*Qu'est-ce que le Tiers-État?* 1789), to whom Schmitt refers in his Constitutional Theory from 1928, comparing it with Spinoza's *natura naturans*. In *Insurgencies: Constituent Power and the Modern State* (Minneapolis: University of Minnesota Press, 2009), Antonio Negri begins with this comparison in order to

propose a genealogy of the "constituent power" that traverses all modernity as an alternative to its dominant trend (in which he is careful not to include both Rousseau and Hegel). Indeed, if one begins again with Sieyès, one cannot avoid the Rousseau-Hegel "line" (this is at least the thesis that I would uphold). Hobbes, however, would not be part of this lineage . . . See also Bruno Bernardi's recent works available on his website: http://rousseau2.wordpress.com/accueil/.

27. In Hegel's *Phenomenology*, there is a pure historical event, entirely negative and unproductive: the revolutionary Terror (*das Schrecken*), which he characterizes as an eruption in the real of abstract freedom. There is also a profound view of the effects of "alienated" subjectivity inherent to the language of objectivity. But there is neither any recognition of how conflict and its dynamic operate at the level of materiality "without spirit" nor any understanding of the autonomization of the "language of commodities" with respect to consciousness (although Marx's description of this language is partly inspired by the Hegelian analysis of "sense-certainty").

28. I decided to separate the two readings of Marx that I offer here (the one on the ultra-subjective "messianic moment" incarnated by the invention of the proletariat as revolutionary agent, the other on the "structure" of objectivation par excellence, associated with the analysis of the general equivalent as *objektive Gedankenform*, which becomes the basis for juridical subjection). Each of these readings go beyond Hegel, but from opposite sides; but, in a sense, everything that Marx ever wrote on the "social relation," sometimes adopting Hegelian terminology for his own purposes (such as *Herrschafts- und Knechtschaftsverhältnis* in *Capital*, Book III, Chapter 47, "The Genesis of Capitalist Ground-Rent"), is inserted somewhere between these two poles.

29. As the author rightly underscores, the singular economy of this title is untranslatable. It can and must be translated as "From right (or law) to transgression" and "Of the right to transgression." The hyphen, in the French text, functions to keep both possible readings (and others) in play.

30. This project began at the behest of MIRE and was directed by Nathalie Robatel.

31. See Étienne Balibar, *Écrits pour Althusser* (Paris: La Découverte, 1991). See also my biographical article "Althusser and the Rue d'Ulm," *New Left Review* 58 (July–August 2009), 91–107.

32. These expressions come respectively from Robert Castel, Michel Foucault (synthesizing the discourse of the new racism of nineteenth-century biopolitics), and Gilles Deleuze. In my essay on crime and madness (Chapter 12), I relied primarily upon Foucault's analyses, and I attempted a formalization of the respective postulates of the "three ideologies" of political modernity: liberalism, conservatism, and anarchism (the theme of the "three ideologies" comes from Immanuel Wallerstein; and the thesis of the primacy or "normality" of liberalism is common to both Foucault and Wallerstein).

33. I invert Althusser's well-known formula, which does not appear to me incompatible with his intentions. Thereby I would like to show that the scheme of "interpellation" should not only serve to think the grip of the community upon individuals by means of a figure of the universal but also the relative autonomization of subjects, which renders their behavior problematic at the heart of the community and for it (which is why he tried to make room for the idea of "subjects" who are "bad subjects").

34. On this point, I would underscore a remarkable *mise en abyme* in the essay by Fredric Jameson that introduced the problematic of the "vanishing mediator" into contemporary "theory": without his own "vanishing" intervention, the relationship between the texts where he identifies this problematic would itself never become noticeable. See "The Vanishing Mediator; or, Max Weber as Storyteller" (1973), in *The Ideologies of Theory: Essays 1971–1986* (Minneapolis: University of Minnesota Press, 1988), 2:3–34.

35. Bruno Berardi, *La fabrique des concepts: Recherches sur l'invention conceptuelle chez Rousseau* (Paris: Honoré Champion, 2006).

36. Étienne Balibar, "The Infinite Contradiction," trans. Jacques Lezra, *Yale French Studies* 88 (1995): 144–146. This text was originally presented as an *exposé de soutenance* toward the Habiliation à Diriger des Recherches, Université de Paris I, Saturday, January 16, 1993.

37. Such classification is standard practice for a philosopher-professor; he does it as well in the *Science of Logic*, at the risk of falling into the trap of "refutation." See Pierre Macherey, *Hegel or Spinoza*, trans. Susan M. Ruddick (Minneapolis: University of Minnesota Press, 2011).

38. Herein lies the program of the *Vocabulaire européen des philosophies* (*Dictionary of Untranslatables*), published in in 2004 under the direction of Barbara Cassin, who conceived and organized its production from beginning to end. See note 14.

39. Friedrich Nietzsche, *The Genealogy of Morality*, trans. Keith Ansell Pearson (Cambridge: Cambridge University Press, 2006), §12.

40. It would be necessary to compare Locke to the thematic of the "double man" in the classical age. See Giovanni Paoletti, ed., *Homo duplex: Filosofia e esperanza della dualità* (Pisa: Edizioni ETS, 2004).

41. On this point, might I underscore my differences with an enterprise such as that of Charles Taylor in *Sources of the Self: The Making of Modern Identity* (Cambridge: Cambridge University Press, 1989), from which there is so much to learn, and that it would be vain to compete with?

42. Hannah Arendt, *The Origins of Totalitarianism* (New York: Harcourt, Brace, and Jovanovich, 1973), Chapter 9, §2, "The Perplexities of the Rights of Man." In Arendt's formulation ("the right to have rights"), I think that it is possible to read a definition of the function fulfilled by individuals belonging to a community of citizens in view of their incorporation into "humanity," but also a problematization of the anthropological relation between citizenship, nationality, and the recognition of personality (and thus the "right to difference") in the modern era.

43. Pierre Macherey, "Aux sources des 'rapports sociaux': Bonald, Saint-Simon, Guizot," *Genèses* 9 (1992): 25–43. Republished in Pierre Macherey, *Études de philosophie "française": De Sieyès à Barni* (Paris: Publications de la Sorbonne, 2013).

44. The "nation," which is not identifiable with the "city" (or city-state), or an "empire," or a "Church," even if it shares with all of these historical institutions certain forms of what Max Weber called "socialization" or "communitarization" (*Vergesellshaftung, Vergemeinschaftung*), is the dominant political community of the bourgeois era but not the single or generalizable form of political community. In fact, the nation only pertains to the dominant region of the modern universe, which coincides with the "center" of a world economy founded upon the colonial expansion of Europe: which is the index of the fact that the constitution of the "civil-bourgeois" universal and its relation to a specific "becoming-subject" are inscribed within a framework or a geographical "distribution" that, with respect to them, have a quasi-transcendental function. When the stability of this distribution or of the interstate framework of its institution is called into question, the problem of "citizenship without community" returns in both affirmative and reactive forms. See Étienne Balibar, *We, People of Europe? Reflections of Transnational Citizenship*, trans. James Swenson (Princeton: Princeton University Press, 2003), 93ff.

45. I am aware that Heidegger also played upon this inversion, especially in the developments that he devotes to the question of the "essence of truth" (which is itself identified with the inexhaustible "questioning" of being). As he writes in *Beiträge zur Philosophie (Vom Ereignis)*, §223, "Un-wesen" must be understood in two senses: that of the determinate negation of an essence (e.g., the representation of truth as exactitude or adequation) and that of a radical negativity that inheres in an originary indetermination (the opening of a presence in which truth manifests itself as remaining essentially veiled). With my play on words, on the contrary, I keep as close as possible to the common usages of the term *Un-wesen* (employed most often in the expression "*sein Unwesen treiben*," to stir up trouble, to cause a ruckus).

46. Herein lies another great historic or historial "play on words," on which, one will see, I conferred a symptomatic value at least equal to that which I started by conferring on the doublet *subjectus/subjectum.*

47. Monique David-Ménard relies upon the term "constructions of the universal" in a book from which I have greatly benefited, *Les constructions de l'universel: Psychanalyse, philosophie* (Paris: Presses Universitaires de France, 1997).

48. Ultimately, I had to wait for another occasion to include, even elliptically, this "case" within the tableau that I am outlining here. I do not exclude the possibility that its inclusion would upset the symmetries that I have established and cast certain conclusions into doubt.

49. Accordingly, subjects of the colony, women, sexual minorities, or criminals and the mad, invoke their internal exclusion at once in the name of the "right to difference" and in the name of "common humanity."

50. The questions that were stirred up in the German university between 1927 and 1930 by Dilthey's disciples (Groethuysen), the phenomenologists (Scheler, Heidegger) and the Neo-Kantians (Cassirer), based on the rediscovery of Kant's formulations on the "fourth critical question" (*Was ist der Mensch?*), reemerged in a new form, more directly linked to ethnology and political theory, both in the United States during the 1940s and 50s (Cassirer, Arendt) and in France during the 1960s and 1970s (Sartre, Lévi-Strauss, Althusser, Derrida); but (unless I am mistaken) it is only in Germany and France that there was any discussion on the question of principle: that of the *possibility* of a "philosophical anthropology" and, at the limit, that of the identification of philosophy with anthropology (which Althusser calls "theoretical humanism"). In order to reconstruct the conjunction that took place in France between the two questions of humanism and anthropology, it is necessary to measure the weight of Heidegger's formulations contained in his "Letter on Humanism" (*Brief an Jean Beaufret*) from 1947. To get an idea of how they were dissociated, it would be necessary to discuss, in particular, the distance that Foucault established between them in the conclusion to *The Order of Things* (1966), which could be read in light of later essays (in particular, his commentary on Kant's "What Is Enlightenment?"). An interesting perspective on these questions, which insists upon the importance of Groethuysen's work as a "*passeur*" between Germany and France, although it is oriented by relations between "forms of life" and "enunciative positions" rather than toward philosophical texts, can be found in Pascal Michon, *Élements d'un histoire du sujet* (Paris: Kimé, 1999). On the Heideggerian treatment of the question, Françoise Dastur's *Heidegger et la question anthropologique* (Leuven: Peeters, 2003) is irreplaceable. On Foucault, see in particular Diogo Sardinha, *Ordre et temps and la philosophie de Michel Foucault* (Paris: L'Harmattan, 2011).

51. I here borrow the phrase that Althusser planned to use as the title for an unfinished essay from 1967. See Louis Althusser, *The Humanist Controversy and Other Texts*, trans. G. M. Goshgarian (New York: Verso, 2003).

52. Here I am drawing upon the work of Bertrand Ogilvie in "Anthropologie du propre à rien," *Passant Ordinaire*, October 2003; *La seconde nature du politique: Essai d'anthropologie negative* (Paris: L'Harmattan, 2012).

53. These questions are, of course, very close to those that Foucault raises (whether it be in his genealogical inquiries that examine the institutions of bourgeois "normality" and "abnormality," in his commentaries on philosophers—in particular, Kant, Hegel, and Nietzsche—that problematize the "reflexive" individualism and "possessive" individualism of the modern citizen, or in his archaeology of the human sciences that is also a theory of the "anthropological moment" in philosophy). However, although my work intersects with Foucault at many points, I attempt to formulate a problematic that does not precisely coincide with his own. On this point, see Sardinha's book on Foucault cited earlier.

54. "Thus things have now come to such a pass that the individuals must appropriate the existing totality of productive forces, not only to manifest their ego, but above all to safeguard

their very existence. This appropriation is first conditioned by the object to be appropriated, the productive forces, which have been developed to the stage of totality and which only exist within the framework of universal exchange." Karl Marx and Friedrich Engels, *The German Ideology*, ed. and trans. C. J. Arthur (New York: International Publishers, 1970), 92. [Translation modified in accordance with the French edition that the author cites.]

55. There is an affinity between this thesis and that which compels one to think the "Enlightenment" not only in relation to the "anti-Enlightenment" but also as a constitutive tension between "knowledge" and "non-knowledge." See Hans Adler and Reiner Gödel, *Formen des Nichtwissens der Aufklärung* (Munich: Wilhelm Fink Verlag, 2010).

56. See Simon Schama, *Citizens: A Chronicle of the French Revolution* (New York: Knopf, 1989), xiii.

CITIZEN SUBJECT: RESPONSE TO JEAN-LUC NANCY'S QUESTION
"WHO COMES AFTER THE SUBJECT?"

This essay was first published in English as "Citizen Subject," in *Who Comes after the Subject?* ed. Eduardo Cadava, Peter Connor, and Jean-Luc Nancy (New York: Routledge, 1991), 33–57. Copyright 1991. Reproduced by permission of Taylor and Francis Group, LLC, a division of Informa plc.

1. Letter by Descartes to Christine, 3 November 1645, *Oeuvres de Descartes*, ed. Charles Adam and Paul Tannery (Paris: J. Vrin, 1969), 4:333. Cited by Jean-Luc Marion, *Sur la théologie blanche de Descartes* (Paris: Presses Universitaires de France, 1981), 411.

2. *Oeuvres de Descartes*, 1: 145.

3. I am aware that is a matter of *opposing* them: but in order to oppose them directly, as the recto and verso, the permanence of a single question (of a single "opening") must be supposed, *beyond* the question of the *subjectus*, which falls into the ashcan of the "history of being."

4. Applying it to Kant himself if need be: for the fate of this problematic—by the very fact that the transcendental subject is a limit, even *the* limit as such, declared to be constitutive is to observe that there always remains some substance or some phenomenality in that it must be *reduced*.

5. As Nancy himself suggests in the considerations of his letter of invitation, from which I reproduce a key passage: "This question can be explained as follows: one of the major characteristics of contemporary thought is the putting into question of the instance of the 'subject,' according to the structure, the meaning, and the value subsumed under this term in modern thought from Descartes to Hegel, if not to Husserl. The inaugurating decisions of contemporary thought . . . have all involved putting subjectivity on trial. A widespread discourse of recent date proclaimed the subject's simple liquidation. Everything seems, however, to point to the necessity, not of a 'return to the subject' . . . but on the contrary, of a move forward toward someone—*some one*—else in his place (this last expression is obviously a mere convenience: the 'place' could not be the same). Who would it be? How would s/he present him/herself? Can we name him/her? Is the question 'who' suitable? . . . In other words: If it is appropriate to assign something like a punctuality, a singularity, or a hereness (*haecceitas*) as the place of emission, reception, or transition (or affect, of action, of language, etc.), how would one designate its specificity? Or would the question need to be transformed—or is it in fact out of place to ask it?" (*Who Comes After the Subject?*, 5).

6. Jacques-Bénigne Bossuet, *Politique tirée de des propres paroles de l'Écriture sainte*, ed. Jacques Le Brun (Geneva: Droz, 1967), 53. Bossuet states: "All men *are born* subjects." Descartes says: There are *innate* ideas, which God has always already planted in my soul, as seeds of truth, whose *nature* (that of being eternal truths) is contemporaneous with *my nature* (for God creates or conserves them at every moment just as he creates or conserves me), and which at bottom are

entirely enveloped in the infinity of that envelops all my true ideas, beginning with the first: my thinking existence.

7. *The Institutes of Gaius*, trans. W. M. Gordon and O. F. Robinson (London: Gerald Duckworth & Co., Ltd., 1988), §48, 45.

8. See Christian Bruschi, "Le droit de cité dans l'Antiquité: Un questionnement pour la citoyenneté aujourd'hui," in *La citoyenneté et les changements de structures sociales et nationales de la population française*, ed. Catherine Wihtol de Wenden, 125–153 (n.p.: Edilig/Fondation Diderot, 1988).

9. Emmanuel Terray suggests to me that this is one of the reasons for Constantine's rallying to Pauline Christianity ("All power comes from God": see *Epistle to the Romans*).

10. On all of these points, see, for example, Walter Ullman, *The Individual and Society in the Middle Ages* (Baltimore: Johns Hopkins University Press, 1966), and *A History of Political Thought: The Middle Ages* (Harmondsworth, UK: Penguin, 1965).

11. On all this, see Ernst Kantorowicz, *Frederick the Second, 1194–1250*, trans. E. O. Lorimer (New York: Ungar, 1957); *The King's Two Bodies* (Princeton: Princeton University Press, 1960); *Selected Studies* (New York: J. J. Augustin, 1965).

12. How does one get from the Roman *servus* to the medieval *serf*? Doubtless by a change in the "mode of production" (even though it is doubtless that, from the strict point of view of production, each of these terms corresponds to *a* single mode). But this change presupposes or implies that the "serf" also has an immortal soul included in the economy of salvation; this is why he is attached to the land rather than to the master.

13. Jean Bodin, *Les six livres de la République*, vol. 1, §6 (Paris: Fayard, 1986), 114.

14. Ibid., 1:112.

15. See Alain Grosrichard, *The Sultan's Court: European Fantasies of the East*, trans. Liz Heron, intro. Mladen Dolar (New York: Verso, 1998).

16. See the frequently developed theme, notably following Proudhon: Rousseau and the French revolutionaries substituted the people for the king of "divine right" without touching the idea of sovereignty, or "archy."

17. In the *Cahiers de doléance* of 1789, one sees the peasants legitimize, by the fact that they are *men*, the claim to equality that they raise: to become citizens (notably by the suppression of the fiscal privileges and seigneurial rights). See Regine Robin, *La société française en 1789: Semur-en-Auxois* (Paris: Plon, 1970).

18. Pierre Richelet, *Dictionnaire de la langue française, ancienne et moderne* (Lyon, 1728), s.v. "citoyen." Cited by Pierre Rétat, "Citoyen-Sujet, Civisme," in *Handbuch politisch-sozialer Grundbegriffe in Frankreich, 1680–1820*, ed. Rolf Reichardt and Eberhard Schmitt (Munich: Oldenbourg, 1988), 9:79.

19. (Anon.), *La liberté du peuple* (Paris, 1789). Cited by Rétat, "Citoyen-Sujet, Civisme," 91.

20. Maximilien Robespierre, *Virtue and Terror*, trans. John Howe, ed. and intro., Slavoj Žižek (New York: Verso, 2007), 5–19.

21. See Rene Fedou, *L'État au Moyen Âge* (Paris: Presses Universitaires de France, 1971), 162–163.

22. See the discussion of apathy evoked by Moses I. Finley, *Democracy, Ancient and Modern* (New Brunswick, N.J.: Rutgers University Press, 1985).

23. See Saint-Just, "Discours sur la Constitution de la France" (24 April 1793): "The general will is indivisible . . . Representation and the law thus have a common principle." *Discours et rapports*, ed. Albert Soboul (Paris: Éditions sociales, 1977), 107.

24. Jean-Jacques Rousseau, *Du contrat social*, 1, 6, in *Oeuvres complètes*, ed. Bernard Gagnebin and Marcel Raymond (Paris: Gallimard, Bibliothèque de la Pléiade, 1964), 3:362.

25. Ibid., I, 7, *Oeuvres complètes*, 3:362–364.

26. During the revolution, a militant grammarian will write: "France is no longer a kingdom, because it is no longer a country in which the king is everything and the people nothing. . . .

What the is France? A new word is needed to express a new thing. . . . We call a country sovereignly ruled by a king a kingdom (*royaume*); I will call a country in which the law along commands a lawdom (*loyaume*)." Urbain Domergeue, *Journal de la langue française*, 1 August 1791. Cited by Sonia Branca-Rosoff, "Le loyaume des mots," in *Lexique* 3 (1985): 47.

27. Louis-Sébastien Mercier and Jean-Louis Carra, *Annales patriotiques*, 18 January 1791. Cited by Rétat, "Citoyen-Sujet, Civisme," 97.

28. Louis-Antoine Saint-Just, *Fragments d'institutions républicaines*, in *Oeuvres complètes*, ed. Michele Duval (Paris: Éditions Gérard Lebovici, 1984), 978. Cited by Rétat, "Citoyen-Sujet, Civisme," 97.

29. The Declaration of Rights of 1789, First Article, immediately following "Men are born and remain free and equal in rights," continues: "Social distinctions can only be founded on common utility." Distinctions are *social*, and whoever says "society," "social bond," says "distinctions" (and not "inequalities," which would contradict the principle). This is why freedom and equality must be predicated of man, and not of the citizen.

30. Maurice Blanchot, "Insurrection, the madness of writing," in *The Infinite Conversation*, trans. Susan Hanson (Minneapolis: University of Minnesota Press, 1993), 217–229.

31. Instead of reciprocal action, today one would say "communication" or "communicative action."

32. *Du contrat social*, I, 6, *Oeuvres complètes*, 3:361.

33. Ibid., I, 5, 3:359.

34. I am entirely in agreement on this point with Robert Derathé's commentary (against Vaughn) on the adjective "moral" in his notes to the Pléiade edition of Rousseau (*Oeuvres complètes*, 3:1446).

35. See Karl Marx, *Capital*, trans. Ben Fowkes (New York: Vintage Books, 1977), 1:292. "The product [of the worker's labor in his workshop] belongs to [the capitalist] just as much as the wine that is the product of the process of fermentation taking place in his cellar."

36. See Étienne Balibar, "Spinoza, l'anti-Orwell: La crainte des masses," *Les temps modernes* 470 (September 1985): 353–394.

37. As Louis Sala-Molins does in *Le Code Noir ou le calvaire de Canaan* (Paris: Presses Universitaires de France, 1987).

38. See Yves Benot, *La révolution française et la fin des colonies* (Paris: La Découverte, 1988).

39. Let us note that this thesis is *not* Kantian: the accent is placed on the citizen and not on the ends of man; the object of the struggle is not anticipated but discovered in the wake of political action; and each given figure is not an approximation of the regulatory ideal of the citizen but an obstacle to effective equality. Nor is this thesis Hegelian: Nothing obliges a new realization of the citizen to be superior to the preceding one.

40. Pierre-François Moreau, *Le récit utopique: Droit naturel et roman de l'État* (Paris: Presses Universitaires de France, 1982).

ANNEX: SUBJECTUS/SUBJECTUM

1. Friedrich Nietzsche, *Jenseits von Gut und Böse/Zur Genealogie der Moral*, Kritische Studienausgabe, ed. Giorgio Colli and Mazzino Montinari (Munich: Deutsche Taschenbuch Verlag, 1999), §19. *Par delà bien et mal*, in *Oeuvres philosophiques complètes*, vol. 7, ed. Giorgio Colli and Mazzino Molinari, trans. Jean Gratien, Cornélius Heim, and Isabelle Hildenbrand (Paris: Gallimard, 1971), §19.

2. Friedrich Nietzsche, *Beyond Good and Evil*, trans. R. J. Hollingdale (New York: Penguin Books, 2003), §19.

3. Georges Bataille, *La Part maudite* III, La Souveraineté, I, 4, in *Oeuvres complètes* 8:83–286; *The Accursed Share*, vol. 3, Sovereignty, 237–241; trans. amended.

4. Martin Heidegger, *Nietzsche*, trans. David Farrell Krell (New York: HarperOne, 1991), 4:123ff.)

5. Joachim Ritter, *Subjectivität* (Berlin: Suhrkamp, 1974).

6. See Alain de Libera's contribution to the article, "Subject," in *The Dictionary of Untranslatables: A Philosophical Lexicon* (Princeton: Princeton University Press, 2014), 1073–1078.

7. Immanuel Kant, *Kritik der reinen Vernunft* (1781/1787) (Hamburg: Felix Meiner Verlag, 1976), B132, 140.

8. Immanuel Kant, *Critique of Pure Reason*, trans. Paul Guyer and Allen W. Wood, Cambridge University Press 1998), Transcendental Logic §16, B 132, 246.

9. Kant, *Kritik der reinen Vernunft* (1781/1787), 371–374.

10. Kant, *Critique of Pure Reason*, Paralogisms of Pure Reason, A342, 343, 345–346.

11. Kant, *Kritik der reinen Vernunft* (1781/1787), 375.

12. Kant, *Critique of Pure Reason*, Paralogisms of Pure Reason, A347. See also Jocelyn Benoist, "La subjectivité," in *Notions de philosophie*, vol. 2, ed. Denis Kambouchner (Paris: Gallimard, 1995).

13. See my article "I/Me/Myself," in *Dictionary of Untranslatables*, 463–476.

14. Yves-Charles Zarka, "L'invention du subjet de droit," *Archives de philosophie* 60 (1997): 531–550, republished in his book *L'autre voie de la subjectivité: Six études sur le sujet et le droit naturel au XVIIᵉ siècle* (Paris: Beauchesne, 2000).

15. Georg Friedrich Puchta, *Cursus der Institutionen (I)* (Leipzig: Breitkopf und Härtel, 1841).

16. "So wird hier die Souveränität, das Wesen des Staats, zuerst als ein selbstständiges Wesen betrachtet, vergegenständlicht. Dann, versteht sich, muß dies Objective wieder Subjekt werden. Dies Subjekt erscheint aber dann als eine Selbstverkörperung der Souveränität, während die Souveränität nichts anders ist als der vergegenständlichte Geist der Staatsubjekte" (Karl Marx, *Kritik der Hegelschen Staatsrecht*, in *Marx-Engels Werke* [Berlin: Dietz Verlag, 1961], 225). "Thus sovereignty, the essence of the state, is first objectified and conceived as something independent. Then, of course, this object must again become a subject. The subject, however, becomes manifest as the self-embodiment of sovereignty, whereas [in fact] sovereignty is nothing but the objectified spirit of the subjects of the state" (Karl Marx, "Critique of Hegel's Doctrine of the State," in *Early Writings*, trans. Rodney Livingstone and Gregor Benton [New York: Penguin Books, 1992], 80).

17. Jean-Jacques Rousseau, *Rêveries du promeneur solitaire*, Dixième Promenade, in *Oeuvres complètes* (Paris: Gallimard, "Bibliothèque de la Pléiade," 1959), 1:1099.

18. Gilles Deleuze, *Empiricism and Subjectivity*, trans. Constantin V. Boundas (New York: Columbia University Press, 2001), 31.

19. Gilles Deleuze and Félix Guattari, *A Thousand Plateaus*, trans. Brian Massumi (Minneapolis: University of Minnesota Press, 1987), 456–457.

20. Jacques Derrida, *Of Grammatology*, trans. Gayatri Chakravorty Spivak (Baltimore: Johns Hopkins University Press, 1974), 281.

21. Jacques Derrida, *Adieu to Emmanuel Lévinas*, trans. Pascale-Anne Brault and Michael Naas (Stanford: Stanford University Press, 1999), 54.

22. Louis Althusser, "On Content in the Thought of G. W. F. Hegel," in *The Spectre of Hegel: Early Writings*, trans. G. M. Goshgarian (New York: Verso, 1997), 90.

23. Louis Althusser, "Ideology and Ideological State Apparatuses," in *Lenin and Philosophy and Other Essays*, trans. Ben Brewster (New York: Monthly Review Press, 2001), 121.

24. Jacques Lacan, *Écrits*, trans. Bruce Fink (New York: Norton, 2006), 525.

25. Ibid., 520. See also Betrand Ogilvie, *Lacan: La formation du concept de sujet (1932–1949)* (Paris: Presses Universitaires de France, 1987); Slavoj Žižek, *Subversions du sujet: Psychanalyse, philosophie, politique* (Rennes: Presses Universitaires de Rennes, 1999).

26. Michel Foucault, *Discipline and Punish: The Birth of the Prison*, trans. Alan Sheridan (New York: Vintage, 1995), 2002.

27. Michel Foucault, "The Subject and Power," *Critical Inquiry* 8, no. 4 (Summer 1982): 777.

28. Michel Foucault, "(Auto)biography: Michel Foucault, 1926–1984," trans. Jackie Urla, in *Michel Foucault: Critical Assessments*, ed. Barry Smart (New York: Routledge, 1995), 7:259.

29. Georges Canguilhem, "The Brain and Thought" [1980], trans. Steven Corcoran and Peter Hallward, *Radical Philosophy* 148 (March–April 2008): 7–18.

1. "*EGO SUM, EGO EXISTO*": DESCARTES ON THE VERGE OF HERESY

The following text corresponds, with the addition of a few insertions and corrections, to the lecture that I delivered to the Société française de philosophie on Saturday, February 22, 1992. The footnotes were either not read or added afterward. The text was first published in the *Bulletin de la Société Française de Philosophie* 86, no. 3 (July–September 1992). The quotation comes from the abstract circulated in advance of the lecture to members of the Société.

1. The two French authors—perhaps not entirely independently of one another—who come closest to recognizing this key are certainly Jacques Derrida and Jean-Luc Marion (see my footnotes below). One of their sources (because no idea is absolutely primary) is perhaps the *Descartes* of Paul Valéry: *Les pages immortelles de Descartes choisies et expliquées par Paul Valéry* (Paris: Éditions Correa, 1941). See, in particular, 34ff.

2. Descartes, *Méditations métaphysiques*, intro. and trans. Michelle Beyssade (Paris: Livre de Poche, 1990). This edition also includes the Latin text and the translation by the Duc de Luynes.

3. The words *Ego sum, ego existo* are printed in italics in the first edition.

4. René Descartes, *Meditations on First Philosophy*, trans. and ed. John Cottingham (Cambridge: Cambridge University Press, 1996), 17

5. *Nunquid ergo saltem ego aliquid sum?* "In that case am not I, at least, something?" *Haud dubie igitur ego etiam sum, si me fallit*: "In that case I too undoubtedly exist, if he is deceiving me." *Nondum vero satis intelligo, quisnam sim ego . . . :* "But I do not yet have a sufficient understanding of who this 'I' is . . ." *Deincepsque cavendum est ne forte quid aliud imprudenter assumam in locum mei*: "So must I be on my guard against carelessly taking something else to be this 'I' [or, against carelessly supposing other in my place]." *Quare jam denuo meditabor quidnam me olim esse crediderim*: "I will therefore go back and meditate on what I formerly believed myself to be."

6. In this "opinion," it is difficult to avoid hearing, thanks to Henri Gouhier, an echo of the Credo. With the *hoc corpus meum esse*, what Gouhier calls the "epistemological Satan" of the Evil Genius, and especially the "arithmetical" profession of faith (as Molière's Signarelli would say) from the preceding paragraph, this formulation participates in a tightly woven and—it must be said—very equivocal (because verging on blasphemy) network of religious allusions in the First and Second Meditations. See Henri Gouhier, *La pensée métaphysique de Descartes* (Paris: Vrin, 1962), 119, 187; and Mariafranca Spallanzani, "Bis bina quatuor," *Rivista di storia della filosofia* 83, no. 2 (August 1991): 301–317.

7. Descartes, *Meditations*, 14.

8. On this point, Françoise Kerleroux reminds me of Benveniste's demonstration (in "The Relation of Persons in the Verb," "The Nature of Pronouns," and "The Antonym and the Pronoun in Modern French," in *Problems of General Linguistics*, trans. Mary Elizabeth Meek [Miami: University of Miami Press, 1973]) that the first and the second persons (I and You), on the one hand, and the third person, on the other, are not "persons" in the same sense. In reality, only the first two persons are persons in the strict sense—that is, they enact or presuppose the self-referentiality of the enunciation. The "third person" has a completely different status: it is, in this sense, a "nonperson." Correlatively, the third person alone comprises a "true" plural. It seems to me that this demonstration is perfectly aligned with my preceding analysis. In his famous 1962 article "Cogito ergo sum: Inference or performance?" (*I* 71, no. 1 [January 1962]: 3–32), Jakko Hintikka also clearly underscores the correlation whose consequences we pursue in what follows.

"The independence of Descartes's insight of introspection is illustrated by the fact that there is a peculiarity about certain sentences in the second person which is closely related to the peculiarities of Descartes's *ego sum, ego existo*. In the same way as it is self-defeating to say 'I don't exist,' it is usually absurd to say, 'You don't exist.' If the latter sentence is true, it is ipso facto empty in that there is no one to whom it could conceivably be addressed" (19). For the moment, I will not dwell on another aspect of this problem (which, one may suspect, has to do with a "Genius" who would be "evil" in quite another sense): the frequency and efficaciousness in everyday life of statements that say, "You do not exist" to certain people rather than others.

9. The confirmation of this can be found in the equivocality of certain demonstratives in the text of Descartes (*hujus*) that lead translators to opposite choices.

Descartes's Latin reads: *Novi me existere: quaero quis sim ego ille quem novi. Certissum est hujus sic praecise sumpti notitiam non pendere ab iis . . .* (1) Luynes translation: "*J'ai reconnu que j'existe; je cherche ce que je suis, moi que j'ai reconnu être. Or il est très certain que cette notion et connaissance de moi-même, ainsi précisément prise, ne dépend point des choses.*" (2) Beyssade translation: "*J'ai reconnu que j'existe; je cherche ce que je suis, moi, ce moi que j'ai reconnu. Il est tout à fait certain que la connaissance de cet être considéré dans ces limites précises ne dépend pas des choses.*" (3) Cottingham translation: "I know that I exist; the question is, what is this 'I' that I know? If the 'I' is understood strictly as we have been taking it, then it is quite certain that knowledge of it does not depend on things of whose existence I am as yet unaware" (18–19).

10. Ovid reprised this trope in his *Art of Love*, II: 1: "*Hoc quoque composui Paelignis natus aquosis,/ Ille ego nequitiae Naso poeta meae . . .*"; and in *Tristia*, IV: 10: "*Ille ego qui fuerim, tenerorum lusor amorum,/ Quem legis, ut noris, accipe, posteritas . . . Editus hic ego sum, nec non, ut tempora noris,/ Cum cecidit fato consul uterque pari . . .*" I owe these references to M. Bardin, on the occasion of the seminar on the History of Materialism directed by Olivier Bloch at the Université de Paris I (Sorbonne), and to my friend Gabriel Albiac. I would also like to thank Jean Plaud, the Honorary Inspector General of National Education, my former teacher, who generously responded in writing to my questions about the comparative syntax of the different sentences under discussion. It goes without saying that I ultimately take sole responsibility for my proposed translations (or nontranslations).

11. Exodus 3: "And Moses was herding the flock of Jethro his father-in-law . . . and came to the mountain of God, to Horeb. And the LORD's messenger appeared to him in a flame of fire from the midst of the bush, and he saw, and look, the bush was burning with fire and the bush was not consumed . . . And the LORD saw that he had turned aside to see, and God called to him from the midst of the bush and said, 'Moses, Moses!' And he said, 'Here I am.' And He said, 'Come no closer here. Take off your sandals from your feet for the place you are standing on is holy ground.' And He said, 'I am the God of your father, the God of Abraham, the God of Isaac, and the God of Jacob.' And Moses hid his face, for he was afraid to look upon God. And the LORD said, 'I indeed have seen the abuse of My people that is in Egypt . . . I know its pain . . . And now, go that I may send you to Pharaoh, and bring My people out of Egypt.' And Moses said to God, 'Who am I that I should go to Pharaoh and that I should bring out the Israelites from Egypt?' and He said: 'For I will be with you. And this is the sign for you that I myself have sent you . . .' And Moses said to God, 'Look, when I come to the Israelites and say to them, "The God of your fathers has sent me to you," and they say to me "What is His name?", what shall I say to them?' And God said to Moses, "Ehyeh-Asher-'Ehyeh, I-Will-Be-Who-I-Will-Be.' And He said, 'Thus shall you say to the Israelites, " 'Ehyeh has sent me to you' " (Robert Alter, *The Five Books of Moses: A Translation and Commentary* [New York: Norton, 2004]).

The problems of translating and interpreting this passage—notably the Hebrew formula *'Ehyeh Asher 'Ehyeh*, translated in the Septuagint as *Egō eimi ho ōon*, and, very differently in the Vulgate as *sum qui sum*, which was, in turn, rendered more or less awkwardly in French as "*Je suis celui qui suis*," "*je suis celui qui est*," "*je suis qui je suis*," etc.—will not be my concern here. See, especially, André Caquot, "Les énigmes d'un héministiche biblique," in *Dieu et l'Être, Exégèses d'Exode 3:14 et de Coran 20: 11–24* (Paris: IEA Institut d'Études Augustiniennes, 1978), 17–26; Georges Madec, "'Ego sum qui sum' de Tertullian à Jérôme," ibid., 121–139. Nonetheless, let us pay some attention to the way in which the haecceity ("Here I am") and the question ("Who am I?") circulate in this dialogue (such that the LORD's "response," which can be interpreted as the transmission of a proper name, could also appear as a manner of turning the question back upon Moses). Among other readers of this passage, one will recall that Louis Althusser referred to this text as the model of any "interpellation of the individual as a subject." See "Ideology and Ideological State Apparatuses," in *Lenin and Philosophy and Other Essays*, trans. Ben Brewster (New York: Monthly Review Press, 1971), 127–186.

12. See, latterly, Étienne Gilson, *Constantes philosophiques de l'Être* (Paris: Vrin, 1983), chaps. VII–VIII. See also Stanislas Breton, *Libres commentaires* (Paris: Éditions du Cerf, 1990), chap. IV.

13. Parodying the terminology of Wittgenstein's *Tractatus*, one might say that this insistence is not spoken or uttered (*sprechen*) but that it is shown (*zeigen*) in the form of the utterance.

14. Whence the "translation" "en abyme" of the *sum qui sum* that Schelling proposes in *The Ages of the World*: "I am he who says: I am." (F. W. J. von Schelling, *The Ages of the World*, trans. Jason M. Wirth [Albany: State University of New York Press, 2000], 45). In "Science and Truth," Lacan applies the same procedure to Descartes's other "canonical" utterance: "I am thinking: 'therefore I am'" (*Écrits*, trans. Bruce Fink [New York: Norton, 2006], 734).

15. "Again he said to them: 'I am going away, and you will search for me, but you will die in your sin. Where I am going you cannot come' . . . 'You are from below, I am from above; you are of this world, I am not of this world. I told you that you would die in your sins, for you will die in your sins unless you believe that I AM.' (*Dixi ergo vobis quia moriemini in peccatis vestris: si enim non credideris quia ego sum, moriemini in peccatis vestris*). They said to him: 'Who are you?' (*Tu quis es?*) Jesus said to them: 'Why do I speak to you at all? . . . [T]he one who sent me is true, and I declare to the world what I have heard from him.' They did not understand that he was speaking to them about the Father. So Jesus said: 'When you have lifted up the Son of Man, then you will realize that I AM, and that I do nothing on my own (*Cum exaltaveritis Filium hominis, tunc cognoscetis qiua ego sum et a meipso facio nihil*), but I speak these things as the Father instructed me. And the one who sent me is with me; he has not left me alone . . . They answered him: 'We are the descendants of Abraham . . . Now we know that you have a demon . . . Who do you claim to be?' Jesus answered: 'If I glorify myself, my glory is nothing. It is my father who glorifies me, he of whom you say, "He is our God," though you do not know him. But I know him; if I would say I do not know him, I would be a liar like you. But I do know him and I keep his word. Your ancestor Abraham rejoiced that he would see my day; he saw it and he was glad.' Then the Jews said to him: 'You are not yet fifty years old, and have you seen Abraham?' Jesus said to them: 'Very truly, I tell you, before Abraham was, I am' (*Amen, amen dico vobis: Antequam Abraham fieret, ego sum*). So they picked up stones to throw at him, but Jesus hid himself and went out of the temple" (*The New Oxford Annotated Bible*, ed. Bruce M. Metzger and Roland E. Murphy [New York: Oxford University Press, 1994], John 8:21–59; I have interpolated the Latin from the Vulgate Bible).

My object here, once again, is not to interpret this text. I simply note the insistence therein of an opposition between the fiction of a "lying" God and the act of bearing witness to the true God that is intimately associated with the reprisal of the "name" I AM.

16. Alain de Libera and Elisabeth zum Brunn, eds., *Celui qui est, Interprétations juives et chrétiennes d'Exode 3, 14* (Paris: Éditions du Cerf, 1986), 217–236.

17. Jean-Christophe Goddard has sent me the manuscript of the lecture "Fichte critique de Spinoza," which he delivered on November 30, 1991, at the Association des Amis de Spinoza in Paris. This text contains remarkable analyses that seem to confirm the pertinence of my own questioning. Notably, Goddard shows how Fichte, formulating and formalizing the "Ich bin" and "Ich bin ich" as the *Grundsatz* of an ontology of activity that he upheld as an alternative to

Spinozist substantialism, was led not only to define the Ego on the basis of the Kantian "I think" but also on the basis of a reformulation of the Cartesian *cogito, ergo sum* as *sum, ergo sum* [*sic*], before resorting to a paraphrase of the Gospel of John in his 1795 lecture *On the Dignity of Man*, at the end of which man—the new Christ—"is distinguished by his ability to say 'I am.'" Goddard also refers to the Rodis-Lewis essay that I mention earlier, focusing on her comparison of Descartes and Spinoza. As for Kant, who is responsible for nominalizing "the *cogito*," he never refers to the "I am"; but, early in his *Anthropology from a Pragmatic Point of View* (1797), he does posit that what is proper to man, which "elevates him above all other living beings on earth," is that "he possesses the 'I' in his representation" (*in seiner Vorstellung das Ich haben*).

18. The most recent and also, by virtue of its scope and subtlety, most impressive elaboration of such an interpretation is, of course, Jean-Luc Marion's analysis of Descartes's "two discourses on the Being of beings" and his "double onto-theology" in *Sur le prisme métaphysique de Descartes* (Paris: Presses Universitaires de France, 1986). I cannot enter into a discussion of this work here because I am concerned with the *Ego sum, ego existo*, whereas, for Marion, Descartes's "first word" is *cogitatio* (and the second is *causa*).

19. This proof from the Third Meditation has also been divided (e.g., Martial Gueroult) into a "first proof by effects" and a "second proof by effects." Other commentators have endeavored to show that the two moments of Descartes's argumentation envelop one another and thus constitute a single "proof."

20. These considerations embolden me to risk the following hypothesis: if there is an utterance in the *Meditations* that should be called *cogito* or *the cogito*, it would be precisely that which affirms that I think all at once, within a single "clear idea," the idea of (infinite) God and the idea of my (finite) self, measuring the imperfection of the second against the perfection of the first (whereas, a decisive point, the reverse is impossible). Not only, therefore, does this *cogito* not have the simple form *cogito me cogitare*, but it is not immediate: it is, on the contrary, constructed in the course of the meditation (which does not prevent the corresponding intellectual modality from being, in the language of the *Regulae*, an "intuition"). On this point, it would be necessary to take up Jean-Marie Beyssade's detailed argumentation in *La philosophie première de Descartes* (Paris: Flammarion, 1979), 272ff.

21. In many respects, I am following the opposite path to that of Annette Baier in her study "The Idea of the True God in Descartes," in *Essays on Descartes's Meditations*, ed. Amelie Oksenberg Rorty (Berkeley: University of California Press, 1986), 359ff.

22. Descartes, *Meditations on First Philosophy*, 35.

23. *Majus illud* ("this Greater Thing" or "this, which is more"—or, in Michelle Beyssade's translation, *cela, qui est plus*), writes Descartes in the same remarkable passage from the Third Meditation (AT 48), where he establishes that he himself, *Ego*, could not be God.

24. That is, in the *Meditations*—which is not to say, in general, that Descartes ignores the problem of the "other" as the problem of the other man (or woman), nor even that there is no path that, by way of dialogue, would lead from the *Ego sum, ego existo* from the Second Meditation to the philosopher of love who, in the letter to Chanut of February 1, 1647, cries with Virgil: *Me, me, adsum qui feci* . . . ["Oh me, oh me, I am here, the one who did it . . . *Aeneid*, 9:427] Jean-Marie Beyssade, who wrote a marvelous commentary on these texts in his introduction to *Correspondance de Descartes avec Elisabeth* (Paris: Garnier-Flammarion, 1989), still insists upon an "extraordinary contrast" between them.

25. Descartes, *Meditations on First Philosophy*, 34; translation modified and emphasis added

26. Ibid., 33.

27. Ibid., 47.

28. On the "violence of tautological propositions," see Stanislas Breton, *Philosophie buissonière* (Grenoble: Éditions Jérôme Millon, 1989), Chapter 9 ("Dieu est Dieu").

29. In a recent analysis that compares the "metaphysics" of the *Discourse on Method* and that of the *Meditationes*, Jean-Luc Marion underscores the fact that the formula from the latter (*Ego sum*,

ego existo), as distinct from the *cogito* as such (from the Discourse), "excluding thought itself, is valid only if an actually thinking thought thinks the formulation of existence" ("What Is the Metaphysics within the Method? The Metaphysical Situation of the Discourse on Method," in *Cartesian Questions* (Chicago: University of Chicago Press, 1999), 33. I will add that this actuality is sufficient for the *Ego* . . . But what is no less striking is the way in which the "ontological" utterance from the Fifth Meditation—so perfectly symmetrical with the other from the Second Meditation that one can no longer think the latter otherwise than as the recurrence of this former—excludes, in its turn, the *Ego* from the knot of *esse* and *existere*.

30. I place "finite" in quotation marks because I suspect that we are dealing here with a true circle: At bottom, the Cartesian concept of the finitude of thought (or the "thinking thing") does not derive from a transcendental category of finitude (common to thought and nonthought). Wouldn't this concept be defined precisely by the enunciation in the first person (I doubt, I am, I exist, I think, I imagine, I am deceived, I write . . .)? Wouldn't "ontological difference" between the finite thinking being and the infinite thinking being, within the stunning ambivalence of its enunciation, rest upon this paradox: to posit the less of being as a more of saying? What is "something intermediary between God and nothingness" if not: I say (that) I am, I am saying I am (every time that I say it)?

[By way of comparison, one might consult the analyses of Jacques Derrida in *Voice and Phenomenon* that, as it should be, I rediscover belatedly: "The appearing of the *I* to itself in the *I am* is therefore originarily the relation to its own possible disappearance. I am means therefore originarily *I am mortal*. *I am immortal* is an impossible proposition. We can therefore go further. Insofar as it is language, 'I am the one who is' is the confession of a mortal. . . . The ideality of the *Bedeutung* has here a value that is structurally testimonial. . . . The statement 'I am living' is accompanied by my being-dead and the statement's possibility requires the possibility that I be dead—and the reverse." *Voice and Phenomenon*, trans. Leonard Lawlor (Evanston, Ill.: Northwestern University Press, 2011), 46, 82–83.]

31. "And now, from this contemplation of the true God [*ab ista contemplatione veri Dei* . . .], in whom all the treasures of wisdom and the sciences lie hidden, I think I can see a way forward to the knowledge of other things" (M, 37); "Thus I see plainly that the certainty and truth of all knowledge depends uniquely on my awareness of the true God [*ab una veri Dei cognitione pendere*], to such an extent that I was incapable of perfect knowledge about anything else until I became aware of him" (M, 49).

32. Descartes, *Meditations on First Philosophy*, 36.

33. Here become visible both Descartes's proximity to and incompatibility with Spinoza, who writes in the *Tractatus Theologico-Politicus* (Chapter 1): "It seems quite alien to reason to assert that a created thing, dependent on God in the same way as other created things, should be able to express or display, factually or verbally, through its own person [*per suam personam*], God's essence or existence, declaring in the first person, 'I am Jehovah your God, etc.' [*Nempe diciendo in prima persona. Ego sum Jehovah Deus tuus etc.*] Granted, when someone utters the words 'I understand,' we all realize that it is the speaker's mind, not his mouth, that understands. But it is because the mouth is identified with the person of the speaker, and also because the hearer knows what it is to understand, that he readily grasps the speaker's meaning through comparison with himself. Now in the case of people who previously knew nothing of God but his name, and desired to speak with him so as to be assured of his existence [*ipsum alloqui cupiebant, et de Ejus Existentia certi fierent*], I fail to see how their need was met through a created thing (which is no more related to God than are other created things, and does not pertain to God's nature) which declared, 'I am the Lord' [*per creaturam . . . quae diceret: Ego sum Deus*]. What if God had manipulated the lips of Moses—but why Moses? the lips of some beast—so as to pronounce the words 'I am the Lord?' Would the people thereby have understood God's existence [*si Deus labia Mosis . . . contorsisset ad eadem pronuntiandum, et dicendum, Ego sum Deus, an inde Dei existentiam intelligerent*]? Again, it is the indisputable meaning

of Scripture that God himself spoke [*Deum ipsum locutum fuisse*] . . ." Baruch Spinoza, *Complete Works*, trans. Samuel Shirley (Indianapolis: Hackett, 2002; translation modified), 397.

34. Let us not stop halfway: if God is not "I" or does not have the capacity to say "I," it becomes very doubtful that we would have, in relation to him, the capacity to say "You" (from the "Who are you, Lord?" to the *nunc dimittis* . . . and to the *fiat voluntas tua* . . .). This might suggest, on the other hand, that our propensity to "hear" God saying "I" is a function, retroactively, of the propensity that drives us to say You to him (you, Lord, command, forgive, hear . . .); but, at this point, we are departing from the texts or, in any event, the texts of Descartes. It would be necessary to take up Jean-Luc Marion's discussion (with and against Heidegger) in "The Ego and Dasein," in *Reduction and Givenness: Investigations of Husserl, Heidegger, and Phenomenology*, trans. Thomas A. Carlson (Evanston, Ill.: Northwestern University Press, 1998), 77–107.

35. Starting from other premises, this is what Georges Canguilhem has proposed: "Thinking is a human practice that requires self-consciousness in presence to the world, not as the representation of the subject I but as its claim or demand, for this presence is vigilance and more exactly sur-veillance . . . In this respect, the surveillant I of the world of things and people is as much the I of Spinoza as the I of Descartes. While Descartes inwardly considers the self-evidence of his *cogito*, Spinoza asserts the impersonal axiom *Homo cogitat*. But when he comes to compose the *Theologico-Political Treatise*, Spinoza is that I who in the last chapter demands, confronted by the Sovereign's acknowledged right to govern over all things in the state concerning the actions of its citizens, 'that all be granted the right to be able to think what they want and to say what they think.' Although Spinoza generally used the modest pronoun 'we,' at the end of this work he could not restrain himself from writing: 'I have thus fulfilled the task that I set myself in this treatise . . . I know that I am a man, and as a man liable to error.' Intentions, mistakes—these, we have argued, are among the marks of thought." Georges Canguilhem, "The Brain and Thought," trans. Steven Corcoran and Peter Hallward, in *Radical Philosophy* 148 (March–April 2008): 16. The First Meditation, with respect to the cause that is responsible in the last instance for the evil of error, especially in the radical form of error about my own being, implicitly proposed three possible responses: God, the Devil, or me who thinks . . . At the end of the *Meditations*, the response becomes known: it is me and me alone. There is no cause to look elsewhere for the principle of Cartesian ethics, also the source of his radically atheological morality.

36. "Here I am, I can do no other" (Martin Luther's famous pronouncement before the Imperial Diet of Worms (1521), resisting the injunction to recant his teachings).

37. Let us recall, for example, Feuerbach's assertion, "What man calls Absolute Being, his God, is his own being," from the Introduction to *The Essence of Christianity*. (Ludwig Feuerbach, *The Fiery Brook: Selected Writings* [New York: Verso Books, 2014], 102). Or that Sartre, in "Cartesian Freedom," attributed precisely to Descartes the intuition of this reappropriation (Jean-Paul Sartre, *Literary and Philosophical Essays*, trans. Annette Michelson [New York: Collier Books, 1962], 181–192).

2. "MY SELF," "MY OWN": VARIATIONS ON LOCKE

Irvine Lectures in Critical Theory, The Critical Theory Institute, University of California, Irvine, Wednesday, February 12, 2003. First published in English in Bill Maurer and Gabrielle Schwab, eds., *Accelerating Possession: Global Futures and Personhood* (New York: Columbia University Press, 2006). The text that appears in the present volume is a translation based on the final French version.

1. The titles and content of innumerable scholarly works would suggest as much. Among them is Charles Taylor's book, *Sources of the Self: The Making of Modern Identity* (Cambridge, Mass.: Harvard University Press, 1992), which I mention here all at once because of the fundamental problems that it poses, because of the problems that its title poses for the French translator, and

because, on the level of method and interpretation, I go almost in the exact opposite direction. I borrow from Renée Balibar the notion and term of colingualism. See *L'Institution du Français, Essai sur le colinguisme des Carolingiens à la République* (Paris: Presses Universitaires de France, 1985); *Le colinguisme* (Paris: Presses Universitaires de France, "Que sais-je?" 1993).

2. Regrettably, I must leave aside the neighboring questions raised by Heidegger's German neologism, *Jemeinigkeit*, which becomes the cornerstone of the phenomenological analyses of *Being and Time* (1927). We would not only be interested in the term itself, which is introduced in §9 of *Being and Time*, and then either "translated" incompletely as the "mineness," or abstractly as the "unsubstitutability," or alternately paraphrased as "the fact of being at each instant mine," which characterizes *Dasein*. More interesting, for us, is the fact that Heidegger immediately neutralizes the construction of this term with the thesis that "when we speak of Dasein, we must always use the personal pronoun along with whatever we say: *Ich bin, Du bist . . . .*" (Martin Heidegger, *Being and Time*, trans. Joan Stambaugh [Albany: SUNY Press, 2010], 42). It is as if the difference between "I" and "You" were inessential (although this difference was just evoked in the *mein*). In any event, all of this completely inscribes Heidegger within the history of what has been called "possessive individualism," to which I will return.

3. Barbara Cassin, ed., *Vocabulaire européen des philosophies* (Paris: Éditions Seuil-Robert, 2004). This volume, today, has become the object of translations (which are, inevitably, adaptions) into various languages, from Arabic to Farsi to Russian by way of English. In the *Vocabulaire*, I myself composed the entries entitled, "Conscience," "Ame-Esprit," "Sujet" (in collaboration with Barbara Cassin and Alain de Libera), "Je-Moi-Soi," "Praxis," and "Agency" (in collaboration with Sandra Laugier), the content of which intersects and develops many aspects of my present discourse.

4. *Identité et différence: Le chapitre II, xxvii de l'Essay Concerning Human Understanding de Locke. L'invention de la conscience*, translated with an introduction and commentary by Étienne Balibar (Paris: Seuil, 1998). Étienne Balibar, *Identity and Difference: John Locke and the Invention of Consciousness*, trans. Stella Sandford, intro. Warren Montag (New York: Verso, 2013). The only French translation (which I included as a parallel text in my edition) available at the time I wrote this book (1998) was still that of Pierre Coste, which was produced under the supervision of Locke himself and published for the first time in 1700 (and was the version used by all the eighteenth-century "continental" readers of Locke—foremost among them, Leibniz, who interpolated extracts from this translation into his own *New Essays on Human Understanding*).

5. I will cite from John Locke, *An Essay Concerning Human Understanding*, ed. and intro. Peter H. Nidditch (Oxford: Oxford University Press, 1975). Among the very numerous commentaries on this text, one might consult in particular: Henry E. Allison, "Locke's Theory of Personal Identity: A Re-Examination," in *Locke on Human Understanding*, ed. J. C. Tipton (Oxford: Oxford University Press, 1977); Michael Ayers, *Locke: Epistemology and Ontology* (London: Routledge, 1991); Cathy Caruth, *Empirical Truths and Critical Fictions: Locke, Wordsworth, Kant, Freud* (Baltimore: Johns Hopkins University Press, 1991); Karl Olivecrona, "Locke's Theory of Appropriation," *Philosophical Quarterly* 24, no. 96 (1974): 220–234; Udo Thiel, "Locke's Concept of the Person," in *John Locke: Symposium Wolfenbüttel 1979*, ed. Reinhard Brandt (Berlin: Walter de Gruyter, 1981). The contemporary work that has done the most to revive the question of the "Lockean criterion of identity" among analytic philosophers is undoubtedly Derek Parfit, *Reasons and Persons* (Oxford: Oxford University Press, 1984). See John McDowell's critique of Parfit, "Reductionism and the First Person," in *Mind, Value, Reality* (Cambridge, Mass.: Harvard University Press, 1998). See also the updated bibliography provided by Stella Stanford in the volume cited earlier.

6. John Locke, *Two Treatises of Government*, ed. and intro. Peter Laslett (Cambridge: Cambridge University Press, 1963). In accord with Stoic ontology, which does not start from the subject and object but privileges the viewpoint of the agent and its functions, Locke exclusively applies the term *appropriate* to *actions*: the play of consciousness and memory is what makes it

possible to "admit as its own," and thus to "impute" them to the subject—which is to say, to the "self." On the other hand, the notion of appropriation is identically that which, in Locke's political works and especially in the *Second Treatise on Government*, makes it possible to define civil personality as that of an individual who is "proprietor of his own person" and ascribes to himself all the goods and rights necessary to his independence through the intermediary of labor (or, more generally, effort):

§27: "Though the earth, and all inferior creatures, be common to all men, yet every man has a *property* in his own *person*: this no body has any right to but himself. The *labour* of his body, and the *work* of his hands, we may say, are properly his. Whatsoever then he removes out of the state that nature hath provided, and left it in, he hath mixed his *labour* with, and joined to it something that is his own, and thereby makes it his *property*."

§44: "[M]an, by being master of himself, and *proprietor of his own person, and the actions or labour of it, had still in himself the foundation of property*; and that, which made up the great part of what he applied to the support or comfort of his being . . . was perfectly his own, and did not belong in common to others."

§§193–194: "The nature whereof is, that without a man's *own consent* [his property] *cannot be taken from him* . . . Their *persons* are *free* by a Native Right, and their *properties*, be they more or less, are *their own, and at their own dispose* . . . or else it is no property."

In order for the terminology of these texts to accord with those of the *Essay*, it is necessary to suppose that there is a reciprocal presupposition between the theory of personal identity, which is founded on the inner continuity of consciousness, and that of self-ownership, which is founded on the material autonomy acquired through labor. One must, it seems to me, go so far as the idea of an "anthropological doublet" of consciousness and labor, which renders obsolete any reference to a substantial union of body and spirit, being immanent to the sphere of action and not attached to the representation of a substratum.

7. C.B. MacPherson, *The Political Theory of Possessive Individualism: Hobbes to Locke* (Oxford: Oxford University Press, 1962). I think that it was MacPherson who introduced the neologism "self-ownership" to replace Locke's more archaic formula, "proprietor of one's own person." This neologism was quickly adopted by all analytic philosophy, both of the "right" and the "left": Robert Nozick, Carole Pateman, Gerald A. Cohen, and so on. See my essay "Le renversement de l'individualisme possessif," in *La propriété: Le propre, l'appropriation*, eds. Hervé Guineret and Arnaud Milanese (Paris: Ellipses, 2004). Reprinted in Étienne Balibar, *Equaliberty: Political Essays*, trans. James Ingram (Durham, N.C.: Duke University Press, 2014), 67–98.

8. This is what Jean-Paul Sartre upholds from a phenomenological viewpoint in *The Transcendence of the Ego: An Existentialist Theory of Consciousness*, trans. Forrest Williams and Robert Kirkpatrick (New York: Hill & Wang, 1960).

9. To these considerations pertaining to the history of the teaching of philosophy in France, I must add a single corrective note: it was from an extraordinary course offered at the Sorbonne in 1960–1961 by Georges Canguilhem on "Origins of Scientific Psychology" that I got the first inkling of Locke's "invention of consciousness" as something that remains *short of* the distinctions between the "psychological" and "transcendental" points of view to which the subsequent philosophical debates of the eighteenth century would lead.

10. In 1690, "consciousness" (defined by Locke as a "the perception of what passes in a Man's own Mind," *Essay*, II, 1, §19) was also a quasi-neologism in English. It was invented by the line leader of the Cambridge "neo-Platonists," Ralph Cudworth, in his monumental and unfinished work from 1678, *The True Intellectual System of the Universe, The First Part: Wherein All the Reason and Philosophy of Atheism is Confuted, and Its Impossibility Demonstrated* (Bristol: Theommes Press, 1995).

11. See Jean Deprun, *La philosophie de l'inquiétude en France au XVIIIe siècle* (Paris: J. Vrin, 1979).

12. I find it revealing, but also ironic, that a recent (and very intelligent) study of Locke's doctrine of personal identity, which typifies the analytical "reconstructive" approach, the author first needed to *retranslate* Locke's original text into a more "modern" and less "literary" English that would make its logic visible (at the risk of blurring the concepts). See Galen Strawson, *Locke on Personal Identity: Consciousness and Concernment* (Princeton: Princeton University Press, 2011). Our two essays thus appear as twin volumes, with a strange familiarity of disjunction, and opposite objectives.

13. Better still, the mutual implication of consciousness and memory, the temporal flux of consciousness that "retains" itself. It would be useful, at this point, to examine the proximity between Locke and Husserl's famous analyses in *Lectures on the Phenomenology of the Consciousness of Internal Time, 1904–1905*, to which I referred, albeit rapidly, in *Identity and Difference: John Locke and the Invention of Consciousness*, along with the analyses of William James. Husserl studied Locke and his influence very closely, as evidenced by his courses on "first philosophy" from 1923–1924. Edmund Husserl, *Erste Philosophie* (1923–24) (Berlin: Springer Verlag, 2013 [reprint of the 1956 edition]).

14. In Locke's text can also be found the apparently redundant composite adjective, *self-same*. Latin speakers would point out that it combines the significations of *idem* (which Paul Ricoeur sought to translate by "*mêmeté*" [sameness]) and *ipse* (which he translates by "*ipséité*" [ipseity]), or, in contemporary English, *sameness* and *selfhood*. In his book subsequent to *Oneself as Another*, Ricoeur refers favorably to the commentary on Locke that I offered in *Identity and Difference*; but I am obliged to say that my reading of Locke precisely falsifies the idea that there is a radical antithesis between these two notions: instead, there is a "overlapping zone" where the reflexive idea of the subject as self is formed. See Paul Ricoeur, *Memory, History, Forgetting*, trans. Kathleen Blamey and David Pellauer (Chicago: University of Chicago Press, 2004), 102–109.

15. On the metaphysical consequences of the properties of the Greek verb, see Emile Benveniste's classic essay, "Categories of Thought and Language," in *Problems of General Linguistics*, trans. Mary Elizabeth Meek (Coral Gables: University of Miami Press, 1971), 55–64, and its critique by Jacques Derrida, "The Supplement of the Copula," in *Margins of Philosophy*, trans. Alan Bass (Chicago: University of Chicago Press, 1984), 175–206. More recently, Barbara Cassin proposed a new interpretation of the problem in her edition of the Poem of Parmenides, *Sur la nature ou sur l'étant: Parménide, La langue de l'être?* (Paris: Seuil, 1998). On the double genealogy of the subject as subjectus and subjectum, see my essay, "Citizen Subject: Response to Jean-Luc Nancy" (Chapter 1 of this volume), as well as my contribution to the article "Subject" in *Dictionary of Untranslatables*.

16. The coherence between the two parts of the doctrine is even more thoroughgoing because there is a rigorous analogy between the process of acquiring knowledge through understanding, under the condition that my consciousness appropriates me to myself, and the process of constituting private property through "personal work," under the condition that I am first of all the "owner of myself" (that is, according to the formula inherited from the English revolutionary tradition, of my "Life, Liberty, and Estates." See C.B. MacPherson, *Democratic Theory: Essays in Retrieval* (Oxford: Oxford University Press, 1973), 24ff. See also Étienne Balibar, "The Reversal of Possessive Individualism."

17. See, in particular, Jacques Derrida, *Spurs: Nietzsche's Styles*, trans. Barbara Harlow (Chicago: University of Chicago Press, 1981).

18. Étienne Balibar, *Identity and Difference*, 118 n. 86, where I correct my initial mistake.

19. Of course, this is where I should have begun. As we learn in school, a citation can never be understood out of context. See Robert Browning, "By the Fire Side," *The Complete Works of Robert Browning*, Volume V, ed. Roma A. King Jr. (Athens: Ohio University Press, 1981), 205–206.

20. As Roman Jakobson asserts, the first person is a *shifter*: Never failing to reproduce a performative contradiction, it both exhibits and annuls the difference between the enunciated

and the enunciation. See Roman Jakobson, "Shifters and Verbal Categories," in *On Language*, ed. Linda R. Waugh and Monique Monville-Burston (Cambridge, Mass.; Harvard University Press, 1995), 386–392.

21. Not added but considerably augmented and transformed in the second edition of 1694. In French, "power" is at once *pouvoir* and *puissance*: impossible to choose one or the other.

22. Locke, *An Essay on Human Understanding*, 233–287. Wim Klever shows the presence in Locke of an occult element of "Spinozism," based on their common belonging to the Radical Enlightenment. See "Locke's Disguised Spinozism," http://www.benedictusdespinoza.nl/lit/ Locke%27s_Disguised_Spinozism.pdf. In my article "Soul" from the *Dictionary of Untranslatables*, I attempted to situate this Lockean uneasiness within another problematic: that of the "residue of soul" to be found in philosophies of the classical age, from the Cartesian "third substance" (the union of the soul and body) to the Kantian schematism of the transcendental imagination ("the hidden art in the depths of the human soul").

23. But let us take care not to oversimplify sociological "substantialism" or "personalism." See Bruno Karsenti, *La société en personnes: Études durkheimiennes* (Paris: Economica, 2006).

24. "I divide myself as it were, into two persons . . ." See *The Theory of Moral Sentiments* (Indianapolis: Liberty Classics, 1969), 247, 352, 371, etc. The "Impartial Spectator," in Smith, is also called the "inner man," or literally, "the man within the breast."

25. George Herbert Mead, *Mind, Self, and Society from the Standpoint of a Social Behaviorist*, ed. and intro. Charles W. Morris (Chicago: University of Chicago Press, 1934), 135–226.

26. See David Lapoujade, *William James: Empiricisme et pragmatisme* (Paris: Presses Universitaires de France, 1997). Another reason to compare Locke and James is the latter's interest in the question of "multiple personalities," to which I will return in a moment.

27. Should I say "sexual" or "erotic" (which might include *auto-erotism*)? I will leave the question open for now.

28. Among the verified examples of multiple personality syndrome, today, there are not only cases of doubling but also with as many as eighteen distinct "personalities" for a single individual. See Mikkel Borch-Jacobsen, "Who's Who? Introducing Multiple Personality," in Joan Copjec, ed., *Supposing the Subject* (New York: Verso, 1994). See also Ian Hacking, *Rewriting the Soul: Multiple Personality and the Sciences of Memory* (Princeton: Princeton University Press, 1995). One of the singular traits of the Locke's writing (as opposed to his predecessor Cudworth) is that he uses the word *consciousness* in the plural nominal to designate individualized and personified *consciousnesses*. On the "metonymy of consciousness," see my article, "Consciousness," in *Dictionary of Untranslatables*.

29. In *Identity and Difference*, I already discussed this aspect of Locke's thought. I here develop further its implications. Since the publication of my book, the great Locke specialist John W. Yolton (d. 2005) reconstituted Locke's entire doctrine of Spirits, *The Two Intellectual Worlds of John Locke: Man, Person, and Spirits in the "Essay"* (Ithaca, N.Y.: Cornell University Press, 2004).

30. James. J. O'Donnell, *The Confessions of Saint Augustine: An Electronic Edition, Text and Commentary*, 1992, Book X, §30.41. I provide the English translation by Henry Chadwick (Oxford: Oxford University Press, 1991): "You command me without question to abstain 'from the lust of the flesh and the lust of the eyes and the ambition of the secular world' (1 John 2: 16). You commanded me to abstain from sleeping with a girl-friend and, in regard to marriage itself, you advised me to adopt a better way of life than you have allowed (1 Cor. 7: 38). And because you granted me strength, this was done even before I became a dispenser of your sacrament. But in my memory of which I have spoken at length, there still live images of acts which were fixed there by my sexual habit. These images attack me. While I am awake they have no force, but in sleep they not only arouse pleasure but even elicit consent, and are very like the actual act. The illusory image within the soul has such force upon my flesh that false dreams have an effect on me when asleep, which the reality could not have when I am awake. During this time of sleep surely it is not my true

self, Lord my God? Yet how great a difference between myself at the time when I am asleep and myself when I return to the waking state. Where then is reason which, when wide-awake, resists such suggestive thoughts, and would remain unmoved if the actual reality were to be presented to it? Surely reason does not shut down as the eyes close. It can hardly fall asleep with the bodily senses. For if that were so, how could it come about that often in sleep we resist and, mindful of our avowed commitment and adhering to it with strict chastity, we give no assent to such seductions? Yet there is a difference so great that, when it happens otherwise than we would wish, when we wake up we return to peace in our conscience. From the wide gulf between the occurrences and our will, we discover that we did not actively do what, to our regret, has somehow been done in us."

31. A Freudian would be tempted to say: for good reason! Since psychical conflicts linked to sexuality are the most violent, or the source of the greatest disturbances, they are also the most deeply repressed . . .

32. Robert Louis Stevenson, *The Strange Case of Dr. Jekyll and Mr. Hyde* (New York: Penguin, 2003), Chapter 10: "Henry Jekyll's Full Statement of the Case," 55–72.

33. From the perspective of "psycho-pathology," the two personalities are dissymmetrical: the one is unconscious of the other's thoughts, but not the inverse, up to the point where this relation of forces is inverted.

34. All of this, which obviously pertains to the fantastic or fantasy, is sustained in the text with a Franco-English play on words that commentators have not failed to notice: Jekyll = Je kill. See, in particular, Masao Miyoshi, "The Divided Self," in *The Definitive Dr. Jekyll and Mr. Hyde Companion*, ed. Harry M. Geduld (New York and London: Garland, 1983), 104–105.

35. At the beginning of his experiment, Jekyll took care to draw up a last will and testament that guarantees, in case of an unhappy accident, that each of his two personalities will benefit from the inheritance of the other. Accordingly, Jekyll ultimately has to write checks to pay off the victims of Hyde's criminal activities that, in turn, have made him rich.

36. "Between the two," we can see, the one who names the subject of enjoyment (*jouissance*) is Jekyll, not Hyde.

37. *Propriety* is the modern equivalent (and thereby the translation, as in the work of Adam Smith) of the Stoic *oikeiosis* or *oikeiotes*, rendered in Latin as *convenientia* (Cicero).

38. The author, in particular, of *Frankenstein: Mythe et philosophie* (Paris: Presses Universitaires de France, 1987); *Philosophy of Nonsense: Intuitions of Victorian Nonsense Literature* (New York: Routledge, 1994); *Interpretation as Pragmatics* (New York: Palgrave, 1999); and *A Marxist Philosophy of Language* (Chicago: Haymarket Books, 2009).

3. *AIMANCES* IN ROUSSEAU: *JULIE OR THE NEW HELOISE* AS TREATISE ON THE PASSIONS

Presentation at the colloquium "Property, Sovereignty, and the Theotropic: Paul de Man's Political Archive," University of California, Irvine, April 24–25, 2009. I thank Erin Obodiac for inviting me to the colloquium, organized alongside her research at the U.C. Irvine library. The French version was adapted for the École d'Été de l'Association Jan Hus, Bratislava, July 8, 2010. [This chapter has been translated anew from the French version.]

1. Letter by Rousseau on *Julie or the New Heloise*. See Jean-Jacques Rousseau, *Oeuvres complètes* (Paris: Gallimard, Bibliothèque de la Pléiade, 1961), vol. II, xxx.

2. Paul de Man, *Allegories of Reading: Figural Language in Rousseau, Nietzsche, Rilke, and Proust* (New Haven: Yale University Press, 1979), 210.

3. Ibid., 205.

4. Ibid., 138–139.

5. See Alain Grosrichard, "L'inoculation de l'amour," in *De l'amour* (Paris: Flammarion, 1999), 73.

6. *Julie or the New Heloise* was composed during the years 1756–1759 and was published in 1761. Prévost's French translation of Clarissa (published in English in 1748) appeared in 1751.

A new edition of the Persian Letters appeared in 1758, after Montesquieu's death. Laurent Versini credits these two works with introducing "polyphony" into the epistolary novel, before Rousseau's masterpiece. See *Le roman épistolaire* (Paris: Presses Universitaires de France, 1979), 71.

7. In Letter I, 24, Saint-Preux offers Julie a commentary upon the story of Héloïse and Abélard that he wishes not to imitate. In 1687, Bussy-Rabutin published an adaptation of the letters of Héloïse and Abélard. See Jean-Jacques Rousseau, *Julie or the New Heloise*, trans. Philip Stewart and Jacques Vaché (Hanover, N.H.: Dartmouth University Press, 1997), 70.

8. F. H. Jacobi, *Allwill* (1775); Pierre Choderlos de Laclos, *Les Liaisons dangereuses* (1782); D. A. F. de Sade, *Aline et Valcour* (1793); Friedrich Hölderlin, *Hyperion* (1797 and 1799); Honoré de Balzac, *Mémoires de deux jeunes mariées* (1842). Goethe's *Werther* (1774), in which Rousseau's influence can be felt, is generally classified among "epistolary novels"; but, revolving around a lone scriptor, it is an equivocal example.

9. Nonetheless, episodes of this type do occur, such as the moment when Julie's mother "happens upon" Saint-Preux's letters, which triggers the novel's first dramatic turn of events: see Part II, Letter XXVIII; and Part III, Letter I.

10. This circle becomes fascinating and enigmatic in its own right, especially if one supposes that Rousseau only wrote to Madame d'Houdetot with the intention of suffusing his novel with the sentimental community and erotic excitation engendered by a flirtation with this *grande dame*, which, in turn, fed upon her admiration for his talent as a writer. See Bernard Guyon, "Introduction," in Jean-Jacques Rousseau, *Oeuvres complètes* (Paris: Pléiade, 1961), vol. II, xlv ff. Accordingly, coming from the opposite direction, some of Rousseau's female readers, who "supposed" him to be the model for Saint-Preux, proposed that he play out the novel's correspondence with them in the roles of Claire and Julie. See James Swenson, *On Jean-Jacques Rousseau Considered as One of the First Authors of the Revolution* (Stanford: Stanford University Press, 2000), 134–135.

11. See the "Second Preface" to *Julie or the New Heloise* in the form of a dialogue: "I put my name at the head of the collection, not to claim it as mine; but to answer for it." (Jean-Jacques Rousseau, *Julie or the New Heloise*, 19). See E. S. Burt's commentary on it, "Rousseau the Scribe," *Studies in Romanticism* 18, no. 4 (Winter 1979).

12. See, in particular, Letters 54 and 55 from Part I, respectively preceding and following sexual relations between Saint-Preux and Julie: "How fortunate to have found ink and paper!" (120).

13. De Man himself repeats, for his own reasons, this old reproach about Rousseau: that his characters lack individuality, that he didn't know how to make them live and to make us imagine their feelings and thoughts like a "true" novelist would have done.

14. I refer to the conclusions that Jean-Marie Beyssade draws in his article, "Jean-Jacques Rousseau: Le pacte social ou la voix du gueux," *Cahiers de Fontenay* 67/68 (September 1992): 31–47.

15. Too many commentators (even Starobinski) in their interpretation of a certain passage (such as the party at the domaine de Clarens) attempt to reduce the *partiality* of the voice that narrates it. Accordingly, it is Saint-Preux (whose instruction has elevated him above his initial condition and allowed him into the inner circle of the masters) who writes to the aristocrat Milord Édouard: "The sweet equality that reigns here restores the order of nature" (Part V, Letter 7). It is not "Jean-Jacques" or the "citizen of Geneva" . . .

16. One of the best explications of this thesis, relating it to the new function of affectivity and sexual difference in bourgeois society, where women are recognized as "subjects" without access to the title (or the proper "virtues") of the "citizen," can be found in Elena Pulcini, *Amour-passion et amour conjugal: Rousseau et l'origine d'un conflit moderne* (Paris: Honoré Champion, 1998). See, in particular, the very beautiful chapter that she devotes to "friendship-love" as a condition of "happiness" (149–191). I am glad to have rediscovered this book after I finished this essay (although, most likely, I was working on the basis of an unconscious memory of it), because it deals with each of the "moments" that I discuss here, often in a much more subtle and detailed fashion than me, inserting them into a very different argument.

17. *The New Heloise* thus ends, in its specific form of writing, with an articulation of the "religious problem," much as *The Social Contract* concludes with "civil religion." In *Emile, or On Education*, the third great book from 1761–62, this development is anticipated by the "Profession of Faith of the Savoyard Vicar." Whence the temptation to uphold *Emile* as the "synthesis" of the two other works at the same time as a theory of education. But Emile is a rational anarchist rather than an active citizen, and his marriage is a failure.

18. The "mystical" (if not edifying) conclusion of Rousseau's novel is a response to the "libertine" conclusion of its English model (*Clarissa*). I thank Françoise Duroux for pointing this out to me. See also, David Marshall, "Fatal Letters: *Clarissa* and the Death of Julie," in *Clarissa and Her Readers: New Essays for the "Clarissa" Project*, ed. Carol Houlihan Flynn and Edward Copeland (New York: AMS Press, 1999).

19. The French term was created in 1926 by the linguist and psychoanalyst Édouard Pichon, but Derrida culled it from the work of his friend Abdelkébir Khatibi. See *The Politics of Friendship*, trans. George Collins (New York: Verso, 1997): "Beyond all ulterior frontiers between love and friendship, but also between the passive and active voices, between the loving and the being-loved, which is at stake is 'lovence' [*aimance*]. You must know how *it can be more worthwhile* to love lovence" (7); "The reader will have sensed that this is what I would be tempted to call 'lovence': love *in* friendship, lovence beyond love and friendship following their determined figures, beyond all this book's trajectories of reading, beyond all ages, cultures and traditions of loving. This does not mean that lovence itself can take place figurelessly: for example, the Greek *philía*, courtly love, such and such a great current (as we call it) of mysticism. But lovence cuts across these figures" (69–70); "This desire ('pure, impure desire') which, in lovence—friendship or love—engages me with a particular him or her rather than with somebody or with all hims or hers, which engages me with these men and women (and not with all of either or just anyone), which engages me with a singular 'who,' be it a certain number of them, a number that is always small . . . this desire of the call to bridge distance (necessarily unbridgeable) is (perhaps) no longer of the order of the common or community, the share taken up or given, participation or sharing. . . . Consequently, if there were a politics of this lovence, it would no longer imply the motifs of community, appurtenance or sharing, whatever the sign assigned to them" (298). See also Abdelkébir Khatibi, "L'aimance et l'invention d'un idiome," in *Oeuvres d'Abdelkébir Khatibi* (Paris: Éditions de la Différence, 2008), 2:125ff.

20. The question of the place that *The New Heloise* occupies within the series of "Treatises on the Passions" from the classical and romantic ages—from Descartes and Spinoza, to Hume, Smith, Stendhal, and Fourier—and of the transformation that it imposes upon their genetic or typological method, arises on the horizon of this essay although I cannot address it as such. In his beautiful book (with a Spinoza-inspired title) *Géométrie des passions. Peur, espoir, bonheur: de la philosophie à l'usage politique*, Remo Bodei only discusses Rousseau to consider the relation between *The Social Contract* and *Emile* to discourses of the French Revolution, thereby leaving aside what, I submit, is most essential.

21. Barbara Cassin, ed., *Dictionary of Untranslatables: A Philosophical Lexicon*, trans. Steven Rendall et al. (Princeton: Princeton University Press, 2014).

22. See also *L'amitié: Dans son harmonie, dans ses dissonances*, ed. Sophie Jankélevitch and Betrand Ogilvie (Paris: Éditions Autrement, 1995). Pierre Macherey's article in this volume, "Le *Lysis* de Platon: Dilemme de l'amitié et de l'amour" (58–75) shows how Rousseau inverts the Platonic schema of the transcendence of friendship (*philia*) in love (*eros*).

23. Étienne Balibar, "What Makes a People a People? Rousseau and Kant," in *Masses, Classes, and the Public Sphere*, ed. Mike Hill and Warren Montag, trans. Erin Post (London: Verso, 2000), 105–131.

24. This experimental structure is clearly elaborated by Fulvia de Luise and Giuseppe Farinetti in the chapter on Rousseau ("Rousseau: una felicità sofferta") from their "history of

happiness." *Storia della felicità: Gli antichi e i moderni* (Turin: Piccola Biblioteca Einaudi, 2001), 401ff.

25. I thank my UC Irvine student Debra Ligorski-Channick, author of a dissertation on "Romantic Emulation and Aesthetic Citizenship," for drawing my attention to the omnipresence of the theme of "emulation" in Rousseau's work and its influence within Romanticism, especially in the works of feminist writers (Madame de Staël, Charlotte Smith, Frances Burney). In his recent book *Living in the End Times* (Verso, 2010), 109ff, Slavoj Žižek proposes a quite different interpretation of *Julie* based on the Lacanian distinction between the "discourse of the master" and the "discourse of the university," placing Wolmar on the side of the "university." Comparing the figures of Wolmar, the "legislator" from the *Social Contract*, and the "master" from *Emile*, I would instead attempt to think how Rousseau worked (successfully) to undermine such a distinction using a "negative" conception of teaching that admits to its manipulative dimension. See also Howard Caygill, "The Master and the Magician," in *Jean-Jacques Rousseau and the Sources of the Self*, ed. Timothy O'Hagen (London: Ashgate, 1997), 16–24.

26. Part IV, Letter XVI.

27. This aspect of Wolmar's "plan," it seems to me, is not noticed often enough: the impossibility of love as passion between he and his wife is thereby not only compensated but also justified and converted into a positive value in the service of another passion in which they are no longer the sole participants.

28. Jean-Jacques Rousseau, *Julie or the New Heloise*, 417. On the ambivalence of this negation of past affect that also secures its repetition, read as a "work of death," see James Swenson, *On Jean-Jacques Rousseau*, 141.

29. In this respect, Rousseau might still be compared to Descartes, for whom (in *The Passions of the Soul*) it is important to show that "all the passions are good in themselves." See Denis Kambouchner's great book, *L'homme des passions: Commentaires sur Descartes*, 2 vols. (Paris: Albin Michel, 1995).

30. It would seem that Rousseau borrowed this expression from La Mettrie: "God of beautiful souls, charming pleasure, do not allow your brush to be prostituted to debased indulgences . . . Begone, shameless courtesans!" (*L'art de jouir*, 1750). According to Alan Speight, the figure of the "beautiful soul" in Hegel's *Phenomenology of Spirit* refers primarily to Jacobi's novel, *Woldemar* (1779), whose title clearly evokes the name of Wolmar from *The New Heloise*. But this does not mean—quite to the contrary—that Hegel was not deeply influenced by Rousseau.

31. See Suzanne Gearhart, *The Interrupted Dialectic: Philosophy, Psychoanalysis, and The Tragic Other* (Baltimore: Johns Hopkins University Press, 1992).

32. Part I, Letter LIII, From Julie to Saint-Preux: "Come then, soul of my heart . . . come be reunited with yourself" (119). In a later letter (Part VI, Letter VII), in declining Julie's offer to marry her cousin, Saint-Preux formalizes the difference between love and friendship: "I rediscover in her and me two friends who love each other tenderly and tell one another so. But do two lovers love each other? No; *you* and *I* are words banished from their language; they are no longer two, they are one" (555). On the basis of these formulations, one might discuss what in *The New Heloise* remains incompatible with the social formation of the idea of community (which comes, in part, from the *Social Contract*) whose constitutive formula Hegel utters in the *Phenomenology of Spirit* (Chapter IV, Introduction): "*Ich, das Wir, und Wir, das Ich ist*" (see Chapter 5).

33. Evidently, for Rousseau, paternal love is no more than the pale counterpart of maternal love, *unless* it is a component of the "rational preference" for the type of just domestic order incarnated by Monsieur de Wolmar.

34. I intentionally adopt Judith Butler's phrase, derived from her reading of Hegel in *The Psychic Life of Power: Theories in Subjection* (Stanford: Stanford University Press, 1997).

35. Or, in Starobinski's terms, a society of "transparency." It is in a letter from Rousseau to Madame de la Tour about his novel that Starobinski finds the word "transparency," which he uses

in general to characterize the "lost paradise" of natural relations between men, thereafter veiled to one another: "If I imagine rightly the hearts of Julie and Claire, they were transparent to one another" (cited in *Jean-Jacques Rousseau: la transparence et l'obstacle* [Paris: Gallimard, 1971], 105). The foundational equivalence of friendship and sincerity (or confidence—the doublet of *confiance*, trust, *pistis* . . .) is articulated in the letter from Julie to Saint-Preux (Part III, Letter XVIII) that marks the turning of love into friendship, or rather proposes it, by "putting love in the past" or deliberately transforming it into a memory. "You have so long been the trustee of all my heart's secrets that there is no way it could now forsake such a lovely habit. On the most important occasion in my life it desires to pour itself out to you. Open yours to it, my gentle friend; take friendship's lengthy discourse into your breast; although friendship may sometimes make the speaking friend prolix, it always makes the listening friend patient" (279).

36. Such a goal, for Rousseau, is not "natural," even if it can be called "libidinal": this is the lesson of the *Discourse on the origin of inequality* and the strict parallel that it establishes between the ownership of goods (which gives rise to competition and war) and the appropriation of women (which gives rise to violence and jealousy).

37. "Little sensible to pleasure and pain, I even experience but weakly that sentiment of interest and humanity that causes us to assimilate the affections of others. If I am pained when I see good people suffer, pity has nothing to do with it, for I feel none when I see the wicked suffer. My only active principle is a natural taste for order. . . . If I have a ruling passion it is that of observation. I like to read what is in men's hearts. . . . I enjoy observing society, not taking part in it. If I could change the nature of my being and become a living eye, I would gladly make that exchange. Thus my indifference for men does not make me independent of them; though I care not about being seen, I need to see them" (IV, 12; 402–403, From Madame de Wolmar to Madame d'Orbe, relaying what Monsieur de Wolmar said to the former lovers). See Jean Staro-binski, *Jean-Jacques Rousseau: La transparence et l'obstacle*, 106 and 138; Judith Shklar, "Rousseau's Images of Authority," *American Political Science Review* 58, no. 4 (Dec. 1964): 919–934.

38. See in Bernard Guyon's notes to the Pléiade edition of *Julie ou la nouvelle Héloïse* (1777ff) his remarks about the tendentiously heretical relationship that Rousseau, as a Protestant, influenced by the "quietism" of Fénelon and Jeanne Guyon, maintained with the Catholic Church.

39. The two "mates," "comrades," or *hetairoi* in Greek, by virtue of their travels across the world are like an opening outside of the community, and they bear witness to another possible development. Readers and critics tend to ignore this possibility because of their exclusive interest in the "domestic" aspect of the novel, which they identify as a study of the "private" world.

40. This is undoubtedly the point at which Jacobi's 1779 novel *Woldemar* decisively diverges from Rousseau: since the misunderstanding between the characters is caused by a *secret* that the protagonists felt they must keep from one another (for moral reasons), it can de dispelled by a confession which brings forgiveness or reconciliation. In Rousseau, it is never possible to identify the source of a loss that remains essentially unbeknown. See Allen Speight, *Hegel, Literature, and the Problem of Agency* (Cambridge: Cambridge University Press, 2001), 112ff.

41. I borrow this idea from Deleuze and Guattari who, in their essay on Kafka, speak of a "field of immanence that will function as a dismantling," to the extent that Kafka himself is always "proliferating doubles" in order to subvert the signification of triangles. *Kafka: Toward a Minor Literature*, trans. Dana Polan (Minneapolis: University of Minnesota Press, 1986), 86. It would be interesting to ask to what degree this topology reached a new level of generality by way of Fourier, albeit at the price of falling back upon a classificatory method.

42. Thomas Kavanagh, *Writing the Truth: Authority and Desire in Rousseau* (Berkeley: University of California Press, 1987).

43. His "superegoic" quality with respect to the latent incest of the triangle is also obvious. At one dramatic moment, it happens that he designates his wife and her old lover, Saint-Preux, as "my children" (Part IV, Letter XII).

44. Julie's "sovereignty" in the "little society" of Clarens is what Elena Pulcini interprets as a *power of love* that is completely "private," and thus subordinated or *subjected* to the public power of men in the "large society" which it can only subvert locally in order to reinforce it globally." But this argument fails to see that, in *Julie or the New Heloise*, the "large society" is either neutralized or utopically envisaged as a possible extension of the small one. Historically speaking, Rousseau contributed to the forging of stereotypes of a bourgeois order divided between "the two governments" (to use the expression of Geneviève Fraisse in *Les deux governements: La famille et la Cité* [Paris: Gallimard, 2000]); but this did not prevent him from constructing an allegorical scene of the superimposition or latent conflict of these two sovereignties, and thus of two ways of thinking "subjection." But one could also say: if there are "two sovereignties" (two places for the what the Roman tradition calls the *sublimis*, no longer those of the temporal and the spiritual sovereign, but of "man" and "woman"), then the place of the "subject" (the *subjectus*) that they dispute can only be a site of indecision, division, and discontent. Besides, *The New Heloise* is a privileged text for studying the circulation of the Lockean theme of *uneasiness* in the classical age, a theme that Rousseau will transmit to Romanticism. See Jean Deprun, *La philosophie de l'inquiétude en France au XVIIIe siècle* (Paris: Vrin, 1979).

45. "Each character in the book must overcome various difficulties before joining this group of communicating souls and extending the zone of transparency. Saint-Preux cannot hide anything. . . . As the book proceeds, secrets are divulged, confidence grows, and the characters' knowledge of one another becomes ever more perfect. . . . After Julie's mother discovers Saint-Preux's letters, which reveal her daughter's guilty passion, cousin Claire writes: 'This odious mystery must be hidden beneath an eternal veil. . . . The secret belongs to six trustworthy people' (Part III, Letter 1). Six! Initially there were only three. While the lovers endure the trial of separation, the number of 'initiates' has increased. Indeed, the more sublimated Saint-Preux's love becomes, the more remote from carnal satisfaction, the more transparent is the gaze of others. . . . As his love gradually becomes pure, it is revealed to more and more witnesses. Perfect trust brings exquisite pleasures to the small group of *belles âmes*. . . . The society of Clarens is based on unanimous consent" (Jean Starobinski, *Transparency and Obstruction*, trans. Arthur Goldhammer [Chicago: University of Chicago Press, 1988], 84–85). Starobinski thus reveals one of the main consequences of the novel's epistolary form: the moral and physical passion of Julie and Saint-Preux, to the extent that we only know of it not through any "realist" narration, but rather through the lovers' correspondence, constitutes a sort of prehistory, the material upon which the veritable intrigue will be built: that of the (once again, epistolary) transformation that this passion undergoes as it is "shared" or "divulged." He also shows how Rousseau "socializes"— I would also say, for my part, "politicizes"—friendship between the sexes by working against the traditional image of friendship. Nonetheless, one might ask why, under such conditions, isn't the relation between Saint-Preux and Milord Édouard (which will also end up being extended to all the other relations) equally valued for its contribution to the constitution of "unanimity." It is undoubtedly the effect of the "preference for the feminine" that Rousseau articulates in his commentary on *Julie*, combined with a "matriarchal" reading of the quasi-familial structure of Clarens. But the real structure is even more complex. It is also politically more significant, since the correspondence between Saint-Preux and Milord Éduoard is the place where we find the critique of morals and forms of paternal authority in the Ancien Régime. See Barbara Carnevali, *Romaticismo e riconoscimento: Figure della conscienza in Rousseau* (Bologna: Il Mulino, 2004), 155.

46. In the end, when Julie is soon to die, Claire will speak openly of her passion for her cousin, and they sleep in the same bed. In his essay on the "L'inoculation de l'amour" (in Alain Badiou et al., *De l'amour* [Paris: Flammarion, 1999], 15–80), Alain Grosrichard underscores the sensuality of the relation between Julie and Claire. Everything is said in advance in the letter (Part I, Letter XXXVIII) where Saint-Preux describes to Julie how he is affected by the spectacle of the caresses that pass between the two cousins: "Ye gods! What a ravishing spectacle or rather what ecstasy, to

behold two such moving Beauties tenderly embracing, the one's face resting on the other's breast, their sweet tears flowing together, and bathing that charming breast as dew from Heaven moistens the freshly bloomed lily! I was jealous of such a tender friendship; it had seemed to me that there was something more engaging about it than love itself, and I resented in a way my own inability to offer you such dear consolations, without troubling them by the turmoil of my transports. No, nothing, nothing on earth has the power to excite such a voluptuous empathy as your mutual caresses" (94). Bernard Guyon, the author of the notes to the Pléiade edition of *Julie*, begs to differ: "Nothing authorizes us to find any equivocal meaning on this page of the novel," especially coming from such an "orthodox" (*sic*) lover as Rousseau would have been.

47. Let us set aside the question of knowing whether there is such a thing as couples, in the absolute—that is, exclusive—sense of the term, without the intervention of supplementary "triangles." However, it is impossible not to remark that other "inhabitants" of the domain are excluded from the system: the *servants*. Unless we consider that Saint-Preux himself (much as Julien Sorel will do) "represents" the intrusion of the plebeians at the heart of the world of the masters, insofar as he is a preceptor and pretender to the love of a high born woman. But it is not in such a capacity that, once granted his independence, he returns to take part in this "little society." The only two letters written by a servant in the novel come from Fanchon Regard-Anet and they are almost absurdly "subaltern." In accordance with a tradition that goes back to Aristotle, the novel discusses the possibility of friendship between masters and servants (Part IV, Letter X): "Subordination of inferiors is complemented by harmony between equals, and this aspect of domestic administration is not the least difficult. . . . This propensity toward concord begins with the choice of Subjects. . . . But every well-regulated house is the image of the master's soul" (379–383). It shows that a house's two concurrent empires do not have the same mainspring or the same amplitude: the empire of the woman, which is more intense within the world of the masters, does not extend to the servants. Comparison with the aporia that concludes Spinoza's *Political Treatise*, shows that Rousseau here undoes the symmetry that he constructed in the *Discourse on the Origin of Inequality*: The bond of friendship dispels the perils of jealousy and lifts the prohibition upon the equality of women, but it changes nothing about the relation of classes. And this relation reestablishes the empire of man. See Françoise Duroux, "Des passions et de la compétence politique: La démonstration spinoziste de l'inopportunité de la présence des femmes au gouvernement d'un État," in *Cahiers du GRIF* 46 (1992): 103–123.

48. Derrida, *The Politics of Friendship*, 290–293.

49. One might take issue with one or another of Carole Pateman's readings of texts in her famous book, *The Sexual Contract* (Stanford: Stanford University Press, 1988); but she undeniably touches upon the fundamental. Pateman argues that the contractualist tradition, from Hobbes to Rousseau ("the leading theorist of the original sexual contract"), if one considers its structural analogy with the Freudian "myth" of the origin of institutions in the brothers' repression of the murder of the primal father, reveals that the contract of citizenship is exclusively sealed among men and presupposes another contract that operates the exclusion of women from the public sphere for the benefit of their fathers, brothers and husbands. Her reading of Rousseau is essentially based upon the correlation between *The Social Contract* and *Emile*. She does not refer to *The New Heloise* except to discern the avowal of weakness with respect to this scenario (without taking into account, it seems to me, that such "avowals" are inscribed within an *epistolary fiction* and thus cannot be directly ascribed to the novel's author; although they might very well spark a reading of Julie as the exposition of *another history*, albeit at the price of the idea that each writer has a "unique doctrine"): "But modesty is a precarious control of sexual desire. The story of Julie in *La Nouvelle Héloïse* shows just how fragile it is, when, despite all Julie's efforts to live an exemplary life as a wife and a mother, she is unable to overcome her illicit passion and takes the only course she can to preserve the haven of family life in Clarens: she goes to her 'accidental' death" (97).

50. The *unanimity* of which Starobinski speaks also evokes the Spinozan definition of political community in Chapter III, §2, of the *Political Treatise*. See my article "*Potentia multitudinis, quae una veluti mente ducitur*," in *Ethik, Recht, und Politik bei Spinoza*, ed. Marcel Senn and Manfred Walther (Zurich: Schulthess, 2001), 105–137.

51. Perhaps the *Émile* opens toward yet a third possibility, that of a *new nature*—or better, a "new savagery" at the heart of society, obtained by virtue of an "education against the grain."

52. Pierre-François Moreau, *Le récit utopique: Droit naturel et roman d'État*.

4. FROM SENSE CERTAINTY TO THE LAW OF GENRE: HEGEL, BENVENISTE, DERRIDA

Address at the conference "Derrida, la tradition de la philosophie," École Normale Supérieure, October 21–22, 2005, the proceedings of which have since been published (without my contribution) with Éditions Galilée. An earlier version of this text was presented within the framework of the Derrida Lectures organized by the Institut Français de Londres and the Birkbeck Institute for the Humanities, University of London (published as *Adieu Derrida*, ed. Costas Douzinas [London: Palgrave MacMillan, 2007]).

1. Jacques Derrida, *Monolingualism of the Other: or, The Prosthesis of Origin*, trans. Patrick Mensah (Stanford: Stanford University Press, 1998), 25.

2. See Benjamin Stora, *Les trois exils: Juifs d'Algérie* (Paris: Stock, 2006), a book that refers to Derrida's testimony and makes it possible to situate it in history.

3. Jacques Derrida, *Monolingualism of the Other*, 19–20.

4. G. W. F. Hegel, *The Phenomenology of Spirit*, trans. A. V. Miller (Oxford: Oxford University Press, 1977), 58–66.

5. In the *Phenomenology*, the "thematic" developments on questions of language and speech occur, on the one hand, in the section devoted to culture (*Bildung*) as an "alienated" (*entfremdete*) form of Spirit (whose extreme actualization is the form of social life dominated by the flattery of the powerful—an eminently Rousseauist theme) (*Phenomenology of Spirit*, §520, 315ff); and, on the other hand, much to the contrary, in the developments on the religious hymn as the elevation of the "religion of art" (*Kunstreligion*) into a "higher element" (higher with respect to the representation of sense experience) (*Phenomenology of Spirit*, §710, 430ff).

6. See Jacques Derrida, *Of Grammatology*, trans. Gayatri Spivak (Baltimore: Johns Hopkins University Press, 141ff, 269ff; *Voice and Phenomenon*, trans. Leonard Lawlor (Evanston, Ill.: Northwestern University Press, 2011), 75ff; "Plato's Pharmacy," in *Dissemination*, trans. Barbara Johnson (Chicago: University of Chicago Press, 1983), 156ff.

7. Émile Benveniste, *Problèmes de linguistique générale*, vol. I (Paris: Gallimard, 1966); vol. II (Paris: Gallimard, 1974). Volume II was compiled by Benveniste's students after his brain accident, and it reprises exactly the same classifications and the same section titles as the first volume. But the synthetic article, "The Formal Apparatus of Enunciation" (Vol. II, Chap. 4, 79–88) was placed in a section on "Communication." These disjunctions are actually quite problematic since the subjacent anthropological thesis (that Derrida will never stop interrogating) basically identifies the two problems: "Intersubjectivity has its own temporality, its terms, its dimensions. Language thus reflects a primordial, constant, and indefinitely reversible relation between the speaker and his partner. In the final analysis, it is always the act of speech in the process of exchange that relays the human experience inscribed in languages" (*Problèmes de linguistique générale*, II, 78).

8. Émile Benveniste, *Problems of General Linguistics* (Coral Gables: University of Miami Press, 1971), 197–198, 199, 221–222.

9. Paul Ricoeur, of course, makes extensive use of this distinction: see, in particular, *Time and Narrative*, vol. 2, trans. Kathleen Blamey and David Pellauer (Chicago: University of Chicago Press, 1988), 61ff ("Games with Time"); vol. 3, 207ff ("Toward a Hermeneutics of Historical Consciousness").

10. Benveniste, *Problems in General Linguistics*, Chap. 22, "Analytic Philosophy and Language," 231–238.

11. Émile Benveniste, "The Formal Apparatus of Enunciation," in *The Discourse Studies Reader: Main Currents in Theory and Analysis*, ed. Johannes Angermuller, Dominique Maingueneau, and Ruth Wodak (Philadelphia: John Benjamins, 2014), 143ff.

12. Étienne Balibar, "Structuralism: A Destitution of the Subject?", *differences* 14, no. 1 (Spring 2003).

13. Aeneas and the Sibyl descend into the underworld: *"Ibant obscuri sola sub nocte per umbram"* (*Aeneid* VI:269); see Jean-Claude Milner, *Le périple structural* (Paris: Verdier, 2008), 121ff.

14. Derrida's references to Benveniste are too numerous to list here (not to mention the "dark continent" of the seminars waiting to be read or published, preserved in the Critical Theory Archive at the University of California, Irvine). These references generally follow a characteristic pattern that consists in borrowing from Benveniste the analysis of an institution (and its ambivalence) which etymology opens up and then contesting the anthropological interpretation of this analysis in the name of a deconstruction to come. See *Margins of Philosophy*, trans. Alan Bass (Chicago: University of Chicago Press, 1982), 177ff; *Given Time, Vol. 1 (Counterfeit Money)*, trans. Peggy Kamuf (Chicago: University of Chicago Press, 1992), 69, 78ff; *The Politics of Friendship*, trans. George Collins (New York: Verso Books, 1997), 96–98; *Of Hospitality: Anne Dufourmentelle Invites Jacques Derrida to Respond*, trans. Rachel Bowlby (Stanford: Stanford University Press, 2000), 27ff; "Poétique et politique du témoignage," in Marie-Louise Mallet and Ginette Michaud, eds., *Derrida* (Paris: Cahiers de l'Herne, 2004), 526ff.

15. Benveniste, "The Formal Apparatus of Enunciation," 141.

16. I will leave aside the question of knowing how much Benveniste might owe to Martin Buber's elaborations in his 1923 work bearing this title. There are undoubtedly more significant "sources," in particular the work of Wilhelm von Humboldt that perhaps gave rise to the expression "man in language." (On this subject, Jean-Claude Milner—whom I here vigorously thank—wrote me the following: "1) The relation between Benveniste and Hegel is not born from Kojève. I agree. Benveniste cites Hegel in German in 1932: I think that he had been reading him (or at least a few words of him) since 1925–26, along with the so-called group of Les Philosophes [Lefebvre, Guterman, etc.], which means even before decent translations were available; 2) I think that Benveniste read Buber. Let us not forget his relationship with the priest Jean de Menasce, who wrote a book on Hassidism, *Quand Israël aime Dieu* [1931, reprinted by Éditions du Cerf in 1992]. His reflections on pronouns also seems to me to owe something to [Georges] Politzer.")

17. Benveniste, "The Formal Apparatus of Enunciation," 143 (translation modified).

18. Jacques Lacan, "The Function and Field of Speech and Language in Psychoanalysis," in *Écrits*, trans. Bruce Fink (New York: Norton, 2006), 246.

19. Jacques Derrida, "Le facteur de la vérité," in *The Post Card: From Socrates to Freud and Beyond*, trans. Alan Bass (Chicago: University of Chicago Press, 1987), 411–496.

20. Jacques Derrida, *Parages*, ed. John P. Leavey, trans. Tom Conley et al. (Stanford: Stanford University Press, 2011), 11.

21. This title can be read in two ways. It oscillates between the name of a thing, such as a house or (why not?) a tree, and a call that means "stay," or "please don't go!" or even, "always come back as if you were already gone!"

22. [The phrase *"ce qui est tu"* is strictly impossible to translate because it hinges upon two possible readings of the word *"tu"*—either as *"tu,"* the second person singular, or as *"tu,"* the past participle of the verb *taire* ("to fall or keep silent"). The phrase can and must be translated in two ways at the same time: "that which is you" and "that which keeps silent"—Trans.]

23. Maurice Blanchot, *The Instant of My Death*/Jacques Derrida, *Demeure: Fiction and Testimony*, trans. Elizabeth Rottenberg (Stanford: Stanford University Press, 2000), 96–97.

24. Ibid., 53–54.

25. Jacques Derrida, *The Post Card: From Socrates to Freud and Beyond*, trans. Alan Bass (Chicago: University of Chicago Press, 1987), 12–13.

26. I borrow the expression, "law of genre," from another well-known Derrida essay: "The Law of Genre," in *Parages*, 217–249.

27. For example, "Avant de poster cette carte je t'aurai appellée" ["Before posting this card I will have called you"] (*La Carte Postale* [Paris: Flammarion, 1980], 14; *The Post Card*, 10).

28. Derrida, *Parages*, 66–67. The reference is to *L'arrêt de mort* [Death Sentence] (1948) and *Celui qui ne m'accompagnait pas* [The One Who was Standing Apart from Me (1953).

29. I am talking about Françoise Kerleroux, who, even as she denies having uttered this exclamation, provides me with an exhaustive article on the way in which different languages distinguish (or not) between genres using different personal pronouns. See Anna Siewierska, "Gender Distinctions in Independent Personal Pronouns," in *The World Atlas of Language Structures*, ed. Martin Haspelmath, Matthew S. Dryer, and David Gil (Oxford: Oxford University Press, 2005). It is notable that, with the exception of certain African languages, there are no examples of languages that decline for gender the personal pronouns of the first two persons but not the third. On the other hand, in "Semitic" languages such as Arabic and Hebrew the second person singular and plural are declined for gender, but not the first person ("I").

30. Derrida, *Parages*, 241–242.

31. On Derrida's elaboration of the category of "exappropriation," see Étienne Balibar, "The Reversal of Possessive Individualism," in *Equaliberty*, trans. James Ingram (Durham, N.C.: Duke University Press, 2014), 67–98. I refer to *Spurs: The Styles of Nietzsche* (1972), *Margins: Of Philosophy* (1972), *Glas* (1974), *The Post Card* (1980), *Specters of Marx* (1993), and *Given Time* (1991).

5. *ICH, DAS WIR, UND WIR, DAS ICH IST:* SPIRIT'S DICTUM

This talk was delivered on Wednesday, May 3, 2006, under the title: "Première modernité, seconde modernité: de Rousseau à Hegel" to the "Philosophie au sens large" working group," directed by Pierre Macherey at the Université de Lille III. The reader may consult the working group's website to see all the contributions to its proceedings.

1. Étienne Balibar, "Séjourner dans la contradiction: L'idée de 'nouvelles Lumières' et les contradictions de l'Universalisme," in *Formen des Nichtwissens der Aufklärung*, ed. Hans Adler-Rainer Gödel (Munich: Wilhelm Fink Verlag, 2010).

2. Dipesh Chakrabarty, *Provincializing Europe: Postcolonial Thought and Historical Difference* (Princeton: Princeton University Press, 2000).

3. This debate is well explained by Nicolà Marcucci in his doctoral dissertation, defended in 2005 at the Università di Pisa: *Le forme dell'ingiustificazione: Relazione sociale/Relazione politica tra prima e tarda modernità*.

4. The term "point of heresy" comes from Michel Foucault, in *The Order of Things*, where he rediscovers a figure of Pascalian argumentation. I have already employed the expression "threshold of modernity," in the singular, in the article "Soul, Spirit, Mind, Wit," which I contributed to *Dictionary of Untranslatables: A Philosophical Lexicon*, ed. Barbara Cassin, trans. Steven Rendall et al. (Princeton: Princeton University Press, 2014),

5. [A. V. Miller's English translation of the sentence reads: " 'I' that is 'We' and 'We' that is 'I' "—Trans.]

6. One might compare what I have just written to what Bruno Karsenti writes in his book, *Politique de l'esprit: Auguste Comte et la naissance de la science sociale* (Paris: Hermann, 2006), 66: "At the moment when Bonald opposes the point of view of the ego to the point of view of the we as two manners of philosophizing (Louis Gabriel Ambroise de Bonald, *Démonstration philosophique du principe constitutif de la société*, 1830), at the moment when the figure of social man rises up against the illusions of the ego in which the psychology of the individual man seems to indulge,

Comte thus seeks to . . . offer his own incisive version of this opposition: that which casts into relief a certain manner of conceiving of the we, in a mode that would itself be desubjectivized." Hegel's project is exactly the inverse; and, from this point of view, Comte's enterprise can only appear as a contradiction in terms. See also Pierre Macherey's article, "Aux sources des rapports sociaux: Bonald, Saint-Simon, Guizot," in *Genèses* 9 (1992), "Conservatisme, libéralisme, socialisme."

7. As I showed in an article entitled, "I/Me/Myself" in the *Dictionary of Untranslatables*, 463–476.

8. Philosophical or psychoanalytic English only has a compromise formation that resorts to Latin: "the *ego*."

9. In order to do complete justice to the singularity of this utterance and its staging within the Hegelian text, it would be necessary to connect it to the question of the phenomenological "for us," which allows Hegel to write in the first person in the "name" of an egalitarian community (or being-in-common); see the chapter entitled "We" in Jean-Luc Nancy, *Hegel: The Restlessness of the Negative*, trans. Steven Miller and Jason E. Smith (Minneapolis: University of Minnesota Press, 2002), 76–79.

10. Hegel could not address the question of the subject, nor a fortiori "make it speak" as Spirit, without having in mind the Kantian critique of transcendental paralogism: as per his usual habit, he will *revindicate*, in the name of an entirely other conception of the dialectic, what Kant wanted to *denounce* as an illusion. In this instance, it is a matter of positing that *one can* (and even that *one must*) confer substantiality upon the subjective function, but only on the condition that one identifies this substantiality with the "community" or "reciprocity" of singular and plural persons.

11. Jean-Pierre Lefebvre proposes another variant in his own translation of the *Phenomenology*: "*Un Je qui est un Nous, un Nous qui est un Je.*" Pierre-Jean Labarrière, for his part, translates between the two: "*Je qui [est] nous, et nous qui est Je.*"

12. Étienne Balibar, "*Ego sum, ego existo*: Descartes au point d'hérésie," lecture delivered at the Société Française de Philosophie on February 22, 1992. See Chapter 2 in this volume.

13. Testimony to the immediate effects of this Fichtian invention can be found in Hölderlin's fragment *Urteil und Sein* (dating probably from 1795): "'*Ich bin Ich' ist das passendste Beispiel zu diesem Begriffe der Urteilung, als theoretischer Urteilung, denn in der praktischen Urteilung setzt es sich dem nicht-Ich, nicht sich selbst entgegen . . . Aber dieses Sein muss nicht mit der Identität verwechselt werden. Wenn Ich sage: Ich bin Ich, so ist das Subjekt (Ich) und das Objeckt (Ich) nicht so vereiniget, dass gar keine Trennung vorgenommen werden kann, ohne das Wesen, desjenigen, was getrennt werden soll, zu verletzen; im Gegenteil: das Ich ist nur durch diese Trennung des Ichs vom Ich möglich. Wie kann Ich sagen: Ich! ohne Selbstbewusstsein? Wie ist aber Selbstbewusstsein möglich? Dadurch, das ich mich selbst entgegensetze*" (Friedrich Hölderlin, *Werke* [Munich: Carl Hanser Verlag, 1990], 597–98). ("'I am I' is the most fitting example for this concept of arche-separation as *theoretical* separation, for in the practical separation it [the "I"] opposes the *non-I, not itself* . . . If I say: I am I, the subject ("I") and the object ("I") are not united in such a way that no separation could be performed without violating the essence of what is to be separated, on the contrary, the I is only possible by means of this separation of the I from the I. How can I say: 'I'! without self-consciousness? Yet how is self-consciousness possible? In opposing myself to myself." Friedrich Hölderlin, *Essays and Letters on Theory*, trans. and ed. Thomas Pfau [Albany: SUNY Press, 1988], 37–38).] See Dieter Heinrich, *Grundlegung aus dem Ich: Untersuchungen zur Vorgeschichte des Idealismus, Tübingen–Jena 1790–1794* (Frankfurt: Suhrkamp, 2004). Translating these locutions into English, it is impossible not to think of the extraordinary precedent or model in Shakespeare's *Richard III*: "O coward conscience, how dost thou afflict me! / . . . Richard loves Richard; that is, I am I" (V.iii).

14. On the syntax and semantics of *Selbst* in German (which should be compared with the very different English word *self*), see Jean-Pierre Lefebvre, "Selbst," in *Dictionary of Untranslatables*, 946–947.

15. This expression can, in fact, be found in the *Phenomenology*, Chapter VIII.

16. On the introduction of the term (rare, but decisive in Hegel) of *Geschichtlichkeit* (that we translate here as *historicity*), see Leonhard von Renthe-Fink, *Geschichtlichkeit: Ihr terminologischer und begrifflicher Ursprung bei Hegel, Haym, Dilthey, und York* (Göttingen: Vandenhoek & Ruprecht, 1964). Renthe-Fink identifies two significant passages in Hegel's *Lectures on the Philosophy of History*—one on the Greeks, the other on the Church Fathers—whence it becomes clear that *Geschichtlichkeit*, whose correlative is *Heimatlichkeit*, refers to the fact that Spirit is "at home" in history: this is, in fact, the sense of the final developments of the *Phenomenology*, even if the word as such never appears there).

17. G. W. F. Hegel, *Phenomenology of Spirit*, 214, §351.

18. Ibid., 252, §418. (translation modified). The transcendental "category" of reason, which expresses the speculative unity of being and thought, is thus transformed, at least in principle, into an active rationality or a work of reason, which is the indivisible operation of "each and all." In very Rousseauistic fashion, starting with the subsequent section, even before communal spirit itself comes on stage, Hegel will present this operation by sketching a comparison between the work of the individual and the work of the State, the latter reducing the former to insignificance. On the "*Sache selbst*" and its interpretation as "*Tun aller und Jeder*," Marcuse usefully recalls the double signification of the Greek *to pragma*, from which *praxis* derives: "thing" and "work" or "operation." See Chapter 7 in this volume.

19. I borrow this formulation from Cassirer, who, in an extraordinary essay, "Sprache und Mythos: Ein Beitrag zum Problem der Götternamen" (1924), in *Wesen und Wirkung des Symbolbegriffs* (Darmstadt: Wissenschaftliche Buchgesellschaft, 1956), 135ff, compares the "*Weg über das Ich*" and "*der Weg über das Sein*" and thus points us toward the antithetical relation of Hegel's text to the theological tradition. On the chart, the page numbers refer to the Hoffmeister edition of the *Phenomenology* followed by those from the A. V. Miller translation, along with the mention of the corresponding chapters. I have left out the many approximate or indirect repetitions, such as "the tautology of consciousness," etc.

20. Alexandre Kojève, *Introduction to the Reading of Hegel*, ed. Allan Bloom, trans. James H. Nichols Jr. (Ithaca, N.Y.: Cornell University Press, 1969), 95.

21. Originally published in 1932 under the title *Hegels Ontologie und Grundlegung einer Theorie der Geschichtlichkeit* and first translated into English by Selya Benhabib in 1987. Herbert Marcuse, *Hegel's Ontology and Theory of Historicity*, trans. Seyla Benhabib (Cambridge, Mass.: MIT Press, 1987).

22. In his second commentary on the *Phenomenology*, published under the title *Phénoménologie de l'esprit de Hegel: Introduction à une lecture* (Paris: Aubier-Montaigne, 1979), Pierre-Jean Labarrière come close, it seems to me, to the guiding thread that I propose here. In a note on page 126, he indicates that "this Fichtian 'Ich bin Ich' . . . always expresses for Hegel the perfection of form; and one might say that the entire *Phenomenology of Spirit* inheres in the movement that permits recognition of this form at the same time as its actual fulfillment (or rather, the awakening to the fact that this form is always already concrete and loaded with actuality). Herein lies a privileged principle for recapitulating the content of the entire work; and it is not surprising to find it in prime position within each of the major developments." However, Labarrière does not consider the "tautology" *Ich =Ich* together with its various transformations—IWWI, SMMS, SIIS—which alone give it an experiential content by opposing the "I" to its others ("We," "They," "Being") wherein it must recognize itself. He sees perfectly well the "structuring function" of the repetition "I = I"; but, astonishingly, he does not see that only upon its final occurrence, in the chapter on absolute knowledge, when it is identified with the reflexivity of the *Selbst*, does this form get "loaded with actuality." In my opinion, it is impossible to claim, as Labarrière does, that this form is always still concrete, when, on the contrary, it is always already abstract, up until the final reversal. Another fascinating commentary is that of Ernst Tugendhat, which combines the

resources of analytic philosophy and a profound familiarity with German Idealism. But he believes that the reciprocity of the "Ich" and the "Wir" is a variant of the relation to the other, which falls under the general law of the "identity of identity and non-identity" formulated in Hegel's *Science of Logic*. See Ernst Tugendhat, *Selbstbewusstsein und Selbstbestimmung: Sprachanalytische Interpretationen* (Frankfurt am Main: Suhrkamp Taschenbuch, 1979), 338.

23. I say "Kant and Fichte" in order to follow Hegel's argument as closely as possible, but it is really Fichte, as we know, "retranslating" into dialectical language the Kant of the transcendental deduction and the paralogism of pure reason. See Heinrich, *Grundlegung aus dem Ich*.

24. One could also say, in a less polemical fashion that might bring us closer to the Spinoza of the *Tractatus Theologico-Politicus*: a *human substitute* for the ever inaudible divine voice (occupying, in a sense, the latter's "place" of utterance: *vicem dei*).

25. Hyppolite translates: "*la confession du mal: 'Voilà ce que je suis . . .'*" J. P. Lefebvre: "*l'aveu du Mal: c'est moi qui a fait ça . . .*" Labarrière: "*l'aveu du mal: c'est moi . . .*" Once again, we are reminded of Shakespeare's *Richard III*: "Is there a murderer here? No. Yes, I am" (V.iii).

26. Personal correspondence.

27. This is what Althusser, in his essay on "Ideology and Ideological State Apparatuses" (1970), calls the "structure of interpellation," referring to Exodus 3:14 on the vision of Moses at Sinai.

28. From a dialectical viewpoint, obviously, this means that the Rousseauist *law*, the sovereign people's "expression of the general will," brings about a negation of the negation in relation to the incarnation (Jesus Christ = *logos* = love), which itself was a negation of the Mosaic *law*. This remark should open a discussion of another aspect of Hegel's discourse that certainly overdetermines his reprisal of the Johannine utterances: that is, the fact that, in his youthful text on the Spirit of Christianity, Hegel offers, as a first version of the "word of spirit," an iteration or symmetrization of John's formula, "God is love"—"*Gott ist Liebe, die Liebe is Gott*," which we might schematize as GLLG (*Hegels Theologische Jugendschriften*, ed. Herman Nohl, 1907, 391). This formulation pertains at once to Hegel's "settling accounts" with Spinozist "pantheism" and to his intimate confrontation with Hölderlin's *Vereinigungsnungsphilosophie*. (Christoph Jamme likens it to the *Deus sive Natura*, such that he can speak of a "Johannine-Spinozist" theme in his book on Hegel and Hölderlin, *Ein ungelehrtes Buch: Die philosophische Gemeinschaft zwischen Hölderlin und Hegel in Frankfurt 1797–1800* (Bonn: Bouvier Verlag, 1983), 180). Of course, this formulation also rediscovers the schema of biblical writing, close to the ritual invocation that is typical of the Gospel of John ("In the beginning was the Word, and the Word was with God, and the Word was God . . ."). See Daniel Weidner, "Gemeinschaft des Geistes und Härte des Buchstabens: Georg W. F. Hegel," in *Bibel und Literatur um 1800* (Munich: Wilhelm Fink Verlag, 2011), 236–245.

29. For the same reason, in the interpretation of Descartes that appears earlier in this volume, I privileged the assertion from the Gospel of John 8: 24, etc.—"I am"—which repeats Exodus 3:14—"I am who I am"—to the detriment of more "theoretical" (or more "onto-theological") considerations on the finite image of the infinite that is supposed to bring the divine model down into man (or to make the latter into the emanation of the former). Instead of pursuing a discussion of why theological models always inevitably give way to secularization, I thereby sought to raise the question of the heretical and blasphemous utterances that mark the outset of modernity.

30. Hegel, *Phenomenology of Spirit*, 408, §670.

31. The First Epistle of John also contains a series of almost identical utterances, developing the idea of "God is Love": "Beloved, let us love one another, for love is from God, and whoever loves has been born of God and knows God. Anyone who does not love does not know God, because God is love . . . In this is love, not that we have loved God but that he loved us and sent his Son to be the propitiation for our sins. . . . God abides in us and his love is perfected in us. By this we know that we abide in him and he in us (*Daran erkennen wir, daß wir in ihm bleiben und er in uns*) . . . and whoever abides in love abides in God, and God abides in him" (1 John 4:7–17).

32. Jean-Jacques Rousseau, *The Social Contract* and the *First and Second Discourses*, ed. and intro. Susan Dunn (New Haven: Yale University Press, 2002), 164. [The italics are in the original French text but not in the English translation, which, instead, features quotation marks. I have restored the italics.—Trans.] One might underscore that Rousseau expresses in terms of the gift and the law what John expresses in terms of love and grace. At the vertical of "grace" that men receive by loving "one another" (*allelous*), in John, is the Father who is the origin of this love and the Son who transmits the commandment. In Rousseau's reduction of this verticality, the place of the origin is not annulled, but there is "no one" to occupy it. Further, from another viewpoint, it is from this very place, vacated by the absence of the Father or the Master, that the collective voice—one and many at the same time—speaks, that the collective gift is "actualized" in the declaration: "Each of us puts in common . . ." This was already, in fact, the case with the Hobbesian performative enunciation of the contract, leading to the absolute subjection to the Sovereign it creates (*Leviathan*, Chap. 17), which Rousseau repeats and subverts. Hegel maintains the horizontality (or the plane of immanence) but now calls "Spirit" that which is mutually declared therein.

33. This is not the place, regretfully, to study two distant and ultimately parodic utterances of sovereignty, between which *The Social Contract* functions as a pivot (the "The State is me," attributed to Louis XIV and the "*Ich, der Staat, bin das Volk*" that Nietzsche fictioned in *Also sprach Zarathustra*. Nor can we study the precursors to Rousseau's formulations of the *Social Contract* in his earlier texts: the *Discourse on Political Economy* reprises the adage, *vox populi, vox dei*; the *Geneva Manuscript* contains a weaker version of the same utterance that upholds the "common self," without italics, not as a form of self-reference, but as a metaphysical principle of life and will). Norbert Elias has attempted a "sociologico-linguistic deduction" of such utterances: "the princes . . . could regard the whole state organization, including the population, as a kind of personal property. They said 'we' not in relation to the population but to themselves. The dictum ascribed to Louis XIV, 'I am the state,' shows a specific fusion of 'we' and 'I' . . . The population, for their part, perceived the autocratic princely state to only a low degree as a layer of their we-groups, and very much as a grouping to be spoken and thought of in the third person, as 'they,' not 'we.' The princes and nobles, we can say, saw the state largely as their own state, as a we-unit confined to themselves, and the mass of the population as people with whom they did not identify themselves. They alone, as the established group, formed the state. The mass of the population were perceived only as 'they' and as outsiders." Norbert Elias, "Changes in the We-I Balance," in *The Society of Individuals* (New York: Continuum Books, 1991), 206. Inversely, the revolutionary narrative or testimony that allows a messenger to become the representative of a whole people's consciousness of oppression confuses the "I" and the "We" in a single utterance effects a transition from private to public (for example: *I, Rigoberta Menchu: An Indian Woman in Guatemala*, trans. Ann Wright (New York: Verso Books, 2010).

34. Jean-Jacques Rousseau, *The Social Contract* and the *First and Second Discourses*, 165.

35. See Étienne Balibar, "Apories rousseauistes," in *L'anthropologie et le politique selon Jean-Jacques Rousseau*, ed. Michèle Cohen-Halimi, *Les Cahiers philosophiques de Strasbourg*, 13:22.

36. Jean-Jacques Rousseau, *The Social Contract*, II.6: "But when the whole people decree concerning the whole people, they consider themselves alone; and if a relation is then constituted, it is between the whole object under one point of view and the whole object under another point of view" (179).

37. Although not without latent contradiction. Let us set aside this point that has to do with patriotism and cosmopolitanism.

38. Jean-Jacques Rousseau, *The Social Contract* and the *First and Second Discourses*, 166. On the passage from naturalist models (in particular, chemical ones) to pragmatic models of the "general will," going by way of a critique of the theological and juridical tradition, see Bruno Berardi, *La fabrique des concepts: Recherches sur l'invention conceptuelle chez Rousseau* (Paris: Honoré Champion, 2006).

39. This means that Rousseau's construction, in Hegel's eyes, is not pure theory; or rather that it is the incursion of pure theory as such into the real of politics and history; it is theory actualizing or realizing itself—that is, "spirit." Indeed, from this viewpoint, Rousseau is for Hegel, as for Louis-Sébastien Mercier, "one of the principal authors of the Revolution"—and even *the* principal author. See James Swenson, *On Jean-Jacques Rousseau: Considered as One of the First Authors of the Revolution* (Stanford: Stanford University Press, 2000).

40. This is a moment that Hegel frequently aligns—at least in his early work—with a Roman, but also Jewish, model of *formalism*. Of course, he will change his mind in *Elements of the Philosophy of Right*.

41. I return to this question in a later essay, "*Zur Sache selbst*: On the Common and the Universal in Hegel's *Phenomenology of Spirit*." See Chapter 7 in this volume.

42. That is, as well, a "mediator" who as such would not be *death* (for men or by them). [As it happens, A. V. Miller's English translation of Hegel's German phrase as "mediating minister" does double duty as a translation of Hyppolite's French translation of the same phrase. See G. W. F. Hegel, *Phenomenology of Spirit*, trans. A. V. Miller, 138.—Trans.]

43. "Death becomes transfigured from its immediate meaning, viz. the non-being of this particular individual, into the universality of the Spirit who dwells in His community, dies in it everyday, and is daily resurrected." G. W. F. Hegel, *Phenomenology of Spirit*, trans. A. V. Miller, 475.

6. THE MESSIANIC MOMENT IN MARX

This text was first published in "Theologies politiques du *Vormärz*: De la doctrine à l'action (1817–1850)," *Revue Germanique Internationale* 8 (2008): 143–160.

1. Heinrich Heine, "Die armen Weber" (Die schlesischen Weber), published June 10, 1844, on the front page of *Vorwärts*. Aristide Bruant is perhaps recalling these lines when, in 1894, he writes a "chant des canuts" (song of the canuts): "*C'est nous les canuts, Nous allons tout nus! / Mais nôtre règne arrivera / Quand votre règne finira. (bis) / Nous tisserons le linceul du vieux monde, / Car on entend déjà la révolte qui gronde! / C'est nous les canuts, Nous n'irons plus nus!*" [The *canuts* were weavers, protagonists of a tragic uprising in Lyons, that took place in 1831 and remained a touchstone of nineteenth-century revolutionary memory].

2. "A Contribution to the Critique of Hegel's Philosophy Right. Introduction (1843–44)," in Karl Marx, *Early Writings*, trans. Rodney Livingstone and Gregor Benton (New York: Penguin Books, 1992), 243–258. Hereafter, for the German text, I will rely upon *Einleitung* in *Marx-Engels Werke* (Berlin: Dietz Verlag, 1970), 1:378–391.

3. Karl Marx, *Zur Kritik des Hegelschen Staatsrecht*, in *Marx-Engels Werke*, 1:201–333; "Critique of Hegel's Doctrine of the State," in *Early Writings*, 57–198. I will cite the first edition of Miguel Abensour's essay, "Marx et le moment machiavélien: 'Vraie démocratie' et modernité," in *Phénoménologie et politique: Mélanges offertes à Jacques Taminiaux* (Brussels: Éditions Ousia, 1989), 17–114. See also *Democracy Against the State: Marx and the Machiavellian Movement*, trans. Max Blechman (Cambridge: Polity Press, 2011).

4. In his article, "Proletariat, Pöbel, Pauperismus," which appears in *Geschichtliche Grundbegriffe: Historisches Lexikon der politisch-sozialen Sprache in Deutschland* (Stuttgart: Klett Verlag, 1972–97), Werner Conze shows how, in Germany, during the years 1835–40, the word "proletariat," imported from the lexicon of the French socialists, replaced Pöbel ("populace"), which Hegel used to designate the masses who went "without" (without property, without domicile, without profession, and without status) or the pauperized class outside the corporate system of "civil-bourgeois society" (*bürgerliche Gesellschaft*). In the context of increasing social antagonisms, the word ends up naming the salaried workers whose interests are opposed to those of manufacturing capital. Conze then compares the way in which two "Hegelians" make use of the word: Lorenz

von Stein (1842), for whom it names the internal enemy of industrial society, and Marx (1844), for whom it becomes the agent of the "decomposition" of the existing order. For his part, Georges Labica, in his article "Proletariat," from the *Dictionnaire critique du marxisme* (Paris: Presses Universitaires de France, 1982), insists upon the role of Moses Hess both in Marx's discovery of the term "proletariat" in his reading of Stein and in his connection of a critique of pauperization with a philosophy of action.

5. Karl Marx, *Early Writings*, 257.

6. Stathis Kouvelakis, in an important study, *Philosophy and Revolution: From Kant to Marx*, trans. G. M. Goshgarian (New York: Verso Books, 2003), refers on several occasions to this "sign" of commonality between Marx and Heine in 1844. He proposes an incontestable conjunctural interpretation that links this sign to the circulation of the revolutionary problematic between France and Germany in the first half of the nineteenth century; but he does not explore the allegorical dimension that will be important to me here.

7. Heinrich Heine, "From the Introduction to 'Kahldorf on the Nobility in Letters to Count M. von Moltke' (1831)," in *On the History of Religion and Philosophy in Germany and Other Writings*, ed. Terry Pinkard (Cambridge: Cambridge University Press, 2007), 130–131. Further testimony to the influence of these sentences on Marx, he evoked them once again in his article from November 12, 1848, in the *Neue Rheinische Zeitung*, addressing the cycle of revolutions and counterrevolutions in Europe: "*Vom Paris aus wird der gallische Hahn noch einmal Europa wachkrähen*" (from Paris the Gallic cock will once again waken Europe). But the work from which Marx primarily derived his conception of the influence of the Lutheran Reformation upon philosophy and of the "revolutionary" meaning common to German idealism (Kant, Fichte, Hegel) and modern French politics is *On the History of Religion and Philosophy in Germany* (1834–35).

8. It behooves us to see the rooster's crowing identified as an eschatological trumpet (*schmettern*) as the condensation of two allegorical lineages. The "Gallic rooster" is a French national symbol invented in the Renaissance, which, during the Revolution, became associated with the idea of fraternity. The Consulate had it imprinted on coins; the July 1830 revolution had it printed on flags; and only later would it be appropriated for use by the military and in sports. The crowing of the rooster that announces the imminence of sunrise is messianic theme both Christian (initially linked to "Saint Peter's denial of Jesus" in the Gospels of Matthew and Luke) and Jewish (going back to the Babylonian exile: see JewishEncyclopedia.com, "Cock").

9. See, in particular, Jean-Pierre Lefebvre, "Marx und Heine," in *Schriften aus dem Karl-Marx Haus* (Trier, 1972); Jacques Grandjonc, *Marx et les communistes allemands à Paris* (Paris: Maspero, 1974); Lucien Calvié, *Le renard et les raisins: La révolution française et les intellectuels allemands (1789–1845)* (Paris: Edi, 1989); Christoph Marx, *Heinrich Heine als politischer Dichter und das Ideologische Verhältnis zu Karl Marx 1843/44* (GRIN Verlag für Akademische Texte, 1997 [ebook]); Stathis Kouvelakis, *Philosophy and Revolution: From Kant to Marx* (New York: Verso, 2003).

10. Karl Marx, *Early Writings*, 244.

11. As we know, Marxists after Engels, and then after Ernst Bloch, will consider this war to be the first historical appearance of the revolutionary proletariat in Germany. The conflict between Luther and Münzer is periodically reactivated within the history of Protestantism, with or without a "political" translation, particularly in the form of an opposition between the "Jesus of History" and the "Christ of the Church." See John Lewis, "The Jesus of History," in *Christianity and the Social Revolution* (New York: Scribner's, 1935).

12. Pierre Leroux, *De l'Humanité: De son principe et son avenir* (1840) (Paris: Corpus des Oeuvres de philosophie en langue française, Fayard, 1985).

13. Hugo Assmann and Franz Hinkelammert, *L'idolâtrie du marché* (Paris: Éditions du Cerf, 1993). See also Michael Löwy's commentary, *Marxism and Liberation Theology* (Amsterdam: International Institute for Research and Education, 1988) and his book *The War of Gods: Religion and Politics in Latin America* (New York: Verso, 1996).

14. "The plan of this work is quite simple. There are three questions that we have to ask of ourselves: 1) What is the Third Estate?—*Everything*; 2) What, until now, has it been in the existing political order?—*Nothing*; 3) What does it want to be?—*Something*." Emmanuel-Joseph Sieyès, *What is the Third Estate?* in *Political Writings*, ed. and trans. Michael Sonenscher (Indianapolis: Hackett, 2003), 92–161. On the importance, for Marx in 1843, of the thought and action of Sieyès, who founded national unity upon the "self-determination of the people," see Jacques Guilhaumou, "Marx, la Révolution française et le *Manuscrit de Kreuznach*," in *Marx démocrate: Le Manuscrit de 1843, de la modernité*, ed. Étienne Balibar and Gérard Raulet (Paris: Presses Universitaires de France, 2001), 79–88; and Antonio Negri, *Insurgencies: Constituent Power and the Modern State*, trans. Maurizia Boscagli (Minneapolis: University of Minnesota Press, 2009). The entire opening couplet of the "Internationale," written in 1871 by Eugène Pottier, is homogenous with Marx's *Einleitung*: "*Debout! les damnés de la terre / Debout! les forçats de la faim / La raison tonne en son cratère: / C'est l'eruption de la fin / Du passé faisons table rase / Foule esclave, debout! debout! / Le monde va changer de base: / Nous ne sommes rien, soyons tout!*" (Arise! the wretched of the earth! / Arise! the prisoners of want! / For Reason in revolt now thunders / It's the eruption of the end / Let's wipe away the past / Enslaved masses, arise! arise! / The world will change its basis / We are nothing, let us be everything).

15. John of the Cross, "The Ascent of Mount Carmel," II.4, in *Selected Writings* (New York: Paulist Press, 1988). See Stanislas Breton, *Esquisses du politique* (Paris: Messidor, 1991), 37–38: "The force of early Marxism, which was both critical and prophetic, lies in the fact that it took, very much against the spirit of the epoch, the supposedly inert mass of humanity and converted it from a "class of nothings" into a transformative force of universal amplitude and unprecedented intensity. Such is, if I am not mistaken, the deep meaning of the "nothing" and the "everything" in their reciprocal implication, which underlies the faith in a new chosen people, after centuries of scorn."

16. On this point, one might read Georges G. M. Cottier's developments, in *L'athéisme du jeune Marx: Ses origines hégéliennes* (Paris: J. Vrin, 1959), on the Christological heritage of "kenosis" in the figure of the proletariat, such as it is characterized, or rather announced, in Marx's *Einleitung*: "The *Proletariat*, shouldering universal suffering, is the echo of the Suffering Servant in Isaiah. He is the Messiah, and, much like the Christ of a certain Lutheran theology, he must, in order to accomplish his redemptive mission, begin as sin and malediction . . . the positive in order to be must *empty* itself into its *other*" (176). Most of all, however, one might examine how the motif of the identification of the proletariat with Christ as the incarnation of universal human suffering follows a trajectory that passes from Ernst Bloch's "utopian Marxism" to the "theology of the Cross" (Moltmann), and from there to the Liberation theologians. See Richard J. Baukham, *Moltmann: Messianic Theology in the Making* (London: Marshall Pickering, 1987). On this point, Jean-Luc Nancy, in his essay, "The Unsacrifiable," considers Marx's text together with that of Hegel. *A Finite Thinking*, trans. Simon Sparks et al. (Stanford: Stanford University Press, 2003), 51–77.

17. Certain philosophers have been particularly sensitive to this ethical dimension of Marx's messianism, linked to the problematic of "absolute wrong." In a crucial passage from his book *The Differend* (Minneapolis: University of Minnesota Press, 1989), Jean-François Lyotard cites Marx's *Einleitung* and shows that its revindication of an emancipation derived from an "absolute wrong" (*Unrecht schlechthin*) entails an abolition of genres and species, and thus opens a communication of humanity with itself in the utterance of its suffering (§§236–237).

18. See, in particular, Gershom Scholem, "The Messianic Idea in Kabbalism," in *The Messianic Idea in Judaism and Other Essays in Jewish Spirituality* (New York: Schocken Books, 1995), 37–48. According to a certain Jewish tradition, the people of Israel in exile from the whole world, whose "reparation" it promises, is itself a "messiah-people" at the service of all humanity; and, for this reason, it could be called the "people of peoples," much like Marx's proletariat is, because of the resolution it brings to the problem of revolution, the "people of the people."

19. Karl Marx and Friedrich Engels, *The Communist Manifesto: A Modern Edition* (New York: Verso Books, 2012). The thematic of the *chains of slavery* (which, with the strange expression, "radical chains," forges the link between the *Einleitung* and the conclusion of the Manifesto, but can also be found in Capital in the form of "invisible chains" that bind the proletariat to the conditions of its exploitation), is a sure sign that Marx's text belongs to the messianic discourse of the "exodus from Egypt." Nonetheless, it would be simplifying too much to rely exclusively upon this reference, because Greco-Roman antiquity also handed down to us a problematic of overturning slavery into sovereignty. The two traditions are fused together in the work of Saint Paul with the idea of an apostle who would make himself the "slave of all." See Dale B. Martin, *Slavery as Salvation: The Metaphor of Slavery in Pauline Christianity* (New Haven: Yale University Press, 1990). For a contemporary echo of the idea of an overturning of slavery into sovereignty, see Jacques Rancière, "The Community of Equals," in *On the Shores of Politics*, trans. Liz Heron (New York: Verso, 2007), 63–92.

20. Enrique Dussel has studied "Marx's theological metaphors" in *Las metaforas de Marx* (Estella: El Verbo Divino, 1993); but his study primarily concerns the theory of "commodity fetishism" and pertains to hermeneutics rather than the history of ideas.

21. See Jacques Droz, "Le socialisme allemande du *Vormärz*," in *Histoire générale du socialisme*, Vol. 1: *Des origines à 1875* (Paris: Presses Universitaires de France, 1972), 424ff; Auguste Cornu, *Karl Marx et Friedrich Engels: Leur vie et leur oeuvre*, Tome 2: *Du libéralisme démocratique au communisme* (Paris: Presses Universitaires de France, 1958), 150ff. On Hess, see Edmund Silberner, *Moses Hess* (Leiden: Brill, 1966).

22. Eric Voegelin, "Marx: The Genesis of Gnostic Socialism," in *From Enlightenment to Revolution* (Durham, N.C.: Duke University Press, 1975), 282.

23. See Étienne Balibar, "Fichte and the Internal Border: On *Addresses to the German Nation*," in *Masses, Classes, Ideas: Studies in Politics and Philosophy Before and After Marx*, trans. James Swenson (New York: Routledge, 1994), 61–84; *The Selected Writings of August Cieskowski*, ed. and trans. André Liebich (Cambridge: Cambridge University Press, 1979). What Fichte calls "nation" or "people" cannot be reduced to what has today become a banal alternative between *demos* and *ethnos*: in order to interpret it, a third category is necessary, that of *laos* (a Homeric word that the Septuagint used to "translate" the Hebrew *'am*, the chosen people of God as opposed to the *goyim*). A general comparative study could not, in any event, be limited to the European context. As Pocock showed in *The Machiavellian Moment* (Princeton: Princeton University Press, 1975), the theme of the "Elect Nation" traveled with the English Puritans to America in the seventeenth century. In the 1840s, then, was forged the terminology of the "manifest destiny" of the American people that made it possible to see it as a "new Israel." See Anders Stephanson, *Manifest Destiny: American Expansionism and the Empire of Right* (New York: Hill and Wang, 1996).

24. One thereby affords oneself the possibility of completing, and perhaps of rectifying, Foucault's brilliant insights in his course at the Collège de France (1975–76) on the theme of "race war" between the seventeenth and nineteenth centuries and the role that it played in the formation of modern discourses of the nation, class, and race. Michel Foucault, *Society Must be Defended: Lectures at the Collège de France, 1975–1976*, trans. David Macey (New York: Picador, 2003).

25. "If we quash servitude even in its last hope for a hiding place, which is heaven; if we rescue the god that dwells on earth, within us, from his abasement; if we become God's redeemers; if we restore dignity to the impoverished people, who have become disinherited of their happiness, and to genius that has been mocked and to beauty that has been desecrated, as our great master have proclaimed in word and song . . . the whole world will become German! It is of this mission and this universal dominion on the part of Germany that I often dream when I wander beneath the oak trees. This is *my* patriotism." Heinrich Heine, *Germany: A Winter's Tale*, trans. Edgar Alfred Bowring (New York: Mondial, 2007), v. See Christoph Marx, *Heinrich Heine als politischer Dichter und das ideologische Verhältnis zu Karl Marx 1843/44* (Munich: GRIN Verlag, 2007), 19. In

Philosophy and Revolution, Stathis Kouvelakis, in my opinion, offers the correct interpretation when he insists upon Heine's overturning of "Teutomaniac" discourse. At the same moment, Engels was discovering the revolutionary disposition and universal humanity of the English proletariat. Friedrich Engels, *The Condition of the Working Class in England*, ed. and intro. David McLellan (Oxford: Oxford University Press, 2009).

26. On the historical references and the uses of the term "emancipation," see Karl Martin Grass and Reinhart Koselleck, "Emanzipation," in *Geschichtliche Grundbegriffe: Historisches Lexikon zur politisch-sozialen Sprache in Deutschland*, eds. Otto Bruner, Werner Conze, and Reiner Koselleck (Stuttgart: Ernst Klett Verlag, 1972); and Gérard Bensussan, "Emancipation," in *Dictionnaire critique du marxisme*, eds. Gérard Bensussan and Georges Labica (Paris: Presses Universitaires de France, 1982).

27. This claim especially applies to the concept of the *proletariat*, which "signs" the *Einleitung*, but which the *Manuscripts of 1844* ignore in favor of *work* and *the worker*—with one exception, which is, in truth, remarkable: "It goes without saying that national economy regards the proletarian . . . as nothing more than a *worker*. . . . It does not consider him, during the time when he is not working, as a human being. It leaves this to criminal law, doctors, religion, statistical tables, politics and the beadle" (Marx, *Early Writings*, 288).

28. On this point, I absolutely concur with Abensour's remark: "at that moment in his development Marx had not yet decided in an unequivocal way on the apparently sovereign direction he attributed retrospectively to the unpublished manuscript of 1843 . . . to the detriment of the tensions and multiple possibilities of this unfinished essay" (Miguel Abensour, *Democracy Against the State*, 40). These virtualities, obviously more interesting today than the systematizations of "Marxism," are what I am seeking to complete with a supplementary element.

29. I will not restate here what I have underscored elsewhere (in *Marx démocrate*), i.e. that the singularity of the writing of Marx's text inserts itself into and thereby reveals the "dialogism" of Hegel's own text.

30. I will not discuss further this ultrasensitive point for appreciating the relation between Marx's thought and the use that his successors made of it. See my *The Philosophy of Marx*, trans. Chris Turner (New York: Verso, reprint edition, 2014).

31. This translation, borrowed from Albert Baraquin, which serves Abensour's project quite well, deserves some discussion. The German text speaks, more precisely, of "moments of the totality of the demos" (*Die Demokratie ist die Wahrheit der Monarchie, die Monarchie is nicht die Wahrheit der Demokratie . . . In der Demokratie erlangt keines der Momente eine andere Bedeutung, als ihm zukommt. Jedes ist wirklich nur Moment des ganzen Demos. In der Monarchie bestimmt ein Teil den Charakter des Ganzen* [Marx-Engels Werke, 1:230]).

32. At this point, of course, one might discuss a number of Abensour's readings. The Marx text that he relies upon (showing very clearly its relation to contemporary French socialist writings, especially Victor Considérant's *Manifesto of Democracy in the 19th Century*, published in 1843) does not evoke "true democracy" as a figure but rather says that "*die neueren Franzosen haben dies so aufgefasst, dass in der wahren Demokratie der politischen Staat untergehe*" (*Mark-Engels Werke*, 1:232). This is to say that, according to the most recent French authors, the political State is extinguished, or abolished, in "veritable democracy," when it truly becomes what it must be. There is no doubt, however, that this perspective corresponds to the hypothesis of a democratic or popular principle at work within the succession of regimes (whose "truth" it constitutes), and leading, at least ideally, toward the withering away of the State as a separate organism. Shlomo Avineri, in *The Social and Political Thought of Karl Marx* (Cambridge: Cambridge University Press, 1968) goes further than Abensour in the hypostasis of the expression "true democracy." His reference point is not the "total demos" but the "universal class," not Machiavelli but Hegel as the thinker of the "political."

33. Miguel Absenour, *Democracy Against the State*, 69.

34. Ibid., 74–75.

35. Frank Fischbach, in his own commentary upon this constellation of texts, "L'agir libéré (Marx)" (in *L'être et l'acte: Enquête sur les fondements de l'ontologie moderne de l'agir* [Paris: Vrin, 2002], 131ff), insists upon Marx's fusion, within the social or transindividual subject of revolutionary transformation, of the determinations of *acting* and *making* (which translates the category of what *The German Ideology* calls *Selbstbetätigung*). It seems to me that this fusion is also the mainspring of what I am here calling the "plenitude" of the political subject. The difficulty is that, to be able to be a *subject*, and thus *a* subject, the "people"—with respect to the class struggle—must be at the same time one "part" (or one "camp") and "virtually" the *whole*. The *Communist Manifesto* will make this claim: at the final stage of capitalist evolution, the proletariat is (as Sieyès's Third Estate once was) the "immense majority." Whereas the 1844 Introduction risks the "mystical" thesis: the proletariat is the "everything" because it is "nothing" anymore.

36. *Marx-Engels Werke*, 1:259: "*damit der Mensch mit Bewusstsein tut, was er sonst ohne Bewusstsein durch die Natur der Sache gezwungen wird zu tun, ist es notwendig, dass die Bewegung der Verfassung, dass der* Fortschritt zum Prinzip der Verfassung *gemacht wird, dass also der wirkliche Träger der Verfassung, das Volk, zum Prinzip der Verfassung gemacht wird.*"

37. "*wo in ihrer Besonderheit als das Herrschende auftrat*" (*Marx-Engels Werke*, 1:260).

38. "Germany, as a world of its own embodying all the deficiencies of the present political age, will not be able to overcome the specifically German limitations without overcoming the limitations of the present political age." Marx, *Early Writings*, 253.

39. One cannot elude the question of an affinity with the way in which Derrida, in *Specters of Marx* (1993), works with the eschatological image of Shakespeare's *Hamlet* in order to interpret the Marxian conception of the communist revolution to come: "The time is out of joint." However, Derrida cites many of Marx's works but never the *Einleitung*. This is because, it seems to me, his interpretation aims to cast into relief the heritage of a "messianicity without messianism," and thus, a fortiori, without a figure of the messiah—which the proletariat of 1844 is par excellence. On this point, at least, there is a contradiction between the two points of view.

40. Marx, *Early Writings*, 257.

41. Auguste Comte, *Discours sur l'esprit positif* (1844): Part 3, "Conditions d'avènement de l'école positive." Comte's project of an "alliance" rests essentially upon a program of "higher" popular education designed to surmount the social division that endangers the pursuit of progress as the development of order, and by gathering the forces opposed to the theological and metaphysical spirit (science, industry) to found the possibility of a new spiritual power, putting an end to the era of revolutions. In this sense, Comte's project is the opposite of Marx's. Pierre Macherey discusses the parallel in his commentary on the expression, "*Im Anfang war die Tat*" and its interpretations (http://stl.recherche.univ-lille3.fr/seminaires/philosophie/macherey/Macherey20012002/Macherey2trimestre1.html).

42. Marx, *Early Writings*, 257. Marx arrives at this formulation at the end of the *Einleitung* after three previous attempts, which it "solves" but also converts into a "slogan" (*Lösung/Losung*): (1) "*Ihr könnt die Philosophie nicht aufheben, ohne sie zu verwicklichen* [you cannot sublate philosophy without realizing it]"; (2) "*Sie glaubte, die Philosophie verwicklichen zu können, ohne sie aufzuheben* [It believed it possible to realize philosophy without sublating it"; (3) "*Die Waffe der Kritik kann allerdings die Kritik der Waffen nicht ersetzen* [The weapon of criticism cannot replace the criticism of weapons]" (Ibid., 250, 251). These formulations approach a transcendental reciprocity in the form: Concepts without intuition are empty, intuitions without concept are blind.

43. Michael Löwy, *La théorie de la révolution chez le jeune Marx* (Paris: Maspero, 1979), 69. I have no intention of diminishing the merits of this book which includes very useful explications, and which its author followed up with fundamental studies on the importance of the "utopian" and "messianic" elements in Marxism.

44. See also Marx's formulations in his correspondence with Ruge, published in the inaugural issue of the *Deutsch-Französische Jahrbücher* (1844), on critique as the world's internalization (*innewerden*) of its own consciousness (*Marx-Engels Werke*, 1:346).

45. Marx, *Early Writings*, 257.

46. Immediately after he composed the *Einleitung*, Marx will find the verification of his thinking in the insurrection of the Silesian weavers. This will provide the occasion for his break with liberal democrats such as Ruge, the coeditor of the *Deutsche-Französische Jahrbücher* (see the *Kritische Randglossen zu dem Artikel "Der König von Preussen une die Sozialreform. Von einem Preussen*, July 31, 1844, *Marx-Engels Werke*, 1:392ff). The fact that the insurgents adopted Heine's poem "Die armen Weber," which he himself published in the *Vorwärts*, as a song of struggle and sorrow, gave Marx proof that the German proletariat is the "most theoretical" in Europe. In this proletariat, the difference between the head and the heart vanishes; the two sides of critical passivity are not really separate; and thus praxis is *already there*.

47. In truth, this conjunction is not absent in Machiavelli himself: not the Machiavelli of the *Discorsi*, who is Abensour's privileged reference, but rather he of *The Prince*, the final chapter of which invokes the coming of a "redeemer" who would save Italy from the dissolutive and antinational action of the Church.

48. Even before the *Communist Manifesto*, in fact, this difficulty was central to Marx's formulations in *The Poverty of Philosophy* (1846) on the "political" character of the "class struggle" between capital and the coalition of proletarians aligned against it, a struggle that opens toward a "total revolution" excluding any "new political power" (Chapter II, §5, "Strikes and Combinations of Workers").

49. Karl Löwith, *Meaning in History: The Theological Implications of the Philosophy of History* (Chicago: University of Chicago Press, 1949), Chapter II: "Marx," 33–51.

7. *ZUR SACHE SELBST*: THE COMMON AND THE UNIVERSAL IN HEGEL'S PHENOMENOLOGY OF SPIRIT

The first part of this chapter first appeared in Irde 52 (2008), a special issue entitled "Bicentenaire de la Phénoménologie de l'esprit de Hegel" (The Bicentennial of Hegel's Phenomenology of Spirit). The entire piece was then presented as a contribution to the conference "200 ans de Phénoménologie de l'esprit" (200 years of Phenomenology of Spirit), December 13–14, Université de Paris IV, organized by Danielle Cohen-Lévinas, Joseph Cohen, and Raphaël Zagury-Ory.

1. Alexandre Kojève, *Introduction to the Reading of Hegel: Lectures on the Phenomenology of Spirit*, ed. Allan Bloom, trans. James H. Nichols (Ithaca, N.Y.: Cornell University Press, 1969), 95; Herbert Marcuse, *Hegel's Ontology and the Theory of Historicity*, trans. Seyla Benhabib (Cambridge, Mass.: MIT Press, 1987), 267ff; Georg Lukács, *The Young Hegel*, trans. Rodney Livingstone (Cambridge, Mass.: MIT Press, 1977), 484ff.

2. Jean-Paul Sartre, *Critique of Dialectical Reason*, Volume 1, trans. Alan Sheridan-Smith (New York: Verso, 2004).

3. Jean-Luc Nancy, *The Inoperative Community*, trans. Peter Connor et al. (Minneapolis: University of Minnesota Press, 1991); Maurice Blanchot, *The Unavowable Community*, trans. Pierre Joris (Barrytown, N.Y.: Station Hill Press, 1988); Jacques Derrida, *The Politics of Friendship*, trans. George Collins (New York: Verso, 1997). A neighboring problematic has been developed in Italy in the work of Roberto Esposito (who is, in any case, perfectly well versed in the French debates), under the heading of the "impolitical." To my knowledge, Esposito does not comment on Hegel directly, but, in an important chapter from his book, *Nove pensieri sulla politica* (Bologna: Il Mulino, 1993), devoted to a commentary on Karl Barth's *The Epistle to the Romans*, he studies the relation between the two theological notions of the world as "work" and as "workable" by man as the "center" of creation, and their inversion within the perspective of negative theology,

thereby suggesting that it would be important to study the Paulinian ancestry of Hegelian questions (which I do not do here).

4. Maurice Blanchot, "La littérature et le droit à la mort," first published in *Critique* in 1948, then as the conclusion to *La part du feu* (Paris: Gallimard, 1949). For an English translation, see Maurice Blanchot, *The Work of Fire*, trans. Charlotte Mandell (Stanford: Stanford University Press, 1995), 300ff. See also James Swenson, "Revolutionary Sentences," *Yale French Studies* 93 (1998): 11–29.

5. See, in particular, Otto Pöggeler, "Die Komposition der Phänomenologie des Geistes," in *Materialien zu Hegels Phänomenologie des Geistes*, ed. Hans Friedrich Fulda and Dieter Heinrich (Berlin: Suhrkamp, 1973), 329–390.

6. On the stylistic particularities of the *Phenomenology*, see Jean-Pierre Lefebvre's "Avant-propos" to his French translation of the work (Paris: Aubier-Montaigne, 1991) and the article, "German," in *Dictionary of Untranslatables: A Philosophical Lexicon*, ed. Barbara Cassin, trans. Steven Rendall et al. (Princeton: Princeton University Press, 2014), 385–391.

7. Françoise Dastur, *Hölderlin: Le retournement natal* (La Versanne: Encre Marine, 1997).

8. G. W. F. Hegel, *System of Ethical Life and First Philosophy of Spirit*, ed. and trans. H. S. Harris and T. M. Knox (Albany: SUNY Press, 1998).

9. One will find the counterproof in the excellent work of Franck Fischbach, *L'être et l'acte: Enquête sur les fondements de l'ontologie moderne de l'agir* (Paris: Vrin, 2002) (Chapter II: "L'esprit en acte: Hegel"). There is no commentary on *TAJ* because the author concentrates on the way in which the later Hegel (the "system-builder" of the *Science of Logic*, the *Philosophy of Right*, and the *Encyclopedia*) fuses the theoretical Idea and the practical Idea within a single doctrine of the "pure activity of the spirit," identified with the ontological necessity of freedom. This is not to say, of course, that such analyses are of no help to the reading of the *Phenomenology*, even if they exacerbate the difference between the points of view. More surprising is the impasse of Bernard Bourgeois in the section of his book, *Hegel: Les actes de l'esprit* (Paris: Vrin, 2001), devoted to "action" (particularly 161–171), in which the question of the "double affirmation of individuality and the universal," insofar as it is distributed "among singular individuals assembling their interaction into a collective individuality," is discussed with reference at once to the *Phenomenology*, the *Logic*, and the *Philosophy of History*. This would seem to be because Bourgeois inscribes the set of these developments on action into the perspective of the constitution of a State ("The communitarian site of action is political life in the state. We know that, for Hegel, the State alone is fully affirmative, because it affirms the one through the other, the freedom of the individual through the authority of the whole"). It is doubtful that this applies to the *Phenomenology*, which is the most "astatist" of Hegel's works (and perhaps the only one—but this is another debate, going on since Rosenzweig's assertions in *Hegel und der Staat* [1920]).

10. On the *Werk* and the "people," see also Silvia Rodeschini, *Costituzione e popolo: Lo stato moderno nella filosofia della storia di Hegel (1818–1831)* (Macerata: Quodlibet, 2005), 123ff.

11. The function of this "play on words" can be found presented in Chapter II of the *Phenomenology*, "Die Wahrnehmung" (literally, "taking-the-true" or "grasping-the-true"): "*Ich muss um der Allgemeinheit der Eigenschaft willen das gegenständliche Wesen vielmehr als eine Gemeinschaft überhaupt nehmen*" (because of the universality—lit. community of all—of the [singular] quality/property, I must, on the contrary, take/perceive/grasp it as an undivided community/property in general). It is also relevant to consult §20 of the *Encyclopedia*: "*Ich ist das an und für sich Allgemeine, und die Gemeinschaftlichkeit ist auch eine, aber eine äusserliche Form der Allgemeinheit.*" See Jean-Luc Nancy's commentary on this passage in *Being Singular Plural*, trans. Robert D. Richardson and Anne E. O'Byrne (Stanford: Stanford University Press, 2000), 30ff.

12. G. W. F. Hegel, *Phenomenology of Spirit*, trans. A. V. Miller (Oxford: Oxford University Press, 1977), §409, 245.

13. Ibid., §417, 251–252 (translation modified).

14. Ibid., §379, 227.

15. Ibid., §§350–51, 212–14. In association with this immediate intuition of unity and the freedom that it promises, Hegel evokes a remarkable utterance, whose variants we will soon discover, that places recognition in the mouth of subjects: "*Ich schaue die freie Einheit mit den Andern in ihnen so an, dass sie wie durch Mich, so durch die Andern selbst ist: Sie als Mich, Mich als Sie*" (I perceive in them the free unity with others in such wise that, just as this unity exists through me, so it exists through the others too—I regard them as myself and myself as them [214]). This is the proper site of the Hegelian "mirror stage."

16. See the development and bibliographical notices by Remo Bodei in his book, *Scomposizioni: Forme dell'individuo moderno* (Turin: Einaudi, 1987), 221: "*Le vene dell'oggettività.*" In this schematic commentary, I am obliged to leave aside a whole (essential) swath of Hegel's reflection, which delves into the relation between the *idion* and the *koinon*: action, insofar as it achieves reality in a "work," only appears to proceed from a foregoing "intention"; or, more precisely, an intention can only be assigned to it on the basis of the result, retroactively. This is why action ultimately makes individual subjectivity depend upon the community represented as its "cause."

17. See Jean-Marie Vaysse, *Hegel: Temps et histoire* (Paris: Presses Universitaires de France, 1998), 100ff.

18. On this point, one should consult not only Lukács's classic work on the young Marx (which tends to train upon Smith the Marxist critique of economic alienation associated with the rereading of Hegel's *Phenomenology* in the "Economic and Philosophic Manuscripts of 1844") but also Laurence Dickey's remarkable study *Hegel:, Religion, Economics, and the Politics of Spirit* (Cambridge: Cambridge University Press, 1987), whose ultimate objective is the interpretation of the chapter from the *Phenomenology* on *Bildung*.

19. It is tempting here to adopt Vincent Descombes's term from the work that bears it as its title, *Les institutions de sens* (Paris: Les Éditions de Minuit, 1996), even if (or precisely because) his entire project is, in order to analyze these institutions, to constitute an alternative solution to that of Hegel.

20. Hegel, *Phenomenology of Spirit*, Sections A and B of Chapter VI.

21. Ibid., §439, 263–264.

22. We will refrain from confusing this "end without end" with "indefinite progress," which, on the contrary, is eminently representable; and which is at most an approximation of the end in mechanical terms. Obviously, it remains to ask whether, in a certain manner, all of Hegel's great works, no matter the disparity of their points of view, would lead to the utterance (or the problem) of such an "end without (the) end" or "infinite end" (in particular, the Logic, by means of what it calls the "absolute method," beyond teleology, as Althusser suggested). Another way to pose the problem of the irreducible but vanishing gap between the two occurrences of the *TAJ*, such as it continues to inform the discourse of "absolute knowledge," would be to show (with and against Blanchot) what the dialectic of the *Sache* and its intrinsic "deception" owes to the model of literature as a typically "modern" social activity, while the vantage point of Geist must begin by seeking its truth in the "substance" of ancient Greek tragedy.

23. Jean Hyppolite, *Genesis and Structure of Hegel's Phenomenology of Spirit*, trans. Samuel Cherniak and John Heckman (Evanston, Ill.: Northwestern University Press, 1974), 321–324.

24. Hegel, *Phenomenology of Spirit*, §177, 110–111. In an earlier study, I attempted to examine in more detail the sources of this formula and to trace it throughout the *Phenomenology*: "Première modernité, seconde modernité: From Rousseau to Hegel" ("La philosophie au sens large," Working Group led by Pierre Macherey, Université de Lille III, session of May 3, 2006). See Chapter 5.

25. See, in particular, Franck Fischbach's comments about this in *L'être et l'acte*.

26. Hegel, *Phenomenology of Spirit*, §418, 252. Translation modified.

27. This is essentially a reformulation of the grand foundational formulas: *tauton gar estin noein te kai einai*, or *ordo et connexio idearum idem est ac ordo et connexio rerum*, or "the conditions

of possibility of our experience of objects are the same as the conditions of possibility of the objects of our experience"—leaving in suspense the question which "us" precisely this "our" refers to.

28. In this schematic presentation, I use both at once "finitude" and "representation" as marks of the historicity of the figures of spirit; or I suggest that the "phenomenological" problem of the development of the concept in the field of representation is none other than the problem of the existence of the infinite within the finite (or better: as finite). The two problems are different without being separable. This must be shown more rigorously, in particular by closely rereading the chapter on "absolute knowledge," which, in fact, revolves around these problems. In any case, it seems to be indubitable that, in the *Phenomenology*, the element of "representation" does not only designate the operations of theoretical reason, but also and above all the institutions of historical spirit and the modality of their "sense," including everything that pertains to Hegel's ultimate critical proposition: that revealed religion institutes a community in which spirit "beholds" itself as subject, and that, nonetheless, this beholding (*Anschauung*) is also what distances it from itself, because it necessarily takes place "in the form of a representation" (*in der Form des Vorstellens für sie*). See the great (and difficult) book by Gérard Lebrun, *La patience du concept: Essai sur le discours hégélien* (Paris: Gallimard, 1972); and Françoise Dastur, *Philosophie et différence* (Chatou: Éditions de la Transparence, 2004).

29. Étienne Balibar, "*Sub specie universitatis,*" *Topoi* 25, nos. 1–2 (September 2006, special issue, "Philosophy: What Is to Be Done?"): 3–16.

30. Hyppolite, *Genesis and Structure*, 600.

31. This figure of the dialectic presents a difficulty for contemporary discussions that found a critique of the "grand narrative" of the philosophy of history upon the convergence of European hegemony, the absolutization of the form of the nation, and the monopoly of the state upon the representation of history; for, on the one hand, it consummates the subordination of all collective formations to the concept of a universality that essentially resides in the *process* of surmounting them; but, on the other hand, it *dissociates* this perspective from any hegemony of the state, even a spiritualized one.

32. There is nothing less "historicist," in fact, than the historicity thought and transcribed by Hegel in the *Phenomenology*. We are no less "contemporaries" of Antigone than of the Enlightenment debates between materialism and idealism, or faith and reason; of the "sovereign of the world" no less than the revolutionary Terror.

33. The idea of a "conflict of universals" and its central function to interpret the dialectic of the common and the universal was suggested to me by Judith Butler's essays, "Restaging the Universal: Hegemony and the Limits of Formalism" and "Competing Universalities," in Judith Butler, Ernesto Laclau, and Slavoj Žižek, *Contingency, Hegemony, Universality: Contemporary Dialogues on the Left* (New York: Verso, 2000).

34. I rediscover, at this point, the same schema of two alternate "paths" that, beginning with the development in the *Phenomenology* on the "struggle of self-consciousnesses for recognition," Franck Fischbach in *Fichte et Hegel: La reconnaissance* (Paris: Presses Universitaires de France, 1999) aligns with the figures of the *bourgeois* and the *citizen* such as the *Philosophy of Right* (1820) presents them as realizations of *Bürgertum* (§190). I differ from Fischbach in that he believes it possible to an identify this alternative with that of the "I" and the "We" in the utterance of spirit, *Ich, das Wir, und Wir, das Ich ist*. I read this utterance as the *common matrix* of the different figures—all problematic—of community (and I readily admit—precisely by virtue of the reversibility of the utterance—that every "community" perceives its antithesis as a *dissolution of the community*, or its reduction to a abstract and unilateral term).

35. Hegel, *Phenomenology of Spirit*, §436, 261.

36. Let us note that Marx, after Hegel, will attempt an wholly other "mediation" of the conflict between the classical modalities of the *Tun aller und jeder*, conceiving the "social contract"

as the expression of a system of equivalence between commodities based on money, and *vice versa.* See Chapter 9 in this volume.

37. G. W. F. Hegel, *Lectures on the Philosophy of World History*, trans. H. B. Nisbet (Cambridge: Cambridge University Press, 1975), 120.

38. Max Weber, *Economy and Society*, trans. Ephraim Fischer et al. (Berkeley: University of California Press, 1978), Part One, Chapter 1, §8, 38ff.

39. Hegel, *Phenomenology of Spirit*, §670, 408.

40. See Étienne Balibar, "Note sur l'origine et les usages du terme 'monotheisme,'" *Critique* 704–705 (January–February 2006).

41. Obviously, I do not use the expression "paradoxical community" without thinking of the "paradoxical class" that Jean-Claude Milner upholds as the negative limit-form of "assembly" in his book, *Les noms indistincts* (Paris: Seuil, 1983).

42. Hegel, *Phenomenology of Spirit*, §784, 475. It is impossible not to evoke here the displacement of this idea in Jean-Luc Nancy's *The Inoperative Community*: "Community no more makes a work out of death than it is itself a work. . . . If community is revealed in the death of others it is because death itself is the true community of the *I*'s that are not *egos*. It is not a communion that fuses *egos* into an *Ego* or a higher *We*. It is a community of *others* . . . it is their impossible communion" (14–15).

43. The word of "reconciliation comes from Saint Paul (Romans 11:15: *katallagè*), but it is difficult to escape the feeling that Hegel is here very specifically inspired by the Gospel of John (for example, 17: 21: "That they all may be one; as thou, Father, art in me, and I in thee, that they also may be one in us . . . And the glory which thou gavest me I have given them; that they may be one, even as we are one: I in them, and thou in me, that they may be made perfect in one"). This is confirmed by rereading the developments in the Frankfurt manuscript (*The Spirit of Christianity and Its Fate*) on the equation: "God is love, love is God."

44. Friedrich Hölderlin, *Hyperion and Selected Poems*, ed. Eric L. Santner (New York: Continuum Books, 1990), 133. See Françoise Dastur, *Hölderlin: Le retourement natal* (Paris: Encre Marine, 1997); Christoph Jamme, *"Ein Ungelehrtes Buch": Die philosophische Gemeinschaft zwischen Hölderlin und Hegel in Frankfurt 1797–1800* (Bonn: Bouvier, 1983).

45. Hegel, *Phenomenology of Spirit*, §785, 476. The "sharing of certainty (Gewissheit)" as an operation effectuated within the interiority of consciousness is obviously a Lutheran idea, opposed both to the intellectualism and institutionalism ("of the State") of the Catholic tradition. If this sharing evokes a Church, it can only be the "invisible church." This reference is necessary in order to understand how, at the end of the great phenomenological cycle and before the final "reflection" of absolute knowledge, Hegel returns to the theme of sense certainty (*sinnliche Gewissheit*) that he began from, on the threshold of the constitution of consciousness. On the Lutheran semantics of faith, certainty, and consciousness, see Philippe Büttgen, *"Conscientia* and *Gewissen* in Luther" and "Glaube" in *The Dictionary of Untranslatables*, 396–397.

46. Derrida has done more than suggest this interpretation in the final pages of *Glas* (Paris: Galilée, 1974) devoted to the paradoxical relation between "absolute religion" and absolute knowledge in the *Phenomenology*. For very good reason, he calls attention to the turn of writing that characterize the section that precedes "absolute knowledge" (and that I would extend to the previous section on morality), that of the reiterated *différance* of the end that might be expressed thus: "do not believe that we have reached the absolute, despite appearances we are not truly there yet."

8. MEN, ARMIES, PEOPLES: TOLSTOY AND THE SUBJECT OF WAR

This chapter was previously published under the title "Sur Guerre et Paix de Tolstoi: Un essai de 'philosophie littéraire,'" in *War and Peace: The Role of Science and Art*, ed. Soraya Nour and Olivier Remaud (Berlin: Duncker & Humboldt, 2010). This volume is based on a conference held at the

Fondation Humboldt in Paris (Institut Goethe), November 19–21, 2007. My heartfelt thanks to S. Nour and O. Remaud for inviting me to participate in this conference. I have made some cuts that do not detract from the main argument of the essay.

1. See, for example, the works published during the last decade by Martin van Creveld, Samuel Huntington, Mary Kaldor, Herfried Münkler, Alain Joxe, and so on.

2. This discussion is sustained, in particular, in Raymond Aron, *Clausewitz: A Philosopher of War*, trans. Christine Booker and Norman Stone (New York: Simon & Schuster, 1986); Herfried Münkler, *Theorie des Krieges* (Baden-Baden: Nomos, 2003); and Emmanuel Terray, *Clausewitz* (Paris: Fayard, 1999).

3. In fact, not so much *Vom Kriege* as Clausewitz's previous work, *The Campaign of 1812*, also posthumous, on the war between Napoleon and the Russian Empire, in which he himself participated on the Russian side.

4. In a strange and perhaps revealing manner, an author who studied the philosophy of war in great detail, W. B. Gallie, in his book *Philosophers of War: Clausewitz, Marx, Engels, and Tolstoy* (Cambridge: Cambridge University Press, 1978), devoted a long chapter to Clausewitz and another to Tolstoy but ignores the relationship between the two authors (with the exception of an allusion to the passage in *War and Peace* in which Tolstoy allegorically figures Clausewitz as an episodic character).

5. In his *Tales from the Caucasus* from 1853, Tolstoy tells the story of the expedition of a irregular force against a Chechen village in the course of which he almost lost his life.

6. One the most interesting aspects of Gallie's work is his attempt to articulate the relation between the phenomenology of war proposed in *War and Peace* and Tolstoy's late doctrine (as it was elaborated especially in *The Kingdom of God Is Within You*, 1891, and *Christianity and Pacifism*, 1894). The pivot, in Gallie's view, is constituted by Prince Andrei's speech on the eve of the battle of Borodino (for him, also an expression of Tolstoy's own thinking) in which, reacting to the "cynical" words of the German officers serving in the tsarist army, he anticipates the horror of the massacres to come and expresses the opinion that the only "just" wars are those in which the participants accept death in advance. See Leo Tolstoy, *War and Peace*, trans. Richard Peavar and Larissa Volokhonsky (New York: Vintage Classics, 2007), 771–777.

7. Pierre Macherey, *The Object of Literature*, trans. David Macey (Cambridge: Cambridge University Press, 1995); "Y-a-t-il une Philosophie littéraire?" *Bulletin de la Société Française de la Philosophie* 98, no. 3 (2004).

8. See Emily Dalgarno's study "A British *War and Peace*? Virginia Woolf Reads Tolstoy," *Modern Fiction Studies* 50, no. 1 (2004): 129–150.

9. Pierre Macherey, "Lenin, Critic of Tolstoy," in *A Theory of Literary Production*, trans. Geoffrey Wall (London: Routledge & Kegan Paul, 1978), 105–118.

10. Gary Saul Morson, *Hidden in Plain View: Narrative and Creative Potentials in War and Peace* (Stanford: Stanford University Press, 1987).

11. Jacques Revel, "Une date, un siècle," paper delivered at the conference "Quelle Europe annonce la bataille d'Austerlitz?" Prague, November 28–29, 2005.

12. It is on this point, in particular, that I take a distance from the scrupulous interpretation of Raymond Aron (which aims to characterize Clausewitz's exact position on the rationality of war and to differentiate it from Hegel and Tolstoy). Aron thinks that Tolstoy's critique of the role of individuals ("great men") in history such as it is imposed by the reality of war (or its "truth") "tends as well to raise up a historical hero, this time a collective one: the Russian People." Raymond Aron, *Penser la guerre, Clausewitz* I: L'âge européen (Paris: Gallimard, 1976), "Note V: Clausewitz et Tolstoy," 386–390. [This lengthy "Note" to Chapter 1 has been omitted from the English translation of Aron's book, *Clausewitz: A Philosopher of War*—Trans.]

13. See Morson, *Hidden in Plain View*, Chapter 6: "Forms of Negative Narration": "The laws of history that Tolstoy advances in *War and Peace* are *negative* laws. They are primarily laws of

ignorance, phrased in the language of absolute negation. No matter how conscientious the historical narrator, the account of historical events must inevitably be false. The more narratable the account and the more it appears to make sense, the more certain it is to be false" (130).

14. Leo Tolstoy, *War and Peace*, III, ii, Chapter 19, 754. This account might be compared to that of Engels in his article, "Borodino," written in 1858 for the *New American Cyclopedia*, in which he upholds the views of Barclay de Tolly against the Russian historiography that exalts Kutuzov (*Marx-Engels Werke* [Berlin: Dietz Verlag, 1969], 14:247–252).

15. "To study the laws of history, we must change completely the object of observation, leave kings, ministers, and generals alone, and study the uniform, infinitesimal elements that govern the masses. No one can tell to what extent it is given to man to achieve in this way an understanding of he laws of history; but it is obvious that the possibility of grasping historical laws lies only on this path, and that on this path human reason bas not yet made one millionth of those efforts the historians have made in describing the deeds of various kings, commanders, and ministers, and in setting forth their reflections on the occasion of those deeds" (Tolstoy, *War and Peace*, 823). Several studies have offered interpretations of Tolstoy's "philosophy of history," and notably his conception of causality: to Isaiah Berlin's famous analysis in *The Hedgehog and the Fox* (Princeton: Princeton University Press, 2013), in my opinion overvalued, I prefer that of Ermanno Bencivenga: "The Causes of War and Peace," *Philosophy and Literature* 30, no. 2 (2006): 484–495.

16. Joseph de Maistre's attempt to reactivate, for the intellectual benefit of modern revolutions, providentialist schemas derived from Saint Augustine (*Les soirées de Saint-Pétersbourg ou Entretiens sur le gouvernement temporel de la Providence*, 1832) figures among Tolstoy's sources; but, in his own *War and Peace*, Pierre-Joseph Proudhon explicitly claims it as a source as well.

17. Tolstoy, *War and Peace*, 1193: "The theory of the transfer of the will of the masses to historical figures is only a paraphrase—only an expression of the words of the question in different words. What is the cause of historical events? Power. What is power? Power is the sum total of wills transferred to one person. On what condition are the wills of the masses transferred to one person? On condition that the person express the will of the whole people. That is, power is power. That is, power is a word the meaning of which we do not understand."

18. Ibid., 1066–1067: "But in essence the process of the flight and decomposition of the French army had not changed in the least. . . . After Vyazma the French army, instead of three columns, pressed together in a single mass, and so went on to the end."

19. The idea of "nonaction" cannot but evoke certain themes of Eastern philosophy or wisdom, notably those of Buddhism. Whence, undoubtedly, the historical convergence that eventually took place between what might be called Tolstoyan "impolitics" and anti-imperialist politics founded on nonviolence (in the thought and work of Gandhi). But—remaining within the cultural context in which Tolstoy's thought was formed—the most interesting intersection (which I am not in a position to document here) would seem to be with the "negative" interpretations of the theology of Saint Paul, such as can be found especially in the work of Karl Barth around the idea of the *Nicht-Handeln* as the originary or "kerygmatic" form of action. See Roberto Esposito, *Nove pensieri sulla politica* (Bologna: Il Mulino, 1993), 148ff.

20. On this point, see Thomas Hippler, *Soldats et citoyens: Naissance du service militaire en France et en Prusse* (Paris: Presses Universitaires de France, 2006)

21. This is the aporia that later theoreticians of popular war such as Mao Zedong will believe that they had solved by replacing the figure of the State, or the army as State apparatus, with that of the revolutionary party, thereby somehow placing the factor of organization on the side of the masses themselves . . . or of their "avant-garde."

22. *War and Peace* as a whole is manifestly structured by the constitution of couples, the experience of their constancy or inconstancy. These couples fall within social and psychological categories: "natural" or "elective" brothers and sisters (André and Marie, Marie and Natasha),

"bad loves" (such as Pierre and Hélène, Anatole and Natasha, or even André and Lise), "impossible loves" (Nicolas and Sonia, André and Natasha, Marie and Anatole), loves of convention or convenience (Boris and Vera), perfect marriages (Nicolas and Marie, and even the old Rostovs), etc. They illustrate relations of power or the effects of historical situations: Alexander and Napoleon are one "couple," much as, on another front, André and Kutuzov, or Pierre and Speransky, or Denisov and Dolokhov. Most of all, these couples enter into systems of oppositions, which can be organized by alternately considering the unions and separations of the principal characters: Natasha with André, with Anatole, and with Pierre; André with his father, with Lise, with Natasha, with Pierre, with his minister. . . . In the final analysis, the couple of Pierre and Platon is, in a certain sense, opposed to all the others, not only those in which the protagonists participate in the course of history (essentially Pierre), but also the couples of "archontes" with whom they have no relation (Napoleon and Alexander, or Alexander and Speranski). This couple exists in another time, so fugitive that its trace remains imperceptible.

9. THE SOCIAL CONTRACT AMONG COMMODITIES: MARX AND THE SUBJECT OF EXCHANGE

The present essay, extracted from a course offered at the Université de Paris X–Nanterre, was first published in the volume *L'argent: Croyance, mesure, speculation*, ed. Marcel Drach (Paris: La Découverte, 2004).

  1. During his lifetime, Marx published the first book of *Capital* (*Das Kapital: Kritik der politischen Ökonomie*, Buch 1: *Der Produktionsprozess des Kapitals*, 1864), which was supposed to have three volumes (or four, according to other plans). Joseph Roy translated it into French on the eve of the Commune. This translation, often quite far from the German text but corrected by Marx, appeared in forty-four installments between 1872 and 1875. Even today, this is the most widely reproduced translation (Editions de Moscou, Pléiade, Garnier-Flammarion, etc.). In 1983, a team of translators directed by Jean-Pierre Lefebvre published a new French translation with Éditions Sociales based on the fourth German edition (the last reviewed by Marx himself). This same translation is now available in the "Quadriges" collection at Presses Universitaires de France, and it is the version to which I refer throughout this chapter.

  2. Karl Marx, *Capital*, trans. Ben Fowkes, intro. Ernest Mandel (New York: Penguin Books, 1990), 1:187.

  3. Ibid., 188.

  4. "It is in the world market that money first functions to its full extent as the commodity whose natural form is also the directly social form of realization of human labor in the abstract. Its mode of existence becomes adequate to its concept" (Ibid., 240–241).

  5. Hegel, *Elements of the Philosophy of Right*, ed. Allen Wood, trans. H. B. Nisbet (Cambridge: Cambridge University Press, 1991), §31 (Remark), 60.

  6. Karl Marx, *A Contribution to the Critique of Political Economy*, trans. S. W. Ryazanskaya (New York: International Publishers, 1970), 206–207.

  7. Marx, *Capital*, 1:209.

  8. Jacques Derrida, *Specters of Marx: The State of Debt, the Work of Mourning, and the New International*, trans. Peggy Kamuf (New York: Routledge, 1994), 55ff, 164ff.

  9. See Suzanne de Brunhoff, *Marx on Money* (New York: Verso, 1976); *Les rapports d'argent* (Grenoble: Presses Universitaires de Grenoble, 1979).

  10. "What Marx designates as the subjectification of the thing is the acquisition by the thing of the function of motor of the process. In the process, this function does not belong to a subject or to the reciprocal action of a subject and an object, but to the relations of production which are radically removed from the space of subject and object in which they can only find supports. . . . It is insofar as the thing inherits the motion that it presents itself as a subject. The concept of the subject designates a function which has its place in an illusory motion." Jacques Rancière, "The

Concept of 'Critique' and the 'Critique of Political Economy' (from the *1844 Manuscript* to *Capital*," *Economy and Society* 5, no. 3 (1976): 362.

11. Marx, *Capital*, 1:178–187.

12. Evgeny Pashukanis, *Law and Marxism: A General Theory*, trans. Barbara Einhorn (London: Pluto Press, 1989).

13. Marx, *Capital*, 1:178.

14. If juridical categories are strictly correlative to economic categories, the question inevitably arises whether we should apply to the former what Marx says about the latter, precisely in the section of *Capital* on fetishism: "They are forms of thought which are socially valid, and therefore objective, for the relations of production belonging to this historically determined mode of social production, i.e. commodity production" (Marx, *Capital*, 1:169). This question results also from the close correspondence between Marx's analysis of exchange and Hegel's presentation of abstract right (that is, juridical personhood, property, and contract). I touched on this question in *The Philosophy of Marx*, trans. Chris Turner (New York: Verso, 1995).

15. On the anthropological dimension of Marx's analyses of "commodity fetishism," see, in particular, Jean-Joseph Goux, *Économie et symbolique: Freud, Marx* (Paris: Seuil, 1973) and *Les iconoclastes* (Paris: Seuil, 1978); and Alfonso Maurizio Iacono, *The History and Theory of Fetishism* (New York: Palgrave MacMillan, 2016).

16. One must speak of the "ensemble" (much as the Sixth Thesis on Feuerbach states that "human essence [*das menschliche Wesen*] is, in its reality [*in seiner Wirklichkeit*], "the ensemble of social relations" [*das ensemble der gesellschaftlichen Verhältnisse*]), because there is no totalization and no imputation of these practices. In like manner, in *The Poverty of Philosophy* (1846), Marx explicitly writes: "society is no one." ("To prove that all labor must leave a surplus, M. Proudhon personifies society; he turns it into a *person*, Society—a society which is not by any means a society of persons, since it has its laws apart, which have nothing in common with the persons of which a society is composed, and 'own intelligence,' which is not the intelligence of the common herd, but an intelligence devoid of common sense." Karl Marx, *The Poverty of Philosophy*, ed. C. P. Dutt and V. Chattopadhaya [London: Martin Lawrence, 1937], 76.)

17. Marx, *Capital*, 1:166.

18. G. W. F. Hegel, *Phenomenology of Spirit*, trans. A. V. Miller (Oxford: Oxford University Press, 1977). See Chapter 7 in this volume.

19. Ibid., 167.

20. This means that political economy does not only "fetishize" the commodity or money but also labor itself (or labor as a commodity), which both functions to dissolve and to confirm appearances. This idea has been developed in Moishe Postone, *Time, Labor and Social Domination: A Reinterpretation of Marx's Critical Theory* (Cambridge: Cambridge University Press, 1993).

21. Marx, *Capital*, 1:158.

22. Ibid., 158–159.

23. Ibid., 159.

24. Ibid., 161.

25. Ibid., 180–181.

26. Karl Marx, *Le Capital: Critique de l'économie politique, Livre Premier: Le developpement de la production capitaliste*, trans. Joseph Roy, entirely revised by the author (Paris: Éditions Sociales, 1959), 147. This passage does not figure within the fourth German edition of *Das Kapital*, but it is unlikely that it could be sheer fabrication of the part of Joseph Roy. Therefore, it is either a sentence from the first German edition that Marx later suppressed, or a gloss that he added upon reading through the translation. In the corresponding passage from *Contribution to the Critique of Political Economy* (1859), he wrote: "As money develops into international money, so the commodity-owner becomes a cosmopolitan. The cosmopolitan relations of men to one another originally comprise only their relations as commodity-owners. Commodities as such are

indifferent to all religious, political, national and linguistic barriers. Their universal language is price and their common bond is money. But together with the development of international money as against national coins, there develops the commodity-owner's cosmopolitanism, a cult of practical reason, in opposition to the traditional religious, national and other prejudices which impede the metabolic process of mankind. The commodity-owner realizes that nationality 'is but the guinea's stamp,' since the same amount of gold that arrives in England in the shape of American eagles is turned into sovereigns, three days later circulates as napoleons in Paris and may be encountered as ducats in Venice a few weeks later. The sublime idea in which for him the whole world merges is that of a market, *the world market*" (152–153). This is already the same idea of a community whose constitutive relations are instituted by the things themselves.

27. In Marx's presentation—which could thus be inserted between Hegel's phenomenology of "sense certainty" and a structuralist theory of the signifying function—the commodities themselves speak in the mouths of their "masters and owners," who are, in turn, reduced to no more than instruments of social ventriloquism: "We see, then, that everything our analysis of the value of commodities previously told us is repeated by the linen itself, as soon as it enters into association with another commodity. . . . In order to inform us that its sublime objectivity as a value differs from its stiff and starchy existence as a body, it says that value has the appearance of a coat, and therefore that in so far as the linen itself is an object of value, it and the coat are as like as two peas" (Marx, *Capital*, 1:20). Luce Irigaray has interrogated this ventriloquism and discovered another implication in the form of expression that Marx describes: the fact the "body" of the commodities put into circulation by money is homologous to that of women "exchanged" between the men who name their qualities ("Women on the Market," in *This Sex Which Is Not One*, trans. Catherine Porter and Carolyn Burke [Ithaca, N.Y.: Cornell University Press, 1985], 170–191).

28. "It is not money that renders the commodities commensurable. Quite the contrary. Because all commodities, as values, are objectified human labour, and therefore in themselves commensurable, their values can be communally measured in one and the same specific commodity, and this commodity can be converted into the common measure of their values, that is into money. Money as a measure of value is the necessary form of appearance of the measure of value which is immanent in commodities, namely labor-time" (Marx, *Capital*, 1:66). Once again, we encounter the figure of the "social contract": It is a social property of commodities, the products of socially necessary labor, which is presented by money; but only money can exhibit universality as such. Compare a recent economic and anthropological analysis based on Mauss's category of the "total social phenomenon": Michel Aglietta and André Orléan, *La monnaie souverain* (Paris: Odile Jacob, 1998); *La monnaie entre violence et confiance* (Paris: Odile Jacob, 2002).

29. Simmel remembers this (as well as Aristotelian "chrematistics" and certain theological themes) when, in *The Philosophy of Money* (1900), he defines money as the "absolute means" or the "means of means." However, to my knowledge, there is no good *philosophical* study comparing the notion of "universal need" in Marx to that of "liquidity preference" in Keynes. Notwithstanding, one might consult Bruno Théret, "L'argent de la mondialization: en quoi pose-t-il des problèmes éthiques?" *Sociétés politiques comparées* 9 (January 2009), fasopo.org.

30. Karl Marx, *Contribution to the Critique of Political Economy*, 207. Marx's developments on the "sovereignty" of money, as the "absolute social actualization of wealth in itself" on a world scale, cannot but evoke the section in Hegel on the generalization of Roman law in the empire, whose sovereign is the "master of the world" and absorbs into himself the whole self-consciousness of his subjects (*Phenomenology of Spirit*, Chapter VI, section c, §606).

31. With Immanuel Wallerstein, we might call this a "world-system" politically structuring historical capitalism. See *The Politics of the World-Economy: The States, the Movements, and the Civilizations* (Cambridge: Cambridge University Press, 1984).

32. The first indication comes when Marx evokes the way in which, "when the production of commodities has attained a certain level and extent, the function of money as means of payment begins to spread out beyond the sphere of the circulation of commodities. It becomes the universal subject-matter of all contracts" (*Capital*, 1:117)—and, consequently, that of the provision of services, taxes, penalties and damages, and so on.

33. The expression "fictitious commodity" does not literally come from Marx but rather from Karl Polanyi, who deploys it as a central category in his 1944 book *The Great Transformation: The Political and Economic Origins of Our Time* (New York: Beacon Press, 2001), 71ff, even as he recuses any resemblance to Marx's theory of "fetishism."

34. This analysis should be continue with a close rereading of the section from *Capital* devoted to salary and its different industrial modalities, in which Marx returns to the question of fetishism as a mode of the "irrational" representation or the "imaginary expression" of the subjection of labor force to the process of (over)valorization. In this same section, Marx also makes an ironic reference to the *contrat social* in relation to Sismondi.

35. These remarks proceed from the discussion that followed my talk on February 24, 2011, at the University of California, Los Angeles (Department of Philosophy), "From Hegel's *Sache selbst* to Marx's fetishism," which combined elements from Chapters 7 and 9 of the present volume. I thank Joseph Almog, John Carriero, and Barbara Herman, as well as their students, for their questions and observations.

36. This expression comes from Louis Althusser, who employs it in the introductory essay in *Reading Capital* (1965).

37. This is the reading that I proposed, in particular, in my little book *The Philosophy of Marx*, trans. Chris Turner (New York: Verso, 1995).

38. It would not be uninteresting, obviously, to return from here to Hobbes's *Leviathan*, and to ask to what extent the allegorical gap between its rational constitution and its mythical figuration (as it is indicated, in particular, by the iconography of the frontispiece that Hobbes himself designed and commissioned) might gain from an interpretation in terms of Marxian "fetishism."

39. The notion of "spirit," whose subjective schema is provided in the key formula, "I that is We and We that is I," comes to the fore with the emergence of the problem of the mutual recognition of "self-consciousnesses" (See the Introduction to Chapter IV of *Phenomenology*, "The Truth of Self-Certainty").

40. The community of "revealed religion," founded on the commonality of the "death of God"; see Chapters 5 and 7 of this volume. At the end of Chapter VII of *Phenomenology*, Hegel denounces the transfiguration (*Verklärung*) implied within the Christian theology of the resurrection as a "representation" (*Vorstellung*), if not a myth.

41. Marx—outside the moments when he voluntarily submits to the constraints of militant utterance that ought (or believes it ought) to announce the "expropriation of the expropriators" as the ineluctable outcome of the historical tendencies of capitalist production (*Capital*, vol. 1, Chapter 24, §7)—evoked in different forms the possibility either of a "real subsumption" of the reproduction of workers and their needs within the logic of accumulation that perpetuates the form of such reproduction ("Results of the Immediate Process of Production," in *Capital*, vol. 1), or as the "surmounting of the mode of capitalist production in the capitalist form itself" that socializes production (or abolishes private property) without thereby instituting it as the common act of the workers (*Capital*, vol. 3, Chapter 27: "The Role of Credit in Capitalist Production"). These "nihilist" issues have been pushed to the margins but remain immensely interesting because they reveal the element of objective and subjective uncertainty that subtends the necessity and linearity of "exoteric" Marxism. By the same token, they inscribe Marx's reflection within an *open* history of collective practice and the institution of community, which is inseparable from its permanent exposure to the annihilation of the political capacity. See my commentary in *Violence and Civility*, trans. G. M. Goshgarian (New York, Columbia University Press, 2015).

10. JUDGING SELF AND OTHERS: ON THE POLITICAL THEORY OF REFLEXIVE INDIVIDUALISM

Paper presented on June 23, 2008, at the École d'Été de L'Association Jan Hus: "Crimes et criminel," Université Blaise-Pascal de Clermont-Ferrand. Now published in the conference proceedings, *Fictions et vérités assassines*, ed. Sylviane Coyault, intro. Jacques Message (Clermont-Ferrand: Presses Universitaires Blaise Pascal, 2013).

1. Michel Foucault, *The Government of Self and Others: Lectures at the Collège de France, 1982–83*, trans. Graham Burchell (New York: Picador, 2011)

2. Paul Ricoeur, *Oneself as Another*, trans. Kathleen Blamey (Chicago: University of Chicago Press, 1995).

3. Immanuel Kant, *Metaphysics of Morals*, trans. Mary Gregor (Cambridge: Cambridge University Press, 1991), 233–235.

4. See Étienne Balibar, "Consciousness," in *Dictionary of Untranslatables: A Philosophical Lexicon*, ed. Barbara Cassin, trans. Steven Rendall et al. (Princeton: Princeton University Press, 2014). [It is important to note that, in addition to its juridical connotations, *for intérieur*, designates the innermost self, the "heart of hearts"—Trans.]

5. In such a genealogy, it would be important to make a special place for the history of eighteenth-century "utilitarian" empiricism, in particular around Adam Smith's elaboration in *Theory of the Moral Sentiments* (1759) of the theory of the "impartial spectator" as a social or "sympathetic" instance at the heart of the ego, and of the analogy of the "three tribunals." See Pierre Macherey, "Sympathy," in *Dictionnaire de philosophie politique*, eds. Philippe Raynaud and Stéphane Rials (Paris: Presses Universitaires de France, 1996); Warren Montag, "'Tumultuous Combinations': Transindividuality in Adam Smith and Spinoza," *Graduate Faculty Philosophy Journal* 28, no. 1 (2007): 117–158; Michael Bray, "Sympathy, Disenchantment, and Authority: Adam Smith and the Constructions of Moral Sentiments," ibid., 159–193.

6. This is actually the first of three successive definitions that Aristotle will propose in a dialectical progression: it is followed (in 1266a) by the definition of citizenship as the alternating exercise of authority (*archein*) and obedience (*archesthai*), then (in 1283b) by the definition of *politeia* ("constitution of citizenship") as the distribution according to merit of the functions of governing and being governed (which the *Nicomachean Ethics* will call "timocracy," of which democracy, to Aristotle, would only be a perversion).

7. On these points, one might reread Jean-Pierre Vernant's analysis of "Le citoyen dans la cité," in *L'homme grec* (Paris: Seuil, 1999).

8. See Jacqueline de Romilly, *Problèmes de la démocratie grecque* (Paris: Hermann, 2006).

9. For an interesting recent elaboration of the political dimensions of the institution of the jury around the contemporary debate about "juries of peers" (*jurys citoyens*), see Yves Sintomer, *Le pouvoir au people* (Paris: La Decouverte, 2007)

10. See Claude Nicolet, *Le métier de citoyen dans la Rome républicaine* (Paris: Gallimard, 1989).

11. See Aldo Schiavone, *The Invention of Law in the West*, trans. Jeremy Carden and Antony Sugaar (Cambridge, Mass.: Harvard University Press, 2012), especially Chapter VII, "The Paradigm of the Law."

12. Paul Ricoeur, *The Just*, trans. David Pellauer (Chicago: University of Chicago Press, 2000), xvii.

13. See C. B. Macpherson, *The Political Theory of Possessive Individualism: Hobbes to Locke* (Oxford: Oxford University Press, 2011).

14. On the theological and canonical origins of the distinction between the internal tribunal (or conscience) (*for intérieur*) and the external tribunal (*for extérieur*), see Paolo Prodi, *Una storia della giustizia: Dal pluralismo dei fori al moderno dualismo tra coscienza e diritto* (Bologna: Il Mulino, 2000).

15. Thomas Hobbes, *Leviathan*, ed. and intro. C. B. MacPherson (New York: Penguin Books, 1968), Chapter XXI, "Of the Liberty of Subjects" (on the confession). What is made politically unacceptable is therefore the *solidarity* without which, in practice, the defense of a claim to individual rights ("subjective" rights) is no more than a pious wish: it is *the right to have rights* understood as the power to gain access to rights. Even our democratic "States of right" do not leave Hobbes far behind on this point . . .

16. Hobbes cites the allegorical formula from the Book of Job that designates the Leviathan as "king of all the children of pride."

17. Immanuel Kant, *Metaphysics of Morals*, "The Doctrine of Right," §49, 128: "A people judges itself through those of its fellow citizens whom it designates as its representatives for this by a free choice and, indeed, designates especially for each act."

18. Ibid., "The Doctrine of Virtue," Part I, Chapter II, Section I. In a quite remarkable fashion, this practical principle is presented in this chapter as the moral foundation of the "know thyself," or of its character as "duty" (in order to judge oneself, one must know oneself and always seek to know oneself better).

19. Immanuel Kant, *Groundwork of The Metaphysics of Morals*, Section II. Compare to §§45–49 of the "Doctrine of Right" as well as the General Remark §E on "On the Right to Punish and Grant Clemency" (*Metaphysics of Morals*, 140–145).

20. These diverse influences remain legible in contemporary French republican discourse. See the commentary of a magistrate about governmental projects to extend the institution of the jury to certain correctional trials (while limiting its place in the court of assize): "Still today, at the moment of the appeal to juries and their eventual recusal, we are witnessing the metamorphosis of a private individual into a citizen. This is the beginning of a moral experience in which each person *becomes* internally the judge of the other, seeing him as his fellow man, and putting himself in his place. Becoming 'oneself as another,' he opens within himself a distance that hones the aptitude for judgment. . . . For the jury, each audience reactualizes the metamorphosis that gives the people a direct responsibility within the decisions of justice. This is why the democratic ritual of drawing lots makes the jury into what is doubtless the most accomplished figure of the citizen" (Denis Salas, "Tocqueville défenseur de la justice populaire," *Libération*, May 9, 2011).

21. See Dominique Schnapper, *La communauté des citoyens: Sur l'idée moderne de nation* (Paris: Gallimard, 1994).

22. From this perspective, his positions are less comparable to Anglo-Saxon liberalism than to those of a French-style "republican" liberalism, whose quasi-contemporary model would be Guizot (see Pierre Rosanvallon, *Le moment Guizot* [Paris: Gallimard, 1985]). See also Domenico Losurdo, *Hegel et les libéraux* (Paris: Presses Universitaires de France, 1992). In *Tocqueville et Marx* (Paris: Presses Universitaires de France, 2012), Nestor Capdevila discusses with great precision this problematic of the "revolution without revolution," which, to a certain extent, liberalism gets from Hegel.

23. One need not insist on the obvious actuality of such a thesis or on the difficulties of application that it entails when it comes to judging "noncitizens," whether they be minors, the disabled, or foreigners. A certain French republican constitutionalism will resolve this difficulty by returning to a Hobbesian inspiration: refusing the authority of the law, the delinquent places himself in the position of an *internal foreigner*, "exiting" the national community without thereby "escaping" its territorial grasp. See Malberg, *Contribution à la théorie générale de l'État* (Paris: CNRS, 1920): "The passive subject of this power is the individual, to the extent that he resists the previously decided upon measures . . . as soon as certain individuals enter into a state of resistance with respect to the law, unity is dissipated and opposition between people arises; the national, in this case, puts itself in a position similar to the one occupied, vis-à-vis the State, by the individual who is foreign to the community. From then on, the relations of the State with this individual member become both relations of power and relations with the other" (250–254).

On the Hegelian conception of the criminal's right to be punished, see Igor Primoratz, *Banquos Geist: Hegels Theorie der Strafe* (Bonn: Bouvier Verlag Grundmann, 1986), especially the chapter "Die Strafe als ein Recht des Verbrechers," 83ff.

24. One will note a new significant silence on Hegel's part at the moment when the logic of his reflection should lead him to pose the question of the *place of women* in the circuit of recognition.

25. On the problems of "translation" posed by this notion, see Philippe Raynaud, "État de droit/Rule of Law," in *The Dictionary of Untranslatables*. On the transition in Hegel from "recognition" to Rule of Law, see Franck Fischbach, *Fichte et Hegel: La reconnaissance* (Paris: Presses Universitaires de France, 1999).

26. I refer to my essay "Private Crime, Public Madness" (Chapter 9 in this volume), where I discuss three theoretically conceivable politics that would conjoin the questions of responsibility and that of criminality. See also Michel Foucault, *Abnormal: Lectures at the Collège de France, 1974–1975*, trans. Graham Burchell (New York: Picador, 2003), whose position seems to be that the conservative identification of the madman and the criminal within the figure of the "dangerous individual" never ceases to haunt the liberal distinction between crime and madness. Later on, Foucault will return to this question in order to evaluate the distance, on this point and others, that separates classical political "liberalism" from contemporary "neoliberalism" dominated by cost-benefit analyses within the management of delinquency. See *The Birth of Biopolitics: Lectures at the Collège de France, 1978–1979*, trans. Graham Burchell (New York: Picador, 2008), Lecture of March 21, 1979, 239–266.

27. In a study published under the title, "The Invention of the Superego: Freud and Kelsen, 1922" (Chapter 12 of this volume), I argue that this elaboration has a precise relationship with Kelsen's elaboration of the internal link between the juridical norm and judicial coercion.

28. One might regret, along with Deleuze and Guattari (*Kafka: Toward a Minor Literature*, trans. Dana Polan [Minneapolis: University of Minnesota Press, 1986], Chapter 5, "Immanence and Desire") that, in Freud's theorization of the Superego, he did not pay as much attention to Kafka (whose work, it is true, remained largely inaccessible to him) as to Dostoevsky: as opposed to an *excessive* internal law, the violence of Kafkaesque law is, on the contrary, always lacking, leading to an incapacity to "believe" in the authority to which the subject must submit.

11. PRIVATE CRIME, PUBLIC MADNESS

This essay was originally a contribution to *Le citoyen fou*, ed. Nathalie Robatel (Paris: Presses Universitaires de France, 1991). Commissioned by the Mission Interministerielle pour Recherche et Expérimentation, this volume contains studies by Jean Bart, Philippe Bernardet, Jean-François Braunstein, Franck Chaumon, Dominique Coujard, Bernard Doray, François Hinker, Michel Miaille, Jacques Michel, Bernard Odier, and Philippe Rappard. I have not updated any of the references for this publication. The legal texts in question (in particular Article 64 of the French Penal Code and the law of 1838) are discussed as they appeared in 1990, before the Evin reforms. Subheadings were added for this republication.

1. Article 64 of the Penal Code of 1810 (retained until 1992) states: "There is no crime or offence if the defendant was in a state of insanity at the time of the action or if he was constrained by a force that he was incapable of resisting." The Law of June 30, 1848 (reformed in 1990) states that individuals declared mentally ill by psychiatric expertise may be committed to a state hospital and placed under tutelage (in cases of "legal incompetence") upon the request of administrative authorities, especially in the aftermath of violence against oneself or against others.

2. The category of *proches* ("intimates") is of crucial importance, as we know, in the treatment of mental illness (e.g., the theoretical and practical modalities of so-called voluntary internment) and in its phenomenology (to the extent that it revolves around a deficit or excess of proximity in

relation to others, self, and things). This category is extraordinarily elastic *and* restrictive. *Proches* might include anyone who, at a given moment, depends upon the "subject" or whom he or she depends upon, whenever such a bond cannot be reduced to any contractual arrangement. In many contexts, the English equivalent would probably be *intimates*; see Erving Goffman, *Stigma: Notes on the Management of Spoiled Identity* (New York: Simon & Schuster, 1963), 51ff.

3. This position appears within the logic of the combat waged—successfully but perhaps not definitively—against the death penalty: see the discussion between Jean Laplanche, Robert Badinter, and Michel Foucault, *Le Nouvel Observateur*, May 30, 1977 [Reprinted in Michel Foucault, *Dits et Écrits*, Vol. III (Paris: Gallimard, 1994), 282ff]. One might well consider the possibility that it is the abolition of the death penalty that also leads to the liberation of the inverse position, as illustrated a some years ago in the Ferraton affair: see Serge Ferraton, *Ferraton, le fou, l'assassin* (Paris: Solin, 1978): refusal of psychiatrization and thus vindication of responsibility against Article 64.

4. See Franck Chaumon and Nicole Vacher, *Psychiatrie et justice* (Paris: La Documentation française, 1988).

5. Herein, it would seem, lies the sense of the main provisions of the reform of the law of 1838 presented in 1989 by Minister for Health Claude Evin in the name of the French government.

6. I use the expression "conflict of the faculties" even though, officially, in France, there were no "faculties" but rather "schools of law" until the end of the nineteenth century (personal communication by Michel Troper).

7. On these different possibilities, see especially Jean Pinatel, *Le phénomène criminel* (Paris: MA Éditions, 1987); and, on the historical origins of this debate, Michèle Perrot et al., *L'impossible prison* (Paris: Seuil, 1980). See also Paul Broussolle, *Délinquance et déviance: Brève histoire de leurs approches psychiatriques* (Toulouse: Privat, 1978).

8. "Psychiatric sector": a reformist system of psychiatric hospitalization created in the 1960s to prevent patients from being consigned to remote hospitals and to help them maintain ties with their world.

9. On this point, see Chaumon and Vacher, *Psychiatrie et justice*.

10. See, especially, Philippe Rappard, "Le procès de la loi de 1838," *Transitions: Revue international du changement psychiatrique et sociale* 15 (1983); "Folie et société civile," in *La folie raisonnée*, ed. Michelle Cadoret (Paris: Presses Universitaires de France, 1989); and his contribution to this volume, "La citoyenneté thérapeutique" (*Le citoyen fou*, 217–240).

11. This "speech" can be an obstinate silence, a refusal or privation that might also be understood as renunciation, protest, demand, or interpellation.

12. Jean Lafont, *Criminel (Comportement)*, *Encyclopedia Universalis*, 1969: "The juridical distinction between crimes (infractions that the laws punish with afflictive or defamatory penalties) and delicts (infractions that the laws punish with correctional penalties) is purely formal and without interest in the psychological or sociological level. Under the same rubric, one also studies both the behavior of those who commit crimes *strico sensu*—such as willful homicide, aggravated forms of theft, and violent attacks upon morals, and the behavior of those who commit delicts, such as simple theft, fraud, and assault. . . . Most criminologists agree to set apart, under various designations, two categories of criminals who pose special problems, the first of a primarily sociological order, the second of a primarily psychiatric order: 'normal' criminals and 'insane' criminals . . ."

13. This is not to annul the imminence of death but rather, quite to the contrary, to underscore its uncertainty, obscured by practices of public order, and disavowed by the formalism of medico-legal expertise. Lucien Bonnafé writes: "Nothing is more dangerous than labeling as 'dangerous' a subject having trouble with human relations, at risk of sinking into madness, and to strike him with a few more or less 'legal' measures, such as internment or restraint. . . . It must not be forgotten that the old coercive measures designed to 'prevent' suicide actually have many

deaths to answer for, because, in fact, they ended up pushing people to commit suicide," *L'Humanité*, November 2, 1989. Other psychiatrists uphold the imminence of death as testimony to the seriousness of their own discipline: "Psychiatry is not a medical gadget. It is a discipline in which there are many deaths" (Dr. Pierre Chabrand, cited in Chaumon and Vacher, *Psychiatrie et justice*, 54).

14. Dominique Coujard, "Problèmes de la legislation spécifique et de l'obligation de soins," in *Le citoyen fou*, 155–160.

15. Certain authors retrospectively project this trace by reading ancient theology as a precursor to criminology. See André Laingui, *Histoire du droit pénal* (Paris: Presses Universitaires de France, 1985), 107: "In the criminal psychology of ancient law, do we find the type of the born criminal, such as he was identified by Lombroso in *Uomo delinquente*, in 1876, predestined to a life of crime by his anatomical, biological, physiological, and psychological constitution, the 'atavistic' resurgence of the prehistorical savage or the prehistorical animal, and even the inferior animal? Evidently not, at least in this form, and even less so considering that classical theology takes a distance from the idea that morbid tendencies, with the exception of original sin, can be inherited. But it is possible to conceive the Lombrosian born criminal in the form of the pervert whom neither the religious moralists nor the criminologists have failed to recognize. It might even be regretted that Lombroso ignored, when he spoke of the 'moral madman,' so similar to the born criminal, Thomas Aquinas's reflections on the morbid dispositions of the body that make evil something loveable for certain individuals." On the mystical dimensions of sociological positivism, see the dossier edited by Clara Gallini and her collaborators at the Instituto Orientale in Naples, "Aspetti del postivismo italiano," *Quaderni* 3, nos. 3–4 (1990).

16. Robert Castel, *La gestion des risques* (Paris: Minuit, 1981).

17. This is also the case elsewhere than in France, although, in this country, the medico-legal apparatus is particularly valorized as a state apparatus. In the United States, as well, technocratic objectivism does not predominate. At the same time, we are told that, in cases of sex crime, some states are introducing or reintroducing the possibility of negotiating a sentence of surgical or chemical castration rather than prison time.

18. See Michel Foucault, "The Dangerous Individual," Address to the Law and Psychiatry Symposium at York University, Toronto, 1978. Reprinted as "About the Concept of the 'Dangerous Individual' in Nineteenth Century Legal Psychiatry," in *Essential Works of Michel Foucault, 1954–1984: Power*, ed. James D. Faubion, trans. Robert Hurley et al. (New York: New Press, 2001), 176–200. Previously, the alternative "insanity or illegality" was most often evoked when the delinquency was less grave; but it subsequently became focused on horrible crimes and then radiated outward into the whole domain of violence.

19. In the fact that the suppression or nullification of responsibility can only ever be its *displacement* (because there is no thing without a master and no action without an author: responsibility, like sovereignty, "never dies") resides perhaps the strongest of continuities between the ancient juridical tradition and the present-day practice of inculpation. Undoubtedly, when Justice, acting upon the advice of experts, dismisses a case because a defendant is not competent to stand trial, because his responsibility is compromised by internal or external coercion, it *derealizes* crime as the act of *such and such* a person; but it does not thereby annul it absolutely; for, this is the way in which—in opposition to the figure of the "scapegoat"—it symbolically *takes this responsibility upon itself.* This is why Justice must make sure to exercise the responsibility that it has taken upon itself (first asking the psychiatric expert to specify the object and consequences of this act), which helps to explain the fact that, after recourse to Article 64 of the Penal Code, in cases of violent acts, the *placement d'office* ("commitment") stipulated in the law of 1838, overseen by another administration, should be basically automatic. Whence the impression that what society has "given" with one hand it has immediately "taken away" with the other, sometimes with usury. However, society also never ceases to define more precisely the modalities of this transfer—for example, dissociating

penal responsibility and civil responsibility; or rather, at the other extreme, reforming the regime of incompetence in order to abolish the strict correlation that reigns over penal responsibility, obligatory treatment, commitment, and civil incompetence (law of 1968). One of the objectives of psychiatric reformism clearly would be to push this process to the limit, to the point of the inverse correlation between *treatment and civil (and civic) responsibility*. But would this correlation not come into contradiction with the juridical form itself—unless, of course, *other transfers* of responsibility are implemented (which orients us inevitably toward the intimates, the family, whose "defect" or "faultiness" are precisely linked most often to the situation of crisis).

20. There are obviously other possible designations (such as *aggressivity*); and, in reality, none are stable. It is significant that the term "deviance," first introduced by the critical bent of Anglo-Saxon "radical criminology," should now be primarily employed within positivism: see Jean Pinatel, *Le phénomène criminel*, 64ff. A similar inversion took place, in other fields, with the notion of "difference."

21. See Jean-François Braunstein, "Droit de punir, responsabilité et défense sociale," in *Le citoyen fou*, 63–80.

22. Michel Foucault, "The Abnormals," in *Ethics: Subjectivity and Truth*, ed. Paul Rabinow, trans. Robert Hurley et al. (New York: New Press, 1997), 51–58.

23. Herein lies a good criteria for appreciating the political vision of the world to which, at a certain moment in his work, a theoretician seeks to adhere: for example, the fact that, in his famous thesis from 1932 on *paranoia*, Jacques Lacan (who, it seems, will subsequently change position) explicitly claims to offer, through the development of an anti-organicist "science" of the personality, a better means of demarcating those violent forms of madness that call for criminal punishment and those that should be exempt from it, clearly places him in the direct lineage of the liberal tradition. See Jacques Lacan, *De la psychose paranoiaque dans des rapports avec la personnalité* (Paris: Seuil, 1975), 276ff, 298ff.

24. Foucault and his collaborators came very close, however, in the admirable volume *I, Pierre Rivière, having slaughtered my mother, my sister, and my brother . . . A Case of Parricide in the 19ᵗʰ century*, trans. Frank Jelinek (Lincoln: University of Nebraska Press, 1982); but the properly political analysis in this text remains dominated by a culturalist perspective. Diving into the breach thereby opened up is Marcel Gauchet and Gladys Swain's heavy-handed effort of revision, *Madness and Democracy: The Modern Psychiatric Universe*, trans. Catherine Porter (Princeton: Princeton University Press, 1999). [Marcel Gauchet also published a very interesting posthumous collection of the articles of Gladys Swain, *Dialogues avec l'insensé: Essais d'histoire et de psychiatrie* (Paris: Gallimard, 1994), contributing a very beautiful preface to the volume, "À la recherche d'une autre histoire de la folie."]

25. See my earlier studies "Response to a Question from Jean-Luc Nancy: 'Who Comes After the Subject?'" (see the "Overture" to this volume); "Rights of Man and Rights of the Citizen: The Modern Dialectic of Equality and Freedom," in *Masses, Classes, Ideas: Studies in Politics and Philosophy before and after Marx* (New York: Routledge, 1993), 39–59; and *Equaliberty: Political Essays* (Durham, N.C.: Duke University Press, 2014).

26. Jean Bart, "La vote du fou"; François Hincker, "La citoyenneté révolutionnaire saisie à travers ses exclus," both in *Le citoyen fou*, 7–28, 29–44.

27. This same "bourgeois" Code, which has always maintained the principle of a "madness" that annuls crime and renders the individual irresponsible, has always excluded the principle of penal responsibility of "moral persons"—that is, collectives and societies. But can it remain so indefinitely and what would be the consequences of a modification on this point? [This is no longer the case—in France—since the Penal Code of 1994.]

28. See the dossier, "Échos de la profession," published after the mass shooting of December 6, 1989: *Sociologie et sociétés* XXII, no. 1 (1990): 193ff. [On December 6, 1989, at the École polytéchnique de Montréal, Marc Lépine, twenty-five years old, opened fire on twenty-eight people,

killing fourteen of them (all women) and wounding fourteen others (four men and ten women) before killing himself.]

12. THE INVENTION OF THE SUPEREGO: FREUD AND KELSEN, 1922

This text is based on a lecture presented on May 20, 2006, at a conference, "La psychanalyse à venir," organized by the Séminaire Inter-Universitaire Européen d'Enseignement et de Recherche en Psychopathologie et Psychanalyse, CHU La Pitié-Salpêtrière. The version printed here benefited from a variety of observations for which I am very grateful, in particular, those of Olivia Custer and Janine Altounian. It was in a special dossier entitled *Le surmoi, genèse politique*, ed. Étienne Balibar, Carlos Herrera, and Bertrand Ogilvie, in *Incidence* 3 (October 2007). I vigorously thank Jonathan Chalier, the journal's editorial assistant, for his help in preparing this collective publication.

1. On the encounter between Freud and Kelsen, see Carlos-Miguel Herrera, *Théorie juridique et politique chez Hans Kelsen* (Paris: Éditions Kimé, 1997), 253–260, which refers to Rudolf A. Métall's biography of Kelsen, *Hans Kelsen: Leben und Werk* (Vienna: Verlag Franz Deuticke, 1969). Enrique Mari, *El Banquete de Platon: El Eros, el vino, los discursos* (Buenos Aires: Editorial Biblos, 2001), II: "La lectura psicoanalítica de *El Banquete*: Freud y Platon; Hans Kelsen y el *Symposium*" (201–288). Among other important references, one might single out: Mario G. Losano, "I rapport fra Kelsen e Freud," *Sociologica del diritto* 1 (1977): 142ff; Antonio A. Martino, "Freud, Kelsen et l'unité de l'État," *Revue interdisciplinaire d'études juridiques* 14 (1985): 119–146. (I owe all of these references to Soraya Dib Nour and thank her for all of her help.)

2. On this point, my reading concurs with the indications in Jean Laplanche and Jean-Bertrand Pontalis, *The Language of Psychoanalysis*, trans. Donald Nicholson-Smith (New York: Norton, 1974), and in Elisabeth Roudinesco and Michel Plon, *Dictionnaire de la psychanalyse* (Paris: Fayard, 1997), which are both confirmed by the index of Freud's *Gesammelte Werke*.

3. I remain faithful to the convention of translating the German word *Ich* into French as *moi* ("me" or "ego"), even if strictly speaking its equivalent should be, in most cases, "I." In fact, no translation of Freud opts for the latter since the nominalization of pronouns in French bears upon the reflexive (*le moi*, and not *Das Ich*). One only says "le Je" in order to cite a linguistic unit as such. Herein lies a properly "untranslatable" difference with considerable philosophical consequences. See my article, "I-Me-Self," in *Dictionary of Untranslatables: A Philosophical Lexicon*, ed. Barbara Cassin, trans. Steven Rendall et al. (Princeton: Princeton University Press, 2014).

4. Rudolf Métall's biography indicates that it was Hanns Sachs—a former lawyer turned psychoanalyst and coeditor of the journal *Imago*—who introduced Kelsen in Freud's private seminar during the war years. He mentions the "vacations in common" of Freud and Kelsen in Seefeld during the summer of 1921 (and thus during the composition of *Massenpsychologie une Ich-Analyse*), thereby correcting Jones's more imprecise report in his Freud biography. See Ernest Jones, *The Life and Work of Sigmund Freud* III.

5. See Jean Clavreul, *L'ordre medical* (Paris: Seuil, 1978). Carlos Herrera's book on Kelsen (cited before) is an exception: He investigates how Kelsen's critique of Marxism might have had an influence on Freud's judgments on communism in his works from the 1920s and 1930s.

6. Freud's only public reaction to Kelsen's presentation, to my knowledge, consists in a note added to the end of Chapter III of *Massenpsychologie und Ich-Analyse* in the 1923 edition, in which he rejects the idea that attributing a "mass soul" (*Massenseele*) to an organization leads to "hypostasizing" the latter—that is, to rendering it autonomous with respect to psychic processes (*seelischen Vorgängen*), as Kelsen had objected in a study that is nonetheless pertinent and incisive (*verständnisvollen end scharfsinnigen*). A reading of the corresponding passage from the *Massenpsychologie*, based upon a "translation" of McDougall's thesis on the individualization of the masses in

terms of the composition of higher organisms, shows that there is, at least, nothing straightforward about this question.

7. One might object that, with the introduction of the idea of *censorship* within the theory of repression elaborated in *The Interpretation of Dreams* (1900), this interference had already taken place. But this is a metaphor whose status will be rethought belatedly, precisely upon the basis provided by the encounter with Kelsen in the 1920s.

8. On the problems posed, in the work of Freud and that of his successors, by the sometimes affirmed and sometimes denied equivalence between the terms "ego-ideal" (*Ich-Ideal*) and "superego" (*über-Ich*), see Laplanche and Pontalis, *The Language of Psychoanalysis.* See also Janine-Chasseguet-Smirgel, *La maladie d'idéalité: Essai psychoanalytique sur l'idéal du moi* (Paris: Éditions Universitaires, 1990); Jean-Luc Donnet, *Le surmoi I: Le concept freudien et la règle fondamentale*; Nadine Amar, Georges Le Gouès, and Georges Pragier, eds. *Le Surmoi II: Les développements post-freudiens* (Paris: Presses Universitaires de France, 1995); Daniel Lagache, "Rapport," *La psychanalyse* 6 (1961): 5–54, to which Lacan responds in "Remarks on Daniel Lagache's Presentation: 'Psychoanalysis and Personality Structure,'" in *Écrits: The First Complete Edition in English*, trans. Bruce Fink (New York: Norton, 2006), 543–574 (see especially 546ff and 571ff). Lacan's own texts dealing with the "superego" are numerous but scattered and do not comprise, to my knowledge, any philological discussion: from his early research on aggressivity, paranoia, and criminality (*De la psychose paranoïaque dans ses rapports à la personnalité*, 1932; "Fonction de la psychanalyse en criminologie," 1950) to *Seminar, Book XX: Encore*, in which the superego is reinterpreted as the imperative of jouissance, in addition to various references to the "obscene and ferocious" figure of the Superego in the *Écrits* ("The Freudian Thing," "Variations on the Standard Treatment"). In *Problématiques (I): l'angoisse* (Paris: Presses Universitaires de France, 1980), 331–363, Jean Laplanche develops an insightful commentary on Freud's texts devoted to the Superego from which, it will become clear, I have borrowed several suggestions. On the philosophical side, we should not forget that Gilles Deleuze also works on the distinction between the ego and the superego in *Masochism: Coldness and Cruelty*, trans. Jean McNeill (New York: Zone Books, 1991). In *Oneself as Another*, trans. Kathleen Blarney (Chicago: University of Chicago Press, 1995), Paul Ricoeur credits Freud with an explication, "legitimate as far as it goes" [*sic*], of the phenomenon of moral conscience as the "speech of ancestors echoing in my head" under the name of the "superego."

9. Or the psychology of *masses*: It is more precise to translate using the word mass or else certain political connotations get lost, but it is impossible to forget that Le Bon's essay, which Freud begins by discussing, and which, as the editors show, he never ceased to mine for formulations, often without saying so, is called in French *La psychologie des foules* (*The Psychology of Crowds*). Freud's chosen term (which appears in the title of Eisler's German translation, from 1912, of Le Bon's book, published in French in 1895) allows him to overcome the antithesis with the English word "group," which designates the object of McDougall's book, *The Group Mind*, which he read upon its publication in 1920 and constitutes the other fundamental "source" of his theorization.

10. The best reconstruction of this great chapter in the history of ideas is, to my knowledge, the second part ("La colonizzazione delle conscienze") of Remo Bodei's book, *L'età della colonizzazione delle conscienze* (Milan: Feltrinelli, 2002).

11. In 1919, in the midst of the torment gripping the countries of central Europe, one of Freud's disciples, Paul Federn, published an essay in *Der Oesterreichische Volkswirt* entitled, "Zur Psychologie der Revolution: Die Vaterlose Gesellschaft" ("Contribution to the Psychology of Revolution: the Fatherless Society"), which was derived from presentations to the Psychoanalytic Society of Vienna and The Monist League (that is, the neo-Darwinist disciples of Haeckel), and was republished the same year as a twenty-nine-page pamphlet. Drawing from the theory of *Totem and Taboo*, he sought to interpret contemporary revolutionary phenomena: the movement of "councils" (*Räte*, the equivalent in Germany, Austria, and Hungary, to the Russian *soviets* and the

Italian *consigli di fabbrica*) and political strikes. The principle of the explication is the disillusionment of subjects with respect to the mediocrity of real fathers compared to the omnipotence of their infantile image. They react to this disillusionment either with the elaboration of an imaginary substitute (paternal figures culminating in the imperial person or the monotheist God, which form the keystone of the institutions of authority—*Obrigkeit*—that are the State and the Church, each buttressing the other) or with a nihilist attitude of opposition and resistance to all power. Federn credits the Austrian socialist party and its leaders, who will come to occupy the place of the father, with having used their influence on the masses to prevent the development of a situation of anarchy comparable to that of the Russian Revolution, the seeds of which are borne by strikes in a situation of penury that threatens the very subsistence of the working class. However, inversely, Federn denounces the hypocrisy of bourgeois critiques of the Soviet revolution that traffic in nostalgia for the paternal order of politico-ecclesiastical power (to which he ascribes the defense of property and inheritance) and proposes a solution (close to that of the "Austro-Marxists") that *constitutionalizes the councils* in order to uphold them as a counterweight to parliamentarianism. This political position is accompanied by a psychoanalytic genealogy of the councils that makes them into a latter-day manifestation of the "fraternal institution" (*Bruderschaft*) that has been repressed since the origin of society by the prevalence of the paternal system. At the moment when this system collapses, or at least is shaken by war and revolution, fraternity emerges as the alternative that must refound society upon an egalitarian basis. Reading this fascinating text, which is indeed the first attempt psychoanalytically to reconstruct political psychology, helps to understand much better the meaning of the displacement that Freud will operate two years later and of his choice to privilege the Army and the Church as institutional prototypes, "eliding" the State.

12. See Freud, "On Narcissism: An Introduction," *SE* 14:73–102.

13. See Horst Bredekamp, *Thomas Hobbes visuelle Strategien: Der Leviathan: Urbild des modernen Staates; Werkillustrationen und Portraits* (Berlin: Akademie Verlag, 1999). Regarding the equally remarkable transposition of these schemas in Marx's "social contract among commodities," see Chapter 9 in this volume.

14. Nonetheless, it is necessary to take into account Freud's suggestion, in "On Narcissism," that what disposes certain individuals to occupy the "place" of the leader is the power of their own narcissism, which renders them "attractive" to the individuals who believe that they have found in them a self-love lost since childhood, reviving this self-love by proxy—that is, by identification. The proper questions about the relation between the thought of Freud and that of Max Weber are still waiting to be framed (but see Pierre Macherey, "Entre Weber et Freud: questions de modernité, modernités en question," *Incidence* 3 [Autumn 2007]).

15. Explicitly evoked in *The Ego and the Id*, Chapter III, *SE* 19:30–31.

16. Kelsen's article appeared in *Imago: Zeitschrift fur Anwendung der Psycho-Analyse auf die Geisteswissenschaften* 8 (1922); it was translated into English and published in January 1924 in *The International Journal of Psychoanalysis* 4, no. 1 (1924), under the title "The Conception of the State and Social Psychology, with Special Reference to Freud's Group Theory."

17. From which he would withdraw a few years later by reason of a change in the rules of designation, but also because of ideological conflicts provoked by his decisions on the question of divorce. See Métall, *Hans Kelsen*, 47–57.

18. Hans Kelsen, *Reine Rechtslehre: Einleitung in die rechtswissenschaftliche Problematik* (Leipzig and Vienna: Franz Deuticke, 1934); *Pure Theory of Law*, trans. Max Knight (Berkeley: University of California Press, 1967).

19. Notably, *Gott und Staat* (God and State), also published in 1922–23. Kelsen's *Der soziologische und der juristische Staatsbegriff, kritische Untersuchung des Verhältnisses von Staat und Recht* was first published in 1922 and then reissued in 1928 (which is the edition that I have consulted). In *Freud et les sciences sociales: psychanalyse et théorie de la culture* (Paris: Armand Colin, 1993), 115–116, Paul-Laurent Assoun has suggested that Kelsen's use of the term *Urnorm* ("originary norm"),

which he will quickly replace with *Grundnorm* ("fundamental norm"), might have been influenced by the Freudian thematic of the *Urvater*. This merits examination, but I would be tempted to suggest the opposite: if Kelsen noticed such a verbal analogy, this is what turned him away from his initial formulation.

20. See, in particular, Chapters 3 and 4 of *Der sociologische und der juristische Staatsbegriff*, in which the author establishes at great length the reciprocity of the two notions, arguing against the unilateral representation of the holders of "State of power" (*Machtstaat*) as well as the theoreticians of the "State of right" (*Rechtstaat*)—which, by extension, determines how to understand the concept of "order." "*Der 'mächtige' Staat und das 'positive' Recht sind so sehr identisch, das man ebensogut von einem positive Staat und einem mächtigen Recht sprechen könnte*" (93). ("The power of the State and the positivity of law are identical to such an extent that it is possible to speak of a positivity of the State and a power of the law".)

21. *Durst nach Unterwerfung*, which one might render, in turn, as "thirst for subjection," or even "abjection," and thus stronger than Le Bon's original that Freud borrows here without saying so, and that Kelsen addresses in the second part (§13) of his essay.

22. Always with the proviso that Freud did speak "metonymically" of the *State* through a comparative analysis of the Army and the Church. If one disputes this reading, the situation changes: Freud's description might then be adapted either to an analysis of what threatens the State as juridical order from within itself, or to an analysis of a "pathological" type of State constructed as a synthesis of militarism and religion that would destroy or neutralize the "State of right." What is interesting to me is that Freud's text does not let itself get locked within such an alternative. Its main concerns are the structures of the *institution* and *belonging* as such, but Kelsen's critique will show Freud that his articulation of them still lacks an essential element. The State-form as reciprocity of coercion and law, and the autonomization of this relation, is not the latent signified of communitarian institutions but rather their vanishing point.

23. Which can be described in philosophical terms as the onto-theologization of the State that lies at the root of all representations of sovereignty as an absolute. Kelsen read and appreciated the contemporary writing of Cassirer on the opposition between "functional concepts" and "substantial concepts" (*Substanzbegriff und Funktionsbegriff*, to which he refers in *Der soziologische und der juristische Staatsbegriff*). He thus anticipates the way in which Cassirer himself, in his final book, will extend these concepts to an analysis of the State and its "imaginary" pathology. See Ernst Cassirer, *The Myth of the State* (New Haven: Yale University Press, 1946).

24. Who, as Althusser would say, circularly interpellates individuals as subjects. The question of the "personality of the State," central to the tradition of juridical positivism since its origins in the Historische Rechtsschule, is the privileged point of application of the idea of "fiction," which Kelsen will approach from a neo-Kantian "critical" perspective inspired by Hans Vaihinger's *Die Philosophie des "Als Ob": System der theoretischen, praktischen and religiösen Fiktionen der Menschheit auf Grund eines idealistischen Positivismus* [*sic*]; *Mit einem Anhang über Kant und Nietzsche* (Berlin, 1911). Enrique Mari offers a remarkable commentary on Kelsen's indebtedness to these formulations, at least in his early work: see his posthumous collection of essays, *La teoria de las ficciones* (Buenos Aires: Editorial Universitaria de Buenos Aires, 2002). For his part, at the end of Chapter V of *The Future of an Illusion* (1927), Freud proposed a critique of Vaihinger as the "modern" and "subtle" transposition of the *credo quia absurdum* which would make it possible to account for the power of religious convictions, *SE* 21:29.

25. This is a recurrent theme in his work since the 1913 article, "Über Staatsunrecht: Zugleich ein Beitrag zur Frage der Deliktsfähigkeit juristischer Personen und zur Lehre vom fehlerhaften Staatsakt" (republished in *Die Wiener Rechtstheoretische Schule: Ausgewählte Schriften von Hans Kelsen, Adolf Julius Merkl und Alfred Verdross* [Vienna: Franz Steiner Verlag, 2010], 1:957–1058).

26. Kelsen, "The Concept of the State and Social Psychology," §§13–14. Kelsen evokes an "antidote" to this fear: the idea of the *self-limitation* (*Selbst-beschränkung*) of State power, on the

model of the "self-limitation of the power of God," which is the object of theodicy (God limits the exercise of his power to the Good or at least avoids any Evil that is not strictly necessary for the actualization of the Good). This is precisely the type of fiction specific to theories of sovereignty that, in Kelsen's eyes, psychoanalysis should make it possible to combat. On Kelsen's critique of the theory of the "State of right" as an effect of self-limitation, see Philippe Raynaud's article "Rule of Right," in *The Dictionary of Untranslatables*.

27. This problem that does not arise when, as Le Bon does (and Plato before him), the idea of a "passion for obedience" is only associated with phenomena of social pathology (such as tyranny) or with revolutionary movements, but that Freud can no longer avoid when the permanence of institutions (even considered in terms of the possibility of their collapse) becomes the object of "social psychology."

28. We know that the schema that Freud transposes here constituted one of the great scientific ideologies of the nineteenth century, organized around Haeckel's formulation of what he called the "fundamental biogenetic law" of the recapitulation of phylogenesis within ontogenesis. The epistemological history of this law as written by Georges Canguilhem, Georges Lapassade, Jacques Piquemal, and Jacques Ullman, in *Du developpement à l'évolution au XIXe siècle* (Paris: Presses Universitaires de France, 1985). Freud derived his argument from this history in order to confer upon the social domestication of the drives a biological ground and scope, and to propose a theory of the way in which the history of the "ancestors" of humanity might continue unconsciously to determine the behavior of "historical" individuals. An excellent discussion of Freud's thought on this point can be found in Richard J. Bernstein, *Freud and the Legacy of Moses* (Cambridge: Cambridge University Press, 1998).

29. In an important commentary on the analogies and symmetries existing between the Hobbesian foundation of the political and its "repetition" by Freud, in the form of an anthropological myth, Giacomo Marramao insists that, for Freud, the two moments that correspond to a "state of nature" and to a "civil state" are not far away from one another but indissociably conjoined (*Dopo il Leviatano. Individuo e communita* [Turin: Bollati Boringhieri, 2000], 315 ff). It is true that one may make the same argument with regard to Hobbes himself by viewing it as the latent truth of his conception of the political order as founded on the omnipresence of fear. On this theme, see also Roberto Esposito, *Communitas: Origin and Destiny of Community, trans. Timothy Campbell* (Stanford: Stanford University Press, 2009), Chapter 1 and appendix.

30. For a discussion of the origins of this formulation in the work of German jurists, of whom Kelsen is a critical heir, which restitutes the whole series of notions from "the monopoly of coercion" (*Zwangsmonopol*), to "the force of coercion" (*Zwangsgewalt*), to "juridical coercion" (*Rechtszwang*), see Catherine Colliot-Thélène, "La fin du monopole de la violence legitime?" *Revue des études comparatives Est-Ouest* 34, no. 1 (2003): 5–31.

31. In his commentary on the Freud-Kelsen encounter, Carlos-Miguel Herrera rightly recalls Kelsen's predilection for Nietzsche's pointed aphorism that condenses this "hypostasis": *Ich, der Staat, bin das Volk* (*Also Sprach Zarathustra*, "Vom neuen Götzen"). The new idol, the State, designates itself as the sovereign people.

32. On the role and positions of Kelsen at the moment of the constitution of the Austrian Republic, see Clemens Jabloner, "Kelsen and His Circle: The Viennese Years," *The European Journal of International Law* 9, no. 2 (1998): 368–385 (which evokes the influence of Freud along with that of Otto Weininger).

33. It was Ferenczi, in particular, who held the chair of psychoanalysis created in Budapest in 1919 by the First Hungarian Republic before it was defeated by the troupes of the "regent" Horthy and gave way to one of the first European fascist regimes. It seems that Freud was shifting his allegiances between Kelsen and Ferenczi. The Freud-Ferenczi letters (as well as his texts from the period, including a remarkable review of *Massenpsychologie*) bear witness to Ferenczi's interest in the problematic of the *Massen*; but the two men observed a strict silence

upon any litigious political matters. In order to complete the political triangulation of psychoanalysts, see also the text of Paul Federn cited before, *Zur Psychologie der Revolution . . .*

34. In the introduction to *Metaphysical first principles to the doctrine of right* (the first part of the *Metaphysics of Morals*), the external coercion inherent to the law is defined as "the obstacle to obstructions of freedom." It is presented, by virtue of the principle of contradiction, as the correlative of the reciprocity of juridical obligations. Immanuel Kant, *Metaphysics of Morals*, trans. Mary Gregor (New York: Cambridge University Press, 1996).

35. A third possibility is irony or derision: this is the path that Kafka explores at the same moment in *The Trial* (and the story detached from it and published separately as "Before the Law"). But this example suffices to show that anxiety is not so easy to dispel. See Michael Löwy's *Franz Kafka, rêveur insoumis* (Paris: Stock, 2004), which insists on Kafka's ties to anarchist groups in Prague and reminds us of the significance of the theme of the "State injustice" (*Staatsunrecht*) in liberal European culture at the turn of the century. Deleuze's commentary on Sacher Masoch goes in the same direction.

36. It is worth recalling that "L'État dans la tête" was a pervasive motto during the Paris upsurge of May 1968, urging participants to liberate themselves from such inner tyranny or conditioning.

37. If we draw all the possible consequences from the theoretical reorientation known as the "second topic," it is essential—although it raises a not at all incidental problem of enunciation—to make sure not to identify the subject with *one or another* of the particular "instances" of the psychic personality. "We" are not the "ego" (or just "ego," "me") any more than "the id" or the "superego" ("id," "superego"); or rather, "we" are all this at once, concurrently and conflictually. The fact that the "ego" is the instance whereby we individualize ourselves by opposing ourselves to "objects" in the external world, in particular to other persons, does not endow it with the privilege to represent the whole personality, of which it remains merely one side in double scission. This logical difficulty never ceased to trouble Freud himself, as can be seen in *Inhibitions, Symptom, Anxiety*, where he returns to the "case" of Little Hans from the perspective of the second topic: there must be a supernumerary designation of the subject besides the three instances of "its" personality (the proper name or its diminutive, as the case may be).

38. Many commentators—for example Peter Gay, in his biography *Freud: A Life for Our Time* (New York: Norton, 1998), 414—are surprised that Freud's 1923 essay is entitled *Das Ich und Das Es* and not *Das Ich, das Es, und das Über-Ich*, since this is truly the object of study, and are not far from viewing this omission as a slip of the pen. The fact is that Freud is very forthcoming about "borrowing" the term "Das Es" from Groddek and his changes to its usage but remains mute on the provenance of "Das Über-Ich," as if this term emerged naturally from the function attributed to it.

39. Respectively translated as transference, overdetermination, overvaluation, and secondary revision.

40. From the moment that the concept was formed, Freud associated the ego-ideal (*Ichideal*) with the idea of a function of observation and critique, and thus with an agency of "censorship": see "On Narcissism: An Introduction," *SE* 13:73–102. This is why it is important to highlight what in the idea of the Superego remains irreducible to it (or in excess of it). Freud's relation to Anglo-Scottish empiricism was the topic of Bernard Burgoyne's unpublished thesis, "Freud et la science," defended in 1995 at the Université de Paris VIII.

41. On this point, Freud was not afraid to let himself get carried away by polysemy of this terms, as his hazardous rapprochement of the "superhuman" figure of the *Urvater der Urhorde*, such as it projected in the imaginary power of chiefs and leaders, to the Nietzschean "superman" (*Übermensch*, where *über* signifies that which "surpasses" the human). See *Group Psychology and the Analysis of the Ego*, *SE* 18:123.

42. The Latinate expression chosen by English translators, "superego," accentuates this second sense. In contemporary jargon, one could easily call it a "super-me."

43. Freud, *The Ego and the Id*, SE 19:1–308.

44. What makes it difficult to clarify Freud's various positions on this point is also his hesitation about how to use the term *Gewissen*, translated in English as "conscience" (and into French as *conscience morale*). For once, the absence of adequate French to render the distinction in German between *Bewusstsein* and *Gewissen* (or, in English, *consciousness* and *conscience*)—both translated into French by the single term *conscience*—helps us to underscore the problem raised by the idea of the *unbewusstes Gewissen*, or the "unconscious morality," discussed in the first chapter of *The Ego and the Id*. It can only be a question of a "hypermorality," a "supermorality," or a "morality beyond morality" (*Übermoral* is a term that appears already in *Totem and Taboo*). . . . On the history of the intersections between *Gewissen* and *Bewusstsein* ("moral conscience" and "psychological conscience"), see my article "Consciousness," in *Dictionary of Untranslatables* (Princeton: Princeton University Press, 2014) as well as H.D. Kittsteiner, *La naissance de la conscience morale au seuil de l'âge moderne* (Paris: Éditions du Cerf, 1997).

45. It is in the essay "On the Economic Problem of Masochism" ("Das Ökonomische Problem des Masochismus," 1924), written as a continuation *The Ego and the Id*, that Freud elaborates this equation between *Schuldgefühl* and *Strafbedürfnis* within the context of his analysis of "moral masochism" (*SE* 19: 155–70). See Suzanne Gearhart's very clarifying reflections on this equation in light of Racinian tragedy from *The Interrupted Dialectic: Philosophy, Psychoanalysis, and Their Tragic Other* (Baltimore: Johns Hopkins University Press, 1992).

46. Allusions in Freud's text to the transferential dimension of the phenomena also suggest that, on the part of the patient, it might not only be a matter of "the need for illness" but also an aggressive desire to put the doctor in the position of tormentor rather than healer.

47. I must cite here the crux of the argument: "An interpretation of the normal, conscious sense of guilt (conscience) [*Gewissen*] presents no difficulties; it is based on the tension between the ego and the ego ideal and is the expression of a condemnation [*Verurteilung*] of the ego by its critical agency [*kritische Instanz*]. The feelings of inferiority so well known in neurotics are presumably not far removed from it. In two very familiar maladies the sense of guilt is over-strongly conscious [*überstark bewusst*]; in them the ego ideal displays particular severity [*Strenge*] and often rages [*wütet*] against the ego in a cruel fashion. . . . In certain forms of obsessional neurosis [*Zwangneurose*] the sense of guilt is over-noisy [*überlaut*] but cannot justify itself [*sich rechtfertigen*] to the ego. Consequently the patient's ego rebels against the imputation of guilt [*die Zumutung, schulding zu sein*]. . . . In melancholia the impression that the super-ego has obtained a hold on consciousness [*Bewusstsein*] is even stronger. But here the ego ventures no objection; it admits its guilt and submits to the punishment [*es bekennt sich schuldig und unterwirft sich den Strafen*] . . . the object to which the super-ego's wrath [*der Zorn des Uber-Ichs*] applies has been taken into the go through identification. . . . One may go further and venture the hypothesis that a great part of the sense of guilt must normally remain unconscious, because the origin of conscience [*die Entstehung des Gewissens*] is intimately connected with the Oedipus complex, which belongs to the unconscious. If anyone were inclined to put forward the paradoxical proposition that the normal man is not only far more immoral than he believes but also far more moral than he knows, psycho-analysis, on whose findings the first half of the assertion rests, would have no object to raise against the second half" (*SE* 19: 50–51). There is a certain ambiguity to this text as a result of the fact that it appears to oscillate between the opposition of the normal and the pathological and the opposition of the conscious and the unconscious. But the ambiguity can be dispelled if one supposes that what characterizes these "maladies" (obsessive-compulsive disorder, melancholia—and in other contexts he would add the perversions: masochism) is that they let pass into consciousness or into overt behavior that which characterizes the unconscious as such.

48. "This diffusion [of the two drives] would be the source of the general character of harshness and cruelty exhibited by the ideal—its dictatorial 'Thou shalt'" (*SE* 19:54–55).

49. *SE* 22:60 (Lecture XXXI).

50. In his later works—especially *Civilization and its Discontents*—Freud, in accordance with a certain sociological and anthropological tradition, will designate "civilization" or "society" as the stratum of premoral and prejuridical normativity governed by the development of the superego and by the extent of its domination. Herein lies another aspect of Freud's research that, within the framework of the hypothesis that orients my present reading, I would prefer to leave aside.

51. Once again, the comparison between Federn's brochure and his psychoanalytic "deduction" of council democracy is very clarifying: for Freud—in no way a libertarian, nor even a radical democrat, in the sense of "participatory" democracy—the figure of the brother belongs to the same schema as the figure of the father; it is a component of this schema much as, in the myth of *Totem and Taboo*, the egalitarianism of the brothers is haunted by guilt for the murder of the father. Freud does not believe that this figure can become autonomous. Nor does he believe in the "juridical dissolution" of the familial complex, except, as we will see, in the form of an antinomian reversal.

52. Jean-Luc Donnet insists upon this point: "the Superego clearly appears as a space for the transit of identifications; it remains 'destined' to be shared. In this sense, for Freud, there is scarcely an 'individual' Superego; and the second topic is trans-subjective and trans-generational"(*Surmoi I: Le concept freudien et la règle fondamentale* [Paris: Presses Universitaires de France, 1995], 40). This is why I insist not on the fact that the superego is "individual" but rather on the fact that it both *produces individuality* by "forcing" the subject to feel guilty—much as the ego-ideal studied in *Group Psychology and The Analysis of the Ego* is not "social" in the sense of a preexisting organism but is rather "shared in common"—and *produces community*. In question each time is the orientation of a vector toward either individualization or communization.

53. In many respects, the counteridentification produced by the superego comes to occupy the place in the final tableau of *Group Psychology* (Chapter XII, "Postscript") that Freud reserves for neurosis as "void" of erotic or hypnotic relations, whereby *it too* proves to correspond to a social formation, but operating in the opposite direction.

54. "Freud: la modernité entre Eros et Thanatos" can be found on the website of the working group, "La philosophie au sens du large" (exposé du 12 octobre 2005, Université de Lille III): http://stl.recherche.univlille3.fr/seminaries/philosophie.macherey/macherey20052006/macherey12102005cadreprincipal.html.

55. It is striking that, in Hobbes's construction, the hierarchy of judicial instances within the framework of sovereignty has as its unassimilated "remainder" or "residue," precisely, the asocial or anti-political "masses," agents of State disintegration, who purport "to do justice themselves": see *Leviathan*, Chapter 22, "Of Systemes Subject, Politicall, and Private." I have offered a commentary on this chapter in my introductory essay to the French translation of Carl Schmitt's book on *Leviathan*, "Le Hobbes de Schmitt, le Schmitt de Hobbes" (Paris: Seuil, 2002). Although situated at the other extreme of the social order, this both residual and menacing figure is not without analogy to the way in which Kelsen distances the "rational" functioning of the institution from the phantasmatic hypostases of State power, in order to propose that the latter be addressed by psychoanalysis.

56. G. W. F. Hegel, *Elements of the Philosophy of Right*, §91.

57. "Das Unrecht is ein solcher Schein, und durch das Verschwinden desselben erhält das Recht die Bestimmung eines Festen und Geltenden" (*Elements of the Philosophy of Right*, § 82, Zusatz). Let us not forget the "democratic" counterpart of this thesis: it is not possible legitimately to judge an individual for his mistakes or crimes except in the name of a law that he, in his capacity as a citizen, has himself helped to formulate, before a tribunal upon which, in principle, he himself could sit.

58. Hans Kelsen, *Théorie pure du droit* (Paris: La Baconniere, 1953), 76. [The French translation that Balibar uses here differs so drastically from the English translation that it is not possible to find the corresponding passage—Trans.]

59. See, for example, *Civilization and Its Discontents,* Chap. VIII (*SE* 21:135).

60. In *The New Introductory Lectures on Psychoanalysis,* Freud uses the expression *Elterninstanz* or "parental agency" (*SE* 22:62, 64).

61. In his commentary on these questions (*Problématiques I: l'angoisse* [Paris: Presses Universitaires de France, 1980], 355ff), Laplanche stresses, in particular, the way in which the alternative between "the father" and "the parents" was influenced by Melanie Klein's intervention, whose observations on the "severity" of the superego Freud must have taken into account—not too graciously. Initially, Freud sustained that this severity for every individual (and consequently, in the end, his choice of either this or that neurotic, melancholic, or perverse "position" etc.) directly depends on the severity or the aggressivity that the parents (and notably the father) bring into the "education" of the child's drives. However, Melanie Klein showed that the violence inherent to the ego/superego relation has nothing to do with empirical history but constitutes an effect that is independent of real behaviors. Independently of her own explication (which emphasizes the projection onto the pre-Oedipal Mother of a destructivity that comes from within from the child himself), one notices that this corrective leads to the reversibility between the "genetic" point of view, which upholds the superego as the "heir to Oedipus," and even to earlier object relations, and the "structural" point of view, which claims that violence and its conversion into guilt is an effect of the infantile ego's dependency upon the "omnipotent" authority figures to whom he is bound by love and by fear.

62. *The Economic Problem of Masochism* (*SE* 19:155–170).

63. This is an idea that is not so much Marxist as it is Rousseauist, as in the *Discourse on the Origin of Inequality.* The fact that these particularly clear formulations appear in one of Freud's texts on war, the first of which was his 1915 essay, *Thoughts for the Times on War and Death* (*SE* 14:273–300) is not incidental. They are completely inscribed within the framework of World War One and the "disillusionment" or a "destruction of illusions" (*Enttäuschung, Zerstörung einer Illusion*) that it wrought with respect to the value of progress and decline of violence in civilization that leads to the hypothesis about the original and thus unavoidable character of the "death drive." See Pierre Macherey: "Freud: La modernité entre Eros et Thanatos"; Samuel Weber, "War Time," in *Violence, Identity, and Self-Determination,* eds. Hent de Vries and Samuel Weber (Stanford: Stanford University Press, 1997), 80–105; René Kaës, "Travail de la mort et théorisation," in Jean Guillaumin et al., *L'invention de la pulsion de mort* (Paris: Dunod, 2000), 89–111.

64. *New Introductory Lectures on Psychoanalysis* in *SE* 22:67.

65. Daniel Lagache, "Rapport," in *La psychanalyse* 6 (1961): 39; Jean Laplanche and Jean-Bertrand Pontalis, *The Language of Psychoanalysis,* trans. Donald Nicholson-Smith (London: Hogarth Press, 1973), 435; Jean-Luc Donnet, *Le Surmoi* I, 36ff.

66. Lacan is not far from such a formulation in a passage from his article for the *Encyclopédie française* on the "familial complexes," except that he makes it into a atypical situation: "A first atypical situation arises from the conflict implied by the Oedipus complex especially in the relations of the son to the father. . . . There have been divergent considerations on the notion of the familial superego: it certainly responds to an intuition of reality. For us, the pathological reinforcement of the superego in the individual is the function of a double cause: 1) the rigors of patriarchal domination and 2) the tyrannical form of the interdictions that arise with the matriarchal structure of any stagnation within domestic bonds. Religious ideals and their social equivalents thus easily act as vehicles of this psychological oppression insofar as they are used to exclusionary ends by the familial body and reduced to signifying the exigencies of the name or the race. At such conjunctures are produced the most striking cases of these neuroses, called neuroses of self-punishment because of the often univocal preponderance in them of the psychic mechanism that goes by this name . . ." (Les complexes familiaux dans la formation de l'individu" [1938], reprinted in Jacques Lacan, *Autres écrits* [Paris: Seuil, 2001], 79–80). See Bertrand Ogilvie, *Lacan: la formation du concept du sujet (1932–1949)* (Paris: Presses Universitaires de France, 2005), 22–27, 76–77, 86–95.

67. The developments in *Civilization and Its Discontents* are clearly marked this overdetermination: "Thus we know of two origins of the sense of guilt: one arising from fear of an authority (*Angst vor der Autorität*), and the other, later on, arising from fear of the super-ego (*Angst vor dem Über-Ich*). The first insists upon a renunciation of instinctual satisfactions; the second, as well as doing this, presses for punishment (*drängt . . . ausserdem zur Bestrafung*), since the continuance of the forbidden wishes cannot be concealed from the super-ego." (*SE* 21:127).

68. See George Canguilhem's classic article "La décadence de l'idée de progrès," in *Revue de Métaphysique et de Morale* 4 (1987).

69. Once again, I must cite at length: "We have there what could, in fact, correspond to the double aspect of the ideal agency . . . without one of theses facets being clearly designated as ideal and the other as super-ego. However, this duplicity, despite everything, is very different from the distinctions suggested by Lagache, and is probably more sensitive to a certain contradiction existing in reality. . . . In Freud, there is not a complementary system (on the one hand, the imperative, and on the other, the ideal, which must be realized in order to act in conformity with the imperative) but two disjointed and equally imperative series: the series of injunctions, 'you must be like your father'—and the series of interdictions, 'you must not be like your father.' Obviously, the series of injunctions is more similar to idealization, since it presents a model, while the negative series is more similar to the super-ego. However, not only is there no *complementarity between the two* . . . but *there is also contradiction* since the two imperatives, positive and negative, concern the same proposition: 'be like the father.' Indeed, one can pretend to resolve this contradiction, one can disjoin it in an effort to conform to logic. . . . In fact, I hold that a resolution of the contradiction is only an illusion, since, most of the time, and not only in clinically proven neurosis, the two series overlap, disjunctions become conjunctions, resulting in these impossible imperatives that correctly characterize unconscious morality, the morality of the super-ego. . . . This contradiction . . . clearly reveals that the superego is not a coherent system, well-ordered. Only in exceptional and ideal . . . cases is it an ordering principle of the inner world. The law it mediates is a contradictory law, where the most contradictory propositions are juxtaposed. At times, it is a pitiless, merciless law. We saw this with obsessional neurosis where guilt is present on both sides, in order and in counterorder: 'you must return this money' and 'you must not return it' are characterized by the same anxiety and guilt; and in melancholia we have also confronted this sort of absolute guilt that cannot be resolved by a simple *demarcation* between interdiction or the permissible. This leads to the conception of the super-ego as an agency that in the most extreme cases appears to place legalism and even the laws that it declares, the semblance of reason, reasoning reason, in the service of the primary process. *In any case, you are guilty*, the super-ego seemingly says" (Jean Laplanche, *Problematiques I: l'angoisse*, 352–353).

70. Once again, there is a comparison to be made with the Nietzsche of *The Genealogy of Morals* but especially with Saint Paul's proposition in *Epistle to the Romans* (7:7) that upholds the revelation of the law (*nomos*) as the condition for the recognition of sin (*hamartia*) insofar as it is opposed to desire (*epithumia*). Whereas Saint Paul challenges the "impossible" *identification* of law and sin (*ho nomos hamartia; mè genoito*), this subversive extremity was completely embraced by the mystical tradition of the Kabbalists (which, at least, Freud knew indirectly) that led the "false messiah" Sabbataï Zevi in the seventeenth century to vindicate his transgression of the law and his right to blasphemy as proof of a redemptive mission. See Gershom Scholem, *Sabbatai Zevi: The Mystical Messiah 1626–1676*, trans. Zwi Werblowsky (Princeton: Princeton University Press, 1975). David Bakan's *Sigmund Freud and the Jewish Mystical Tradition* (New York: Van Nostrand & Co., 1958) does not actually shed any new light on this matter since the correspondences that it discusses between Freud and Sabbateanism are not founded upon documentary evidence but rather only upon inferences (even if certain of them are suggestive).

71. See in particular, Freud's essay from 1915, "The Unconscious" (*SE* 14:159–209); and *New Introductory Lectures on Psychoanalysis* (*SE* 22:1–82). In the case of "obsessional neurosis"

(*Zwangneurose*) constituted by the Rat Man, Freud explicitly evokes to the identification of opposites in the unconscious (*SE* 10:153–251).

72. Sigmund Freud, "Dostoevsky and Parricide" (1928), *SE* 21:189–190.

73. It is no simple matter, despite his frequent clarifications, to attribute to Freud a consistent position with regard to the distinction between the "normal" and the "pathological." Undoubtedly, the same goes, *mutatis mutandis*, for the relation between juridico-political "order" and psychic "disorder."

74. Kelsen, *Reine Rechtslehre*, 31ff.

75. Here, I summarize Kelsen's developments in Chapter III of *The Pure Theory of Law*, 70–107.

76. In the *Critique of Pure Reason* (1781), Kant famously wrote: "Concepts that are not filled with intuitions are empty, intuitions that are not subsumed under concepts are blind." He outlines the construction of such a schematism of the rule of law through a twofold rejection of its "exceptions" that, as such, fall outside the jurisdiction of a tribunal—those of *equity* and *necessity* (or *force majeure*). See Immanuel Kant, "Appendix to the Introduction to the Doctrine of Right," in *The Metaphysics of Morals*, trans. Mary Gregor (Cambridge: Cambridge University Press, 1991), 59–61.

77. Fundamentally, Kelsen's presentation concerns the behaviors that obstruct the freedom of others: Therein we recognize Kant's definition of freedom. All behavior directly or indirectly falls under an interdict insofar as it is a violation of the other's right to do what is not interdicted.

13. BLANCHOT'S INSUBORDINATION: ON THE WRITING OF THE *MANIFESTO OF THE 121*

Presentation at the conference, "Maurice Blanchot," directed by Christophe Bident, Centre Culturel international de Cerisy-la-Salle, July 2–9, 2007 (revised and corrected version). The conference proceedings have since been published. See *Blanchot dans son siècle: Colloque de Cerisy*, ed. Monique Antelme, Gisèle Berkman, Christophe Bident, Jonathan Degenève (Lyon: Parangon, 2009). The *Manifesto of the 121* (in French: *Déclaration sur le droit à l'insoumission dans la guerre d'Algérie*) was an open letter signed by 121 intellectuals and published on September 6, 1960, in the magazine *Verité-Liberté*. It called upon the French government and the public to recognize the Algerian War as a legitimate struggle for independence, denouncing the use of torture by the Army, and calling for French conscientious objectors (and deserters) to be respected by the authorities.

1. Christophe Bident, *Maurice Blanchot partenaire invisible* (Paris: Champ Vallon, 1998), 394. The phrase "called up" (*appelé*), which is not devoid of evangelical resonances, primarily refers to the historical conjuncture: It is the technical term used for military service in wartime.

2. See ibid., 391–402; *Lignes* 33, "Avec Dionys Mascolo du Manifeste des 121 à Mai 68" (March 1998), 84. See also Jérôme Duwa's detailed study "La Déclaration des 121: Un texte fait par tous et non par un," in Antelme et al., *Blanchot dans son siècle*, 274–288. Relying upon the Mascolo archives at IMEC, Duwa examines the transformation of the initial version of the Declaration through its twelve successive versions, each annotated by the drafters.

3. The "success" in question is the failure of the "Week of Barricades" organized in January 1960 by the extremist colonizers and some rebel soldiers against the self-determination proposed by de Gaulle.

4. René Rémond, *Notre siècle 1918–1988* (Paris: Fayard, 1988), 594–595.

5. It was Sartre of whom de Gaulle would utter, upon giving up the indictment that his government had undertaken, the much-anthologized dictum, "One does not imprison Voltaire."

6. See the irreplaceable—and today almost impossible to find—volume published in 1961 by François Maspero (himself a signatory of the Declaration, along with other militant publishers), confiscated and republished outside France in order to avoid censorship, *Le droit à l'insoumission (le dossier des "121")* (Paris: Maspero, Cahiers libres 14, 1961).

7. Pierre Vidal-Naquet, *Mémoires 2: Le trouble et la lumière 1955–1998* (Paris: Seuil/La Découverte, 1995), 137–139.

8. Compare the formulations in Bident, *Maurice Blanchot partenaire invisible*, 392.

9. Vangelis Bitsoris, "Blanchot, Derrida: du droit à la mort au droit à la vie," in *Blanchot dans son siècle*, 179–193.

10. Maurice Blanchot, "The Main Impropriety (Excerpts)," trans. June Guicaharnaud, *Yale French Studies* 39 (1967): 50–63.

11. The study of the historico-literary "genre" of the "Manifesto" is indispensable in order to understand the regime of ideas and discourses in modernity. See Martin Puchner's beautiful book *Poetry of the Revolution: Marx, Manifestos, and the Avant-gardes* (Princeton: Princeton University Press, 2005).

12. This is not the place to rewrite the history of the "end" of the Algerian War. It is generally accepted that General de Gaulle, even as he played a canny double game with the army and the *pieds-noirs*, recognized the ineluctability of independence and made preparations for it. But he wanted it to occur on his schedule and on his conditions, which meant that he considered any support for the liberation struggle as treason and any expression of opinion in favor of peace and independence as an unacceptable pressure—not to mention, of course, his will to cover up war crimes committed in Algeria and at home by the army and the police. In order to pull out of Algeria while preserving the means to retain post-colonial control over it, it would be necessary to "win the war" (which, as it happens, the French army will always claim to have accomplished).

13. See the edited volume *Le droit à la résistance au XII–XX siècle*, ed. Jean-Claude Zancarini (Fontenay-St. Cloud: ENS Éditions, 1999), which historicizes and discusses the opposition between the two views of the resistance as the historical antinomy of sovereignty and as the limitation of power. I will return to this opposition in my conclusion.

14. On the difference between the cause of "self" and the cause of the "other" and its importance within the solidarity inspired by the Algerians' struggle, see Jacques Rancière, "La cause de l'autre," in *Lignes* 30, "Algérie-France: Regards croisés" (February 1997): 36–49. In the trial to which he was called as witness, the novelist Claude Simon, not an especially Marxist signatory of the Declaration, cites Marx's formula, "A people that oppresses another people cannot be free" (*Le droit à l'insoumission*, 84). Bident also reports the following declaration from Blanchot: "for the first time a word rises from the intimacy of the people in order to claim a *right not to oppress* with the same force that previously drove all peoples to claim a right *not to be oppressed*" (Bident, *Maurice Blanchot partenaire invisible*, 395).

15. In this sense, insubordination would be distinguished from "desertion," even if an internal discussion among the signatories led them to consider that the second might be implicated within the former. In relation to the onset of war in 1939, René Rémond writes: "The mobilization proceeded apace . . . the proportion of insubordinates never exceeded 1.5%" (*Notre siècle*, 270).

16. This semantics, with the different levels or modalities of negation that it entails, will be deployed later by Foucault (in what is to me obviously an anamnesis of the *Manifesto* and the event it constituted for all its contemporaries) in his elaboration of the question of "counter-conduct." *Security, Territory, Population: Lectures at the Collège de France, 1977–78*, trans. Graham Burchell (New York: Palgrave MacMillan, 2007). See, in particular, the lecture from March 1, 1978, in which he forges the neologism, "*s'insoumettre au pouvoir*" ["to refuse submission to power"].

17. Dante, *Inferno*, Canto III, 58–60: "*Poscia ch'io v'ebbi alcun riconosciuto, / vidi e conobbi l'ombra di colui / che fece per viltade il gran rifiuto.*" See Maurice Blanchot, "Refusal," in *Political Writings, 1953–1993*, trans. Zakir Paul (New York: Fordham University Press, 2010), 7–8 [originally published in the journal *14 juillet* in 1958]; "The Great Refusal," in *The Infinite Conversation*, trans. Susan Hanson (Minneapolis: University of Minnesota Press, 1993), 33–48 [this section of the book comprises two articles, grouped under the title of the first, which appeared respectively

in October and November 1959 in the *Nouvelle Revue Française*). See Christophe Bident's commentary on these texts in *Maurice Blanchot partenaire invisible*. It would be necessary to study how Herbert Marcuse "relays" this expression when he introduces it in the conclusion to *One Dimensional Man* (1964) in order to synthesize the radical opposition to advanced capitalist society whose repressive mechanisms have enabled it to neutralize all internal opposition (*The Great Refusal*). It will then become the slogan of revolutionary student movements, especially those in Germany, that will open the way for the revolt of May '68. Marcuse cites Blanchot's 1958 article and endows it with a general application (opposing the pure form of negation to the pure form of domination). "What we refuse is not without value or importance. This is precisely why refusal is necessary. There is a kind of reason that we will no longer accept, there is an appearance of wisdom that horrifies us, there is an offer of agreement and compromise that we will not hear. A rupture has occurred. We have been brought back to this frankness that does not tolerate complicity any longer" (Blanchot, "Refusal," cited in Herbert Marcuse, *One-Dimensional Man: Studies in the Ideology of Advanced Industrial Society* [New York: Routledge, 2007], 259–260). Earlier, in *Eros and Civilization* (1955), the same Marcuse had ascribed the expression to a passage from Alfred North Whitehead's *Science and the Modern World* (1925)—wherein it designates the spontaneous protest of life, relayed by art, against the "non necessary repression" of instincts and the anxiety that it generates—and associates it with a neo-Freudian myth of Orpheus and Narcissus as heroes of resistance to erotic normality. See Herbert Marcuse, *Eros and Civilization* (New York: Beacon Press, 1955), 149, 160ff.

18. The French edition of *Écrits politiques 1958–1993* does not specify if, where, or when this "update" was published. [Neither does the English translation.]

19. Republished in *Lignes* 33: 79–83.

20. Compare Sartre, "The Republic of Silence" (1944), in *The Aftermath of War*, trans. Chris Turner (Calcutta: Seagull Books, 2008), 3: "Never were we freer than under the German Occupation" (but it should be noted that, in 1958, Sartre was no less radical in his condemnation of the illegitimacy of the Gaullist regime instituted after the Algiers putsch).

21. [The reader might recall that Charles de Gaulle returned to power in May 1958 as consequence of a military coup by elements of the army and secret "Gaullist" organizations in Algiers. This political transformation, at the origin of the Fifth Republic, was legitimized ex post facto through the referendum of September 28, 1958.—Trans.]

22. One will recall the title of François Mitterand's book *Le coup d'état permanent* (Paris: Plon, 1964).

23. Maurice Blanchot, *Political Writings, 1953–1993*, 16 [translation slightly modified]. It has been reported that the introduction of the word "like" (*comme*) was due to Blanchot's own intervention. See Bident, *Maurice Blanchot partenaire invisible*, 395 n. 3 (and the report is confirmed and developed by Jérôme Duwa in his essay on the Manifesto).

24. One will recall the fifth couplet—often repressed—of the *Internationale*: "Kings get us drunk on smoke, Peace among us, war on tyrants! Let armies go on strike, lay down their weapons, and break ranks. If these cannibals, if they keep on making us heroes, we'll show them our bullets are for our own generals . . ." The text by the physician Jean-Pierre Vigier, then a member of the PCF (Parti Communiste Français) central committee (republished in Maspero's dossier on the 121) expresses a personal solidarity with the indicted militants and intellectuals even as he recalls what he presents as the Leninist position: Communists join the army in order to prepare from inside the transformation of imperialist war into socialist revolution.

25. Blanchot, *Political Writings, 1953–1993*, 34.

26. Ibid., 16.

27. This sentence would seem to come straight from Hegel's analyses of the "beautiful soul" in the *Phenomenology of Spirit* (Chapter VI, C).

28. Ibid., 34.

29. Philippe Mesnard, *Maurice Blanchot et le sujet de l'engagement* (Paris: L'Harmattan, 1996), 16–20.

30. [Ordre Nouveau was the name of one of the protofascist organizations created in France in the 1930s, of which Blanchot had been a member or sympathizer.—Trans.]

31. "The principle of all sovereignty essentially resides in the nation," *Déclaration des droits de l'homme et du citoyen* (DDHC), Article 3.

32. "X without X" (e.g. "community without community") is an oxymoronic syntagm, linked to the idea of the "neuter," that Blanchot frequently employed and that Jean-Luc Nancy or Jacques Derrida would later adopt as an instrument of "deconstruction."

33. Significantly, it was only with the third revolutionary Déclaration—the "Thermidorian constitution" from 1795, that which marked the triumph of the idea of property—that the form of a "declaration of the rights and duties of man and the citizen" will be reintroduced, in ephemeral fashion. On all of this, see Florence Gauthier, *Triomphe et mort du droit naturel en révolution, 1789–1802* (Paris: Presses Universitaires de France, 1992).

34. Étienne Balibar, "Citizen Subject: Response to a Question from Jean-Luc Nancy" (see the Overture in this volume).

35. Étienne Balibar, "(De)constructing the Human as Human Institution: A Reflection on the Coherence of Hannah Arendt's Practical Philosophy" (paper presented at the conference, *Hidden Tradition—Untimely Actuality? Hannah Arendt 1906–2006*, October 5–7, 2006, Heinrich Böll Foundation, Berlin). Reprinted as "Hannah Arendt, the Right to Have Rights, and Civic Disobedience," in Étienne Balibar, *Equaliberty*, trans. James Ingram (Durham, N.C.: Duke University Press, 2014), 165–186.

36. Christophe Bident, *Maurice Blanchot partenaire invisible*, 385–386; Étienne Balibar, "État d'urgence démocratique," article from February 19, 1997, reprinted as "On la désobeissance civique," in *Droit de cité* (Paris: Éditions de l'Aube, 1998), 17–22.

37. Christophe Bident, *Maurice Blanchot partenaire invisible*, 283ff (on *The Madness of the Day*, "a new status for speech"). I recall that "inflexible" is one of the accepted translations of the Greek word *omos*, the adjective whereby Sophocles qualifies the character of Antigone, and of which Lacan proposes an interpretation in his 1959–60 seminar "The Ethics of Psychoanalysis." (In her biography *Jacques Lacan: Outline of a Life, History of a System of Thought*, trans. Barbara Bray [New York: Columbia University Press, 1997], Elisabeth Roudinesco suggests that one of the reasons why Lacan chose this object was the imprisonment of the psychoanalyst Laurence Bataille, his stepdaughter, for aiding the FLN.)

38. Reprinted in *La part du feu* (Paris: Gallimard, 1949), 293–331. Maurice Blanchot, *The Work of Fire*, trans. Charlotte Mandell (Stanford: Stanford University Press, 1995), 300–344.

39. Maurice Blanchot, *The Infinite Conversation*, trans. Susan Hanson (Minneapolis: University of Minnesota Press, 1993), 45 ("The Great Refusal," 2: "How to discover the obscure?); and once again, 179 ("Reflections on Hell" 2: "Logical victory over 'the absurd,'" a critical commentary on Albert Camus).

40. Ibid, 33.

41. Ibid, 35.

42. Everything that I say here proceeds from James Swenson's admirable explication in "Revolutionary Sentences," *Yale French Studies* 93 (1998): 11–29.

43. *Déclaration des droits de la femme* (1791), Article X (first complete publication on Olympe de Gouges, *Morceaux choisis* [Paris: Benoîte Groult éditions, 1986]). De Gouges's idea is that if woman can be sentenced to death as a citizen, she must also be entitled to represent the people and speak in the Assembly. Dying and speaking are corollary rights.

44. Philippe Lacoue-Labarthe, *Poétique de l'histoire* (Paris: Galilée, 2002).

45. Étienne Balibar, "Zur Sache selbst: Sur la dialectique de la communauté et de l'universalité dans la *Phénomenologie de l'esprit*." See Chapter 7 of this volume.

46. Maurice Blanchot, "Literature and the Right to Death," 330.

47. Ibid., 314.

48. Ibid., 330.

49. Ibid., 337.

50. Ibid., 335.

51. This sentence thus reprises Nietzsche's exergue from *Also Sprach Zarathustra: Ein Buch für Alle und Keinen*. It is also the inversion of the Hegelian formulation that defines the "thing itself" as *the action of all and each*: see "Literature and the Right to Death," 321. Behind each of these utterances, it is difficult not to discern Rousseau's statement from *Social Contract*: "each who gives himself to everyone does not give himself to anyone."

52. Blanchot, "Insurrection, the madness of writing," in *The Infinite Conversation*, 225. For a detailed critique of the way in which Blanchot identifies the discourses of Sade and Saint-Just (and consequently their conceptions of the relation between insurrection and institution), see Miguel Abensour, *Rire des lois, du magistrate et des dieux: L'impulsion Saint-Just* (Paris: Éditions Horlieu, 2005). Abensour insists in particular on the absence in Saint-Just of any "sovereign" identity between *crime* and *virtue*, because of his "heroic" conception of revolutionary energy in which irony becomes the weapon that destroys the old order, whose injustice it critiques, but not the law as such. Gilles Deleuze, however, in the pages from *Masochism: Coldness and Cruelty*, trans. Jean McNeil (New York: Zone Books, 1991) that he devotes to opposition between the schemas of the institution and the contract, without explicitly naming Blanchot, reiterates his question and proposes that we see Sade's discourse as the ironic inversion of the revolutionary problem posed by Saint-Just, in which the sexualization of the institution is "to challenge any attempt to think of politics in legalistic or contractual terms" (79).

53. Ibid., 222.

54. See *Le droit à la résistance XII–XX siècle*, 12.

55. See, in particular, Karl Marx and Friedrich Engels, "Address of the Central Authority to the League, March 1850" (*Ansprache der Zentralbehörde an den Bund von März 1850*): "While the democratic petty bourgeois wish to bring the revolution to a conclusion as quickly as possible, and with the achievement, at most, of the above demands, it is our interest and our task to make the revolution permanent, until all more or less possessing classes have been forced out of their position of dominance, the proletariat has conquered state power, and the association of proletarians, not only in one country but in all the dominant countries of the world, has advanced so far that competition among the proletarians in these countries has ceased and that at least the decisive productive forces are concentrated in the hands of the proletarians" (Karl Marx and Friedrich Engels, *Collected Works*, Volume 10, *Marx and Engels, 1849–1851* [New York: International Publishers, 1978], 281).

56. Blanchot, *Infinite Conversation*, 222–223.

57. Whence the invocation of *justice* at the heart of the great discourse in which Robespierre theorizes the Terror ("On the Principles of Political Morality that Should Guide the National Convention in the Domestic Administration of the Republic"): "These precautions should be taken in good time to place the destinies of liberty in the hands of truth which is eternal, rather than of men who pass on, in such a way that if the government forgets the people's interests, of falls into the hands of corrupt men, in the natural course of things, the light of acknowledged principles would expose its betrayals, and any new faction would die at the very thought of crime" (Maximilien Robespierre, *Virtue and Terror*, intro. Slavoj Žižek, trans. John Howe [New York: Verso, 2007], 109).

58. Maurice Blanchot, *The Infinite Conversation*, 224.

59. Ibid., 222–229.

60. There is also Blanchot's statement on the concentration camps, cited by Christophe Bident, that responsibilities for them also lies with "those who did not know how to prefer disobedience in reason to obedience in madness."

61. Maurice Blanchot, "*Humankind*," in *The Infinite Conversation*, 130–135.

14. BOURGEOIS UNIVERSALITY AND ANTHROPOLOGICAL DIFFERENCES

1. Pamphlet, "The Liberty of the People," 1789. See my essay "Citizen Subject," contained in this volume.

2. Karl Marx, "Debates on the Law on Thefts of Wood," in *The Complete Works of Karl Marx and Friedrich Engels* (Moscow: Progress Publishers, 1975), 1:236.

3. I attempted to raise this question for the first time twenty years ago in "Citizen Subject—A Response to a Question from Jean-Luc Nancy: Who Comes After the Subject?" I have already touched on the question of "anthropological differences," but never in a systematic fashion. I returned to it in an article written at the friendly behest of Michel Naepels. "L'introuvable humanité du sujet moderne. L'universalité 'civique-bourgeoise' et la question des différences anthropologiques," *L'Homme. Revue française d'anthropologie* 203–204 (2012): 19–50. The present chapter borrows several developments from the latter essay and benefited from seminars that I offered in 2010 and 2011 at the University of Pittsburgh, University of Essex, Universiteit Utrecht, Columbia University, and University of California at Irvine, in addition to presentations in the seminars of Bertrand Ogilvie and Nestor Capdevila at the Université de Paris-Ouest.

4. Jürgen Habermas, "Modernity—An Incomplete Project," trans. Seyla Benhabib, in *The Anti-Aesthetic*, ed. Hal Foster (New York: The New Press, 1983), 3–15. The thesis of this essay is also developed in *The Philosophical Discourse of Modernity*, trans. Frederick G. Lawrence (Cambridge, Mass.: MIT Press, 1990).

5. Hannah Arendt, *The Origins of Totalitarianism* (New York: Harcourt, Brace, and Jovanovich, 1973), 296–302. An extension of Arendt's analysis can be found in Alessandro dal Lago's book *Non Persone: L'esclusione dei migranti in una società globale* (Milan: Feltrinelli, 1999). In the final analysis, the very idea of a "nonperson" derives from the institution of slavery; but its history remains complex because Roman law includes slaves among "dependent" *personae* (*alieni iuris*). The term *manus*—which designates the master's power over the slave—also applies to the power of a husband over his wife. Although the slave trade developed in antiquity, it was the expansion of this trade within the framework of "world capitalist economy" that gave rise to the concept of the "human thing"—whose obviously contradictory character would become the cornerstone of abolitionist discourse. On the casuistry that entails the necessity of considering the slave both as a nonperson, a thing to be used, and as a "subject" in order to make him accountable to religion and the penal code, see Louis Sala-Molins, *Le Code Noir ou le calvaire de Canaan* (Paris: Presses Universitaires de France, 1987). Roberto Esposito recently published a genealogical study of the whole set of registers comprising "personalism" from the perspective of a critique of immunity conceived as the other or other side of community. *Third Person: Politics of Life and Philosophy of the Impersonal*, trans. Zakiya Hanafi (New York: Polity, 2012). I will have to discuss this book elsewhere.

6. On the way in which this critique operates in the context of "critiques of the rights of man" that postdate the French and American revolutions, see Bertrand Binoche, *Critiques des droits de l'homme* (Paris: Presses Universitaires de France, 1989).

7. Karl Marx, "On the Jewish Question," in *Early Writings* (New York: Penguin Books, 1992), 211–242; *Marx-Engels Werke* (Berlin: Dietz Verlag, 1961), 1:363–370.

8. This term is notoriously difficult to translate because it conjoins two ideas that Hegel developed and that Marx turns against him: the idea of a universe of economic and juridical "private relations," which is distinguished from the State and its institutions that function to "represent" the common interest, and the idea of a mode of appropriation founded upon competition between individual commodity owners. In his stand-alone edition of the section from Hegel's *Elements of the Philosophy of Right* on *Bürgerliche Gesellschaft*, Lefebvre proposes that we translate the term as "civil-bourgeois society." See G. W. F. Hegel, *La société civile-bourgeoise*, trans. and intro. Jean-Pierre Lefebvre (Paris: Maspero, 1975).

9. C. B. MacPherson, *The Political Theory of Possessive Individualism: Hobbes to Locke* (Oxford: Oxford University Press, 1962). On the emergence of the notion of individualism from that of egoism during the 1840s, see Étienne Balibar, "Le renversement de l'individualisme possessif," in *La proposition de l'égaliberté* (Paris: Presses Universitaires de France, 2010), 91–126. In Kant's *Anthropology from a Pragmatic Point of View*, "egoism" (defined as a tendency to "enclose the entire world within oneself" that derives from the disposition of the *I*) is opposed to "pluralism" ("comporting oneself as a simple citizen of the world"). It is de Tocqueville who, it seems, substitutes one term for the other. See *Democracy in America*, Volume Two, Part Two, Chapter 2: "Individualism in Democratic Countries."

10. Jacques Rancière, *Disagreement*, trans. Julie Rose (Minneapolis: University of Minnesota Press, 2004), 82.

11. Ibid., 83.

12. The same amphibology can be found in *Capital* when Marx extends his analysis of the "fetishism of the commodity" to the category of the "person." See the postscriptum to Chapter 9 in this volume.

13. But this is also true for the entire series of texts that emerge between the "Manuscript of 1843" (which Michel Abensour designates as Marx's "Machiavellian moment"), in which human emancipation is conceived as the "consequential" upsurge of the immanent tendency of democracy as the sovereignty of the "total *demos*," and the *Manifesto of the Communist Party* of 1847–48 (in which the "party" is nothing other than the set of forces and claims leading to a classless society through the "conquest of democracy").

14. The "language games" that Marx practices by means of these two languages obviously come from Hegel who, from the Jena texts to the "Remarks" in *Elements of a Philosophy of Right*, interpolated the French nouns *citoyen* and *bourgeois*, thereby breaking open the category of the *Bürger* in order to mark the "ethical" consequences of the contemporary (political and industrial) revolutions. Carl Schmitt comments on this disjunction in *Der Begriff des Politischen* (*The Concept of the Political*, trans. George Schwab [Chicago: University of Chicago Press, 2007]), finding in it the germ of the liberal dissolution of the political as the institution of sovereignty. See Jean-François Kervégan, "Le citoyen contre le bourgeois? La quête de *l'espirit de tout*," in *L'effectif et le rationnel: Hegel et l'espirit positif* (Paris: Vrin, 2005), 151–175. Kervégan elaborates and comments on the complete genealogy of the debate within German philosophy that surrounds the French revolution. See also Franck Fischbach, *Fichte et Hegel: La reconnaissance* (Paris: Presses Universitaires de France, 1999).

15. For a detailed history of the notion of the "bourgeois" (*Bürger*) and its relation to the successive forms of "civil-bourgeois society" (*bürgerliche Gesellschaft*), see, in particular, Manfred Riedel's articles "Bürger, Bürgertum" and "Bürgerliche Gesellschaft" in *Geschichtliche Grundbegriffe, Historisches Lexikon zur politisch-sozialen Sprache in Deutschland*, ed. Werner von Otto Brunner, Werner Conze, and Reinhart Koselleck (Stuttgart: Ernst Klett Verlag, 1972). See also, of course, Max Weber, *The City*, trans. Gertrud Neuwirth (New York: Free Press, 1966).

16. Or, more likely, constitutes it. If this transformation is not stripped of historical presuppositions, we can see that it represents something other than a passage from nature to culture or to artifice: instead, it would be, according Bertrand Ogilvie's thesis, a "second nature within primary nature." See "Anthropologie du propre à rien," in *La seconde nature du politique: Essai d'anthropologie négative* (Paris: L'Harmattan, 2012).

17. The concept of "character," which can serve to subsume the anthropological differences proper to the "civil-bourgeois" era, was generalized in the seventeenth and eighteenth centuries in Europe. Kant uses it in his *Anthropology from a Pragmatic Point of View* in order to systematize the differences and appurtenances that furnish, in a contradictory fashion, both the matter of and the obstacle to the exercise of morality. Character is thus the example par excellence of an

"empirico-transcendental" construction—to the extent that the latter requires a formation that, in its turn, distributes individuals into "classes" and "types" at the heart of the human race.

18. Max Weber, *Economy and Society*, ed. Gunther Roth and Claus Wittich (Berkeley: University of California Press, 1978).

19. *Anthropology* and *pedagogy*, for Kant, constitute two sides of the same "pragmatic" apparatus whose primary objective is to confront the problems posed by the "pathological" aspects of subjectivity—that is, those aspects which, at the heart of freedom, turn the will away from obedience to the categorical imperative and subject it to egoistic and thus non-universalizable "interests." In Bourdieu, whose terminology of the habitus I have borrowed here, the pedagogical dimension is no less evident; but, in his case, it has two levels. The visible "formation" of the individual (in school) is doubled by an invisible social preformation (that is, an archiformation). The latter, which is the true matrix of subjectivities and their differences, conditions the success or failure of the former just as the "body" materially conditions the "spirit."

20. "As we proceed to develop our investigation, we shall find, in general, that the characters who appear on the economic stage are merely personifications of economic relations; it is as the bearers of these economic relations that they come into contact with one another." Karl Marx, *Capital*, Vol. 1, trans. Ben Fowkes (New York: Penguin Books, 1992), 179. But later the mask comes off in order to give voice to demands for the rights that will subvert the law of exchange: "Suddenly, however, there arises the voice of the worker which had previously been stifled in the sound and fury of the production process" (ibid., 342). And the evocation of this voice is followed by a transcription of the declaration tendered by London construction workers on strike to reduce the working day to nine hours.

21. I concur upon this point, at least in part, with Rancière's analysis cited earlier. See Rancière, *Disagreement*, 82.

22. Consequently, it would be necessary at this juncture to open a deep discussion with the ironic thesis that Gayatri Spivak makes the cornerstone of her deconstruction of colonial narratives of subjectivity in "The Subaltern Cannot Speak." Gayatri Chakravorty Spivak, *A Critique of Postcolonial Reason* (Cambridge, Mass.: Harvard University Press, 1999).

23. In 1790, Mary Wollstonecraft published *A Vindication of the Rights of Men*, one of the principal "replies" to Edmund Burke's pamphlet, *Reflections on the Revolution in France*, which founded the conservative "critique of the rights of man." Upon reflection, the disparity makes sense: if *Men* is in the plural, this could well be a measure to include a diversity of genders (although, today, this plural would have the effect, against the intention of the author, of connoting the community of males); if *Woman* appears in the singular, it is undoubtedly because she wants to describe the condition and demands of woman as a gender and excluded as such—although, as in Lacan, this genderedness is ultimately "barred," producing the effect of a "not all." See Joan Copjec, *Imagine There is No Woman: Ethics and Sublimation* (Cambridge, Mass.: MIT Press, 2004). Wollstonecraft's logical violence often recalls that of Virginian Woolf in *Three Guineas* (1938). See Françoise Duroux, ed., *Virginia Woolf: Identité, politique, écriture* (Paris: Indigo, 2008).

24. This same decision is at the origin of Olympe de Gouges's *Declaration des droits de la femme*, which will lead her to the guillotine. See William H. Sewell, "Le Citoyen, La Citoyenne: Activity, Passivity and the French Revolutionary Concept of Citizenship," in *The French Revolution and the Creation of Modern Political Culture*, ed. Colin Lucas (Oxford: Pergamon Press, 1988), 2:105–125.

25. Wollstonecraft will say later that the education of girls transforms women into *abject slaves*. And she coins the now famous definition of bourgeois marriage as "legal prostitution." See Geneviève Fraisse's classic, *Muse de la raison: La démocratie exclusive et la difference des sexes* (Paris: Éditions Alinéa, 1989). It is very interesting to compare Wollstonecraft to Kant. In the passages from *Anthropology from a Pragmatic Point of View*, which was published in 1798 but dates from the

1770s, where Kant discusses "the character of sex" (almost never discussing men since, presumably, they don't really have a "character"), he appropriates all the misogynist stereotypes about the coquetry of women and how they use it to become mistresses of their lord and master. However, in *The Doctrine of Right* from 1796, he proposes a definition of marriage—which Hegel called "scandalous"—that evacuates all distinction between man and woman (since it construes marriage as "equality of possession," the "superiority" of the man only belatedly coming into play in a pragmatic argument about the protection of house and home). See Immanuel Kant, *The Metaphysics of Morals*, ed. Mary J. Gregor (Cambridge: Cambridge University Press, 1996), 62–63. The moment of egalitarian materialism causes Carole Pateman considerable trouble in her discussions of Kant in *The Sexual Contract* (Stanford: Stanford University Press, 1988), 168–173.

26. Mary Wollstonecraft, *A Vindication of the Rights of Woman* (Oxford: Oxford University Press, 2008), 74–75.

27. See Marie-Lise Paoli's different interpretation of the same passage in terms of the "rhetoric of sincerity." "Les mots et les choses in *A Vindication of the Rights of Woman*," in *Lectures d'une oeuvre: "A Vindication of the Rights of Woman" de Mary Wollstonecraft*, ed. Marie-Lise Paoli (Paris: Éditions du Temps, 1999), 119–133.

28. It is essential to remember that "feminism," synonymous with a demand for equality, is not a recent phenomenon in bourgeois "nations of citizens." Feminism is, in fact, coextensive with the history of these nations, particularly at revolutionary moments, when it becomes the target of especially intense repression. This is the history which, in France, is symbolized by the names Olympe de Gouges and Théroigne de Méricourt. See Joan Wallach Scott, *Only Paradoxes to Offer: French Feminists and the Rights of Man* (Cambridge, Mass.: Harvard University Press, 1997).

29. Or, as Geneviève Fraisse writes, women are relegated to the function of "minister," which is to say assistant. *Les deux governements: La famille et la Cité* (Paris: Gallimard, 2000).

30. The starting point for Monique David-Ménard's *Les Constructions de l'universel: Psychanalyse, philosophie* (Paris: Presses Universitaires de France, 1997) is precisely the critique (that is, an attempt to analyze the "logic") of the representation of woman as the one to whom the universal fails to apply, to the precise extent to which it supposes her, because she supports it, in a sort of originary torsion in the metaphysics of the "subject."

31. Colette Guillaumin, "Masculin banal/masculin général," *Le genre humain* 10 (1984).

32. This book was first published in 1952, the same year as other fundamental texts on "race" and "racism." Among them, I would single out Claude-Lévi Strauss's essay *Race and History*, whose contrast with Fanon's work is all the more striking since their philosophical background overlaps in significant respects.

33. Fanon's description of this instrumentalization of language is profoundly ironic because, even as he expresses the suffering that results from it and the feelings of failure that it provokes in the colonized subject, it borrows liberally from the great Martiniquais poet, Léon-Gontran Damas (the author of *Hoquet*), and uses his language to flagellate the paranoia of some and the neurosis of others.

34. In order for such humanity to appear as such, the barbarism of colonization—much more real than that imputed to the black man—must inspire in whites an admiration for "negro" culture (jazz, African sculpture) and give rise to the desire to identify with it.

35. See Gayatri Chakravorty Spivak, "Can the Subaltern Speak?" in *Marxism and the Interpretation of Culture*, ed. Lawrence Grossberg and Cary Nelson (Bloomington: University of Illinois Press, 1988), 271–315.

36. Frantz Fanon, *Black Skin, White Masks*, trans. Richard Philcox (New York: Grove Press, 2008), xii–xiii.

37. Ibid., 206.

38. Ibid.

39. A great Hegelian, Fanon could not ignore the dialectic of "sense-certainty" that opens *The Phenomenology of Spirit*. To the problem that Hegel poses—how to get beyond the abstraction of an utterance or an "I speak" that either belongs to no one or designates anyone—Fanon responds in the form of a short circuit: to overcome this abstraction, no more is required than to consider that the sounding voice itself is *already* the expression of a struggle for recognition. In other words, the dialectic of master and slave does not represent an ulterior *consequence* of the education of consciousness but always already *precedes* the modalities of its access to language (and thus to experience). Or perhaps: *before* the undifferentiated state that allows everyone to appropriate language "equally," there is an *inequality* in the differential incorporation of voices.

40. See the humorous formulation of Karl Valentin (one of Brecht's teachers): *"fremd ist der Fremd nur in der Fremde"* (the foreigner is only foreign in a foreign land). This figure entails an intrinsic ambivalence: the object of fear, hatred or merely surprise, it can also engender attraction, love, solicitude, and so on. And the corresponding subjective configurations are no less complex; see the analyses of Simmel and his successors (Alfred Schutz, Zygmunt Bauman) on the condition of being a foreigner, the typical scene of which is not an encounter across borders but the experience of expatriation that produces a large group of "internal foreigners" to the precise extent that they are no longer entirely foreign. In the "diasporic cosmopolitanism" of late modernity, the foreigner becomes the "mediator" whereby the universal can be reconstructed as the universality of differences.

41. Emmanuel Sieyès, *What Is the Third Estate?* In *Political Writings*, ed. and trans. Michael Sonenscher (Indianapolis: Hackett, 2003), 92–162. See Foucault's commentary on this text in *Society Must be Defended: Lectures at the Collège de France, 1975–76*, trans. David Macey (New York: Picador, 2003), the session from March 10, 1976. On the mutation of the "nation" in the course of the revolutionary process, see Florence Gauthier, *Triomphe et mort du droit naturel en revolution, 1789–1795–1802* (Paris: Presses Universitaires de France, 1992).

42. See Étienne Balibar, "Fichte and the Internal Border," in *Masses, Classes, Ideas* (New York: Routledge, 1994), 61–84; as well as *"Homo Nationalis*: An Anthropological Sketch of the Nation-Form," in *We, The People of Europe?* trans. James Swenson (Princeton: Princeton University Press, 2003), 11–31.

43. In historical terms, a "culture"; in political terms, a "national education"; in philosophical terms, an "intersubjectivity" that creates the language and is created by it: *"indem weitmehr die Menschen von der Sprache gebildet werden, denn die Sprache von den Menschen"* (*Addresses to the German Nation*, Fourth Address). It is on this point that one would have to assess carefully what brings Humboldt ever so close to Fichte but ultimately separates them.

44. Uli Bielefeld, *Nation und Gesellschaft: Selbstthematisierungen in Frankreich und Deutschland* (Hamburg: Hamburger Edition, 2003). This book develops three parallels: Fichte and Barrès, Weber and Durkheim, Céline and Ernst von Salomon.

45. Contemporary postcolonial thought has subverted the concept by forging the paradoxical notion of hybridity without "purity" (or without "roots"). See Stuart Hall, "New Ethnicities," in *"Race," Culture, and Difference*, ed. James Donald and Ali Rattansi (London: Sage Publications, 1992); and Homi Bhabha, *The Location of Culture* (New York: Routledge, 1994).

46. See Étienne Balibar, "Is There a Neo-Racism?" in Étienne Balibar and Immanuel Wallerstein, *Race, Nation, Class: Ambiguous Identities* (New York: Verso, 1991), 17–28; Pierre-André Tanguieff, *La force du préjugé: Essai sur le racisme et ses doubles* (Paris: La Découverte, 1988).

47. Hence the ambivalence of the notion of "multiculturalism"—for some the purveyor of neoracism, for others the antidote to the essentialization of cultures. See David Theo Goldberg, ed., *Multiculturalism: A Reader* (Oxford: Blackwell, 1994).

48. See Jean-Loup Amselle and Elikia M'Bokolo, eds., *Au coeur de l'ethnie: Ethnies, tribalisme et état en Afrique* (Paris: La Découverte, 1985),

49. The situation is actually circular, because if one asks, "What is ethnic difference?" there is no choice but to draw upon various combinations of references to race or population, to

languages, to alliances, to traditions, or the like. The evolution of Claude Lévi-Strauss's work from *Race and History* (1952) to *Race and Culture* (1972), which provoked intense controversy, revolves around two points: (1) the rectification of pure "culturalism" in favor of the idea that cultural distance fulfills the "biological" (or bio-ecological) function of promoting the preservation of populations; (2) the rectification of the idea that cultures are always already given, and that they must ineluctably decrease in number, in favor of the idea of a (hypothetical) regeneration of cultural diversity on the basis of resistance to globalization. Privileging one viewpoint or the other yields differing readings of Lévi-Strauss's ever reiterated thesis: that a culture is inseparable from an "ethnocentrism" that protects its particularity but takes the form of an illusory universality (every culture—whether it be that of the Greeks or the Bororos—upholds itself as the sole "human" culture). See Wiktor Stoczkowski, "Controverse sur la diversité humaine," *Sciences Humaines* 8 (November–December 2008): 48–52. It is interesting to compare this thesis with Fanon's exactly contemporary analyses: the functioning of the "color line" proves to be incompatible, as I showed earlier, with this fixation of the border between any given humanity and its "outside." The obvious conclusion, then, is that postslavery (and even postcolonial) "race" does not adhere to an "ethnic" model" or that "ethnicity" and "culture" alike are fictions. Each of these two great Frenchmen has an American precursor: Boas for Lévi-Strauss and Du Bois for Fanon.

50. Within the framework of these strategies, I attribute special meaning to the reconduction of the genealogical schema—that is, to the idea of a both individual and collective "transmission" whereby characteristics pass from one generation to another either to be identically reproduced or substantially conserved or to be altered or lost (left to reemerge long after the fact). The genealogical schema has theological and, what is most important, aristocratic origins (race as "blood" or "lineage"), but went on to become the basis for the representation of peoples (in particular, those who consider themselves historically as the "masters" of other peoples) or cultures, and for the history of humanity itself. It always prevails when the naturalized descendents of foreigners are considered as "immigrants" of the second or third generation, which is a manner of immediately designating them as "foreign bodies," or of drawing an internal border between "them" and "us." But the justifications of this schema are always transforming, passing from lineage to genetics, or to the classification of civilizations and individuals by the measure of "progress"—whose underside is an obsession with "decadence," the return to "barbarism."

51. Which means that "the somatic" cannot be separated from representations of the "masculine," the "feminine," and their "aberrations." This is what Fanon demonstrated, combining a dialectic of recognition inherited from Hegel and Sartre with a phenomenology of "double consciousness" close to that of W. E. B. Du Bois to produce what remains today one of the purest definitions of the subject as "nonbeing" or relational negativity. See Lewis R, Gordon, *Fanon and the Crisis of European Man: An Essay on Philosophy and the Human Sciences* (New York: Routledge, 1995).

52. Michel Foucault, *Abnormal: Lectures at the Collège de France 1974–1975*, trans. Graham Burchill (New York: Picador, 2004); "The Dangerous Individual," in *Politics, Philosophy, Culture: Interviews and Other Writings, 1977–1984* (New York: Routledge, 1988), 125–151. Foucault undertook his work on "abnormals," which succeeded his course on "psychiatric power" and was contemporary with *Discipline and Punish* (*Surveiller et punir*, 1975), soon after the activities of the "groupe d'informations sur les prisons" (GIP), the creation of the Syndicat de la Magistrature, and the rise of antipsychiatry that called into question the opposition between the "normal" and the "pathological." It is also contemporary with the revelation that Soviet authorities used psychiatric internment as a means of political repression (the Pliouchtch affair in 1974).

53. See also Michel Foucault, *Discipline and Punish: The Birth of the Prison*, trans. Alan Sheridan (New York: Vintage Books, 1995), 303. "But it is perhaps more important to ask the reverse question: how were people made to accept the power to punish, or quite simply, when punished, tolerate being so?" One will note the syntactical equivocity of the phrase "to accept the power to

punish": this acceptance applies both to those who exercise such power (but might have to submit to it) and to those who submit to it (but who might ideally exercise it once they have been "rehabilitated"). Aristotle, we know, considered this type reversibility between the *archein* and the *archesthai* as the essence of citizenship (see *Politics*, 1277a).

54. Guillaume Le Blanc, *L'esprit des sciences humaines* (Paris: Vrin, 2005), 135: "The invention of normality is, in fact, the secret project of the human sciences." One would have to examine the "overturning" that Foucault imposed upon the arguments of the French school of sociology about anomie and, at the same time, to elucidate his relation to Canguilhem's conception of the "norm" (to which his course on the abnormal makes explicit reference). See Stéphane Legrand, *Les normes chez Foucault* (Paris: Presses Universitaires de France, 2007) and Pierre Macherey, *De Canguilhem à Foucault, la force des normes* (Paris: La Fabrique, 2009). These texts might also be compared to Erving Goffman's analysis in *Stigma: Notes on the Management of Spoiled Identity* (New York: Touchstone, 1986), in which he shows how normative identity, which allows the members of a "majority" to recognize one another as "We, the Normals," is never routed through a "positive" mark of direct belonging, but rather through a potentially infinite series of "negations of the negation" that furnish subjects of the majority with a guarantee that they are *not* "abnormal"— not, for example, a handicap, a deviant, or a monster, and so on.

55. See *Discipline and Punish*, 304: "The judges of normality are present everywhere [=in our society]. We are in the society of the teacher-judge, the doctor-judge, the educator-judge, the 'social worker'-judge; it is on them that the universal reign of the normative is based."

56. That is to say, a subject incapable of resisting "the desire to transgress the law." See *Abnormal*, Session of January 8, 1975; *Discipline and Punish*, 252ff. on the "introduction of the 'biographical'" that "establishes the 'criminal' as existing before the crime."

57. *Abnormal*, Session of February 12, 1975. In this context, Foucault does not explicitly discuss the "doublet" of (medical) perversion and (moral) perversity, but it seems obvious that it is one of the bases for his critique.

58. For Foucault, this analysis doubles as a genealogy of psychoanalysis. See, in particular, his study of the bourgeois obsession with infantile masturbation and the need to repress it, whereby he offers an institutional and social history of one of the features of infantile sexuality that Freud upheld as a source of the "castration complex."

59. *Abnormal*, Session of January 15, 1975. This is why the description of judiciary institutions is an integral part of what, somewhat later, Foucault will call a "political history of truth."

60. *Omnes et singulatim*: Foucault used this phrase as the title for a now famous lecture from 1979, subtitled "toward a critique of political reason." See Michel Foucault, *The Essential Works of Michel Foucault, 1954–1984: Power*, ed. James Faubion (New York: New Press, 2000), 298–325. He does not designate the provenance of the phrase. In the session of February 8, 1978, from his course "Security, Territory, Population," offers no further clarification, but it does make explicit its relation to the thematic of sacrifice for the salvation of the community: "the sacrifice of one for all, and the sacrifice of all for one, which will be at the absolute heart of the Christian problematic of the pastorate." Michel Foucault, *Security, Territory, Population: Lectures at the Collège de France, 1977–1978*, trans. Graham Burchell (New York: Picador, 2007), 129. Would it be possible to determine if, at this moment, he was thinking of Hegel's formulations from the *Phenomenology of Spirit* (*das Tun aller und jeder*) whereby the function of the sovereign is transposed into the "law" of the community of subjects?

61. See Immanuel Wallerstein, "Trois idéologies ou une seule? La problématique de la modernité," *Genèses* 9 (1992), *Conservatisme, libéralisme, socialisme*.

62. The type of such determinism remains Lombroso's criminology (*L'uomo delinquente*, 1876), revived in today's theories that "predicate" delinquency on the basis of "erratic" behavior in children that the school is expected to detect as early as possible. Foucault clearly thought that, in the nineteenth century, the project of "social defense" tends to suffuse the "microphysics" of

power as soon as liberalism becomes dominant at the level of constitutional principles. He did not develop his analysis of the relationship between the theme of the "dangerous individual" and that of "dangerous classes" (evoked in *Discipline and Punish*, "Illegalities and Delinquency," 257ff). Whence the equivocity of the category of abnormals and the procedure of *isolating individuals* that makes it possible to conjure away the *collectivization* of social struggles or, more simply, subversive forms of behavior.

63. Étienne Balibar, "Private Crime, Public Madness," Chapter 11 in this volume.

64. See the alarm sounded by Dr. Allen Frances, the former president of the commission tasked in 1994 with producing the DSM-IV, about what he considered to be the "excesses" and "risks" of the forthcoming DSM-V ("It's Not Too Late to Save 'Normal,'" *Los Angeles Times*, March 1, 2010) as well as the intense reactions to the French government's projects to create a "judiciary psychiatric record" and to impose psychiatric care as a substitute or complement to incarceration for first time sexual offenders and recidivists. See Dr. Daniel Zagury, "La loi sur la psychiatrie est l'indice d'un État qui préfère punir que guérir," *Le Monde*, March 22, 2011.

65. [The subheading comes from] Honoré de Balzac, *Père Goriot* (1835) (the inscription on the pediment of "Vauquer house" where the hero takes up residence).

66. On the fluctuations of the terminology of "sex," "sexuality," and "gender" (*genre*) following the importation into French of this last term modeled on American usage, see Elsa Dorlin, *Sexe, genre et sexualités: introduction à la théorie féministe* (Paris: Presses Universitaires de France, 2007); Nicole-Claude Mathieu, "Sexe et genre," in Héléna Hirata et al., eds. *Dictionnaire critique du féminisme* (Paris: Presses Universitaires de France, 2000); and, more recently, Geneviève Fraisse, *À côté du genre* (Bordeaux: Éditions du bord de l'eau, 2011).

67. Sigmund Freud, *The Ego and the Id*, *SE* XIX, 3–66. See also, "A Child Is Being Beaten" (1919, *SE* XVII, 179–204); "Psychogenesis of a Case of Homosexuality in a Woman" (1920, *SE* XVIII, 147–172); "Neurotic Mechanisms in Jealousy, Paranoia, and Homosexuality" (1922, *SE* XVIII, 221–232); "The Genital Organization of the Libido" (1923, *SE* XIX, 140–145); "The Economic Problem of Masochism" (1924, *SE* XIX, 159–170); "The Dissolution of the Oedipus Complex" (1924, *SE* XIX, 172–179); and "Fetishism" (1927, *SE* XXI, 152–157).

68. *SE* XIX, 31.

69. *SE* XIX, 32.

70. To simplify a little bit, one could say that, for Freud, the transposition from an original "bisexuality" to an acceptance of both homosexual and heterosexual object choice is much more "normal" for women than for men, in whom one of the two tendencies necessarily represses the other. See Freud, "A Child Is Being Beaten" (1919) and "Psychogenesis of a Case of Homosexuality in a Woman" (1920). Perhaps this is Freud's own "uncle fantasy."

71. See, in particular, the chapter in *New Introductory Lectures* (1933) on "Femininity," where, in the space of a few pages, Freud seems to transition from one thesis to the other: the "feminine character" *is and is not* the same thing as "passivity." It seems that this disjunction is essential to Freud's central thesis that *there are not two libidos*, one "masculine" and one "feminine," because the oscillation from active to passive (much as the ambivalence of love-hate) is part of the *same* evolution of the drive. But this thesis is also occasionally articulated in the form, "the only libido is masculine" (see, in particular, *Three Essays*).

72. This is the object of Freud's controversy with Adler, whose theory revolves around the idea that what constitutes the different sexuality of the two sexes are the (unequal) possibilities of acceptance and refusal, confidence and anxiety that result from the social devalorization of the "feminine." See Alfred Adler, "The Myth of Female Inferiority" (1927).

73. See "Some Neurotic Mechanisms in Jealousy, Paranoia, and Homosexuality" (1922), *SE* XVIII, 221ff.

74. See Bertrand Ogilvie, *Lacan: La formation du concept de sujet* (1932–1949) (Paris: Presses Universitaires de France, 1987).

75. See Jacques Lacan, *Encore, The Seminar of Jacques Lacan, Book XX: On Feminine Sexuality, the Limits of Love and Knowledge*, trans. Bruch Fink (New York: Norton, 1999). Among the commentaries on Lacan's formalism, I use, in particular, Monique David-Ménard, *Les constructions de l'universel* (Paris: Presses Universitaires de France, 1997), and Joan Copjec, "Sex and the Euthanasia of Reason," in *Read My Desire: Lacan Among the Historicists* (Cambridge, Mass.: MIT Press, 1994), both of which base their readings upon detailed comparisons of Lacan with Kant's elaboration of the antinomies of pure reason.

76. Lacan, *Encore*, 80. Lacan forges the portmanteau word "*parlêtre*" (speaking being) that, in this context also appears, necessarily, as a "*malêtre*" (ill-being).

77. In his own manner, Lacan thus rediscovers the thesis that Hegel derives from his interpretation of Antigone: femininity, "the eternal irony of community." See the discussion of this aspect of Lacan's work in *Lacan avec les philosophes* (Paris: Albin Michel, 1991), 19–66 (with contributions from Philippe Lacoue-Labarthe, Françoise Duroux, Nicole Loraux, Samuel Weber, and Patrick Guyomard).

78. Michel Tort, "Quelques conséquences de la différence 'psychanalytique' des sexes," *Les Temps Modernes* 55, no. 609 (Summer 2000): 176–215; *Fin du dogme paternal* (Paris: Aubier, 2005); Joan Copjec, "Sex and the Euthanasia of Reason."

79. There is, of course, a whole group of feminist challenges to Lacan that attempt to identify an "alternative symbolic function," which would also be supported by the presence or absence of a typically "feminine" organ (belly or uterus, vagina, lips, etc.). Here we have a discursive mirror formation, because Seminar XX is already, very explicitly, an attempted "response" to the feminist challenge, and notably to the discourse of the Movement de libération des femmes (MLF) (Antoinette Fouque). It would be more difficult, but also highly interesting, to know something about the "competition" between Lacan's work leading up to Seminar XX and the teaching of Luce Irigaray in the Département de Psychanalyse at the Université de Vincennes (Paris VIII) between 1970 and 1974, when *Speculum of the Other Woman* was published in France, leading to her expulsion from the Department.

80. Judith Butler, *Gender Trouble: Feminism and the Subversion of Sexual Identity* (New York: Routledge, 1990); *Bodies That Matter: On the Discursive Limits of "Sex"* (New York: Routledge, 1993); *Undoing Gender* (New York: Routledge, 2004).

81. This expression is used in another context by Giacomo Marramao in *The Passage West: Philosophy After the Age of the Nation-State* (New York: Verso, 2012). But Patrice Maniglier, who derives from it an entirely *relational* "metaphysics of sex," does not say anything different: "humanity is nothing beyond this diversity." See "Bien plus que cinq sexes: par-delà masculin et féminin," http://www.lemonde.fr/savoirs-et-connaissances/son/2007/12/06/patrice-maniglier -bien-plus-que-cinq-sexes-par-dela-masculin-et-feminin_986359_3328.html.

82. See Butler, *Undoing Gender*, 179, 190–191.

83. This is what Butler calls "passionate attachment." *The Psychic Life of Power* (Stanford: Stanford University Press, 1997), 6ff. Later, in relation to "bodily subjection," passionate attachment is also called "stubborn." More recently, she has reformulated this theory within the framework of a theory of vulnerability as an originary characteristic of the subject—which is not without relation to Bataille's "principle of incompleteness." See *Excitable Speech* (New York: Routledge, 1997); *Precarious Life* (New York: Verso, 2004).

84. Accordingly, what the philosophical tradition calls the "proper" body is always essentially "foreign" (*fremd, unheimlich*). See "Melancholia and the Limits of Performance," in *Bodies That Matter*, 233ff.

85. See Butler's remarks on the "butch-femme" couple, which suddenly conjoins the third and first persons by means of a slash: "There are many ways of approaching the issue of desire and gender. We could immediately blame the butch community, and say that they/we are simply antifeminine or that we have disavowed a primary femininity, but then we would be left with

the quandary that for the most part (not exclusively) butches are deeply, if not fatally, attracted to the feminine and, in this sense, love the feminine" (*Undoing Gender*, 197). Isn't "feminine," here, always a "non-man" who, for this very reason, might represent the alterity of "sex"?

86. It would be necessary, at this point, to take up once again the phenomenology of the "subjective couple" (or *personal-real*, as Kant said about marriage in *The Metaphysics of Morals*), which, in the modern era, runs at least from Rousseau to Simmel and to Derrida: a strange figure, upon reflection, because not only does it permanently oscillate between the polarities of conflict and contract, love and friendship, fear and hatred, but also it never stops compensating for its tendency toward dissemination by adjoining "thirds" or "supplements" (fathers, mothers, children, students, servants, lovers, confessors, lawyers, and therapists, but also houses check- books, domestic animals, gardens, workbenches and drills, computers and televisions, books, postcards . . .) whose interposition both *destroys the relation* and *constructs* it.

87. See his comparison of the "model of the plague" and the "model of leprosy" in *Abnormal* (January 15, 1975) and (notably contained in the collection, *L'impossible prison*, 48ff) his revision of the formula that he advanced in *Discipline and Punish*: "Is it surprising that prisons resemble factories, schools, barracks, hospitals, which all resemble prisons?" (228).

88. Here I am thinking of Sidi Mohammed Barkat, *Le corps d'exception: Les artifices du pouvoir colonial et la destruction de la vie* (Paris: Éditions Amsterdam, 2005).

89. The colonial metaphor of the "dark continent" that Freud used in 1926 (in *The Question of Lay Analysis*) in order to characterize female sexuality derives, it would seem, from the explorer Henry M. Stanley's bestseller *Through the Dark Continent* (London: Sampson Low, Marston & Co., 1878).

90. In counterpoint to the work of Fernand Deligny, Bertrand Ogilvie systematically explores the overlapping and exchange between these different figures, compressed into the most violated and institutional figure of difference: that of childhood. See "Deligny, une anthropologie infinie," in *Oeuvres de Fernand Deligny* (Paris: L'Arachnéen, 2007). Between what Ogilvie calls the improper and what I call ill-being or the monster, there is an affinity and a difference that we have yet to discuss.

91. What Goffman calls the "normal deviant" is the complex character constructed by the mimetic relation between stigmatized types and their normalized counterpart. In his account, the "normal" individual in North American society would be characterized thus: "For example, in an important sense there is only one complete unblushing male in America: a young, married, white, urban, Northern, heterosexual, Protestant father of college education, fully employed, of good complexion, weight, and height, and a recent record in sports. Every American male tends to look out upon the world from this perspective, this constituting one sense in which one can speak of a common value system in America" (*Stigma*, 153).

92. This is Kant's proposition from his 1784 essay, "An Answer to the Question: 'What Is Enlightenment?'" See Immanuel Kant, *Practical Philosophy*, trans. and ed. Mary J. Gregor (Cambridge: Cambridge University Press, 1999), 11.

93. On this parallel, see Étienne Balibar, "Cosmopolitisme et internationalisme: deux modèles, deux héritages," in *Philosophie politique et horizon cosmopolitique. La mondalisation et les apories d'une cosmopolitique de la paix, de la citoyenneté et des actions*, under the direction of Francisco Naishtat (Geneva: UNESCO, 2006).

94. Gilles Deleuze and Félix Guattari, *A Thousand Plateaus*, trans. Brian Massumi (Minneapo- lis: University of Minnesota Press, 1987), 232–234.

95. On the combination of these traditions in the genealogy of the modern idea of the "subject," see Alain de Libera's contribution to our co-written entry ("subject") in *The Dictionary of Untranslatables* and, more recently, the two volumes of his *Archéologie du sujet* (Paris: Vrin, 2007 and 2008). The "residence of abstraction" that Marx speaks of (*innewohnend*) cannot not resonate with Saint Augustine's formulation from *De vera religione*: *In interiore homine habitat veritas*. See Charles Taylor's commentary on it in *Sources of the Self*, 127ff.

96. This reciprocal action is what Marx, in *The German Ideology*, calls the "commerce" among men (*Verkehr*). In the analysis that he proposes, geared toward explaining how the universalization of the division of labor forms the preconditions for communism, *Verkehr* is the correlate of the historical configurations of the mode of production. However, without excluding this "materialist" orientation, the *Theses on Feuerbach* confer upon "the ensemble of social relations" a potentially indefinite extension, on condition that they always refer back to *practice* (which, for the Marx of 1845, is a veritable name of the "subject"). It is true that, symptomatically, this extension forecloses sexual difference, which tends to falsify Marx's entire representation of the history of forms of domination. This foreclosure also leads him to misrecognize that which, in Feuerbach, despite the omnipresence of the category of species or genre (*Gattung*), does not derive from the imposition of an abstract idea of isolated individuals but rather, precisely, from an anthropology of *relation*—the identification of human essence with "the love of man for man" (that is, essentially, love of man and woman).

97. Étienne Balibar, *The Philosophy of Marx*, trans. Chris Turner (New York: Verso Reprint Edition, 2014), 32–33. See also Pierre Macherey's detailed commentary in *Marx 1845: Les "Theses" sur Feuerbach* (Paris: Éditions Amsterdam, 2008), 137–160, which concludes upon the fact that Marx's "critique of essence" transforms essence into "nonessence" (which could well be translated as *Un-wesen*).

98. What *Religion Within the Boundaries of Mere Reason* (1793) calls "radical evil" is the transcendental interiority of the pathological, attaching it to an allegorical interpretation of the "fall." See Immanuel Kant, *Religion and Rational Theology*, trans. and ed. Allen Wood and George di Giovanni (Cambridge: Cambridge University Press, 1996), 69ff.

Commonalities

Timothy C. Campbell, series editor

Roberto Esposito, *Terms of the Political: Community, Immunity, Biopolitics.* Translated by Rhiannon Noel Welch. Introduction by Vanessa Lemm.

Maurizio Ferraris, *Documentality: Why It Is Necessary to Leave Traces.* Translated by Richard Davies.

Dimitris Vardoulakis, *Sovereignty and Its Other: Toward the Dejustification of Violence.*

Anne Emmanuelle Berger, *The Queer Turn in Feminism: Identities, Sexualities, and the Theater of Gender.* Translated by Catherine Porter.

James D. Lilley, *Common Things: Romance and the Aesthetics of Belonging in Atlantic Modernity.*

Jean-Luc Nancy, *Identity: Fragments, Frankness.* Translated by François Raffoul.

Miguel Vatter, *Between Form and Event: Machiavelli's Theory of Political Freedom.*

Miguel Vatter, *The Republic of the Living: Biopolitics and the Critique of Civil Society.*

Maurizio Ferraris, *Where Are You? An Ontology of the Cell Phone.* Translated by Sarah De Sanctis.

Irving Goh, *The Reject: Community, Politics, and Religion after the Subject.*

Kevin Attell, *Giorgio Agamben: Beyond the Threshold of Deconstruction.*

J. Hillis Miller, *Communities in Fiction.*

Remo Bodei, *The Life of Things, the Love of Things.* Translated by Murtha Baca.

Gabriela Basterra, *The Subject of Freedom: Kant, Levinas.*

Roberto Esposito, *Categories of the Impolitical.* Translated by Connal Parsley.

Roberto Esposito, *Two: The Machine of Political Theology and the Place of Thought.* Translated by Zakiya Hanafi.

Akiba Lerner, *Redemptive Hope: From the Age of Enlightenment to the Age of Obama.*

Adriana Cavarero and Angelo Scola, *Thou Shalt Not Kill: A Political and Theological Dialogue.* Translated by Margaret Adams Groesbeck and Adam Sitze.

Massimo Cacciari, *Europe and Empire: On the Political Forms of Globalization.* Edited by Alessandro Carrera, Translated by Massimo Verdicchio.

Emanuele Coccia, *Sensible Life: A Micro-ontology of the Image.* Translated by Scott Stuart, Introduction by Kevin Attell.

Timothy C. Campbell, *The Techne of Giving: Cinema and the Generous Forms of Life.*

Étienne Balibar, *Citizen Subject: Foundations for Philosophical Anthropology.* Translated by Steven Miller. Foreword by Emily Apter.

Ashon T. Crawley, *Blackpentecostal Breath: The Aesthetics of Possibility.*

Terrion L. Williamson, *Scandalize My Name: Black Feminist Practice and the Making of Black Social Life.*

Jean-Luc Nancy, *The Disavowed Community.* Translated by Philip Armstrong.

This page represents a continuation of the copyright page.

Library of Congress Cataloging-in-Publication Data

Names: Balibar, Étienne, 1942– author.
Title: Citizen subject : foundations for philosophical anthropology / Étienne
    Balibar ; translated by Steven Miller.
Description: New York, NY : Fordham University Press, 2017. | Series:
    Commonalities | Includes bibliographical references and index.
Identifiers: LCCN 2016027230 | ISBN 9780823273607 (cloth : alk. paper) |
    ISBN 9780823273614 (pbk. : alk. paper)
Subjects: LCSH: Philosophical anthropology. | Subject (Philosophy)
Classification: LCC BD450 .B25613 2017 | DDC 128—dc23
LC record available at https://lccn.loc.gov/2016027230

www.ingramcontent.com/pod-product-compliance
Lightning Source LLC
Chambersburg PA
CBHW080925050426
42334CB00056B/2863